Statistical Concepts

A Second Course

Fourth Edition

Statistical Concepts

A Second Course

Fourth Edition

Richard G. Lomax
The Ohio State University

Debbie L. Hahs-Vaughn
University of Central Florida

Routledge
Taylor & Francis Group
New York   London

Routledge
Taylor & Francis Group
711 Third Avenue
New York, NY 10017

Routledge
Taylor & Francis Group
27 Church Road
Hove, East Sussex BN3 2FA

© 2012 by Taylor & Francis Group, LLC
Routledge is an imprint of Taylor & Francis Group, an Informa business

Printed in the United States of America on acid-free paper
Version Date: 20120106

International Standard Book Number: 978-0-415-88007-7 (Paperback)

**Visit the Taylor & Francis Web site at
http://www.taylorandfrancis.com**

**and the Psychology Press Web site at
http://www.psypress.com**

Printed and bound in the United States of America by
Edwards Brothers Malloy on sustainably sourced paper

This book is dedicated to our families

and to all of our former students.

Contents

Preface

Approach

We know, we know! We've heard it a million times before. When you hear someone at a party mention the word *statistics* or *statistician*, you probably say "I hate statistics" and turn the other cheek. In the many years that we have been in the field of statistics, it is extremely rare when someone did not have that reaction. Enough is enough. With the help of this text, we hope that "statistics hating" will become a distant figment of your imagination.

As the title suggests, this text is designed for a second course in statistics for students in education and the behavioral sciences. We begin with the most basic analysis of variance in the first chapter and proceed through regression analysis. The text is designed for you to become a better prepared researcher and a more intelligent consumer of research. We do not assume that you have extensive or recent training in mathematics. Many of you have only had algebra, perhaps some time ago. We do assume, however, that you have had an introductory statistics course. Rest assured; you will do fine.

We believe that a text should serve as an effective instructional tool. You should find this text to be more than a reference book; you might actually use it to learn statistics. (What an oxymoron that a statistics book can actually teach you something.) This text is not a theoretical statistics book, nor is it a cookbook on computing statistics or a statistical software manual. Recipes have to be memorized; consequently, you tend not to understand how or why you obtain the desired product. As well, knowing how to run a statistics package without understanding the concepts or the output is not particularly useful. Thus, concepts drive the field of statistics.

Goals and Content Coverage

Our goals for this text are lofty, but the effort and its effects will be worthwhile. First, the text provides a comprehensive coverage of topics that could be included in an undergraduate or graduate level second course in statistics. The text is flexible enough so that instructors can select those topics that they desire to cover as they deem relevant in their particular discipline. In other words, chapters and sections of chapters from this text can be included in a statistics course as the instructor sees fit. Most of the popular as well as many of the lesser-known procedures and models are described in the text. A particular feature is a thorough and up-to-date discussion of assumptions, the effects of their violation, and how to deal with their violation.

Chapters 1 through 6 cover all of the basic analysis of variance (ANOVA) models. In Chapters 7 through 9, we go on to examine various regression models.

Second, the text communicates a conceptual, intuitive understanding of statistics, which requires only a rudimentary knowledge of basic algebra and emphasizes the important concepts in statistics. The most effective way to learn statistics is through the conceptual approach. Statistical concepts tend to be easy to learn because (a) concepts can be simply stated, (b) concepts can be made relevant through the use of real-life examples, (c) the same concepts are shared by many procedures, and (d) concepts can be related to one another.

This text will help you to reach these goals. The following indicators will provide some feedback as to how you are doing. First, there will be a noticeable change in your attitude toward statistics. Thus, one outcome is for you to feel that "statistics is not half bad," or "this stuff is OK." Second, you will feel comfortable using statistics in your own work. Finally, you will begin to "see the light." You will know when you have reached this highest stage of statistics development when suddenly, in the middle of the night, you wake up from a dream and say, "now I get it!" In other words, you will begin to *think* statistics rather than think of ways to get out of doing statistics.

Pedagogical Tools

The text contains several important pedagogical features to allow you to attain these goals. First, each chapter begins with an outline (so you can anticipate what will be covered), and a list of key concepts (which you will need in order to understand what you are doing). Second, realistic examples from education and the behavioral sciences are used to illustrate the concepts and procedures covered in each chapter. Each of these examples includes an initial vignette, an examination of the relevant procedures and necessary assumptions, how to run SPSS and develop an APA style write-up, as well as tables, figures, and annotated SPSS output to assist you. Third, the text is based on the conceptual approach. That is, material is covered so that you obtain a good understanding of statistical concepts. If you know the concepts, then you know statistics. Finally, each chapter ends with three sets of problems, computational, conceptual, and interpretive. Pay particular attention to the conceptual problems as they provide the best assessment of your understanding of the concepts in the chapter. We strongly suggest using the example data sets and the computational and interpretive problems for additional practice through available statistics software. This will serve to reinforce the concepts covered. Answers to the odd-numbered problems are given at the end of the text.

New to the Fourth Edition

A number of changes have been made in the fourth edition based on the suggestions of reviewers, instructors, teaching assistants, and students. These improvements have been made in order to better achieve the goals of the text. You will note the addition of a coauthor to this edition, Debbie Hahs-Vaughn, who has contributed greatly to the further development of this text. The changes include the following: (a) additional end of chapter problems have been included; (b) more information on power has been added, particularly use of the

G*Power software with screenshots; (c) content has been updated and numerous additional references have been provided; (d) the final chapter on logistic regression has been added for a more complete presentation of regression models; (e) numerous SPSS (version 19) screenshots on statistical techniques and their assumptions have been included to assist in the generation and interpretation of output; (f) more information has been added to most chapters on SPSS; (g) research vignettes and templates have been added to the beginning and end of each chapter, respectively; (h) a discussion of expected mean squares has been folded into the analysis of variance chapters to provide a rationale for the formation of proper F ratios; and (i) a website for the text that provides students and instructors access to detailed solutions to the book's odd-numbered problems; chapter outlines; lists of key terms for each chapter; and SPSS datasets that correspond to the chapter examples and end-of-chapter problems that can be used in SPSS and other packages such as SAS, HLM, STATA, and LISREL. Only instructors are granted access to the PowerPoint slides for each chapter that include examples and APA style write ups, chapter outlines, and key terms; multiple-choice (approximately 25 for each chapter) and short answer (approximately 5 for each chapter) test questions; and answers to the even-numbered problems. This material is available at: http://www.psypress.com/statistical-concepts-9780415880077.

Acknowledgments

There are many individuals whose assistance enabled the completion of this book. We would like to thank the following individuals whom we studied with in school: Jamie Algina, Lloyd Bond, Amy Broeseker, Jim Carlson, Bill Cooley, Judy Giesen, Brian Gray, Harry Hsu, Mary Nell McNeese, Camille Ogden, Lou Pingel, Rod Roth, Charles Stegman, and Neil Timm. Next, numerous colleagues have played an important role in our personal and professional lives as statisticians. Rather than include an admittedly incomplete listing, we just say "thank you" to all of you. You know who you are.

Thanks also to all of the wonderful people at Lawrence Erlbaum Associates (LEA), in particular, to Ray O'Connell for inspiring this project back in 1986, and to Debra Riegert (formerly at LEA and now at Routledge) for supporting the development of subsequent texts and editions. We are most appreciative of the insightful suggestions provided by the reviewers of this text over the years, and in particular the reviewers of this edition: Robert P. Conti, Sr. (Mount Saint Mary College), Feifei Ye (University of Pittsburgh), Nan Thornton (Capella University), and one anonymous reviewer. A special thank you to all of the terrific students that we have had the pleasure of teaching at the University of Pittsburgh, the University of Illinois–Chicago, Louisiana State University, Boston College, Northern Illinois University, the University of Alabama, The Ohio State University, and the University of Central Florida. For all of your efforts, and the many lights that you have seen and shared with us, this book is for you. We are most grateful to our families, in particular to Lea and Kristen, and to Mark and Malani. It is because of your love and understanding that we were able to cope with such a major project. Thank you one and all.

Richard G. Lomax
Debbie L. Hahs-Vaughn

1

One-Factor Analysis of Variance: Fixed-Effects Model

Chapter Outline

Key Concepts

1. Between- and within-groups variability
2. Sources of variation
3. Partitioning the sums of squares
4. The ANOVA model
5. Expected mean squares

The first six chapters are concerned with different analysis of variance (ANOVA) models. In this chapter, we consider the most basic ANOVA model, known as the one-factor ANOVA model. Recall the independent *t* test from Chapter 7 of *An Introduction to Statistical Concepts*, Third Edition where the means from two independent samples were compared. What if you wish to compare more than two means? The answer is to use the **analysis of variance**. At this point, you may be wondering why the procedure is called the analysis of variance rather than the analysis of means, because the intent is to study possible mean differences. One way of comparing a set of means is to think in terms of the variability among those means. If the sample means are all the same, then the variability of those means would be 0. If the sample means are not all the same, then the variability of those means would be somewhat greater than 0. In general, the greater the mean differences are, the greater is the variability of the means. Thus, mean differences are studied by looking at the variability of the means; hence, the term analysis of variance is appropriate rather than analysis of means (further discussed in this chapter).

We use X to denote our single **independent variable**, which we typically refer to as a **factor**, and Y to denote our **dependent** (or **criterion**) **variable**. Thus, the one-factor ANOVA is a bivariate, or two-variable, procedure. Our interest here is in determining whether mean differences exist on the dependent variable. Stated another way, the researcher is interested in the influence of the independent variable on the dependent variable. For example, a researcher may want to determine the influence that method of instruction has on statistics achievement. The independent variable, or factor, would be method of instruction and the dependent variable would be statistics achievement. Three different methods of instruction that might be compared are large lecture hall instruction, small-group instruction, and computer-assisted instruction. Students would be randomly assigned to one of the three methods of instruction and at the end of the semester evaluated as to their level of achievement in statistics. These results would be of interest to a statistics instructor in determining the most effective method of instruction (where "effective" is measured by student performance in statistics). Thus, the instructor may opt for the method of instruction that yields the highest mean achievement.

There are a number of new concepts introduced in this chapter as well as a refresher of concepts that have been covered in your introductory course. The concepts addressed in this chapter include the following: independent and dependent variables; between- and within-groups variability; fixed and random effects; the linear model; partitioning of the sums of squares; degrees of freedom, mean square terms, and *F* ratios; the ANOVA summary table; expected mean squares; balanced and unbalanced models; and alternative ANOVA procedures. Our objectives are that by the end of this chapter, you will be able to (a) understand the characteristics and concepts underlying a one-factor ANOVA, (b) generate and interpret the results of a one-factor ANOVA, and (c) understand and evaluate the assumptions of the one-factor ANOVA.

X = independent variable
Y = dependent variable

1.1 Characteristics of One-Factor ANOVA Model

We are following Marie, our very capable educational research graduate student, as she develops her statistical skills. As we will see, Marie is embarking on a very exciting research adventure of her own.

Marie is enrolled in an independent study class. As part of the course requirement, she has to complete a research study. In collaboration with the statistics faculty in her program, Marie designs an experimental study to determine if there is a mean difference in student attendance in the statistics lab based on the attractiveness of the statistics lab instructor. Marie's research question is: *Is there a mean difference in the number of statistics labs attended by students based on the attractiveness of the lab instructor?* Marie determined that a one-way ANOVA was the best statistical procedure to use to answer her question. Her next task is to collect and analyze the data to address her research question.

This section describes the distinguishing characteristics of the one-factor ANOVA model. Suppose you are interested in comparing the means of two independent samples. Here the independent *t* test would be the method of choice (or perhaps the Welch *t'* test). What if your interest is in comparing the means of more than two independent samples? One possibility is to conduct multiple independent *t* tests on each pair of means. For example, if you wished to determine whether the means from five independent samples are the same, you could do all possible pairwise *t* tests. In this case, the following null hypotheses could be evaluated: $\mu_1 = \mu_2, \mu_1 = \mu_3, \mu_1 = \mu_4, \mu_1 = \mu_5, \mu_2 = \mu_3, \mu_2 = \mu_4, \mu_2 = \mu_5, \mu_3 = \mu_4, \mu_3 = \mu_5$, and $\mu_4 = \mu_5$. Thus, we would have to carry out 10 different independent *t* tests. The number of possible pairwise *t* tests that could be done for *J* means is equal to $\frac{1}{2}[J(J - 1)]$.

Is there a problem in conducting so many *t* tests? Yes; the problem has to do with the probability of making a Type I error (i.e., α), where the researcher incorrectly rejects a true null hypothesis. Although the α level for each *t* test can be controlled at a specified nominal α level that is set by the researcher, say .05, what happens to the overall α level for the entire set of tests? The overall α level for the entire set of tests (i.e., α_{total}), often called the **experimentwise Type I error rate,** is larger than the α level for each of the individual *t* tests.

In our example, we are interested in comparing the means for 10 pairs of groups (again, these would be $\mu_1 = \mu_2, \mu_1 = \mu_3, \mu_1 = \mu_4, \mu_1 = \mu_5, \mu_2 = \mu_3, \mu_2 = \mu_4, \mu_2 = \mu_5, \mu_3 = \mu_4, \mu_3 = \mu_5$, and $\mu_4 = \mu_5$). A *t* test is conducted for each of the 10 pairs of groups at $\alpha = .05$. Although each test controls the α level at .05, the overall α level will be larger because the risk of a Type I error accumulates across the tests. For each test, we are taking a risk; the more tests we do, the more risks we are taking. This can be explained by considering the risk you take each day you drive your car to school or work. The risk of an accident is small for any 1 day; however, over the period of a year, the risk of an accident is much larger.

For *C* independent (or orthogonal) tests, the experimentwise error is as follows:

$$\alpha_{total} = 1 - (1 - \alpha)^C$$

Assume for the moment that our 10 tests are independent (although they are not because within those 10 tests, each group is actually being compared to another group in four different instances). If we go ahead with our 10 *t* tests at $\alpha = .05$, then the experimentwise error rate is

$$\alpha_{total} = 1 - (1 - .05)^{10} = 1 - .60 = .40$$

Although we are seemingly controlling our α level at the .05 level, the probability of making a Type I error across all 10 tests is .40. In other words, in the long run, if we conduct 10 independent *t* tests, 4 times out of 10, we will make a Type I error. For this reason, we do not want to do all possible *t* tests. Before we move on, the experimentwise error rate for *C* dependent tests α_{total} (which would be the case when doing all possible pairwise *t* tests, as in our example) is more difficult to determine, so let us just say that

$$\alpha \leq \alpha_{total} \leq C\alpha$$

Are there other options available to us where we can maintain better control over our experimentwise error rate? The optimal solution, in terms of maintaining control over our overall α level as well as maximizing power, is to conduct one overall test, often called an **omnibus test**. Recall that power has to do with the probability of correctly rejecting a false null hypothesis. The omnibus test could assess the equality of all of the means simultaneously and is the one used in ANOVA. The one-factor ANOVA then represents an extension of the independent *t* test for two or more independent sample means, where the experimentwise error rate is controlled.

In addition, the one-factor ANOVA has only one independent variable or factor with two or more levels. The independent variable is a discrete or grouping variable, where each subject responds to only one level. The levels represent the different samples or groups or treatments whose means are to be compared. In our example, method of instruction is the independent variable with three levels: large lecture hall, small-group, and computer-assisted. There are two ways of conceptually thinking about the selection of levels. In the fixed-effects model, all levels that the researcher is interested in are included in the design and analysis for the study. As a result, generalizations can only be made about those particular levels of the independent variable that are actually selected. For instance, if a researcher is only interested in these three methods of instruction—large lecture hall, small-group, and computer-assisted—then only those levels are incorporated into the study. Generalizations about other methods of instruction cannot be made because no other methods were considered for selection. Other examples of fixed-effects independent variables might be SES, gender, specific types of drug treatment, age group, weight, or marital status.

In the random-effects model, the researcher randomly samples some levels of the independent variable from the population of levels. As a result, generalizations can be made about all of the levels in the population, even those not actually sampled. For instance, a researcher interested in teacher effectiveness may have randomly sampled history teachers (i.e., the independent variable) from the population of history teachers in a particular school district. Generalizations can then be made about other history teachers in that school district not actually sampled. The random selection of levels is much the same as the random selection of individuals or objects in the random sampling process. This is the nature of inferential statistics, where inferences are made about a population (of individuals, objects, or levels) from a sample. Other examples of random-effects independent variables might be randomly selected classrooms, types of medication, animals, or time (e.g., hours, days). The remainder of this chapter is concerned with the fixed-effects model. Chapter 5 discusses the random-effects model in more detail.

In the fixed-effects model, once the levels of the independent variable are selected, subjects (i.e., persons or objects) are randomly assigned to the levels of the independent variable. In certain situations, the researcher does not have control over which level a subject is assigned to. The groups may already be in place when the researcher arrives on the scene. For instance, students may be assigned to their classes at the beginning of the year by the school administration. Researchers typically have little input regarding class assignments.

In another situation, it may be theoretically impossible to assign subjects to groups. For example, as much as we might like, researchers cannot randomly assign individuals to an age level. Thus, a distinction needs to be made about whether or not the researcher can control the assignment of subjects to groups. Although the analysis will not be altered, the interpretation of the results will be. When researchers have control over group assignments, the extent to which they can generalize their findings is greater than for those researchers who do not have such control. For further information on the differences between **true experimental designs** (i.e., with random assignment) and **quasi-experimental designs** (i.e., without random assignment), take a look at Campbell and Stanley (1966), Cook and Campbell (1979), and Shadish, Cook, and Campbell (2002).

Moreover, in the model being considered here, each subject is exposed to only one level of the independent variable. Chapter 5 deals with models where a subject is exposed to multiple levels of an independent variable; these are known as **repeated-measures models**. For example, a researcher may be interested in observing a group of young children repeatedly over a period of several years. Thus, each child might be observed every 6 months from birth to 5 years of age. This would require a repeated-measures design because the observations of a particular child over time are obviously not independent observations.

One final characteristic is the measurement scale of the independent and dependent variables. In ANOVA, because this is a test of means, a condition of the test is that the scale of measurement on the dependent variable is at the interval or ratio level. If the dependent variable is measured at the ordinal level, then the nonparametric equivalent, the Kruskal–Wallis test, should be considered (discussed later in this chapter). If the dependent variable shares properties of both the ordinal and interval levels (e.g., grade point average [GPA]), then both the ANOVA and Kruskal–Wallis procedures could be considered to cross-reference any potential effects of the measurement scale on the results. As previously mentioned, the independent variable is a grouping or discrete variable, so it can be measured on any scale.

However, there is one caveat to the measurement scale of the independent variable. Technically the condition is that the independent variable be a grouping or discrete variable. Most often, ANOVAs are conducted with independent variables which are categorical— nominal or ordinal in scale. ANOVAs can also be used in the case of interval or ratio values that are discrete. Recall that discrete variables are variables that can only take on certain values and that arise from the counting process. An example of a discrete variable that could be a good candidate for being an independent variable in an ANOVA model is number of children. What would make this a good candidate? The responses to this variable would likely be relatively limited (in the general population, it may be anticipated that the range would be from zero children to five or six—although outliers may be a possibility), and each discrete value would likely have multiple cases (with fewer cases having larger numbers of children). Applying this is obviously at the researcher's discretion; at some point, the number of discrete values can become so numerous as to be unwieldy in an ANOVA model. Thus, while at first glance we may not consider it appropriate to use interval or ratio variables as independent variables in ANOVA models, there are situations where it is feasible and appropriate.

In summary, the characteristics of the one-factor ANOVA fixed-effects model are as follows: (a) control of the experimentwise error rate through an omnibus test; (b) one independent variable with two or more levels; (c) the levels of the independent variable are fixed by the researcher; (d) subjects are randomly assigned to these levels; (e) subjects are exposed to only one level of the independent variable; and (f) the dependent

TABLE 1.1

Layout for the One-Factor ANOVA Model

	Level of the Independent Variable					
	1	2	3	...	J	
	Y_{11}	Y_{12}	Y_{13}	...	Y_{1J}	
	Y_{21}	Y_{22}	Y_{23}	...	Y_{2J}	
	Y_{31}	Y_{32}	Y_{33}	...	Y_{3J}	
	.	.	.	.	.	
	.	.	.	.	.	
	Y_{n1}	Y_{n2}	Y_{n3}	...	Y_{nJ}	
Means	$\bar{Y}_{.1}$	$\bar{Y}_{.2}$	$\bar{Y}_{.3}$	...	$\bar{Y}_{.J}$	$\bar{Y}_{..}$

variable is measured at least at the interval level, although the Kruskal–Wallis one-factor ANOVA can be considered for an ordinal level dependent variable. In the context of experimental design, the one-factor ANOVA is often referred to as the **completely randomized design**.

1.2 Layout of Data

Before we get into the theory and analysis of the data, let us examine one tabular form of the data, known as the layout of the data. We designate each observation as Y_{ij}, where the j subscript tells us what group or level the observation belongs to and the i subscript tells us the observation or identification number within that group. For instance, Y_{34} would mean this is the third observation in the fourth group, or level, of the independent variable. The first subscript ranges over $i = 1,\ldots, n$, and the second subscript ranges over $j = 1,\ldots, J$. Thus, there are J levels (or categories or groups) of the independent variable and n subjects in each group, for a total of $Jn = N$ total observations. For now, presume there are n subjects (or cases or units) in each group in order to simplify matters; this is referred to as the **equal n's** or **balanced case**. Later on in this chapter, we consider the **unequal n's** or **unbalanced case**.

The layout of the data is shown in Table 1.1. Here we see that each column represents the observations for a particular group or level of the independent variable. At the bottom of each column are the sample group means ($\bar{Y}_{.j}$), with the overall sample mean ($\bar{Y}_{..}$) to the far right. In conclusion, the layout of the data is one form in which the researcher can think about the data.

1.3 ANOVA Theory

This section examines the underlying theory and logic of ANOVA, the sums of squares, and the ANOVA summary table. As noted previously, in ANOVA, mean differences are tested by looking at the variability of the means. Here we show precisely how this is done.

1.3.1 General Theory and Logic

We begin with the hypotheses to be tested in ANOVA. In the two-group situation of the independent t test, the null and alternative hypotheses for a two-tailed (i.e., nondirectional) test are as follows:

$$H_0: \mu_1 = \mu_2$$

$$H_1: \mu_1 \neq \mu_2$$

In the multiple-group situation (i.e., more than two groups), we have already seen the problem that occurs when multiple independent t tests are conducted for all pairs of population means (i.e., increased likelihood of a Type I error). We concluded that the solution was to use an *omnibus test* where the equality of all of the means could be assessed simultaneously. The hypotheses for the omnibus ANOVA test are as follows:

$$H_0: \mu_1 = \mu_2 = \mu_3 = \cdots = \mu_J$$

$$H_1: \text{not all the } \mu_j \text{ are equal}$$

Here H_1 is purposely written in a general form to cover the multitude of possible mean differences that could arise. These range from only two of the means being different to all of the means being different from one another. Thus, because of the way H_1 has been written, only a nondirectional alternative is appropriate. If H_0 were to be rejected, then the researcher might want to consider a multiple comparison procedure (MCP) so as to determine which means or combination of means are significantly different (we cover this in greater detail in Chapter 2).

As was mentioned in the introduction to this chapter, the analysis of mean differences is actually carried out by looking at variability of the means. At first, this seems strange. If one wants to test for mean differences, then do a test of means. If one wants to test for variance differences, then do a test of variances. These statements should make sense because logic pervades the field of statistics. And they do for the two-group situation. For the multiple-group situation, we already know things get a bit more complicated.

Say a researcher is interested in the influence of amount of daily study time on statistics achievement. Three groups were formed based on the amount of daily study time in statistics, half an hour, 1 hour, and 2 hours. Is there a differential influence of amount of time studied on subsequent mean statistics achievement (e.g., statistics final exam)? We would expect that the more one studied statistics, the higher the statistics mean achievement would be. One possible situation in the population is where the amount of study time does not influence statistics achievement; here the population means will be equal. That is, the null hypothesis of equal group means is actually true. Thus, the three groups are really three samples from the same population of students, with mean μ. The means are equal; thus, there is no variability among the three group means. A second possible situation in the population is where the amount of study time does influence statistics achievement; here the population means will not be equal. That is, the null hypothesis is actually false. Thus, the three groups are not really three samples from the same population of students, but rather, each group represents a sample from a distinct population of students receiving that particular amount of study time, with mean μ_j. The means are not equal, so there is variability among the three group means. In summary, the statistical question becomes whether the difference between the sample means is due to the usual sampling variability expected from a single population, or the result of a true difference between the sample means from different populations.

We conceptually define **within-groups variability** as the variability of the observations within a group combined across groups (e.g., variability on test scores within children in the same proficiency level, such as low, moderate, and high, and then combined across all proficiency levels), and **between-groups variability** as the variability between the groups (e.g., variability among the test scores from one proficiency level to another proficiency level). In Figure 1.1, the columns represent low and high variability *within* the groups. The rows represent low and high variability *between* the groups. In the upper left-hand plot, there is low variability both within and between the groups. That is, performance is very consistent, both within each group as well as across groups. We see that there is little variability *within* the groups since the individual distributions are not very spread out and little variability *between* the groups because the distributions are not very distinct, as they are nearly lying on top of one another. Here within- and between-group variability are both low, and it is quite unlikely that one would reject H_0. In the upper right-hand plot, there is high variability within the groups and low variability between the groups. That is, performance is very consistent across groups (i.e., the distributions largely overlap) but quite variable within each group. We see high variability *within* the groups because the spread of each individual distribution is quite large and low variability *between* the groups because the distributions are lying so closely together. Here within-groups variability exceeds between-group variability, and again it is quite unlikely that one would reject H_0. In the lower left-hand plot, there is low variability within the groups and high variability between the groups. That is, performance is very consistent within each group but quite variable across groups. We see low variability *within* the groups because each distribution is very compact with little spread to the data and high variability *between* the groups because each distribution is nearly isolated from one another with very little overlap. Here between-group variability exceeds within-groups variability, and it is quite

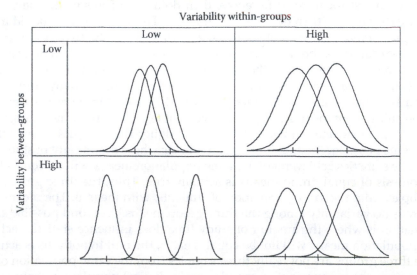

FIGURE 1.1
Conceptual look at between- and within-groups variability.

likely that one would reject H_0. In the lower right-hand plot, there is high variability both within and between the groups. That is, performance is quite variable within each group, as well as across the groups. We see high variability *within* groups because the spread of each individual distribution is quite large and high variability *between* groups because of the minimal overlap from one distribution to another. Here within- and between-group variability are both high, and depending on the relative amounts of between- and within-groups variability, one may or may not reject H_0. In summary, the optimal situation when seeking to reject H_0 is the one represented by high variability between the groups and low variability within the groups.

1.3.2 Partitioning the Sums of Squares

The partitioning of the sums of squares in ANOVA is a new concept in this chapter, which is also an important concept in regression analysis (from Chapters 7 and 8). In part, this is because ANOVA and regression are both forms of the same general linear model (GLM) (to be further discussed). Let us begin with the total sum of squares in Y, denoted as SS_{total}. The term SS_{total} represents the amount of total variation in Y. The next step is to partition the total variation into variation between the groups (i.e., the categories or levels of the independent variable), denoted by SS_{betw}, and variation within the groups (i.e., units or cases within each category or level of the independent variable), denoted by SS_{with}. In the one-factor ANOVA, we therefore partition SS_{total} as follows:

$$SS_{total} = SS_{betw} + SS_{with}$$

or

$$\sum_{i=1}^{n}\sum_{j=1}^{J}(Y_{ij} - \bar{Y}_{..})^2 = \sum_{i=1}^{n}\sum_{j=1}^{J}(\bar{Y}_{.j} - \bar{Y}_{..})^2 + \sum_{i=1}^{n}\sum_{j=1}^{J}(Y_{ij} - \bar{Y}_{.j})^2$$

where

SS_{total} is the total sum of squares due to variation among all of the observations without regard to group membership

SS_{betw} is the between-groups sum of squares due to the variation between the groups

SS_{with} is the within-groups sum of squares due to the variation within the groups combined across groups

We refer to this particular formulation of the partitioned sums of squares as the **definitional** (or **conceptual**) **formula** because each term literally defines a form of variation.

Due to computational complexity and the likelihood of a computational error, the definitional formula is rarely used with real data. Instead, a **computational formula** for the partitioned sums of squares is used for hand computations. However, since nearly all data analysis at this level utilizes computer software, we defer to the software to actually perform an ANOVA (SPSS details are provided toward the end of this chapter). A complete example of the one-factor ANOVA is also considered later in this chapter.

1.3.3 ANOVA Summary Table

An important result of the analysis is the **ANOVA summary table**. The purpose of the summary table is to literally summarize the ANOVA. A general form of the summary table is shown in Table 1.2. The first column lists the sources of variation in the model. As we already know, in the one-factor model, the total variation is partitioned into between-groups variation and within-groups variation. The second column notes the sums of squares terms computed for each source (i.e., SS_{betw}, SS_{with}, and SS_{total}).

The third column gives the degrees of freedom for each source. Recall that, in general, the degrees of freedom have to do with the number of observations that are free to vary. For example, if a sample mean and all of the sample observations except for one are known, then the final observation is not free to vary. That is, the final observation is predetermined to be a particular value. For instance, say the mean is 10 and there are three observations, 7, 11, and an unknown observation. Based on that information, first, the sum of the three observations must be 30 for the mean to be 10. Second, the sum of the known observations is 18. Therefore, the unknown observation must be 12. Otherwise the sample mean would not be exactly equal to 10.

For the between-groups source, the definitional formula is concerned with the deviation of each group mean from the overall mean. There are J group means (where J represents the number of groups or categories or levels of the independent variable), so the df_{betw} (also known as the degrees of freedom numerator) must be $J - 1$. Why? If we have J group means and we know the overall mean, then only $J - 1$ of the group means are free to vary. In other words, if we know the overall mean and all but one of the group means, then the final unknown group mean is predetermined. For the within-groups source, the definitional formula is concerned with the deviation of each observation from its respective group mean. There are n observations (i.e., cases or units) in each group; consequently, there are $n - 1$ degrees of freedom in each group and J groups. Why are there $n - 1$ degrees of freedom in each group? If there are n observations in each group, then only $n - 1$ of the observations are free to vary. In other words, if we know one group mean and all but one of the observations for that group, then the final unknown observation for that group is predetermined. There are J groups, so the df_{with} (also known as the degrees of freedom denominator) is $J(n - 1)$, or more simply as $N - J$. Thus, we lose one degree of freedom for each group. For the total source, the definitional formula is concerned with the deviation of each observation from the overall mean. There are N total observations; therefore, the df_{total} must be $N - 1$. Why? If there are N total observations and we know the overall mean, then only $N - 1$ of the observations are free to vary. In other words, if we know the overall mean and all but one of the N observations, then the final unknown observation is predetermined.

Why is the number of degrees of freedom important in the ANOVA? Suppose two researchers have conducted similar studies, except Researcher A uses 20 observations per group and Researcher B uses 10 observations per group. Each researcher obtains a SS_{with} value of 15. Would it be fair to say that this particular result for the two studies is the same?

TABLE 1.2

ANOVA Summary Table

Source	SS	df	MS	F
Between groups	SS_{betw}	$J - 1$	MS_{betw}	MS_{betw}/MS_{with}
Within groups	SS_{with}	$N - J$	MS_{with}	
Total	SS_{total}	$N - 1$		

Such a comparison would be unfair because SS_{with} is influenced by the number of observations per group. A fair comparison would be to weight the SS_{with} terms by their respective number of degrees of freedom. Similarly, it would not be fair to compare the SS_{betw} terms from two similar studies based on different numbers of groups. A fair comparison would be to weight the SS_{betw} terms by their respective number of degrees of freedom. The method of weighting a sum of squares term by the respective number of degrees of freedom on which it is based yields what is called a **mean squares** term. Thus, $MS_{betw} = SS_{betw}/df_{betw}$ and $MS_{with} = SS_{with}/df_{with}$, as shown in the fourth column of Table 1.2. They are referred to as mean squares because they represent a summed quantity that is weighted by the number of observations used in the sum itself, like the mean. The mean squares terms are also variance estimates because they represent the sum of the squared deviations from a mean divided by their degrees of freedom, like the sample variance s^2.

The last column in the ANOVA summary table, the *F* value, is the summary test statistic of the summary table. The *F* value is computed by taking the ratio of the two mean squares or variance terms. Thus, for the one-factor ANOVA fixed-effects model, the *F* value is computed as $F = MS_{betw}/MS_{with}$. When developed by Sir Ronald A. Fisher in the 1920s, this test statistic was originally known as the variance ratio because it represents the ratio of two variance estimates. Later, the variance ratio was renamed the *F* ratio by George W. Snedecor (who worked out the table of *F* values, discussed momentarily) in honor of Fisher (*F* for Fisher).

The *F* ratio tells us whether there is more variation *between* groups than there is *within* groups, which is required if we are to reject H_0. Thus, if there is more variation *between* groups than there is *within* groups, then MS_{betw} will be larger than MS_{with}. As a result of this, the *F* ratio of MS_{betw}/MS_{with} will be greater than 1. If, on the other hand, the amount of variation *between* groups is about the same as there is *within* groups, then MS_{betw} and MS_{with} will be about the same, and the *F* ratio will be approximately 1. Thus, we want to find large *F* values in order to reject the null hypothesis. The *F* test statistic is then compared with the *F* critical value so as to make a decision about the null hypothesis. The critical value is found in the *F* table of Table A.4 as $_\alpha F_{(J-1, N-J)}$. Thus, the degrees of freedom are $df_{betw} = J - 1$ for the numerator of the *F* ratio and $df_{with} = N - J$ for the denominator of the *F* ratio. The significance test is a one-tailed test in order to be consistent with the alternative hypothesis. The null hypothesis is rejected if the *F* test statistic exceeds the *F* critical value. This is the omnibus *F* test which, again, simply provides evidence of the extent to which there is at least one statistically significant mean difference between the groups.

If the *F* test statistic exceeds the *F* critical value, and there are more than two groups, then it is not clear where the differences among the means lie. In this case, some MCP should be used to determine where the mean differences are in the groups; this is the topic of Chapter 2. When there are only two groups, it is obvious where the mean difference falls, that is, between groups 1 and 2. A researcher can simply look at the descriptive statistics to determine which group had the higher mean relative to the other group. For the two-group situation, it is also interesting to note that the *F* and *t* test statistics follow the rule of $F = t^2$, for a nondirectional alternative hypothesis in the independent *t* test. In other words, the one-way ANOVA with two groups and the independent *t* test will generate the same conclusion such that $F = t^2$. This result occurs when the numerator degrees of freedom for the *F* ratio is 1. In an actual ANOVA summary table (shown in the next section), except for the source of variation column, it is the values for each of the other entries generated from the data that are listed in the table. For example, instead of seeing SS_{betw}, we would see the computed value of SS_{betw}.

1.4 ANOVA Model

In this section, we introduce the ANOVA linear model, the estimation of parameters of the model, effect size measures, confidence intervals (CIs), power, and an example, and finish up with expected mean squares.

1.4.1 Model

The one-factor ANOVA fixed-effects model can be written in terms of population parameters as

$$Y_{ij} = \mu + \alpha_j + \varepsilon_{ij}$$

where
   Y is the observed score on the dependent (or criterion) variable for individual i in group j
   μ is the overall or grand population mean (i.e., regardless of group designation)
   α_j is the group effect for group j
   ε_{ij} is the random residual error for individual i in group j

The residual error can be due to individual differences, measurement error, and/or other factors not under investigation (i.e., other than the independent variable X). The population group effect and residual error are computed as

$$\alpha_j = \mu_{.j} - \mu$$

and

$$\varepsilon_{ij} = Y_{ij} - \mu_{.j}$$

respectively, and $\mu_{.j}$ is the population mean for group j, where the initial dot subscript indicates we have averaged across all i individuals in group j. That is, the group effect is equal to the difference between the population mean of group j and the overall population mean. The residual error is equal to the difference between an individual's observed score and the population mean of the group that the individual is a member of (i.e., group j). The group effect can also be thought of as the average effect of being a member of a particular group. A positive group effect implies a group mean greater than the overall mean, whereas a negative group effect implies a group mean less than the overall mean. Note that in a one-factor fixed-effects model, the population group effects sum to 0. The residual error in ANOVA represents that portion of Y not accounted for by X.

1.4.2 Estimation of the Parameters of the Model

Next we need to estimate the parameters of the model μ, α_j, and ε_{ij}. The sample estimates are represented by $\bar{Y}_{.}$, a_j, and e_{ij}, respectively, where the latter two are computed as

$$a_j = \bar{Y}_{.j} - \bar{Y}_{..}$$

and

$$e_{ij} = Y_{ij} - \bar{Y}_{.j}$$

respectively. Note that $\bar{Y}_{..}$ represents the overall sample mean, where the double dot subscript indicates we have averaged across both the i and j subscripts, and $\bar{Y}_{.j}$ represents the sample mean for group j, where the initial dot subscript indicates we have averaged across all i individuals in group j.

1.4.3 Effect Size Measures, Confidence Intervals, and Power

1.4.3.1 Effect Size Measures

There are various effect size measures to indicate the strength of association between X and Y, that is, the relative strength of the group effect. Let us briefly examine η^2, ω^2, and Cohen's (1988) f. First, η^2 (eta squared), ranging from 0 to +1.00, is known as the correlation ratio (generalization of R^2) and represents the proportion of variation in Y explained by the group mean differences in X. An eta squared of 0 suggests that *none* of the total variance in the dependent variable is due to differences between the groups. An eta squared of 1.00 indicates that *all* the variance in the dependent variable is due to the group mean differences. We find η^2 to be as follows:

$$\eta^2 = \frac{SS_{betw}}{SS_{total}}$$

It is well known that η^2 is a positively biased statistic (i.e., overestimates the association). The bias is most evident for n's (i.e., group sample sizes) less than 30.

Another effect size measure is ω^2 (omega squared), interpreted similarly to eta squared (specifically proportion of variation in Y explained by the group mean differences in X) but which is less biased than η^2. We determine ω^2 through the following formula:

$$\omega^2 = \frac{SS_{betw} - (J-1)MS_{with}}{SS_{total} + MS_{with}}$$

A final effect size measure is f developed by Cohen (1988). The effect f can take on values from 0 (when the means are equal) to an infinitely large positive value. This effect is interpreted as an approximate correlation index but can also be interpreted as the standard deviation of the standardized means (Cohen, 1988). We compute f through the following:

$$f = \sqrt{\frac{\eta^2}{1-\eta^2}}$$

COHEN's F

We can also use f to compute the effect size d, which you recall from the t test is interpreted as the standardized mean difference. The formulas for translating f to d are dependent on whether there is minimum, moderate, or maximum variability between the means of the groups. Interested readers are referred to Cohen (1988).

IMP.

These are the most common measures of effect size used for ANOVA models, both in statistics software and in print. Cohen's (1988) subjective standards can be used as follows to interpret these effect sizes: small effect, $f = .1$, η^2 or $\omega^2 = .01$; medium effect, $f = .25$, η^2 or $\omega^2 = .06$; and large effect, $f = .40$, η^2 or $\omega^2 = .14$. Note that these are subjective standards developed for the behavioral sciences; your discipline may use other standards. For further discussion, see Keppel (1982), O'Grady (1982), Wilcox (1987), Cohen (1988), Keppel and Wickens (2004), and Murphy, Myors, and Wolach (2008; which includes software).

1.4.3.2 Confidence Intervals

CI procedures are often useful in providing an interval estimate of a population parameter (i.e., mean or mean difference); these allow us to determine the accuracy of the sample estimate. One can form CIs around any sample group mean from an ANOVA (provided in software such as SPSS), although CIs for means have more utility for MCPs, as discussed in Chapter 2. CI procedures have also been developed for several effect size measures (Fidler & Thompson, 2001; Smithson, 2001).

1.4.3.3 Power

As for power (the probability of correctly rejecting a false null hypothesis), one can consider either planned power (a priori) or observed power (post hoc), as discussed in *Introduction to Statistical Concepts*, Third Edition. In the ANOVA context, we know that power is primarily a function of α, sample size, and effect size. For planned power, one inputs each of these components either into a statistical table or power chart (nicely arrayed in texts such as Cohen, 1988, or Murphy et al., 2008), or into statistical software (such as Power and Precision, Ex-Sample, G*Power, or the software contained in Murphy et al., 2008). Planned power is most often used by researchers to determine adequate sample sizes in ANOVA models, which is highly recommended. Many disciplines recommend a minimum power value, such as .80. Thus, these methods are a useful way to determine the sample size that would generate a desired level of power. Observed power is determined by some statistics software, such as SPSS, and indicates the power that was actually observed in a completed study.

1.4.4 Example

Consider now an example problem used throughout this chapter. Our dependent variable is the number of times a student attends statistics lab during one semester (or quarter), whereas the independent variable is the attractiveness of the lab instructor (assuming each instructor is of the same gender and is equally competent). The researcher is interested in whether the attractiveness of the instructor influences student attendance at the statistics lab. The attractiveness groups are defined as follows:

- Group 1, unattractive
- Group 2, slightly attractive
- Group 3, moderately attractive
- Group 4, very attractive

TABLE 1.3

Data and Summary Statistics for the Statistics Lab Example

	Number of Statistics Labs Attended by Group				
	Group 1: Unattractive	Group 2: Slightly Unattractive	Group 3: Moderately Attractive	Group 4: Very Attractive	Overall
	15	20	10	30	
	10	13	24	22	
	12	9	29	26	
	8	22	12	20	
	21	24	27	29	
	7	25	21	28	
	13	18	25	25	
	3	12	14	15	
Means	11.1250	17.8750	20.2500	24.3750	18.4063
Variances	30.1250	35.2679	53.0714	25.9821	56.4425

Students were randomly assigned to one group at the beginning of the semester, and attendance was taken by the instructor. There were 8 students in each group for a total of 32. Students could attend a maximum of 30 lab sessions. In Table 1.3, we see the raw data and sample statistics (means and variances) for each group and overall (far right).

The results are summarized in the ANOVA summary table as shown in Table 1.4. The test statistic, $F = 6.1877$, is compared to the critical value, $_{.05}F_{3,28} = 2.95$ obtained from Table A.4, using the .05 level of significance. To use the F table, find the numerator degrees of freedom, df_{betw}, which are represented by the columns, and then the denominator degrees of freedom, df_{with}, which are represented by the rows. The intersection of the two provides the F critical value. The test statistic exceeds the critical value, so we reject H_0 and conclude that level of attractiveness is related to mean differences in statistics lab attendance. The exact probability value (p value) given by SPSS is .001.

Next we examine the group effects and residual errors. The group effects are estimated as follows where the grand mean (irrespective of the group membership; here 18.4063) is subtracted from the group mean (e.g., 11.125 for group 1). The subscript of a indicates the level or group of the independent variable (e.g., 1 = unattractive; 2 = slightly attractive; 3 = moderately attractive; 4 = very attractive). A negative group effect indicates that group had a smaller mean than the overall average and thus exerted a negative effect on the dependent variable (in our case, lower attendance in the statistics lab). A positive group effect indi-

TABLE 1.4

ANOVA Summary Table—Statistics Lab Example

Source	SS	df	MS	F
Between groups	738.5938	3	246.1979	6.8177[a]
Within groups	1011.1250	28	36.1116	
Total	1749.7188	31		

[a] $_{.05}F_{3,28} = 2.95$.

cates that group had a larger mean than the overall average and thus exerted a positive effect on the dependent variable (in our case, higher attendance in the statistics lab):

$$a_1 = \bar{Y}_{.1} - \bar{Y}_{..} = 11.125 - 18.4063 = -7.2813$$

$$a_2 = \bar{Y}_{.2} - \bar{Y}_{..} = 17.875 - 18.4063 = -.5313$$

$$a_3 = \bar{Y}_{.3} - \bar{Y}_{..} = 20.250 - 18.4063 = +1.8437$$

$$a_4 = \bar{Y}_{.4} - \bar{Y}_{..} = 24.375 - 18.4063 = +5.9687$$

Thus, group 4 *(very attractive)* has the largest *positive* group effect (i.e., higher attendance than average), while group 1 *(unattractive)* has the largest *negative* group effect (i.e., lower attendance than average). In Chapter 2, we use the same data to determine which of these group means, or combination of group means, are statistically different. The residual errors (computed as the difference between the observed value and the group mean) for each individual by group are shown in Table 1.5 and discussed later in this chapter.

Finally we determine the effect size measures. For illustrative purposes, all effect size measures that were previously discussed have been computed. In practice, only one effect size is usually computed and interpreted. First, the correlation ratio η^2 is computed as follows:

$$\eta^2 = \frac{SS_{betw}}{SS_{total}} = \frac{738.5938}{1749.7188} = .4221$$

Next ω^2 is found to be the following:

$$\omega^2 = \frac{SS_{betw} - (J-1)MS_{with}}{SS_{total} + MS_{with}} = \frac{738.5938 - (3)36.1116}{1749.7188 + 36.1116} = .3529$$

Lastly f is computed as follows:

$$f = \sqrt{\frac{\eta^2}{1-\eta^2}} = \sqrt{\frac{.4221}{1-.4221}} = .8546$$

TABLE 1.5

Residuals for the Statistics Lab Example by Group

Group 1	Group 2	Group 3	Group 4
3.875	2.125	−10.250	5.625
−1.125	−4.875	3.750	−2.375
.875	−8.875	8.750	1.625
−3.125	4.125	−8.250	−4.375
9.875	6.125	6.750	4.625
−4.125	7.125	.750	3.625
1.875	.125	4.750	.625
−8.125	−5.875	−6.250	−9.375

Recall Cohen's (1988) subjective standards that can be used to interpret these effect sizes: small effect, $f = .1$, η^2 or $\omega^2 = .01$; medium effect, $f = .25$, η^2 or $\omega^2 = .06$; and large effect, $f = .40$, η^2 or $\omega^2 = .14$. Based on these effect size measures, all measures lead to the same conclusion: there is a large effect size for the influence of instructor attractiveness on lab attendance. Examining η^2 or ω^2, we can also state that 42% or 35%, respectively, of the variation in Y (attendance at the statistics lab) can be explained by X (attractiveness of the instructor). The effect f suggests a strong correlation.

In addition, if we rank the instructor group means from unattractive (with the lowest mean) to very attractive (with the highest mean), we see that the more attractive the instructor, the more inclined the student is to attend lab. While visual inspection of the means suggests descriptively that there are differences in statistics lab attendance by group, we examine MCPs with these same data in Chapter 2 to determine which groups are statistically significantly different from each other.

1.4.5 Expected Mean Squares

There is one more theoretical concept called **expected mean squares** to introduce in this chapter. The notion of expected mean squares provides the basis for determining what the appropriate error term is when forming an F ratio (recall this ratio is $F = MS_{betw}/MS_{with}$). That is, when forming an F ratio to test a certain hypothesis, how do we know which source of variation to use as the error term in the denominator? For instance, in the one-factor fixed-effects ANOVA model, how did we know to use MS_{with} as the error term in testing for differences between the groups? There is a good rationale, as becomes evident.

Before we get into expected mean squares, consider the definition of an expected value. An expected value is defined as the average value of a statistic that would be obtained with repeated sampling. Using the sample mean as an example statistic, the expected value of the mean would be the average value of the sample means obtained from an infinite number of samples. The expected value of a statistic is also known as the mean of the sampling distribution of that statistic. In this case, the expected value of the mean is the mean of the sampling distribution of the mean.

An expected mean square for a particular source of variation represents the average mean square value for that source obtained if the same study were to be repeated an infinite number of times. For instance, the expected value of MS_{betw}, denoted by $E(MS_{betw})$, is the average value of MS_{betw} over repeated samplings. At this point, you might be asking, "why not only be concerned about the values of the mean square terms for my own little study"? Well, the mean square terms from your little study do represent a sample from a population of mean square terms. Thus, sampling distributions and sampling variability are as much a concern in ANOVA as they are in other situations previously described in this text.

Now we are ready to see what the expected mean square terms actually look like. Consider the two situations of H_0 actually being true and H_0 actually being false. If H_0 is actually *true*, such that there really are *no* differences between the population group means, then the *expected mean squares* [represented in statistical notation as either $E(MS_{betw})$ or $E(MS_{with})$] are as follows:

$$E(MS_{betw}) = \sigma_\varepsilon^2$$

$$E(MS_{with}) = \sigma_\varepsilon^2$$

and thus the ratio of expected mean squares is as follows:

$$E(MS_{betw}) / E(MS_{with}) = 1$$

where the expected value of F is then $E(F) = df_{with}/(df_{with} - 2)$, and σ_ε^2 is the population variance of the residual errors. What this tells us is the following: if H_0 is actually true, then each of the J samples really comes from the same population with mean μ.

If H_0 is actually *false*, such that there really *are* differences between the population group means, then the expected mean squares are as follows:

$$E(MS_{betw}) = \sigma_\varepsilon^2 + \left(n \sum_{j=1}^{J} \alpha_j^2 \right) / (J-1)$$

$$E(MS_{with}) = \sigma_\varepsilon^2$$

and thus the ratio of the expected mean squares is as follows:

$$E(MS_{betw}) / E(MS_{with}) > 1$$

where $E(F) > df_{with}/(df_{with} - 2)$. If H_0 is actually false, then the J samples do really come from different populations with different means μ_j.

There is a difference in the expected mean square between [i.e., $E(MS_{betw})$] when H_0 is actually true as compared to when H_0 is actually false, as in the latter situation, there is a second term. The important part of this second term is $\sum_{j=1}^{J} \alpha_j^2$, which represents the sum of the squared group effects. The larger this part becomes, the larger MS_{betw} is, and thus the larger the F ratio becomes. In comparing the two situations, we also see that $E(MS_{with})$ is the same whether H_0 is actually true or false and thus represents a reliable estimate of σ_ε^2. This term is mean-free because it does not depend on group mean differences. Just to cover all of the possibilities, F could be less than 1 [or technically less than $df_{with}/(df_{with} - 2)$] due to sampling error, nonrandom samples, and/or assumption violations. For a mathematical proof of the E(MS) terms, see Kirk (1982, pp. 66–71).

Finally let us try to put all of this information together. In general, the F ratio represents the following:

$$F = (\text{systematic variability} + \text{error variability}) / (\text{error variability})$$

where, for the one-factor fixed-effects model, *systematic variability* is variability *between* the groups and *error variability* is variability *within* the groups. The F ratio is formed in a particular way because we want to isolate the systematic variability in the numerator. For this model, the only appropriate F ratio is MS_{betw}/MS_{with} because it does serve to isolate the systematic variability (i.e., the variability between the groups). That is, the appropriate error term for testing a particular effect (e.g., mean differences between groups) is the mean square that is identical to the mean square of that effect, except that it lacks a term due to the effect of interest. For this model, the appropriate error term to use for testing differences between groups is the mean square identical to the numerator MS_{betw}, except it lacks a term due to the between groups effect [i.e., $\left(n \sum_{j=1}^{J} \alpha_j^2 \right) / (J-1)$]; this, of course, is MS_{with}. It should also be noted that the F ratio is a ratio of two independent variance estimates, here being MS_{betw} and MS_{with}.

1.5 Assumptions and Violation of Assumptions

There are three standard assumptions made in ANOVA models, which we are already familiar with from the independent t test. We see these assumptions often in the remainder of this text. The assumptions are concerned with independence, homogeneity of variance, and normality. We also mention some techniques appropriate to use in evaluating each assumption.

1.5.1 Independence

The first assumption is that observations are independent of one another (both within samples and across samples). In general, the assumption of independence for ANOVA designs can be met by (a) keeping the assignment of individuals to groups separate through the design of the experiment (specifically random assignment—not to be confused with random selection), and (b) keeping the individuals separate from one another through experimental control so that the scores on the dependent variable Y for group 1 do not influence the scores for group 2 and so forth for other groups of the independent variable. Zimmerman (1997) also stated that independence can be violated for supposedly independent samples due to some type of matching in the design of the experiment (e.g., matched pairs based on gender, age, and weight).

The use of independent random samples is crucial in ANOVA. The F ratio is very sensitive to violation of the independence assumption in terms of increased likelihood of a Type I and/or Type II error (e.g., Glass, Peckham, & Sanders, 1972). This effect can sometimes even be worse with larger samples (Keppel & Wickens, 2004). A violation of the independence assumption may affect the standard errors of the sample means and thus influence any inferences made about those means. One purpose of random assignment of individuals to groups is to achieve independence. If each individual is only observed once and individuals are randomly assigned to groups, then the independence assumption is usually met. If individuals work together during the study (e.g., through discussion groups or group work), then independence may be compromised. Thus, a carefully planned, controlled, and conducted research design is the key to satisfying this assumption.

The simplest procedure for assessing independence is to examine residual plots by group. If the independence assumption is satisfied, then the residuals should fall into a random display of points for each group. If the assumption is violated, then the residuals will fall into some type of pattern. The Durbin–Watson statistic (1950, 1951, 1971) can be used to test for autocorrelation. Violations of the independence assumption generally occur in three situations: (1) when observations are collected over time, (2) when observations are made within blocks, or (3) when observation involves replication. For severe violations of the independence assumption, there is no simple "fix" (e.g., Scariano & Davenport, 1987). For the example data, a plot of the residuals by group is shown in Figure 1.2, and there does appear to be a random display of points for each group.

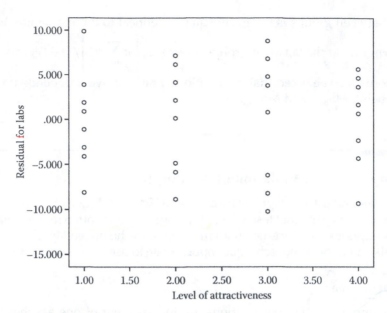

FIGURE 1.2
Residual plot by group for statistics lab example.

1.5.2 Homogeneity of Variance

The second assumption is that the variances of each population are equal. This is known as the assumption of **homogeneity of variance** or **homoscedasticity**. A violation of the homogeneity assumption can lead to bias in the SS_{with} term, as well as an increase in the Type I error rate and possibly an increase in the Type II error rate. Two sets of research studies have investigated violations of this assumption, classic work and more modern work.

The classic work largely resulted from Box (1954a) and Glass et al. (1972). Their results indicated that the effect of the violation was small with equal or nearly equal n's across the groups. There is a more serious problem if the larger n's are associated with the smaller variances (actual observed $\alpha >$ nominal α, which is a liberal result; for example, if a researcher desires a nominal alpha of .05, the alpha actually observed will be greater than .05), or if the larger n's are associated with the larger variances (actual observed $\alpha <$ nominal α, which is a conservative result). [Note that Bradley's (1978) criterion is used in this text, where the actual α should not exceed 1.1–1.5 times the nominal α.] Thus, the suggestion from the classic work was that heterogeneity was only a concern when there were unequal n's. However, the classic work only examined minor violations of the assumption (the ratio of largest variance to smallest variance being relatively small), and unfortunately, has been largely adapted in textbooks and by users.

There has been some research conducted since that time by researchers such as Brown and Forsythe (1974) and Wilcox (1986, 1987, 1988, 1989) and nicely summarized by Coombs, Algina, and Ottman (1996). In short, this more modern work indicates that the effect of heterogeneity is more severe than previously thought (e.g., poor power; α can be greatly affected), even with equal n's (although having equal n's does reduce the magnitude of the problem). Thus, F is not even robust to heterogeneity with equal n's (equal n's are sometimes referred to as a balanced design). Suggestions for dealing with such a violation include (a) using alternative procedures such as the Welch, Brown–Forsythe, and

James procedures (e.g., Coombs et al., 1996; Glass & Hopkins, 1996; Keppel & Wickens, 2004; Myers & Well, 1995; Wilcox, 1996, 2003); (b) reducing α and testing at a more stringent alpha level (e.g., .01 rather than the common .05) (e.g., Keppel & Wickens, 2004; Weinberg & Abramowitz, 2002); or (c) transforming Y (such as $\sqrt{Y}$, $1/Y$, or log Y) (e.g., Keppel & Wickens, 2004; Weinberg & Abramowitz, 2002). The alternative procedures will be more fully described later in this chapter.

In a plot of residuals versus each value of X, the consistency of the variance of the conditional residual distributions may be examined simply by eyeballing the plot. Another method for detecting violation of the homogeneity assumption is the use of formal statistical tests, as discussed in Chapter 9 of *An Introduction to Statistical Concepts*, Third Edition. The traditional homogeneity tests (e.g., Levene's test) are commonly available in statistical software, but are not robust to nonnormality. Unfortunately the more robust homogeneity tests are not readily available. For the example data, the residual plot of Figure 1.2 shows similar variances across the groups, and Levene's test suggests the variances are not different [$F(3, 28) = .905, p = .451$].

1.5.3 Normality

The third assumption is that each of the populations follows the normal distribution (i.e., there is normality of the dependent variable for each category or group or level of the independent variable). The F test is relatively robust to moderate violations of this assumption (i.e., in terms of Type I and II error rates). Specifically, effects of the violation will be minimal except for small n's, for unequal n's, and/or for extreme nonnormality. Violation of the normality assumption may be a result of outliers. The simplest outlier detection procedure is to look for observations that are more than two or three standard deviations from their respective group mean. We recommend (and will illustrate later) inspection of residuals for examination of evidence of normality. Formal procedures for the detection of outliers are now available in many statistical packages.

The following graphical techniques can be used to detect violations of the normality assumption: (a) the frequency distributions of the scores or the residuals for each group (through stem-and-leaf plots, boxplots, histograms, or residual plots), (b) the normal probability or quantile–quantile (Q–Q) plot, or (c) a plot of group means versus group variances (which should be independent of one another). There are also several statistical procedures available for the detection of nonnormality [e.g., the Shapiro–Wilk (S–W) test, 1965]. Transformations can also be used to normalize the data. For instance, a nonlinear relationship between X and Y may result in violations of the normality and/or homoscedasticity assumptions. Readers interested in learning more about potential data transformations are referred to sources such as Bradley (1982), Box and Cox (1964), or Mosteller and Tukey (1977).

In the example data, the residuals shown in Figure 1.2 appear to be somewhat normal in shape, especially considering the groups have fairly small n's. This is suggested by the random display of points. In addition, for the residuals overall, skewness = $-.2389$ and kurtosis = $-.0191$, indicating a small departure from normality. Thus, it appears that all of our assumptions have been satisfied for the example data. We will delve further into examination of assumptions later as we illustrate how to use SPSS to conduct a one-way ANOVA.

A summary of the assumptions and the effects of their violation for the one-factor ANOVA design are presented in Table 1.6. Note that in some texts, the assumptions are written in terms of the residuals rather than the raw scores, but this makes no difference for our purposes.

TABLE 1.6

Assumptions, Evidence to Examine, and Effects of Violations: One-Factor ANOVA Design

Assumption	Evidence to Examine	Effect of Assumption Violation
Independence	• Scatterplot of residuals by group	Increased likelihood of a Type I and/or Type II error in the F statistic; influences standard errors of means and thus inferences about those means
Homogeneity of variance	• Scatterplot of residuals by X • Formal test of equal variances (e.g., Levene's test)	Bias in SS_{with}; increased likelihood of a Type I and/or Type II error; less effect with equal or nearly equal n's; effect decreases as n increases
Normality	• Graphs of residuals (or scores) by group (e.g., boxplots, histograms, stem-and-leaf plots) • Skewness and kurtosis of residuals • Q–Q plots of residuals • Formal tests of normality of residuals • Plot of group means by group variances	Minimal effect with moderate violation; effect less severe with large n's, with equal or nearly equal n's, and/or with homogeneously shaped distributions

1.6 Unequal n's or Unbalanced Procedure

Up to this point in the chapter, we have only considered the equal n's or balanced case where the number of observations is equal for each group. This was done only to make things simple for presentation purposes. However, we do not need to assume that the n's must be equal (as some textbooks incorrectly do). This section briefly describes the **unequal n's or unbalanced case.** For our purposes, the major statistical software can handle the analysis of this case for the one-factor ANOVA model without any special attention. Thus, interpretation of the analysis, the assumptions, and so forth are the same as with the equal n's case. However, once we get to factorial designs in Chapter 3, things become a bit more complicated for the unequal n's or unbalanced case.

1.7 Alternative ANOVA Procedures

There are several alternatives to the parametric one-factor fixed-effects ANOVA. These include the Kruskal and Wallis (1952) one-factor ANOVA, the Welch (1951) test, the Brown and Forsythe (1974) procedure, and the James (1951) procedures. You may recognize the Welch and Brown–Forsythe procedures as similar alternatives to the independent t test.

1.7.1 Kruskal–Wallis Test

The Kruskal–Wallis test makes no normality assumption about the population distributions, although it assumes similar distributional shapes, but still assumes equal population variances across the groups (although heterogeneity does have some effect on this test, it is less than with the parametric ANOVA). When the normality assumption is met, or nearly so (i.e., with mild nonnormality), the parametric ANOVA is slightly more powerful than the Kruskal–Wallis test (i.e., less likelihood of a Type II error). Otherwise the Kruskal–Wallis test is more powerful.

The Kruskal–Wallis procedure works as follows. First, the observations on the dependent measure are rank ordered, regardless of group assignment (the ranking is done by the computer). That is, the observations are ranked from highest to lowest, disregarding group membership. The procedure essentially tests whether the mean ranks are different across the groups such that they are unlikely to represent random samples from the same population. Thus, according to the null hypothesis, the mean rank is the same for each group, whereas for the alternative hypothesis, the mean rank is not the same across groups. The test statistic is denoted by H and is compared to the critical value $_\alpha\chi^2_{J-1}$. The null hypothesis is rejected if the test statistic H exceeds the χ^2 critical value.

There are two situations to consider with this test. First, the χ^2 critical value is really only appropriate when there are at least three groups and at least five observations per group (i.e., the χ^2 is not an exact sampling distribution of H). The second situation is that when there are tied ranks, the sampling distribution of H can be affected. Typically a midranks procedure is used, which results in an overly conservative Kruskal–Wallis test. A correction for ties is commonly used. Unless the number of ties is relatively large, the effect of the correction is minimal.

Using the statistics lab data as an example, we perform the Kruskal–Wallis ANOVA. The test statistic $H = 13.0610$ is compared with the critical value $_{.05}\chi^2_3 = 7.81$, from Table A.3, and the result is that H_0 is rejected ($p = .005$). Thus, the Kruskal–Wallis result agrees with the result of the parametric ANOVA. This should not be surprising because the normality assumption apparently was met. Thus, we would probably not have done the Kruskal–Wallis test for the example data. We merely provide it for purposes of explanation and comparison.

In summary, the Kruskal–Wallis test can be used as an alternative to the parametric one-factor ANOVA under nonnormality and/or when data on the dependent variable are ordinal. Under normality and with interval/ratio dependent variable data, the parametric ANOVA is more powerful than the Kruskal–Wallis test and thus is the preferred method.

1.7.2 Welch, Brown–Forsythe, and James Procedures

Next we briefly consider the following procedures for the heteroscedasticity condition: the Welch (1951) test, the Brown and Forsythe (1974) procedure, and the James (1951) first- and second-order procedures (more fully described by Coombs et al., 1996; Myers & Well, 1995; Wilcox, 1996, 2003). These procedures do not require homogeneity. Current research suggests that (a) under homogeneity, the F test is slightly more powerful than any of these procedures, and (b) under heterogeneity, each of these alternative procedures is more powerful than the F, although the choice among them depends on several conditions, making a recommendation among these alternative procedures somewhat complicated (e.g., Clinch & Keselman, 1982; Coombs et al., 1996; Tomarken & Serlin, 1986). The Kruskal–Wallis test is widely available in the major statistical software, and the Welch and Brown–Forsythe procedures are available in the SPSS one-way ANOVA module. Wilcox (1996, 2003) also provides assistance for these alternative procedures.

1.8 SPSS and G*Power

Next we consider the use of SPSS for the statistics lab example. Instructions for determining the one-way ANOVA using SPSS are presented first, followed by additional steps for examining the assumptions for the one-way ANOVA. Next, instructions for computing the Kruskal–Wallis and Brown and Forsythe are presented. Finally we return to G*Power for this model.

One-Way ANOVA

Note that SPSS needs the data to be in a specific form for any of the following analyses to proceed, which is different from the layout of the data in Table 1.1. ==For a one-factor ANOVA, the dataset must consist of at least two variables or columns.== One column or variable indicates the levels or categories of the independent variable, and the second is for the dependent variable. Each row then represents one individual, indicating the level or group that individual is a member of (1, 2, 3, or 4 in our example), and their score on the dependent variable. Thus, we wind up with two long columns of group values and scores as shown in the following screenshot.

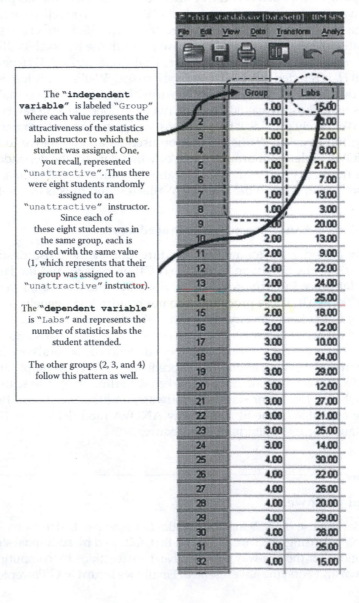

The "**independent variable**" is labeled "Group" where each value represents the attractiveness of the statistics lab instructor to which the student was assigned. One, you recall, represented "unattractive". Thus there were eight students randomly assigned to an "unattractive" instructor. Since each of these eight students was in the same group, each is coded with the same value (1, which represents that their group was assigned to an "unattractive" instructor).

The "**dependent variable**" is "Labs" and represents the number of statistics labs the student attended.

The other groups (2, 3, and 4) follow this pattern as well.

	Group	Labs
1	1.00	15.00
2	1.00	5.00
3	1.00	2.00
4	1.00	8.00
5	1.00	21.00
6	1.00	7.00
7	1.00	13.00
8	1.00	3.00
9	2.00	20.00
10	2.00	13.00
11	2.00	9.00
12	2.00	22.00
13	2.00	24.00
14	2.00	25.00
15	2.00	18.00
16	2.00	12.00
17	3.00	10.00
18	3.00	24.00
19	3.00	29.00
20	3.00	12.00
21	3.00	27.00
22	3.00	21.00
23	3.00	25.00
24	3.00	14.00
25	4.00	30.00
26	4.00	22.00
27	4.00	26.00
28	4.00	20.00
29	4.00	29.00
30	4.00	28.00
31	4.00	25.00
32	4.00	15.00

Step 1. To conduct a one-way ANOVA, go to "Analyze" in the top pulldown menu, then select "General Linear Model," and then select "Univariate." Following the screenshot (step 1) as follows produces the "Univariate" dialog box.

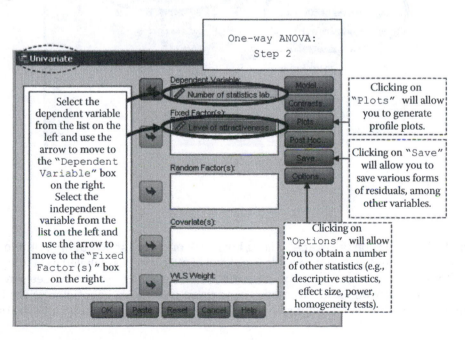

Step 2. Click the dependent variable (e.g., number of statistics labs attended) and move it into the "Dependent Variable" box by clicking the arrow button. Click the independent variable (e.g., level of attractiveness) and move it into the "Fixed Factors" box by clicking the arrow button. Next, click on "Options."

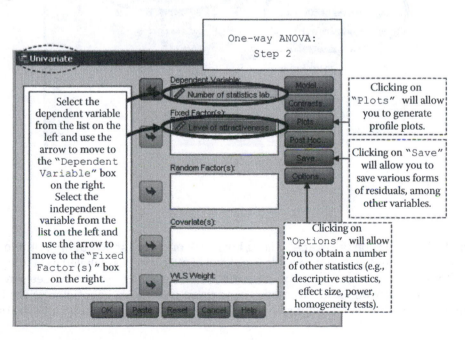

Step 3. Clicking on "Options" will provide the option to select such information as "Descriptive Statistics," "Estimates of effect size," "Observed power," and "Homogeneity tests" (i.e., Levene's test for equal variances) (those are the options that we typically utilize). Click on "Continue" to return to the original dialog box.

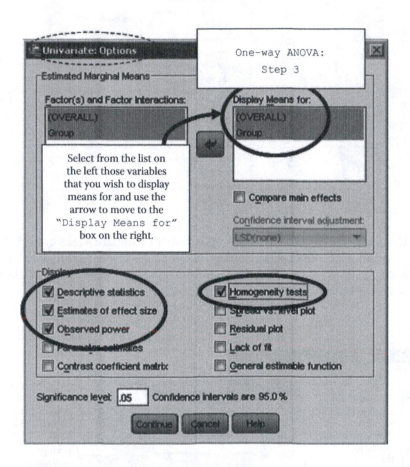

Step 4. From the "Univariate" dialog box, click on "Plots" to obtain a profile plot of means. Click the independent variable (e.g., level of attractiveness labeled as "Group") and move it into the "Horizontal Axis" box by clicking the arrow button (see screenshot step 4a). Then click on "Add" to move the variable into the "Plots" box at the bottom of the dialog box (see screenshot step 4b). Click on "Continue" to return to the original dialog box.

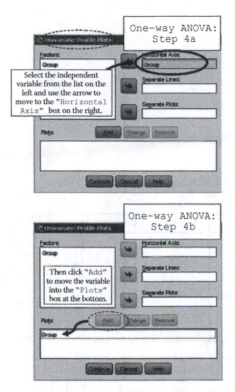

Step 5. From the "Univariate" dialog box, click on "Save" to select those elements that you want to save (in our case, we want to save the unstandardized residuals which will be used later to examine the extent to which normality and independence are met). From the "Univariate" dialog box, click on "OK" to return to generate the output.

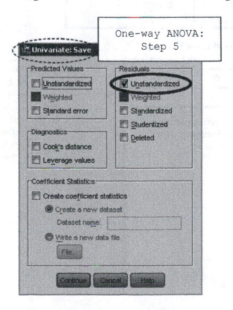

Interpreting the output: Annotated results are presented in Table 1.7, and the profile plot is shown in Figure 1.3.

TABLE 1.7

Selected SPSS Results for the Statistics Lab Example

Between-Subjects Factors

		Value Label	N
Level of attractiveness	1.00	Unattractive	8
	2.00	Slightly attractive	8
	3.00	Moderately attractive	8
	4.00	Very attractive	8

The table labeled "Between-Subjects Factors" provides sample sizes for each of the categories of the independent variable (recall that the independent variable is the "between subjects factor").

Descriptive Statistics
Dependent Variable: Number of Statistics Labs Attended

Level of Attractiveness	Mean	Std. Deviation	N
Unattractive	11.1250	5.48862	8
Slightly attractive	17.8750	5.93867	8
Moderately attractive	20.2500	7.28501	8
Very attractive	24.3750	5.09727	8
Total	18.4062	7.51283	32

The table labeled "Descriptive Statistics" provides basic descriptive statistics (means, standard deviations, and sample sizes) for each group of the independent variable.

Levene's Test of Equality of Error Variances[a]
Dependent Variable: Number of Statistics Labs Attended

F	$df1$	$df2$	Sig.
.905	3	28	.451

Tests the null hypothesis that the error variance of the dependent variable is equal across groups.
[a] Design: intercept + group

The F test (and associated p value) for Levene's Test for Equality of Error Variances is reviewed to determine if equal variances can be assumed. In this case, we meet the assumption (as p is greater than α). Note that $df1$ is degrees of freedom for the numerator (calculated as $J-1$) and $df2$ are the degrees of freedom for the denominator (calculated as $N-J$).

TABLE 1.7 (continued)

Selected SPSS Results for the Statistics Lab Example

The row labeled "**GROUP**" is the independent variable or between-groups variable. The *between-groups mean square* (246.198) tells how much the group means vary. The degrees of freedom for between groups is $J - 1$ (3 in this example).

The omnibus F test is computed as:

$$F = \frac{MS_{betw}}{MS_{with}} = \frac{246.198}{36.112} = 6.818$$

The p value for the omnibus F test is .001. This indicates there is a statistically significant difference in the mean number of statistics labs attended based on attractiveness of the instructor. The probability of observing these mean differences or more extreme mean differences by chance if the null hypothesis is really true (i.e., if the means really are equal) is substantially less than 1%. We reject the null hypothesis that all the population means are equal. For this example, this provides evidence to suggest that number of stats labs attended differs based on attractiveness of the instructor.

Partial eta squared is one measure of effect size:

$$\eta_p^2 = \frac{SS_{betw}}{SS_{total}} = \frac{738.594}{1749.719} = .422$$

We can interpret this to mean that approximately 42% of the variation in the dependent variable (in this case, number of statistics labs attended) is accounted for by the attractiveness of the statistics lab instructor.

Tests of Between-Subjects Effects

Dependent Variable: Number of Statistics Labs Attended

Source	Type III Sum of Squares	df	Mean Square	F	Sig.	Partial Eta Squared	Noncent. Parameter	Observed Power[b]
Corrected model	738.594[a]	3	246.198	6.818	.001	.422	20.453	.956
Intercept	10841.281	1	10841.281	300.216	.000	.915	300.216	1.000
Group	738.594	3	246.198	6.818	.001	.422	20.453	.956
Error	1011.125	28	36.112					
Total	12591.000	32						
Corrected total	1749.719	31						

[a] R squared = .422 (adjusted R squared = .360).

[b] Computed using alpha = .05.

R squared is listed as a footnote underneath the table. R squared is the ratio of sum of squares between divided by sum of squares total:

$$R^2 = \frac{SS_{betw}}{SS_{total}} = \frac{738.594}{1749.719} = .422$$

and, in the case of one-way ANOVA, is also the simple bivariate Pearson correlation between the independent variable and dependent variable squared.

The row labeled "**Error**" is within groups. The within groups mean square tells us how much the observations within the groups vary (i.e., 36.112). The degrees of freedom for within groups is $(N - J)$ or the total sample size minus the number of levels of the independent variable. The row labeled "corrected total" is the sum of squares total. The degrees of freedom for the total is $(N - 1)$ or the total sample size minus 1.

Observed power tells whether our test is powerful enough to detect mean differences if they really exist. Power of .956 indicates that the probability of rejecting the null hypothesis if it is really false is about 96%; this represents strong power.

(continued)

TABLE 1.7 (continued)

Selected SPSS Results for the Statistics Lab Example

Estimated Marginal Means

1. Grand Mean

Dependent Variable: Number of Statistics Labs Attended

Mean		95% Confidence Interval	
	Std. Error	Lower Bound	Upper Bound
18.406	1.062	16.230	20.582

> The "Grand Mean" (in this case, 18.406) represents the overall mean, regardless of group membership, on the dependent variable. The 95% CI represents the CI of the grand mean.

2. Level of Attractiveness

Dependent Variable: Number of Statistics Labs Attended

Level of Attractiveness	Mean	Std. Error	95% Confidence Interval	
			Lower Bound	Upper Bound
Unattractive	11.125	2.125	6.773	15.477
Slightly attractive	17.875	2.125	13.523	22.227
Moderately attractive	20.250	2.125	15.898	24.602
Very attractive	24.375	2.125	20.023	28.727

> The table labeled "**Level of attractiveness**" provides descriptive statistics for each of the categories of the independent variable (notice that these are the same means reported previously). In addition to means, the *SE* and 95% CI of the means are reported.

Test Statistics[a,b]

	dv
Chi-square	13.061
df	3
Asymp. sig.	.005

[a] Kruskal–Wallis test.
[b] Grouping variable: group.

> The Kruskal–Wallis procedure is shown here. The *p* value (denoted here as Asymp. sig. for asymptotic significance) is less than α, therefore the null hypothesis is also rejected for this nonparametric test.

dv   Robust Tests of Equality of Means

	Statistic[a]	df1	df2	Sig.
Welch	7.862	3	15.454	.002
Brown–Forsythe	6.818	3	25.882	.002

[a] Asymptotically *F* distributed.

> The Welch and Brown–Forsythe robust ANOVA procedures are shown here. For both tests, the *p* value is less than α, therefore the null hypothesis is also rejected for these robust tests.

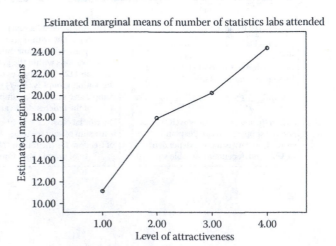

Estimated marginal means of number of statistics labs attended

FIGURE 1.3
Profile plot for statistics lab example.

Examining Data for Assumptions

Normality

	Group	Labs	RES_1
1	1.00	15.00	3.88
2	1.00	10.00	-1.13
			.88
			-3.13
			9.88
			-4.13
			1.88
			-8.13
			2.13
			-4.88
			-8.88
			4.13
			6.13
			7.13
			.13
			-5.88
			-10.25
18	3.00	24.00	3.75
19	3.00	29.00	8.75
20	3.00	12.00	-8.25
21	3.00	27.00	6.75
22	3.00	21.00	.75
23	3.00	25.00	4.75
24	3.00	14.00	-6.25
25	4.00	30.00	5.63
26	4.00	22.00	-2.38
27	4.00	26.00	1.63
28	4.00	20.00	-4.38
29	4.00	29.00	4.63
30	4.00	28.00	3.63
31	4.00	25.00	.63
32	4.00	15.00	-9.38

The residuals are computed by subtracting the group mean from the dependent variable value for each observation.
For example, the mean number of labs attended for group 1 was 11.125. The residual for person 1 is then $(15 - 11.125 = 3.88)$.

As we look at our raw data, we see a new variable has been added to our dataset labeled **RES_1**. This is our residual.

The residual will be used to review the assumptions of normality and independence.

Generating normality evidence: As alluded to earlier in the chapter, understanding the distributional shape, specifically the extent to which normality is a reasonable assumption, is important. For the one-way ANOVA, the distributional shape for the residuals should be a normal distribution. We can again use "Explore" to examine the extent to which the assumption of normality is met.

The general steps for accessing "Explore" have been presented in *Introduction to Statistical Concepts*, Third Edition and will not be repeated here. Click the residual and move it into the "Dependent List" box by clicking on the arrow button. The procedures for selecting normality statistics were also presented in Chapter 6 of *An Introduction to Statistical Concepts*, Third Edition and remain the same here: Click on "Plots" in the upper right corner. Place a checkmark in the boxes for "Normality plots with tests" and also for "Histogram." Then click "Continue" to return to the main "Explore" dialog box. Then click "OK" to generate the output.

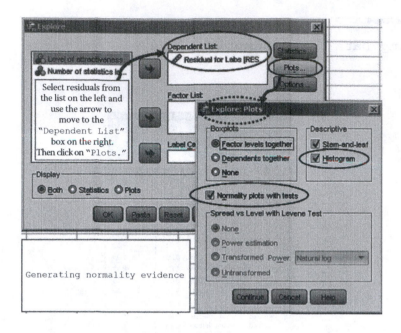

Interpreting normality evidence: We have already developed a good under-standing of how to interpret some forms of evidence of normality including skewness and kurtosis, histograms, and boxplots.

Descriptives

			Statistic	Std. Error
Residual for labs	Mean		.0000	1.00959
	95% Confidence interval	Lower bound	−2.0591	
	for mean	Upper bound	2.0591	
	5% Trimmed mean		.0260	
	Median		.8125	
	Variance		32.617	
	Std. deviation		5.71112	
	Minimum		−10.25	
	Maximum		9.88	
	Range		20.13	
	Interquartile range		9.25	
	Skewness		−.239	.414
	Kurtosis		−1.019	.809

The skewness statistic of the residuals is −.239 and kurtosis is −1.019—both within the range of an absolute value of 2.0, suggesting some evidence of normality.

The histogram of residuals is not exactly what most researchers would consider a classic normally shaped distribution, but it approaches a normal distribution and there is nothing to suggest normality may be an unreasonable assumption.

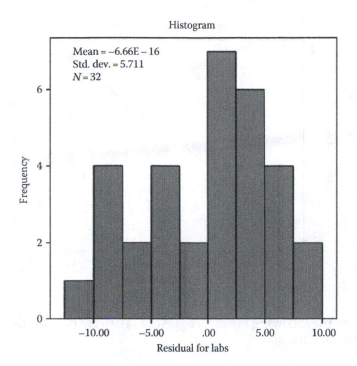

Histogram

Mean = −6.66E − 16
Std. dev. = 5.711
N = 32

There are a few other statistics that can be used to gauge normality. The formal test of normality, the S–W test (*SW*) (Shapiro & Wilk, 1965), provides evidence of the extent to which our sample distribution is statistically different from a normal distribution. The output for the S–W test is presented in the following and suggests that our sample distribution for residuals is not statistically significantly different than what would be expected from a normal distribution ($SW = .958$, $df = 32$, $p = .240$).

Tests of Normality

	Kolmogorov–Smirnov[a]			Shapiro–Wilk		
	Statistic	*df*	Sig.	Statistic	*df*	Sig.
Residual for labs	.112	32	.200	.958	32	.240

[a] Lilliefors significance correction.

* This is a lower bound of the true significance.

Q–Q plots are also often examined to determine evidence of normality. Q–Q plots are graphs that plot quantiles of the theoretical normal distribution against quantiles of the sample distribution. Points that fall on or close to the diagonal line suggest evidence of normality. The Q–Q plot of residuals shown in the following suggests relative normality.

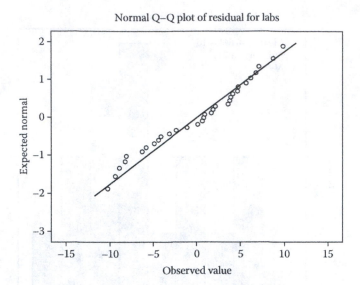

Examination of the following boxplot suggests a relatively normal distributional shape of residuals and no outliers.

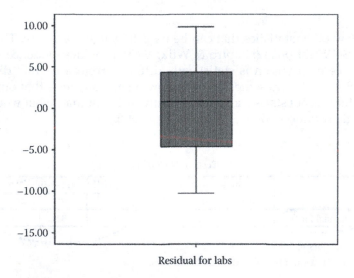

Residual for labs

Considering the forms of evidence we have examined, skewness and kurtosis statistics, the S–W test, the Q–Q plot, and the boxplot, all suggest normality is a reasonable assumption. We can be reasonably assured we have met the assumption of normality of the dependent variable for each group of the independent variable.

Independence

The only assumption we have not tested for yet is independence. If subjects have been randomly assigned to conditions (in other words, the different levels of the independent variable), the assumption of independence has been met. In this illustration, students were randomly assigned to instructor, and thus, the assumption of independence was met. However, we often use independent variables that do not allow random assignment, such as preexisting characteristics such as education level (high school diploma, bachelor's, master's, or terminal degrees). We can plot residuals against levels of our independent variable using a scatterplot to get an idea of whether or not there are patterns in the data and thereby provide an indication of whether we have met this assumption. Remember that these variables were added to the dataset by saving the unstandardized residuals when we generated the ANOVA model.

Please note that some researchers do not believe that the assumption of independence can be tested. If there is not a random assignment to groups, then these researchers believe this assumption has been violated—period. The plot that we generate will give us a general idea of patterns, however, in situations where random assignment was not performed.

The general steps for generating a simple scatterplot through "Scatter/dot" have been presented in Chapter 10 of *An Introduction to Statistical Concepts*, Third Edition, and they will not be reiterated here. From the "Simple Scatterplot" dialog screen, click the residual variable and move it into the "Y Axis" box by clicking on the arrow. Click the independent variable (e.g., level of attractiveness) and move it into the "X Axis" box by clicking on the arrow. Then click "OK."

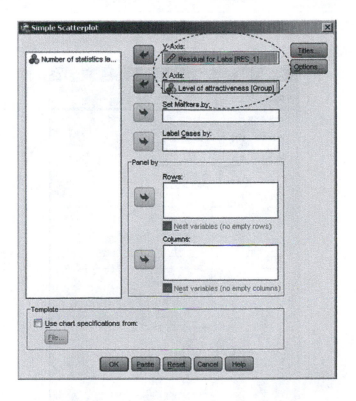

Double click on the graph in the output to activate the chart editor.

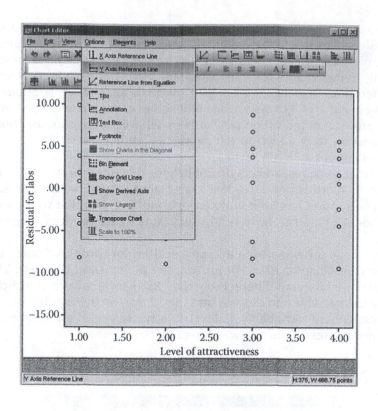

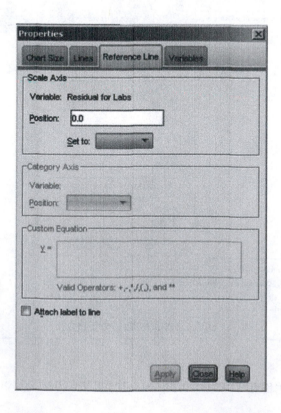

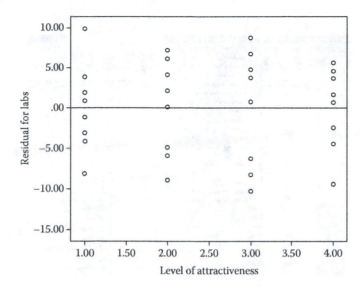

Interpreting independence evidence: In examining the scatterplot for evidence of independence, the points should be falling relatively randomly above and below the reference line. In this example, our scatterplot suggests evidence of independence with a relatively random display of points above and below the horizontal line at 0. Thus, had we not met the assumption of independence through random assignment of cases to groups, this would have provided evidence that independence was a reasonable assumption.

Nonparametric Procedures

Results from some of the recommended alternative procedures can be obtained from two other SPSS modules. Here we discuss the Kruskal–Wallis, Welch, and Brown–Forsythe procedures.

Kruskal–Wallis

Step 1: To conduct a Kruskal–Wallis test, go to the "Analyze" in the top pulldown menu, then select "Nonparametric Tests," then select "Legacy Dialogs," and finally select "K Independent Samples." Following the screenshot (step 1) as follows produces the "Tests for Several Independent Samples" dialog box.

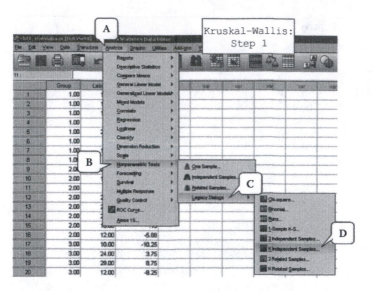

Step 2: Next, from the main "`Tests for Several Independent Samples`" dialog box, click the dependent variable (e.g., number of statistics labs attended) and move it into the "`Test Variable List`" box by clicking on the arrow button. Next, click the grouping variable (e.g., attractiveness of instructor) and move it into the "`Grouping Variable`" box by clicking on the arrow button. You will notice that there are two question marks next to the name of your grouping variable. This is SPSS letting you know that you need to define (numerically) which categories of the grouping variable you want to include in the analysis (this must be done by identifying a range of values for all groups of interest). To do that, click on "`Define Range.`" We have four groups or levels of our independent variable (labeled 1, 2, 3, and 4 in our raw data); thus, enter 1 as the minimum and 4 as the maximum. In the lower left portion of the screen under "`Test Type,`" check "`Kruskal-Wallis H`" to generate this nonparametric test. Then click on "`OK`" to generate the results presented as follows.

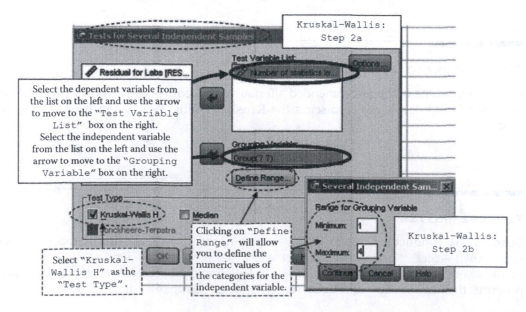

Interpreting the output: The Kruskal–Wallis is literally an ANOVA of ranks. Thus, the null hypothesis is that the mean ranks of the groups of the independent variable will not be significantly different. In this example, the results ($p = .005$) suggest statistically significant differences in the mean ranks of the dependent variable by group of the independent variable.

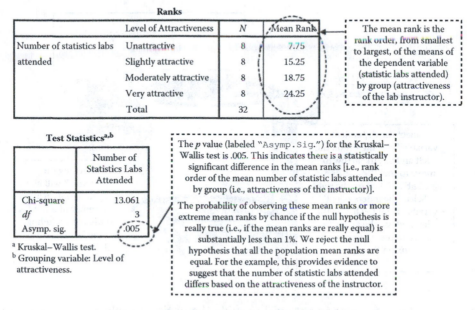

Ranks

	Level of Attractiveness	N	Mean Rank
Number of statistics labs attended	Unattractive	8	7.75
	Slightly attractive	8	15.25
	Moderately attractive	8	18.75
	Very attractive	8	24.25
	Total	32	

> The mean rank is the rank order, from smallest to largest, of the means of the dependent variable (statistic labs attended) by group (attractiveness of the lab instructor).

Test Statistics[a,b]

	Number of Statistics Labs Attended
Chi-square	13.061
df	3
Asymp. sig.	.005

[a] Kruskal–Wallis test.
[b] Grouping variable: Level of attractiveness.

> The p value (labeled "Asymp.Sig.") for the Kruskal–Wallis test is .005. This indicates there is a statistically significant difference in the mean ranks [i.e., rank order of the mean number of statistic labs attended by group (i.e., attractiveness of the instructor)].
>
> The probability of observing these mean ranks or more extreme mean ranks by chance if the null hypothesis is really true (i.e., if the mean ranks are really equal) is substantially less than 1%. We reject the null hypothesis that all the population mean ranks are equal. For the example, this provides evidence to suggest that the number of statistic labs attended differs based on the attractiveness of the instructor.

Welch and Brown-Forsythe

Step 1: To conduct the Welch and Brown–Forsythe procedures, go to the "Analyze" in the top pulldown menu, then select "Compare Means," and then select "One-way ANOVA." Following the screenshot (step 1) as follows produces the "One-way ANOVA" dialog box.

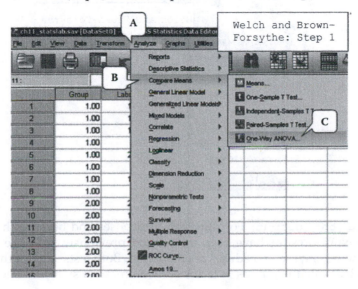

Welch and Brown-Forsythe: Step 1

Step 2: Click the dependent variable (e.g., number of stats labs attended) and move it into the "Dependent List" box by clicking the arrow button. Click the independent variable (e.g., level of attractiveness) and move it into the "Factor" box by clicking the arrow button. Next, click on "Options."

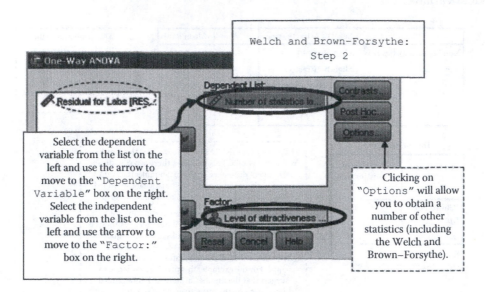

Step 3: Clicking on "Options" will provide the option to select such information as "Descriptive," "Homogeneity of variance test" (i.e., Levene's test for equal variances), "Brown-Forsythe," "Welch," and "Means plot." **Click** on "Continue" to return to the original dialog box. From the "One-way ANOVA" dialog box, click on "OK" to return and to generate the output.

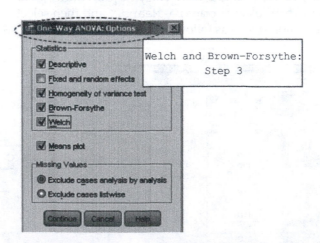

Interpreting the output: For illustrative purposes and because the remainder of the one-way ANOVA results have been interpreted previously, only the results for the Welch and Brown–Forsythe procedures are displayed. Both tests suggest there are statistical differences between the groups in terms of the number of stats labs attended.

Robust Tests of Equality of Means

Number of Statistics Labs Attended

	Statistic[a]	df1	df2	Sig.
Welch	7.862	3	15.454	.002
Brown–Forsythe	6.818	3	25.882	.002

[a] Asymptotically *F* distributed.

The *p* values for the Welch and Brown–Forsythe tests are .002. These indicate there is a statistically significant difference in the mean number of statistics labs attended per group (i.e., attractiveness of the instructor). The probability of observing the *F* statistics (7.862 and 6.818) or larger by chance if the means of the groups are really equal is substantially less than 1%. We reject the null hypothesis that all the population means are equal. For this example, this provides evidence to suggest that the number of statistic labs attended differs based on attractiveness of the instructor.

For further details on the use of SPSS for these procedures, be sure to examine books such as Page, Braver, and MacKinnon (2003), or Morgan, Leech, Gloeckner, and Barrett (2011).

A priori and post hoc power can again be determined using the specialized software described previously in this text (e.g., G*Power), or you can consult a priori power tables (e.g., Cohen, 1988). As an illustration, we use G*Power to compute the post hoc power of our test.

Post Hoc Power for One-Way ANOVA Using G*Power

The first thing that must be done when using G*Power for computing post hoc power is to select the correct test family. In our case, we conducted a one-way ANOVA. To find the one-way ANOVA, we will select "Tests" in the top pulldown menu, then "Means," and then "Many groups: ANOVA: One-way (one independent variable)." Once that selection is made, the "Test family" automatically changes to "F tests."

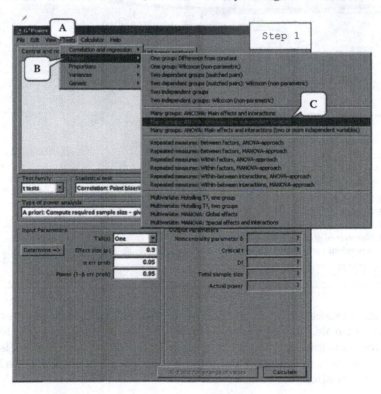

The "Type of Power Analysis" desired then needs to be selected. To compute post hoc power, we need to select "Post hoc: Compute achieved power—given α, sample size, and effect size."

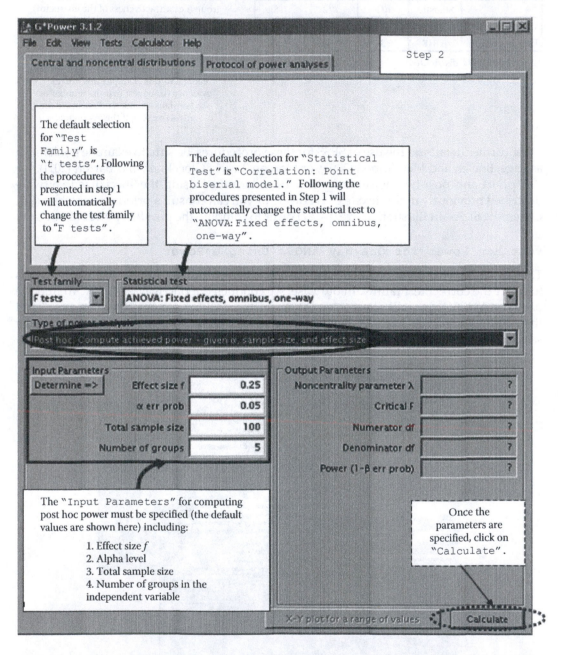

The "Input Parameters" must then be specified. The first parameter is the effect size, *f*. In our example, the computed *f* effect size was .8546. The alpha level we used was .05, the total sample size was 32, and the number of groups (i.e., levels of the independent variable) was 4. Once the parameters are specified, click on "Calculate" to find the power statistics.

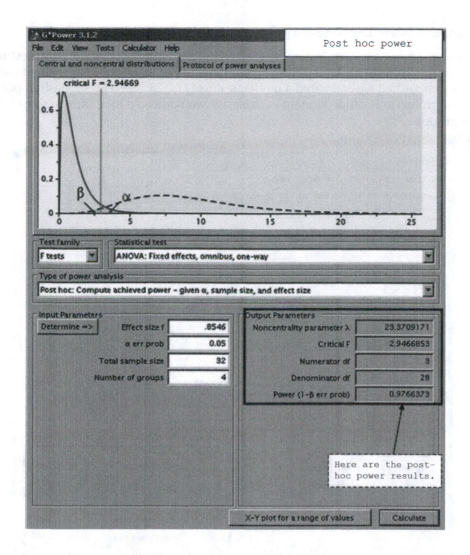

The "Output Parameters" provide the relevant statistics given the input just specified. In this example, we were interested in determining post hoc power for a one-way ANOVA with a computed effect size f of .8546, an alpha level of .05, total sample size of 32, and 4 groups (or categories) in our independent variable.

Based on those criteria, the post hoc power was .98. In other words, with a one-way ANOVA, computed effect size f of .8546, alpha level of .05, total sample size of 32, and 4 groups (or categories) in our independent variable, the post hoc power of our test was .98—the probability of rejecting the null hypothesis when it is really false (in this case, the probability that the means of the dependent variable would be equal for each level of the independent variable) was 98%, which would be considered more than sufficient power (sufficient power is often .80 or above). Note that this value is slightly different than the observed value reported in SPSS. Keep in mind that conducting power analysis a priori is recommended so that you avoid a situation where, post hoc, you find that the sample size was not sufficient to reach the desired level of power (given the observed parameters).

A Priori Power for One-Way ANOVA Using G*Power

For a priori power, we can determine the total sample size needed given an estimated effect size f, alpha level, desired power, and number of groups of our independent variable. In this example, had we estimated a moderate effect f of .25, alpha of .05, desired power of .80, and 4 groups in the independent variable, we would need a total sample size of 180 (or 45 per group).

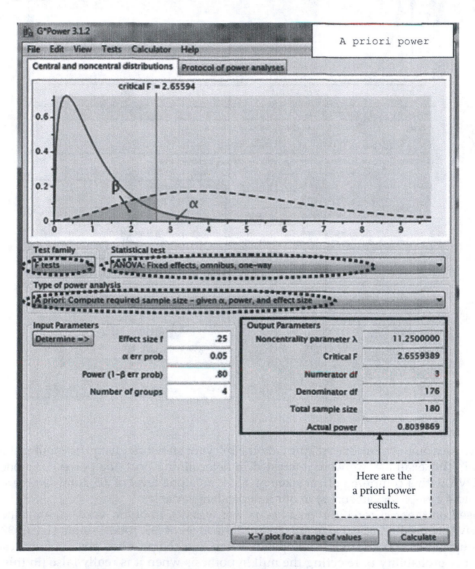

1.9 Template and APA-Style Write-Up

Finally we come to an example paragraph of the results for the statistics lab example. Recall that our graduate research assistant, Marie, was working on a research project for an independent study class to determine if there was a mean difference in the number of statistics labs attended based on the attractiveness of the lab instructor. Her research question was as follows: *Is there a mean difference in the number of statistics labs students attend based on the attractiveness of the lab instructor?* Marie then generated a one-way ANOVA as the test of inference. A template for writing a research question for a one-way ANOVA is presented as follows. Please note that it is important to ensure the reader understands the levels or groups of the independent variable. This may be done parenthetically in the actual research question, as an operational definition, or specified within the methods section. In this example, parenthetically we could have stated the following: *Is there a mean difference in the number of statistics labs students attend based on the attractiveness of the lab instructor (unattractive, slightly attractive, moderately attractive, very attractive)?*

```
Is there a mean difference in [dependent variable] between [indepen-
dent variable]?
```

It may be helpful to preface the results of the one-way ANOVA with information on an examination of the extent to which the assumptions were met (recall there are three assumptions: normality, homogeneity of variance, and independence). This assists the reader in understanding that you were thorough in data screening prior to conducting the test of inference.

```
A one-way ANOVA was conducted to determine if the mean number
of statistics labs attended by students differed on the level of
attractiveness of the statistics lab instructor. The assumption of
normality was tested and met via examination of the residuals.
Review of the S-W test for normality (SW = .958, df = 32, p = .240)
and skewness (-.239) and kurtosis (-1.019) statistics suggested that
normality was a reasonable assumption. The boxplot suggested a rela-
tively normal distributional shape (with no outliers) of the residu-
als. The Q-Q plot and histogram suggested normality was reasonable.
According to Levene's test, the homogeneity of variance assumption
was satisfied [F(3, 28) = .905, p = .451]. Random assignment of indi-
viduals to groups helped ensure that the assumption of independence
was met. Additionally, a scatterplot of residuals against the levels
of the independent variable was reviewed. A random display of points
around 0 provided further evidence that the assumption of indepen-
dence was met.
```

Here is an APA-style example paragraph of results for the one-way ANOVA (remember that this will be prefaced by the previous paragraph reporting the extent to which the assumptions of the test were met).

```
From Table 1.7, we see that the one-way ANOVA is statistically signif-
icant (F = 6.818, df = 3, 28, p = .001), the effect size is rather large
(η² = .422; suggesting about 42% of the variance of number of sta-
tistics labs attended is due to differences in the attractiveness of
the instructor), and observed power is quite strong (.956). The means
and standard deviations of the number of statistics labs attended for
each group of the independent variable were as follows: 11.125 (SD =
5.489) for the unattractive level, 17.875 (SD = 5.939) for the slightly
attractive level, 20.250 (SD = 7.285) for the moderately attractive
```

level, and 24.375 (*SD* = 5.097) for the very attractive level. The means and profile plot (Figure 1.3) suggest that with increasing instructor attractiveness, there was a corresponding increase in mean lab attendance. For completeness, we also conducted several alternative procedures. The Kruskal-Wallis test (χ^2 = 13.061, *df* = 3, *p* = .005), the Welch procedure (F_{asymp} = 7.862, *df1* = 3, *df2* = 15.454, *p* = .002), and the Brown-Forsythe procedure (F_{asymp} = 6.818, *df1* = 3, *df2* = 25.882, *p* = .002) also indicated a statistically significant effect of instructor attractiveness on statistics lab attendance, providing further support for the assumptions being satisfied.

1.10 Summary

In this chapter, methods involving the comparison of multiple group means for a single independent variable were considered. The chapter began with a look at the characteristics of the one-factor fixed-effects ANOVA including (a) control of the experimentwise error rate through an omnibus test, (b) one independent variable with two or more fixed levels, (c) individuals are randomly assigned to levels or groups and then exposed to only one level of the independent variable, and (d) the dependent variable is measured at least at the interval level. Next, a discussion of the theory underlying ANOVA was conducted. Here we examined the concepts of between- and within-groups variability, sources of variation, and partitioning the sums of squares. The ANOVA model was examined. Some discussion was also devoted to the ANOVA assumptions, their assessment, and how to deal with assumption violations. Finally, alternative ANOVA procedures were described. At this point, you should have met the following objectives: (a) be able to understand the characteristics and concepts underlying the one-factor ANOVA, (b) be able to determine and interpret the results of a one-factor ANOVA, and (c) be able to understand and evaluate the assumptions of the one-factor ANOVA. Chapter 2 considers a number of MCPs for further examination of sets of means. Chapter 3 returns to ANOVA and discusses models which have more than one independent variable.

Problems

Conceptual Problems

1.1   Data for three independent random samples, each of size 4, are analyzed by a one-factor ANOVA fixed-effects model. If the values of the sample means are all equal, what is the value of MS_{betw}?

a.   0

b.   1

c.   2

d.   3

1.2 For a one-factor ANOVA fixed-effects model, which of the following is always true?

a. $df_{betw} + df_{with} = df_{total}$ no?

b. $SS_{betw} + SS_{with} = SS_{total}$ ✓

c. $MS_{betw} + MS_{with} = MS_{total}$ no?

d. All of the above

e. Both a and b

1.3 Suppose $n_1 = 19$, $n_2 = 21$, and $n_3 = 23$. For a one-factor ANOVA, the df_{with} would be

a. 2

b. 3

c. 60

d. 62

1.4 Suppose $n_1 = 19$, $n_2 = 21$, and $n_3 = 23$. For a one-factor ANOVA, the df_{betw} would be

a. 2

b. 3

c. 60

d. 62

1.5 Suppose $n_1 = 19$, $n_2 = 21$, and $n_3 = 23$. For a one-factor ANOVA, the df_{total} would be

a. 2

b. 3

c. 60

d. 62

1.6 Suppose $n_1 = 19$, $n_2 = 21$, and $n_3 = 23$. For a one-factor ANOVA, the df for the numerator of the F ratio would be which one of the following?

a. 2

b. 3

c. 60

d. 62

1.7 In a one-factor ANOVA, H_0 asserts that

a. All of the population means are equal.

b. The between-groups variance estimate and the within-groups variance estimate are both estimates of the same population residual variance.

c. The within-groups sum of squares is equal to the between-groups sum of squares.

d. Both a and b.

1.8 For a one-factor ANOVA comparing three groups with $n = 10$ in each group, the F ratio has degrees of freedom equal to

a. 2, 27

b. 2, 29

c. 3, 27

d. 3, 29

1.9   For a one-factor ANOVA comparing five groups with $n = 50$ in each group, the F ratio has degrees of freedom equal to

   a. 4, 245
   b. 4, 249
   c. 5, 245
   d. 5, 249

1.10   Which of the following is not necessary in ANOVA?

   a. Observations are from random and independent samples.
   b. The dependent variable is measured on at least the interval scale.
   c. Populations have equal variances.
   d. Equal sample sizes are necessary.

1.11   If you find an F ratio of 1.0 in a one-factor ANOVA, it means that

   a. Between-groups variation exceeds within-groups variation.
   b. Within-groups variation exceeds between-groups variation.
   c. Between-groups variation is equal to within-groups variation.
   d. Between-groups variation exceeds total variation.

1.12   Suppose students in grades 7, 8, 9, 10, 11, and 12 were compared on absenteeism. If ANOVA were used rather than multiple t tests, then the probability of a Type I error will be less. True or false?

1.13   Mean square is another name for variance or variance estimate. True or false?

1.14   In ANOVA, each independent variable is known as a level. True or false?

1.15   A negative F ratio is impossible. True or false?

1.16   Suppose that for a one-factor ANOVA with $J = 4$ and $n = 10$, the four sample means are all equal to 15. I assert that the value of MS_{with} is necessarily equal to 0. Am I correct?

1.17   With $J = 3$ groups, I assert that if you reject H_0 in the one-factor ANOVA, you will necessarily conclude that all three group means are different. Am I correct?

1.18   The homoscedasticity assumption is that the populations from which each of the samples are drawn are normally distributed. True or false?

1.19   When analyzing mean differences among more than two samples, doing independent t tests on all possible pairs of means

   a. Decreases the probability of a Type I error
   b. Does not change the probability of a Type I error
   c. Increases the probability of a Type I error
   d. Cannot be determined from the information provided

1.20   Suppose for a one-factor fixed-effects ANOVA with $J = 5$ and $n = 15$, the five sample means are all equal to 50. I assert that the F test statistic cannot be significant. Am I correct?

1.21   The independence assumption in ANOVA is that the observations in the samples do not depend on one another. True or false?

1.22   For $J = 2$ and $\alpha = .05$, if the result of the independent t test is significant, then the result of the one-factor fixed-effects ANOVA is uncertain. True or false?

1.23   A statistician conducted a one-factor fixed-effects ANOVA and found the F ratio to be less than 0. I assert this means the between-groups variability is less than the within-groups variability. Am I correct?

Computational Problems

1.1   Complete the following ANOVA summary table for a one-factor ANOVA, where there are 4 groups receiving different headache medications, each with 16 observations, and $\alpha = .05$.

Source	SS	df	MS	F	Critical Value and Decision
Between	9.75	—	—	—	
Within	—	—	—		
Total	18.75	—			

1.2   A social psychologist wants to determine if type of music has any effect on the number of beers consumed by people in a tavern. Four taverns are selected that have different musical formats. Five people are randomly sampled in each tavern and their beer consumption monitored for 3 hours. Complete the following one-factor ANOVA summary table using $\alpha = .05$.

Source	SS	df	MS	F	Critical Value and Decision
Between	—	—	7.52	5.01	
Within	—	—	—		
Total	—	—			

1.3   A psychologist would like to know whether the season (fall, winter, spring, and summer) has any consistent effect on people's sexual activity. In the middle of each season, a psychologist selects a random sample of $n = 25$ students. Each individual is given a sexual activity questionnaire. A one-factor ANOVA was used to analyze these data. Complete the following ANOVA summary table ($\alpha = .05$).

Source	SS	df	MS	F	Critical Value and Decision
Between	—	—	—	5.00	
Within	960	—	—		
Total	—	—			

1.4 The following five independent random samples are obtained from five normally distributed populations with equal variances. The dependent variable is the number of bank transactions in 1 month, and the groups are five different banks.

Group 1	Group 2	Group 3	Group 4	Group 5
16	16	2	5	7
5	10	9	8	12
11	7	11	1	14
23	12	13	5	16
18	7	10	8	11
12	4	13	11	9
12	23	9	9	19
19	13	9	9	24

Use SPSS to conduct a one-factor ANOVA to determine if the group means are equal using $\alpha = .05$. Test the assumptions, plot the group means, consider an effect size, interpret the results, and write an APA-style summary.

1.5 The following three independent random samples are obtained from three normally distributed populations with equal variances. The dependent variable is starting hourly wage, and the groups are the types of position (internship, co-op, work study).

Group 1: Internship	Group 2: Co-op	Group 3: Work Study
10	9	8
12	8	9
11	10	8
11	12	10
12	9	8
10	11	9
10	12	9
13	10	8

Use SPSS to conduct a one-factor ANOVA to determine if the group means are equal using $\alpha = .05$. Test the assumptions, plot the group means, consider an effect size, interpret the results, and write an APA-style summary.

Interpretive Problems

1.1 Using the survey 1 dataset from the website, use SPSS to conduct a one-factor fixed-effects ANOVA, including effect size, where political view is the grouping variable (i.e., independent variable) ($J = 5$) and the dependent variable is a variable of interest to you [the following variables look interesting: books, TV, exercise, drinks, GPA, GRE-Quantitative (GRE-Q), CDs, hair appointment]. Then write an APA-style paragraph describing the results.

1.2 Using the survey 1 dataset from the website, use SPSS to conduct a one-factor fixed-effects ANOVA, including effect size, where hair color is the grouping variable (i.e., independent variable) ($J = 5$) and the dependent variable is a variable of interest to you (the following variables look interesting: books, TV, exercise, drinks, GPA, GRE-Q, CDs, hair appointment). Then write an APA-style paragraph describing the results.

2

Multiple Comparison Procedures

Chapter Outline

Key Concepts

1. Contrast
2. Simple and complex contrasts
3. Planned and post hoc comparisons
4. Contrast- and family-based Type I error rates
5. Orthogonal contrasts

In this chapter, our concern is with **multiple comparison procedures** (MCPs) that involve comparisons among the group means. Recall from Chapter 1 the one-factor analysis of variance (ANOVA) where the means from two or more samples were compared. What do we do if the omnibus F test leads us to reject H_0? First, consider the situation where there are only two samples (e.g., assessing the effectiveness of two types of medication), and H_0 has already been rejected in the omnibus test. Why was H_0 rejected? The answer should be obvious. Those two sample means must be significantly different as there is no other way that the omnibus H_0 could have been rejected (e.g., one type of medication is significantly more effective than the other based on an inspection of the means).

Second, consider the situation where there are more than two samples (e.g., three types of medication), and H_0 has already been rejected in the omnibus test. Why was H_0 rejected? The answer is not so obvious. This situation is one where a multiple comparison procedure (MCP) would be quite informative. Thus, for situations where there are at least three groups and the ANOVA H_0 has been rejected, some sort of MCP is necessary to determine which means or combination of means are different. Third, consider the situation where the researcher is not even interested in the ANOVA omnibus test but is only interested in comparisons involving particular means (e.g., certain medications are more effective than a placebo). This is a situation where an MCP is useful for evaluating those specific comparisons.

If the ANOVA omnibus H_0 has been rejected, why not do all possible independent t tests? First let us return to a similar question from Chapter 1. There we asked about doing all possible pairwise independent t tests rather than an ANOVA. The answer there was to do an omnibus F test. The reasoning was related to the probability of making a Type I error (i.e., α), where the researcher incorrectly rejects a true null hypothesis. Although the α level for each t test can be controlled at a specified nominal level, say .05, what would happen to the overall α level for the set of t tests? The overall α level for the set of tests, often called the family-wise Type I error rate, would be larger than the α level for each of the individual t tests. The optimal solution, in terms of maintaining control over our overall α level as well as maximizing power, is to conduct one overall omnibus test. The omnibus test assesses the equality of all of the means simultaneously.

Let us apply the same concept to the situation involving multiple comparisons. Rather than doing all possible pairwise independent t tests, where the family-wise error rate could be quite large, one should use a procedure that controls the family-wise error rate in some way. This can be done with MCPs. As pointed out later in the chapter, there are two main methods for taking the Type I error rate into account.

This chapter is concerned with several important new concepts, such as a contrast, planned versus post hoc comparisons, the Type I error rate, and orthogonal contrasts. The remainder of the chapter consists of selected MCPs, including when and how to apply them. The terms **comparison** and **contrast** are used here synonymously. Also, MCPs are only applicable for comparing levels of an independent variable that are fixed, in other words, for fixed-effects independent variables and not for random-effects independent variables. Our objectives are that by the end of this chapter, you will be able to (a) understand the concepts underlying the MCPs, (b) select the appropriate MCP for a given research situation, and (c) determine and interpret the results of MCPs.

2.1 Concepts of Multiple Comparison Procedures

In the previous chapter, Marie, our very capable educational researcher graduate student, was embarking on a very exciting research adventure of her own. She continues to work toward completion of this project.

Marie is enrolled in an independent study class. As part of the course requirement, she has to complete a research study. In collaboration with the statistics faculty in her program, Marie designs an experimental study to determine if there is a mean difference in student attendance in the statistics lab based on the attractiveness of the statistics lab instructor. Marie's research question is as follows: *Is there a mean difference in the number of statistics labs attended by students based on the attractiveness of the lab instructor?* Marie determined that a one-way ANOVA was the best statistical procedure to use to answer her question. Marie has collected the data to analyze her research question and has conducted a one-way ANOVA, where she rejected the null hypothesis. Now, her task is to determine which groups (recall there were four statistics labs, each with an instructor with a different attractiveness rating) are statistically different on the outcome (i.e., number of statistics labs attended).

This section describes the most important characteristics of the MCPs. We begin by defining a contrast and then move into planned versus post hoc contrasts, the Type I error rates, and orthogonal contrasts.

2.1.1 Contrasts

A **contrast** is a weighted combination of the means. For example, one might wish to form contrasts involving the following means: (a) group 1 with group 2 and (b) the combination (or average) of groups 1 and 2 with group 3. Statistically a contrast is defined as

$$\psi_i = c_1 \mu_{.1} + c_2 \mu_{.2} + \ldots + c_J \mu_{.J}$$

where the c_j represents contrast coefficients (or weights), which are positive, zero, and negative values used to define a particular contrast ψ_i, and the $\mu_{.j}$ represents population group means. In other words, a contrast is simply a particular combination of the group means, depending on which means the researcher is interested in comparing. It should also be noted that to form a fair or legitimate contrast, $\Sigma c_j = 0$ for the equal n's or balanced case, and $\Sigma(n_j c_j) = 0$ for the unequal n's or unbalanced case.

For example, suppose we wish to compare the means of groups 1 and 3 for $J = 4$ groups or levels, and we call this contrast 1. The contrast would be written as

$$\psi_1 = c_1 \mu_{.1} + c_2 \mu_{.2} + c_3 \mu_{.3} + c_4 \mu_{.4}$$

$$= (+1) \mu_{.1} + (0) \mu_{.2} + (-1) \mu_{.3} + (0) \mu_{.4}$$

$$= \mu_{.1} - \mu_{.3}$$

What hypotheses are we testing when we evaluate a contrast? The null and alternate hypotheses of any specific contrast can be written, respectively, simply as

$$H_0: \psi_i = 0$$

and

$$H_1: \psi_i \neq 0$$

Thus we are testing whether a particular combination of means, as defined by the contrast coefficients, are different. How does this relate back to the omnibus F test? The null and alternate hypotheses for the omnibus F test can be written in terms of contrasts as

$$H_0: \text{all } \psi_i = 0$$

$$H_1: \text{at least one } \psi_i \neq 0$$

Here the omnibus test is used to determine whether any contrast that could be formulated for the set of J means is significant or not.

Contrasts can be divided into simple or pairwise contrasts, and complex or nonpairwise contrasts. A simple or pairwise contrast is a comparison involving only two means. Take as an example the situation where there are $J = 3$ groups. There are three possible distinct pairwise contrasts that could be formed: (a) $\mu_{.1} - \mu_{.2} = 0$ (comparing the mean of group 1 to the mean of group 2), (b) $\mu_{.1} - \mu_{.3} = 0$ (comparing the mean of group 1 to the mean of group 3), and (c) $\mu_{.2} - \mu_{.3} = 0$ (comparing the mean of group 2 to the mean of group 3). It should be obvious that a pairwise contrast involving groups 1 and 2 is the same contrast whether it is written as $\mu_{.1} - \mu_{.2} = 0$ or as $\mu_{.2} - \mu_{.1} = 0$.

In terms of contrast coefficients, these three contrasts could be written in the form of a table as follows:

	c_1	c_2	c_3
$\psi_1: \mu_{.1} - \mu_{.2} = 0$	+1	−1	0
$\psi_2: \mu_{.1} - \mu_{.3} = 0$	+1	0	−1
$\psi_3: \mu_{.2} - \mu_{.3} = 0$	0	+1	−1

where each contrast (i.e., ψ_1, ψ_2, ψ_3) is read across the table (left to right) to determine its contrast coefficients (i.e., c_1, c_2, c_3). For example, the first contrast, ψ_1, does not involve group 3 because that contrast coefficient is 0 (see c_3 for ψ_1), but does involve groups 1 and 2 because those contrast coefficients are not 0 (see c_1 and c_2 for ψ_1). The contrast coefficients are +1 for group 1 (see c_1) and −1 for group 2 (see c_2); consequently we are interested in examining the difference between the means of groups 1 and 2.

Written in long form so that we can see where the contrast coefficients come from, the three contrasts are as follows:

$$\psi_1 = (+1)\mu_{.1} + (-1)\mu_{.2} + (0)\mu_{.3} = \mu_{.1} - \mu_{.2}$$

$$\psi_2 = (+1)\mu_{.1} + (0)\mu_{.2} + (-1)\mu_{.3} = \mu_{.1} - \mu_{.3}$$

$$\psi_3 = (0)\mu_{.1} + (+1)\mu_{.2} + (-1)\mu_{.3} = \mu_{.2} - \mu_{.3}$$

An easy way to remember the number of possible unique pairwise contrasts that could be written is $\frac{1}{2}[J(J - 1)]$. Thus for $J = 3$, the number of possible unique pairwise contrasts is 3, whereas for $J = 4$, the number of such contrasts is 6 (or $1/2[4 (4 - 1)] = 1/2(4)(3) = 1/2(12) = 6$).

A complex contrast is a comparison involving more than two means. Continuing with the example of $J = 3$ groups, we might be interested in testing the contrast of $\mu_{.1} - (\frac{1}{2})$ $(\mu_{.2} + \mu_{.3})$ $\left[\text{which could also be written as } \mu_{.1} - \left(\frac{(\mu_{.2} + \mu_{.3})}{2}\right)\right]$. This contrast is a comparison of the mean for group 1 (i.e., $\mu_{.1}$) with the average of the means for groups 2 and 3 $\left[\text{i.e., } \left(\frac{(\mu_{.2} + \mu_{.3})}{2}\right)\right]$. In terms of contrast coefficients, this contrast would be written as seen here:

	c_1	c_2	c_3
$\psi_4: \mu_{.1} - \frac{\mu_{.2}}{2} - \frac{\mu_{.3}}{2} = 0$	+1	−1/2	−1/2

Written in long form so that we can see where the contrast coefficients come from, this complex contrast is as follows:

$$\psi_4 = (+1)\mu_{.1} + (-1/2)\mu_{.2} + (-1/2)\mu_{.3} = \mu_{.1} - (1/2)\mu_{.2} - (1/2)\mu_{.3} = \mu_{.1} - \frac{\mu_{.2}}{2} - \frac{\mu_{.3}}{2} = 0$$

The number of unique complex contrasts is greater than $\frac{1}{2}[J(J-1)]$ when J is at least 4. In other words, the number of such contrasts that could be formed can be quite large when there are more than three groups. It should be noted that the total number of unique pairwise and complex contrasts is $[1 + \frac{1}{2}(3^J - 1) - 2^J]$ (Keppel, 1982). Thus for $J = 4$, one could form 25 total contrasts.

Many of the MCPs are based on the same test statistic, which we introduce here as the "standard t." The standard t ratio for a contrast is given as follows:

$$t = \frac{\psi'}{s_{\psi'}}$$

where $s_{\psi'}$ = represents the standard error of the contrast as follows:

$$s_{\psi'} = \sqrt{MS_{error} \sum_{j=1}^{J}\left(\frac{c_j^2}{n_j}\right)}$$

where the prime (i.e., ') indicates that this is a sample estimate of the population value of the contrast (i.e., based on sample data), and n_j refers to the number of observations in group j.

2.1.2 Planned Versus Post Hoc Comparisons BEFORE

This section examines specific types of contrasts or comparisons. One way of classifying contrasts is whether the contrasts are formulated prior to the research or following a significant omnibus F test. **Planned contrasts** (also known as specific or a priori contrasts) involve particular comparisons that the researcher is interested in examining *prior* to data collection. These planned contrasts are generally based on theory, previous research, and/or specific hypotheses. Here the researcher is interested in certain specific contrasts a priori, where the number of such contrasts is usually small. Planned contrasts are done without regard to the result of the omnibus F test (i.e., whether or not the overall F test is statistically significant). In other words, the researcher is interested in certain specific contrasts, but not in the omnibus F test that examines all possible contrasts. In this situation, the researcher could care less about the multitude of possible contrasts and need not even examine the overall F test, but rather the concern is only with a few contrasts of substantive interest. In addition, the researcher may not be as concerned with the family-wise error rate for planned comparisons because only a few of them will actually be carried out. Fewer planned comparisons are usually conducted (due to their specificity) than post hoc comparisons (due to their generality), so planned contrasts generally yield narrower confidence intervals (CIs), are more powerful, and have a higher likelihood of a Type I error than post hoc comparisons.

Post hoc contrasts are formulated such that the researcher provides no advance specification of the actual contrasts to be tested. This type of contrast is done *only* following a statistically significant omnibus F test. Post hoc is Latin for "after the fact," referring to contrasts tested after a statistically significant omnibus F in the ANOVA. Here the researcher may want to take the family-wise error rate into account somehow to achieve better overall Type I error protection. Post hoc contrasts are also known as unplanned, a posteriori, or postmortem contrasts. It should be noted that most MCPs are not derived or based on finding a statistically significant F in the ANOVA.

2.1.3 Type I Error Rate

How does the researcher deal with the family-wise Type I error rate? Depending on the MCP selected, one may either set α for each contrast or set α for a family of contrasts. In the former category, α is set for each individual contrast. The MCPs in this category are known as **contrast-based**. We designate the α level for contrast-based procedures as α_{pc}, as it represents the **per contrast** Type I error rate. Thus α_{pc} represents the probability of making a Type I error for that particular contrast. In the latter category, α is set for a family or set of contrasts. The MCPs in this category are known as **family-wise**. We designate the α level for family-wise procedures as α_{fw}, as it represents the **family-wise** Type I error rate. Thus α_{fw} represents the probability of making at least one type I error in the family or set of contrasts.

For **orthogonal** (or independent or unrelated) contrasts, the following property holds:

$$\alpha_{fw} = 1 - (1 - \alpha_{pc})^c$$

where $c = J - 1$ orthogonal contrasts (as defined in the next section). For nonorthogonal (or related or oblique) contrasts, this property is more complicated, so we simply say the following:

$$\alpha_{fw} \leq c\alpha_{pc}$$

These properties should be familiar from the discussion in Chapter 1, where we were looking at the probability of a Type I error in the use of multiple independent t tests.

2.1.4 Orthogonal Contrasts

Let us begin this section by defining orthogonal contrasts. A set of contrasts is *orthogonal* if they represent nonredundant and independent (if the usual ANOVA assumptions are met) sources of variation. For J groups, you will only be able to construct $J - 1$ orthogonal contrasts in a set. However, more than one set of orthogonal contrasts may exist. Note that although the contrasts within each set are orthogonal, contrasts across such sets may not be orthogonal.

For purposes of simplicity, we first consider the equal n's or balanced case (in other words, the sample sizes are the same for each group). With equal observations per group, two contrasts are defined to be orthogonal if the products of their contrast coefficients sum to 0. That is, two contrasts are orthogonal if the following holds:

$$\sum_{j=1}^{J}(c_j c_{j'}) = c_1 c_{1'} + c_2 c_{2'} + \dots + c_J c_{J'} = 0$$

where j and j' represent two distinct contrasts. Thus we see that orthogonality depends on the contrast coefficients, the c_j, and *not* the group means, the $\mu_{.j}$.

For example, if $J = 3$, then we can form a set of two orthogonal contrasts. One such set is as follows. In this set of contrasts, the first contrast (ψ_1) compares the mean of group 1 ($c_1 = +1$) to the mean of group 2 ($c_2 = -1$). The second contrast (ψ_2) compares the average of the means of group 1 ($c_1 = +1/2$) and group 2 ($c_2 = +1/2$) to the mean of group 3 ($c_3 = -1$):

	c_1	c_2	c_3
ψ_1: $\mu_{.1} - \mu_{.2} = 0$	+1	−1	0
ψ_2: $(1/2)\mu_{.1} + (1/2)\mu_{.2} - \mu_{.3} = 0$	+1/2	+1/2	−1
$\sum_{j=1}^{J}(c_j c_{j'}) =$	+1/2	−1/2	0 = 0

Thus, plugging these values into our equation produces the following:

$$\sum_{j=1}^{J}(c_j c_{j'}) = c_1 c_{1'} + c_2 c_{2'} + c_3 c_{3'} = (+1)(+1/2) + (-1)(+1/2) + (0)(-1) = (+1/2) + (-1/2) + 0 = 0$$

If the sum of the contrast coefficient products for a set of contrasts is equal to 0, then we define this as an orthogonal set of contrasts.

A set of two contrasts that are *not* orthogonal is the following, where we see that the set of contrasts does not sum to 0:

	c_1	c_2	c_3
ψ_3: $\mu_{.1} - \mu_{.2} = 0$	+1	−1	0
ψ_4: $\mu_{.1} - \mu_{.3} = 0$	+1	0	−1
$\sum_{j=1}^{J}(c_j c_{j'}) =$	+1	0	0 = +1

Thus, plugging these values into our equation produces the following, where we see that the product of the contrasts also does not sum to 0:

$$\sum_{j=1}^{J}(c_j c_{j'}) = c_1 c_{1'} + c_2 c_{2'} + c_3 c_{3'} = (+1)(+1)+(-1)(0)+(0)(-1)=(+1)+0+0=+1$$

Consider a situation where there are three groups and we decide to form three pairwise contrasts, knowing full well that they cannot all be orthogonal to one another. For this set of contrasts, the first contrast (ψ_1) compares the mean of group 1 ($c_1 = +1$) to the mean of group 2 ($c_2 = -1$). The second contrast (ψ_2) compares the mean of group 2 ($c_2 = +1$) to the mean of group 3 ($c_3 = -1$), and the third contrast compares the mean of group 1 ($c_1 = +1$) to the mean of group 3 ($c_3 = -1$).

	c_1	c_2	c_3
ψ_1: $\mu_{.1} - \mu_{.2} = 0$	+1	−1	0
ψ_2: $\mu_{.2} - \mu_{.3} = 0$	0	+1	−1
ψ_3: $\mu_{.1} - \mu_{.3} = 0$	+1	0	−1

Say that the group population means are $\mu_{.1} = 30$, $\mu_{.2} = 24$, and $\mu_{.3} = 20$. We find $\psi_1 = 6$ for the first contrast (i.e., ψ_1: $\mu_{.1} - \mu_{.2} = 30 - 24 = 6$) and $\psi_2 = 4$ for the second contrast (i.e., ψ_2: $\mu_{.2} - \mu_{.3} = 24 - 20 = 4$). Because these three contrasts are not orthogonal and contain totally redundant information about these means, $\psi_3 = 10$ for the third contrast by definition (i.e., ψ_3: $\mu_{.1} - \mu_{.3} = 30 - 20 = 10$). Thus the third contrast contains no additional information beyond that contained in the first two contrasts.

Finally, for the unequal n's or unbalanced case, two contrasts are orthogonal if the following holds:

$$\sum_{j=1}^{J}\left[\frac{c_j\, c_{j'}}{n_j}\right] = 0$$

The denominator n_j makes it more difficult to find an orthogonal set of contrasts that is of any interest to the applied researcher (see Pedhazur, 1997, for an example).

2.2 Selected Multiple Comparison Procedures (mostly planned) comp

This section considers a selection of MCPs. These represent the "best" procedures in some sense, in terms of ease of utility, popularity, and control of Type I and Type II error rates. Other procedures are briefly mentioned. In the interest of consistency, each procedure is discussed in the hypothesis testing situation based on a test statistic. Most, but not all, of these procedures can also be formulated as CIs (sometimes called a **critical difference**), although these will not be discussed here. The first few procedures discussed are for planned comparisons, whereas the remainder of the section is devoted to post hoc comparisons. For each MCP, we describe its major characteristics and then present the test statistic with an example using the data from Chapter 1.

Unless otherwise specified, each MCP makes the standard assumptions of normality, homogeneity of variance, and independence of observations. Some of the procedures do have additional restrictions, such as equal n's per group. Throughout this section, we also presume that a two-tailed alternative hypothesis is of interest, although some of the MCPs can also be used with a one-tailed alternative hypothesis. In general, the MCPs are fairly robust to nonnormality (but not for extreme cases), but are not as robust to departures from homogeneity of variance or from independence (see Pavur, 1988).

2.2.1 Planned Analysis of Trend

Trend analysis is a planned MCP useful when the groups represent different quantitative levels of a factor (i.e., an interval or ratio level independent variable). Examples of such a factor might be age, drug dosage, and different amounts of instruction, practice, or trials. Here the researcher is interested in whether the sample means vary with a change in the amount of the independent variable. We define **trend analysis** in the form of orthogonal polynomials and assume that the levels of the independent variable are equally spaced (i.e., same distances between the levels of the independent variable, such as 100, 200, 300, and 400cc) and that the number of observations per group is the same. This is the standard case; other cases are briefly discussed at the end of this section.

Orthogonal polynomial contrasts use the standard t test statistic, which is compared to the critical values of $\pm_{\alpha/2} t_{df(error)}$ obtained from the t table in Table A.2. The form of the contrasts is a bit different and requires a bit of discussion. Orthogonal polynomial contrasts incorporate two concepts, orthogonal contrasts (recall these are unrelated or independent contrasts) and polynomial regression. For J groups, there can be only $J - 1$ orthogonal contrasts in a set. In polynomial regression, we have terms in the model for a linear trend, a quadratic trend, a cubic trend, and so on. For example, linear trend is represented by a straight line (no bends), quadratic trend by a curve with one bend (e.g., U or upside-down U shapes), and cubic trend by a curve with two bends (e.g., S shape).

Now put those two ideas together. A set of orthogonal contrasts can be formed where the first contrast evaluates a linear trend, the second a quadratic trend, the third a cubic trend, and so forth. Thus for J groups, the highest order polynomial that can be formed is $J - 1$. With four groups, for example, one could form a set of three orthogonal contrasts to assess linear, quadratic, and cubic trends.

You may be wondering just how these contrasts are formed? For $J = 4$ groups, the contrast coefficients for the linear, quadratic, and cubic trends are as follows:

	c_1	c_2	c_3	c_4
ψ_{linear}	-3	-1	$+1$	$+3$
$\psi_{quadratic}$	$+1$	-1	-1	$+1$
ψ_{cubic}	-1	$+3$	-3	$+1$

where the contrasts can be written out as follows:

$$\psi_{linear} = (-3)\mu_{.1} + (-1)\mu_{.2} + (+1)\mu_{.3} + (+3)\mu_{.4}$$

$$\psi_{quadratic} = (+1)\mu_{.1} + (-1)\mu_{.2} + (-1)\mu_{.3} + (+1)\mu_{.4}$$

$$\psi_{cubic} = (-1)\mu_{.1} + (+3)\mu_{.2} + (-3)\mu_{.3} + (+1)\mu_{.4}$$

These contrast coefficients, for a number of different values of J, can be found in Table A.6. If you look in the table of contrast coefficients for values of J greater than 6, you see that the coefficients for the higher-order polynomials are not included. As an example, for J = 7, coefficients only up through a quintic trend are included. Although they could easily be derived and tested, these higher-order polynomials are usually not of interest to the researcher. In fact, it is rare to find anyone interested in polynomials beyond the cubic because they are difficult to understand and interpret (although statistically sophisticated, they say little to the applied researcher as the results must be interpreted in values that are highly complex). The contrasts are typically tested sequentially beginning with the linear trend and proceeding to higher-order trends (cubic then quadratic).

Using the example data on the attractiveness of the lab instructors from Chapter 1, let us test for linear, quadratic, and cubic trends. Trend analysis may be relevant for these data because the groups do represent different quantitative levels of an attractiveness factor. Because J = 4, we can use the contrast coefficients given previously.

The following are the computations, based on these mean values, to test the trend analysis. The critical values (where df_{error} is calculated as $N - J$, or $32 - 4 = 28$) are determined to be as follows:

$$\pm_{\alpha/2} t_{df(error)} = \pm_{.025} t_{28} = \pm 2.048$$

The standard error for **linear trend** is computed as follows (where $n_j = 8$ for each of the J = 4 groups; MS_{error} was computed in the previous chapter and found to be 36.1116). Recall that the contrast equation for the linear trend is $\psi_{linear} = (-3)\mu_{.1} + (-1)\mu_{.2} + (+1)\mu_{.3} + (+3)\mu_{.4}$, and thus these are the c_j values in the following equation (-3, -1, +1, and +3, respectively):

$$s_{\psi'} = \sqrt{MS_{error} \sum_{j=1}^{J}\left(\frac{c_j^2}{n_j}\right)} = \sqrt{36.1116\left(\frac{(-3)^2}{8} + \frac{(-1)^2}{8} + \frac{1^2}{8} + \frac{3^2}{8}\right)}$$

$$= \sqrt{36.1116\left(\frac{9}{8} + \frac{1}{8} + \frac{1}{8} + \frac{9}{8}\right)} = 9.5015$$

The standard error for **quadratic trend** is determined similarly. Recall that the contrast equation for the quadratic trend is $\psi_{quadratic} = (+1)\mu_{.1} + (-1)\mu_{.2} + (-1)\mu_{.3} + (+1)\mu_{.4}$, and thus these are the c_j values in the following equation (+1, -1, -1, and +1, respectively):

$$s_{\psi'} = \sqrt{MS_{error} \sum_{j=1}^{J}\left(\frac{c_j^2}{n_j}\right)} = \sqrt{36.1116\left(\frac{1^2}{8} + \frac{(-1)^2}{8} + \frac{(-1)^2}{8} + \frac{1^2}{8}\right)}$$

$$= \sqrt{36.1116\left(\frac{1}{8} + \frac{1}{8} + \frac{1}{8} + \frac{1}{8}\right)} = 4.2492$$

The standard error for **_cubic trend_** is computed similarly. Recall that the contrast equation for the cubic trend is $\psi_{cubic} = (-1)\mu_{.1} + (+3)\mu_{.2} + (-3)\mu_{.3} + (+1)\mu_{.4}$, and thus these are the c_j values in the following equation (-1, $+3$, -3, and $+1$, respectively):

$$s_{\psi'} = \sqrt{MS_{error} \sum_{j=1}^{J} \left(\frac{c_j^2}{n_j} \right)} = \sqrt{36.1116 \left(\frac{(-1)^2}{8} + \frac{3^2}{8} + \frac{(-3)^2}{8} + \frac{1^2}{8} \right)}$$

$$= \sqrt{36.1116 \left(\frac{1}{8} + \frac{9}{8} + \frac{9}{8} + \frac{1}{8} \right)} = 9.5015$$

Recall the following means for each group (as presented in the previous chapter):

	Number of Statistics Labs Attended by Group				
	Group 1: Unattractive	Group 2: Slightly Unattractive	Group 3: Moderately Attractive	Group 4: Very Attractive	Overall
	15	20	10	30	
	10	13	24	22	
	12	9	29	26	
	8	22	12	20	
	21	24	27	29	
	7	25	21	28	
	13	18	25	25	
	3	12	14	15	
Means	11.1250	17.8750	20.2500	24.3750	18.4063
Variances	30.1250	35.2679	53.0714	25.9821	56.4425

Thus, using the contrast coefficients (represented by the constant c values in the numerator of each term) and the values of the means for each of the four groups (represented by $\bar{Y}_{.1}, \bar{Y}_{.2}, \bar{Y}_{.3}, \bar{Y}_{.4}$), the test statistics are computed as follows:

$$t_{linear} = \frac{-3\bar{Y}_{.1} - 1\bar{Y}_{.2} + 1\bar{Y}_{.3} + 3\bar{Y}_{.4}}{s_{\psi'}} = \frac{-3(11.1250) - 1(17.8750) + 1(20.2500) + 3(24.3750)}{9.5015} = 4.4335$$

$$t_{quadratic} = \frac{1\bar{Y}_{.1} - 1\bar{Y}_{.2} - 1\bar{Y}_{.3} + 1\bar{Y}_{.4}}{s_{\psi'}} = \frac{1(11.1250) - 1(17.8750) - 1(20.2500) + 1(24.3750)}{4.2492} = -0.6178$$

$$t_{cubic} = \frac{-1\bar{Y}_{.1} + 3\bar{Y}_{.2} - 3\bar{Y}_{.3} + 1\bar{Y}_{.4}}{s_{\psi'}} = \frac{-1(11.1250) + 3(17.8750) - 3(20.2500) + 1(24.3750)}{9.5015} = 0.6446$$

The t test statistic for the linear trend exceeds the t critical value. Thus we see that there is a statistically significant *linear trend* in the means but no significant *higher-order* trend (in other words, no significant quadratic or cubic trend). This should not be surprising as shown in the profile plot of the means of Figure 2.1, where there is a very strong linear

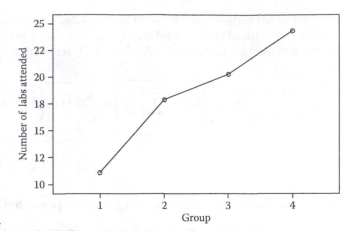

FIGURE 2.1
Profile plot for statistics lab example.

trend, and that is about it. In other words, there is a steady increase in mean attendance as the level of attractiveness of the instructor increases. Always plot the means so that you can interpret the results of the contrasts.

Let us make some final points about orthogonal polynomial contrasts. First, be particularly careful about extrapolating beyond the range of the levels investigated. The trend may or may not be the same outside of this range; that is, given only those sample means, we have no way of knowing what the trend is outside of the range of levels investigated. Second, in the unequal n's or unbalanced case, it becomes difficult to formulate a set of orthogonal contrasts that make any sense to the researcher. See the discussion in the next section on planned orthogonal contrasts, as well as Kirk (1982). Third, when the levels are not equally spaced, this needs to be taken into account in the contrast coefficients (see Kirk, 1982).

2.2.2 Planned Orthogonal Contrasts

Planned orthogonal contrasts (POC) are an MCP where the contrasts are defined ahead of time by the researcher (i.e., planned) and the set of contrasts are orthogonal (or unrelated). The POC method is a contrast-based procedure where the researcher is not concerned with control of the family-wise Type I error rate across the set of contrasts. The set of contrasts are orthogonal, so the number of contrasts should be small, and concern with the family-wise error rate is lessened.

Computationally, planned orthogonal contrasts use the standard t test statistic that is compared to the critical values of $\pm_{\alpha/2} t_{df(error)}$ obtained from the t table in Table A.2. Using the example dataset from Chapter 1, let us find a set of orthogonal contrasts and complete the computations. Since $J = 4$, we can find at most a set of three (or $J-1$) orthogonal contrasts. One orthogonal set that seems reasonable for these data is as follows:

	c_1	c_2	c_3	c_4
$\psi_1: \left(\dfrac{\mu_{.1}+\mu_{.2}}{2}\right)-\left(\dfrac{\mu_{.3}+\mu_{.4}}{2}\right)=0$	+1/2	+1/2	−1/2	−1/2
$\psi_2: \mu_{.1}-\mu_{.2}=0$	+1	−1	0	0
$\psi_3: \mu_{.3}-\mu_{.4}=0$	0	0	+1	−1

Here we see that the first contrast compares the average of the two least attractive groups (i.e., unattractive and slightly attractive) with the average of the two most attractive groups (i.e., moderately attractive and very attractive), the second contrast compares the means of the two least attractive groups (i.e., unattractive and slightly attractive), and the third contrast compares the means of the two most attractive groups (moderately attractive and very attractive). Note that the design is balanced (i.e., the equal n's case as all groups had a sample size of 8). What follows are the computations. The critical values are as follows:

$$\pm_{\alpha/2}t_{df(error)} = \pm_{.025}t_{28} = \pm 2.048$$

The standard error for contrast 1 is computed as follows (where $n_j = 8$ for each of the $J = 4$ groups; MS_{error} was computed in the previous chapter and found to be 36.1116). The equation for contrast 1 is ψ_1: $\left(\dfrac{\mu_{.1} + \mu_{.2}}{2}\right) - \left(\dfrac{\mu_{.3} + \mu_{.4}}{2}\right) = 0$, and thus these are the c_j values in the following equation (+1/2, +1/2, –1/2, –1/2, respectively, and these values are then squared, which results in the value of .25):

$$s_{\psi'} = \sqrt{MS_{error} \sum_{j=1}^{J}\left(\frac{c_j^2}{n_j}\right)} = \sqrt{36.1116\left(\frac{.25}{8} + \frac{.25}{8} + \frac{.25}{8} + \frac{.25}{8}\right)} = 2.1246$$

Similarly, the standard errors for contrasts 2 and 3 are computed as follows:

$$s_{\psi'} = \sqrt{MS_{error} \sum_{j=1}^{J}\left(\frac{c_j^2}{n_j}\right)} = \sqrt{36.1116\left(\frac{1}{8} + \frac{1}{8}\right)} = 3.0046$$

The test statistics are computed as follows:

$$t_1 = \frac{+\frac{1}{2}\overline{Y}_{.1} + \frac{1}{2}\overline{Y}_{.2} - \frac{1}{2}\overline{Y}_{.3} - \frac{1}{2}\overline{Y}_{.4}}{s_{\psi'}}$$

$$= \frac{+\frac{1}{2}(11.1250) + \frac{1}{2}(17.8750) - \frac{1}{2}(20.2500) - \frac{1}{2}(24.3750)}{2.1246} = -3.6772$$

$$t_2 = \frac{\overline{Y}_{.1} - \overline{Y}_{.2}}{s_{\psi'}} = \frac{11.1250 - 17.8750}{3.0046} = -2.2466$$

$$t_3 = \frac{\overline{Y}_{.3} - \overline{Y}_{.4}}{s_{\psi'}} = \frac{20.2500 - 24.3750}{3.0046} = -1.3729$$

The result for contrast 1 is that the combined less attractive groups have statistically significantly lower attendance, on average, than the combined more attractive groups. The result for contrast 2 is that the two less attractive groups are statistically significantly different from one another, on average. The result for contrast 3 is that the means of the two more attractive groups are not statistically significantly different from one another.

There is a practical problem with this procedure because (a) the contrasts that are of interest to the researcher may not necessarily be orthogonal, or (b) the researcher may not be interested in all of the contrasts of a particular orthogonal set. Another problem already mentioned occurs when the design is unbalanced, where an orthogonal set of contrasts may be constructed at the expense of meaningful contrasts. Our advice is simple:

1. If the contrasts you are interested in are not orthogonal, then use another MCP.
2. If you are not interested in all of the contrasts of an orthogonal set, then use another MCP.
3. If your design is not balanced and the orthogonal contrasts formed are not meaningful, then use another MCP.

In each case, you need a different *planned* MCP. We recommend using one of the following procedures discussed later in this chapter: the Dunnett, Dunn (Bonferroni), or Dunn–Sidak procedure.

We defined the POC as a contrast-based procedure. One could also consider an alternative family-wise method where the α_{pc} level is divided among the contrasts in the set. This procedure is defined by $\alpha_{pc} = \alpha_{fw}/c$, where c is the number of orthogonal contrasts in the set (i.e., $c = J - 1$). As we show later, this borrows a concept from the Dunn (Bonferroni) procedure. If the variances are not equal across the groups, several approximate solutions have been proposed that take the individual group variances into account (see Kirk, 1982).

2.2.3 Planned Contrasts with Reference Group: Dunnett Method

A third method of planned comparisons is attributed to Dunnett (1955). It is designed to test pairwise contrasts where a reference group (e.g., a control or baseline group) is compared to each of the other $J - 1$ groups. Thus a family of prespecified pairwise contrasts is to be evaluated. The Dunnett method is a family-wise MCP and is slightly more powerful than the Dunn procedure (another planned family-wise MCP). The test statistic is the standard t except that the standard error is simplified as follows:

$$s_{\psi'} = \sqrt{MS_{error}\left[\frac{1}{n_c} + \frac{1}{n_j}\right]}$$

where c is the reference group and j is the group to which it is being compared. The test statistic is compared to the critical values $\pm_{\alpha/2}t_{df(error),J-1}$ obtained from the Dunnett table located in Table A.7.

Using the example dataset, compare group 1, the unattractive group (used as a reference or baseline group), to each of the other three groups. The contrasts are as follows:

	c_1	c_2	c_3	c_4
$\psi_1: \mu_{.1} - \mu_{.2} = 0$	+1	−1	0	0
$\psi_2: \mu_{.1} - \mu_{.3} = 0$	+1	0	−1	0
$\psi_3: \mu_{.1} - \mu_{.4} = 0$	+1	0	0	−1

The following are the computations. The critical values are as follows: $\pm_{\alpha/2}t_{df(error),J-1} = \pm_{.025}t_{28,3} \approx \pm 2.48$

The standard error is computed as follows (where $n_c = 8$ for the reference group; $n_j = 8$ for each of the other groups; MS_{error} was computed in the previous chapter and found to be 36.1116):

$$s_{\psi'} = \sqrt{MS_{error}\left[\frac{1}{n_c}+\frac{1}{n_j}\right]} = \sqrt{36.1116\left[\frac{1}{8}+\frac{1}{8}\right]} = 3.0046$$

The test statistics for the three contrasts (i.e., group 1 to group 2, group 1 to group 3, and group 1 to group 4) are computed as follows:

Unnattractive to slightly attractive: $t_1 = \dfrac{\bar{Y}_1 - \bar{Y}_2}{s_{\psi'}} = \dfrac{11.1250 - 17.8750}{3.0046} = -2.2466$

Unnattractive to moderately attractive: $t_2 = \dfrac{\bar{Y}_1 - \bar{Y}_3}{s_{\psi'}} = \dfrac{11.1250 - 20.2500}{3.0046} = -3.0370$

Unnattractive to very attractive: $t_3 = \dfrac{\bar{Y}_1 - \bar{Y}_4}{s_{\psi'}} = \dfrac{11.1250 - 24.3750}{3.0046} = -4.4099$

Comparing the test statistics to the critical values, we see that the second group (i.e., slightly attractive) is not statistically significantly different from the baseline group (i.e., unattractive), but the third (moderately attractive) and fourth (very attractive) more attractive groups are significantly different from the baseline group.

If the variance of the reference group is different from the variances of the other $J - 1$ groups, then a modification of this method is described in Dunnett (1964). For related procedures that are less sensitive to unequal group variances, see Wilcox (1987) or Wilcox (1996) (e.g., variation of the Dunnett T3 procedure). *— widely used*

2.2.4 Other Planned Contrasts: Dunn (or Bonferroni) and Dunn–Sidak Methods

The Dunn (1961) procedure (commonly attributed to Dunn as the developer is unknown), also often called the Bonferroni procedure (because it is based on the Bonferroni inequality), is a planned family-wise MCP. It is designed to test either pairwise or complex contrasts for balanced or unbalanced designs. Thus this MCP is very flexible and may be used to test any planned contrast of interest. The Dunn method uses the standard t test statistic with one important exception. The α level is split up among the set of planned contrasts. Typically the per contrast α level (denoted as α_{pc}) is set at α/c, where c is the number of contrasts. That is, $\alpha_{pc} = \alpha_{fw}/c$. According to this rationale, the family-wise Type I error rate (denoted as α_{fw}) will be maintained at α. For example, if $\alpha_{fw} = .05$ is desired and there are five contrasts to be tested, then each contrast would be tested at the .01 level of significance (.05/5 = .01). We are reminded that α need not be distributed equally among the set of contrasts, as long as the sum of the individual α_{pc} terms is equal to α_{fw} (Keppel & Wickens, 2004; Rosenthal & Rosnow, 1985).

Computationally, the Dunn method uses the standard t test statistic, which is compared to the critical values of $\pm_{\alpha/c}t_{df(error)}$ for a two-tailed test obtained from the table in Table A.8. The table takes the number of contrasts into account without requiring you to physically split up the α. Using the example dataset from Chapter 1, for comparison purposes, let us test the same set of three orthogonal contrasts we evaluated with the POC method. These contrasts are as follows:

	c_1	c_2	c_3	c_4
$\psi_1: \left(\dfrac{\mu_{.1}+\mu_{.2}}{2}\right)-\left(\dfrac{\mu_{.3}+\mu_{.4}}{2}\right)=0$	+1/2	+1/2	−1/2	−1/2
$\psi_2: \mu_{.1}-\mu_{.2}=0$	+1	−1	0	0
$\psi_3: \mu_{.3}-\mu_{.4}=0$	0	0	+1	−1

Following are the computations, with the critical values

$$\pm_{\alpha/c}t_{df(error)}=\pm_{.05/3}t_{28}\approx\pm2.539$$

The standard error for contrast 1 is computed as follows:

$$s_{\psi'}=\sqrt{MS_{error}\sum_{j=1}^{J}\left(\frac{c_j^2}{n_j}\right)}=\sqrt{36.1116\left(\frac{.25}{8}+\frac{.25}{8}+\frac{.25}{8}+\frac{.25}{8}\right)}=2.1246$$

Similarly, the standard error for contrasts 2 and 3 is computed as follows:

$$s_{\psi'}=\sqrt{MS_{error}\sum_{j=1}^{J}\left(\frac{c_j^2}{n_j}\right)}=\sqrt{36.1116\left(\frac{1}{8}+\frac{1}{8}\right)}=3.0046$$

The test statistics are computed as follows:

$$t_1=\frac{+\frac{1}{2}\bar{Y}_{.1}+\frac{1}{2}\bar{Y}_{.2}-\frac{1}{2}\bar{Y}_{.3}-\frac{1}{2}\bar{Y}_{.4}}{s_{\psi'}}$$

$$=\frac{+\frac{1}{2}(11.1250)+\frac{1}{2}(17.8750)-\frac{1}{2}(20.2500)-\frac{1}{2}(24.3750)}{2.1246}=-3.6772$$

$$t_2=\frac{\bar{Y}_{.1}-\bar{Y}_{.2}}{s_{\psi'}}=\frac{11.1250-17.8750}{3.0046}=-2.2466$$

$$t_3=\frac{\bar{Y}_{.3}-\bar{Y}_{.4}}{s_{\psi'}}=\frac{20.2500-24.3750}{3.0046}=-1.3729$$

Notice that the test statistic values have not changed from the POC, but the critical value *has* changed. For this set of contrasts then, we see the same results as were obtained via the POC procedure with the exception of contrast 2, which is now nonsignificant (i.e., only contrast 1 is significant). The reason for this difference lies in the critical values used, which were ±2.048 for the POC method and ±2.539 for the Dunn method. Here we see the conservative nature of the Dunn procedure because the critical value is larger than with the POC method, thus making it a bit more difficult to reject H_0.

The Dunn procedure is slightly conservative (i.e., not as powerful) in that the true α_{fw} may be less than the specified nominal α level. For example, if the nominal alpha (specified by the researcher) is .05, then the true alpha may be less than .05. Thus when using the Dunn, you may be less likely to reject the null hypothesis (i.e., less likely to find a statistically significant contrast). A less conservative (i.e., more powerful) modification is known as the Dunn–Sidak procedure (Dunn, 1974; Sidak, 1967) and uses slightly different critical values. For more information, see Kirk (1982), Wilcox (1987), and Keppel and Wickens (2004). The Bonferroni modification can also be applied to other MCPs.

2.2.5 Complex Post Hoc Contrasts: Scheffé and Kaiser–Bowden Methods

Another early MCP due to Scheffé (1953) is quite versatile. The Scheffé procedure can be used for any possible type of comparison, orthogonal or nonorthogonal, pairwise or complex, planned or post hoc, where the family-wise error rate is controlled. The Scheffé method is so general that the tests are quite conservative (i.e., less powerful), particularly for the pairwise contrasts. This is so because the family of contrasts for the Scheffé method consists of all possible linear comparisons. To control the Type I error rate for such a large family, the procedure has to be conservative (i.e., making it less likely to reject the null hypothesis if it is really true). Thus we recommend the Scheffé method only for complex post hoc comparisons.

The Scheffé procedure is the only MCP that is necessarily consistent with the results of the F ratio in ANOVA. If the F ratio is statistically significant, then this means that at least one contrast in the entire family of contrasts will be significant with the Scheffé method. Do not forget, however, that this family can be quite large and you may not even be interested in the contrast(s) that wind up being significant. If the F ratio is not statistically significant, then none of the contrasts in the family will be significant with the Scheffé method.

The test statistic for the Scheffé method is the standard t again. This is compared to the critical value $\sqrt{(J-1)(\alpha F_{J-1, df(error)})}$ taken from the F table in Table A.4. In other words, the square root of the F critical value is adjusted by $J-1$, which serves to increase the Scheffé critical value and make the procedure a more conservative one.

Consider a few example contrasts with the Scheffé method. Using the example dataset from Chapter 1, for comparison purposes, we test the same set of three orthogonal contrasts that were evaluated with the POC method. These contrasts are again as follows:

	c_1	c_2	c_3	c_4
$\psi_1: \left(\dfrac{\mu_{.1}+\mu_{.2}}{2}\right) - \left(\dfrac{\mu_{.3}+\mu_{.4}}{2}\right) = 0$	+1/2	+1/2	−1/2	−1/2
$\psi_2: \mu_{.1}-\mu_{.2}=0$	+1	−1	0	0
$\psi_3: \mu_{.3}-\mu_{.4}=0$	0	0	+1	−1

The following are the computations. The critical value is as follows:

$$\sqrt{(J-1)(\alpha F_{J-1, df(error)})} = \sqrt{(3)(_{.05}F_{3,28})} = \sqrt{(3)(2.95)} = 2.97$$

Standard error for contrast 1:

$$s_{\psi'} = \sqrt{MS_{error} \sum_{j=1}^{J} \left(\frac{c_j^2}{n_j} \right)} = \sqrt{36.1116\,(.25/8 + .25/8 + .25/8 + .25/8)} = 2.1246$$

Standard error for contrasts 2 and 3:

$$s_{\psi'} = \sqrt{MS_{error} \left[\frac{1}{n_j} + \frac{1}{n_{j'}} \right]} = \sqrt{36.1116 \left[\frac{1}{8} + \frac{1}{8} \right]} = 3.0046$$

The test statistics are computed as follows:

$$t_1 = \frac{+\frac{1}{2}\bar{Y}_{.1} + \frac{1}{2}\bar{Y}_{.2} - \frac{1}{2}\bar{Y}_{.3} - \frac{1}{2}\bar{Y}_{.4}}{s_{\psi'}}$$

$$= \frac{+\frac{1}{2}(11.1250) + \frac{1}{2}(17.8750) - \frac{1}{2}(20.2500) - \frac{1}{2}(24.3750)}{2.1246} = -3.6772$$

$$t_2 = \frac{\bar{Y}_{.1} - \bar{Y}_{.2}}{s_{\psi'}} = \frac{11.1250 - 17.8750}{3.0046} = -2.2466$$

$$t_3 = \frac{\bar{Y}_{.3} - \bar{Y}_{.4}}{s_{\psi'}} = \frac{20.2500 - 24.3750}{3.0046} = -1.3729$$

Using the Scheffé method, these results are precisely the same as those obtained via the Dunn procedure. There is somewhat of a difference in the critical values, which were 2.97 for the Scheffé method, 2.539 for the Dunn method, and 2.048 for the POC method. Here we see that the Scheffé procedure is even more conservative than the Dunn procedure, thus making it a bit more difficult to reject H_0.

For situations where the group variances are unequal, a modification of the Scheffé method less sensitive to unequal variances has been proposed by Brown and Forsythe (1974). Kaiser and Bowden (1983) found that the Brown-Forsythe procedure may cause the actual α level to exceed the nominal α level, and thus we recommend the Kaiser–Bowden modification. For more information, see Kirk (1982), Wilcox (1987), and Wilcox (1996).

2.2.6 Simple Post Hoc Contrasts: Tukey HSD, Tukey–Kramer, Fisher LSD, and Hayter Tests

Tukey's (1953) honestly significant difference (HSD) test is one of the most popular post hoc MCPs. The HSD test is a family-wise procedure and is most appropriate for considering all pairwise contrasts with equal n's per group (i.e., a balanced design). The HSD test is sometimes referred to as the **studentized range test** because it is based on the sampling distribution of the studentized range statistic developed by William Sealy Gosset (forced to use the pseudonym "Student" by his employer, the Guinness brewery). For the traditional approach, the first step in the analysis is to rank order the means from largest $(\bar{Y}_{.1})$ to smallest $(\bar{Y}_{.J})$. The test statistic, or studentized range statistic, is computed as follows:

$$q_i = \frac{\bar{Y}_{.j} - \bar{Y}_{.j'}}{s_{\psi'}}$$

where

$$s_{\psi'} = \sqrt{\frac{MS_{error}}{n}}$$

where

   i identifies the specific contrast
   j and j' designate the two group means to be compared
   n represents the number of observations per group (equal n's per group is required)

The test statistic is compared to the critical value $\pm_\alpha q_{df(error),J}$, where df_{error} is equal to $J(n-1)$. The table for these critical values is given in Table A.9.

The first contrast involves a test of the largest pairwise difference in the set of J means (q_1) (i.e., largest vs. smallest means). If these means are not significantly different, then the analysis stops because no other pairwise difference could be significant. If these means are different, then we proceed to test the second pairwise difference involving the largest mean (i.e., q_2). Contrasts involving the largest mean are continued until a nonsignificant difference is found. Then the analysis picks up with the second largest mean and compares it with the smallest mean. Contrasts involving the second largest mean are continued until a nonsignificant difference is detected. The analysis continues with the next largest mean and the smallest mean, and so on, until it is obvious that no other pairwise contrast could be significant.

Finally, consider an example using the HSD procedure with the attractiveness data. The following are the computations. The critical values are as follows:

$$\pm_\alpha q_{df(error),J} = \pm_{.05} q_{28,4} \approx \pm 3.87$$

The standard error is computed as follows where n represents the sample size per group:

$$s_{\psi'} = \sqrt{\frac{MS_{error}}{n}} = \sqrt{\frac{36.1116}{8}} = 2.1246$$

The test statistics are computed as follows:

Very attractive to unattractive: $q_1 = \dfrac{\bar{Y}_4 - \bar{Y}_{.1}}{s_{\psi'}} = \dfrac{24.3750 - 11.1250}{2.1246} = 6.2365$

Very attractive to slightly attractive: $q_2 = \dfrac{\bar{Y}_4 - \bar{Y}_2}{s_{\psi'}} = \dfrac{24.3750 - 17.8750}{2.1246} = 3.0594$

Moderately attractive to unattractive: $q_3 = \dfrac{\bar{Y}_3 - \bar{Y}_{.1}}{s_{\psi'}} = \dfrac{20.2500 - 11.1250}{2.1246} = 4.2949$

Moderately attractive to slightly attractive: $q_4 = \dfrac{\bar{Y}_3 - \bar{Y}_2}{s_{\psi'}} = \dfrac{20.2500 - 17.8750}{2.1246} = 1.1179$

Slightly attractive to unattractive: $q_5 = \dfrac{\bar{Y}_2 - \bar{Y}_1}{s_{\psi'}} = \dfrac{17.8750 - 11.1250}{2.1246} = 3.1771$

Comparing the test statistic values to the critical value, these results indicate that the group means are significantly different for groups 1 (unattractive) and 4 (very attractive) and for groups 1 (unattractive) and 3 (moderately attractive). Just for completeness, we examine the final possible pairwise contrast involving groups 3 and 4. However, we already know from the results of previous contrasts that these means cannot possibly be significantly different. The test statistic result for this contrast is as follows:

Very attractive to moderately attractive: $q_6 = \dfrac{\bar{Y}_4 - \bar{Y}_3}{s_{\psi'}} = \dfrac{24.3750 - 20.2500}{2.1246} = 1.9415$

Occasionally researchers need to summarize the results of their pairwise comparisons. Table 2.1 shows the results of Tukey HSD contrasts for the example data. For ease of interpretation, the means are ordered from lowest to highest. The first row consists of the results for those contrasts that involve group 1. Thus the mean for group 1 (unattractive) is statistically different from those of groups 3 (moderately attractive) and 4 (very attractive) only. None of the other pairwise contrasts were shown to be significant. Such a table could also be developed for other pairwise MCPs.

The HSD test has exact control of the family-wise error rate assuming normality, homogeneity, and equal n's (better than Dunn or Dunn–Sidak). The HSD procedure is more powerful than the Dunn or Scheffé procedure for testing all possible pairwise contrasts, although Dunn is more powerful for less than all possible pairwise contrasts. The HSD technique is the recommended MCP as a pairwise method in the equal n's situation. The HSD test is reasonably robust to nonnormality, but not in extreme cases, and is not as robust as the Scheffé MCP.

There are several alternatives to the HSD for the unequal n's case. These include the Tukey–Kramer modification (Kramer, 1956; Tukey, 1953), which assumes normality and homogeneity. The Tukey–Kramer test statistic is the same as the Tukey HSD except that the standard error is computed as follows (*note that when requesting Tukey in SPSS, the program knows which standard error to calculate*):

$$ s_{\psi'} = \sqrt{MS_{error}\left[\frac{1}{2}\left(\frac{1}{n_1} + \frac{1}{n_2}\right)\right]} $$

The critical value is determined in the same way as with the Tukey HSD procedure.

TABLE 2.1

Tukey HSD Contrast Test Statistics and Results

	Group 1: Unattractive	Group 2: Slightly Unattractive	Group 3: Moderately Attractive	Group 4: Very Attractive
Group 1 (mean = 11.1250)	—	3.1771	4.2949*	6.2365*
Group 2 (mean = 17.8750)		—	1.1179	3.0594
Group 3 (mean = 20.2500)			—	1.9415
Group 4 (mean = 24.3750)				—

*$p < .05$; $_{.05}q_{28,4} = 3.87$.

Fisher's (1949) least significant difference (LSD) test, also known as the protected t test, was the first MCP developed and is a pairwise post hoc procedure. It is a sequential procedure where a significant ANOVA F is followed by the LSD test in which all (or perhaps some) pairwise t tests are examined. The standard t test statistic is compared with the critical values of $\pm_{\alpha/2}t_{df(error)}$. The LSD test has precise control of the family-wise error rate for the three-group situation, assuming normality and homogeneity; but for more than three groups, the protection deteriorates rather rapidly. In that case, a modification due to Hayter (1986) is suggested for more adequate protection. The Hayter test appears to have more power than the Tukey HSD and excellent control of family-wise error (Keppel & Wickens, 2004).

2.2.7 Simple Post Hoc Contrasts for Unequal Variances: Games–Howell, Dunnett T3 and C Tests

When the group variances are unequal, several alternative procedures are available. These alternatives include the Games and Howell (1976), and Dunnett T3 and C (1980) procedures. According to Wilcox (1996, 2003), T3 is recommended for $n < 50$ and Games–Howell for $n > 50$, and C performs about the same as Games-Howell. For further details on these methods, see Kirk (1982), Wilcox (1987, 1996, 2003), Hochberg (1988), and Benjamini and Hochberg (1995).

2.2.8 Follow-Up Tests to Kruskal–Wallis

Recall from Chapter 1 the nonparametric equivalent to ANOVA, the Kruskal–Wallis test. Several post hoc procedures are available to follow up a statistically significant overall Kruskal–Wallis test. The procedures discussed here are the nonparametric equivalents to the Scheffé and Tukey HSD methods. One may form pairwise or complex contrasts as in the parametric case. The test statistic is Z and computed as follows:

$$Z = \frac{\psi_i'}{s_{\psi'}}$$

where the standard error in the denominator is computed as

$$s_{\psi'} = \sqrt{\frac{N(N+1)}{12} \sum_{j=1}^{J} \left(\frac{c_j^2}{n_j} \right)}$$

and where N is the total number of observations. For the Scheffé method, the test statistic Z is compared to the critical value $\sqrt{_\alpha \chi_{J-1}}$ obtained from the χ^2 table in Table A.3. For the Tukey HSD procedure, the test statistic Z is compared to the critical value $_\alpha q_{df(error),J}/\sqrt{2}$ obtained from the table of critical values for the studentized range statistic in Table A.9.

Let us use the attractiveness data to illustrate. Do not forget that we use the ranked data as described in Chapter 1. The rank means for the groups are as follows: group 1 (unattractive) = 7.7500, group 2 (slightly attractive) = 15.2500, group 3 (moderately attractive) = 18.7500, and group 4 (very attractive) = 24.2500. Here we only examine two contrasts and then compare the results for both the Scheffé and Tukey HSD methods. The first contrast compares the two low-attractiveness groups (i.e., groups 1 and 2), whereas the second contrast compares the two low-attractiveness groups with the two high-attractiveness groups (i.e., groups 3 and 4). In other words, we examine a pairwise contrast and a complex contrast, respectively. The results are given here. The critical values are as follows:

$$\text{Scheffé } \sqrt{_\alpha \chi_{J-1}} = \sqrt{_{.05}\chi_3} = \sqrt{7.8147} = 2.7955$$

$$\text{Tukey } _\alpha q_{df(error),J}/\sqrt{2} = {_{.05}}q_{28,4}/\sqrt{2} \approx 3.87/\sqrt{2} \approx 2.7365$$

The standard error for contrast 1 is computed as

$$s_{\psi'} = \sqrt{\frac{N(N+1)}{12}\sum_{j=1}^{J}\left(\frac{c_j^2}{n_j}\right)} = \sqrt{\left[\frac{32(33)}{12}\right]\left[\frac{1}{8}+\frac{1}{8}\right]} = 4.6904$$

The standard error for contrast 2 is calculated as follows:

$$s_{\psi'} = \sqrt{\frac{N(N+1)}{12}\sum_{j=1}^{J}\left(\frac{c_j^2}{n_j}\right)} = \sqrt{\left[\frac{32(33)}{12}\right]\left[\frac{.25}{8}+\frac{.25}{8}+\frac{.25}{8}+\frac{.25}{8}\right]} = 3.3166$$

The test statistics are computed as follows:

$$Z_1 = \frac{\bar{Y}_{.1}-\bar{Y}_{.2}}{s_{\psi'}} = \frac{7.75-15.25}{4.6904} = -1.5990$$

$$Z_2 = \frac{+\frac{1}{2}\bar{Y}_{.1}+\frac{1}{2}\bar{Y}_{.2}-\frac{1}{2}\bar{Y}_{.3}-\frac{1}{2}\bar{Y}_{.4}}{s_{\psi'}} = \frac{+\frac{1}{2}(7.75)+\frac{1}{2}(15.25)-\frac{1}{2}(18.75)-\frac{1}{2}(24.25)}{3.3166} = -3.0151$$

For both procedures, we find a statistically significant difference with the second contrast but not with the first. These results agree with most of the other parametric procedures for these particular contrasts. That is, the less attractive groups are not significantly different (only significant with POC), whereas the two less attractive groups are significantly different from the two more attractive groups (significant with all procedures). One could also devise nonparametric equivalent MCPs for methods other than the Scheffé and Tukey procedures.

2.3 SPSS

In our last section, we examine what SPSS has to offer in terms of MCPs. Here we use the general linear model module (although the one-way ANOVA module can also be used). The steps for requesting a one-way ANOVA were presented in the previous chapter and will not be reiterated here. Rather, we will assume all the previously mentioned options have been selected. The last step, therefore, is selection of one or more planned (a priori) or post hoc MCPs. For purposes of this illustration, the Tukey will be selected. However, you are encouraged to examine other MCPs for this dataset.

Step 1: From the "Univariate" dialog box, click on "Post Hoc" to select various post hoc MCPs or click on "Contrasts" to select various planned MCPs (see screenshot step 1).

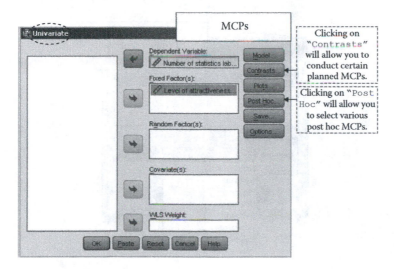

Step 2 (post hoc MCP): Click on the name of independent variable in the "Factor(s)" list box in the top left and move to the "Post Hoc Tests for" box in the top right by clicking on the arrow key. Check an appropriate MCP for your situation by placing a checkmark in the box next to the desired MCP. In this example, we will select "Tukey." Click on "Continue" to return to the original dialog box. Click on "OK" to return to generate the output.

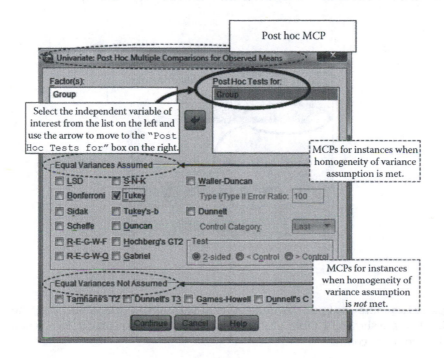

Step 3a (planned MCP): To obtain trend analysis contrasts, click the "Contrasts" button from the "Univariate" dialog box (see screenshot step 1). From the "Contrasts" dialog box, click the "Contrasts" pulldown and scroll down to "Polynomial."

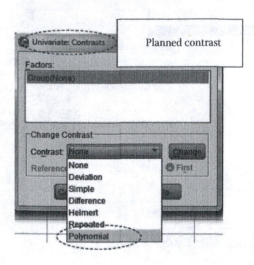

Step 3b: Click "Change" to select "Polynomial" and move it to be displayed in parentheses next to the independent variable. Recall that this type of contrast will allow testing of linear, quadratic, and cubic contrasts. Other specific planned contrasts are also available. Then click "Continue" to return to the "Univariate" dialog box.

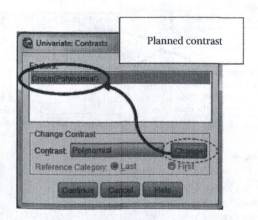

Interpreting the output: Annotated results from the Tukey HSD procedure, as one example MCP, are shown in Table 2.2. Note that CIs around a mean difference of 0 are given to the right for each contrast.

TABLE 2.2

Tukey HSD SPSS Results for the Statistics Lab Example

Descriptive Statistics

Dependent Variable: Number of Statistics Labs Attended

Level of Attractiveness	Mean	Std. Deviation	N
Unattractive	11.1250	5.48862	8
Slightly attractive	17.8750	5.93867	8
Moderately attractive	20.2500	7.28501	8
Very attractive	24.3750	5.09727	8
Total	18.4062	7.51283	32

Recall the means of the groups as presented in the previous chapter.

"Mean difference" is simply the difference between the means of the two groups compared. For example, the mean difference of group 1 and group 2 is calculated as $11.1250 - 17.8750 = -6.7500$

Number of Statistics Labs Attended   **Multiple Comparisons**

Tukey HSD

(I) Level of Attractiveness	(J) Level of Attractiveness	Mean Difference (I–J)	Std. Error	Sig.	95% Confidence Interval	
					Lower Bound	Upper Bound
Unattractive	Slightly attractive	−6.7500	3.00465	.135	−14.9536	1.4536
	Moderately attractive	−9.1250*	3.00465	.025	−17.3286	−.9214
	Very attractive	−13.2500*	3.00465	.001	−21.4536	−5.0464
Slightly attractive	Unattractive	6.7500	3.00465	.135	−1.4536	14.9536
	Moderately attractive	−2.3750	3.00465	.858	−10.5786	5.8286
	Very attractive	−6.5000	3.00465	.158	−14.7036	1.7036
Moderately attractive	Unattractive	9.1250*	3.00465	.025	.9214	17.3286
	Slightly attractive	2.3750	3.00465	.858	−5.8286	10.5786
	Very attractive	−4.1250	3.00465	.526	−12.3286	4.0786
Very attractive	Unattractive	13.2500*	3.00465	.001	5.0464	21.4536
	Slightly attractive	6.5000	3.00465	.158	−1.7036	14.7036
	Moderately attractive	4.1250	3.00465	.526	−4.0786	12.3286

Based on observed means.

The error term is Mean Square(error) = 36.112.

The standard error calculated in SPSS uses the harmonic mean (Tukey-Kramer modification):

$$S_{\Psi'} = \sqrt{MS_{error}\left[\frac{1}{2}\left(\frac{1}{n_1}+\frac{1}{n_2}\right)\right]}$$

$$S_{\Psi'} = \sqrt{36.112\left[\frac{1}{2}\left(\frac{1}{8}+\frac{1}{8}+\frac{1}{8}+\frac{1}{8}\right)\right]}$$

$$S_{\Psi'} = \sqrt{9.028} = 3.00465$$

"Sig." denotes the observed p value and provides the results of the contrasts. There are only two statistically significant contrasts. There is a statistically significant mean difference between: (1) group 1 (unattractive) and group 3 (moderately attractive); and (2) between group 1 (unattractive) and group 4 (very attractive). Note that there are only 6 unique contrast results:

$$½[J(J-1)] = ½[4(4-1)] = ½(12) = 6.$$

However there are redundant results presented in the table. For example, the comparison of group 1 and 2 (presented in results row 1) is the same as the comparison of group 2 and 1 (presented in results row 2).

2.4 Template and APA-Style Write-Up

In terms of an APA-style write-up, the MCP results for the Tukey HSD test for the statistics lab example are as follows.

Recall that our graduate research assistant, Marie, was working on a research project for an independent study class to determine if there was a mean difference in the number of statistics labs attended based on the attractiveness of the lab instructor. Her research question was the following: *Is there a mean difference in the number of statistics labs students attended based on the attractiveness of the lab instructor?* Marie then generated a one-way ANOVA as the test of inference. The APA-style example paragraph of results for the one-way ANOVA, prefaced by the extent to which the assumptions of the test were met, was presented in the previous chapter. Thus only the results of the MCP (specifically the Tukey HSD) are presented here.

Post hoc analyses were conducted given the statistically significant omnibus ANOVA F test. Specifically, Tukey HSD tests were conducted on all possible pairwise contrasts. The following pairs of groups were found to be significantly different ($p < .05$): groups 1 (unattractive; $M = 11.125$, $SD = 5.4886$) and 3 (moderately attractive; $M = 20.2500$, $SD = 7.2850$), and groups 1 (unattractive) and 4 (very attractive; $M = 24.3750$, $SD = 5.0973$). In other words, students enrolled in the least attractive instructor group attended statistically significantly fewer statistics labs than students enrolled in either of the two most attractive instructor groups.

2.5 Summary

In this chapter, methods involving the comparison of multiple group means for a single independent variable were considered. The chapter began with a look at the characteristics of multiple comparisons including (a) the definition of a contrast, (b) planned and post hoc comparisons, (c) contrast-based and family-wise Type I error rates, and (d) orthogonal contrasts. Next, we moved into a lengthy discussion of recommended MCPs.

Figure 2.2 is a flowchart to assist you in making decisions about which MCP to use. Not every statistician will agree with every decision on the flowchart as there is not total consensus about which MCP is appropriate in every single situation. Nonetheless, this is simply a guide. Whether you use it in its present form or adapt it for your own needs, we hope you find the figure to be useful in your own research.

At this point, you should have met the following objectives: (a) be able to understand the concepts underlying the MCPs, (b) be able to select the appropriate MCP for a given research situation, and (c) be able to determine and interpret the results of MCPs. Chapter 3 returns to ANOVA again and discusses models for which there is more than one independent variable.

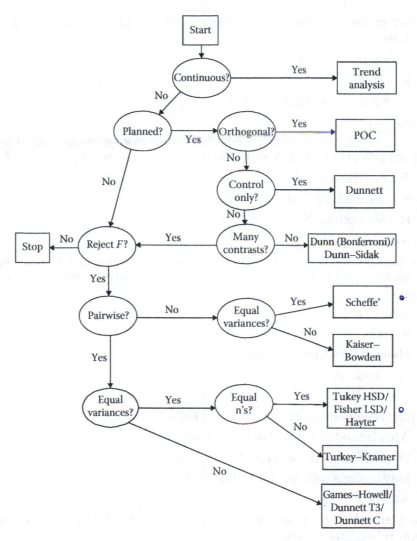

FIGURE 2.2
Flowchart of recommended MCPs.

Problems

Conceptual Problems

2.1 The Tukey HSD procedure requires equal n's and equal means. True or false?

2.2 Applying the Dunn procedure, given a nominal family-wise error rate of .10 and two contrasts, what is the per contrast alpha? $A_{fw} = .10$

    a. .01

    b. .05

    c. .10

    d. .20

2.3 Which of the following linear combinations of population means is not a legitimate contrast?

a. $(\mu_{.1} + \mu_{.2} + \mu_{.3})/3 - \mu_{.4}$

b. $\mu_{.1} - \mu_{.4}$

c. $(\mu_{.1} + \mu_{.2})/2 - (\mu_{.3} + \mu_{.4})$

d. $\mu_{.1} - \mu_{.2} + \mu_{.3} - \mu_{.4}$

2.4 When a one-factor fixed-effects ANOVA results in a significant F ratio for $J = 2$, one should follow the ANOVA with which one of the following procedures?

a. Tukey HSD method

b. Scheffé method *no*

c. Hayter method *※*

d. None of the above

2.5 If a family-based error rate for α is desired, and hypotheses involving all pairs of means are to be tested, which method of multiple comparisons should be selected?

a. Tukey HSD

b. Scheffé

c. Planned orthogonal contrasts

d. Trend analysis

e. None of the above

2.6 A priori comparisons are which one of the following?

a. Are planned in advance of the research ✓

b. Often arise out of theory and prior research ✓

c. May be done without examining the F ratio

d. All of the above

2.7 For planned contrasts involving the control group, the Dunn procedure is most appropriate. True or false?

2.8 Which is not a property of planned orthogonal contrasts?

a. The contrasts are independent. ✓

b. The contrasts are post hoc. *no*

c. The sum of the cross products of the contrast coefficients equals 0. ✓

d. If there are J groups, there are $J - 1$ orthogonal contrasts. ✓

2.9 Which MCP is most flexible in the contrasts that can be tested?

a. Planned orthogonal contrasts

b. Newman–Keuls

c. Dunnett

d. Tukey HSD

e. Scheffé

2.10 Post hoc tests are necessary after an ANOVA given which one of the following?

    a. H_0 is rejected. *yes ?*

    b. There are more than two groups.

    c. H_0 is rejected and there are more than two groups. ←

    d. You should always do post hoc tests after an ANOVA. *no*

2.11 Post hoc tests are done after ANOVA to determine why H_0 was not rejected. True or false?

HELP!

2.12 Holding the α level and the number of groups constant, as the df_{error} increases, the critical value of the q decreases. True or false?

2.13 The Tukey HSD procedure maintains the family-wise Type I error rate at α. True or false?

2.14 The Dunnett procedure assumes equal numbers of observations per group. True or false?

2.15 For complex post hoc contrasts with unequal group variances, which of the following MCPs is most appropriate?

    a. Kaiser–Bowden

    b. Dunnett

    c. Tukey HSD

    d. Scheffé

2.16 The number of levels of the independent variable is 6. How many orthogonal contrasts can be tested?

    a. 1

    b. 3

    c. 5 —

    d. 6

2.17 A researcher is interested in testing the following contrasts in a $J = 6$ study: group 1 versus 2, group 3 versus 4, and group 5 versus 6. I assert that these contrasts are orthogonal. Am I correct?

2.18 I assert that rejecting H_0 in a one-factor fixed-effects ANOVA with $J = 3$ indicates that all three pairs of group means are necessarily statistically significantly different using the Scheffé procedure. Am I correct?

2.19 For complex post hoc contrasts with equal group variances, which of the following MCPs is most appropriate?

    a. Planned orthogonal contrasts

    b. Dunnett

    c. Tukey HSD

HELP!

    d. Scheffé

2.20 A researcher finds a statistically significant omnibus F test. For which one of the following will there be at least one statistically significant MCP?

    a. Kaiser–Bowden

    b. Dunnett

    c. Tukey HSD

    d. Scheffé

2.21   If the difference between two sample means is 1000, I assert that H_0 will necessarily be rejected with the Tukey HSD. Am I correct?

2.22   Suppose all $J = 4$ of the sample means are equal to 100. I assert that it is possible to find a significant contrast with some MCP. Am I correct?

Computational Problems

2.1   A one-factor fixed-effects ANOVA is performed on data for 10 groups of unequal sizes, and H_0 is rejected at the .01 level of significance. Using the Scheffé procedure, test the contrast that

$$\bar{Y}_{.2} - \bar{Y}_{.5} = 0$$

at the .01 level of significance given the following information: $df_{with} = 40$, $\bar{Y}_{.2} = 10.8$, $n_2 = 8$, $\bar{Y}_{.5} = 15.8$, $n_5 = 8$, and $MS_{with} = 4$.

2.2   A one-factor fixed-effects ANOVA is performed on data from three groups of equal size ($n = 10$), and H_0 is rejected at the .01 level. The following values were computed: $MS_{with} = 40$ and the sample means are $\bar{Y}_{.1} = 4.5$, $\bar{Y}_{.2} = 12.5$, and $\bar{Y}_{.3} = 13.0$. Use the Tukey HSD method to test all possible pairwise contrasts.

2.3   A one-factor fixed-effects ANOVA is performed on data from three groups of equal size ($n = 20$), and H_0 is rejected at the .05 level. The following values were computed: $MS_{with} = 60$ and the sample means are $\bar{Y}_{.1} = 50$, $\bar{Y}_{.2} = 70$, and $\bar{Y}_{.3} = 85$. Use the Tukey HSD method to test all possible pairwise contrasts.

2.4   Using the data from Chapter 1, Computational Problem 4, conduct a trend analysis at the .05 level.

2.5   Consider the situation where there are $J = 4$ groups of subjects. Answer the following questions:

   a.   Construct a set of orthogonal contrasts and show that they are orthogonal.

   b.   Is the following contrast legitimate? Why or why not?

$$H_0: \mu_{.1} - (\mu_{.2} + \mu_{.3} + \mu_{.4})$$

   c.   Using the same means, how might the contrast in part (b) be altered to yield a legitimate contrast?

Interpretive Problems

2.1   For the interpretive problem you selected in Chapter 1 (using the survey 1 dataset on the website), select an a priori MCP, apply it using SPSS, and write an APA-style paragraph describing the results.

2.2   For the interpretive problem you selected in Chapter 1 (using the survey 1 dataset on the website), select a post hoc MCP, apply it using SPSS, and write an APA-style paragraph describing the results.

3

Factorial Analysis of Variance: Fixed-Effects Model

Chapter Outline

Key Concepts

1. Main effects

2. Interaction effects

3. Partitioning the sums of squares

4. The ANOVA model

5. Main-effects contrasts and simple and complex interaction contrasts

6. Nonorthogonal designs

The last two chapters have dealt with the one-factor analysis of variance (ANOVA) model and various multiple comparison procedures (MCPs) for that model. In this chapter, we continue our discussion of ANOVA models by extending the one-factor case to the two- and three-factor models. This chapter seeks an answer to the following question: What should we do if there are multiple factors for which we want to make comparisons of the means? In other words, the researcher is interested in the effect of two or more independent variables or factors on the dependent (or criterion) variable. This chapter is most concerned with two- and three-factor models, but the extension to more than three factors, when warranted, is fairly simple.

For example, suppose that a researcher is interested in the effects of textbook choice and time of day on statistics achievement. Thus, one independent variable would be the textbook selected for the course, and the second independent variable would be the time of day the course was offered. The researcher hypothesizes that certain texts may be more effective in terms of achievement than others and that student learning may be greater at certain times of the day. For the time-of-day variable, one might expect that students would not do as well in an early morning section or a late evening section than at other times of the day. In the example study, say that the researcher is interested in comparing three textbooks (A, B, and C) and three times of the day (early morning, mid-afternoon, and evening sections). Students would be randomly assigned to sections of statistics based on a combination of textbook and time of day. One group of students might be assigned to the section offered in the evening using textbook A. These results would be of interest to statistics instructors for selecting a textbook and optimal time of the day.

Most of the concepts used in this chapter are the same as those covered in Chapters 1 and 2. In addition, new concepts include main effects, interaction effects, MCPs for main and interaction effects, and nonorthogonal designs. Our objectives are that by the end of this chapter, you will be able to (a) understand the characteristics and concepts underlying factorial ANOVA, (b) determine and interpret the results of factorial ANOVA, and (c) understand and evaluate the assumptions of factorial ANOVA.

3.1 Two-Factor ANOVA Model

Marie, the educational research graduate student that we have been following, successfully conducted an experiment and used (as we saw in a previous chapter) one-way ANOVA to answer her research question. As we will see in this chapter, Marie will be extending her analysis to include an additional independent variable.

As we learned in Chapter 1, Marie is enrolled in an independent study class. As part of the course requirement, she was required to complete a research study. In collaboration with the statistics faculty in her program, Marie designed an experimental study to determine if there was a mean difference in student attendance in the statistics lab based on the attractiveness of the statistics lab instructor. Marie had also included an additional component to this experiment—time of day that the course was taken (afternoon or evening)—and she is now ready to examine these data. Marie's research question is the following: *Is there a mean difference in the number of statistics labs attended by students based on the attractiveness of the lab instructor and time of day that the course is offered?* With two independent variables, Marie determines that a factorial ANOVA is the best statistical procedure to use to answer her question. Her next task is to collect and analyze the data to address her research question.

This section describes the distinguishing characteristics of the two-factor ANOVA model, the layout of the data, the linear model, main effects and interactions, assumptions of the model and their violation, partitioning the sums of squares, the ANOVA summary table, MCPs, effect size measures, confidence intervals (CIs), power, an example, and expected mean squares.

3.1.1 Characteristics of the Model

factorial design = more than one factor

The first characteristic of the two-factor ANOVA model should be obvious by now; this model considers the effect of two factors or independent variables on a dependent variable. Each factor consists of two or more levels (or categories). This yields what we call a **factorial design** because more than a single factor is included. We see then that the two-factor ANOVA is an extension of the one-factor ANOVA. Why would a researcher want to complicate things by considering a second factor? Three reasons come to mind. First, the researcher may have a genuine interest in studying the second factor. Rather than studying each factor separately in two analyses, the researcher includes both factors in the same analysis. This allows a test not only of the effect of each individual factor, known as **main effects**, but of the effect of both factors collectively. This latter effect is known as an **interaction effect** and provides information about whether the two factors are operating independent of one another (i.e., no interaction exists) or whether the two factors are operating together to produce some additional impact (i.e., an interaction exists). If two separate analyses were conducted, one for each independent variable, no information would be obtained about the interaction effect. As becomes evident, assuming a factorial ANOVA with two independent variables, the researcher will test three hypotheses: one for each factor or main effect individually and a third for the interaction between the factors. Factorial ANOVA models with more than two independent variables will, accordingly, test for additional main effects and interactions. This chapter spends considerable time discussing interactions.

A second reason for including an additional factor is an attempt to reduce the error (or within-groups) variation, which is variation that is unexplained by the first factor. The use of a second factor provides a more precise estimate of error variance. For this reason, a two-factor design is generally more powerful than two one-factor designs, as the second factor and the interaction serve to control for additional extraneous variability. A third reason for considering two factors simultaneously is to provide greater generalizability of the results and to provide a more efficient and economical use of observations and resources. Thus, the results can be generalized to more situations, and the study will be more cost efficient in terms of time and money.

In addition, for the two-factor ANOVA, every level of the first factor (hereafter known as factor A) is paired with every level of the second factor (hereafter known as factor B). In other words, every combination of factors A and B is included in the design of the study, yielding what is referred to as a **fully crossed design**. If some combinations are not included, then the design is not fully crossed and may form some sort of a nested design (see Chapter 6). Individuals (or objects or subjects) are randomly assigned to one combination of the two factors. In other words, each individual responds to only one combination of the factors. If individuals respond to more than one combination of the factors, this would be some sort of repeated measures design, which we examine in Chapter 5. In this chapter, we only consider models where all factors are fixed. Thus, the overall design is known as a fixed-effects model. If one or both factors are random, then the design is not a fixed-effects model, which we discuss in Chapter 5. It is also a condition for factorial ANOVA that the dependent variable is measured at least at the interval level and the independent variables are categorical (either nominal or ordinal).

In this section of the chapter, for simplicity sake, we impose the restriction that the number of observations is the same for each factor combination. This yields what is known as an orthogonal design, where the effects due to the factors (separately and collectively) are independent or unrelated. We leave the discussion of the unequal *n*'s factorial ANOVA until later in this chapter. In addition, there must be at least two observations per factor combination so as to have within-groups variation.

In summary, the characteristics of the two-factor ANOVA fixed-effects model are as follows: (a) two independent variables (both of which are categorical) each with two or more levels, (b) the levels of both independent variables are fixed by the researcher, (c) subjects are randomly assigned to only one combination of these levels, (d) the two factors are fully crossed, and (e) the dependent variable is measured at least at the interval level. In the context of experimental design, the two-factor ANOVA is often referred to as the **completely randomized factorial design**.

3.1.2 Layout of Data

Y_{ijk} = each observation

Before we get into the theory and analysis of the data, let us examine one form in which the data can be placed, known as the layout of the data. We designate each observation as Y_{ijk}, where the *j* subscript tells us what level (or category) of factor A (e.g., textbook) the observation belongs to, the *k* subscript tells us what level of factor B (e.g., time of day) the observation belongs to, and the *i* subscript tells us the observation or identification number within that combination of factor A and factor B. For instance, Y_{321} would mean that this is the third observation in the second level of factor A and the first level of factor B. The first subscript ranges over $i = 1, \ldots, n$; the second subscript ranges over $j = 1, \ldots, J$; and the third subscript ranges over $k = 1, \ldots, K$. Note also that the latter two subscripts denote the cell of an observation. Using the same example, we are referring to the third observation in the 21 cell. Thus, there are *J* levels of factor A, *K* levels of factor B, and *n* subjects in each cell, for a total of $JKn = N$ observations. For now, we consider the case where there are *n* subjects in each cell in order to simplify matters; this is referred to as the equal *n*'s case. Later in this chapter, we consider the unequal *n*'s case.

The layout of the sample data is shown in Table 3.1. Here we see that each row represents the observations for a particular level of factor A (textbook) and that each column represents the observations for a particular level of factor B (time). At the bottom of each column are the column means ($\overline{Y}_{.k.}$), to the right of each row are the row means ($\overline{Y}_{.j.}$), and in the lower right-hand corner is the overall mean ($\overline{Y}_{...}$). We also need the cell means ($\overline{Y}_{.jk}$), which are shown at the bottom of each cell. Thus, the layout is one form in which to think about the data.

3.1.3 ANOVA Model

This section introduces the ANOVA linear model, as well as estimation of the parameters of the model. The two-factor ANOVA model is a form of the general linear model (GLM) like the one-factor ANOVA model of Chapter 1. The two-factor ANOVA fixed-effects model can be written in terms of population parameters as

$$Y_{ijk} = \mu + \alpha_j + \beta_k + (\alpha\beta)_{jk} + \varepsilon_{ijk}$$

where
   Y_{ijk} is the observed score on the criterion (i.e., dependent) variable for individual *i* in level *j* of factor A (e.g., text) and level *k* of factor B (e.g., time) (or in the *jk* cell)
   μ is the overall or grand population mean (i.e., regardless of cell designation)
   α_j is the main effect for level *j* of factor A (row or text effect)

TABLE 3.1

Layout for the Two-Factor ANOVA

Level of Factor A	Level of Factor B				Row Mean
	1	2	...	K	
1	Y_{111}	Y_{112}	...	Y_{11K}	$\bar{Y}_{.1.}$
	.	.	...		
	.	.	...		
	.	.	...		
	Y_{n11}	Y_{n12}	...	Y_{n1K}	
	$\bar{Y}_{.11}$	$\bar{Y}_{.12}$	...	$\bar{Y}_{.1K}$	
2	Y_{121}	Y_{122}	...	Y_{12K}	$\bar{Y}_{.2.}$
	.	.	...	.	
	.	.	...	.	
	.	.	...	.	
	Y_{n21}	Y_{n22}	...	Y_{n2K}	
	$\bar{Y}_{.21}$	$\bar{Y}_{.22}$	...	$\bar{Y}_{.2K}$	
	.	.	...	.	
J	Y_{1j1}	Y_{1j2}	...	Y_{1jK}	$\bar{Y}_{.j.}$
	.	.	...	.	
	.	.	...	.	
	Y_{nj1}	Y_{nj2}	...	Y_{njK}	
	$\bar{Y}_{.j1}$	$\bar{Y}_{.j2}$	...	$\bar{Y}_{.jK}$	
Column mean	$\bar{Y}_{..1}$	$\bar{Y}_{..2}$		$\bar{Y}_{..K}$	$\bar{Y}_{...}$

β_k is the main effect for level k of factor B (column or time effect)

$(\alpha\beta)_{jk}$ is the interaction effect for the combination of level j of factor A and level k of factor B

ε_{ijk} is the random residual error for individual i in cell jk

The residual error can be due to individual differences, measurement error, and/or other factors not under investigation.

The population effects and residual error can be computed as follows:

$$\begin{cases} \alpha_j = \mu_{.j.} - \mu \\ \beta_k = \mu_{..k} - \mu \\ (\alpha\beta)_{jk} = \mu_{.jk} - (\mu_{.j.} + \mu_{..k} - \mu) \\ \varepsilon_{ijk} = Y_{ijk} - \mu_{.jk} \end{cases}$$

[a] That is, the row effect is equal to the difference between the population mean of level j of factor A (a particular text) and the overall population mean, the column effect is equal to the difference between the population mean of level k of factor B (a particular time) and the overall population mean, the interaction effect is the effect of being in a certain combination of the levels of factor A and factor B (a particular text used at a particular time), whereas the residual error is equal to the difference between an individual's observed

score and the population mean of cell jk. The row, column, and interaction effects can also be thought of as the average effect of being a member of a particular row (i.e., a student who is assigned to textbook A, B, or C), column (i.e., a student who attends class in the afternoon or evening), or cell (i.e., a student assigned to textbook A, B, or C who attends class in the afternoon or evening), respectively. It should also be noted that the sum of the row effects is equal to 0, the sum of the column effects is equal to 0, and the sum of the interaction effects is equal to 0 (both across rows and across columns). This implies, for example, that if there are any nonzero row effects, then the row effects will balance out around 0 with some positive and some negative effects.

You may be wondering why the interaction effect looks a little different than the main effects. We have given you the version that is solely a function of population means. A more intuitively convincing conceptual version of this effect is as follows:

$$(\alpha\beta)_{jk} = \mu_{.jk} - \alpha_j - \beta_k - \mu$$

which is written in similar fashion to the row and column effects. Here we see that the interaction effect $[(\alpha\beta)_{jk}]$ is equal to the population cell mean $(\mu_{.jk})$ minus the following: (a) the row effect, (α_j); (b) the column effect, (β_k); and (c) the overall population mean, (μ). In other words, the interaction is solely a function of cell means without regard to, or controlling for, its row effect, column effect, or the overall mean.

To estimate the parameters of the model $[\mu, \alpha_j, \beta_k, (\alpha\beta)_{jk}, \text{and } \varepsilon_{ijk}]$, the least squares method of estimation is used as the most appropriate for GLMs (e.g., regression, ANOVA). These sample estimates are represented by $\bar{Y}_{...}, a_j, b_k, (ab)_{jk}, \text{and } e_{ijk}$, respectively, where the latter four are computed as follows, respectively:

$$a_j = \bar{Y}_{.j.} - \bar{Y}_{...}$$

$$b_k = \bar{Y}_{..k} - \bar{Y}_{...}$$

$$(ab)_{jk} = \bar{Y}_{.jk} - (\bar{Y}_{.j.} + \bar{Y}_{..k} - \bar{Y}_{...})$$

$$e_{ijk} = Y_{ijk} - \bar{Y}_{.jk}$$

Note that

$\bar{Y}_{...}$ represents the overall sample mean

$\bar{Y}_{.j.}$ represents the sample mean for level j of factor A (a particular text)

$\bar{Y}_{..k}$ represents the sample mean for level k of factor B (a particular time)

$\bar{Y}_{.jk}$ represents the sample mean for cell jk (a particular text at a particular time)

For the two-factor ANOVA model, there are three sets of hypotheses, one for each of the main effects and one for the interaction effect. The null and alternative hypotheses, respectively, for testing the main effect of factor A (text) are as follows:

$$H_{01}: \mu_{.1.} = \mu_{.2.} = \ldots = \mu_{.J.}$$

$$H_{11}: \text{not all the } \mu_{.j.} \text{ are equal}$$

The hypotheses for testing the main effect of factor B (time) are noted as follows:

$$H_{02}: \mu_{..1} = \mu_{..2} = \ldots = \mu_{..K}$$

$$H_{12}: \text{not all the } \mu_{..k} \text{ are equal}$$

Finally, the hypotheses for testing the interaction effect (text with time) are as follows:

$$H_{03}: (\mu_{.jk} - \mu_{.j.} - \mu_{..k} + \mu) = 0 \text{ for all } j \text{ and } k$$

$$H_{13}: \text{not all the } (\mu_{.jk} - \mu_{.j.} - \mu_{..k} + \mu) = 0$$

The null hypotheses can also be written in terms of row, column, and interaction effects (which may make more intuitive sense to you) as

$$H_{01}: \alpha_1 = \alpha_2 = \ldots = \alpha_J = 0$$

$$H_{02}: \beta_1 = \beta_2 = \ldots = \beta_K = 0$$

$$H_{03}: (\alpha\beta)_{jk} = 0 \text{ for all } j \text{ and } k$$

As in the one-factor model, all of the alternative hypotheses are written in a general form to cover the multitude of possible mean differences that could arise. These range from only two of the means being different to all of the means being different from one another. Also, because of the way the alternative hypotheses have been written, only a nondirectional alternative is appropriate. If one of the null hypotheses is rejected, then consider an MCP so as to determine which means, or combination of means, are significantly different (discussed later).

3.1.4 Main Effects and Interaction Effects

Finally we come to a formal discussion of main effects and interaction effects. A **main effect** of factor A (text) is defined as the effect of factor A, averaged across the levels of factor B (time), on the dependent variable Y (achievement). More precisely, it represents the unique effect of factor A on the outcome Y, controlling statistically for factor B. A similar statement may be made for the main effect of factor B.

As far as the concept of interaction is concerned, things are a bit more complex. An **interaction** can be defined in any of the following ways: An interaction is said to exist if (a) certain combinations of the two factors produce effects beyond the effects of the two factors when those two factors are considered separately; (b) the mean differences among the levels of factor A are not constant across, and thus depend on, the levels of factor B; (c) there is a joint effect of factors A and B on Y; or (d) there is a unique effect that could not be predicted from knowledge of only the main effects. Let us mention two fairly common examples of interaction effects. The first is known as an aptitude-treatment interaction (ATI). This means that the effectiveness of a particular treatment depends on the aptitude of the individual. In other words, some treatments are more effective for individuals with a high aptitude, and other treatments are more effective for those with a low aptitude. A second example is an interaction between treatment and gender. Here some treatments may be more effective for males, and others may be more effective for females. This is often considered in gender studies research.

For some graphical examples of main and interaction effects, take a look at the various plots in Figure 3.1. Each plot represents the graph of a particular set of cell means (the mean of the dependent variable for a cell—the combination of a particular category of factor A and a particular category of factor B), sometimes referred to as a **profile plot**. On the X axis are the levels of factor A (text), the Y axis provides the cell means on the dependent variable Y (achievement), and the separate lines in the body of the plot represent the levels of factor B (time) (although the specific placement of the two factors here is arbitrary;

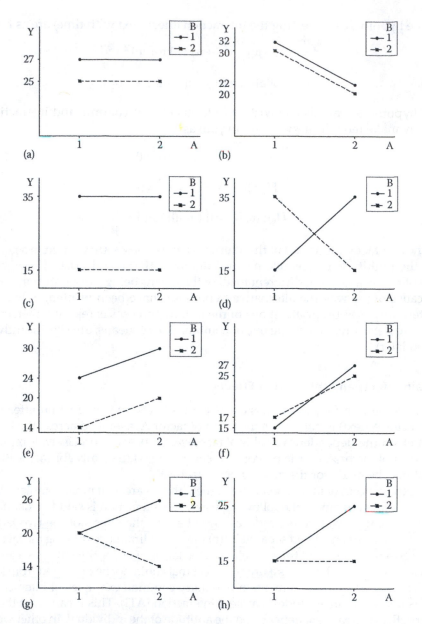

FIGURE 3.1
Display of possible two-factor ANOVA effects.

alternatively factor B could be plotted on the X axis, and factor A, as the separate lines). Profile plots provide information about the possible existence of a main effect for A, a main effect for B, and/or an interaction effect. A main effect for factor A can be examined by taking the means for each level of A and averaging them across the levels of B. If these marginal means for the levels of A are the same or nearly so, this would indicate no main effect for factor A. A main effect for factor B can be assessed by taking the means for each level of B and averaging them across the levels of A. If these marginal means for the levels of B are the same or nearly so, this would imply no main effect for factor B. An interaction effect is determined by whether the cell means for the levels of A are constant across the levels of B (or vice versa). This is easily viewed in a profile plot by checking to see whether or not the lines are parallel. Parallel lines indicate no interaction, whereas nonparallel lines suggest that an interaction may exist. Of course, the statistical significance of the main and interaction effects is a matter to be determined by the *F* test statistics (coming up). The profile plots only give you a rough idea as to the possible existence of the effects. For instance, lines that are nearly parallel will probably not show up as a significant interaction. It is suggested that the plot can be simplified if the factor with the most levels is shown on the *X* axis. This cuts down on the number of lines drawn.

The plots shown in Figure 3.1 represent the eight different sets of results possible for a two-factor design, that is, from no effects to all three effects being evident. To simplify matters, only two levels of each factor are used. Figure 3.1a indicates that there is no main effect either for factor A or B, and there is no interaction effect. The lines are horizontal (no A effect), lie nearly on top of one another (no B effect), and are parallel (no interaction effect). Figure 3.1b suggests the presence of an effect due to factor A only (the lines are not horizontal because the mean for A_1 is greater than the mean for A_2), but are nearly on top of one another (no B effect) and are parallel (no interaction). In Figure 3.1c, we see a separation between the lines for the levels of B (B_1 being greater than B_2); thus, a main effect for B is likely, but the lines are horizontal (no A effect) and are parallel (no interaction).

For Figure 3.1d, there are no main effects (the means for the levels of A are the same, and the means for the levels of B are the same), but an interaction is indicated by the lack of parallel lines. Figure 3.1e suggests a main effect for both factors as shown by mean differences (A_1 less than A_2, and B_1 greater than B_2), but no interaction (the lines are parallel). In Figure 3.1f, we see a main effect for A (A_1 less than A_2) and an interaction effect, but no main effect for B (little separation between the lines for factor B). For Figure 3.1g, there appear to be a main effect for B (B_1 greater than B_2) and an interaction, but no main effect for A. Finally, in Figure 3.1h, we see the likelihood of two main effects (A_1 less than A_2, and B_1 greater than B_2) and an interaction. Although these are clearly the only possible outcomes from a two-factor design, the precise pattern will differ depending on the obtained cell means. In other words, if your study yields a significant effect only for factor A, your profile plot need not look exactly like Figure 3.1b, but it will retain the same general pattern and interpretation.

In many statistics texts, a big deal is made about the type of interaction shown in the profile plot. They make a distinction between an ordinal interaction and a disordinal interaction. An ordinal interaction is said to exist when the lines are not parallel and they do not cross; ordinal here means the same relative order of the cell means is maintained across the levels of one of the factors. For example, the means for level 1 of factor B are always greater than the means for level 2 of B, regardless of the level of factor A. A disordinal interaction is said to exist when the lines are not parallel and they do cross. For example, the mean for B_1 is greater than the mean for B_2 at A_1, but the opposite is true at A_2. Dwelling on the distinction between the two types of interaction is not recommended as it can depend on how the plot is drawn (i.e., which factor is plotted on the *X* axis). That is, when factor A is plotted on the *X* axis, a disordinal interaction may be shown, and when factor B is plotted on the *X* axis, an ordinal interaction may be shown. The purpose of the profile plot is to simplify interpretation of the results; worrying about the type of interaction may merely serve to confuse that interpretation.

Let us take a moment to discuss how to deal with an interaction effect. Consider two possible situations, one where there is a significant interaction effect and one where there is no such effect. If there is no significant interaction effect, then the findings regarding the main effects can be generalized with greater confidence. In this situation, the main effects are known as **additive effects**, and an additive linear model with no interaction term could actually be used to describe the data. For example, the results might be that for factor A, the level 1 means always exceed those of level 2 by 10 points, across all levels of factor B. Thus, we can make a blanket statement about the constant added benefits of A_1 over A_2, regardless of the level of factor B. In addition, for the no-interaction situation, the main effects are statistically independent of one another; that is, each of the main effects serves as an independent predictor of Y.

If there is a significant interaction effect, then the findings regarding the main effects cannot be generalized with such confidence. In this situation, the main effects are not additive, and the interaction term must be included in the linear model. For example, the results might be that (a) the mean for A_1 is greater than A_2 when considering B_1, but (b) the mean for A_1 is less than A_2 when considering B_2. Thus, we cannot make a blanket statement about the constant added benefits of A_1 over A_2, because it depends on the level of factor B. In addition, for the interaction situation, the main effects are not statistically independent of one another; that is, each of the main effects does not serve as an independent predictor of Y. In order to predict Y well, information is necessary about the levels of factors A and B. Thus, in the presence of a significant interaction, generalizations about the main effects must be qualified. A profile plot should be examined so that a proper graphical interpretation of the interaction and main effects can be made. A significant interaction serves as a warning that one cannot generalize statements about a main effect for A over all levels of B. If you obtain a significant interaction, this is an important result. Do not ignore it and go ahead to interpret the main effects.

3.1.5 Assumptions and Violation of Assumptions

In Chapter 1, we described in detail the assumptions for the one-factor ANOVA. In the two-factor model, the assumptions are again concerned with independence, homogeneity of variance, and normality. A summary of the effects of their violation is provided in Table 3.2. The same methods for detecting violations described in Chapter 1 can be used for this model.

There are only two different wrinkles for the two-factor model as compared to the one-factor model. First, as the effect of heterogeneity is small with balanced designs

TABLE 3.2

Assumptions and Effects of Violations for the Two-Factor ANOVA Design

Assumption	Effect of Assumption Violation
1. Independence	• Increased likelihood of a Type I and/or Type II error in the F statistic • Influences standard errors of means and thus inferences about those means
2. Homogeneity of variance	• Bias in SS_{with} • Increased likelihood of a Type I and/or Type II error • Less effect with balanced or nearly balanced design • Effect decreases as n increases
3. Normality	• Minimal effect with moderate violation • Minimal effect with balanced or nearly balanced design • Effect decreases as n increases

(equal n's per cell) or nearly balanced designs, and/or with larger n's, this is a reason to strive for such a design. Unfortunately, there is very little research on this problem, except the classic Box (1954b) article for a no-interaction model with one observation per cell. There are limited solutions for dealing with a violation of the homogeneity assumption, such as the Welch (1951) test, the Johansen (1980) procedure, and variations described by Wilcox (1996, 2003). Transformations are not usually used, as they may destroy an additive linear model and create interactions that did not previously exist. Nonparametric techniques are not commonly used with the two-factor model, although see the description of the Brunner, Dette, and Munk (1997) procedure in Wilcox (2003). Second, the effect of nonnormality seems to be the same as heterogeneity (Miller, 1997).

3.1.6 Partitioning the Sums of Squares

As pointed out in Chapter 1, partitioning the sums of squares is an important concept in ANOVA. We will illustrate with a two-factor model, but this can be extended to more than two factors. Let us begin with the total sum of squares in Y, denoted here as SS_{total}. The term SS_{total} represents the amount of total variation among all of the observations without regard to row, column, or cell membership. The next step is to partition the total variation into variation between the levels of factor A (denoted by SS_A), variation between the levels of factor B (denoted by SS_B), variation due to the interaction of the levels of factors A and B (denoted by SS_{AB}), and variation within the cells combined across cells (denoted by SS_{with}). In the two-factor ANOVA, then, we can partition SS_{total} into

$$SS_{total} = SS_A + SS_B + SS_{AB} + SS_{with}$$

interaction of the levels of factors

Then computational formulas are used by statistical software to actually compute these sums of squares.

3.1.7 ANOVA Summary Table

The next step is to assemble the ANOVA summary table. The purpose of the summary table is to simply summarize ANOVA. A general form of the summary table for the two-factor model is shown in Table 3.3. The first column lists the sources of variation in the model. We note that the total variation is divided into a within-groups source, and a general between-groups source, which is then subdivided into sources due to A, B, and the AB interaction. This is in keeping with the spirit of the one-factor model, where total variation was divided into a between-groups source (just one effect because there is only one factor and no interaction term) and a within-groups source. The second column provides the computed sums of squares.

TABLE 3.3

Two-Factor ANOVA Summary Table

Source	SS	df	MS	F
A	SS_A	$J-1$	MS_A	MS_A/MS_{with}
B	SS_B	$K-1$	MS_B	MS_B/MS_{with}
AB	SS_{AB}	$(J-1)(K-1)$	MS_{AB}	MS_{AB}/MS_{with}
Within	SS_{with}	$N-JK$	MS_{with}	
Total	SS_{total}	$N-1$		

The third column gives the degrees of freedom for each source. As always, degrees of freedom have to do with the number of observations that are free to vary in a particular context. Because there are J levels of factor A, then the number of degrees of freedom for the A source is equal to $J - 1$. As there are J means and we know the overall mean, then only $J - 1$ of the means are free to vary. This is the same rationale we have been using throughout this text. As there are K levels of factor B, there are $K - 1$ degrees of freedom for the B source. For the AB interaction source, we take the product of the degrees of freedom for the main effects. Thus, we have as degrees of freedom for AB the product $(J - 1)(K - 1)$. The degrees of freedom within groups are equal to the total number of observations minus the number of cells, $N - JK$. Finally, the degrees of freedom total can be written simply as $N - 1$.

Next, the sum of squares terms are weighted by the appropriate degrees of freedom to generate the mean squares terms. Thus, for instance, $MS_A = SS_A/df_A$. Finally, in the last column of the ANOVA summary table, we have the F values, which represent the summary statistics for ANOVA. There are three hypotheses that we are interested in testing, one for each of the two main effects and one for the interaction effect, so there will be three F test statistics. For the factorial fixed-effects model, each F value is computed by taking the MS for the source that you are interested in testing and dividing it by MS_{with}. Thus, for each hypothesis, the same error term is used in forming the F ratio (i.e., MS_{with}). We return to the two-factor model for cases where the effects are not fixed in Chapter 5.

Each of the F test statistics is then compared with the appropriate F critical value so as to make a decision about the relevant null hypothesis. These critical values are found in the F table of Table A.4 as follows: for the test of factor A as $_\alpha F_{J-1, N-JK}$; for the test of factor B as $_\alpha F_{K-1, N-JK}$; and for the test of the interaction as $_\alpha F_{(J-1)(K-1), N-JK}$. Thus, with a two-factor model, testing two main effects and one interaction, there are three F tests and three decisions that must be made. Each significance test is one-tailed so as to be consistent with the alternative hypothesis. The null hypothesis is rejected if the F test statistic exceeds the F critical value.

Recall that these F tests are omnibus tests that tell only if there is an overall main effect or interaction effect. If the F test statistic does exceed the F critical value, and there is more than one degree of freedom for the source being tested, then it is not clear precisely why the null hypothesis was rejected. For example, if there are three levels of factor A and the null hypothesis for A is rejected, then we are not sure where the mean differences lie among the levels of A. In this case, some MCP should be used to determine where the mean differences are; this is the topic of the next section.

3.1.8 Multiple Comparison Procedures

In this section, we extend the concepts related to multiple comparison procedures (MCPs) covered in Chapter 2 to the two-factor ANOVA model. This model includes main and interaction effects; consequently you can examine contrasts of both main and interaction effects. In general, the procedures described in Chapter 2 can be applied to the two-factor situation. Things become more complicated as we have row and column means (i.e., marginal means) and cell means. Thus, we have to be careful about which means are being considered.

Let us begin with contrasts of the main effects. If the effect for factor A is significant, and there are more than two levels of factor A, then we can form contrasts that compare the levels of factor A ignoring factor B. Here we would be comparing the means for the levels of factor A, which are marginal means as opposed to cell means. Considering each factor separately is strongly advised; considering the factors simultaneously is to be avoided. Some statistics texts suggest that you consider the design as a one-factor model with JK

levels when using MCPs to examine main effects. This is inconsistent with the design and the intent of separating effects, and is not recommended.

For contrasts involving the interaction, our recommendation is to begin with a complex interaction contrast if there are more than four cells in the model. Thus, for example, in a 4×4 design that consists of four levels of factor A (method of instruction) and four levels of factor B (instructor), one possibility is to test both 4×2 complex interaction contrasts. An example of one such contrast is as follows [where, e.g., $(\bar{Y}_{.11} + \bar{Y}_{.21} + \bar{Y}_{.31} + \bar{Y}_{.41})$ is the sum of the cell means of each level of factor A for level 1 of factor B and $(\bar{Y}_{.12} + \bar{Y}_{.22} + \bar{Y}_{.32} + \bar{Y}_{.42})$ is the sum of the cell means of each level of factor A for level 2 of factor B]:

$$\Psi' = \frac{(\bar{Y}_{.11} + \bar{Y}_{.21} + \bar{Y}_{.31} + \bar{Y}_{.41})}{4} - \frac{(\bar{Y}_{.12} + \bar{Y}_{.22} + \bar{Y}_{.32} + \bar{Y}_{.42})}{4}$$

with a standard error of the following:

$$s_{\Psi'} = \sqrt{MS_{\text{with}} \left(\sum_{j=1}^{J} \sum_{k=1}^{K} \frac{c_{jk}^2}{n_{jk}} \right)}$$

$\{ n_{j,k} = $ # of observations in cell jk $\}$

where n_{jk} is the number of observations in cell *jk*. This contrast would examine the interaction between the four methods of instruction and the first two instructors. A second complex interaction contrast could consider the interaction between the four methods of instruction and the other two instructors.

If the complex interaction contrast is significant, then follow this up with a simple interaction contrast that involves only four cell means. This is a single degree of freedom contrast because it involves only two levels of each factor (known as a **tetrad difference**). An example of such a contrast is the following:

$$\Psi' = (\bar{Y}_{.11} - \bar{Y}_{.21}) - (\bar{Y}_{.12} - \bar{Y}_{.22})$$

with a similar standard error term. Using the same example, this contrast would examine the interaction between the first two methods of instruction and the first two instructors.

Most of the MCPs described in Chapter 2 can be used for testing main effects and interaction effects (although there is some debate about the appropriate use of interaction contrasts; see Boik, 1979; Marascuilo & Levin, 1970, 1976). Keppel and Wickens (2004) consider interaction contrasts in much detail. Finally, some statistics texts suggest the use of simple main effects in testing a significant interaction. These involve comparing, for example, the levels of factor A at a particular level of factor B and are generally conducted by further partitioning the sums of squares. However, the simple main effects sums of squares represent a portion of a main effect plus the interaction effect. Thus, the simple main effect does not really help us to understand the interaction, and is not recommended here.

3.1.9 Effect Size Measures, Confidence Intervals, and Power

Various measures of effect size have been proposed. Let us examine two commonly used measures, which assume equal variances across the cells. First is partial eta squared, η^2, which represents the proportion of variation in Y explained by the effect of interest (i.e., by factor A or factor B or the AB interaction). This is the estimate of effect size that can be requested when using SPSS for factorial ANOVA. We determine partial η^2 as follows:

$$partial\ \eta_A^2 = \frac{SS_A}{SS_A + SS_{with}}$$

$$partial\ \eta_B^2 = \frac{SS_B}{SS_B + SS_{with}}$$

$$partial\ \eta_{AB}^2 = \frac{SS_{AB}}{SS_{AB} + SS_{with}}$$

Another effect size measure is the omega squared statistic, ω^2. We can determine ω^2 as follows:

$$\omega_A^2 = \frac{SS_A - (J-1)MS_{with}}{SS_{total} + MS_{with}}$$

$$\omega_B^2 = \frac{SS_B - (K-1)MS_{with}}{SS_{total} + MS_{with}}$$

$$\omega_{AB}^2 = \frac{SS_{AB} - (J-1)(K-1)MS_{with}}{SS_{total} + MS_{with}}$$

Using Cohen's (1988) subjective standards, these effect sizes can be interpreted as follows: small effect, η^2 or ω^2 = .01; medium effect, η^2 or ω^2 = .06; and large effect, η^2 or ω^2 = .14. For further discussion, see Keppel (1982), O'Grady (1982), Wilcox (1987), Cohen (1988), Fidler and Thompson (2001), Keppel and Wickens (2004), and Murphy, Myors, and Wolach (2008; with software).

As mentioned in Chapter 1, CIs can be used for providing interval estimates of a population mean or mean difference; this gives us information about the accuracy of a sample estimate. In the case of the two-factor model, we can form CIs for row means, column means, cell means, the overall mean, as well as any possible contrast formed through an MCP. Note also that CIs have been developed for η^2 and ω^2 (Fidler & Thompson, 2001; Smithson, 2001).

As also mentioned in Chapter 1, power can be determined either in the planned (a priori) or observed (post hoc) power context. For planned power, we typically use tables or power charts (e.g., Cohen, 1988, or Murphy et al., 2008) or software (e.g., Power and Precision, Ex-Sample, G*Power, or Murphy et al. software, 2008). These are particularly useful in terms of determining adequate sample sizes when designing a study. Observed power is reported by statistics software, such as SPSS, to indicate the actual power in a given study.

3.1.10 Example

Consider the following illustration of the two-factor design. Here we expand on the example presented in Chapter 1 by adding a second factor to the model. Our dependent variable will again be the number of times a student attends statistics lab during one semester (or quarter), factor A is the attractiveness of the lab instructor (assuming each instructor is of the same gender and is equally competent), and factor B is the time of day the lab is offered. Thus, the researcher is interested in whether the attractiveness of the instructor, the time of day, or the interaction of attractiveness and time influences student attendance in the statistics lab. The attractiveness levels are defined again as (a) unattractive, (b) slightly attractive, (c) moderately attractive, and (d) very attractive. The time of day levels are defined as (a) afternoon lab and (b) evening lab. Students were randomly assigned to a combination of lab instructor and lab time at the beginning of the semester, and attendance was taken by the instructor. There were four students in each cell and eight cells (four levels of attractiveness and two categories of time, thus 4 × 2 or eight combinations of instructor and time) for a total of 32 observations. Students could attend a maximum of 30 lab sessions. Table 3.4 depicts the raw data and sample means for each cell (given beneath each cell), column, row, and overall.

The results are summarized in the ANOVA summary table as shown in Table 3.5. The F test statistics are compared to the following critical values obtained from Table A.4 (α = .05): $_{.05}F_{3,24}$ = 3.01 for the A (i.e., attractiveness) and AB (i.e., attractiveness-time of day) effects, and $_{.05}F_{1,24}$ = 4.26 for the B (time of day) effect. The test statistics exceed the critical values for the A and B effects only, so we can reject these H_0 and conclude that both the level of attractiveness and the time of day are related to mean differences in statistics lab attendance. The interaction was shown not to be a significant effect. If you would like to see an example of a two-factor design where the interaction is significant, take a look at the end of chapter problems, Computational Problem 3.5.

TABLE 3.4

Data for the Statistics Lab Example: Number of Statistics Labs Attended, by Level of Attractiveness and Time of Day

Level of Attractiveness	Time of Day Afternoon	Evening	Row Mean
Unattractive	15	10	11.1250
	12	8	
	21	7	
	13	3	
	15.2500	7.0000	
Slightly attractive	20	13	17.8750
	22	9	
	24	18	
	25	12	
	22.7500	13.0000	
Moderately attractive	24	10	20.2500
	29	12	
	27	21	
	25	14	
	26.2500	14.2500	
Very attractive	30	22	24.3750
	26	20	
	29	25	
	28	15	
	28.2500	20.5000	
Column mean	23.1250	13.6875	18.4063 (*overall mean*)

TABLE 3.5

Two-Factor ANOVA Summary Table—Statistics
Lab Example

Source	SS	df	MS	F
A	738.5938	3	246.1979	21.3504[a]
B	712.5313	1	712.5313	61.7911[b]
AB	21.8438	3	7.2813	0.6314[a]
Within	276.7500	24	11.5313	
Total	1749.7188	31		

[a] $_{.05}F_{3,24} = 3.01.$
[b] $_{.05}F_{1,24} = 4.26.$

Next we estimate the main and interaction effects. The main effects for the levels of A are estimated to be the following:

Unattractive: $a_1 = \bar{Y}_{1.} - \bar{Y}_{..} = 11.1250 - 18.4063 = -7.2813$

Slightly attractive: $a_2 = \bar{Y}_{.2.} - \bar{Y}_{...} = 17.8750 - 18.4063 = -0.5313$

Moderately attractive: $a_3 = \bar{Y}_{.3.} - \bar{Y}_{...} = 20.2500 - 18.4063 = 1.8437$

Very attractive: $a_4 = \bar{Y}_{.4.} - \bar{Y}_{...} = 24.3750 - 18.4063 = 5.9687$

The main effects for the levels of B (time of day) are estimated to be as follows:

Afternoon: $b_1 = \bar{Y}_{..1} - \bar{Y}_{...} = 23.1250 - 18.4063 = 4.7187$

Evening: $b_2 = \bar{Y}_{..2} - \bar{Y}_{...} = 13.6875 - 18.4063 = -4.7187$

Finally, the interaction effects for the combinations of the levels of factors A (attractiveness) and B (time of day) are as follows:

$$(ab)_{11} = \bar{Y}_{11} - (\bar{Y}_{1.} + \bar{Y}_{.1} - \bar{Y}_{..}) = 15.2500 - (11.1250 + 23.1250 - 18.4063) = -0.5937$$

$$(ab)_{12} = \bar{Y}_{12} - (\bar{Y}_{1.} + \bar{Y}_{.2} - \bar{Y}_{..}) = 7.0000 - (11.1250 + 13.6875 - 18.4063) = 0.5938$$

$$(ab)_{21} = \bar{Y}_{21} - (\bar{Y}_{2.} + \bar{Y}_{.1} - \bar{Y}_{..}) = 22.7500 - (17.8750 + 23.1250 - 18.4063) = 0.1563$$

$$(ab)_{22} = \bar{Y}_{22} - (\bar{Y}_{2.} + \bar{Y}_{.2} - \bar{Y}_{..}) = 13.0000 - (17.8750 + 13.6875 - 18.4063) = -0.1562$$

$$(ab)_{31} = \bar{Y}_{31} - (\bar{Y}_{3.} + \bar{Y}_{.1} - \bar{Y}_{..}) = 26.2500 - (20.2500 + 23.1250 - 18.4063) = 1.2813$$

$$(ab)_{32} = \bar{Y}_{32} - (\bar{Y}_{3.} + \bar{Y}_{.2} - \bar{Y}_{..}) = 14.2500 - (20.2500 + 13.6875 - 18.4063) = -1.2813$$

$$(ab)_{41} = \bar{Y}_{41} - (\bar{Y}_{4.} + \bar{Y}_{.1} - \bar{Y}_{..}) = 28.2500 - (24.3750 + 23.1250 - 18.4063) = -0.8437$$

$$(ab)_{42} = \bar{Y}_{42} - (\bar{Y}_{4.} + \bar{Y}_{.2} - \bar{Y}_{..}) = 20.5000 - (24.3750 + 13.6875 - 18.4063) = 0.8438$$

The profile plot shown in Figure 3.2 graphically depicts these effects. The main effect for attractiveness (factor A) was statistically significant and has more than two levels, so let us

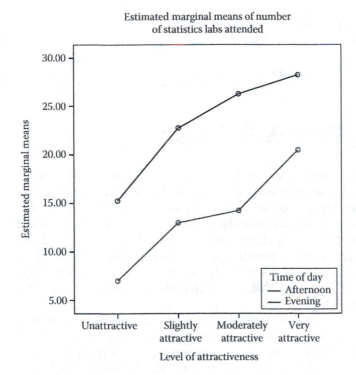

Estimated marginal means of number
of statistics labs attended

FIGURE 3.2
Profile plot for example data.

consider one example of an MCP, the Tukey HSD test. Recall from Chapter 2 that the HSD test is a family-wise procedure most appropriate for considering all pairwise contrasts with a balanced design (which is the case for these data). The following are the computations:

Critical value (obtained from Table A.9):

$$_\alpha q_{df(\text{with}),J} =_{.05} q_{24,4} = 3.901$$

Standard error:

$$s_{\psi'} = \sqrt{\frac{MS_{\text{with}}}{n}} = \sqrt{\frac{11.5313}{8}} = 1.2006$$

Test statistics:

$$q_1 = \frac{\bar{Y}_{.4.} - \bar{Y}_{.1.}}{s_{\psi'}} = \frac{24.3750 - 11.1250}{1.2006} = 11.0361$$

$$q_2 = \frac{\bar{Y}_{.4.} - \bar{Y}_{.2.}}{s_{\psi'}} = \frac{24.3750 - 17.8750}{1.2006} = 5.4140$$

$$q_3 = \frac{\bar{Y}_{.4.} - \bar{Y}_{.3.}}{s_{\psi'}} = \frac{24.3750 - 20.2500}{1.2006} = 3.4358$$

$$q_4 = \frac{\bar{Y}_{3.} - \bar{Y}_{1.}}{s_{\psi'}} = \frac{20.2500 - 11.1250}{1.2006} = 7.6004$$

$$q_5 = \frac{\bar{Y}_{3.} - \bar{Y}_{2.}}{s_{\psi'}} = \frac{20.2500 - 17.8750}{1.2006} = 1.9782$$

$$q_6 = \frac{\bar{Y}_{2.} - \bar{Y}_{1.}}{s_{\psi'}} = \frac{17.8750 - 11.1250}{1.2006} = 5.6222$$

Recall that we compare the test statistic value to the critical value to make our hypothesis testing decision. If the test statistic value exceeds the critical value, we reject the null hypothesis and conclude that those means differ. For these tests, the results indicate that the means for the levels of factor A (attractiveness) are statistically significantly different for levels 1 and 4 (i.e., the test statistic value is 11.0361, and the critical value is 3.901), 2 and 4, 1 and 3, and 1 and 2. Thus, level 1 (unattractive) is significantly different from the other three levels of attractiveness, and levels 2 and 4 (slightly unattractive vs. very attractive) are also significantly different. The only levels that are not statistically different are levels 2 and 3 ($q_5 = 1.9782$) and levels 3 and 4 ($q_3 = 3.4358$).

These results are somewhat different than those found with the one-factor model in Chapters 1 and 2 (where the significantly different levels were only 1 vs. 4 and 1 vs. 3). The MS_{with} has been reduced with the introduction of the second factor from 36.1116 to 11.5313 because SS_{with} has been reduced from 1011.1250 to 276.7500. Although the SS and MS for the attractiveness factor remain unchanged, this resulted in the F test statistic being considerably larger (increased from 6.8177 to 21.3504), although observed power was quite high in both models. Recall that this is one of the benefits we mentioned earlier about the use of additional factors in the model. Also, although the effect of factor B (time of day) was significant, there are only two levels of time of day, and, thus, we need not carry out any multiple comparisons (attendance is better in the afternoon section). Finally, since the interaction was not significant, it is not necessary to consider any related contrasts.

Finally we can estimate the effect size measures. The partial η^2's are determined to be the following:

$$\eta_A^2 = \frac{SS_A}{SS_A + SS_{with}} = \frac{738.5938}{738.5938 + 276.7500} = 0.7274$$

$$\eta_B^2 = \frac{SS_B}{SS_B + SS_{with}} = \frac{712.5313}{712.5313 + 276.7500} = 0.7203$$

$$\eta_{AB}^2 = \frac{SS_{AB}}{SS_{AB} + SS_{with}} = \frac{21.8438}{21.8438 + 276.7500} = 0.0732$$

We calculate ω^2 to be the following:

$$\omega_A^2 = \frac{SS_A - (J-1)MS_{with}}{SS_{total} + MS_{with}} = \frac{738.5938 - (3)11.5313}{1749.7188 + 11.5313} = 0.3997$$

$$\omega_B^2 = \frac{SS_B - (K-1)MS_{\text{with}}}{SS_{\text{total}} + MS_{\text{with}}} = \frac{712.5313 - (1)11.5313}{1749.7188 + 11.5313} = 0.3980$$

$$\omega_{AB}^2 = \frac{SS_{AB} - (J-1)(K-1)MS_{\text{with}}}{SS_{\text{total}} + MS_{\text{with}}} = \frac{21.8438 - (3)11.5313}{1749.7188 + 11.5313} = 0$$

Based on these effect size measures, one would conclude that there is a large effect for instructor attractiveness and for time of day, but no effect for the time-attractiveness interaction.

3.1.11 Expected Mean Squares ✳

As we asked in Chapter 1 for the one-factor fixed-effects model, for the two-factor fixed-effects model being considered here, we again ask the question, *"How do we know which source of variation to use as the error term in the denominator"*? That is, for the two-factor fixed-effects ANOVA model, how did we know to use MS_{with} as the error term in testing for the main effects and the interaction effect? As we learned in Chapter 1, an expected mean square for a particular source of variation represents the average mean square value for that source obtained if the same study were to be replicated an infinite number of times. For instance, the expected value of MS_A, denoted by $E(MS_A)$, is the average value of MS_A over repeated samplings.

Let us examine what the expected mean square terms actually look like for our two-factor fixed-effects model. Consider the two situations of (a) all of the H_0 actually being true and (b) all of the H_0 actually being false. If all of the H_0 are actually *true*, such that there really are no main effects or an interaction effect, then the expected mean squares are as follows:

$$E(MS_A) = \sigma_\varepsilon^2$$

$$E(MS_B) = \sigma_\varepsilon^2$$

$$E(MS_{AB}) = \sigma_\varepsilon^2$$

$$E(MS_{\text{with}}) = \sigma_\varepsilon^2$$

and thus using MS_{with} as the error term will produce F values around 1.

If all of the H_0 are actually *false*, such that there really are main effects and an interaction effect, then the expected mean squares are as follows:

$$E(M_A) = \sigma_\varepsilon^2 + \left(nK \sum_{j=1}^{J} \alpha_j^2 \right) / (J-1)$$

$$E(MS_B) = \sigma_\varepsilon^2 + \left(nJ \sum_{k=1}^{K} \beta_k^2 \right) / (K-1)$$

$$E\left(MS_{AB}\right) = \sigma_\varepsilon^2 + \left[n\sum_{j=1}^{J}\sum_{k=1}^{K}(\alpha\beta)_{jk}^2\right]/(J-1)(K-1)$$

$$E\left(MS_{\text{with}}\right) = \sigma_\varepsilon^2$$

and thus using MS_{with} as the error term will produce F values greater than 1.

There is a difference in the main and interaction effects between when H_0 is actually true as compared to when H_0 is actually false because in the latter situation, there is a second term. The important parts of this second term are α, β, and $\alpha\beta$, which represent the effects for A, B, and AB, respectively. The larger this part becomes, the larger the F ratio becomes. In comparing the two situations, we also see that $E(MS_{\text{with}})$ is the same whether H_0 is actually true or false, and thus represents a reliable estimate of σ_ε^2. This term is mean-free because it does not depend on any mean differences.

Finally let us put all of this information together. In general, the F ratio represents

$$F = (\text{systematic variability} + \text{error variability}) / (\text{error variability})$$

where, for the two-factor fixed-effects model, systematic variability is variability due to the main or interaction effects (i.e., between sources) and error variability is variability within. The F ratio is formed in a particular way because we want to isolate the systematic variability in the numerator. For this model, the only appropriate error term to use for each F ratio is MS_{with} because it does serve to isolate the systematic variability.

3.2 Three-Factor and Higher-Order ANOVA

3.2.1 Characteristics of the Model

All of the characteristics we discussed for the two-factor model apply to the three-factor model, with one obvious exception. There are three factors rather than two. This will result in three main effects (one for each factor, known as A, B, and C), three two-way interactions (known as AB, AC, and BC), and one three-way interaction (known as ABC). The only new concept is the three-way interaction, which may be stated as follows: "Is the AB interaction constant across all levels of factor C"? This may also be stated as "AC across the levels of B" or as "BC across the levels of A." These each have the same interpretation as there is only one way of testing the three-way interaction. In short, the three-way interaction can be thought of as the two-way interaction behaving differently across the levels of the third factor.

We do not explicitly consider models with more than three factors (cf., Keppel & Wickens, 2004; Marascuilo & Serlin, 1988; Myers & Well, 1995). However, be warned that such models do exist and that they will necessitate more main effects, more two-way interactions, more three-way interactions, as well as higher-order interactions—and thus more complex interpretations. Conceptually, the only change is to add these additional effects to the model.

3.2.2 ANOVA Model

The model for the three-factor design is

$$Y_{ijkl} = \mu + \alpha_j + \beta_k + \gamma_l + (\alpha\beta)_{jk} + (\alpha\gamma)_{jl} + (\beta\gamma)_{kl} + (\alpha\beta\gamma)_{jkl} + \varepsilon_{ijkl}$$

where
- Y_{ijkl} is the observed score on the criterion (i.e., dependent) variable for individual i in level j of factor A, level k of factor B, and level l of factor C (or in the jkl cell)
- μ is the overall or grand population mean (i.e., regardless of cell designation)
- α_j is the effect for level j of factor A
- β_k is the effect for level k of factor B
- γ_l is the effect for level l of factor C
- $(\alpha\beta)_{jk}$ is the interaction effect for the combination of level j of factor A and level k of factor B
- $(\alpha\gamma)_{jl}$ is the interaction effect for the combination of level j of factor A and level l of factor C
- $(\beta\gamma)_{kl}$ is the interaction effect for the combination of level k of factor B and level l of factor C
- $(\alpha\beta\gamma)_{jkl}$ is the interaction effect for the combination of level j of factor A, level k of factor B, and level l of factor C
- ε_{ijkl} is the random residual error for individual i in cell jkl

Given that there are three main effects, three two-way interactions, and one three-way interaction, there will be accompanying null and alternative hypotheses for each of these effects. At this point in your statistics career, the hypotheses should be obvious (simply expand on the hypotheses at the beginning of this chapter).

3.2.3 ANOVA Summary Table and Example

The ANOVA summary table for the three-factor model is shown in Table 3.6, with the usual columns for sources of variation, sums of squares, degrees of freedom, mean squares, and F. A quick three-factor example dataset and the resulting ANOVA summary table from SPSS are shown in Table 3.7. Note that the only statistically significant effects are the main effect for B and the AC interaction ($p < .01$).

TABLE 3.6

Three-Factor ANOVA Summary Table

Source	SS	df	MS	F
A	SS_A	$J - 1$	MS_A	MS_A/MS_{with}
B	SS_B	$K - 1$	MS_B	MS_B/MS_{with}
C	SS_C	$L - 1$	MS_C	MS_C/MS_{with}
AB	SS_{AB}	$(J - 1)(K - 1)$	MS_{AB}	MS_{AB}/MS_{with}
AC	SS_{AC}	$(J - 1)(L - 1)$	MS_{AC}	MS_{AC}/MS_{with}
BC	SS_{BC}	$(K - 1)(L - 1)$	MS_{BC}	MS_{BC}/MS_{with}
ABC	SS_{ABC}	$(J - 1)(K - 1)(L - 1)$	MS_{ABC}	MS_{ABC}/MS_{with}
Within	SS_{with}	$N - JKL$	MS_{with}	
Total	SS_{total}	$N - 1$		

TABLE 3.7

Three-Factor Analysis of Variance Example–Raw Data and SPSS ANOVA Summary Table

Raw Data:

$A_1B_1C_1$: 8, 10, 12, 9
$A_1B_1C_2$: 23, 17, 21, 19
$A_1B_2C_1$: 22, 19, 16, 24
$A_1B_2C_2$: 33, 31, 27, 30
$A_2B_1C_1$: 16, 19, 21, 24
$A_2B_1C_2$: 6, 8, 11, 13
$A_2B_2C_1$: 27, 30, 31, 33
$A_2B_2C_2$: 16, 19, 21, 25

SPSS ANOVA Summary Table:

The row labeled **"A"** is the first independent variable or factor or between groups variable. The *between groups mean square* for factor A (.031) provides an indication of the variation in the dependent variable attributable to factor A.

The degrees of freedom for the sum of squares between groups for factor A is $J-1$ ($df = 1$ in this example indicating 2 levels for factor A).

Similar interpretations are made for the other main effects and interactions.

The omnibus F test for the main effect for factor A (and computed similarly for the other main effects and interactions) is computed as

$$F = \frac{MS_A}{MS_{with}} = \frac{.031}{8.698} = .004$$

The p value for the omnibus F test of the main effect for factor A is .953. This indicates there is not a statistically significant difference in the dependent variable based on factor A, averaged across the levels of Factors B and C. In other words, there is not a unique effect of factor A on the dependent variable, controlling for factors B and C. The probability of observing these mean differences or more extreme mean differences by chance if the null hypothesis is really true (i.e., if the population means really are equal) is about 95%. We fail to reject the null hypothesis that the population means of factor A are equal. For this example, this provides evidence to suggest that the dependent variable does not differ, on average, across the levels of factor A, when controlling for factors B and C.

Source	Type III Sum of Squares	df	Mean Square	F	Sig.
A	.031	1	.031	.004	.953
B	871.531	1	871.531	100.200	.000
C	.031	1	.031	.004	.953
A * B	.031	1	.031	.004	.953
A * C	830.281	1	830.281	95.457	.000
B * C	.031	1	.031	.004	.953
A * B * C	.281	1	.281	.032	.859
Error	208.750	24	8.698		
Corrected total	1910.969	31			

The row labeled **"Error"** is within groups. The within groups sum of squares tells us how much variation there is within the cells combined across the cells (i.e., 208.750). The degrees of freedom for the sum of squares within groups is $(N - JKL)$ or the sample size minus the number of levels of the independent variables [i.e., $32 - (2)(2)(2) = 24$].

The row labeled **"corrected total"** is the sum of squares total. The degrees of freedom for the total is $(N - 1)$ or the sample size minus one.

3.2.4 Triple Interaction

Everything else about the three-factor design follows from the two-factor model. The assumptions are the same, MS_{with} is the error term used for testing each of the hypotheses in the fixed-effects model, and the MCPs are easily utilized. The main new feature is the three-way interaction. If this interaction is significant, then this means that the two-way interaction is different across the levels of the third factor. This result will need to be taken into account prior to interpreting the two-way interactions and the main effects.

Although the inclusion of additional factors in the design should result in a reduction in MS_{with}, there is a price to pay for the study of additional factors. Although the analysis is simple for the computer, you must consider the possibility of significant higher-order interactions. If you find, for example, that the four-way interaction is significant, how do you deal with it? First you have to interpret this interaction, which could be difficult if it is unexpected. Then you may have difficulty in dealing with the interpretation of your other effects. Our advice is simple. Do not include additional factors just because they sound interesting. Only include those factors that are theoretically or empirically important. Then if a significant higher-order interaction occurs, you will be in a better position to understand it because you will have already thought about its consequences. Reporting that an interaction is significant, but not interpretable, is not sound research (for additional discussion on this topic, see Keppel & Wickens, 2004).

3.3 Factorial ANOVA With Unequal *n*'s

Up until this point in the chapter, we have only considered the equal *n*'s or balanced case. That is, the model used was where the number of observations in each cell was equal. This served to make the formulas and equations easier to deal with. However, we do not need to assume that the *n*'s are equal. In this section, we discuss ways to deal with the unequal *n*'s (or unbalanced) case for the two-factor model, although these notions can be transferred to higher-order models as well.

When *n*'s are unequal, things become a bit trickier as the main effects and the interaction effect are not orthogonal. In other words, the sums of squares cannot be partitioned into independent effects, and, thus, the individual SS do not necessarily add up to the SS_{total}. As a result, several computational approaches have been developed. In the old days, prior to the availability of high-speed computers, the standard approach was to use unweighted means analysis. This is essentially an analysis of means, rather than raw scores, which are unweighted by cell size. This approach is only an approximate procedure. Due to the availability of quality statistical software, the unweighted means approach is no longer necessary. A rather silly approach, and one that we do not condone, is to delete enough data until you have an equal *n*'s model.

There are three more modern approaches to this case. Each of these approaches really tests different hypotheses and thus may result in different results and conclusions: (a) the **sequential approach** (also known as the hierarchical sums of squares approach), (b) the **partially sequential approach** (also known as the partially hierarchical, or experimental design, or method of fitting constants approach), and (c) the **regression approach** (also known as the marginal means or unique approach). There has been considerable debate over the years about the relative merits of each approach (e.g., Applebaum & Cramer, 1974; Carlson & Timm, 1974; Cramer & Applebaum, 1980; Overall, Lee, & Hornick, 1981; Overall & Spiegel, 1969; Timm & Carlson, 1975). In the following, we describe what each approach is actually testing.

In the sequential approach, the effects being tested are as follows:

$$\alpha \mid \mu$$

$$\beta \mid \mu, \alpha$$

$$\alpha\beta \mid \mu, \alpha, \beta$$

This indicates, for example, that the effect for factor B (β) is adjusted or controls for (as denoted by the vertical line) the overall mean (μ) and the main effect due to factor A (α). Thus, each effect is adjusted for prior effects in the sequential order given (i.e., α, β, $\alpha\beta$). Here the α effect is given theoretical or practical priority over the β effect. In SAS and SPSS, this is the *Type I sum of squares* method.

In the partially sequential approach, the effects being tested are as follows:

$$\alpha \mid \mu, \beta$$

$$\beta \mid \mu, \alpha$$

$$\alpha\beta \mid \mu, \alpha, \beta$$

There is difference here because each main effect controls for the other main effect, but not for the interaction effect. In SAS and SPSS, this is the *Type II sum of squares* method. This is the only one of the three methods where the sums of squares will add up to the total sum of squares. Notice in the sequential and partially sequential approaches that the interaction is not taken into account in estimating the main effects, which is only fine if there is no interaction effect.

In the regression approach, the effects being tested are as follows:

$$\alpha \mid \mu, \beta, \alpha\beta$$

$$\beta \mid \mu, \alpha, \alpha\beta$$

$$\alpha\beta \mid \mu, \alpha, \beta$$

In this approach, each effect controls for each of the other effects. In SAS and SPSS, this is the *Type III sum of squares* method (and is the default selection in SPSS). Many statisticians (e.g., Glass & Hopkins, 1996; Keppel & Wickens, 2004; Mickey, Dunn, & Clark, 2004), including the authors of this text, recommend exclusive use of the regression approach because each effect is estimated taking the other effects into account. The hypotheses tested in the sequential and partially sequential approaches are seldom of interest and are difficult to interpret (Carlson & Timm, 1974; Kirk, 1982; Overall et al., 1981; Timm and Carlson, 1975). The regression approach seems to be conceptually closest to the traditional ANOVA in that each effect is estimated controlling for all other effects. When the n's are equal, each of these three approaches tests the same hypotheses and yields the same results.

3.4 SPSS and G*Power

Next we consider the use of SPSS for the statistics lab example. Instructions for determining the factorial ANOVA using SPSS are presented first, followed by additional steps for examining the assumptions for factorial ANOVA. Finally we examine a priori and post hoc power for this model using G*Power.

Factorial ANOVA

In this section, we take a look at SPSS for the statistics lab example. As already noted in Chapter 1, SPSS needs the data to be in a specific form for the analysis to proceed, which is different from the layout of the data in Table 3.1. For a two-factor ANOVA, the dataset must consist of three variables or columns, one for the level of factor A, one for the level of factor B, and the third for the dependent variable. Each row still represents one individual, indicating the levels of factors A and B that individual is a member of, and their score on the dependent variable. As seen in the following screenshot, for a two-factor ANOVA, the SPSS data are in the form of two columns that represent the group values (i.e., the two independent variables) and one column that represents the scores or values of the dependent variable.

The **first independent variable** is labeled "Group" where each value represents the attractiveness of the statistics lab instructor to which the student was assigned. Group 1, you recall, represented "unattractive". Thus there were eight students randomly assigned to an "unattractive" instructor. Since each of these eight students was in the same group, each is coded with the same value (1, which represents that they were assigned to an "unattractive" instructor). The other groups (2, 3, and 4) follow this pattern as well.

The second **independent variable** is labeled "Time" where each value represents the time of day of the course. One represents "afternoon" and two represents "evening."

The **dependent variable** is "Labs" and represents the number of statistics labs the student attended.

	Group	Time	Labs
1	1.00	1.00	15.00
2	1.00	2.00	10.00
3	1.00	1.00	12.00
4	1.00	2.00	8.00
5	1.00	1.00	21.00
6	1.00	2.00	7.00
7	1.00	1.00	13.00
8	1.00	2.00	3.00
9	2.00	1.00	20.00
10	2.00	2.00	13.00
11	2.00	2.00	9.00
12	2.00	1.00	22.00
13	2.00	1.00	24.00
14	2.00	1.00	25.00
15	2.00	2.00	18.00
16	2.00	2.00	12.00
17	3.00	2.00	10.00
18	3.00	1.00	24.00
19	3.00	1.00	29.00
20	3.00	2.00	12.00
21	3.00	1.00	27.00
22	3.00	2.00	21.00
23	3.00	1.00	25.00
24	3.00	2.00	14.00
25	4.00	1.00	30.00
26	4.00	2.00	22.00
27	4.00	1.00	26.00
28	4.00	2.00	20.00
29	4.00	1.00	29.00
30	4.00	1.00	28.00
31	4.00	2.00	25.00
32	4.00	2.00	15.00

Step 1: To conduct a factorial ANOVA, go to "Analyze" in the top pulldown menu, then select "General Linear Model," and then select "Univariate." Following the screen-shot (Step 1) that follows produces the "Univariate" dialog box.

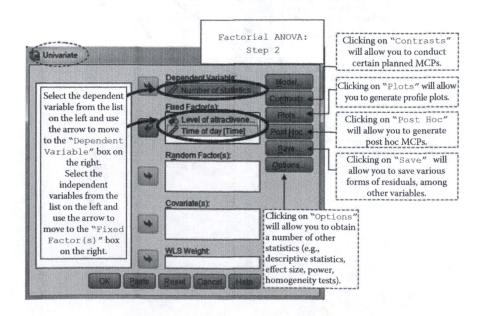

Step 2: Click the dependent variable (e.g., number of statistics labs attended) and move it into the "Dependent Variable" box by clicking the arrow button. Click the first independent variable (e.g., level of attractiveness) and move it into the "Fixed Factors" box by clicking the arrow button. Follow this same step to move the second independent variable into the "Fixed Factors" box. Next, click on "Options."

Step 3: Clicking on "Options" will provide the option to select such information as "Descriptive Statistics," "Estimates of effect size," "Observed power," "Homogeneity tests" (i.e., Levene's test for equal variances), and "Spread versus level plots" (those are the options that we typically utilize). Click on "Continue" to return to the original dialog box.

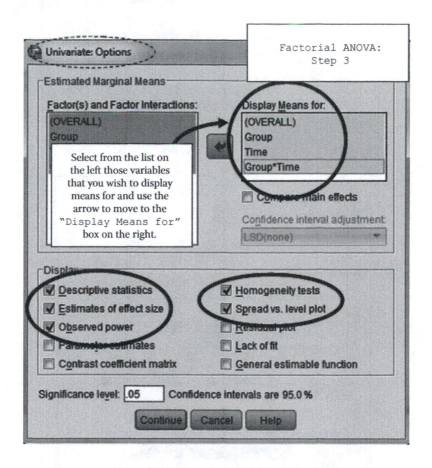

Step 4: From the "Univariate" dialog box, click on "Plots" to obtain a profile plot of means. Click the independent variable (e.g., level of attractiveness labeled as "Group") and move it into the "Horizontal Axis" box by clicking the arrow button (see screenshot step 4a). (*Tip: Placing the independent variable that has the most categories or levels on the horizontal axis of the profile plots will make for easier interpretation of the graph.*) Then click the second independent variable (e.g., "Time") and move it into the "Separate Lines" box by clicking the arrow button (see screenshot Step 4a). Then click on "Add" to move the variable into the "Plots" box at the bottom of the dialog box (see screenshot Step 4b). Click on "Continue" to return to the original dialog box.

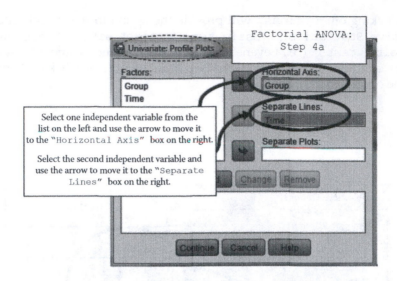

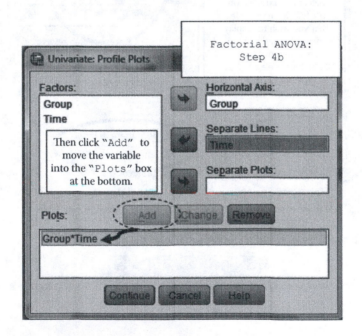

Step 5: From the "Univariate" dialog box, click on "Post Hoc" to select various post hoc MCPs or click on "Contrasts" to select various planned MCPs (see screenshot Step 1). From the "Post Hoc Multiple Comparisons for Observed Means" dialog box, click on the names of the independent variables in the "Factor(s)" list box in the top left (e.g., "Group" and "Time") and move them to the "Post Hoc Tests for" box in the top right by clicking on the arrow key. Check an appropriate MCP for your situation by placing a checkmark in the box next to the desired MCP. In this example, we will select "Tukey." Click on "Continue" to return to the original dialog box.

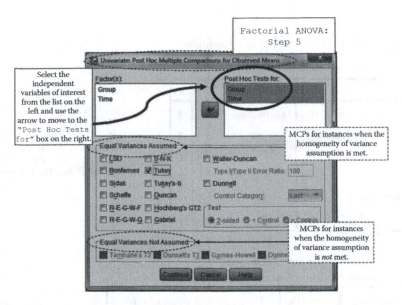

Step 6: From the "Univariate" dialog box, click on "Save" to select those elements that you want to save (in our case, we want to save the unstandardized residuals which will be used later to examine the extent to which normality and independence are met). From the "Univariate" dialog box, click on "OK" to return to generate the output.

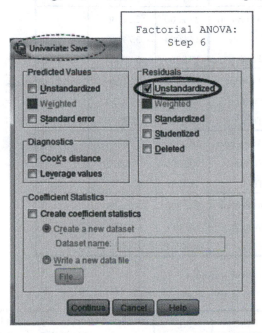

Interpreting the output: Annotated results are presented in Table 3.8, and the profile plot is shown in Figure 3.2. Note that in order to test interaction contrasts in SPSS, syntax is required rather than the use of point-and-click features used primarily in this text (cf., Page, Braver, & MacKinnon, 2003). Note also that the SPSS ANOVA summary table will include additional sources of variation that we find not to be useful (i.e., corrected model, intercept, total); thus, they are not annotated in Table 3.8.

TABLE 3.8

Selected SPSS Results for the Statistics Lab Example

Between-Subjects Factors

		Value Label	N
Level of attractiveness	1.00	Unattractive	8
	2.00	Slightly attractive	8
	3.00	Moderately attractive	8
	4.00	Very attractive	8
Time of day	1.00	Afternoon	16
	2.00	Evening	16

The table labeled "Between-Subjects Factors" provides sample sizes for each of the categories of the independent variables (recall that the independent variables are the "between subjects factors").

Descriptive Statistics

Dependent Variable: Number of Statistics Labs Attended

Level of Attractiveness	Time of Day	Mean	Std. Deviation	N
Unattractive	Afternoon	15.2500	4.03113	4
	Evening	7.0000	2.94392	4
	Total	11.1250	5.48862	8
Slightly attractive	Afternoon	22.7500	2.21736	4
	Evening	13.0000	3.74166	4
	Total	17.8750	5.93867	8
Moderately attractive	Afternoon	26.2500	2.21736	4
	Evening	14.2500	4.78714	4
	Total	20.2500	7.28501	8
Very attractive	Afternoon	28.2500	1.70783	4
	Evening	20.5000	4.20317	4
	Total	24.3750	5.09727	8
Total	Afternoon	23.1250	5.65538	16
	Evening	13.6875	6.09611	16
	Total	18.4062	7.51283	32

The table labeled "Descriptive Statistics" provides basic descriptive statistics (means, standard deviations, and sample sizes) for each cell of the design.

Levene's Test of Equality of Error Variances[a]

Dependent Variable: Number of Statistics Labs Attended

F	df1	df2	Sig.
.579	7	24	.766

Note: Tests the null hypothesis that the error variance of the dependent variable is equal across groups.

[a] Design: Intercept + Group + Time + Group*Time.

The F test (and associated p value) for Levene's Test for Equality of Error Variances is reviewed to determine if equal variances can be assumed.

In this case, we meet the assumption (as p is greater than α). Note that $df1$ is calculated as $(JK-1)$ and $df2$ is calculated as $(N-JK)$.

TABLE 3.8 (continued)

Selected SPSS Results for the Statistics Lab Example

The omnibus F test for the main effect for "Group" (i.e., attractiveness) (and computed similarly for the other main effects and interactions) is computed as

$$F = \frac{MS_A}{MS_{with}} = \frac{246.198}{11.531} = 21.350$$

The p value for the omnibus F test for the main effect for attractiveness is .000. This indicates there is a statistically significant difference in the dependent variable based on attractiveness, averaged across time of day (afternoon and evening). In other words, there is a unique effect of attractiveness on the number of stat labs attended, controlling for time of day. The probability of observing these mean differences or more extreme mean differences by chance if the null hypothesis is really true (i.e., if the population means are really equal) is less than 1%. We reject the null hypothesis that the population means of attractiveness are equal. For our example, this provides evidence to suggest that the number of stat labs differs, on average, across the levels of attractiveness, when controlling for time of day.

Tests of Between-Subjects Effects

Dependent Variable: Number of Statistics Labs Attended

Source	Type III Sum of Squares	df	Mean Square	F	Sig.	Partial Eta Squared	Noncent. Parameter	Observed Power[b]
Corrected model	1472.969[a]	7	210.424	18.248	.000	.842	127.737	1.000
Intercept	10841.281	1	10841.281	940.165	.000	.975	940.165	1.000
Group	738.594	3	246.198	21.350	.000	.727	64.051	1.000
Time	712.531	1	712.531	61.791	.000	.720	61.791	1.000
Group * Time	21.844	3	7.281	.631	.602	.073	1.894	.162
Error	276.750	24	11.531					
Total	12591.000	32						
Corrected total	1749.719	31						

[a] R squared = .842 (adjusted R squared = .796).

[b] Computed using alpha = .05.

R squared is listed as a footnote underneath the table. R squared is the ratio of sum of squares between (i.e., combined SS for main effects and for the interaction) divided by sum of squares total:

$$R^2 = \frac{SS_{betw}}{SS_{total}} = \frac{738.594 + 712.531 + 21.844}{1749.719} = .842$$

The row labeled "**Error**" is for within groups. The within groups sum of squares tells us how much variation there is within the cells combined across the cells (i.e., 276.750). The degrees of freedom for within groups is $(N - JK)$ or the sample size minus the independent variables [i.e., $32 - (4)(2) = 24$]. The row labeled "**Corrected Total**" is the sum of squares total. The degrees of freedom for the total is $(N - 1)$ or the total sample size -1.

Observed power tells whether our test is powerful enough to detect mean differences if they really exist. Power of 1.000 indicates the maximum probability of rejecting the null hypothesis if it is really false (i.e., very strong power).

(continued)

TABLE 3.8 (continued)

Selected SPSS Results for the Statistics Lab Example

1. Grand Mean

Dependent Variable: Number of Statistics Labs Attended

Mean	Std. Error	95% Confidence Interval	
		Lower Bound	Upper Bound
18.406	.600	17.167	19.645

The **"Grand Mean"** (in this case, 18.406) represents the overall mean, regardless of group membership, on the dependent variable. The 95% CI represents the CI of the grand mean.

2. Level of Attractiveness

Dependent Variable: Number of Statistics Labs Attended

Level of Attractiveness	Mean	Std. Error	95% Confidence Interval	
			Lower Bound	Upper Bound
Unattractive	11.125	1.201	8.647	13.603
Slightly attractive	17.875	1.201	15.397	20.353
Moderately attractive	20.250	1.201	17.772	22.728
Very attractive	24.375	1.201	21.897	26.853

The table labeled **"Level of attractiveness"** provides descriptive statistics for each of the categories of the first independent variable. In addition to means, the *SE* and 95% CI of the means are reported.

3. Time of Day

Dependent Variable: Number of Statistics Labs Attended

Time of Day	Mean	Std. Error	95% Confidence Interval	
			Lower Bound	Upper Bound
Afternoon	23.125	.849	21.373	24.877
Evening	13.688	.849	11.935	15.440

The table labeled **"Time of day"** provides descriptive statistics for each of the categories of the second independent variable. In addition to means, the *SE* and 95% CI of the means are reported.

4. Level of Attractiveness * Time of Day

Dependent Variable: Number of Statistics Labs Attended

Level of Attractiveness	Time of Day	Mean	Std. Error	95% Confidence Interval	
				Lower Bound	Upper Bound
Unattractive	Afternoon	15.250	1.698	11.746	18.754
	Evening	7.000	1.698	3.496	10.504
Slightly attractive	Afternoon	22.750	1.698	19.246	26.254
	Evening	13.000	1.698	9.496	16.504
Moderately attractive	Afternoon	26.250	1.698	22.746	29.754
	Evening	14.250	1.698	10.746	17.754
Very attractive	Afternoon	28.250	1.698	24.746	31.754
	Evening	20.500	1.698	16.996	24.004

The table labeled **"Level of attractiveness * Time of day"** provides descriptive statistics for each of the categories of the first independent variable by the second independent variable (i.e., cell means) (notice that these are the same means reported previously). In addition to means, the *SE* and 95% CI of the means are reported.

TABLE 3.8 (continued)

Selected SPSS Results for the Statistics Lab Example

> "Mean difference" is simply the difference between the means of the two levels of attractiveness being compared. For example, the mean difference of level 1 and level 2 is calculated as 11.1250 − 17.8750 = −6.7500.

Number of Statistics Labs Attended
Tukey HSD

Multiple Comparisons

(I) Level of Attractiveness	(J) Level of Attractiveness	Mean Difference (I − J)	Std. Error	Sig.	95% Confidence Interval	
					Lower Bound	Upper Bound
Unattractive	Slightly attractive	−6.7500*	1.69788	.003	−11.4338	−2.0662
	Moderately attractive	−9.1250*	1.69788	.000	−13.8088	−4.4412
	Very attractive	−13.2500*	1.69788	.000	−17.9338	−8.5662
Slightly attractive	Unattractive	6.7500*	1.69788	.003	2.0662	11.4338
	Moderately attractive	−2.3750	1.69788	.512	−7.0588	2.3088
	Very attractive	−6.5000*	1.69788	.004	−11.1838	−1.8162
Moderately attractive	Unattractive	9.1250*	1.69788	.000	4.4412	13.8088
	Slightly attractive	2.3750	1.69788	.512	−2.3088	7.0588
	Very attractive	−4.1250	1.69788	.098	−8.8088	.5588
Very attractive	Unattractive	13.2500*	1.69788	.000	8.5662	17.9338
	Slightly attractive	6.5000*	1.69788	.004	1.8162	11.1838
	Moderately attractive	4.1250	1.69788	.098	−.5588	8.8088

Note: Based on observed means.
The error term is mean square(error) = 11.531.
* The mean difference is significant at the .05 level.

> The standard error calculated in SPSS uses the harmonic mean (Tukey–Kramer modification):
>
> $$S_{\Psi'} = \sqrt{MS_{error}\left[\frac{1}{2}\left(\frac{1}{n_1} + \frac{1}{n_2}\right)\right]}$$
>
> $$S_{\Psi'} = \sqrt{11.531\left[\frac{1}{2}\left(\frac{1}{8} + \frac{1}{8} + \frac{1}{8} + \frac{1}{8}\right)\right]}$$
>
> $$S_{\Psi'} = \sqrt{2.88275} = 1.69788$$

> "Sig." denotes the observed *p* values and provides the results of the contrasts. There are four statistically significant mean differences between: (1) group 1 (unattractive) and group 2 (slightly attractive); (2) group 1 (unattractive) and group 3 (moderately attractive); (3) group 1 (unattractive) and group 4 (very attractive); and (4) group 2 (slightly attractive) and 4 (very attractive).
>
> Note that there are only six unique contrast results:
>
> $$\frac{1}{2}[J\,(J-1)] = \frac{1}{2}[4(4-1)] = \frac{1}{2}(12) = 6.$$
>
> Thus there are redundant results presented in the table. For example, the comparison of group 1 and 2 (presented in results row 1) is the same as the comparison of group 2 and 1 (presented in results row 2).

(continued)

TABLE 3.8 (continued)

Selected SPSS Results for the Statistics Lab Example

Tukey HSD[a][b]   **Number of Statistics Labs Attended**

Level of Attractiveness	N	Subset		
		1	2	3
Unattractive	8	11.1250		
Slightly attractive	8		17.8750	
Moderately attractive	8		20.2500	20.2500
Very attractive	8			24.3750
Sig.		1.000	.512	.098

Means for groups in homogeneous subsets are displayed

> This table displays the means for the groups that are not statistically significantly different. For example, in subset 2 the means for group 2 (slightly attractive) and group 3 (moderately attractive) are displayed, indicating that those group means are "homogeneous" or not significantly different.

Note: Based on observed means.
The error term is mean square(error) = 11.531.
[a] Uses Harmonic Mean Sample Size = 8.000.
[b] Alpha = .05.

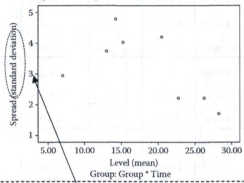

Spread vs. level plot of number of statistics labs attended

> Spread vs. level plots are plots of the dependent variable standard deviations (or variances) against the cell means. These plots can be used to determine what to do when the homogeneity of variance assumption has been violated (remember, we already have evidence of meeting the homogeneity of variance assumption). In addition to Levene's test, homogeneity is suggested when the spread vs. level plots provide a random display of points (i.e., no systematic pattern).
>
> If the plot suggests a linear relationship between the standard deviation and mean, transforming the data by taking the log of the dependent variable values may be a solution to the heterogeneity (since the calculation of logarithms requires positive values, this assumes all the data values are positive).
>
> If there is a linear relationship between the variance and mean, transforming the data by taking the square root of the dependent variable values may be a solution to the heterogeneity (since the calculation of square roots requires positive values, this assumes all the data values are positive).

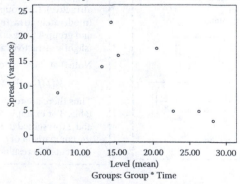

Spread vs. level plot of number on statistics labs attended

Examining Data for Assumptions

Normality

We will use the residuals (which were requested and created through the "Save" option when generating our factorial ANOVA) to examine the extent to which normality was met.

	Group	Time	Labs	RES_1
1	1.00	1.00	15.00	-.25
2	1.00	2.00	10.00	3.00
3	1.00	1.00	12.00	-3.25
4			8.00	1.00
5			21.00	5.75
6			7.00	.00
7			13.00	-2.25
8			3.00	-4.00
9			20.00	-2.75
10			13.00	.00
11			9.00	-4.00
12			22.00	-.75
13			24.00	1.25
14			25.00	2.25
15			18.00	5.00
16			12.00	-1.00
17	3.00	2.00	10.00	-4.25
18	3.00	1.00	24.00	-2.25
19	3.00	1.00	29.00	2.75
20	3.00	2.00	12.00	-2.25
21	3.00	1.00	27.00	.75
22	3.00	2.00	21.00	6.75
23	3.00	1.00	25.00	-1.25
24	3.00	2.00	14.00	-.25
25	4.00	1.00	30.00	1.75
26	4.00	2.00	22.00	1.50
27	4.00	1.00	26.00	-2.25
28	4.00	2.00	20.00	-.50
29	4.00	1.00	29.00	.75
30	4.00	1.00	28.00	-.25
31	4.00	2.00	25.00	4.50
32	4.00	2.00	15.00	-5.50

> The residuals are computed by substracting the cell mean from the dependent variable value for each observation. For example, the cell mean for time 1 group 1 was 15.25. Thus the residual for the first person is: $(15 - 15.25 = -.25)$.
>
> As we look at our raw data, we see a new variable has been added to our dataset labeled RES_1. This is our residual.
>
> The residual will be used to review the assumptions of normality and independence.

Generating normality evidence: As alluded to earlier in the chapter, understanding the distributional shape, specifically the extent to which normality is a reasonable assumption, is important. For factorial ANOVA, the distributional shape for the residuals should be a normal distribution. We can again use "Explore" to examine the extent to which the assumption of normality is met.

The general steps for accessing "Explore" have been presented in *Introduction to Statistical Concepts*, Third Edition, and will not be repeated here. Click the residual and move it into the "Dependent List" box by clicking on the arrow button. The procedures for selecting normality statistics were also presented in Chapter 6 of *An Introduction to Statistical Concepts*, Third Edition, and remain the same here: Click on "Plots" in the upper right corner. Place a checkmark in the boxes for "Normality plots with tests" and also for "Histogram." Then click "Continue" to return to the main "Explore" dialog box. Then click "OK" to generate the output.

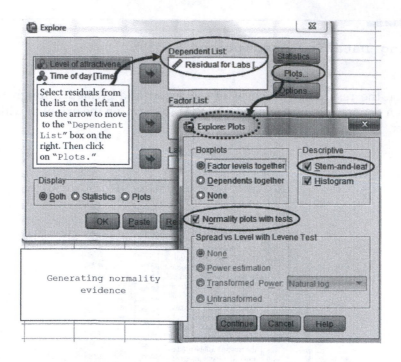

Interpreting normality evidence: We have already developed a good understanding of how to interpret some forms of evidence of normality including skewness and kurtosis, histograms, and boxplots.

Descriptives

			Statistic	Std. Error
Residual for labs	Mean		.0000	.52819
	95% Confidence interval for mean	Lower bound	−1.0772	
		Upper bound	1.0772	
	5% Trimmed mean		−.0747	
	Median		−.2500	
	Variance		8.927	
	Std. deviation		2.98788	
	Minimum		−5.50	
	Maximum		6.75	
	Range		12.25	
	Interquartile range		3.94	
	Skewness		.400	.414
	Kurtosis		−.162	.809

The skewness statistic of the residuals is .400 and kurtosis is −.162—both within the range of an absolute value of 2.0, suggesting some evidence of normality.

As suggested by the skewness statistic, the histogram of residuals is slightly positively skewed, but it approaches a normal distribution and there is nothing to suggest normality may be an unreasonable assumption.

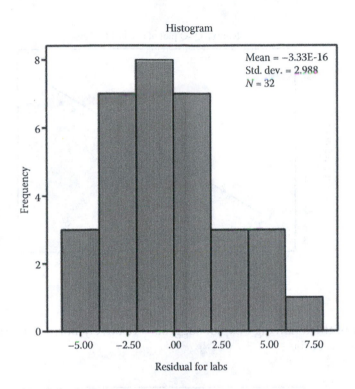

There are a few other statistics that can be used to gauge normality. The formal test of normality, the Shapiro–Wilk (S–W) test (*SW*) (Shapiro & Wilk, 1965), provides evidence of the extent to which our sample distribution is statistically different from a normal distribution. The output for the S–W test is presented as follows and suggests that our sample distribution for residuals is not statistically significantly different than what would be expected from a normal distribution ($SW = .977$, $df = 32$, $p = .701$).

Tests of Normality

	Kolmogorov–Smirnov[a]			Shapiro–Wilk		
	Statistic	df	Sig.	Statistic	df	Sig.
Residual for labs	.094	32	.200	.977	32	.701

[a] Lilliefors significance correction.
*This is a lower bound of the true significance.

Quantile–quantile (Q–Q) plots are also often examined to determine evidence of normality. Q–Q plots are graphs that plot quantiles of the theoretical normal distribution against quantiles of the sample distribution. Points that fall on or close to the diagonal line suggest evidence of normality. The Q–Q plot of residuals shown as follows suggests relative normality.

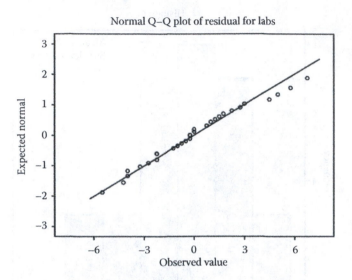

Normal Q–Q plot of residual for labs

Examination of the following boxplot suggests a relatively normal distributional shape of residuals and no outliers.

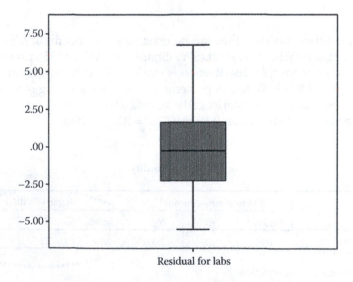

Residual for labs

Considering the forms of evidence we have examined, skewness and kurtosis statistics, the S–W test, the Q–Q plot, and the boxplot, all suggest normality is a reasonable assumption. We can be reasonably assured that we have met the assumption of normality of the dependent variable for each group of the independent variable.

Independence

The only assumption we have not tested for yet is independence. As we discussed in reference to the one-way ANOVA, if subjects have been randomly assigned to conditions (or to the different combinations of the levels of the independent variables in a factorial ANOVA), the assumption of independence has been met. In this illustration, students were randomly assigned to instructor and time of day, and, thus, the assumption of independence was met. However, we often use independent variables that do not allow random assignment, such as preexisting characteristics such as education level (high school diploma, bachelor's, master's, or doctoral degrees). We can plot residuals against levels of our independent variables in a scatterplot to get an idea of whether or not there are patterns in the data and thereby provide an indication of whether we have met this assumption. Given we have multiple independent variables in the factorial ANOVA, we will split the scatterplot by levels of one independent variable ("Group") and then generate a bivariate scatterplot for "Time" by residual. Remember that the residual was added to the dataset by saving it when we generated the factorial ANOVA model.

Please note that some researchers do not believe that the assumption of independence can be tested. If there is not random assignment to groups, then these researchers believe this assumption has been violated—period. The plot that we generate will give us a general idea of patterns, however, in situations where random assignment was not performed or not possible.

Splitting the file: The first step is to split our file by the levels of one of our independent variables (e.g., "Group"). To do that, go to "Data" in the top pulldown menu and then select "Split File."

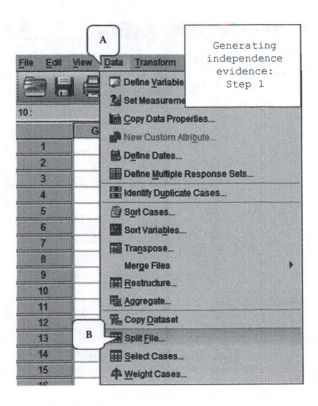

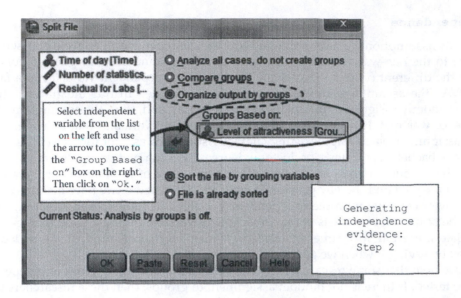

Generating the scatterplot: The general steps for generating a simple scatter-plot through "Scatter/dot" have been presented in Chapter 10 of *An Introduction to Statistical Concepts,* Third Edition, and they will not be reiterated here. From the "Simple Scatterplot" dialog screen, click the residual variable and move it into the "Y Axis" box by clicking on the arrow. Click the independent variable that was not used to split the file (e.g., "Time") and move it into the "X Axis" box by clicking on the arrow. Then click "OK."

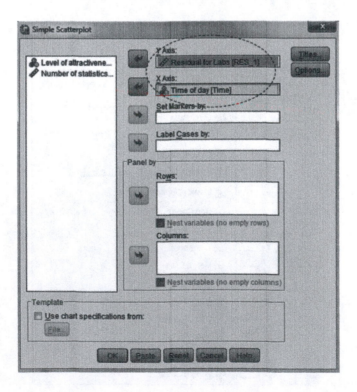

Interpreting independence evidence: In examining the scatterplots for evidence of independence, the points should fall relatively randomly above and below a horizontal line at 0. (You may recall in Chapter 1 that we added a reference line to the graph using Chart Editor. To add a reference line, double click on the graph in the output to activate the chart editor. Select "Options" in the top pulldown menu, then "Y axis reference line." This will bring up the "Properties" dialog box. Change the value of the position to be "0." Then click on "Apply" and "Close" to generate the graph with a horizontal line at 0.)

In this example, our scatterplot for each level of attractiveness generally suggests evidence of independence with a relatively random display of residuals above and below the horizontal line at 0 for each category of time. Thus, had we not met the assumption of independence through random assignment of cases to groups, this would have provided evidence that independence was a reasonable assumption.

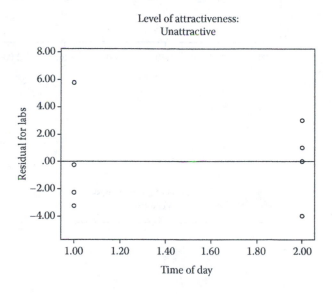

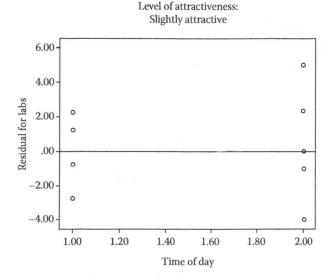

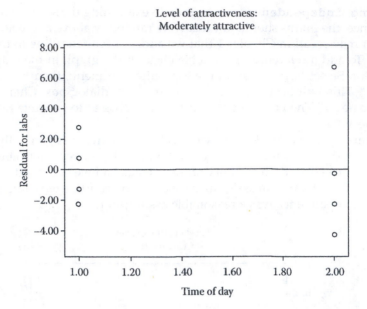

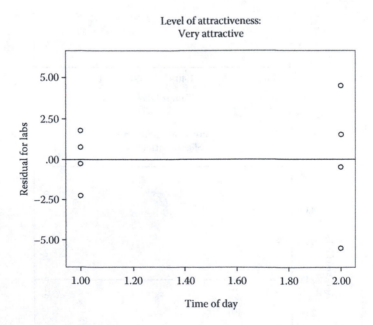

Post Hoc Power for Factorial ANOVA Using G*Power

Main effects: When there are multiple independent variables, G*Power must be calculated for each main effect and for each interaction. We will illustrate the main effect for attractiveness of instructor, but note that computing post hoc power for the other main effect(s) and interaction(s) is similarly obtained.

The first thing that must be done when using G*Power for computing post hoc power is to select the correct test family. In our case, we conducted a factorial ANOVA. To find the factorial ANOVA, we select "Tests" in the top pulldown menu, then "Means," and then "Many groups: ANOVA: Main effects and interactions (two or more independent variables)." Once that selection is made, the "Test family" automatically changes to "F tests."

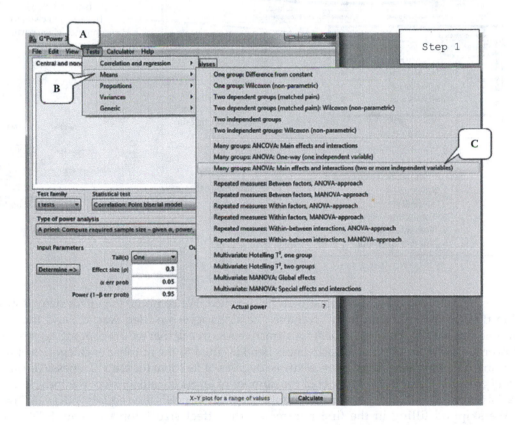

The "Type of Power Analysis" desired then needs to be selected. To compute post hoc power, we need to select "Post hoc: Compute achieved power—given α, sample size, and effect size."

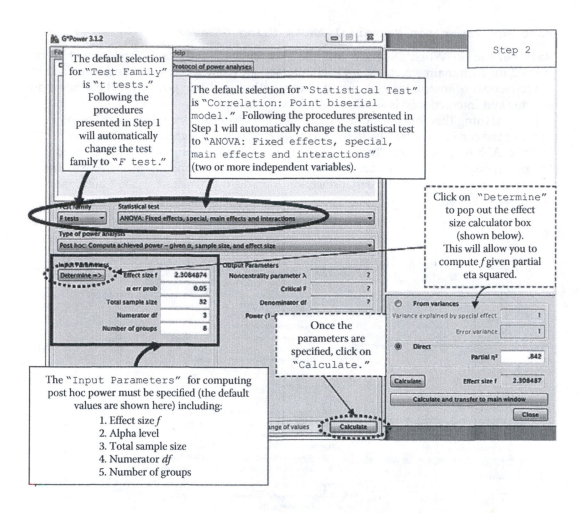

The "Input Parameters" must then be specified. We compute the effect size *f* last, so skip that for the moment. In our example, the alpha level we used was .05, and the total sample size was 32. The *numerator df* for attractiveness (recall that we are computing post hoc power for the main effect of attractiveness here) is equal to the number of categories of this variable (i.e., 4) minus 1; thus, there are three degrees of freedom for attractiveness. The *number of groups* is equal to the product of the number of levels or categories of the independent variables or (*J*)(*K*). In this example, the number of groups or cells then equals (*J*)(*K*) = (4)(2) = 8.

We skipped filling in the first parameter, the effect size *f*, for a reason. SPSS only provided a partial eta squared effect size. Thus, we will use the pop-out effect size calculator in G*Power to compute the effect size *f* (we saved this parameter for last as the calculation is based on the previous values just entered). To pop out the effect size calculator, click on "Determine" which is displayed under "Input Parameters." In the pop-out effect size calculator, click on the radio button for "Direct" and then enter the partial eta squared value for attractiveness that was calculated in SPSS (i.e., .842). Clicking on "Calculate" in the pop-out effect size calculator will calculate the effect size *f*. Then click on "Calculate and Transfer to Main Window" to transfer the calculated effect size (i.e., 2.3084874) to the "Input Parameters." Once the parameters are specified, click on "Calculate" to find the power statistics.

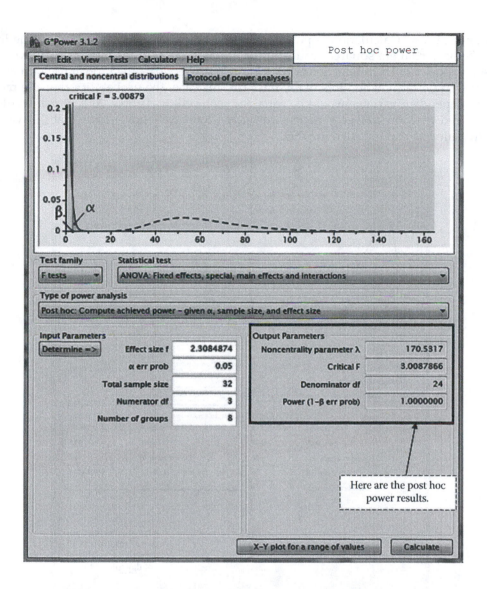

The "Output Parameters" provide the relevant statistics given the input just specified. In this example, we were interested in determining post hoc power for a two-factor ANOVA with a computed effect size f of 2.308, an alpha level of .05, total sample size of 32, numerator degrees of freedom of 3, and 8 groups or cells.

Based on those criteria, the post hoc power for the main effect of attractiveness was 1.00. In other words, with a factorial ANOVA, computed effect size f of 2.308, alpha level of .05, total sample size of 32, numerator degrees of freedom of 3, and 8 groups (or cells), the post hoc power of our main effect was 1.00—the probability of rejecting the null hypothesis when it is really false (in this case, the probability that the means of the dependent variable would be equal for each level of the independent variable) was 1.00, which would be considered maximum power (sufficient power is often .80 or above). Note that this value is the same as that reported in SPSS. Keep in mind that conducting power analysis a priori is recommended so that you avoid a situation where, post hoc, you find that the sample size was not sufficient to reach the desired level of power (given the observed parameters).

Interactions: Calculation of power for interactions is conducted similarly. The input of .075 for partial eta squared results in the following output for interaction power. The post hoc power of the interaction effect for this test was .204—the probability of rejecting the null hypothesis when it is really false (in this case, the probability that the means of the dependent variable would be equal for each cell) was about 20%, which would be considered very low power (sufficient power is often .80 or above). Note that this value is not the same as that reported in SPSS.

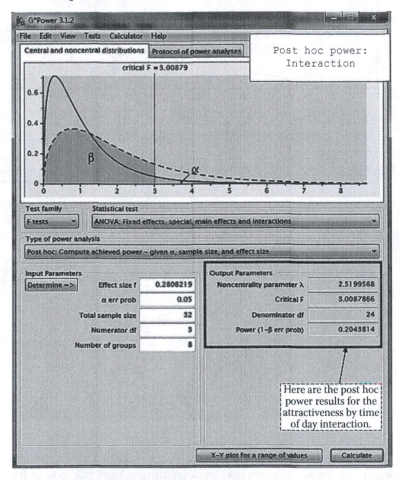

A Priori Power for Factorial ANOVA Using G*Power

For a priori power, we can determine the total sample size needed for the main effects and/or interactions given an estimated effect size f, alpha level, desired power, numerator degrees of freedom (i.e., number of categories of our independent variable or interaction, depending on which a priori power is of interest), and number of groups or cells (i.e., the product of the number of levels of the independent variables). We follow Cohen's (1988) conventions for effect size (i.e., small, $f = .10$; moderate, $f = .25$; large, $f = .40$). In this example, had we estimated a moderate effect f of .25, alpha of .05, desired power of .80, numerator degrees of freedom of 3 (four groups in attractiveness, two levels of time of day, thus $4 - 1 \times 2 - 1 = 3$), and number of groups of 8 (i.e., four categories of attractiveness and two levels in time of day or $4 \times 2 = 8$), we would need a total sample size of 179 (or about 22 or 23 individuals per cell).

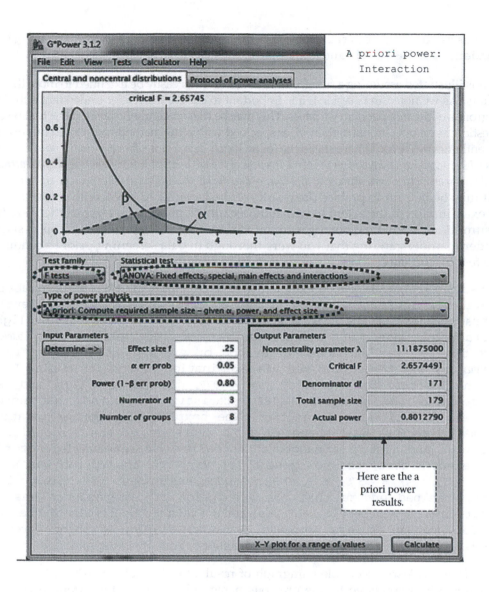

3.5 Template and APA-Style Write-Up

Finally we come to an example paragraph of the results for the two-factor statistics lab example. Recall that our graduate research assistant, Marie, was working on a research project for an independent study class to determine if there was a mean difference in the number of statistics labs attended based on the attractiveness of the lab instructor (four categories) and time of day the lab was attended (afternoon or evening). Her research question was the following: *Is there a mean difference in the number of statistics labs students attended based on the attractiveness of the lab instructor and time of day the lab was attended?* Marie then generated a factorial ANOVA as the test of inference. A template for writing a research question for a factorial ANOVA is presented as follows;

Is there a mean difference in [dependent variable] based on [independent variable 1] and [independent variable 2]?

This is illustrated assuming a two-factor model, but it can easily be extended to more than two factors. As we noted in Chapter 1, it is important to ensure the reader understands the levels or groups of the independent variables. This may be done parenthetically in the actual research question, as an operational definition, or specified within the methods section. In this example, parenthetically we could have stated the following: *Is there a mean difference in the number of statistics labs students attend based on the attractiveness of the lab instructor (unattractive, slightly attractive, moderately attractive, very attractive) and time of day the lab was attended (afternoon or evening)?*

It may be helpful to preface the results of the factorial ANOVA with information on an examination of the extent to which the assumptions were met (recall there are three assumptions: normality, homogeneity of variance, and independence). This assists the reader in understanding that you were thorough in data screening prior to conducting the test of inference:

A factorial ANOVA was conducted to determine if the mean number of statistics labs attended by students differed based on the level of attractiveness of the statistics lab instructor (unattractive, slightly attractive, moderately attractive, very attractive) and the time of day the lab was attended (afternoon or evening). The assumption of normality was tested and met via examination of the residuals. Review of the S-W test for normality (SW = .977, df = 32, p = .701) and skewness (.400) and kurtosis (-.162) statistics suggested that normality was a reasonable assumption. The boxplot suggested a relatively normal distributional shape (with no outliers) of the residuals. The Q-Q plot and histogram suggested normality was reasonable. According to Levene's test, the homogeneity of variance assumption was satisfied [$F(7, 24)$ = .579, p = .766]. Random assignment of individuals to groups helped ensure that the assumption of independence was met. Additionally, scatterplots of residuals against the levels of the independent variables were reviewed. A random display of points around 0 provided further evidence that the assumption of independence was met.

Here is an APA-style example paragraph of results for the factorial ANOVA (remember that this will be prefaced by the previous paragraph reporting the extent to which the assumptions of the test were met):

From Table 3.8, we see that the interaction of attractiveness by time of day is not statistically significant, but there are statistically significant main effects for both attractiveness and time of day ($F_{attract}$ = 21.350, df = 3, 24, p = .001; F_{time} = 61.791, df = 1, 24, p = .001). Effect sizes are large for both attractiveness and time (partial $\eta^2_{attract}$ = .727; partial η^2_{time} = .720), and observed power for attractiveness and time is maximal (i.e., 1.000).

Post hoc analyses were conducted given the statistically significant omnibus ANOVA F tests. The profile plot (Figure 3.2) summarizes these differences. Tukey HSD tests were conducted on all possible pairwise contrasts. For the main effect of attractiveness, Tukey HSD post hoc comparisons revealed that the unattractive level had statistically significantly lower attendance than all the other levels of attractiveness and that the slightly attractive level had statistically significantly lower attendance than the very attractive level. More specifically, the following pairs of groups were found to be significantly different ($p < .05$):

- Groups 1 (unattractive; $M = 11.125$, $SD = 5.4886$) and 2 (slightly attractive; $M = 17.875$, $SD = 5.9387$)
- Groups 1 (unattractive) and 3 (moderately attractive; $M = 20.2500$, $SD = 7.2850$)
- Groups 1 (unattractive) and 4 (very attractive; $M = 24.3750$, $SD = 5.0973$)
- Groups 2 (slightly attractive) and 4 (very attractive)

In other words, students enrolled in the least attractive instructor group attended statistically significantly fewer statistics labs than students enrolled in any of the three more attractive instructor groups. For the main effect of time of day, Tukey HSD post hoc comparisons revealed that the students enrolled in the afternoon ($M = 23.125$, $SD = 5.655$) had statistically significantly higher statistics lab attendance than students in the evening ($M = 13.688$, $SD = 6.096$).

3.6 Summary

This chapter considered methods involving the comparison of means for multiple independent variables. The chapter began with a look at the characteristics of the factorial ANOVA, including (a) two or more independent variables each with two or more fixed levels; (b) subjects are randomly assigned to cells and then exposed to only one combination of the independent variables; (c) the factors are fully crossed such that all possible combinations of the factors' levels are included in the design; and (d) the dependent variable measured at the interval level or better. The ANOVA model was examined and followed by a discussion of main effects and, in particular, the interaction effect. Some discussion was also devoted to the ANOVA assumptions. The ANOVA summary table was shown along with partitioning the sums of squares. MCPs were then extended to factorial models. Then effect size measures, CIs, power, and expected mean squares were considered. Finally, several approaches were given for the unequal n's case with factorial models. At this point, you should have met the following objectives: (a) be able to understand the characteristics and concepts underlying factorial ANOVA, (b) be able to determine and interpret the results of factorial ANOVA, and (c) be able to understand and evaluate the assumptions of factorial ANOVA. In Chapter 4, we introduce the analysis of covariance.

Problems

Conceptual Problems

3.1 You are given a two-factor design with the following cell means (cell 11 = 25; cell 12 = 75; cell 21 = 50; cell 22 = 50; cell 31 = 75; cell 32 = 25). Assume that the within-cell variation is small. Which one of the following conclusions seems most probable?

 a. The row means are significantly different.

 b. The column means are significantly different.

 c. The interaction is significant.

 d. All of the above.

3.2 In a two-factor ANOVA, one independent variable has five levels and the second has four levels. If each cell has seven observations, what is df_{with}?

 a. 20

 b. 120

 c. 139

 d. 140

3.3 In a two-factor ANOVA, one independent variable has three levels or categories and the second has three levels or categories. What is df_{AB}, the interaction degrees of freedom?

 a. 3

 b. 4

 c. 6

 d. 9

3.4 Which of the following conclusions would result in the greatest generalizability of the main effect for factor A across the levels of factor B? The interaction between the independent variables A and B was...

 a. Not significant at the .25 level

 b. Significant at the .10 level

 c. Significant at the .05 level

 d. Significant at the .01 level

 e. Significant at the .001 level

3.5 In a two-factor fixed-effects ANOVA tested at an alpha of .05, the following p values were found: main effect for factor A, $p = .06$; main effect for factor B, $p = .09$; and interaction AB, $p = .02$. What can be interpreted from these results?

 a. There is a statistically significant main effect for factor A.

 b. There is a statistically significant main effect for factor B.

 c. There is a statistically significant main effect for factors A and B.

 d. There is a statistically significant interaction effect.

3.6   In a two-factor fixed-effects ANOVA, $F_A = 2$, $df_A = 3$, $df_B = 6$, $df_{AB} = 18$, and $df_{with} = 56$. The null hypothesis for factor A can be rejected

   a. At the .01 level

   b. At the .05 level, but not at the .01 level

   HELP!

   c. At the .10 level, but not at the .05 level

   d. None of the above

3.7   In ANOVA, the interaction of two factors is certainly present when

   a. The two factors are positively correlated.

   b. The two factors are negatively correlated.

   c. Row effects are not consistent across columns.

   d. Main effects do not account for all of the variation in Y.

   e. Main effects do account for all of the variation in Y.

3.8   For a design with four factors, how many interactions will there be?

   a. 4

   b. 8

   HELP!

   c. 11

   d. 12

   e. 16

3.9   Degrees of freedom for the AB interaction are equal to which one of the following?

   a. $df_A - df_B$

   b. $(df_A)(df_B)$

   c. $df_{with} - (df_A + df_B)$

   d. $df_{total} - df_{with}$

3.10 A two-factor experiment means that the design necessarily includes which one of the following?

   a. Two independent variables ✓

   HELP!

   b. Two dependent variables

   c. An interaction between the independent and dependent variables —

   d. Exactly two separate groups of subjects

3.11 Two independent variables are said to interact when which one of the following occurs?

   a. Both variables are equally influenced by a third variable.

   b. These variables are differentially affected by a third variable.

   c. Each factor produces a change in the subjects' scores.

   d. The effect of one variable depends on the second variable.

3.12 If there is an interaction between the independent variables textbook and time of day, this means that the textbook used has the same effect at different times of the day. True or false?

3.13 If the AB interaction is significant, then at least one of the two main effects must be significant. True or false?

3.14 I assert that a two-factor experiment (factors A and B) yields no more information than two one-factor experiments (factor A in experiment 1 and factor B in experiment 2). Am I correct?

3.15 For a two-factor fixed-effects model, if the degrees of freedom for testing factor A = 2, 24, then I assert that the degrees of freedom for testing factor B will necessarily be = 2, 24. Am I correct?

Questions 3.16 through 3.18 are based on the following ANOVA summary table (fixed-effects):

Source	df	MS	F
A	2	45	4.5
B	1	70	7.0
AB	2	170	17.0
Within	60	10	

3.16 For which source of variation is the null hypothesis rejected at the .01 level of significance?

    a. A

    b. B

    c. AB

    d. All of the above

3.17 How many cells are there in the design?

    a. 1

    b. 2

    c. 3

    d. 5

    e. None of the above

3.18 The total sample size for the design is which one of the following?

    a. 66

    b. 68

    c. 70

    d. None of the above

Questions 3.19 through 3.21 are based on the following ANOVA summary table (fixed effects):

Source	df	MS	F
A	2	164	5.8
B	1	80	2.8
AB	2	68	2.4
Within	9	28	

3.19 For which source of variation is the null hypothesis rejected at the .01 level of significance?

   a. A

   b. B

   c. AB

   d. All of the above

3.20 How many cells are there in the design?

   a. 1

   b. 2

   c. 3

   d. 6

   e. None of the above

3.21 The total sample size for the design is which one of the following?

   a. 10

   b. 15

   c. 20

   d. 25

Computational Problems

3.1 Complete the following ANOVA summary table for a two-factor fixed-effects ANOVA, where there are two levels of factor A (drug) and three levels of factor B (dosage). Each cell includes 26 students and $\alpha = .05$.

Source	SS	df	MS	F	Critical Value	Decision
A	6.15	—	—	—	—	—
B	10.60	—	—	—	—	—
AB	9.10	—	—	—	—	—
Within	—	—	—			
Total	250.85	—				

3.2 Complete the following ANOVA summary table for a two-factor fixed-effects ANOVA, where there are three levels of factor A (program) and two levels of factor B (gender). Each cell includes four students and $\alpha = .01$.

(12)

Source	SS	df	MS	F	Critical Value	Decision
A	3.64	—	—	—	—	—
B	.57	—	—	—	—	—
AB	2.07	—	—	—	—	—
Within	—	—	—			
Total	8.18	—				

3.3   Complete the following ANOVA summary table for a two-factor fixed-effects ANOVA, where there are two levels of factor A (undergraduate vs. graduate) and two levels of factor B (gender). Each cell includes four students and $\alpha = .05$.

Source	SS	df	MS	F	Critical Value	Decision
A	14.06	—	—	—	—	—
B	39.06	—	—	—	—	—
AB	1.56	—	—	—	—	—
Within	—	—	—			
Total	723.43	—				

3.4   Conduct a two-factor fixed-effects ANOVA to determine if there are any effects due to A (task type), B (task difficulty), or the AB interaction ($\alpha = .01$). Conduct Tukey HSD post hoc comparisons, if necessary. The following are the scores from the individual cells of the model:

A_1B_1: 41, 39, 25, 25, 37, 51, 39, 101
A_1B_2: 46, 54, 97, 93, 51, 36, 29, 69
A_1B_3: 113, 135, 109, 96, 47, 49, 68, 38   — (8 ppl per cell)
A_2B_1: 86, 38, 45, 45, 60, 106, 106, 31
A_2B_2: 74, 96, 101, 124, 48, 113, 139, 131
A_2B_3: 152, 79, 135, 144, 52, 102, 166, 155

3.5   An experimenter is interested in the effects of strength of reinforcement (factor A), type of reinforcement (factor B), and sex of the adult administering the reinforcement (factor C) on children's behavior. Each factor consists of two levels. Thirty-two children are randomly assigned to eight cells (i.e., four per cell), one for each of the factor combinations. Using the scores from the individual cells of the model that follow, conduct a three-factor fixed-effects ANOVA ($\alpha = .05$). If there are any significant interactions, graph and interpret the interactions.

$A_1B_1C_1$: 3, 6, 3, 3
$A_1B_1C_2$: 4, 5, 4, 3
$A_1B_2C_1$: 7, 8, 7, 6
$A_1B_2C_2$: 7, 8, 9, 8
$A_2B_1C_1$: 1, 2, 2, 2
$A_2B_1C_2$: 2, 3, 4, 3
$A_2B_2C_1$: 5, 6, 5, 6
$A_2B_2C_2$: 10, 10, 9, 11

3.6   A replication study dataset of the example from this chapter is given as follows (A = attractiveness, B = time; same levels). Using the scores from the individual cells of the model that follow, conduct a two-factor fixed-effects ANOVA ($\alpha = .05$). Are the results different as compared to the original dataset?

A_1B_1: 10, 8, 7, 3
A_1B_2: 15, 12, 21, 13
A_2B_1: 13, 9, 18, 12
A_2B_2: 20, 22, 24, 25

A_3B_1: 24, 29, 27, 25

A_3B_2: 10, 12, 21, 14

A_4B_1: 30, 26, 29, 28

A_4B_2: 22, 20, 25, 15

Interpretive Problem

3.1 Building on the interpretive problem from Chapter 1, utilize the survey 1 dataset from the website. Use SPSS to conduct a two-factor fixed-effects ANOVA, including effect size, where political view is factor A (as in Chapter 1, $J = 5$), gender is factor B (a new factor, $K = 2$), and the dependent variable is the same one you used previously in Chapter 1. Then write an APA-style paragraph summarizing the results.

3.2 Building on the interpretive problem from Chapter 1, use the survey 1 dataset from the website. Use SPSS to conduct a two-factor fixed-effects ANOVA, including effect size, where hair color is factor A (i.e., one independent variable) ($J = 5$), gender is factor B (a new factor, $K = 2$), and the dependent variable is a variable of interest to you (the following variables look interesting: books, TV, exercise, drinks, GPA, GRE-Q, CDs, hair appointment). Then write an APA-style paragraph describing the results.

4

Introduction to Analysis of Covariance: One-Factor Fixed-Effects Model With Single Covariate

Chapter Outline

Key Concepts

1. Statistical adjustment

2. Covariate

3. Adjusted means

4. Homogeneity of regression slopes

5. Independence of the covariate and the independent variable

We have now considered several different analysis of variance (ANOVA) models. As we moved through Chapter 3, we saw that the inclusion of additional factors helped to reduce the residual or uncontrolled variation. These additional factors served as "experimental design controls" in that their inclusion in the design helped to reduce the uncontrolled variation. In fact, this could be the reason an additional factor is included in a factorial design.

In this chapter, a new type of variable, known as a covariate, is incorporated into the analysis. Rather than serving as an "experimental design control," the covariate serves as a "statistical control" where uncontrolled variation is reduced statistically in the analysis. Thus, a model where a covariate is used is known as **analysis of covariance** (ANCOVA). We are most concerned with the one-factor fixed-effects model here, although this model can be generalized to any of the other ANOVA designs considered in this text. That is, any of the ANOVA models discussed in the text can also include a covariate and thus become an ANCOVA model.

Most of the concepts used in this chapter have already been covered in the text. In addition, new concepts include statistical adjustment, covariate, adjusted means, and two important assumptions: homogeneity of regression slopes and independence of the covariate and the independent variable. Our objectives are that by the end of this chapter, you will be able to (a) understand the characteristics and concepts underlying ANCOVA; (b) determine and interpret the results of ANCOVA, including adjusted means and multiple comparison procedures (MCPs); and (c) understand and evaluate the assumptions of ANCOVA.

4.1 Characteristics of the Model

In previous chapters, we have been following Marie, the educational research graduate student who, as part of her independent study course, conducted an experiment to examine statistics lab attendance. She has examined attendance based on attractiveness of instructor (Chapters 1 and 2) and based on attractiveness and time of day (Chapter 3). As we will see in this chapter, Marie will be continuing to examine data generated from a different experiment of students enrolled in statistics courses, now controlling for aptitude.

As we learned in previous chapters, Marie is enrolled in an independent study class. Her previous study was so successful that Marie, again in collaboration with the statistics faculty in her program, has designed another experimental study to determine if there was a mean difference in statistics quiz performance based on the teaching method utilized (traditional lecture method or innovative instruction). Twelve students were randomly assigned to two different sections of the same class. One section was taught using traditional lecture methods, and the second was taught with more innovative instruction which included, for example, small-group and self-directed instruction. Prior to random assignment to sections, participants were also measured on aptitude toward statistics. Marie is now ready to examine these data. Marie's research question is the following: *Is there a mean difference in statistics quiz scores based on teaching method, controlling for aptitude toward statistics*? With one independent variable and one covariate for which to control, Marie determines that an ANCOVA is the best statistical procedure to use to answer her question. Her next task is to analyze the data to address her research question.

In this section, we describe the distinguishing characteristics of the one-factor fixed-effects ANCOVA model. However, before we begin an extended discussion of these characteristics, consider the following example (a situation similar to which we find Marie). Imagine a situation where a statistics professor is scheduled to teach two sections of introductory statistics. The professor, being a cunning researcher, decides to perform a little experiment where Section 4.1 is taught using the traditional lecture method and Section 4.2 is taught with more innovative methods using extensive graphics, computer simulations, and computer-assisted and calculator-based instruction, as well as using mostly small-group and self-directed instruction. The professor is interested in which section performs better in the course.

Before the study/course begins, the professor thinks about whether there are other variables related to statistics performance that should somehow be taken into account in the design. An obvious one is ability in quantitative methods. From previous research and experience, the professor knows that ability in quantitative methods is highly correlated with performance in statistics and decides to give a measure of quantitative ability in the first class and use that as a covariate in the analysis. A **covariate** (e.g., quantitative ability) is defined as a source of variation not controlled for in the design of the experiment but that the researcher believes to affect the dependent variable (e.g., course performance). The covariate is used to statistically adjust the dependent variable. For instance, if Section 4.1 has higher quantitative ability than Section 4.2 going into the study, then it would be wise to take this into account in the analysis. Otherwise Section 4.1 might outperform Section 4.2 due to their higher quantitative ability rather than due to the method of instruction. This is precisely the point of the ANCOVA. Some of the more typical examples of covariates in education and the behavioral sciences are pretest (where the dependent variable is the posttest), prior achievement, weight, IQ, aptitude, age, experience, previous training, motivation, and grade point average (GPA).

Let us now begin with the characteristics of the ANCOVA model. The first set of characteristics is obvious because they carry over from the one-factor fixed-effects ANOVA model. There is a single independent variable or factor with two or more levels or categories (thus the independent variable continues to be either nominal or ordinal in measurement scale). The levels of the independent variable are fixed by the researcher rather than randomly sampled from a population of levels. Once the levels of the independent variable are selected, subjects or individuals are somehow assigned to these levels or groups. Each subject is then exposed to only one level of the independent variable (although ANCOVA with repeated measures is also possible, but is not discussed here). In our example, method of statistics instruction is the independent variable with two levels or groups, the traditional lecture method and the cutting-edge method.

Situations where the researcher is able to randomly assign subjects to groups are known as **true experimental designs**. Situations where the researcher does not have control over which level a subject is assigned to are known as **quasi-experimental designs**. This lack of control may occur for one of two reasons. First, the groups may be already in place when the researcher arrives on the scene; these groups are referred to as **intact groups** (e.g., based on class assignments made by students at the time of registration). Second, it may be theoretically impossible for the researcher to assign subjects to groups (e.g., income level). Thus, a distinction is typically made about whether or not the researcher can control the assignment of subjects to groups. The distinction between the use of ANCOVA in true and quasi-experimental situations has been quite controversial over the past few decades; we look at it in more detail later in this chapter. For further information on true experimental designs and quasi-experimental designs, we suggest you consider Campbell and Stanley (1966), Cook and Campbell (1979), and Shadish, Cook, and Campbell (2002). In our example again, if assignment of students to sections is random, then we have a true experimental design. If assignment of students to sections is not random, perhaps already assigned at registration, then we have a quasi-experimental design.

One final item in the first set of characteristics has to do with the measurement scales of the variables. In the ANCOVA, it is assumed the dependent variable is measured at the interval level or better. If the dependent variable is measured at the ordinal level, then nonparametric procedures described toward the end of this chapter should be considered. It is also assumed that the covariate is measured at the interval level or better. Lastly, as indicated previously, the independent variable must be a grouping or categorical variable.

The remaining characteristics have to do with the uniqueness of the ANCOVA. As already mentioned, the ANCOVA is a form of statistical control developed specifically to reduce unexplained error variation. The covariate (sometimes known as a *concomitant variable*, as it accompanies or is associated with the dependent variable) is a source of variation not controlled for in the design of the experiment but believed to affect the dependent variable. In a factorial design, for example, a factor could be included to reduce error variation. However, this represents an experimental design form of control as it is included as a factor in the model.

In ANCOVA, the dependent variable is adjusted statistically to remove the effects of the portion of uncontrolled variation represented by the covariate. The group means on the dependent variable are adjusted so that they now represent groups with the same means on the covariate. The ANCOVA is essentially an ANOVA on these "adjusted means." This needs further explanation. Consider first the situation of the randomized true experiment where there are two groups. Here it is unlikely that the two groups will be statistically different on any variable related to the dependent measure. The two groups should have roughly equivalent means on the covariate, although 5% of the time, we would expect a significant difference due to chance at $\alpha = .05$. Thus, we typically do not see preexisting differences between the two groups on the covariate in a true experiment—that is the value and beauty of random assignment, especially as it relates to ANCOVA. However, the relationship between the covariate and the dependent variable is important. If these variables are linearly related (discussed later), then the use of the covariate in the analysis will serve to reduce the unexplained variation in the model. The greater the magnitude of the correlation, the more uncontrolled variation can be removed, as shown by a reduction in mean square error.

Consider next the situation of the quasi-experiment, that is, without randomization. Here it is more likely that the two groups will be statistically different on the covariate as well as other variables related to the dependent variable. Thus, there may indeed be a preexisting difference between the two groups on the covariate. If the groups do differ on the covariate and we ignore it by conducting an ANOVA, our ability to get a precise estimate of the group effects will be reduced as the group effect will be confounded with the effect of the covariate. For instance, if a significant group difference is revealed by the ANOVA, we would not be certain if there was truly a group effect or whether the effect was due to preexisting group differences on the covariate, or some combination of group and covariate effects. The ANCOVA takes the covariate mean difference into account as well as the linear relationship between the covariate and the dependent variable.

Thus, the covariate is used to (a) reduce error variation, (b) take any preexisting group mean difference on the covariate into account, (c) take into account the relationship between the covariate and the dependent variable, and (d) yield a more precise and less

TABLE 4.1

Layout for the One-Factor ANCOVA

	Level of the Independent Variable						
	1		**2**		**...**	**J**	
Y_{11}	X_{11}	Y_{12}	X_{12}	...	Y_{1J}	X_{1J}
Y_{21}	X_{21}	Y_{22}	X_{22}	...	Y_{2J}	X_{2J}
...	...	...	...	...	...	...
Y_{n1}	X_{n1}	Y_{n2}	X_{n2}	...	Y_{nJ}	X_{nJ}
$\bar{Y}_{.1}$	$\bar{X}_{.1}$	$\bar{Y}_{.2}$	$\bar{X}_{.2}$	...	$\bar{Y}_{.J}$	$\bar{X}_{.J}$

biased estimate of the group effects. If error variation is reduced, the ANCOVA will be more powerful and require smaller sample sizes than the ANOVA (Keppel & Wickens, 2004; Mickey, Dunn, & Clark, 2004; Myers & Well, 1995). If error variation is not reduced, the ANOVA is more powerful. A more extensive comparison of ANOVA versus ANCOVA is given in Chapter 6. In addition, as shown later, one degree of freedom is lost from the error term for each covariate used. This results in a larger critical value for the F test and makes it a bit more difficult to find a statistically significant F test statistic. This is the major cost of using a covariate. If the covariate is not effective in reducing error variance, then we are worse off than if we had ignored the covariate. Important references on ANCOVA include Elashoff (1969) and Huitema (1980).

4.2 Layout of Data

Before we get into the theory and subsequent analysis of the data, let us examine the layout of the data. We designate each observation on the dependent or criterion variable as Y_{ij}, where the j subscript tells us what group or level the observation belongs to and the i subscript tells us the observation or identification number within that group. The first subscript ranges over $i = 1, \ldots, n_j$, and the second subscript ranges over $j = 1, \ldots, J$. Thus, there are J levels of the independent variable and n_j subjects in group j. We designate each observation on the covariate as X_{ij}, where the subscripts have the same meaning.

The layout of the data is shown in Table 4.1. Here we see that each pair of columns represents the observations for a particular group or level of the independent variable on the dependent variable (i.e., Y) and the covariate (i.e., X). At the bottom of the pair of columns for each group j are group means ($\bar{Y}_{.j}, \bar{X}_{.j}$). Although the table shows there are n observations for each group, we need not make such a restriction, as this was done only for purposes of simplifying the table.

4.3 ANCOVA Model

The ANCOVA model is a form of the general linear model (GLM), much like the models shown in previous chapters of this text. The one-factor ANCOVA fixed-effects model can be written in terms of population parameters as follows:

$$Y_{ij} = \mu_Y + \alpha_j + \beta_w(X_{ij} - \mu_X) + \varepsilon_{ij}$$

where

Y_{ij} is the observed score on the dependent variable for individual i in group j

μ_Y is the overall or grand population mean (i.e., regardless of group designation) for the dependent variable Y

α_j is the group effect for group j

β_w is the within-groups regression slope from the regression of Y on X (i.e., the covariate)

X_{ij} is the observed score on the covariate for individual i in group j

μ_X is the overall or grand population mean (i.e., regardless of group designation) for the covariate X

ε_{ij} is the random residual error for individual i in group j

The residual error can be due to individual differences, measurement error, and/or other factors not under investigation. As you would expect, the least squares sample estimators for each of these parameters are as follows: $\bar{Y}$ for μ_Y, $\bar{X}$ for μ_X, a_j for α_j, b_w for β_w, and e_{ij} for ε_{ij}. Just like in the ANOVA, the sum of the group effects is equal to 0. This implies that if there are any nonzero group effects, then the group effects will balance out around 0 with some positive and some negative effects.

The hypotheses consist of testing the equality of the adjusted means (defined by $\mu_{\cdot j}$ and discussed later) as follows:

$H_0: \mu_{\cdot 1} = \mu_{\cdot 2} = \ldots = \mu_{\cdot J}$

$H_1:$ not all the $\mu_{\cdot j}$ are equal

4.4 ANCOVA Summary Table

We turn our attention to the familiar summary table, this time for the one-factor ANCOVA model. A general form of the summary table is shown in Table 4.2. Under the first column, you see the following sources: adjusted between-groups variation, adjusted within-groups variation, variation due to the covariate, and total variation. The second column notes the sums of squares terms for each source (i.e., $SS_{betw(adj)}$, $SS_{with(adj)}$, SS_{cov}, and SS_{total}). Recall that the *between* source represents the independent variable being systematically studied and the *within* source represents the error or residual.

The third column gives the degrees of freedom for each source. For the adjusted between-groups source (i.e., the independent variable controlling for the covariate), because there are J group means, the $df_{betw(adj)}$ is $J - 1$, the same as in the one-factor ANOVA model. For the adjusted within-groups source, because there are N total observations and J groups, we

TABLE 4.2

One-Factor ANCOVA Summary Table

Source	SS	df	MS	F
Between adjusted	$SS_{betw(adj)}$	$J - 1$	$MS_{betw(adj)}$	$MS_{betw(adj)}/MS_{with(adj)}$
Within adjusted (i.e., error)	$SS_{with(adj)}$	$N - J - 1$	$MS_{with(adj)}$	
Covariate	SS_{cov}	1	MS_{cov}	$MS_{cov}/MS_{with(adj)}$
Total	SS_{total}	$N - 1$		

would expect the degrees of freedom within to be $N - J$, because that was the case in the one-factor ANOVA model. However, as we pointed out earlier in the characteristics of the ANCOVA model, a price is paid for the use of a covariate. The price here is that we lose one degree of freedom from the within term for a single covariate, so that $df_{\text{with(adj)}}$ is $N - J - 1$. For multiple covariates, we lose one degree of freedom for each covariate used (see later discussion). This degree of freedom has gone to the covariate source such that df_{cov} is equal to 1. Finally, for the total source, as there are N total observations, the df_{total} is the usual $N - 1$.

The fourth column gives the mean squares for each source of variation. As always, the mean squares represent the sum of squares weighted by their respective degrees of freedom. Thus, $[MS_{\text{betw(adj)}} = SS_{\text{betw(adj)}}/(J - 1)]$, $[MS_{\text{with(adj)}} = SS_{\text{with(adj)}}/(N - J - 1)]$, and $[MS_{\text{cov}} = SS_{\text{cov}}/1]$. The last column in the ANCOVA summary table is for the F values. Thus, for the one-factor fixed-effects ANCOVA model, the F value tests for differences between the adjusted means (i.e., to test for differences in the mean of the dependent variable based on the levels of the independent variable when controlling for the covariate) and is computed as $F = MS_{\text{betw(adj)}}/MS_{\text{with(adj)}}$. A second F value, which is obviously not included in the ANOVA model, is the test of the covariate. To be specific, this F statistic is actually testing the hypothesis of H_0: $\beta_w = 0$. If the slope is equal to 0, then the covariate and the dependent variable are unrelated. This F value is equal to $F = MS_{\text{cov}}/MS_{\text{with(adj)}}$. If the F test for the covariate is *not* statistically significant (and has a negligible effect size), the researcher may want to consider removing that covariate from the model.

The critical value for the test of difference between the adjusted means is $_{\alpha}F_{J-1, N-J-1}$. The critical value for the test of the covariate is $_{\alpha}F_{1, N-J-1}$. The null hypotheses in each case are rejected if the F test statistic exceeds the F critical value. The critical values are found in the F table of Table A.4.

If the F test statistic for the adjusted means exceeds the F critical value, and there are more than two groups, then it is not clear exactly how the means are different. In this case, some MCP may be used to determine which means are different (see later discussion). For the test of the covariate (i.e., the within-groups regression slope), we hope that the F test statistic does exceed the F critical value. Otherwise the power and precision of the test of the adjusted means in ANCOVA will be lower than the test of the unadjusted means in ANOVA because the covariate is not significantly related to the dependent variable. [As stated previously, if the F test for the covariate is *not* statistically significant (and has a negligible effect size), the researcher may want to consider removing that covariate from the model.]

4.5 Partitioning the Sums of Squares

As seen already, the partitioning of the sums of squares is the backbone of all GLMs, whether we are dealing with an ANOVA model, an ANCOVA model, or a linear regression model. As always, the first step is to partition the total variation into its relevant parts or sources of variation. As we have learned from the previous section, the sources of variation for the one-factor ANCOVA model are adjusted between groups (i.e., the independent variable), adjusted within groups (i.e., error), and the covariate. This is written as

$$SS_{\text{total}} = SS_{\text{betw(adj)}} + SS_{\text{with(adj)}} + SS_{\text{cov}}$$

From this point, the statistical software is used to handle the remaining computations.

4.6 Adjusted Means and Related Procedures

In this section, we formally define the adjusted mean, briefly examine several MCPs, and very briefly consider power, confidence intervals (CIs), and effect size measures.

We have spent considerable time already discussing the analysis of the adjusted means. Now it is time to define them. The adjusted mean is denoted by $\bar{Y}'_{.j}$ and estimated by

$$\bar{Y}'_{.j} = \bar{Y}_{.j} - b_w(\bar{X}_{.j} - \bar{X}_{..})$$

Here it should be noted that the adjusted mean is simply equal to the unadjusted mean (i.e., $\bar{Y}_{.j}$) minus the adjustment [i.e., $b_w(\bar{X}_{.j} - \bar{X}_{..})$]. The adjustment is a function of the within-groups regression slope (i.e., b_w) and the difference between the group mean and the overall mean for the covariate (i.e., the difference being the group effect, $\bar{X}_{.j} - \bar{X}_{..}$). No adjustment will be made if (a) $b_w = 0$ (i.e., X and Y are unrelated), or (b) the group means on the covariate are all the same. Thus, in both cases, $\bar{Y}_{.j} = \bar{Y}'_{.j}$. In all other cases, at least some adjustment will be made for some of the group means (although not necessarily for all of the group means).

You may be wondering how this adjustment actually works. Let us assume the covariate and the dependent variable are positively correlated such that b_w is also positive, and there are two treatment groups with equal n's that differ on the covariate. If group 1 has a higher mean on *both* the covariate and the dependent variable than group 2, then the adjusted means will be closer together than the unadjusted means. For our first example, we have the following conditions:

$$b_w = 1, \quad \bar{Y}_{.1} = 50, \quad \bar{Y}_{.2} = 30, \quad \bar{X}_{.1} = 20, \quad \bar{X}_{.2} = 10, \quad \bar{X}_{..} = 15$$

The adjusted means are determined as follows:

$$\bar{Y}'_{.1} = \bar{Y}_{.1} - b_w(\bar{X}_{.1} - \bar{X}_{..}) = 50 - 1(20-15) = 45$$

$$\bar{Y}'_{.2} = \bar{Y}_{.2} - b_w(\bar{X}_{.2} - \bar{X}_{..}) = 30 - 1(10-15) = 35$$

This is shown graphically in Figure 4.1a. In looking at the covariate X, we see that group 1 has a higher mean ($\bar{X}_{.1} = 20$) than group 2 ($\bar{X}_{.2} = 10$) by 10 points. The vertical line represents the overall mean on the covariate ($\bar{X}_{..} = 15$). In looking at the dependent variable Y, we see that group 1 has a higher mean ($\bar{Y}_{.1} = 50$) than group 2 ($\bar{Y}_{.2} = 30$) by 20 points. The diagonal lines represent the regression lines for each group, with $b_w = 1.0$. The points at which the regression lines intersect (or cross) the vertical line ($\bar{X}_{..} = 15$) represent on the Y scale the values of the adjusted means. Here we see that the adjusted mean for group 1 ($\bar{Y}'_{.1} = 45$) is larger than the adjusted mean for group 2 ($\bar{Y}'_{.2} = 35$) by 10 points. Thus, because of the preexisting difference on the covariate, the adjusted means here are somewhat closer together than the unadjusted means (10 points vs. 20 points, respectively).

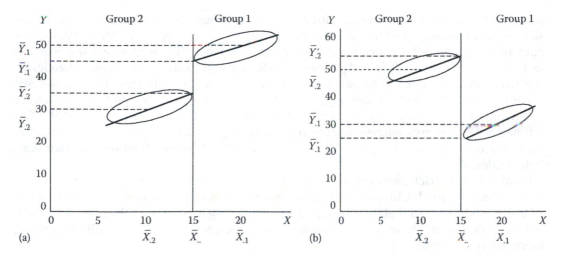

FIGURE 4.1
Graphs of ANCOVA adjustments.

If group 1 has a higher mean on the covariate and a lower mean on the dependent variable than group 2, then the adjusted means will be further apart than the unadjusted means. As a second example, we have the following slightly different conditions:

$$b_w = 1, \quad \bar{Y}_{.1} = 30, \quad \bar{Y}_{.2} = 50, \quad \bar{X}_{.1} = 20, \quad \bar{X}_{.2} = 10, \quad \bar{X}_{..} = 15$$

Then the adjusted means become as follows:

$$\bar{Y}'_{.1} = \bar{Y}_{.1} - b_w(\bar{X}_{.1} - \bar{X}_{..}) = 30 - 1(20 - 15) = 25$$

$$\bar{Y}'_{.2} = \bar{Y}_{.2} - b_w(\bar{X}_{.2} - \bar{X}_{..}) = 50 - 1(10 - 15) = 55$$

This is shown graphically in Figure 4.1b, where the unadjusted means differ by 20 points and the adjusted means differ by 30 points. There are obviously other possible situations.

Let us briefly examine MCPs for use in the ANCOVA situation. Most of the procedures described in Chapter 2 can be adapted for use with a covariate, although a few procedures are not mentioned here as critical values do not currently exist. The adapted procedures involve a different form of the standard error of a contrast. The contrasts are formed based on adjusted means, of course. Let us briefly outline just a few procedures. Each of the test statistics has as its numerator the contrast, ψ', such as $\psi' = \bar{Y}'_1 - \bar{Y}'_2$. The standard errors do differ somewhat depending on the specific MCP, just as they do in ANOVA.

The example procedures briefly described here are easily translated from the ANOVA context into the ANCOVA context. The Dunn (or the Bonferroni) method is appropriate to use for a small number of planned contrasts (still utilizing the critical values from Table A.8). The Scheffé procedure can be used for unplanned complex contrasts with equal group variances (again based on the F table in Table A.4). The Tukey HSD test is most desirous for unplanned pairwise contrasts with equal n's per group. There has been some discussion in the literature about the appropriateness of this test in ANCOVA. Most statisticians currently argue that the procedure is only appropriate when the covariate is fixed, when in fact it is almost always random. As a result, the Bryant and Paulson (1976) generalization of the Tukey procedure has been developed for the random covariate case. The test statistic is compared to the critical value $_\alpha q_{X, df(error), J}$ taken from Table A.10, where X is the number of covariates. If the group sizes are unequal, the harmonic mean can be used in ANCOVA (Huitema, 1980). A generalization of the Tukey-Bryant procedure for unequal n's ANCOVA was developed by Hochberg and Varon-Salomon (1984) (also see Hochberg & Tamhane, 1987; Miller, 1997).

Finally a very brief comment about power, CIs, and effect size measures for the one-factor ANCOVA model. In short, these procedures work exactly the same as in the factorial ANOVA model, except that they are based on adjusted means (Cohen, 1988), and as we will see in SPSS, partial eta squared is still the effect size computed. There really is nothing more to say than that.

4.7 Assumptions and Violation of Assumptions

The introduction of a covariate requires several assumptions beyond the traditional ANOVA assumptions. For the familiar assumptions (e.g., independence of observations, homogeneity, and normality), the discussion is kept to a minimum as these have already been described in Chapters 1 and 3. The new assumptions are as follows: (a) linearity, (b) independence of the covariate and the independent variable, (c) the covariate is measured without error, and (d) homogeneity of the regression slopes. In this section, we describe each assumption, how each assumption can be evaluated, the effects that a violation of the assumption might have, and how one might deal with a serious violation. Later in the chapter, when we illustrate how to use SPSS to generate ANCOVA, we will specifically test for the assumptions of independence of observations, homogeneity of variance, normality, linearity, independence of the covariate and the independent variable, and homogeneity of regression slopes.

4.7.1 Independence

As we learned previously, the assumption of independence of observations can be met by (a) keeping the assignment of individuals to groups (i.e., to the levels or categories of the independent variable) separate through the design of the experiment (specifically random assignment—not to be confused with random selection), and (b) keeping the individuals separate from one another through experimental control so that the scores on the dependent variable Y are independent across subjects (both within and across groups).

As in previous ANOVA models, the use of independent random samples is also crucial in the ANCOVA. The F ratio is very sensitive to violation of the independence assumption in terms of increased likelihood of a Type I and/or Type II error. A violation of the independence assumption may affect the standard errors of the sample adjusted means and thus influence any inferences made about those means. One purpose of random assignment of individuals to groups is to achieve independence. If each individual is only observed once and individuals are randomly assigned to groups, then the independence assumption is usually met. Random assignment is important for valid interpretation of both the F test and MCPs. Otherwise, the F test and adjusted means may be biased.

The simplest procedure for assessing independence is to examine residual plots by group. If the independence assumption is satisfied, then the residuals should fall into a random display of points. If the assumption is violated, then the residuals will fall into some type of cyclical pattern. As discussed in Chapter 1, the Durbin and Watson statistic (1950, 1951, 1971) can be used to test for autocorrelation. Violations of the independence assumption generally occur in the three situations we mentioned in Chapter 1: time series data, observations within blocks, or replication. For severe violations of the independence assumption, there is no simple "fix," such as the use of transformations or nonparametric tests (see Scariano & Davenport, 1987).

4.7.2 Homogeneity of Variance

The second assumption is that the variances of each population are the same, known as the homogeneity of variance assumption. A violation of this assumption may lead to bias in the SS_{with} term, as well as an increase in the Type I error rate, and possibly an increase in the Type II error rate. A summary of Monte Carlo research on ANCOVA assumption violations by Harwell (2003) indicates that the effect of the violation is negligible with equal or nearly equal n's across the groups. There is a more serious problem if the larger n's are associated with the smaller variances (actual or observed $\alpha >$ nominal or stated α selected by the researcher, which is a liberal result), or if the larger n's are associated with the larger variances (actual $\alpha <$ nominal α, which is a conservative result).

In a plot of Y versus the covariate X for each group, the variability of the distributions may be examined for evidence of the extent to which this assumption is met. Another method for detecting violation of the homogeneity assumption is the use of formal statistical tests (e.g., Levene's test), as discussed in Chapter 1 and as we illustrate using SPSS later in this chapter. Several solutions are available for dealing with a violation of the homogeneity assumption. These include the use of variance-stabilizing transformations or other ANCOVA models that are less sensitive to unequal variances, such as nonparametric ANCOVA procedures (described at the end of this chapter).

4.7.3 Normality

The third assumption is that each of the populations follows the normal distribution. Based on the classic work by Box and Anderson (1962) and Atiqullah (1964), as well as the summarization of modern Monte Carlo work by Harwell (2003), the F test is relatively robust to nonnormal Y distributions, "minimizing the role of a normally distributed X" (Harwell, 2003, p. 62). Thus, we need only really be concerned with serious nonnormality (although "serious nonnormality" is a subjective call made by the researcher).

The following graphical techniques can be used to detect violation of the normality assumption: (a) frequency distributions (such as stem-and-leaf plots, boxplots, or histograms) or (b) normal probability plots. There are also several statistical procedures available for the detection of nonnormality [e.g., the Shapiro–Wilk (S–W) test, 1965]. If the assumption of normality is violated, transformations can also be used to normalize the data, as previously discussed in Chapter 1. In addition, one can use one of the rank ANCOVA procedures previously mentioned.

4.7.4 Linearity

The next assumption is that the regression of Y (i.e., the dependent variable) on X (i.e., the covariate) is linear. If the relationship between Y and X is not linear, then use of the usual ANCOVA procedure is not appropriate, just as linear regression (see Chapter 7) would not be appropriate in cases of nonlinearity. In ANCOVA (as well as in correlation and linear regression), we fit a straight line to the data points in a scatterplot. When the relationship is nonlinear, a straight line will not fit the data particularly well. In addition, the magnitude of the linear correlation will be smaller. If the relationship is not linear, the estimate of the group effects will be biased, and the adjustments made in SS_{with} and SS_{betw} will be smaller.

Violations of the linearity assumption can generally be detected by looking at scatterplots of Y versus X, overall and for each group or category of the independent variable. Once a serious violation of the linearity assumption has been detected, there are two alternatives that can be used, transformations and nonlinear ANCOVA. Transformations on one or both variables can be used to achieve linearity (Keppel & Wickens, 2004). The second option is to use nonlinear ANCOVA methods as described by Huitema (1980) and Keppel and Wickens (2004).

4.7.5 Fixed Independent Variable

The fifth assumption states that the levels of the independent variable are fixed by the researcher. This results in a fixed-effects model rather than a random-effects model. As in the one-factor ANOVA model, the one-factor ANCOVA model is the same computationally in the fixed- and random-effects cases. The summary of Monte Carlo research by Harwell (2003) indicates that the impact of a random-effect on the F test is minimal.

4.7.6 Independence of the Covariate and the Independent Variable

A condition of the ANCOVA model (although not an assumption) requires that the covariate and the independent variable be independent. That is, the covariate is not influenced by the independent or treatment variable. If the covariate is affected by the treatment itself, then the use of the covariate in the analysis either (a) may remove part of the treatment effect or produce a spurious (inflated) treatment effect or (b) may alter the covariate scores as a result of the treatment being administered prior to obtaining the covariate data. The obvious solution to this potential problem is to obtain the covariate scores prior to the administration of the treatment. In other words, be alert prior to the study for possible covariate candidates. There are many researchers who argue that, because of this assumption, ANCOVA is only appropriate in the case of a true experiment where random assignment of cases to groups was performed. Thus, in a true experiment, the treatment (i.e., independent variable) and covariate are not related by default of random assignment, and, thereby, the assumption of independence of the covariate and independent variable is met. If randomization is not possible, closely matching participants on the covariate may also help to ensure the assumption is not violated.

Let us consider an example where this condition is obviously violated. A psychologist is interested in which of several hypnosis treatments is most successful in reducing or eliminating cigarette smoking. A group of heavy smokers is randomly assigned to the hypnosis treatments. After the treatments have been completed, the researcher suspects that some patients are more susceptible to hypnosis (i.e., are more suggestible) than others. By using suggestibility as a covariate after the study is completed, the researcher would not be able to determine whether group differences were a result of hypnosis treatment, suggestibility, or some combination. Thus, the measurement of suggestibility after the hypnosis treatments have been administered would be ill-advised. An extended discussion of this condition is given in Maxwell and Delaney (1990).

Evidence of the extent to which this assumption is met can be done by examining mean differences on the covariate across the levels of the independent variable. If the independent variable has only two levels, an independent t test would be appropriate. If the independent variable has more than two categories, a one-way ANOVA would suffice. If the groups are not statistically different on the covariate, then that lends evidence that the assumption of independence of the covariate and the independent variable has been met. If the groups are statistically different on the covariate, then the groups are not likely to be equivalent.

4.7.7 Covariate Measured Without Error

An assumption that we have not yet discussed in this text is that the covariate is measured without error. This is of special concern in education and the behavioral sciences where variables are often measured with considerable measurement error. In randomized experiments, b_w (i.e., the within-groups regression slope from the regression of the dependent variable, Y, on the covariate, X) will be underestimated so that less of the covariate effect is removed from the dependent variable (i.e., the adjustments will be smaller). In addition, the reduction in the unexplained variation will not be as great, and the F test will not be as powerful. The F test is generally conservative in terms of Type I error (the actual observed α will be less than the nominal α which was selected by the researcher—the nominal alpha is often .05). However, the treatment effects will not be biased. In quasi-experimental designs, b_w will also be underestimated with similar effects. However, the treatment effects may be seriously biased. A method by Porter (1967) is suggested for this situation.

There is considerable discussion about the effects of measurement error (e.g., Cohen & Cohen, 1983; Huitema, 1980; Keppel & Wickens, 2004; Lord, 1960, 1967, 1969; Mickey et al. 2004; Pedhazur, 1997; Porter, 1967; Reichardt, 1979; Weisberg, 1979). Obvious violations of this assumption can be detected by computing the reliability of the covariate prior to the study or from previous research. This is the minimum that should be done. One may also want to consider the validity of the covariate as well, where validity may be defined as the extent to which an instrument measures what it was intended to measure. While this is the first mention in the text of measurement error, it is certainly important that all measures included in a model—regardless of which statistical procedure is being conducted—are measured such that the scores provide high reliability and validity.

4.7.8 Homogeneity of Regression Slopes

The final assumption puts forth that the slope of the regression line between the dependent variable and covariate is the same for each category of the independent variable. Here we assume that $\beta_1 = \beta_2 = \ldots = \beta_J$. This is an important assumption because it allows us to use b_w, the sample estimator of β_w, as the within-groups regression slope. Assuming that the group slopes are parallel allows us to test for group intercept differences, *which is all we are really doing when we test for differences among the adjusted means.* Without this assumption of homogeneity of regression slopes, groups can differ on *both* the regression slope and intercept, and β_w cannot legitimately be used. If the slopes differ, then the regression lines interact in some way. As a result, the size of the group differences in Y (i.e., the dependent variable) will depend on the value of X (i.e., the covariate). For example, treatment 1 may be most effective on the dependent variable for low values of the covariate, treatment 2 may be most effective on the dependent variable for middle values of the covariate, and treatment 3 may be most effective on the dependent variable for high values of the covariate. Thus, we do not have constant differences on the dependent variable between the groups of the independent variable across the values of the covariate. A straightforward interpretation is not possible, which is the same situation in factorial ANOVA when the interaction between factor A and factor B is found to be significant. Thus, unequal slopes in ANCOVA represent a type of interaction.

There are other potential outcomes if this assumption is violated. Without homogeneous regression slopes, the use of β_w can yield biased adjusted means and can affect the F test. Earlier simulation studies by Peckham (1968) and Glass, Peckham, and Sanders (1972) suggest that for the one-factor fixed-effects model, the effects will be minimal. Later analytical research by Rogosa (1980) suggests that there is little effect on the F test for balanced designs with equal variances, but the F is less robust for mild heterogeneity. However, a summary of modern Monte Carlo work by Harwell (2003) indicates that the effect of slope heterogeneity on the F test is (a) negligible with equal n's and equal covariate means (randomized studies), (b) modest with equal n's and unequal covariate means (nonrandomized studies), and (c) modest with unequal n's.

A formal statistical procedure is often conducted to test for homogeneity of slopes using statistical software such as SPSS (discussed later in this chapter), although the eyeball method (i.e., see if the slopes look about the same by reviewing scatterplots of the dependent variable and covariate for each category of the independent variable) can be a good starting point. Some alternative tests for equality of slopes when the variances are unequal are provided by Tabatabai and Tan (1985).

Several alternatives are available if the homogeneity of slopes assumption is violated. The first is to use the concomitant variable not as a covariate but as a blocking variable. This will work because this assumption is not made for the randomized block design (see Chapter 6). A second option, and not a very desirable one, is to analyze each group separately with its own slope or subsets of the groups having equal slopes. A third possibility is to utilize interaction terms between the covariate and the independent variable and conduct a regression analysis (see Agresti & Finlay, 1986). A fourth option is to use the Johnson and Neyman (1936) technique, whose purpose is to determine the values of X (i.e., the covariate) that are related to significant group differences on Y (i.e., the dependent variable). This procedure is beyond the scope of this text, and the interested reader is referred to Huitema (1980) or Wilcox (1987). A fifth option is to use more-modern robust methods (e.g., Maxwell & Delaney, 1990; Wilcox, 2003).

A summary of the ANCOVA assumptions is presented in Table 4.3.

TABLE 4.3

Assumptions and Effects of Violations—One-Factor ANCOVA

Assumption	Effect of Assumption Violation
1. Independence	• Increased likelihood of a Type I and/or Type II error in F • Affects standard errors of means and inferences about those means
2. Homogeneity of variance	• Bias in SS_{with}; increased likelihood of a Type I and/or Type II error • Negligible effect with equal or nearly equal n's • Otherwise more serious problem if the larger n's are associated with the smaller variances (increased α) or larger variances (decreased α)
3. Normality	• F test relatively robust to nonnormal Y, minimizing the role of nonnormal X
4. Linearity	• Reduced magnitude of r_{XY} • Straight line will not fit data well • Estimate of group effects biased • Adjustments made in SS smaller
5. Fixed-effect	• Minimal impact
6. Covariate and factor are independent	• May reduce/increase group effects; may alter covariate scores

7. Covariate measured without error	• True experiment:
	  • b_w underestimated
	  • Adjustments smaller
	  • Reduction in unexplained variation smaller
	  • F less powerful
	  • Reduced likelihood of Type I error
	• Quasi-experiment:
	  • b_w underestimated
	  • Adjustments smaller
	  • Group effects seriously biased

8. Homogeneity of slopes	• Negligible effect with equal n's in true experiment • Modest effect with equal n's in quasi-experiment • Modest effect with unequal n's

4.8 Example

Consider the following illustration of what we have covered in this chapter. Our dependent variable is the score on a statistics quiz (with a maximum possible score of 6), the covariate is the score on an aptitude test for statistics taken at the beginning of the course (with a maximum possible score of 10), and the independent variable is the section of statistics taken (where group 1 receives the traditional lecture method and group 2 receives the modern innovative method that includes components such as small-group and self-direction instruction). Thus, the researcher is interested in whether the method of instruction influences student performance in statistics, controlling for statistics aptitude (assume we have developed an aptitude measure that is relatively error-free). Students are randomly assigned to one of the two groups at the beginning of the semester when the measure of statistics aptitude is administered. There

TABLE 4.4

Data and Summary Statistics for the Statistics Instruction Example

Statistic	Group 1 Quiz (Y)	Group 1 Aptitude (X)	Group 2 Quiz (Y)	Group 2 Aptitude (X)	Overall Quiz (Y)	Overall Aptitude (X)
	1	4	1	1		
	2	3	2	3		
	3	5	4	2		
	4	6	5	4		
	5	7	6	5		
	6	9	6	7		
Means	3.5000	5.6667	4.0000	3.6667	3.7500	4.6667
Variances	3.5000	4.6667	4.4000	4.6667	3.6591	5.3333
b_{YX}	0.8143		0.8143		0.5966	
r_{XY}	0.9403		0.8386		0.7203	
Adjusted means	2.6857		4.8143			

are 6 students in each group for a total of 12. The layout of the data is shown in Table 4.4, where we see the data and sample statistics (means, variances, slopes, and correlations).

The results are summarized in the ANCOVA summary table as shown in the top panel of Table 4.5. The ANCOVA test statistics are compared to the critical value $_{.05}F_{1,9} = 5.12$ obtained from Table A.4, using the .05 level of significance. Both test statistics exceed the critical value, so we reject H_0 in each case. We conclude that (a) the quiz score means do differ for the two statistics groups when adjusted (or controlling) for aptitude in statistics, and (b) the slope of the regression of Y (i.e., dependent variable) on X (i.e., covariate) is statistically significantly different from 0 (i.e., the test of the covariate). Just to be complete, the results for the ANOVA on Y are shown in the bottom panel of Table 4.5. We see that in the analysis of the unadjusted means (i.e., the ANOVA), there is no significant group differ-ence. Thus, the adjustment (i.e., ANCOVA which controlled for aptitude toward statistics) yielded a different statistical result. The covariate also "did its thing" in that a reduction

TABLE 4.5

One-Factor ANCOVA and ANOVA Summary Tables—Statistics Instruction Example

Source	SS	df	MS	F
ANCOVA				
Between adjusted	10.8127	1	10.8127	11.3734[a]
Within adjusted	8.5560	9	0.9507	
Covariate	20.8813	1	20.8813	21.9641[a]
Total	40.2500	11		
ANOVA				
Between	0.7500	1	0.7500	0.1899[b]
Within	39.5000	10	3.9500	
Total	40.2500	11		

[a] $_{.05}F_{1,9} = 5.12$ (critical value).
[b] $_{.05}F_{1,10} = 4.96$ (critical value).

in MS_{with} resulted due to the strong relationship between the covariate and the dependent variable (i.e., $r_{XY} = 0.7203$ overall).

Let us next examine the group quiz score means, as shown in Table 4.4. Here we see that with the unadjusted quiz score means (i.e., prior to controlling for the covariate), there is a 0.5000 point difference in favor of group 2 (the innovative teaching method), whereas for the adjusted quiz score means (i.e., the ANCOVA results which controlled for aptitude), there is a 2.1286 point difference in favor of group 2. In other words, the adjustment (i.e., controlling for statistics aptitude) in this case resulted in a greater difference between the adjusted quiz score means than between the unadjusted quiz score means. Since there are only two groups, an MCP is unnecessary (although we illustrate this in the SPSS section).

4.9 ANCOVA Without Randomization

As referenced previously in the discussion of assumptions, there has been a great deal of discussion and controversy over the years, particularly in education and the behavioral sciences, about the use of the ANCOVA in situations where randomization is not conducted. **Randomization** is defined as an experiment where individuals are randomly assigned to groups (or cells in a factorial design). In the Campbell and Stanley (1966) system of experimental design, these designs are known as **true experiments**. (Do not confuse random assignment with random selection, the latter of which deals with how the cases are sampled from the population.)

In certain situations, randomization either has not occurred or is not possible due to circumstances in the study. The best example is the situation where there are **intact groups**, which are groups that have been formed prior to the researcher arriving on the scene. Either the researcher chooses not to randomly assign these individuals to groups through a reassignment (e.g., it is just easier to keep the groups in their current form) or the researcher cannot randomly assign them (legally, ethically, or otherwise). When randomization does not occur, the resulting designs are known as **quasi-experimental**. For instance, in classroom research, the researcher is almost never able to come into a school and randomly assign students to groups. Once students are given their class assignments at the beginning of the year, this cannot be altered. On occasion, the researcher might be able to pull a few students out of several classrooms, randomly assign them to small groups, and conduct a true experiment. In general, this is possible only on a very small scale and for short periods of time.

Let us briefly consider the issues as it relates to ANCOVA, as not all statisticians agree. In true experiments (i.e., with randomization), there is no cause for concern (except for dealing with the statistical assumptions). The ANCOVA is more powerful and has greater precision for true experiments than for quasi-experiments. So if you have a choice, go with a true experimental situation (which is a big *if*). In a true experiment, the probability that the groups differ on the covariate or any other concomitant variable is equal to α. That is, the likelihood that the group means will be different on the covariate is small, and, thus, the adjustment in the group means may be small. The payoff is in the possibility that the error term will be greatly reduced.

In quasi-experiments, as it relates to ANCOVA, there are several possible causes for concern. Although this is the situation where the researcher needs the most help, this is also the situation where less help is available. Here it is more likely that there will be statistically significant differences among the group means on the covariate. Thus, the adjustment in the group means can be substantial (assuming that b_w is different from 0).

Because there are significant mean differences on the covariate, any of the following may occur: (a) it is likely that the groups may be different on other important characteristics as well, which have not been controlled for either statistically or experimentally; (b) the homogeneity of regression slopes assumption is less likely to be met; (c) adjusting for the covariate may remove part of the treatment effect; (d) equating groups on the covariate may be an extrapolation beyond the range of possible values that occur for a particular group (e.g., the examples by Lord, 1967, 1969, on trying to equate men and women, or by Ferguson & Takane, 1989, on trying to equate mice and elephants; these groups should not be equated on the covariate because their distributions on the covariate do not overlap); (e) although the slopes may be equal for the range of Xs obtained, when extrapolating beyond the range of scores, the slopes may not be equal; (f) the standard errors of the adjusted means may increase, making tests of the adjusted means not significant; and (g) there may be differential growth in the groups confounding the results (e.g., adult vs. child groups).

Although one should be cautious about the use of ANCOVA in quasi-experiments, this is not to suggest that ANCOVA should never be used in such situations. Just be extra careful and do not go too far in terms of interpreting your results. If at all possible, replicate your study. For further discussion, see Huitema (1980), or Porter and Raudenbush (1987).

4.10 More Complex ANCOVA Models

The one-factor ANCOVA model can be extended to more-complex models in the same way as we expanded the one-factor ANOVA model. Thus, we can consider ANCOVA designs that involve any of the following characteristics: (a) factorial designs (i.e., having more than one factor or independent variable); (b) fixed-, random-, and mixed-effects designs; (c) repeated measures and split-plot (mixed) designs; (d) hierarchical designs; and (e) randomized block designs. Conceptually there is nothing new for these types of ANCOVA designs, and you should have no trouble getting a statistical package to do such analyses. For further information on these designs, see Huitema (1980), Keppel (1982), Kirk (1982), Myers and Well (1995), Page, Braver, and MacKinnon (2003), or Keppel and Wickens (2004). One can also utilize multiple covariates in an ANCOVA design; for further information, see Huitema (1980), Kirk (1982), Myers and Well (1995), Page et al. (2003), or Keppel and Wickens (2004).

4.11 Nonparametric ANCOVA Procedures

In situations where the assumptions of normality, homogeneity of variance, and/or linearity have been seriously violated, one alternative is to consider nonparametric ANCOVA procedures. Some rank ANCOVA procedures have been proposed by Quade (1967), Puri and Sen (1969), Conover and Iman (1982), and Rutherford (1992). For a description of such procedures, see these references as well as Huitema (1980), Harwell (2003), or Wilcox (2003).

4.12 SPSS and G*Power

Next we consider SPSS for the statistics instruction example. As noted in previous chapters, SPSS needs the data to be in a specific form for the analysis to proceed, which is different from the layout of the data in Table 4.1. For a one-factor ANCOVA with a single covariate, the dataset must contain three variables or columns: one for the level of the factor or independent variable, one for the covariate, and a third for the dependent variable. The following screenshot presents an example of the dataset for the statistics quiz score example. Each row still represents one individual, displaying the level of the factor (or independent variable) for which they are a member, as well as their scores on the covariate and the scores for the dependent variable.

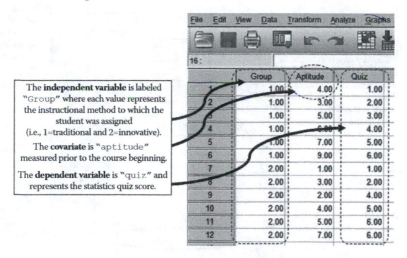

The **independent variable** is labeled "Group" where each value represents the instructional method to which the student was assigned (i.e., 1=traditional and 2=innovative).

The **covariate** is "aptitude" measured prior to the course beginning.

The **dependent variable** is "quiz" and represents the statistics quiz score.

Step 1: To conduct an ANCOVA, go to "Analyze" in the top pulldown menu, then select "General Linear Model," and then select "Univariate." Following the screenshot (step 1) that follows produces the "Univariate" dialog box.

Step 2: From the "Univariate" dialog box (see screenshot step 2), click the dependent variable (e.g., quiz score) and move it into the "Dependent Variable" box by clicking the arrow button. Click the independent variable (e.g., group) and move it into the "Fixed Factor(s)" box by clicking the arrow button. Click the covariate (e.g., aptitude) and move it into the "Covariate(s)" box by clicking the arrow button. Next, click on "Options."

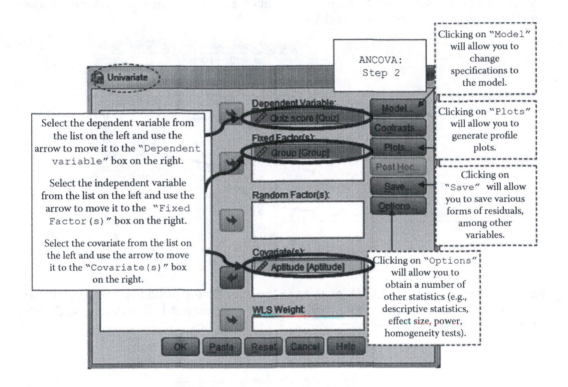

Step 3: Clicking on "Options" will provide the option to select such information as "Descriptive Statistics," "Estimates of effect size," "Observed power," and "Homogeneity tests." While there, move the items that are listed in the "Factor(s) and Factor Interactions:" box into the "Display Means for:" box to generate adjusted means. Also, check the box "Compare Main Effects," then click the pulldown for "Confidence interval adjustment" to choose among the LSD, Bonferroni, or Sidak MCPs of the adjusted means. For this illustration, we select the "Bonferonni." Notice that the "Post Hoc" option button from the main "Univariate" dialog box (see step 2) is not active; thus, you are restricted to the three MCPs just mentioned that are accessible from this "Options" screen. Click on "Continue" to return to the original dialog box.

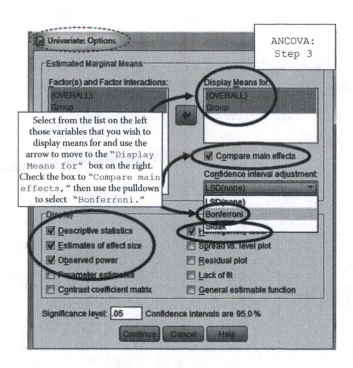

Step 4: From the "Univariate" dialog box (see step 2), click on "Plots" to obtain a profile plot of means. Click the independent variable (e.g., statistics course section, "Group") and move it into the "Horizontal Axis" box by clicking the arrow button (see screenshot step 4a). Then click on "Add" to move the variable into the "Plots" box at the bottom of the dialog box (see screenshot step 4b). Click on "Continue" to return to the original dialog box.

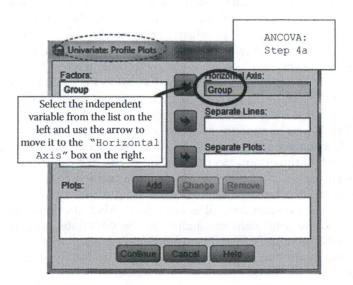

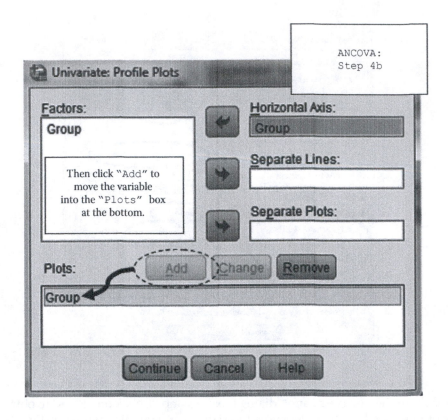

Step 5: Finally, in order to generate the appropriate sources of variation and results as recommended in this chapter, from the main "Univariate" dialog box (see step 2), you need to click on the "Model" button. Then select "Type I" from the "Sum of squares" pull-down menu. Click on "Continue" to return to the original dialog box.

You may be asking yourself why we need to utilize the Type I sum of squares, as up until this point in the text, we have always recommended the Type III (which is the default in SPSS). In a study conducted by Li and Lomax (2011), the following were confirmed with SPSS (as well as with SAS). First, when generating the Type I sum of squares, the covariate is extracted first, then the treatment is estimated controlling for the covariate. The Type I sum of squares will also correctly add up to the total sum of squares. Second, when generating the Type III sum of squares, each effect is estimated controlling for each of the other effects. In other words, the covariate is computed controlling for the treatment, and the treatment is determined controlling for the covariate. The former is not of interest as the treatment is administered after the covariate has been measured; thus, no such control is necessary. Also, the Type III sum of squares will not add up to the total sum of squares as the covariate sum of squares will be different than when using Type I. Thus, you do not want to estimate the covariate controlling for the treatment, and, thus, you want to use the Type I, not Type III, in the ANCOVA context.

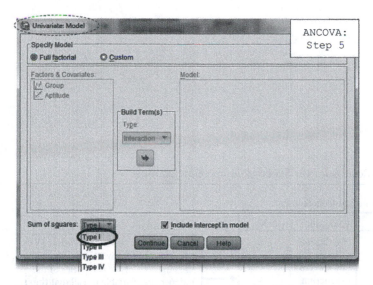

Step 6: From the "Univariate" dialog box (see step 2), click on "Save" to select those elements that you want to save (here we want to save the unstandardized residuals for later use in order to examine the extent to which normality and independence are met). Click on "Continue" to return to the original dialog box. From the "Univariate" dialog box, click on "OK" to return to generate the output.

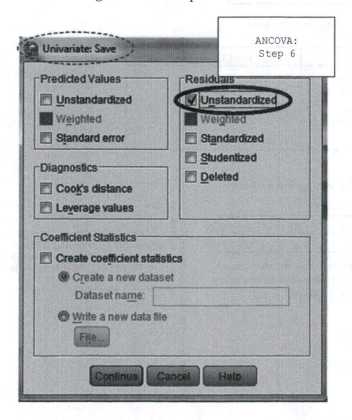

Interpreting the output: Annotated results are presented in Table 4.6.

TABLE 4.6

Selected SPSS Results for the Statistics Instruction Example

Between-subjects factors

		Value label	N
Group	1.00	Traditional lecture method of instruction	6
	2.00	Small group and self-directed instruction	6

The table labeled "Between-Subjects Factors" provides sample sizes for each of the categories of the independent variable (recall that the independent variable is the 'between subjects factor').

Descriptive statistics

Dependent variable: Quiz score

Group	Mean	Std. Deviation	N
Traditional lecture method of instruction	3.5000	1.87083	6
Small group and self-directed instruction	4.0000	2.09762	6
Total	3.7500	1.91288	12

The table labeled "Descriptive Statistics" provides basic descriptive statistics (means, standard deviations, and sample sizes) for each level of the independent variable.

Levene's Test of Equality of Error Variances[a]

Dependent variable: Quiz score

F	df1	df2	Sig.
6.768	1	10	.026

Tests the null hypothesis that the error variance of the dependent variable is equal across groups.

[a] Design: Intercept + aptitude + group

The F test (and associated p value) for Levene's Test for Equality of Error Variances is reviewed to determine if equal variances can be assumed.

In this case, we meet the assumption (as p is greater than α). Note that $df1$ is degrees of freedom for the numerator (calculated as $J - 1$) and $df2$ are the degrees of freedom for the denominator (calculated as $N - J$).

TABLE 4.6 (continued)

Selected SPSS Results for the Statistics Instruction Example

The row labeled **"GROUP"** is the independent variable or between groups variable. The *between groups mean square* (10.812) tells how much observations vary between groups. The degrees of freedom for between groups is $J-1$ (or 2-1 = 1 here).

The omnibus F test is computed as

$$F = \frac{MS_{betw}}{MS_{with}} = \frac{10.812}{.951} = 11.37$$

The p value for the independent variable F test is .008. This indicates there is a statistically significant difference in quiz scores based on instructional method, controlling for aptitude. The probability of observing these mean differences or more extreme mean differences by chance if the null hypothesis is really true (i.e., if the means really are equal) is substantially less than 1%. We reject the null hypothesis that all the population adjusted means are equal. The p value for the covariate F test is .001. This indicates there is a statistically significant relationship between the covariate (aptitude) and quiz score.

Partial eta squared is one measure of effect size:

$$\eta_p^2 = \frac{SS_{betw}}{SS_{betw} + SS_{error}} = \frac{10.812}{10.812 + 8.557} = .558$$

We can interpret this to say that approximately 56% of the variation in the dependent variable (in this case, statistics quiz score) is accounted for by the instructional method when controlling for aptitude.

Tests of Between-Subjects Effects

Dependent variable: Quiz score

Source	Type I Sum of Squares	df	Mean Square	F	Sig.	Partial Eta Squared	Noncent. Parameter	Observed Power[b]
Corrected model	31.693[a]	2	15.846	16.667	.001	.787	33.333	.993
Intercept	168.750	1	168.750	177.483	.000	.952	177.483	1.000
Aptitude	20.881	1	20.881	21.961	.001	.709	21.961	.986
Group	10.812	1	10.812	11.372	.008	.558	11.372	.850
Error	8.557	9	.951					
Total	209.000	12						
Corrected total	40.250	11						

[a] R Squared = .787 (Adjusted R Squared = .740)

[b] Computed using alpha = .05

R squared is listed as a footnote underneath the table. R squared is the ratio of SS between and SS covariate divided by sum of squares total:

$$R^2 = \frac{SS_{betw} + SS_{cov}}{SS_{total}}$$

$$R^2 = \frac{10.812 + 20.881}{40.250} = .787$$

The row labeled **"Error"** is within groups. The within groups mean square tells us how much the observations within the groups vary (i.e., .951). The degrees of freedom for within groups is $(N - J - 1)$ or the sample size minus the number of levels of the independent variable minus one covariate.

The row labeled "corrected total" is the sum of squares total. The degrees of freedom for the total is $(N - 1)$ or the sample size minus one.

Observed power tells whether our test is powerful enough to detect mean differences if they really exist. Power of .850 indicates that the probability of rejecting the null hypothesis if it is really false is about 85%, strong power.

(continued)

TABLE 4.6 (continued)

Selected SPSS Results for the Statistics Instruction Example

Estimated Marginal Means

1. Grand Mean

Dependent variable: Quiz score

Mean	Std. Error	95% Confidence Interval	
		Lower Bound	Upper Bound
3.750[a]	.281	3.113	4.387

The 'Grand Mean' (in this case, 3.750) represents the overall mean, regardless of group membership in the independent variable. The 95% CI represents the CI of the grand mean.

[a] Covariates appearing in the model are evaluated at the following values: Aptitude = 4.6667.

2. Group

Estimates

Dependent variable: Quiz score

Group	Mean	Std. Error	95% Confidence Interval	
			Lower Bound	Upper Bound
Traditional lecture method of instruction	2.686[a]	.423	1.729	3.642
Small group and self-directed instruction	4.814[a]	.423	3.858	5.771

The table labeled **"Group"** provides descriptive statistics for each of the categories of the independent variable, controlling for the covariate (notice that these are NOT the same means reported previously; also note the table footnote). In addition to means, the *SE* and 95% CI of the means are reported.

[a] Covariates appearing in the model are evaluated at the following values: Aptitude = 4.6667.

TABLE 4.6 (continued)

Selected SPSS Results for the Statistics Instruction Example

> 'Mean difference' is simply the difference between the adjusted group means of the two groups compared. For example, the mean difference of group 1 and group 2, controlling for the covariate, is calculated as 2.686−4.814 = −2.128 (rounded).
>
> Because there are only two groups of the independent variable, the values in the table are the same (in absolute value) for row 1 as compared to row 2 (the exception is that the CI for the difference is switched).

Pairwise Comparisons

Dependent variable: Quiz score

(I) Group	(J) Group	Mean Difference (I–J)	Std. Error	Sig.[a]	95% Confidence interval for difference[a] Lower Bound	95% Confidence interval for difference[a] Upper Bound
Traditional lecture method of instruction	Small group and self-directed instruction	−2.129*	.631	.008	−3.556	−701
Small group and self-directed instruction	Traditional lecture method of instruction	2.129*	.631	.008	.701	3.556

Based on estimated marginal means

*The mean difference is significant at the .05 level.

[a] Adjustment for multiple comparisons: Bonferroni.

> 'Sig.' denotes the observed p value and provides the results of the Bonferroni post hoc procedure. There is a statistically significant adjusted mean difference between traditional instruction and innovative instruction (i.e., controlling for aptitude).
>
> Because we had only two groups, requesting post hoc results really was not necessarily. We could have reviewed the F test and then the adjusted means to determine which group had the higher adjusted mean. The pairwise comparison results will become more valuable when the ANCOVA includes independent variables with more than two categories.

(continued)

TABLE 4.6 (continued)

Selected SPSS Results for the Statistics Instruction Example

> The table labeled **"Univariate Tests"** is simply another version of the omnibus *F* test. In the case of one independent variable, the row labeled "Contrast" provides the same results for the independent variable as that presented in the summary table previously. The results from this table suggest there is a statistically significant difference in adjusted mean quiz score based on instructional method when controlling for aptitude.

Univariate Tests

Dependent variable: Quiz score

	Sum of Squares	df	Mean Square	F	Sig.	Partial Eta Squared	Noncent. Parameter	Observed Power[a]
Contrast	10.812	1	10.812	11.372	.008	.558	11.372	.850
Error	8.557	9	.951					

The F tests the effect of Group. This test is based on the linearly independent pairwise comparisons among the estimated marginal means.

[a] Computed using alpha = .05

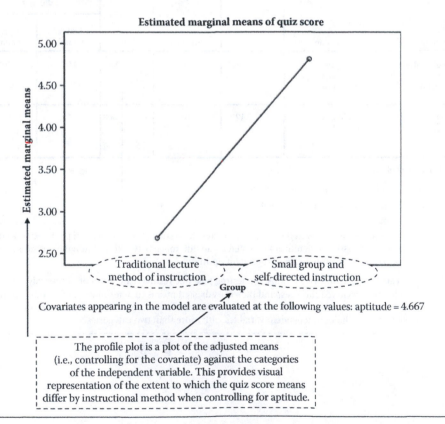

Estimated marginal means of quiz score

Covariates appearing in the model are evaluated at the following values: aptitude = 4.667

> The profile plot is a plot of the adjusted means (i.e., controlling for the covariate) against the categories of the independent variable. This provides visual representation of the extent to which the quiz score means differ by instructional method when controlling for aptitude.

Examining Data for Assumptions

The assumptions that we will test for in our ANCOVA model include (a) independence of observations, (b) homogeneity of variance (this was previously generated; thus, you can examine Table 4.6 for this assumption as it will not be reiterated here), (c) normality, (d) linearity, (e) independence of the covariate and the independent variable, and (f) homogeneity of regression slopes. We will examine the assumptions after generating the ANCOVA results. This is because many of the tests for assumptions are based on examination of the residuals, which were requested when generating the ANCOVA.

Independence

If subjects have been randomly assigned to conditions (in other words, the different levels of the independent variable), the assumption of independence has been met. In this illustration, students were randomly assigned to instructional method (i.e., traditional or innovative), and, thus, the assumption of independence was met. As we have learned in previous chapters, however, we often use independent variables that do not allow random assignment (e.g., intact groups). We can plot residuals against levels of the independent variable in a scatterplot to get an idea of whether or not there are patterns in the data and thereby provide an indication of the extent to which we have met this assumption. Remember that these variables were added to the dataset by saving the unstandardized residuals when we generated the ANCOVA model.

Note that some researchers do not believe that the assumption of independence can be tested. If there is not random assignment to groups, then these researchers believe this assumption has been violated—period. The plot that we generate will give us a general idea of patterns, however, in situations where random assignment was not performed.

The general steps for generating a simple scatterplot through "Scatter/dot" have been presented in Chapter 10 of *An Introduction to Statistical Concepts*, Third Edition, and they will not be reiterated here. From the "Simple Scatterplot" dialog screen, click the residual variable and move it into the "Y Axis" box by clicking on the arrow. Click the independent variable (e.g., group) and move it into the "X Axis" box by clicking on the arrow. Then click "OK."

Interpreting independence evidence: In examining the scatterplot for evidence of independence, the points should fall relatively randomly above and below the horizontal reference line at 0. In this example, the scatterplot does suggest evidence of independence with relative randomness of points above and below the horizontal line at 0.

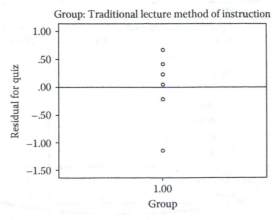

Normality

Generating normality evidence: As alluded to earlier in the chapter, understanding the distributional shape, specifically the extent to which normality is a reasonable assumption, is important. For the ANCOVA, the distributional shape for the residuals should be a normal distribution. We can again use "Explore" to examine the extent to which the assumption of normality is met.

The general steps for accessing "Explore" have been presented in previous chapters, and will not be repeated here. From the "Explore" dialog menu (see following screenshot), click the residual and move it into the "Dependent List" box by clicking on the arrow button. The procedures for selecting normality statistics were presented in Chapter 6 of *An Introduction to Statistical Concepts*, Third Edition, and remain the same here: Click on "Plots" in the upper right corner. Place a checkmark in the boxes for "Normality plots with tests" and also for "Histogram." Then click "Continue" to return to the main "Explore" dialog box. Then click "OK" to generate the output.

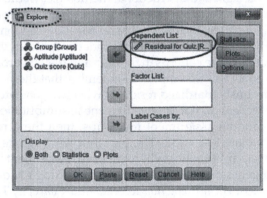

Interpreting normality evidence: We have already developed a good understanding of how to interpret some forms of evidence of normality including skewness and kurtosis, histograms, and boxplots. Here we examine the output for these statistics again.

The skewness statistic of the residuals is −.237 and kurtosis is −1.024—both are within the range of an absolute value of 2.0, suggesting some evidence of normality (see "descriptives" output as follows).

Descriptives

		Statistic	Std. Error
Residual for quiz Mean		.0000	.25461
95% Confidence interval	Lower bound	−.5604	
for mean	Upper bound	.5604	
5% Trimmed mean		.0056	
Median		.1357	
Variance		.778	
Std. deviation		.88200	
Minimum		−1.46	
Maximum		1.36	
Range		2.81	
Interquartile range		1.51	
Skewness		−.237	.637
Kurtosis		−1.024	1.232

The histogram of residuals is not what most would consider normal in shape, and this is largely an artifact of the small sample size. Because of this, we will rely more heavily on the other forms of normality evidence.

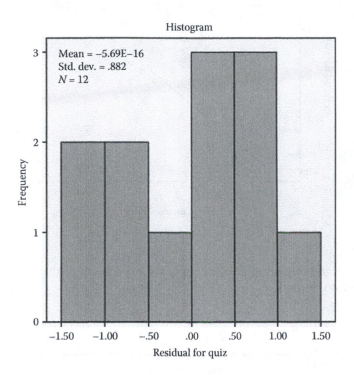

There are a few other statistics that can be used to gauge normality. The formal test of normality, the S–W test (*SW*) (Shapiro & Wilk, 1965), provides evidence of the extent to which our sample distribution is statistically different from a normal distribution. The output for the S–W test is presented as follows and suggests that our sample distribution for residuals is not statistically significantly different than what would be expected from a normal distribution ($SW = .965$, $df = 12$, $p = .854$).

Tests of Normality

	Kolmogorov–Smirnov[a]			Shapiro–Wilk		
	Statistic	df	Sig.	Statistic	df	Sig.
Residual for quiz	.124	12	.200	.965	12	.854

[a] Lilliefors significance correction.
*This is a lower bound of the true significance.

Quantile–quantile (Q–Q) plots are also often examined to determine evidence of normality. Q–Q plots are graphs that plot quantiles of the theoretical normal distribution against quantiles of the sample distribution. Points that fall on or close to the diagonal line suggest evidence of normality. The Q–Q plot of residuals shown as follows suggests relative normality.

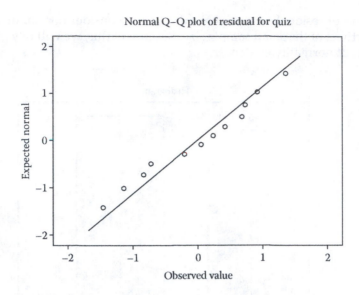

Normal Q–Q plot of residual for quiz

Examination of the following boxplot suggests a relatively normal distributional shape of residuals and no outliers.

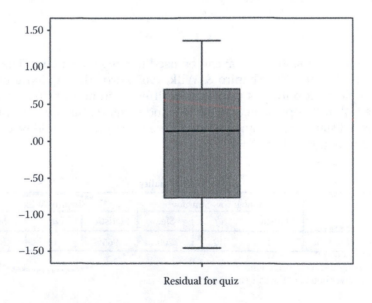

Residual for quiz

Considering the forms of evidence we have examined, skewness and kurtosis statistics, histogram, the S–W test, the Q–Q plot, and the boxplot, all suggest normality is a reasonable assumption. We can be reasonably assured we have met the assumption of normality of the dependent variable for each group of the independent variable.

Linearity

Recall that the assumption of linearity means that the regression of the dependent variable (i.e., "quiz" in this illustration) on the covariate (i.e., "aptitude") is linear. Evidence of the extent to which this assumption is met can be done by examining scatterplots of the dependent variable versus the covariate—both overall and also for each category or group of the independent variable.

Linearity evidence: Overall. The general steps for generating a simple scatterplot through "Scatter/dot" have been presented in Chapter 10 of *An Introduction to Statistical Concepts*, Third Edition, and they will not be reiterated here. To generate the overall scatterplot, from the "Simple Scatterplot" dialog screen, click the dependent variable and move it into the "Y Axis" box by clicking on the arrow. Click the covariate (e.g., aptitude) and move it into the "X Axis" box by clicking on the arrow. Then click "OK."

Interpreting independence of linearity (overall): In examining the scatterplot for overall evidence of linearity, the points should fall relatively linearly (in other words, we should not be seeing a curvilinear or some other nonlinear relationship). In this example, our scatterplot suggests we have evidence of overall linearity as there is a relatively clear pattern of points which suggest a positive and linear relationship between the dependent variable and covariate.

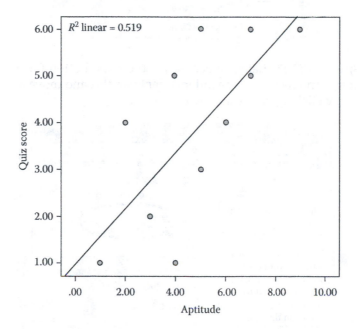

Linearity evidence: By group of independent variable. To generate the scatterplot of the dependent variable and covariate for each group of the independent variable, we must first split the data file. To do this, go to "Data" in the top pulldown menu. Then select "Split File."

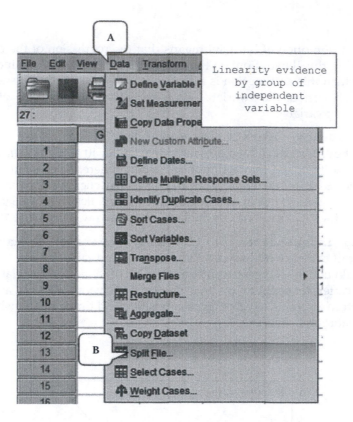

From the "Split File" dialog screen, select the radio button for "Organize output by groups," and then click the independent variable and move it into the "Groups Based on" box by clicking on the arrow. Then click "OK."

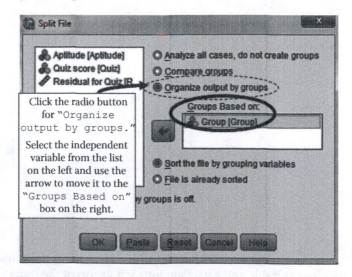

After splitting the file, the next step is to generate the scatterplot of the dependent variable by covariate. Because we have split the file, there will be two scatterplots generated: one for the traditional teaching method and one for the innovative teaching method. The general steps for generating a simple scatterplot through "Scatter/dot" have been presented in Chapter 10 of *An Introduction to Statistical Concepts*, Third Edition, and they will not be repeated here. Because we have just generated the overall scatterplot, the selections made previously will remain, and, thus, from the "Simple Scatterplot" dialog screen, simply click "OK" to generate the output.

Interpreting evidence of linearity (by group of independent variable): In examining the scatterplot for evidence of linearity by group of the independent variable, our interpretation should remain the same: the points should fall relatively linearly (in other words, we should not see a curvilinear or some other nonlinear relationship). In this example, our scatterplots suggest we have evidence of linearity by group of the independent variable as there is a relatively clear pattern of points which suggest a positive and linear relationship between the dependent variable and covariate for each group of the independent variable.

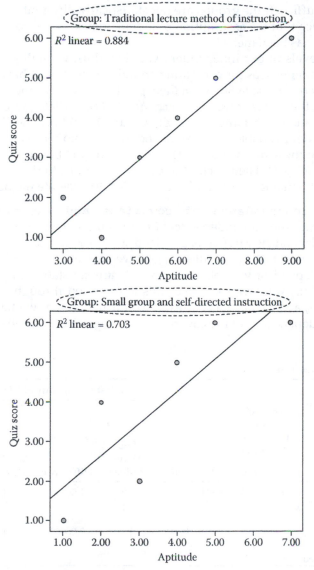

Independence of Covariate and Independent Variable

Recall the assumption of independence of the covariate and independent variable. In other words, the levels of the independent variable should not differ on the covariate. If subjects have been randomly assigned to conditions (in other words, the different levels of the independent variable), the assumption of independence of the covariate and independent variable has likely been met. In this illustration, students were randomly assigned to teaching method (i.e., traditional or innovative), and, thus, the assumption of independence of the covariate and independent variable was likely met. As we have learned in previous chapters, however, we often use independent variables that do not allow random assignment. Evidence of the extent to which this assumption is met can be done by examining mean differences on the covariate based on the independent variable. If the independent variable has only two levels, an independent t test would be appropriate. If the independent variable has more than two categories, a one-way ANOVA would suffice. If the groups are not statistically different on the covariate, then that lends evidence that the assumption of independence of the covariate and the independent variable has been met.

We have two levels of our independent variable; thus, we will generate an independent t test. The general steps for generating an independent t test have been presented in Chapter 8 of *An Introduction to Statistical Concepts*, Third Edition, and they will not be reiterated here. From the "Independent Samples T Test" dialog screen, click the covariate (e.g., aptitude) and move it into the "Test Variable(s)" box by clicking on the arrow. Click the independent variable (e.g., group) and move it into the "Grouping Variable" box by clicking on the arrow. Click the "Define Groups" box and enter "1" for "Group 1" and "2" for "Group 2." Then click "Continue" to return to the main "Independent Samples T Test" dialog screen, and click on "OK" to generate the output.

Interpreting independence of covariate and independent variable evidence: In examining the independent t test results, evidence of independence of the covariate and independent variable is provided when the test results are *not* statistically significant. In this example, our results suggest we have evidence of independence of the covariate and independent variable as the results are *not* statistically significant, $t(10) = 1.604$, $p = .140$. Thus, we have likely met this assumption through random assignment of cases to groups, and this provides further confirmation that we have not violated the assumption of independence of the covariate and independent variable.

Independent Samples Test

		Levene's Test for Equality of Variances		*t*-Test for Equality of Means					95% Confidence Interval of the Difference	
		F	Sig.	t	df	Sig. (Two-Tailed)	Mean Difference	Std. Error Difference	Lower	Upper
Aptitude	Equal variances assumed	.000	1.000	1.604	10	.140	2.00000	1.24722	−.77898	4.77898
	Equal variances not assumed			1.604	10.000	.140	2.00000	1.24722	−.77898	4.77898

Homogeneity of Regression Slopes

Step 1: In order to test the homogeneity of slopes assumption, you will need to rerun the ANCOVA analysis. Keep every screen the same as before, *with one exception*. Return to the main "Univariate" dialog box (see step 2) and click on "Model." From the "Model" dialog box, click on the "Custom" button to build a custom model to include the interaction between the independent and covariate variables. To do this, under the "Build Terms" pulldown in the middle of the dialog box, select "Main effects."

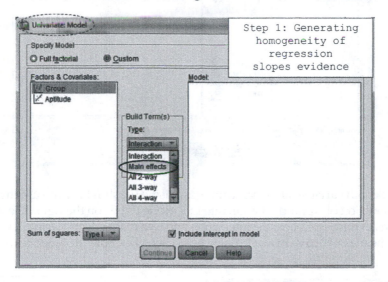

Step 2: Click the independent variable and move it into the "Model" box by clicking on the arrow button. Next, click the covariate and move it into the "Model" box by clicking on the arrow button. This will place "Group" and "Aptitude" in the "Model" box on the right of the screen.

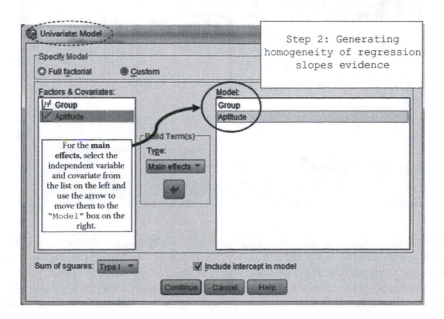

Step 3: Then from the "Build Terms" pulldown menu, select "Interaction."

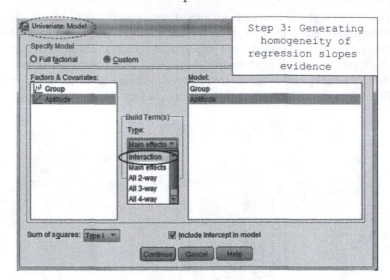

Step 4: Click both variables at the same time (e.g., using the shift key) and use the arrow key to move the interaction of Aptitude*Group into the "Model" box on the right. There should now be three terms in the Model box: the interaction and two main effects. Then click "Continue" to return to the main "Univariate" dialog box. Then click "OK" to generate the output.

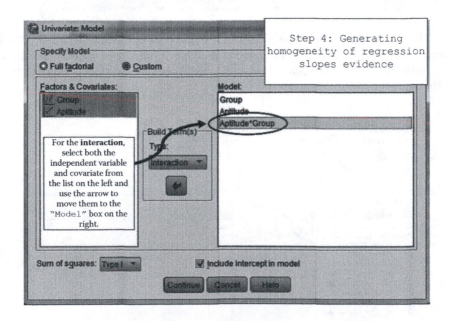

Interpreting homogeneity of regression slopes evidence: Selected results, specifically the ANCOVA summary table which presents the results for the homogeneity of slopes test, are presented as follows. Here the only thing that we care about is the test of the interaction, which we want to be nonsignificant [and we find this to be the case: $F(1, 8) = .000$, $p = 1.000$]. This indicates that we have met the homogeneity of regression slopes assumption.

Dependent Variable: Quiz Score   **Tests of Between-Subjects Effects**

Source	Type I Sum of Squares	df	Mean Square	F	Sig.	Partial Eta Squared	Noncent Parameter	Observed Power[b]
Corrected model	31.693[a]	3	10.564	9.876	.005	.787	29.629	.955
Intercept	168.750	1	168.750	157.763	.000	.952	157.763	1.000
Group	.750	1	.750	.701	.427	.081	.701	.115
Aptitude	30.943	1	30.943	28.928	.001	.783	28.928	.997
Group*Aptitude	.000	1	.000	.000	1.000	.000	.000	.050
Error	8.557	8	1.070					
Total	209.000	12						
Corrected total	40.250	11						

[a] R squared = .787 (adjusted R squared = .708).

[b] Computed using alpha = .05.

Post Hoc Power for ANCOVA Using G*Power

Generating power analysis for ANCOVA models follows similarly to that for ANOVA and factorial ANOVA. In particular, if there is more than one independent variable, we must test for main effects and interactions separately. Because we only have one independent variable for our ANCOVA model, our illustration assumes only one main effect. If there were additional independent variables and/or interactions, we would have followed these steps for those as well.

The first thing that must be done when using G*Power for computing post hoc power is to select the correct test family. In our case, we conducted an ANCOVA. To find ANCOVA, we will select "Tests" in the top pulldown menu, then "Means," and then "Many groups: ANCOVA: Main effects and interactions." Once that selection is made, the "Test family" automatically changes to "F tests."

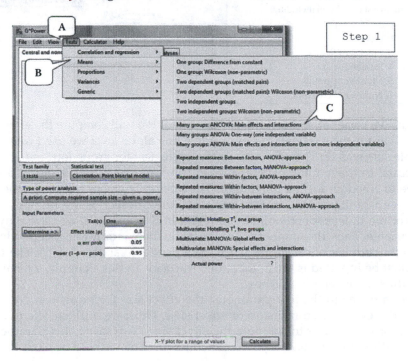

The "Type of Power Analysis" desired then needs to be selected. To compute post hoc power, we need to select "Post hoc: Compute achieved power—given α, sample size, and effect size."

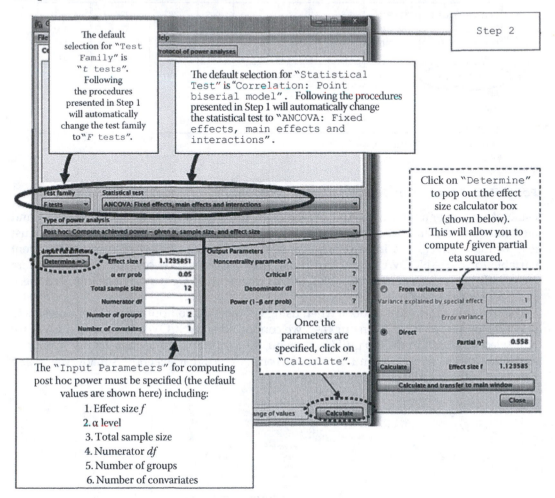

The "Input Parameters" must then be specified. We will compute the effect size *f* last, so we skip that for the moment. In our example, the alpha level we used was .05, and the total sample size was 12. The *numerator degrees of freedom* for group (our independent variable) are equal to the number of categories of this variable (i.e., 2) minus 1; thus, there is one degree of freedom for the numerator. The *number of groups* equals, in the case of an ANCOVA with multiple independent variables, the product of the number of levels or categories of the independent variables or $(J)(K)$. In this example, we have only one independent variable. Thus, the number of groups when there is only one independent variable is equal to the number of categories of this independent variable (i.e., 2). The last parameter that must be inputted is the number of covariates. In this example, we have only one covariate; thus, we enter 1 in this box.

We skipped filling in the first parameter, the effect size *f*, for a reason. SPSS only provides a partial eta squared measure of effect size. Thus, we will use the pop-out effect size calculator in G*Power to compute the effect size *f* (we saved this parameter for last as the calculation is based on the previous values just entered). To pop out the effect size calculator, click on "Determine" which is displayed under "Input Parameters." In the pop-out effect size calculator, click on the radio button for "Direct" and then enter the partial eta squared value for group that was calculated in SPSS (i.e., .558). Clicking on "Calculate" in the pop-out effect size calculator will calculate the effect size *f.* Then click on "Calculate and Transfer to Main window" to transfer the calculated effect size (i.e., 1.1235851) to the "Input Parameters." Once the parameters are specified, click on "Calculate" to find the power statistics.

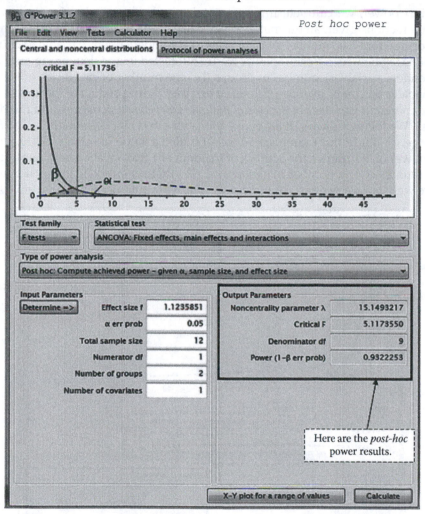

The "Output Parameters" provide the relevant statistics given the input just specified. In this example, we were interested in determining post hoc power for an ANCOVA with a computed effect size *f* of 1.1235851, an alpha level of .05, total sample size of 12, numerator degrees of freedom of 1, two groups, and one covariate.

Based on those criteria, the post hoc power for the main effect of instructional method (i.e., our only independent variable) was .93. In other words, with an ANCOVA, computed effect size *f* of 1.124, alpha level of .05, total sample size of 12, numerator degrees of freedom of 1, two groups, and one covariate, the post hoc power of our main effect for this test was .93— the probability of rejecting the null hypothesis when it is really false (in this case, the probability that the adjusted means of the dependent variable would be equal for each level of the independent variable, controlling for the covariate) was about 93%, which would be considered more than sufficient power (sufficient power is often .80 or above). Note that this value differs slightly than that reported in SPSS. Keep in mind that conducting power analysis a priori is recommended so that you avoid a situation where, post hoc, you find that the sample size was not sufficient to reach the desired level of power (given the observed parameters).

A Priori Power for ANCOVA Using G*Power

For a priori power, we can determine the total sample size needed for the main effects and/or interactions given an estimated effect size f, alpha level, desired power, numerator degrees of freedom (i.e., number of categories of our independent variable and/or interaction, depending on which a priori power we are interested in and depending on the number of independent variables), number of groups (i.e., the number of categories of the independent variable *in the case of only one independent variable* OR the product of the number of levels of the independent variables *in the case of multiple independent variables*), and the number of covariates. We follow Cohen's (1988) conventions for effect size (i.e., small, $f = .10$; moderate, $f = .25$; large, $f = .40$). In this example, had we estimated a moderate effect f of .25, alpha of .05, desired power of .80, numerator degrees of freedom of 1 (two categories in our independent variable thus $2 - 1 = 1$), number of groups of 2 (i.e., there is only one independent variable, and there were two categories), and one covariate, we would need a total sample size of 9.

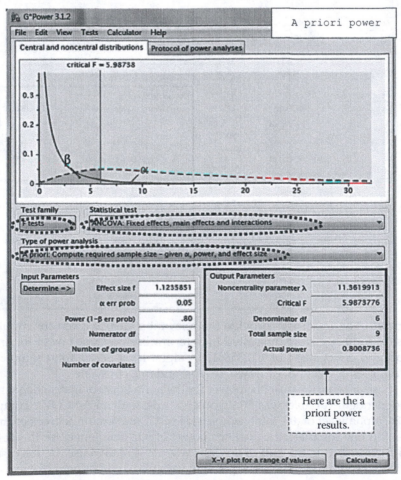

Here are the a priori power results.

4.13 Template and APA-Style Paragraph

Finally we come to an example paragraph of the results for the statistics instruction example. Recall that our graduate research assistant, Marie, was building on work that she had conducted as part of a research project for an independent study class and had now conducted a second experiment. She was looking to see if there was a mean difference in statistics quiz scores based on the instructional method of the class (two categories: traditional or innovative) while controlling for aptitude. Her research question was the following: *Is there a mean difference in statistics quiz scores based on teaching method, controlling for aptitude?* Marie then generated an ANCOVA as the test of inference. A template for writing a research question for ANCOVA is presented as follows:

```
Is there a mean difference in [dependent variable] based on [inde-
pendent variable], controlling for [covariate]?
```

This is illustrated assuming a one-factor (i.e., one independent variable) model, but it can easily be extended to two or more factors. As we noted in previous chapters, it is important to be sure the reader understands the levels or groups of the independent variables. This may be done parenthetically in the actual research question, as an operational definition, or specified within the methods section. In this example, parenthetically we could have stated the following: *Is there a mean difference in statistics quiz scores based on teaching method (traditional vs. innovative), controlling for aptitude?*

It may be helpful to preface the results of the ANCOVA with information on an examination of the extent to which the assumptions were met (recall there are several assumptions that we tested: (a) independence of observations, (b) homogeneity of variance, (c) normality, (d) linearity, (e) independence of the covariate and the independent variable, and (f) homogeneity of regression slopes):

An ANCOVA was conducted to determine if the mean statistics quiz score differed based on the instructional method of the statistics course (traditional vs. innovative) while controlling for aptitude. **Independence of observations** was met by random assignment of students to instructional method. This assumption was also confirmed by review of a scatterplot of residuals against the levels of the independent variable. A random display of points around 0 provided further evidence that the assumption of independence was met. According to Levene's test, the **homogeneity of variance** assumption was not satisfied [$F(1, 10) = 6.768$, $p = .026$]. However, research suggests that violation of homogeneity is minimal when the groups of the independent variable are equal in size (Harwell, 2003), as in the case of this study. The assumption of **normality** was tested and met via examination of the residuals. Review of the S-W test for normality ($SW = .965$, $df = 12$, $p = .854$) and skewness ($-.237$) and kurtosis (-1.024) statistics suggested that normality was a reasonable assumption. The boxplot and histogram suggested a relatively normal distributional shape (with no outliers) of the residuals. The Q-Q plot suggested normality was reasonable. In general, there is evidence that normality has been met. **Linearity** of the dependent variable with the covariate was examined with scatterplots, both overall and by group of the independent variable. Overall, the scatterplot of the dependent variable with the covariate suggested a positive linear relationship. This same pattern was present for the scatterplot of the dependent variable with the covariate when disaggregated by the categories of the independent variables. **Independence of the covariate and independent variable** was met by random assignment of students to instructional method. This assumption was also confirmed by an independent t test which examined the mean difference on the covariate (i.e., aptitude) by independent variable (i.e., teaching method). The results were not statistically significant, $t(10) = 1.604$, $p = .140$, which further confirms evidence of independence of the covariate and independent variable. There was not a mean difference in statistics aptitude based on teaching method. **Homogeneity of regression slopes** was suggested by similar regression lines evidenced in the scatterplots of the dependent variable and covariates by group (reported earlier as evidence for linearity). This assumption was confirmed by a nonstatistically significant interaction of aptitude by group, $F(1, 8) = .000$, $p = 1.000$.

Here is an APA-style example paragraph of results for the ANCOVA (remember that this will be prefaced by the previous paragraph reporting the extent to which the ANCOVA assumptions were met):

The results of the ANCOVA suggest a statistically significant effect of the covariate, aptitude, on the dependent variable, statistics quiz score ($F_{aptitude} = 21.961$; $df = 1,9$; $p = .001$). More importantly, there is a statistically significant effect for instructional method ($F_{group} = 11.372$; $df = 1,9$; $p = .008$), with a large effect size and strong power (partial $\eta^2_{group} = .558$, observed power = .850). The effect size suggests that about 56% of the variance in statistics quiz scores can be accounted for by teaching method when controlling for aptitude.

The *unadjusted* group statistics quiz score mean (i.e., prior to controlling for aptitude) was larger for the innovative instruction group ($M = 4.00$, $SD = 2.10$) as compared to the traditional lecture method ($M = 3.50$, $SD = 1.87$) by only .50. However, the *adjusted mean* for the innovative instruction group ($M = 4.814$, $SE = .423$) as compared to the traditional lecture method ($M = 2.686$, $SE = .423$) was larger by 2.128. Thus, the use of the covariate resulted in a large significant difference between the instructional groups. In summary, students assigned to the innovative teaching method outperformed students in the traditional lecture method on the statistics quiz score when controlling for statistics aptitude.

If our independent variable had more than two groups, we would have needed to evaluate and report the results of a post hoc MCP when generating SPSS (recall that we asked for Bonferroni post hoc results). The following provides a template for how these results may have been written, had our analyses required them:

Follow-up tests were conducted to evaluate the pairwise differences among the adjusted means of [dependent variable] based on [independent variable]. The [post hoc procedure selected, e.g., Bonferroni] was applied to control for the risk of increased Type I error across all pairwise comparisons. Pairwise comparisons revealed [report specific results, including means and standard deviations here].

4.14 Summary

In this chapter, methods involving the comparison of adjusted group means for a single independent variable were considered. The chapter began with a look at the unique characteristics of the ANCOVA, including (a) statistical control through the use of a covariate, (b) the dependent variable means adjusted by the covariate, (c) the covariate used to reduce error variation, (d) the relationship between the covariate and the dependent variable taken into account in the adjustment, and (e) the covariate measured at least at the interval level. The layout of the data was shown, followed by an examination of the ANCOVA model, and the ANCOVA summary table. Next estimation of the adjusted means was considered along with several different MCPs. Some discussion was also devoted to the ANCOVA assumptions, their assessment, and how to deal with assumption violations. We illustrated the use of the ANCOVA by looking at an example. Finally, we finished off the chapter by briefly examining (a) some cautions about the use of ANCOVA in situations without randomization, (b) ANCOVA for models having multiple factors and/or multiple covariates, (c) nonparametric ANCOVA procedures, and (d) SPSS and G*Power. At this point, you should have met the following objectives: (a) be able to understand the characteristics and concepts underlying ANCOVA; (b) be able to determine and interpret the results of ANCOVA, including adjusted means and MCPs; and (c) be able to understand and evaluate the assumptions of ANCOVA. Chapter 5 takes us beyond the fixed-effects models we have discussed thus far and considers random- and mixed-effects models.

Problems

Conceptual Problems

4.1 Malani wants to determine whether children whose preschool classroom has a window differ in their receptive vocabulary as compared to children whose classroom does not have a window. At the beginning of the school year, Malani randomly assigns 10 children at Rainbow Butterfly Preschool to one of two different classrooms: one classroom has a window that looks out onto a grassy area, and the other classroom has no windows. At the end of the school year, Malani measures children on their receptive vocabulary. Is ANCOVA appropriate given this scenario?

4.2 Joe wants to determine whether the time to run the Magic Mountain Marathon (ratio level variable) differs, on average, for nonprofessional athletes who complete a 12 week endurance training program as compared to those who complete a 4 week endurance training program. Joe randomly assigns nonprofessional athletes to one of the two training programs. In conducting this experiment, Joe also wants to control for the number of prior marathons in which the participant has run. Is ANCOVA appropriate given this scenario?

4.3   Tami has generated an ANCOVA. In testing the assumptions, she reviews a scatterplot of the residuals for each category of the independent variable. For which assumption is Tami likely reviewing evidence?

    a. Homogeneity of regression slopes

    b. Homogeneity of variance

    c. Independence of observations

    d. Independence of the covariate and the independent variable

    e. Linearity

4.4   Wesley has generated an ANCOVA. In his model, there is one independent variable which has three categories (type of phone: Blackberry, iPhone, and Droid) and one covariate (amount of time spent on desktop or laptop computer). In testing the assumptions, he reviews a one-way ANOVA, the dependent variable being amount of time spent on desktop or laptop computer and the independent variable being type of phone. For which assumption is Wesley likely reviewing evidence?

    a. Homogeneity of regression slopes

    b. Homogeneity of variance

    c. Independence of observations

    d. Independence of the covariate and the independent variable

    e. Linearity

4.5   If the correlation between the covariate X and the dependent variable Y differs markedly in the two treatment groups, it seems likely that

    a. The assumption of normality is suspect.

    b. The assumption of homogeneity of slopes is suspect.

    c. A nonlinear relation exists between X and Y.

    d. The adjusted means for Y differ significantly.

4.6   If for both the treatment and control groups the correlation between the covariate X and the dependent variable Y is substantial but negative, the error variation for ANCOVA as compared to that for ANOVA is

    a. Less

    b. About the same

    c. Greater

    d. Unpredictably different

4.7   An experiment was conducted to compare three different instructional strategies. Fifteen subjects were included in each group. The same test was administered prior to and after the treatments. If both pretest and IQ are used as covariates, what are the degrees of freedom for the error term?

    a. 2

    b. 40

    c. 41

    d. 42

✓ **4.8** The effect of a training program concerned with educating heart attack patients to the benefits of moderate exercise was examined. A group of recent heart attack patients was randomly divided into two groups; one group received the training program and the other did not. The dependent variable was the amount of time taken to jog three laps, with the weight of the patient after the program used as a covariate. Examination of the data after the study revealed that the covariate means of the two groups differed. Which of the following assumptions is most clearly violated?

    a. Linearity ✗

    b. Homogeneity of slopes

    c. Independence of the treatment and the covariate

    d. Normality

4.9 In ANCOVA, the covariate is a variable which should have a

    a. Low, positive correlation with the dependent variable

    b. High, positive correlation with the independent variable

    c. High, positive correlation with the dependent variable

    d. Zero correlation with the dependent variable

✓ **4.10** In ANCOVA, how will the correlation of 0 between the covariate and the dependent variable appear?

    a. Unequal group means on the dependent variable

    b. Unequal group means on the covariate

    c. Regression of the dependent variable on the covariate with $b_w = 0$

    d. Regression of the dependent variable on the covariate with $b_w = 1$

4.11 Which of the following is not a necessary requirement for using ANCOVA?

    a. Covariate scores are not affected by the treatment.

    b. There is a linear relationship between the covariate and the dependent variable.

    c. The covariate variable is the same measure as the dependent variable.

    d. Regression slopes for the groups are similar.

4.12 Which of the following is the most desirable situation to use ANCOVA?

    a. The slope of the regression line equals 0.

    b. The variance of the dependent variable for a specific covariate score is relatively large.

    c. The correlation between the covariate and the dependent variable is –.95. ✗

    d. The correlation between the covariate and the dependent variable is .60. ✗

4.13 A group of students were randomly assigned to one of three instructional strategies. Data from the study indicated an interaction between slope and treatment group. It seems likely that

    a. The assumption of normality is suspect.

    b. The assumption of homogeneity of slopes is suspect.

    c. A nonlinear relation exists between X and Y.

    d. The covariate is not independent of the treatment.

4.14 If the mean on the dependent variable GPA (Y) for persons of middle social class (X) is higher than for persons of lower and higher social classes, one would expect that

   a. The relationship between X and Y is curvilinear.

   b. The covariate X contains substantial measurement error.

   c. GPA is not normally distributed.

   d. Social class is not related to GPA.

4.15 If both the covariate and the dependent variable are assessed after the treatment has been concluded, and if both are affected by the treatment, the use of ANCOVA for these data would likely result in

   a. An inflated F ratio for the treatment effect

   b. An exaggerated difference in the adjusted means

   c. An underestimate of the treatment effect

   d. An inflated value of the slope b_w

4.16 When the covariate correlates $+.5$ with the dependent variable, I assert that the adjusted MS_{with} from the ANCOVA will be less than the MS_{with} from the ANOVA. Am I correct?

4.17 For each of two groups, the correlation between the covariate and the dependent variable is substantial, but negative in direction. I assert that the error variance for ANCOVA, as compared to that for ANOVA, is greater. Am I correct?

4.18 In ANCOVA, X is known as a factor. True or false?

4.19 A study was conducted to compare six types of diets. Twelve subjects were included in each group. Their weights were taken prior to and after treatment. If pre-weight is used as a covariate, what are the degrees of freedom for the error term?

   a. 5

   b. 65

   c. 66

   d. 71

4.20 A researcher conducts both a one-factor ANOVA and a one-factor ANCOVA on the same data. In comparing the adjusted group means to the unadjusted group means, they find that for each group, the adjusted mean is equal to the unadjusted mean. I assert that the researcher must have made a computational error. Am I correct?

4.21 The correlation between the covariate and the dependent variable is 0. I assert that ANCOVA is still preferred over ANOVA. Am I correct?

4.22 If there is a nonlinear relationship between the covariate X and the dependent variable Y, then it is very likely that

   a. There will be less reduction in SS_{with}.

   b. The group effects will be biased.

   c. The correlation between X and Y will be smaller in magnitude.

   d. All of the above.

Computational Problems

4.1 Consider the ANCOVA situation where the dependent variable Y is the posttest of an achievement test and the covariate X is the pretest of the same test. Given the data that follow, where there are three groups, (a) calculate the adjusted Y values assuming that $b_w = 1.00$, and (b) determine what effects the adjustment had on the posttest results.

Group	X	$\bar{X}$	Y	$\bar{Y}$
	40		120	
1	50 > 50		125 > 125	
	150 — 60		130	
	70		140	
2	75 > 75		150 > 150	
	225 — 80		160	
	90		160	
3	100 ⁄ 100		175 > 175	
	110		190	

(handwritten annotation: divide these by 3 = 150)

4.2 Malani wants to determine whether children whose preschool classroom has a window differ in their receptive vocabulary as compared to children whose classroom does not have a window. At the beginning of the school year, Malani randomly assigns 10 children at Rainbow Butterfly Preschool to one of two different classrooms: one classroom which has a window that looks out onto a grassy area or another classroom that has no windows. At the end of the school year, Malani measures children on their receptive vocabulary. In the following are two independent random samples (classroom with and without window) of paired values on the covariate (X; receptive vocabulary measured at beginning of school year) and the dependent variable essay score (Y; receptive vocabulary measured at the end of the school year). Conduct an ANOVA on Y, an ANCOVA on Y using X as a covariate, and compare the results ($\alpha = .05$). Determine the unadjusted and adjusted means.

Classroom with Window		Classroom Without Window	
X	Y	X	Y
80	105	80	95
75	100	85	100
85	105	90	105
70	100	85	100
90	110	95	105

4.3 In the following are four independent random samples (different methods of instruction) of paired values on the covariate IQ (X) and the dependent variable essay score (Y). Conduct an ANOVA on Y, an ANCOVA on Y using X as a covariate, and compare the results ($\alpha = .05$). Determine the unadjusted and adjusted means.

Group 1		Group 2		Group 3		Group 4	
X	Y	X	Y	X	Y	X	Y
94	14	80	38	92	55	94	24
96	19	84	34	96	53	94	37
98	17	90	43	99	55	98	22
100	38	97	43	101	52	100	43
102	40	97	61	102	35	103	49
105	26	112	63	104	46	104	24
109	41	115	93	107	57	104	41
110	28	118	74	110	55	108	26
111	36	120	76	111	42	113	70
130	66	120	79	118	81	115	63

4.4 A communications researcher wants to know which of five versions of commercials for a new television show is most effective in terms of viewing likelihood. Each commercial is viewed by six students. A one-factor ANCOVA was used to analyze these data where the covariate was amount of television previously viewed per week. Complete the following ANCOVA summary table ($\alpha = .05$):

Source	SS	df	MS	F	Critical Value	Decision
Between adjusted	96	—	—	—	—	—
Within adjusted	192	—	—			
Covariate	—	—	—	—	—	—
Total	328	—				

Interpretive Problems

4.1 The first interpretive problem in Chapter 1 requested the following: "Using the survey 1 dataset from the website, use SPSS to conduct a one-factor fixed-effects ANOVA, including effect size, where political view is the grouping variable (i.e., independent variable) ($J = 5$) and the dependent variable is a variable of interest to you [the following variables look interesting: books, TV, exercise, drinks, GPA, GRE-Quantitative (GRE-Q), CDs, hair appointment]." Using these same data, select an appropriate covariate and then generate a one-factor ANCOVA (including testing the assumptions of both the ANOVA and ANCOVA). Compare and contrast the results of the ANOVA and ANCOVA. Which method would you select and why?

4.2 The second interpretive problem in Chapter 1 requested the following: "Using the survey 1 dataset from the website, use SPSS to conduct a one-factor fixed-effects ANOVA, including effect size, where hair color is the grouping variable (i.e., independent variable) ($J = 5$) and the dependent variable is a variable of interest to you (the following variables look interesting: books, TV, exercise, drinks, GPA, GRE-Q, CDs, hair appointment)." Using these same data, select an appropriate covariate and then generate a one-factor ANCOVA (including testing the assumptions of both the ANOVA and ANCOVA). Compare and contrast the results of the ANOVA and ANCOVA. Which method would you select and why?

5

Random- and Mixed-Effects Analysis of Variance Models

Chapter Outline

Key Concepts

1. Fixed-, random-, and mixed-effects models

2. Repeated measures models

3. Compound symmetry/sphericity assumption

4. Friedman repeated measures test based on ranks

5. Split-plot or mixed designs (i.e., both between- and within-subjects factors)

In this chapter, we continue our discussion of the analysis of variance (ANOVA) by considering models in which there is a random-effects factor, previously introduced in Chapter 1. These models include the one-factor and factorial designs, as well as repeated measures designs. As becomes evident, repeated measures designs are used when there is at least one factor where each individual is exposed to all levels of that factor. This factor is referred to as a **repeated factor**, for obvious reasons. This chapter is mostly concerned with one- and two-factor random-effects models, the two-factor mixed-effects model, and one- and two-factor repeated measures designs.

It should be noted that effect size measures, power, and confidence intervals (CIs) can be determined in the same fashion for the models in this chapter as for previously described ANOVA models. The standard effect size measures already described are applicable (i.e., ω^2 and η^2), although the intraclass correlation coefficient, ρ_I, can be utilized for random effects (similarly interpreted). For additional discussion of these issues in the context of this chapter, see Cohen (1988), Fidler and Thompson (2001), Keppel and Wickens (2004), Murphy, Myors, and Wolach (2008), and Wilcox (1996, 2003).

Many of the concepts used in this chapter are the same as those covered in Chapters 1 through 4. In addition, the following new concepts are addressed: random- and mixed-effects factors, repeated measures factors, the compound symmetry/sphericity assumption, and mixed designs. Our objectives are that by the end of this chapter, you will be able to (a) understand the characteristics and concepts underlying random- and mixed-effects ANOVA models, (b) determine and interpret the results of random- and mixed-effects ANOVA models, and (c) understand and evaluate the assumptions of random- and mixed-effects ANOVA models.

5.1 One-Factor Random-Effects Model

Through the previous chapters, we have learned about many statistical procedures as Marie has assisted others and conducted studies of her own. What is in store for Marie now?

For the past few chapters, we have followed Marie, a graduate student enrolled in an educational research program who, as part of her independent study course, examined various questions related to measures drawn from students enrolled in statistics courses. Knowing the success that Marie achieved in analysis of data from her independent study course, Marie's faculty advisor feels confident that Marie can assist another faculty member at the university. Marie is working with Mark, the coordinator of the English program. Mark has conducted an experiment in which eight students were randomly assigned to one of two instructors. Each student was then assessed on writing by four raters. Mark wants to know the following: if there is a mean difference in writing based on instructor, if there is a mean difference in writing based on rater, and if there is a mean difference in writing based on the rater by instructor interaction. The research questions presented to Mark from Marie's include the following:

- *Is there a mean difference in writing based on instructor?*
- *Is there a mean difference in writing based on rater?*
- *Is there a mean difference in writing based on rater by instructor?*

With one between-subjects independent variable (i.e., instructor) and one within-subjects factor (i.e., rating on writing task), Marie determines that a two-factor split-plot ANOVA is the best statistical procedure to use to answer Mark's question. Her next task is to assist Mark in analyzing the data.

This section describes the distinguishing characteristics of the one-factor random-effects ANOVA model, the linear model, the ANOVA summary table and expected mean squares, assumptions and their violation, and multiple comparison procedures (MCPs).

5.1.1 Characteristics of the Model

The characteristics of the one-factor *fixed-effects* ANOVA model have already been covered in Chapter 1. These characteristics include (a) one factor (or independent variable) with two or more levels, (b) all levels of the factor of interest are included in the design (i.e., a fixed-effects factor), (c) subjects are randomly assigned to one level of the factor, and (d) the dependent variable is measured at least at the interval level. Thus, the overall design is a fixed-effects model, where there is one factor and the individuals respond to only one level of the factor. If individuals respond to more than one level of the factor, then this is a repeated measures design, as shown later in this chapter.

The characteristics of the one-factor *random-effects* ANOVA model are the same with one obvious exception. This has to do with the selection of the levels of the factor. In the fixed-effects case, researchers select all of the levels of interest because they are only interested in making generalizations (or inferences) about those particular levels. Thus, in replications of this design, each replicate would use precisely the same levels. Considering analyses that are conducted on individuals, examples of factors that are typically fixed include SES, gender, specific types of drug treatment, age group, weight, or marital status.

In the random-effects case, researchers randomly select levels from the population of levels because they are interested in making generalizations (or inferences) about the entire population of levels, not merely those that have been sampled. Thus, in replications of this design, each replicate need not have the same levels included. The concept of random selection of factor levels from the population of levels is the same as the random selection of subjects from the population. Here the researcher is making an inference from the sampled levels to the population of levels, instead of making an inference from the sample of individuals to the population of individuals. In a random-effects design then, a random sample of factor levels is selected in the same way as a random sample of individuals is selected.

For instance, a researcher interested in teacher effectiveness may have randomly sampled history teachers (i.e., the independent variable) from the population of history teachers in a particular school district. Generalizations can then be made about all history teachers in that school district that could have been sampled. Other examples of factors that are typically random include *randomly selected* classrooms, types of medication, observers or raters, time (seconds, minutes, hours, days, weeks, etc.), animals, students, or schools. It should be noted that in educational settings, the random selection of schools, classes, teachers, and/or students is not often possible as that decision is not under the researcher's control. Here we would need to consider such factors as fixed rather than random effects.

 ### 5.1.2 ANOVA Model

The one-factor ANOVA random-effects model is written in terms of population parameters as

$$Y_{ij} = \mu + a_j + \varepsilon_{ij}$$

where
Y_{ij} is the observed score on the dependent variable for individual i in level j of factor A
μ is the overall or grand population mean
a_j is the random effect for level j of factor A
ε_{ij} is the random residual error for individual i in level j

The residual error can be due to individual differences, measurement error, and/or other factors not under investigation. Note that we use a_j to designate the random effects to differentiate them from α_j in the fixed-effects model.

Because the random-effects model consists of only a sample of the effects from the population, the sum of the sampled effects is not necessarily 0. For instance, we may select a sample having only positive effects (e.g., all very effective teachers). If the entire population of effects were examined, then the sum of those effects would indeed be 0.

For the one-factor *random-effects* ANOVA model, the hypotheses for testing the effect of factor A are written in terms of equality of the variances among the means of the random levels, as follows (i.e., the means for each level are about the same, and, thus, the variability among those means is about 0). It should be noted that the sign for the alternative hypothesis is "greater than," reflecting the fact that the variance cannot be negative:

$$H_0: \sigma_a^2 = 0$$

$$H_1: \sigma_a^2 > 0$$

Recall for the one-factor *fixed-effects* ANOVA model that the hypotheses for testing the effect of factor A are written in terms of equality of the means of the groups (as presented here):

$$H_0: \mu_{.1} = \mu_{.2} = \ldots = \mu_{.J}$$

$$H_1: \text{not all the } \mu_{.j} \text{ are equal}$$

This reflects the difference in the inferences made in the random- and fixed-effects models. In the fixed-effects case, the null hypothesis is about specific population means; in the random-effects case, the null hypothesis is about variation among the entire population of means. As becomes evident, the difference in the models is reflected in the MCPs. *random effects hypothesis*

5.1.3 ANOVA Summary Table and Expected Mean Squares

Here there are very few differences between the one-factor random-effects and one-factor fixed-effects models. The sources of variation are still A (or between), within, and total. The sums of squares, degrees of freedom, mean squares, F test statistic, and critical value are determined in the same way as in the fixed-effects case. Obviously then, the ANOVA summary table looks the same as well. Using the example from Chapter 1, assuming the model is now a random-effects model, we obtain a test statistic $F = 6.8177$, which is again significant at the .05 level.

As in Chapters 1 and 3, the formation of a proper F ratio is related to the expected mean squares. If H_0 is actually *true*, then the *expected mean squares* are as follows:

$$E(MS_A) = \sigma_\varepsilon^2$$

$$E(MS_{\text{with}}) = \sigma_\varepsilon^2$$

• sources of variation are the same
• SS, df, ms, f + critical value are the same

and thus the ratio of expected mean squares is as follows:

$$\frac{E(MS_A)}{E(MS_{\text{with}})} = 1$$

where
the expected value of F is $E(F) = df_{\text{with}}/(df_{\text{with}} - 2)$
σ_ε^2 is the population variance of the residual errors

If H_0 is actually *false*, then the expected mean squares are as follows:

$$E(MS_A) = \sigma_\varepsilon^2 + n\sigma_a^2$$

$$E(MS_{\text{with}}) = \sigma_\varepsilon^2$$

and thus the ratio of the expected mean squares is as follows:

$$\frac{E(MS_A)}{E(MS_{\text{with}})} > 1$$

where $E(F) > df_{\text{with}}/(df_{\text{with}} - 2)$ and σ_a^2 is the population variance of the levels of factor A. Thus, the important part of $E(MS_A)$ is the magnitude of the second term, $n\sigma_a^2$.

As in previous ANOVA models, the proper F ratio should be formed as follows:

$$F = (\text{systematic variability} + \text{error variability})/(\text{error variability})$$

For the one-factor random-effects model, the only appropriate F ratio is MS_A/MS_{with} because it does serve to isolate the systematic variability (i.e., the variability between the levels or groups in factor A, the independent variable). That is, the within term must be utilized as the error term in the F ratio.

5.1.4 Assumptions and Violation of Assumptions

In Chapter 1, we described the assumptions for the one-factor fixed-effects model. The assumptions are nearly the same for the one-factor random-effects model, and we need not devote much attention to them here. In short, the assumptions are again concerned with the distribution of the dependent variable scores, specifically that scores are random and independent, coming from normally distributed populations with equal population variances. The effect of assumption violations and how to deal with them have been thoroughly discussed in Chapter 1 (although see Wilcox, 1996, 2003, for alternative procedures when variances are unequal).

Additional assumptions must be made for the random-effects model. These assumptions deal with the effects for the levels of the independent variable, the a_j. First, here are a few words about the a_j. The random group effects a_j are computed, in the population, by the following:

$$a_j = \mu_{\cdot j} - \mu_{\cdot\cdot}$$

For example, a_3 represents the effect for being a member of group 3. If the overall mean $\mu_{\cdot\cdot}$ is 60 and the mean of group 3 (i.e., $\mu_{\cdot 3}$) is 100, then the group effect would be

$$a_3 = \mu_{\cdot 3} - \mu_{\cdot\cdot} = 100 - 60 = 40$$

In other words, the effect for being a member of group 3 is an increase of 40 points over the overall mean. The assumptions are that the a_j group effects are randomly and independently sampled from the normally distributed population of group effects, with a population mean of 0 and a population variance of σ_a^2. Stated another way, there is a population of group effects out there from which we are taking a random sample. For example, with teacher as the factor of interest, we are interested in examining the effectiveness of teachers as measured by academic performance of students in their class. We take a random sample of teachers from the population of second-grade teachers. For these teachers, we measure their effectiveness in the classroom via student performance and generate an effect for each teacher (i.e., the a_j). These effects indicate the extent to which a particular teacher is more or less effective than the population average of teachers. Their effects are known as random effects as the teachers are randomly selected. In selecting teachers, each teacher is selected independently of all other teachers to prevent a biased sample.

TABLE 5.1

Assumptions and Effects of Violations: One-Factor Random-Effects Model

Assumption	Effect of Assumption Violation
Independence	• Increased likelihood of a Type I and/or Type II error in F • Affects standard errors of means and inferences about those means
Homogeneity of variance	• Bias in SS_{with}; increased likelihood of a Type I and/or Type II error • Small effect with equal or nearly equal n's; otherwise effect decreases as n increases
Normality	• Minimal effect with equal or nearly equal n's

The effects of the violation of the assumptions about the a_j are the same as with the dependent variable scores. The F test is quite robust to nonnormality of the a_j terms and unequal variances of the a_j terms. However, the F test is quite sensitive to nonindependence among the a_j terms, with no known solutions. A summary of the assumptions and the effects of their violation for the one-factor random-effects model is presented in Table 5.1.

5.1.5 Multiple Comparison Procedures

Let us think for a moment about the use of MCPs for the random-effects model. In general, the researcher is not usually interested in making inferences about just the levels of A that were sampled. Thus, estimation of the a_j terms does not provide us with any information about the a_j terms that were not sampled. Also, the a_j terms cannot be summarized by their mean, as they do not necessarily sum to 0 for the levels sampled, only for the population of levels.

5.2 Two-Factor Random-Effects Model

In this section, we describe the distinguishing characteristics of the two-factor random-effects ANOVA model, the linear model, the ANOVA summary table and expected mean squares, assumptions of the model and their violation, and MCPs.

5.2.1 Characteristics of the Model

The characteristics of the one-factor random-effects ANOVA model have already been covered in this chapter, and of the two-factor fixed-effects model, in Chapter 3. Here we extend and combine these characteristics to form the two-factor random-effects model. These characteristics include (a) two factors (or independent variables) each with two or more levels, (b) the levels of each of the factors are randomly sampled from the population of levels (i.e., two random-effects factors), (c) subjects are randomly assigned to one combination of the levels of the two factors, and (d) the dependent variable is measured at least at the interval level. Thus, the overall design is a random-effects model, with two factors, and the individuals respond to only one combination of the levels of the two factors (note that this is not a popular model in education and the behavioral sciences; in factorial designs, we typically see a random-effects factor with a fixed-effects factor). If individuals respond to more than one combination of the levels of the two factors, then this is a repeated measures design (discussed later in this chapter).

5.2.2 ANOVA Model

The two-factor ANOVA random-effects model is written in terms of population parameters as

$$Y_{ijk} = \mu + a_j + b_k + (ab)_{jk} + \varepsilon_{ijk}$$

where
  Y_{ijk} is the observed score on the dependent variable for individual i in level j of factor A
      and level k of factor B (or in the jk cell)
  μ is the overall or grand population mean (i.e., regardless of cell designation)
  a_j is the random effect for level j of factor A (row effect)
  b_k is the random effect for level k of factor B (column effect)
  $(ab)_{jk}$ is the interaction random effect for the combination of level j of factor A and level k
      of factor B ·
  ε_{ijk} is the random residual error for individual i in cell jk

The residual error can be due to individual differences, measurement error, and/or other factors not under investigation. Note that we use a_j, b_k, and $(ab)_{jk}$ to designate the random effects to differentiate them from the α_j, β_k, and $(\alpha\beta)_{jk}$ in the fixed-effects model. Finally, there is no requirement that the sum of the main or interaction effects is equal to 0 as only a sample of these effects are taken from the population of effects.

There are three sets of hypotheses, one for each of the two main effects and one for the interaction effect. The null and alternative hypotheses, respectively, for testing the main effect of factor A (i.e., independent variable A) follows. The null hypothesis tests whether the variance among the means for the random effect of independent variable A is equal to 0 (i.e., the means for each level of factor A are about the same; thus, the variability among those means is about 0). It should be noted that the sign for the alternative hypothesis is "greater than," reflecting the fact that the variance cannot be negative:

$$H_{01}: \sigma_a^2 = 0$$

$$H_{11}: \sigma_a^2 > 0$$

The hypotheses for testing the main effect of factor B (i.e., independent variable B) similarly test whether the variance among the means for the random effect of independent variable B is equal to 0 (i.e., the means for each level of factor B are about the same, and, thus, the variability among those means is about 0). It should be noted that the sign for the alternative hypothesis is "greater than," reflecting the fact that the variance cannot be negative:

$$H_{02}: \sigma_b^2 = 0$$

$$H_{12}: \sigma_b^2 > 0$$

Finally, the hypotheses for testing the interaction effect are presented next. In this case, the null hypothesis tests whether the variance among the means for the interaction of the random effects of factors A and B is equal to 0 (i.e., the means for each AB cell are about the same, and, thus, the variability among those means is about 0). It should be noted that the sign for the alternative hypothesis is "greater than," reflecting the fact that the variance cannot be negative:

$$
\begin{cases}
H_{03}: \sigma_{ab}^2 = 0 \\[2em]
H_{13}: \sigma_{ab}^2 > 0
\end{cases}
$$

These hypotheses again reflect the difference in the inferences made in the random- and fixed-effects models. In the fixed-effects case, the null hypotheses are about means, whereas in the random-effects case, the null hypotheses are about *variation* among the means.

5.2.3 ANOVA Summary Table and Expected Mean Squares (DIFFERENCES) — F and critical value)

Here there are very few differences between the two-factor fixed-effects and random-effects models. The sources of variation are still A, B, AB, within, and total. The sums of squares, degrees of freedom, and mean squares are determined the same as in the fixed-effects case. However, the F test statistics are different due to the expected mean squares, as are the critical values used. The F test statistics are formed for the test of factor A (i.e., the main effect for independent variable A) as follows:

$$
\begin{cases}
F = \dfrac{MS_A}{MS_{AB}}
\end{cases}
$$

for the test of factor B (i.e., the main effect for independent variable B) as presented here:

$$
F = \frac{MS_B}{MS_{AB}}
$$

and for the test of the AB interaction as indicated:

$$
F = \frac{MS_{AB}}{MS_{with}}
$$

Recall that in the fixed-effects model, the MS_{with} was used as the error term for all three hypotheses. However, in the random-effects model, the MS_{with} is used as the error term *only* for the test of the interaction. The MS_{AB} is used as the error term for the tests of both main effects. The critical values used are those based on the degrees of freedom for the numerator and denominator of each hypothesis tested. Thus, using the example from Chapter 3, assuming that the model is now a random-effects model, we obtain the following as our test statistic for the test of factor A (i.e., the main effect for independent variable A):

$$F_A = \frac{MS_A}{MS_{AB}} = \frac{246.1979}{7.2813} = 33.8124$$

for the test of factor B, the test statistic is computed as follows:

$$F_B = \frac{MS_B}{MS_{AB}} = \frac{712.5313}{7.2813} = 97.8577$$

and for the test of the AB interaction, we find the following:

$$F_{AB} = \frac{MS_{AB}}{MS_{with}} = \frac{7.2813}{11.5313} = 0.6314$$

The critical value for the test of factor A is found in the F table of Table A.4 as $_\alpha F_{J-1,\,(J-1)(K-1)}$, which for the example is $_{.05}F_{3,3} = 9.28$, and is significant at the .05 level. The critical value for the test of factor B is found in the F table as $_\alpha F_{K-1,(J-1)(K-1)}$, which for the example is $_{.05}F_{1,3} = 10.13$, and is significant at the .05 level. The critical value for the test of the interaction is found in the F table as $_\alpha F_{(J-1)(K-1),N-JK}$, which for the example is $_{.05}F_{3,24} = 3.01$, and is not significant at the .05 level. It just so happens for the example data that the results for the random- and fixed-effects models are the same. This will not always be the case.

The formation of the proper F ratios is again related to the expected mean squares. Recall that our hypotheses for the two-factor random-effects model are based on variation among the means of the random effects (rather than the means as seen in the fixed-effects case). If H_0 is actually *true* (i.e., there is no variation among the means of the random effects), then the *expected mean squares* are as follows:

$$E(MS_A) = \sigma_\varepsilon^2$$

$$E(MS_B) = \sigma_\varepsilon^2$$

$$E(MS_{AB}) = \sigma_\varepsilon^2$$

$$E(MS_{with}) = \sigma_\varepsilon^2$$

where σ_ε^2 is the population variance of the residual errors.

If H_0 is actually *false* (i.e., there *is* variation among the means of the random effects), then the expected mean squares are as follows:

$$E(MS_A) = \sigma_\varepsilon^2 + n\sigma_{ab}^2 + Kn\sigma_a^2$$

$$E(MS_B) = \sigma_\varepsilon^2 + n\sigma_{ab}^2 + Jn\sigma_b^2$$

$$E(MS_{AB}) = \sigma_\varepsilon^2 + n\sigma_{ab}^2$$

$$E(MS_{with}) = \sigma_\varepsilon^2$$

where σ_a^2, σ_b^2, and σ_{ab}^2 are the population variances of A, B, and AB, respectively.

As in previous ANOVA models, the proper *F* ratio should be formed as follows:

$$F = (\text{systematic variability} + \text{error variability}) / (\text{error variability})$$

For the two-factor random-effects model, the appropriate error term for the main effects is MS_{AB} and the appropriate error term for the interaction effect is MS_{with}.

5.2.4 Assumptions and Violation of Assumptions

Previously we described the assumptions for the one-factor random-effects model. The assumptions are nearly the same for the two-factor random-effects model, and we need not devote much attention to them here. As before, the assumptions are concerned with the distribution of the dependent variable scores, and of the random-effects (sampled levels of the independent variables, the a_j, b_k, and their interaction $(ab)_{jk}$). However, there are a few new wrinkles. Little is known about the effect of unequal variances (i.e., heteroscedasticity) or dependence (i.e., violation of the assumption of independence) for this random-effects model, although we expect the effects to be the same as for the fixed-effects model. For violation of the normality assumption, effects are known to be substantial. A summary of the assumptions and the effects of their violation for the two-factor random-effects model is presented in Table 5.2.

5.2.5 Multiple Comparison Procedures

The story of multiple comparisons for the two-factor random-effects model is the same as that for the one-factor random-effects model. In general, the researcher is not usually interested in making inferences about just the levels of A, B, or AB that were sampled, and thus performing MCPs in a two-factor random-effects model is a moot point. Thus, estimation of the a_j, b_k, or $(ab)_{jk}$ terms does not provide us with any information about the a_j, b_k, or $(ab)_{jk}$ terms that were not sampled. Also, the a_j, b_k, or $(ab)_{jk}$ terms cannot be summarized by their means as they will not necessarily sum to 0 for the levels sampled, only for the population of levels.

TABLE 5.2

Assumptions and Effects of Violations: Two-Factor Random-Effects Model

Assumption	Effect of Assumption Violation
Independence	Little is known about the effects of dependence; however, based on the fixed-effects model, we might expect the following:
	• Increased likelihood of a Type I and/or Type II error in *F* • Affects standard errors of means and inferences about those means
Homogeneity of variance	Little is known about the effects of heteroscedasticity; however, based on the fixed-effects model, we might expect the following:
	• Bias in SS_{with} • Increased likelihood of a Type I and/or Type II error • Small effect with equal or nearly equal *n*'s • Otherwise effect decreases as *n* increases
Normality	• Minimal effect with equal or nearly equal *n*'s • Otherwise substantial effects

5.3 Two-Factor Mixed-Effects Model

This section describes the distinguishing characteristics of the two-factor *mixed-effects* ANOVA model, the linear model, the ANOVA summary table and expected mean squares, assumptions of the model and their violation, and MCPs.

5.3.1 Characteristics of the Model

The characteristics of the two-factor random-effects ANOVA model have already been covered in the preceding section, and of the two-factor fixed-effects model, in Chapter 3. Here we combine these characteristics to form the two-factor mixed-effects model. These characteristics include (a) two factors (or independent variables) each with two or more levels, (b) the levels for one of the factors are randomly sampled from the population of levels (i.e., the random-effects factor) and all of the levels of interest for the second factor are included in the design (i.e., the fixed-effects factor), (c) subjects are randomly selected and assigned to one combination of the levels of the two factors, and (d) the dependent variable is measured at least at the interval level. Thus, the overall design is a mixed-effects model, with one fixed-effects factor and one random-effects factor, and individuals respond to only one combination of the levels of the two factors. If individuals respond to more than one combination, then this is a repeated measures design.

5.3.2 ANOVA Model

There are actually two variations of the two-factor mixed-effects model, one where factor A is fixed and factor B is random and the other where factor A is random and factor B is fixed. The labeling of a factor as A or B is arbitrary, so we only consider the former variation where A is fixed and B is random. For the latter variation, merely switch the labels of the factors. The two-factor ANOVA mixed-effects model is written in terms of population parameters as

$$Y_{ijk} = \mu + \alpha_j + b_k + (\alpha b)_{jk} + \varepsilon_{ijk}$$

where
  Y_{ijk} is the observed score on the dependent variable for individual i in level j of factor A and level k of factor B (or in the jk cell)
  μ is the overall or grand population mean (i.e., regardless of cell designation)
  α_j is the fixed effect for level j of factor A (row effect)
  b_k is the random effect for level k of factor B (column effect)
  $(\alpha b)_{jk}$ is the interaction mixed effect for the combination of level j of factor A and level k of factor B
  ε_{ijk} is the random residual error for individual i in cell jk

The residual error can be due to individual differences, measurement error, and/or other factors not under investigation. Note that we use b_k and $(\alpha b)_{jk}$ to designate the random and mixed effects, respectively, to differentiate them from β_k and $(\alpha\beta)_{jk}$ in the fixed-effects model.

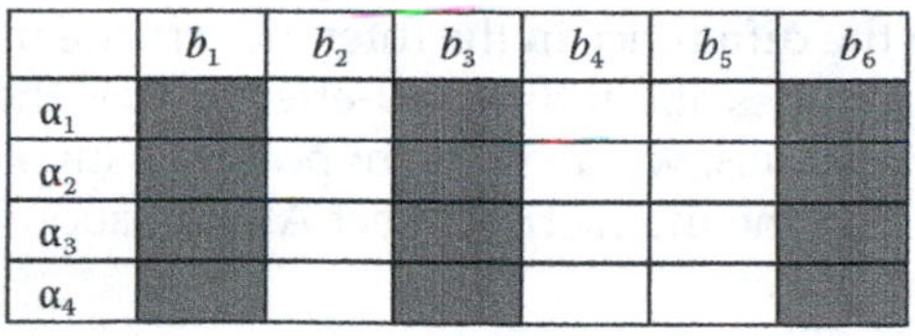

	b_1	b_2	b_3	b_4	b_5	b_6
α_1						
α_2						
α_3						
α_4						

FIGURE 5.1
Conditions for the two-factor mixed-effects model: although all four levels of factor A are selected by the researcher (A is fixed), only three of the six levels of factor B are selected (B is random). If the levels of B selected are 1, 3, and 6, then the design will only consist of the shaded cells. In each cell of the design are row, column, and cell effects. If we sum these effects for a given column, then the effects will sum to 0. If we sum these effects for a given row, then the effects will not sum to 0 (due to missing cells).

As shown in Figure 5.1, due to the nature of the mixed-effects model, only some of the columns are randomly selected for inclusion in the design. Each cell of the design will include row (α), column (b), and interaction (αb) effects. With an equal n's model, if we sum these effects for a given column, then the effects will sum to 0. However, if we sum these effects for a given row, then the effects will not sum to 0, as some columns were not sampled.

The null and alternative hypotheses, respectively, for testing the effect of factor A are presented as follows. These hypotheses reflect testing the equality of means of the levels of independent variable A (the fixed effect):

$$H_{01}: \mu_{.1.} = \mu_{.2.} = \ldots = \mu_{.J.}$$

$$H_{11}: \text{not all the } \mu_{.j.} \text{ are equal}$$

The hypotheses for testing the effect of factor B, the random effect, follow. The null hypothesis tests whether the variance among the means for the random effect of independent variable B is equal to 0 (i.e., the means for each level of factor B are about the same, and, thus, the variability among those means is about 0). It should be noted that the sign for the alternative hypothesis is "greater than," reflecting the fact that the variance cannot be negative:

$$H_{02}: \sigma_b^2 = 0$$

$$H_{12}: \sigma_b^2 > 0$$

Finally, the hypotheses for testing the interaction effect are presented next. In this case, the null hypothesis tests whether the variance among the means for the interaction of the random effects of factors A and B is equal to 0 (i.e., the means for each AB cell are about the same, and, thus, the variability among those means is about 0). It should be noted that the sign for the alternative hypothesis is "greater than," reflecting the fact that the variance cannot be negative:

$$H_{03}: \sigma_{\alpha b}^2 = 0$$

$$H_{13}: \sigma_{\alpha b}^2 > 0$$

These hypotheses reflect the difference in the inferences made in the mixed-effects model. Here we see that the hypotheses about the fixed-effect A (i.e., the main effect for independent variable A) are about *means*, whereas the hypotheses involving the random-effect B (i.e., the main effect of B and the interaction effect AB) are about *variation among the means* as these involve a random effect.

5.3.3 ANOVA Summary Table and Expected Mean Squares

There are very few differences between the two-factor fixed-effects, random-effects, and mixed-effects models. The sources of variation for the mixed-effects model are again A (the fixed effect), B (the random effect), AB (the interaction effect), within, and total. The sums of squares, degrees of freedom, and mean squares are determined the same as in the fixed-effects case. However, the F test statistics are different in each of these models, as well as the critical values used. The F test statistics are formed for the test of factor A, the fixed effect, as seen here:

$$F_A = \frac{MS_A}{MS_{AB}}$$

for the test of factor B, the random effect, is computed as follows:

$$F_B = \frac{MS_B}{MS_{\text{with}}}$$

and for the test of the AB interaction, the mixed effect, as indicated here:

$$F_{AB} = \frac{MS_{AB}}{MS_{\text{with}}}$$

Recall that in the fixed-effects model, the MS_{with} is used as the error term for all three hypotheses. However, in the random-effects model, the MS_{with} is used as the error term only for the test of the interaction, and the MS_{AB} is used as the error term for the tests of both main effects. Finally, in the mixed-effects model, the MS_{with} is used as the error term for the test of factor B (the random effect) and the interaction (i.e., AB), whereas the MS_{AB} is used as the error term for the test of factor A (the fixed effect). The critical values used are those based on the degrees of freedom for the numerator and denominator of each hypothesis tested.

Thus, using the example from Chapter 3, let us assume the model is now a mixed-effects model where factor A, the fixed effect, is the level of attractiveness (four categories). Factor B, the random effect, is time of day (two randomly selected categories). We obtain as our test statistic for the test of factor A, the fixed effect of level of attractiveness, as follows:

$$F_A = \frac{MS_A}{MS_{AB}} = \frac{246.1979}{7.2813} = 33.8124$$

for the test of factor B, the random effect of time of day, the test statistic is computed as follows:

$$F_B = \frac{MS_B}{MS_{with}} = \frac{712.5313}{11.5313} = 61.7911$$

and for the test of the AB (fixed by random effect, levels of attractiveness by time of day) interaction, we find a test statistic as follows:

$$F_{AB} = \frac{MS_{AB}}{MS_{with}} = \frac{7.2813}{11.5313} = 0.6314$$

The critical value for the test of factor A (the fixed effect, level of attractiveness) is found in the F table as $_\alpha F_{J-1,\,(J-1)(K-1)}$, which for the example is $_{.05}F_{3,3} = 9.28$, and is statistically significant at the .05 level. The critical value for the test of factor B (the random effect, time of day) is found in the F table as $_\alpha F_{K-1,N-JK}$, which for the example is $_{.05}F_{1,24} = 4.26$, and is significant at the .05 level. The critical value for the test of the interaction between level of attractiveness and time of day is found in the F table as $_\alpha F_{(J-1)(K-1),\,N-JK}$, which for the example is $_{.05}F_{3,24} = 3.01$, and is not significant at the .05 level. It just so happens for the example data that the results for the mixed-, random-, and fixed-effects models are the same. This is not always the case.

The formation of the proper F ratio is again related to the expected mean squares. If H_0 is actually *true* (i.e., the variance among the means is 0), then the *expected mean squares* are as follows:

$$E(MS_A) = \sigma_\varepsilon^2$$

$$E(MS_B) = \sigma_\varepsilon^2$$

$$E(MS_{AB}) = \sigma_\varepsilon^2$$

$$E(MS_{with}) = \sigma_\varepsilon^2$$

where σ_ε^2 is the population variance of the residual errors.

If H_0 is actually *false* (the variance among the means is *not* equal to 0), then the expected mean squares are as follows:

$$E(MS_A) = \sigma_\varepsilon^2 + n\sigma_{ab}^2 + Kn\left[\sum_{j=1}^{J} \alpha_j^2/(J-1)\right]$$

$$E(MS_B) = \sigma_\varepsilon^2 + Jn\sigma_b^2$$

$$E(MS_{AB}) = \sigma_\varepsilon^2 + n\sigma_{ab}^2$$

$$E(MS_{with}) = \sigma_\varepsilon^2$$

where all terms have been previously defined.

As in previous ANOVA models, the proper F ratio should be formed as follows:

$$F = (\text{systematic variability} + \text{error variability}) / (\text{error variability})$$

For the two-factor mixed-effects model, MS_{AB} must be used as the error term for the test of A, and MS_{with} must be used as the error term for the test of B and for the interaction test.

5.3.4 Assumptions and Violation of Assumptions

Previously we described the assumptions for the two-factor random-effects model. The assumptions are nearly the same for the two-factor mixed-effects model, and we need not devote much attention to them here. As before, the assumptions are concerned with the distribution of the dependent variable scores and of the random effects. However, note that not much is known about the effects of dependence or heteroscedasticity for random effects, although we expect the effects are the same as for the fixed-effects case. A summary of the assumptions and the effects of their violation for the two-factor mixed-effects model is presented in Table 5.3.

5.3.5 Multiple Comparison Procedures

For multiple comparisons in the two-factor mixed-effects model, the researcher is not usually interested in making inferences about just the levels of the random-effects factor (i.e., B) or the interaction (i.e., AB) that were randomly sampled. Thus, estimation of the b_k or $(\alpha b)_{jk}$ terms does not provide us with any information about the b_k or $(\alpha b)_{jk}$ terms not sampled. Also, the b_k or $(\alpha b)_{jk}$ terms cannot be summarized by their means as they will not necessarily sum to 0 for the levels sampled, only for the population of levels. However, inferences about the fixed-factor A can be made in the same way they were made for the two-factor fixed-effects model. We have already used the example data to look at some MCPs in Chapter 3.

TABLE 5.3

Assumptions and Effects of Violations: Two-Factor Mixed-Effects Model

Assumption	Effect of Assumption Violation
Independence	Little is known about the effects of dependence; however, based on the fixed-effects model, we might expect the following: • Increased likelihood of a Type I and/or Type II error in F • Affects standard errors of means and inferences about those means
Homogeneity of variance	Little is known about the effects of heteroscedasticity; however, based on the fixed-effects model, we might expect the following: • Bias in SS_{with} • Increased likelihood of a Type I and/or Type II error • Small effect with equal or nearly equal n's • Otherwise effect decreases as n increases
Normality	• Minimal effect with equal or nearly equal n's • Otherwise substantial effects

This concludes our discussion of random- and mixed-effects models for the one- and two-factor designs. For three-factor designs, see Keppel (1982) or Keppel and Wickens (2004). In the major statistical software, the analysis of random effects can be treated as follows: in SAS PROC general linear model (GLM), use the RANDOM statement to designate random effects; in SPSS GLM, random effects can also be designated, either in the point-and-click mode (by using the "Random Factor(s)" box) or in the syntax mode to designate random effects.

5.4 One-Factor Repeated Measures Design

In this section, we describe the distinguishing characteristics of the one-factor repeated measures ANOVA model, the layout of the data, the linear model, assumptions of the model and their violation, the ANOVA summary table and expected mean squares, MCPs, alternative ANOVA procedures, and an example.

5.4.1 Characteristics of the Model

The one-factor repeated measures model is the logical extension to the dependent t test. Although in the dependent t test there are only two measurements for each subject (e.g., the same individuals measured prior to an intervention and then again after an intervention), in the one-factor repeated measures model, two *or more* measurements can be examined. The characteristics of the one-factor repeated measures ANOVA model are somewhat similar to the one-factor fixed-effects model, yet there are a number of obvious exceptions. The first unique characteristic has to do with the fact that each subject responds to each level of factor A. This is in contrast to the nonrepeated case where each subject is exposed to only one level of factor A. This design is often referred to as a **within-subjects design**, as each subject responds to each level of factor A. Thus, subjects serve as their own controls such that individual differences are taken into account. This was not the case in any of the previously discussed ANOVA models. As a result, subjects' scores are not independent across the levels of factor A. Compare this design to the one-factor fixed-effects model where total variation was decomposed into variation due to A (or between) and due to the residual (or within). In the one-factor repeated measures design, residual variation is further decomposed into variation due to subjects and variation due to the interaction between A and subjects. The reduction in the residual sum of squares yields a more powerful design as well as more precision in estimating the effects of A and thus is more economical in that less subjects are necessary than in previously discussed models (Murphy, Myors, & Wolach, 2008).

The one-factor repeated measures design is also a mixed model. The subjects factor is a random effect, whereas the A factor is almost always a fixed effect. For example, if time is the fixed effect, then the researcher can examine phenomena over time. Finally, the one-factor repeated measures design is similar in some ways to the two-factor mixed-effects design except with one subject per cell. In other words, the one-factor repeated measures design is really a special case of the two-factor mixed-effects design with $n = 1$ per cell. Unequal n's can only happen when subjects miss the administration of one or more levels of factor A.

On the down side, the repeated measures design includes some risk of carryover effects from one level of A to another because each subject responds to all levels of A. As examples of the carryover effect, subjects' performance may be altered due to fatigue (decreased performance), practice (increased performance), or sensitization (increased performance) effects. These effects may be minimized by (a) counterbalancing the order of administration of the levels of A so that each subject does not receive the same order of the levels of A (this can also minimize problems with the compound symmetry assumption; see subsequent discussion), (b) allowing some time to pass between the administration of the levels of A, or (c) matching or blocking similar subjects with the assumption of subjects within a block being randomly assigned to a level of A. This last method is a type of randomized block design (see Chapter 6).

5.4.2 Layout of Data

The layout of the data for the one-factor repeated measures model is shown in Table 5.4. Here we see the columns designated as the levels of factor A and the rows as the subject. Thus, the columns or "levels" of factor A represent the different measurements. An example is measuring children on reading performance before, immediately after, and 6 months after they participate in a reading intervention. Row, column, and overall means are also shown in Table 5.4, although the subject means are seldom of any utility (and thus are not reported in research studies). Here you see that the layout of the data looks the same as the two-factor model, although there is only one observation per cell.

5.4.3 ANOVA Model

The one-factor repeated measures ANOVA model is written in terms of population parameters as

$$Y_{ij} = \mu + \alpha_j + s_i + (s\alpha)_{ij} + \varepsilon_{ij}$$

where

Y_{ij} is the observed score on the dependent variable for individual i responding to level j of factor A
μ is the overall or grand population mean
α_j is the fixed effect for level j of factor A
s_i is the random effect for subject i of the subject factor
$(s\alpha)_{ij}$ is the interaction between subject i and level j
ε_{ij} is the random residual error for individual i in level j

The residual error can be due to measurement error and/or other factors not under investigation. From the model, you can see this is similar to the two-factor model only with one

TABLE 5.4

Layout for the One-Factor Repeated Measures ANOVA

Level of Factor S	Level of Factor A (Repeated Factor)				Row Mean
	1	2	...	J	
1	Y_{11}	Y_{12}	...	Y_{1J}	$\bar{Y}_{1.}$
2	Y_{21}	Y_{22}	...	Y_{2J}	$\bar{Y}_{2.}$
...	...	...	...	...	...
n	Y_{n1}	Y_{n2}		Y_{nJ}	$\bar{Y}_{n.}$
Column mean	$\bar{Y}_{.1}$	$\bar{Y}_{.2}$	...	$\bar{Y}_{.J}$	$\bar{Y}_{..}$

observation per cell. Also, the fixed effect is denoted by α and the random effect by s; thus, we have a mixed-effects model. Lastly, for the equal n's model, the effects for α and $s\alpha$ sum to 0 for each subject (or row).

The hypotheses for testing the effect of factor A are as follows. The null hypothesis indicates that the means for each measurement are the same:

$$H_{01}: \mu_{.1} = \mu_{.2} = \ldots = \mu_{.J}$$

$$H_{11}: \text{not all the } \mu_{.j} \text{ are equal}$$

The hypotheses are written in terms of means because factor A is a fixed effect (i.e., all sampled cases have been measured).

5.4.4 Assumptions and Violation of Assumptions

COMPOUND SYMMETRY

Previously we described the assumptions for the two-factor mixed-effects model. The assumptions are nearly the same for the one-factor repeated measures model (since it is similar to the two-factor mixed-effects model) and are again mainly concerned with the distribution of the dependent variable scores and of the random effects.

A new assumption is known as **compound symmetry** and states that the covariances between the scores of the subjects across the levels of the repeated factor A are constant. In other words, the covariances for all pairs of levels of the fixed factor are the same across the population of random effects (i.e., the subjects). The analysis of variance (ANOVA) is not particularly robust to a violation of this assumption. In particular, the assumption is often violated when factor A is time, as the relationship between adjacent levels of A is stronger than when the levels are farther apart. For example, consider the previous illustration of children measured in reading performance before, after, and 6 months after intervention. The means of the pre- and immediate post-reading performance will likely be more similar than the means of the pre- and 6 months post-reading performance. If the assumption is violated, three alternative procedures are available. The first is to limit the levels of factor A (i.e., the repeated measures factor) either to those that meet the assumption, or to limit the number of repeated measures to 2 (in which case, there would be only one covariance and thus nothing to assume). The second and more plausible alternative is to use adjusted F tests. These are reported shortly. The third is to use multivariate analysis of variance (MANOVA), MANOVA which makes no compound symmetry assumption, but is slightly less powerful. For readers interested in MANOVA, there are a number of excellent multivariate textbooks that can be referred to (e.g., Hair, Black, Babin, Anderson, & Tatham, 2006; Tabachnick & Fidell, 2007).

Huynh and Feldt (1970) showed that the compound symmetry assumption is a sufficient but not necessary condition for the validity of the F test. Thus, the F test may also be valid under less stringent conditions. The necessary and sufficient condition for the validity of the F test is known as **sphericity**. This assumes that the variance of the difference scores for each pair of factor levels is the same (e.g., with $J = 3$ levels, the variance of the difference score between levels 1 and 2 is the same as the variance of the difference score between levels 1 and 3, which is the same as the variance of the difference score between levels 2 and 3; thus, another type of homogeneity of variance assumption). Further discussion of sphericity is beyond the scope of this text (see Keppel, 1982; Kirk, 1982; or Myers & Well, 1995). A summary of the assumptions and the effects of their violation for the one-factor repeated measures design is presented in Table 5.5.

TABLE 5.5

Assumptions and Effects of Violations: One-Factor Repeated Measures Model

Assumption	Effect of Assumption Violation
Independence	Little is known about the effects of dependence; however, based on the fixed-effects model, we might expect the following: • Increased likelihood of a Type I and/or Type II error in F • Affects standard errors of means and inferences about those means
Homogeneity of variance	Little is known about the effects of heteroscedasticity; however, based on the fixed-effects model, we might expect the following: • Bias in SS_{SA} • Increased likelihood of a Type I and/or Type II error • Small effect with equal or nearly equal n's • Otherwise effect decreases as n increases
Normality	• Minimal effect with equal or nearly equal n's • Otherwise substantial effects
Sphericity	• F not particularly robust • Consider usual F test, Geisser–Greenhouse conservative F test, and adjusted (Huynh–Feldt) F test, if necessary

5.4.5 ANOVA Summary Table and Expected Mean Squares

The sources of variation for this model are similar to those for the two-factor model, except that there is no within-cell variation. The ANOVA summary table is shown in Table 5.6, where we see the following sources of variation: A (i.e., the repeated measure), subjects (denoted by S), the SA interaction, and total. The test of subject differences is of no real interest. Quite naturally, we expect there to be variation among the subjects. From the table, we see that although three mean square terms can be computed, only one F ratio results for the test of factor A; thus, the subjects effect cannot be tested anyway as there is no appropriate error term. This is subsequently shown through the expected mean squares.

Next we need to consider the sums of squares for the one-factor repeated measures model. If we take the total sum of squares and decompose it, we have

$$SS_{\text{total}} = SS_A + SS_S + SS_{SA}$$

These three terms can then be computed by statistical software. The degrees of freedom, mean squares, and F ratio are determined as shown in Table 5.6.

TABLE 5.6

One-Factor Repeated Measures ANOVA Summary Table

Source	SS	df	MS	F
A	SS_A	$J-1$	MS_A	MS_A/MS_{SA}
S	SS_S	$n-1$	MS_S	
SA	SS_{SA}	$(J-1)(n-1)$	MS_{SA}	
Total	SS_{total}	$N-1$		

The formation of the proper F ratio is again related to the expected mean squares. If H_0 is actually *true* (in other words, the means are the same for each of the measures), then the *expected mean squares* are as follows:

$$E(MS_A) = \sigma_\varepsilon^2$$

$$E(MS_S) = \sigma_\varepsilon^2$$

$$E(MS_{SA}) = \sigma_\varepsilon^2$$

where σ_ε^2 is the population variance of the residual errors.

If H_0 is actually *false* (i.e., the means are not the same for each of the measures), then the expected mean squares are as follows:

$$E(MS_A) = \sigma_\varepsilon^2 + \sigma_{s\alpha}^2 + n\left[\sum_{j=1}^{J} \alpha_j^2/(J-1)\right]$$

$$E(MS_S) = \sigma_\varepsilon^2 + J\sigma_s^2$$

$$E(MS_{SA}) = \sigma_\varepsilon^2 + \sigma_{s\alpha}^2$$

where σ_s^2 and $\sigma_{s\alpha}^2$ represent variability due to subjects and to the interaction of factor A and subjects, respectively, and other terms are as before.

As in previous ANOVA models, the proper F ratio should be formed as follows:

$$F = (\text{systematic variability} + \text{error variability})/(\text{error variability})$$

For the one-factor repeated measures model, MS_{SA} must be used as the error term for the test of A, and there is no appropriate error term for the test of S or the test of SA (although that is fine as we are not really interested in those tests anyway since they refer to the individual cases).

As noted earlier in the discussion of assumptions for this model, the F test is not very robust to violation of the compound symmetry assumption. This assumption is often violated in education and the behavioral sciences; consequently, statisticians have spent considerable time studying this problem. Research suggests that the following sequential procedure be used in the test of factor A. First, do the usual F test that is quite liberal in terms of rejecting H_0 too often. If H_0 is not rejected, then stop. If H_0 is rejected, then continue with step 2, which is to use the Geisser and Greenhouse (1958) conservative F test. For the model being considered here, the degrees of freedom for the F critical value are adjusted to be 1 and $n - 1$. If H_0 is rejected, then stop. This would indicate that both the liberal and conservative tests reached the same conclusion to reject H_0. If H_0 is not rejected, then the two tests did not reach the same conclusion, and a further test (a tiebreaker) should be undertaken. Thus, in step 3, an adjusted F test is conducted. The adjustment is known as Box's (1954b) correction (usually referred to as the Huynh and Feldt [1970] procedure). Here the numerator degrees of freedom are $(J - 1)\varepsilon$, and the denominator degrees of freedom are $(J - 1)(n - 1)\varepsilon$, where ε is a correction factor (not to be confused with the residual term ε). The correction factor is quite complex and is not shown here (see Keppel & Wickens, 2004; Myers, 1979; Myers & Well, 1995; or Wilcox, 1987). Most major statistical software conducts the Geisser–Greenhouse and Huynh–Feldt tests. The Huynh–Feldt test is recommended due to greater power (Keppel & Wickens, 2004; Myers & Well, 1995); thus, when available, you can simply use the Huynh–Feldt procedure rather than the previously recommended sequence.

5.4.6 Multiple Comparison Procedures

If the null hypothesis for repeated factor (i.e., factor A) is rejected and there are more than two levels of the factor, then the researcher may be interested in which means or combinations of means are different (in other words, which measurement means differ from one other). This could be assessed, as we have seen in previous chapters, by the use of some MCP. In general, most of the MCPs outlined in Chapter 2 can be used in the one-factor repeated measures model (see additional discussion in Keppel & Wickens, 2004; Mickey, Dunn, & Clark, 2004).

It has been shown that these MCPs are seriously affected by a violation of the compound symmetry assumption. In this situation, two alternatives are recommended. The first alternative is, rather than using the same error term for each contrast (i.e., MS_{SA}), to use a separate error term for each contrast tested. Then many of the MCPs previously covered in Chapter 2 can be used. This complicates matters considerably (see Keppel, 1982; Keppel & Wickens, 2004; or Kirk, 1982). A second alternative, recommended by Maxwell (1980) and Wilcox (1987), involves the use of multiple dependent t tests where the α level is adjusted much like the Bonferroni procedure. Maxwell concluded that this procedure is better than many of the other MCPs. For other similar procedures, see Hochberg and Tamhane (1987).

5.4.7 Alternative ANOVA Procedures (Friedman test)

There are several alternative procedures to the one-factor repeated measures ANOVA model. These include the Friedman (1937) test, as well as others, such as the Agresti and Pendergast (1986) test. The Friedman test, like the Kruskal–Wallis test, is a nonparametric procedure based on ranks. However, the Kruskal–Wallis test cannot be used in a repeated measures model as it assumes that the individual scores are independent. This is obviously not the case in the one-factor repeated measures model where each individual is exposed to all levels of factor A.

Let us outline how the Friedman test is conducted. First, scores are ranked within subject. For instance, if there are $J = 4$ levels of factor A, then the scores for each subject would be ranked from 1 to 4. From this, one can compute a mean ranking for each level of factor A. The null hypothesis essentially becomes a test of whether the mean rankings for the levels of A are equal. The test statistic is a χ^2 statistic. In the case of tied ranks, either the available ranks can be averaged, or a correction factor can be used as done with the Kruskal–Wallis test (see Chapter 1). The test statistic is compared to the critical value of $_{\alpha}\chi^2_{J-1}$ (see Table A.3). The null hypothesis that the mean rankings are the same for the levels of factor A will be rejected if the test statistic exceeds the critical value.

You may also recall from the Kruskal–Wallis test the problem with small n's in terms of the test statistic not being precisely distributed as χ^2. The same problem exists with the Friedman test when $J < 6$ and $n < 6$, so we suggest you consult the table of critical values in Marascuilo and McSweeney (1977, Table A-22, p. 521). The Friedman test, like the Kruskal–Wallis test, assumes that the population distributions have the same shape (although not necessarily normal) and variability and that the dependent measure is continuous. For a discussion of other alternative nonparametric procedures, see Agresti and Pendergast (1986), Myers and Well (1995), and Wilcox (1987, 1996, 2003). For information on more advanced within-subjects ANOVA models, see Cotton (1998), Keppel and Wickens (2004), and Myers and Well (1995).

Various MCPs can be used for the Friedman test. For the most part, these MCPs are analogs to their parametric equivalents. In the case of planned (or a priori) pairwise comparisons, one may use multiple matched-pair Wilcoxon tests (i.e., a form of the Kruskal–Wallis test for two groups) in a Bonferroni form (i.e., taking the number of contrasts into account through an adjustment of the α level; for example, if there are six contrasts with an alpha of .05, the adjusted alpha would be .05/6, or .008). For post hoc comparisons, numerous parametric analogs are available. For additional discussion on MCPs for this model, see Marascuilo and McSweeney (1977).

5.4.8 Example

Let us consider an example to illustrate the procedures used for this model. The data are shown in Table 5.7, where there are eight subjects, each of whom has been evaluated by four raters on a task of writing assessment. First, let us take a look at the results for the parametric ANOVA model, as shown in Table 5.8. The F test statistic is compared to the usual F test critical value of $_{.05}F_{3,21} = 3.07$, which is significant. For the Geisser–Greenhouse conservative procedure, the test statistic is compared to the critical value of $_{.05}F_{1,7} = 5.59$, which is also significant. The two procedures both yield a statistically significant result; thus, we need not be concerned with a violation of the compound symmetry assumption. As an example MCP, the Bonferroni procedure determined that all pairs of raters are significantly different from one another, except for rater 1 versus rater 2.

Finally, let us take a look at the Friedman test. The test statistic is $\chi^2 = 22.9500$. This test statistic is compared to the critical value $_{.05}\chi^2_3 = 7.8147$, which is significant. Thus, the conclusions for the parametric ANOVA and nonparametric Friedman tests are the same here. This will not always be the case, particularly when ANOVA assumptions are violated.

TABLE 5.7

Data for the Writing Assessment Example One-Factor Design: Raw Scores and Rank Scores on the Writing Assessment Task by Subject and Rater

Subject	Rater 1		Rater 2		Rater 3		Rater 4	
	Raw	Rank	Raw	Rank	Raw	Rank	Raw	Rank
1	3	1	4	2	7	3	8	4
2	6	2	5	1	8	3	9	4
3	3	1	4	2	7	3	9	4
4	3	1	4	2	6	3	8	4
5	1	1	2	2	5	3	10	4
6	2	1	3	2	6	3	10	4
7	2	1	4	2	5	3	9	4
8	2	1	3	2	6	3	10	4

TABLE 5.8

One-Factor Repeated Measures ANOVA Summary Table for the Writing Assessment Example

Source	SS	df	MS	F
Within subjects				
Rater (A)	198.125	3	66.042	73.477[a]
Error (SA)	18.875	21	.899	
Between subjects				
Error (S)	14.875	7	2.125	
Total	231.875	31		

[a] $_{.05}F_{3,21} = 3.07$.

5.5 Two-Factor Split-Plot or Mixed Design

In this section, we describe the distinguishing characteristics of the two-factor split-plot or mixed ANOVA design, the layout of the data, the linear model, assumptions and their violation, the ANOVA summary table and expected mean squares, MCPs, and an example.

5.5.1 Characteristics of the Model

The characteristics of the two-factor split-plot or mixed ANOVA design are a combination of the characteristics of the one-factor repeated measures and the two-factor fixed-effects models. It is unique because there are two factors, only one of which is repeated. For this reason, the design is often called a **mixed design**. Thus, one of the factors is a *between*-subjects factor, the other is a *within*-subjects factor, and the result is known as a **split-plot design** (from agricultural research). Each subject then responds to every level of the repeated factor but to only one level of the nonrepeated factor. Subjects then serve as their own controls for the repeated factor but not for the nonrepeated factor. The other characteristics carry over from the one-factor repeated measures model and the two-factor model.

5.5.2 Layout of Data

The layout of the data for the two-factor split-plot or mixed design is shown in Table 5.9. Here we see the rows designated as the levels of factor A, the between-subjects or nonrepeated factor, and the columns as the levels of factor B, the within-subjects or repeated factor. Within each factor level combination or cell are the subjects. Notice that the same subjects appear at all levels of factor B (the within-subjects factor, the repeated measure) but only at one level of factor A (the between-subjects factor). Row, column, cell, and overall means are also shown. Here you see that the layout of the data looks much the same as the two-factor model.

TABLE 5.9

Layout for the Two-Factor Split-Plot or Mixed ANOVA

Level of Factor A (Nonrepeated Factor)	Level of Factor A (Repeated Factor)				Row Mean
	1	2	...	K	
1	Y_{111}	Y_{112}	...	Y_{11K}	
	.	.	...	.	$\bar{Y}_{.1.}$
	.	.	...	.	
	Y_{n11}	Y_{n12}	...	Y_{n1K}	
	$\bar{Y}_{.11}$	$\bar{Y}_{.12}$		$\bar{Y}_{.1K}$	
2	Y_{121}	Y_{122}	...	Y_{12K}	
	.	.	...	.	$\bar{Y}_{.2.}$
	.	.	...	.	
	.	.	...	.	
	Y_{n21}	Y_{n22}	...	Y_{n2K}	
	$\bar{Y}_{.21}$	$\bar{Y}_{.22}$	...	$\bar{Y}_{.2K}$	
	.	.	...	.	.
	.	.	...	.	.
	.	.	...	.	.
J	Y_{1J1}	Y_{1J2}	...	Y_{1JK}	
	.	.	...	.	$\bar{Y}_{.J.}$
	.	.	...	.	
	Y_{nJ1}	Y_{nJ2}	...	Y_{nJK}	
	$\bar{Y}_{.J1}$	$\bar{Y}_{.J2}$	...	$\bar{Y}_{.JK}$	
Column Mean	$\bar{Y}_{..1}$	$\bar{Y}_{..2}$		$\bar{Y}_{..K}$	$\bar{Y}_{...}$

Note: Each subject is measured at all levels of factor B, but at only one level of factor A.

5.5.3 ANOVA Model

The two-factor split-plot model can be written in terms of population parameters as

$$Y_{ijk} = \mu + \alpha_j + s_{i(j)} + \beta_k + (\alpha\beta)_{jk} + (\beta s)_{ki(j)} + \varepsilon_{ijk}$$

where

Y_{ijk} is the observed score on the dependent variable for individual i in level j of factor A (the between-subjects factor) and level k of factor B (i.e., the jk cell, the within-subjects factor or repeated measure)

μ is the overall or grand population mean (i.e., regardless of cell designation)

α_j is the effect for level j of factor A (row effect for the nonrepeated factor)

$s_{i(j)}$ is the effect of subject i that is nested within level j of factor A (i.e., $i(j)$ denotes that i is nested within j)

β_k is the effect for level k of factor B (column effect for the repeated factor)

$(\alpha\beta)_{jk}$ is the interaction effect for the combination of level j of factor A and level k of factor B

$(\beta s)_{ki(j)}$ is the interaction effect for the combination of level k of factor B (the within-subjects factor, the repeated measure) and subject i that is nested within level j of factor A (the between-subjects factor)

ε_{ijk} is the random residual error for individual i in cell jk

We use the terminology "subjects are nested within factor A" to indicate that a particular subject s_i is only exposed to one level of factor A (the between-subjects factor), level j. This observation is then denoted in the subjects effect by $s_{i(j)}$ and in the interaction effect by $(\beta s)_{ki(j)}$. This is due to the fact that not all possible combinations of subject with the levels of factor A are included in the model. A more extended discussion of designs with nested factors is given in Chapter 6. The residual error can be due to individual differences, measurement error, and/or other factors not under investigation. We assume for now that A and B are fixed-effects factors and that S is a random-effects factor.

It should be mentioned that for the equal n's model, the sum of the row effects, the sum of the column effects, and the sum of the interaction effects are all equal to 0, both across rows and across columns. This implies, for example, that if there are any nonzero row effects, then the row effects will balance out around 0 with some positive and some negative effects.

The hypotheses to be tested here are exactly the same as in the nonrepeated two-factor ANOVA model (see Chapter 3). For the two-factor ANOVA model, there are three sets of hypotheses, one for each of the main effects and one for the interaction effect. The null and alternative hypotheses, respectively, for testing the main effect of factor A (between-subjects factor) are as follows:

$$H_{01}:\ \mu_{.1.} = \mu_{.2.} = \ldots = \mu_{.J.}$$

$$H_{11}:\ \text{not all the } \mu_{.j.} \text{ are equal}$$

The hypotheses for testing the main effect of factor B (within-subjects factor, i.e., the repeated measure) are noted as follows:

$$H_{02}:\ \mu_{..1} = \mu_{..2} = \ldots = \mu_{..K}$$

$$H_{12}:\ \text{not all the } \mu_{..k} \text{ are equal}$$

Finally, the hypotheses for testing the interaction effect (between by within factors) are as follows:

$$H_{03}:\ (\mu_{.jk} - \mu_{.j.} - \mu_{..k} + \mu) = 0 \text{ for all } j \text{ and } k$$

$$H_{13}:\ \text{not all the } (\mu_{.jk} - \mu_{.j.} - \mu_{..k} + \mu) = 0$$

If one of the null hypotheses is rejected, then the researcher may want to consider an MCP so as to determine which means or combination of means are significantly different (discussed later in this chapter).

TABLE 5.10

Assumptions and Effects of Violations: Two-Factor Split-Plot or Mixed Model

Assumption	Effect of Assumption Violation
Independence	• Increased likelihood of a Type I and/or Type II error in F • Affects standard errors of means and inferences about those means
Homogeneity of variance	• Bias in error terms • Increased likelihood of a Type I and/or Type II error • Small effect with equal or nearly equal n's • Otherwise effect decreases as n increases
Normality	• Minimal effect with equal or nearly equal n's • Otherwise substantial effects
Sphericity	• F not particularly robust • Consider usual F test, Geisser–Greenhouse conservative F test, and adjusted (Huynh–Feldt) F test, if necessary

5.5.4 Assumptions and Violation of Assumptions

Previously we described the assumptions for the different two-factor models and the one-factor repeated measures model. The assumptions for the two-factor split-plot or mixed design are actually a combination of these two sets of assumptions.

The assumptions can be divided into two sets of assumptions, one for the between-subjects factor and one for the within-subjects (or repeated measures) factor. For the between-subjects factor, we have the usual assumptions of population scores being random, independent, and normally distributed with equal variances. For the within-subjects factor (i.e., the repeated measure), the assumption is the already familiar compound symmetry assumption. For this design, the assumption involves the population covariances for all pairs of the levels of the within-subjects factor (i.e., k and k') being equal, at each level of the between-subjects factor (for all levels j). To deal with this assumption, we look at alternative F tests in the next section. A summary of the assumptions and the effects of their violation for the two-factor split-plot or mixed design is presented in Table 5.10.

5.5.5 ANOVA Summary Table and Expected Mean Squares

The ANOVA summary table is shown in Table 5.11, where we see the following sources of variation: A, S, B, AB, BS, and total. The table is divided into within-subjects sources and between-subjects sources. The between-subjects sources are A and S, where S will be used as the error term for the test of factor A. The within-subjects sources are B, AB, and BS, where BS will be used as the error term for the test of factor B and of the AB interaction. This will become clear when we examine the expected mean squares shortly.

Next we need to consider the sums of squares for the two-factor mixed design. Taking the total sum of squares and decomposing it yields

$$SS_{\text{total}} = SS_A + SS_S + SS_B + SS_{AB} + SS_{BS}$$

We leave the computation of these five terms for statistical software. The degrees of freedom, mean squares, and F ratios are computed as shown in Table 5.11.

TABLE 5.11

Two-Factor Split-Plot or Mixed Model ANOVA
Summary Table

Source	SS	df	MS	F
Between subjects				
A	SS_A	$J - 1$	MS_A	MS_A/MS_S
S	SS_S	$J(n - 1)$	MS_S	
Within subjects				
B	SS_B	$K - 1$	MS_B	MS_B/MS_{BS}
AB	SS_{AB}	$(J - 1)(K - 1)$	MS_{AB}	MS_{AB}/MS_{BS}
BS	SS_{BS}	$(K - 1)J(n - 1)$	MS_{BS}	
Total	SS_{total}	$N - 1$		

The formation of the proper F ratio is again related to the expected mean squares. If H_0 is actually *true* (i.e., the means are really equal), then the *expected mean squares* are as follows:

$$E(MS_A) = \sigma_\varepsilon^2$$

$$E(MS_S) = \sigma_\varepsilon^2$$

$$E(MS_B) = \sigma_\varepsilon^2$$

$$E(MS_{AB}) = \sigma_\varepsilon^2$$

$$E(MS_{BS}) = \sigma_\varepsilon^2$$

where σ_ε^2 is the population variance of the residual errors.

If H_0 is actually *false* (i.e., the means are really not equal), then the expected mean squares are as follows:

$$E(MS_A) = \sigma_\varepsilon^2 + K\sigma_s^2 + nK\left[\sum_{j=1}^{J} \alpha_j^2/(J-1)\right]$$

$$E(MS_S) = \sigma_\varepsilon^2 + K\sigma_s^2$$

$$E(MS_B) = \sigma_\varepsilon^2 + \sigma_{\beta s}^2 + nJ\left[\sum_{k=1}^{K} \beta_k^2/(K-1)\right]$$

$$E(MS_{AB}) = \sigma_\varepsilon^2 + \sigma_{\beta s}^2 + n\left[\sum_{j=1}^{J}\sum_{k=1}^{K} (\alpha\beta)_{jk}^2/(J-1)(K-1)\right]$$

$$E\left(MS_{BS}\right) = \sigma_{\varepsilon}^2 + \sigma_{\beta s}^2$$

where $\sigma_{\beta s}^2$ represents variability due to the interaction of factor B (the within-subjects or repeated measures factor) and subjects, and the other terms are as before.

As in previous ANOVA models, the proper F ratio should be formed as follows:

$$F = (\text{systematic variability} + \text{error variability}) / (\text{error variability})$$

For the two-factor split-plot design, the error term for the proper test of factor A (the between-subjects factor) is the S term, whereas the error term for the proper tests of factor B (the within-subjects or repeated measures factor) and the AB interaction is the BS interaction. For models where factors A and B are not both fixed-effects factors, see Keppel (1982).

As the compound symmetry assumption is often violated, we again suggest the following sequential procedure to test for B (the repeated measure) and for AB (the within- by between-subjects factor interaction). First, do the usual F test, which is quite liberal in terms of rejecting H_0 too often. If H_0 is not rejected, then stop. If H_0 is rejected, then continue with step 2, which is to use the Geisser and Greenhouse (1958) conservative F test. For the model under consideration here, the degrees of freedom for the F critical values are adjusted to be 1 and $J(n-1)$ for the test of B, and $J-1$ and $J(n-1)$ for the test of the AB interaction. There is no conservative test necessary for factor A, the between-subjects or nonrepeated factor, as the assumption does not apply; thus, the usual test is all that is necessary for the test of A. If H_0 for B and/or AB is rejected, then stop. This would indicate that both the liberal and conservative tests reached the same conclusion to reject H_0. If H_0 is not rejected, then the two tests did not yield the same conclusion, and an adjusted F test is conducted. The adjustment is known as Box's (1954b) correction (or the Huynh and Feldt [1970] procedure). Most major statistical software conducts the Geisser–Greenhouse and Huynh–Feldt tests.

5.5.6 Multiple Comparison Procedures

Consider the situation where the null hypothesis for any of the three hypotheses is rejected (i.e., for A, B, and/or AB). If there is more than one degree of freedom in the numerator for any of these hypotheses, then the researcher may be interested in which means or combinations of means are different. This could be assessed again by the use of some MCP. Thus, the procedures outlined in Chapter 3 (i.e., for main effects and for simple and complex interaction contrasts) for the regular two-factor ANOVA model can be adapted to this model.

However, it has been shown that the MCPs involving the repeated factor are seriously affected by a violation of the compound symmetry assumption. In this situation, two alternatives are recommended. The first alternative is, rather than using the same error term for each contrast involving the repeated factor (i.e., MS_B or MS_{AB}), to use a separate error term for each contrast tested. Then many of the MCPs previously covered in Chapter 2 can be used. This complicates matters considerably (see Keppel, 1982; Keppel & Wickens, 2004; or Kirk, 1982). The second and simpler alternative is suggested by Shavelson (1988). He recommended that the appropriate error terms be used in MCPs involving the main effects, but for interaction contrasts, both error terms be pooled (or added) together (this procedure is conservative yet simpler than the first alternative).

5.5.7 Example

Consider now an example problem to illustrate the two-factor mixed design. Here we expand on the example presented earlier in this chapter by adding a second factor to the model. The data are shown in Table 5.12, where there are eight subjects, each of whom has been evaluated by four raters on a task of writing assessment (rater is the within-subjects factor as each individual has been evaluated by four raters). Ratings on the writing assessment can range from 1 (lowest rating) to 10 (highest rating). Each student was also randomly assigned to one of two instructors. Thus, factor A represents the instructors of English composition, where we see that four subjects are randomly assigned to level 1 of factor A (i.e., instructor 1) and the remaining four to level 2 of factor A (i.e., instructor 2). Thus, factor B (i.e., rater) is repeated (the within-subjects factor), and factor A (i.e., instructor) is not repeated (the between-subjects factor). The ANOVA summary table is shown in Table 5.13.

The test statistics are compared to the following usual F test critical values: for factor A (the between-subjects factor that tests mean differences based on instructor), $_{.05}F_{1,6} = 5.99$, which is not statistically significant; for factor B (the within-subjects factor that tests mean differences based on repeated ratings), $_{.05}F_{3,18} = 3.16$, which is significant; and for AB, $_{.05}F_{3,18} = 3.16$, which is also statistically significant. For the Geisser–Greenhouse conservative procedure, the test statistics are compared to the following critical values: for factor A (i.e., instructor), no conservative procedure is necessary; for factor B (i.e., repeated measure rater), $_{.05}F_{1,6} = 5.99$, which is also significant; and for the interaction AB (instructor by rater), $_{.05}F_{1,6} = 5.99$, which is also significant. The usual and Geisser–Greenhouse procedures both yield a statistically significant result for factor B (rater) and for the interaction AB (instructor by rater);

TABLE 5.12

Data for the Writing Assessment Example Two-Factor Design: Raw Scores on the Writing Assessment Task by Instructor and Rater

Factor A (Nonrepeated Factor)		Factor B (Repeated Factor)			
Instructor	Subject	Rater 1	Rater 2	Rater 3	Rater 4
1	1	3	4	7	8
	2	6	5	8	9
	3	3	4	7	9
	4	3	4	6	8
2	5	1	2	5	10
	6	2	3	6	10
	7	2	4	5	9
	8	2	3	6	10

TABLE 5.13

Two-Factor Split-Plot ANOVA Summary Table
for the Writing Assessment Example

Source	SS	df	MS	F
Between subjects				
Instructor (A)	6.125	1	6.125	4.200[b]
Error (S)	8.750	6	1.458	
Within subjects				
Rater (B)	198.125	3	66.042	190.200[a]
Instructor × rater	12.625	3	4.208	12.120[a]
Error (BS)	6.250	18	.347	
Total	231.875	31		

a $_{.05}F_{3,18} = 3.16$.
b $_{.05}F_{1,6} = 5.99$.

thus, we need not be concerned with a violation of the sphericity assumption. A profile plot of the interaction is shown in Figure 5.2.

There is a significant AB (i.e., instructor by rater) interaction, so we should follow this up with simple interaction contrasts, each involving only four cell means. As an example of an MCP, consider the contrast

$$\psi' = \frac{(\bar{Y}_{.11} - \bar{Y}_{.21}) - (\bar{Y}_{.14} - \bar{Y}_{.24})}{4} = \frac{(3.7500 - 1.7500) - (8.5000 - 9.7500)}{4} = .8125$$

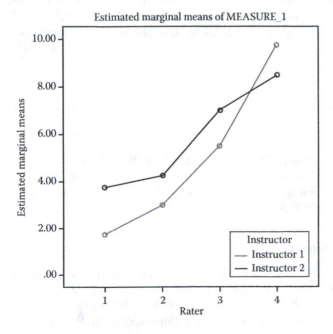

FIGURE 5.2
Profile plot for example writing data.

with a standard error computed as follows:

$$se_{\psi'} = \sqrt{MS_{BS}\left(\frac{\displaystyle\sum_{j=1}^{J}\sum_{k=1}^{K}c_{jk}^2}{n_{jk}}\right)} = \sqrt{0.3472\frac{(1/16+1/16+1/16+1/16)}{4}} = 0.1473$$

Using the Scheffé procedure, we formulate the following as the test statistic:

$$t = \frac{\psi'}{se_{\psi'}} = \frac{0.8125}{0.1473} = 5.5160$$

This is compared with the critical value presented here:

$$\sqrt{(J-1)(K-1)_{\alpha}F_{(J-1)(K-1),(K-1)J(n-1)}} = \sqrt{3(_{.05}F_{3,18})} = \sqrt{3(3.16)} = 3.0790$$

Thus, we may conclude that the tetrad interaction difference between the first and second levels of factor A (instructor) and the first and fourth levels of factor B (rater, the repeated measure) is significant. In other words, rater 1 finds better writing among the students of instructor 1 than instructor 2, whereas rater 4 finds better writing among the students of instructor 2 than instructor 1.

Although we have only considered the basic repeated measures designs here, more complex repeated measures designs also exist. For further information, see Myers (1979), Keppel (1982), Kirk (1982), Myers and Well (1995), Glass and Hopkins (1996), Cotton (1998), Keppel and Wickens (2004), as well as alternative ANOVA procedures described by Wilcox (2003) and McCulloch (2005). To analyze repeated measures designs in SAS, use the GLM procedure with the REPEATED statement. In SPSS GLM, use the repeated measures program.

5.6 SPSS and G*Power

Next we consider SPSS for the models presented in this chapter. Note that all of the designs in this chapter are discussed in the SPSS context by Page, Braver, and MacKinnon (2003). This is followed by an illustration of the use of G*Power for post hoc and a priori power analysis for the two-factor split-plot ANOVA.

One-Factor Random-Effects ANOVA

To conduct a one-factor random-effects ANOVA analysis, there are only two differences from the one-factor fixed-effects ANOVA (Chapter 1). Otherwise, the form of the data and the conduct of the analyses are exactly the same. In terms of the form of the data, one column or variable indicates the levels or categories of the independent variable (i.e., the random factor), and the second is for the dependent variable. Each row then represents one individual, indicating the level or group that individual is a member of (1, 2, 3, or 4 in our example; recall that for the one-factor random-effects ANOVA, these categories are randomly selected from the population of categories), and their score on the dependent variable. Thus, we wind up with two long columns of group values and scores as shown in the following screenshot. We will use the data from Chapter 1 to illustrate, this time assuming the independent variable is a random factor rather than fixed.

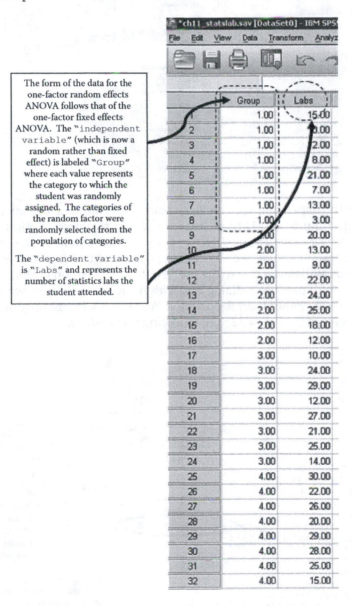

The form of the data for the one-factor random effects ANOVA follows that of the one-factor fixed effects ANOVA. The "independent variable" (which is now a random rather than fixed effect) is labeled "Group" where each value represents the category to which the student was randomly assigned. The categories of the random factor were randomly selected from the population of categories.

The "dependent variable" is "Labs" and represents the number of statistics labs the student attended.

Step 1: To conduct a one-factor random-effects ANOVA, go to "Analyze" in the top pulldown menu, then select "General Linear Model," and then select "Univariate." Following the screenshot (step 1) as follows produces the "Univariate" dialog box.

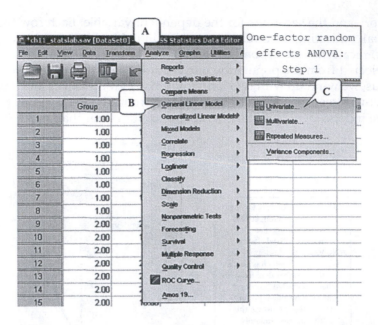

Step 2: Click the dependent variable (e.g., number of statistics labs attended) and move it into the "Dependent Variable" box by clicking the arrow button. Click the independent variable (e.g., level of attractiveness; this is the random-effects factor) and move it into the "Random Factors" box by clicking the arrow button. On this "Univariate" dialog screen, you will notice that while the "Post hoc" option button is active, clicking on "Post hoc" will produce a dialog box with no active options as we are now dealing with a random factor rather than fixed factor. Post hoc MCPs are only available from the "Options" screen as we will see in the following screenshots.

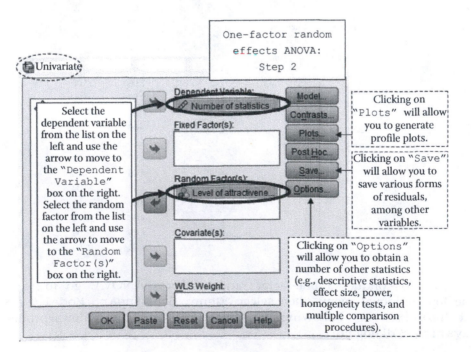

Step 3: Clicking on "Options" provides the option to select such information as "Descriptive Statistics," "Estimates of effect size," "Observed power," and "Homogeneity tests" (i.e., Levene's test for equal variances). Click on "Continue" to return to the original dialog box. *Note that if you are interested in an MCP, post hoc MCPs are only available from the* "Options" *screen.* To select a post hoc procedure, click on "Compare main effects" and use the toggle menu to reveal the Tukey LSD, Bonferroni, and Sidak procedures. However, we have already mentioned that MCPs are not generally of interest for this model.

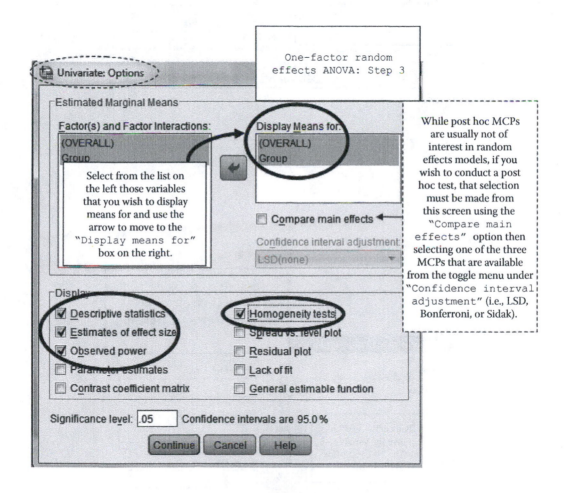

Step 4: From the "Univariate" dialog box, click on "Plots" to obtain a profile plot of means. Click the random factor (e.g., level of attractiveness labeled as "Group") and move it into the "Horizontal Axis" box by clicking the arrow button (see screenshot step 4a). Then click on "Add" to move the variable into the "Plots" box at the bottom of the dialog box (see screenshot step 4b). Click on "Continue" to return to the original dialog box.

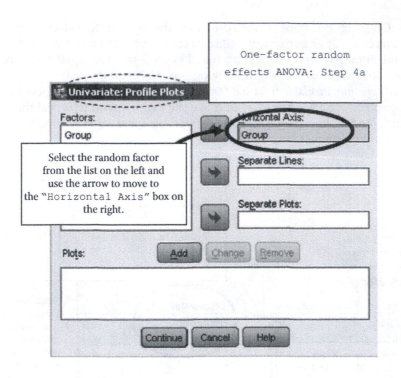

One-factor random effects ANOVA: Step 4a

Select the random factor from the list on the left and use the arrow to move to the "Horizontal Axis" box on the right.

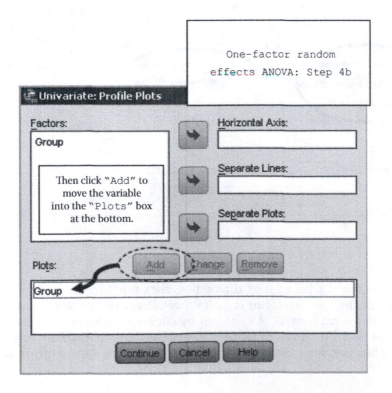

One-factor random effects ANOVA: Step 4b

Then click "Add" to move the variable into the "Plots" box at the bottom.

Step 5: From the "Univariate" dialog box (see screenshot step 2), click on "Save" to select those elements that you want to save. In our case, we want to save the unstandardized residuals which will be used later to examine the extent to which normality and independence are met. Thus, place a checkmark in the box next to "Unstandardized." Click "Continue" to return to the main "Univariate" dialog box. From the "Univariate" dialog box, click on "Ok" to return to generate the output.

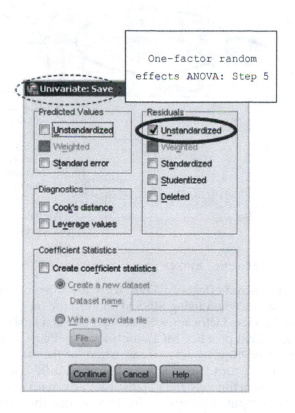

Two-Factor Random-Effects ANOVA

To run a two-factor random-effects ANOVA model, there are the same two differences from the two-factor fixed-effects ANOVA (covered in Chapter 3). First, on the GLM screen (shown in the following screenshot), click both factor names into the "Random Factor(s)" box rather than the "Fixed Factor(s)" box. Second, the same situation exists with MCPs: if you are interested in an MCP, post hoc MCPs are only available from the "Options" screen. However, we have already mentioned that MCPs are not generally of interest for this model. For brevity, the subsequent screenshots are not presented.

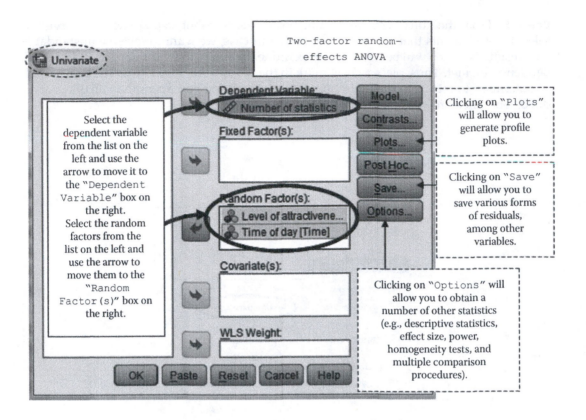

Two-Factor Mixed-Effects ANOVA

To conduct a two-factor mixed-effects ANOVA, there are three differences from the two-factor fixed-effects ANOVA when using SPSS to analyze the model. The first is that both a random- and a fixed-effects factor must be defined (see screenshot step 2 that follows). The second difference is that post hoc MCPs for the fixed-effects factor are available from either the "Post Hoc" or "Options" screens, while for the random-effects factor, they are only available from the "Options" screen. The third difference is related to the output provided by SPSS. Unfortunately the F statistic for any main effect that is random in a mixed-effects model is computed incorrectly in SPSS because the wrong error term is used when implementing the SPSS point-and-click mode. As described in Lomax and Surman (2007) and extended by Li and Lomax (2011), you need to (a) compute the F statistics by hand from the MS values (which are correct), (b) use SPSS syntax where the user indicates the proper error terms, or (c) use a different software package (e.g., SAS, where the user also provides the proper error terms). These options are not presented here. Rather, readers are referred to the appropriate references. For the purpose of this illustration, we will use the statistics lab data. The dependent variable remains the same—the number of statistics labs attended. The level of attractiveness will be a fixed factor, and the time of day will be a random factor.

Step 1: To conduct a one-factor fixed-effects ANOVA, go to "Analyze" in the top pull-down menu, then select "General Linear Model," and then select "Univariate." Following screenshot step 1 for the one-factor random-effects ANOVA presented previously produces the "Univariate" dialog box.

Step 2: Per screenshot step 2 that follows, click the dependent variable (e.g., number of statistics labs attended) and move it into the "Dependent Variable" box by clicking the arrow button. Click the fixed factor (e.g., level of attractiveness) and move it into the "Fixed Factors" box by clicking the arrow button. Click the random factor (e.g., time of day) and move it into the "Random Factors" box by clicking the arrow button. Next, click on "Options." Please note that post hoc MCPs for the fixed-effects factor (in this case, level of attractiveness) are available from either the "Post Hoc" or "Options" screens, while for the random-effects factor, they are only available from the "Options" screen. Because these steps have been presented in previous screenshots (e.g., Chapter 2 for MCPs and the one-factor random-effects previously shown in this chapter), they are not repeated here.

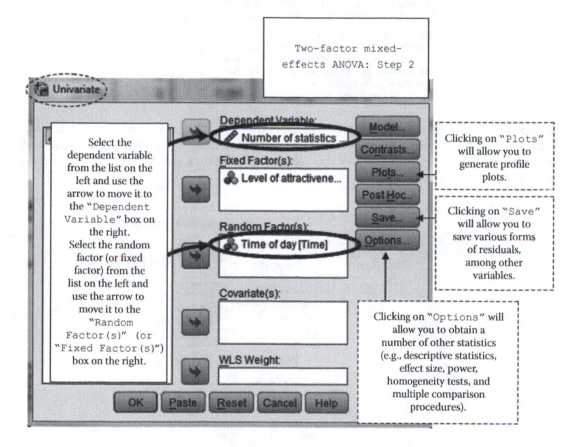

One-Factor Repeated Measures ANOVA

In order to run a one-factor repeated measures ANOVA model, the data have to be in the form suggested by the following screenshot. Each row represents one person in our sample. All of the scores for each subject must be in one row of the dataset, and each level of the repeated factor is a separate variable (represented by the columns). For example, if there are four raters who assess each student's essay, there will be variables for each rater (e.g., rater 1 through rater 4; example dataset on the website). In this illustration, we have both raw scores and ranked data for each of the four raters. When using ANOVA for repeated measures, we will apply the raw scores. The ranked scores will only be of value when computing the nonparametric version of ANOVA (i.e., the Friedman test) which will be covered later in this chapter.

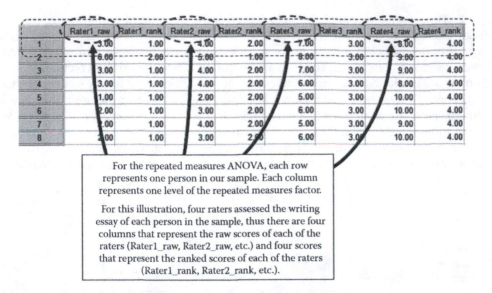

	Rater1_raw	Rater1_rank	Rater2_raw	Rater2_rank	Rater3_raw	Rater3_rank	Rater4_raw	Rater4_rank
1	3.00	1.00	4.00	2.00	7.00	3.00	8.00	4.00
2	6.00	2.00	5.00	1.00	8.00	3.00	9.00	4.00
3	3.00	1.00	4.00	2.00	7.00	3.00	9.00	4.00
4	3.00	1.00	4.00	2.00	6.00	3.00	8.00	4.00
5	1.00	1.00	2.00	2.00	5.00	3.00	10.00	4.00
6	2.00	1.00	3.00	2.00	6.00	3.00	10.00	4.00
7	2.00	1.00	4.00	2.00	5.00	3.00	9.00	4.00
8	2.00	1.00	3.00	2.00	6.00	3.00	10.00	4.00

For the repeated measures ANOVA, each row represents one person in our sample. Each column represents one level of the repeated measures factor.

For this illustration, four raters assessed the writing essay of each person in the sample, thus there are four columns that represent the raw scores of each of the raters (Rater1_raw, Rater2_raw, etc.) and four scores that represent the ranked scores of each of the raters (Rater1_rank, Rater2_rank, etc.).

Step 1: To conduct a one-factor repeated measures ANOVA, go to "Analyze" in the top pulldown menu, then select "General Linear Model," and then select "Repeated Measures." Following the screenshot (step 1) as follows produces the "Repeated Measures" dialog box.

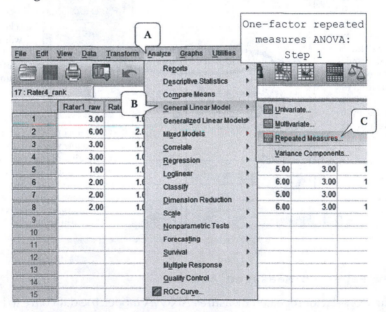

One-factor repeated measures ANOVA: Step 1

Step 2: The "Repeated Measures Define Factor(s)" dialog box will appear (see screenshot step 2). In the box under "Within-Subject Factor Name," enter the name you wish to call the repeated factor. For this illustration, we will label the repeated measure "Rater." It is necessary to define a name for the repeated factor as there is no single variable representing this factor (recall that the columns in the dataset represent the repeated measures); in the dataset, there is one variable for each level of the factor (in other words, one variable for each different rater or measurement). Again, in our example, there are four levels of raters (i.e., four raters) and thus four variables. Thus, we name the within-subjects factor "Rater." The "Number of Levels" indicates the number of measurements of the repeated measure. In this example, there were four raters, and, thus, the "Number of Levels" of the factor is 4 (e.g., 4).

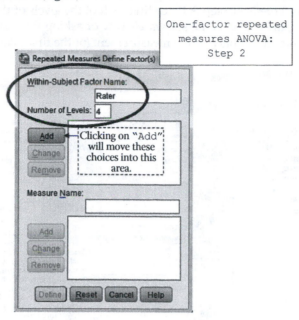

One-factor repeated measures ANOVA: Step 2

Step 3: After we have defined the "Within-Subject Factor Name" and the "Number of Levels," click on "Add" to move this information into the middle box. In screenshot step 3, we see our newly defined repeated measures factor (i.e., Rater) with "4" indicating that there are four levels: Rater(4). Finally, click on "Define" to open the main "Repeated Measures" dialog box.

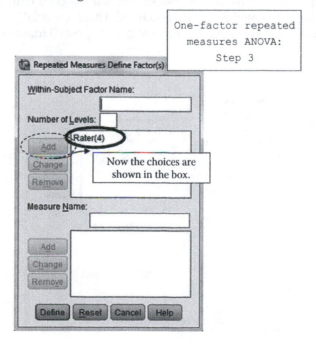

One-factor repeated measures ANOVA: Step 3

Step 4a: From the "Repeated Measures" dialog box (see screenshot step 4a), we see a heading called "Within-Subjects Variables" with the newly defined factor rater in parentheses. In this illustration, the values of 1 through 4 represent each one of the four raters that we just defined through screenshot step 3. Preceding each of the levels of the repeated factor are lines with question marks. This is the software's way of asking us to define which variable from the list on the left represents the first measurement (or the first rater in our illustration).

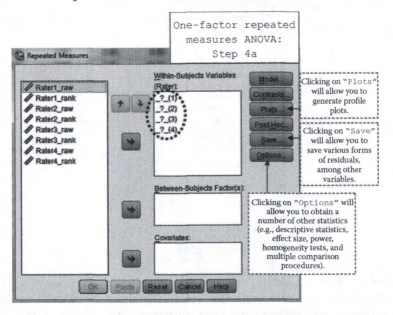

Step 4b: Move the appropriate variables from the variable list on the left into the "Within-Subjects Variables" box on the right. It is important to make sure that the first measurement is matched up with "1," the second measurement is matched with "2," and so forth so that the correct order of repeated measures is defined. This is especially critical when there is some temporal order to the repeated measures (e.g., pre-, post-, 3 months after post-).

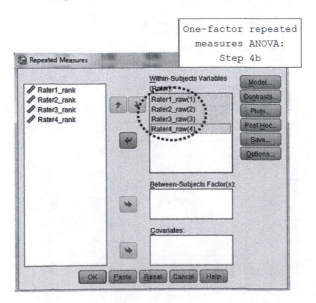

Step 5: From the "Univariate" dialog box (see screenshot step 4a), clicking on "Options" will provide the option to select such information as "Descriptive Statistics," "Estimates of effect size," "Observed power," and "Homogeneity tests." For the one-factor repeated measures ANOVA, the "Options" dialog box is the proper place to obtain post hoc MCPs including the Tukey LSD, Bonferroni, and Sidak procedures. Click on "Continue" to return to the original dialog box.

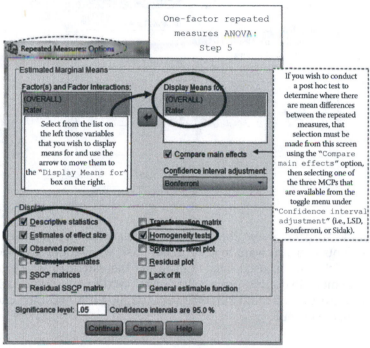

Step 6: From the "Univariate" dialog box (see screenshot step 4a), click on "Plots" to obtain a profile plot of means. Click the repeated measure factor (e.g., "Rater") and move it into the "Horizontal Axis" box by clicking the arrow button (see screenshot step 6a). Then click on "Add" to move the variable into the "Plots" box at the bottom of the dialog box (see screenshot step 6b). Click on "Continue" to return to the original dialog box.

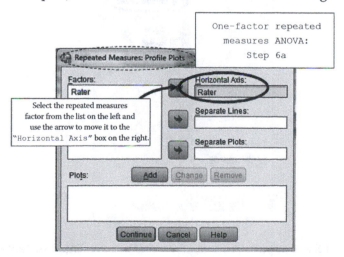

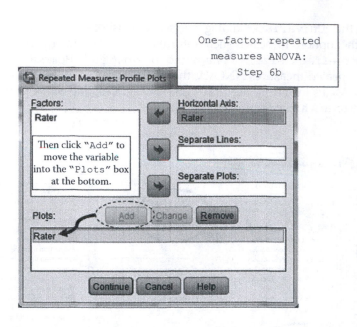

Step 7: From the "Univariate" dialog box (see screenshot step 4a), click on "Save" to select those elements that you want to save (in our case, we want to save the unstandardized residuals which will be used later to examine the extent to which normality and independence are met). To do this, place a checkmark next to "Unstandardized." Click "Continue" to return to the main "Univariate" dialog box and then click on "Ok" to return to generate the output.

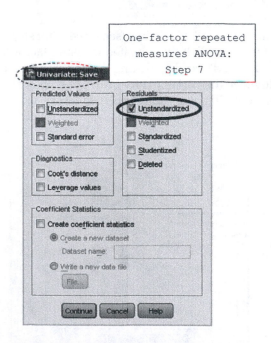

Interpreting the output: Annotated results are presented in Table 5.14.

TABLE 5.14

One-Factor Repeated Measures ANOVA SPSS Results for the Writing Assessment Example

Descriptive Statistics

	Mean	Std. Deviation	N
Rater1_raw	2.7500	1.48805	8
Rater2_raw	3.6250	.91613	8
Rater3_raw	6.2500	1.03510	8
Rater4_raw	9.1250	.83452	8

The table labeled "`Descriptive Statistics`" provides basic descriptive statistics (means, standard deviations, and sample sizes) for each group of the repeated measure.

Multivariate Tests[a]

Effect		Value	F	Hypothesis df	Error df	Sig.	Partial Eta Squared	Noncent. Parameter	Observed Power[b]
Rater	Pillai's trace	.967	48.650[c]	3.000	5.000	.000	.967	145.949	1.000
	Wilks' lambda	.033	48.650[c]	3.000	5.000	.000	.967	145.949	1.000
	Hotelling's trace	29.190	48.650[c]	3.000	5.000	.000	.967	145.949	1.000
	Roy's largest root	29.190	48.650[c]	3.000	5.000	.000	.967	145.949	1.000

[a] Design: intercept.
[b] Computed using alpha = .05.
[c] Exact statistic.
Within-subjects design: rater.

The table labeled "`Multivariate Tests`" provides results for the multivariate test of mean differences between the repeated measures. Multivariate tests are provided when there are three or more levels of the within-subjects factor. These results are generally more conservative than the univariate results (in other words, you may be less likely to find statistically significant multivariate results as compared to univariate results). *Note that the multivariate tests do not require meeting the assumption of sphericity.* Thus if the assumption of sphericity is met, reporting univariate results is recommended.
If results for the multivariate tests are reported, of the four test results, Wilks' lambda is recommended. In this example, all four multivariate criteria produce the same results—specifically that there is a statistically significant multivariate mean difference (as noted by p less than α.)

"`Epsilon`" is a gauge of differences in the variances of the repeated measures and is used to adjust the degrees of freedom when sphericity is violated. The closer the epsilon value is to 1.0, the more homogenous are the variances. Complete heterogeneity of variances is specified by the "Lower bound" and is computed as $1/(K-1)$ where K is the number of within subjects factors. For this example, with four raters, the lower bound is $1/(4-1)$ or .333.

"`Mauchly's Test of Sphericity`" can be reviewed to determine if the assumption of sphericity is met. If the p value is larger than α (as in this illustration), we have met the assumption of sphericity.

Measure: MEASURE_1   **Mauchly's Test of Sphericity[a]**

Within-Subjects Effect	Mauchly's W	Approx. Chi-Square	df	Sig.	Epsilon[b]		
					Geisser–Greenhouse	Huynh–Feldt	Lower Bound
Rater	.155	10.679	5	.062	.476	.564	.333

Tests the null hypothesis that the error covariance matrix of the orthonormalized transformed dependent variables is proportional to an identity matrix.
[a] Design: intercept.
[b] May be used to adjust the degrees of freedom for the averaged tests of significance. Corrected tests are displayed in the tests of within-subjects effects table.
Within-subjects design: rater.

(continued)

TABLE 5.14 (continued)

One-Factor Repeated Measures ANOVA SPSS Results for the Writing Assessment Example

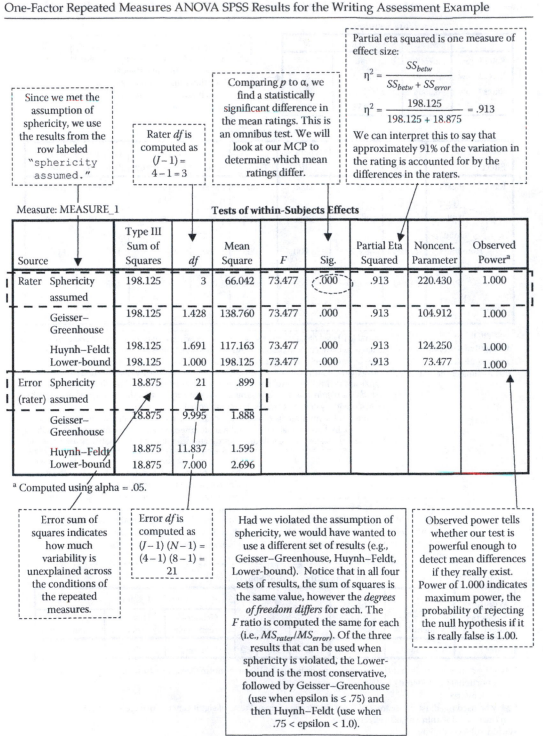

Since we met the assumption of sphericity, we use the results from the row labeled "sphericity assumed."

Rater *df* is computed as $(J-1) = 4-1 = 3$

Comparing *p* to α, we find a statistically significant difference in the mean ratings. This is an omnibus test. We will look at our MCP to determine which mean ratings differ.

Partial eta squared is one measure of effect size:

$$\eta^2 = \frac{SS_{betw}}{SS_{betw} + SS_{error}}$$

$$\eta^2 = \frac{198.125}{198.125 + 18.875} = .913$$

We can interpret this to say that approximately 91% of the variation in the rating is accounted for by the differences in the raters.

Measure: MEASURE_1

Tests of within-Subjects Effects

Source		Type III Sum of Squares	df	Mean Square	F	Sig.	Partial Eta Squared	Noncent. Parameter	Observed Power[a]
Rater	Sphericity assumed	198.125	3	66.042	73.477	.000	.913	220.430	1.000
	Geisser–Greenhouse	198.125	1.428	138.760	73.477	.000	.913	104.912	1.000
	Huynh–Feldt	198.125	1.691	117.163	73.477	.000	.913	124.250	1.000
	Lower-bound	198.125	1.000	198.125	73.477	.000	.913	73.477	1.000
Error (rater)	Sphericity assumed	18.875	21	.899					
	Geisser–Greenhouse	18.875	9.995	1.888					
	Huynh–Feldt	18.875	11.837	1.595					
	Lower-bound	18.875	7.000	2.696					

[a] Computed using alpha = .05.

Error sum of squares indicates how much variability is unexplained across the conditions of the repeated measures.

Error *df* is computed as $(J-1)(N-1) = (4-1)(8-1) = 21$

Had we violated the assumption of sphericity, we would have wanted to use a different set of results (e.g., Geisser–Greenhouse, Huynh–Feldt, Lower-bound). Notice that in all four sets of results, the sum of squares is the same value, however the *degrees of freedom differs* for each. The *F* ratio is computed the same for each (i.e., MS_{rater}/MS_{error}). Of the three results that can be used when sphericity is violated, the Lower-bound is the most conservative, followed by Geisser–Greenhouse (use when epsilon is ≤ .75) and then Huynh–Feldt (use when .75 < epsilon < 1.0).

Observed power tells whether our test is powerful enough to detect mean differences if they really exist. Power of 1.000 indicates maximum power, the probability of rejecting the null hypothesis if it is really false is 1.00.

TABLE 5.14 (continued)

One-Factor Repeated Measures ANOVA SPSS Results for the Writing Assessment Example

> The output from the "Tests of within-Subjects Contrasts" will not be used. Polynomial contrasts do not make sense for the rater factor.

Measure: MEASURE_1   **Tests of within-Subjects Contrasts**

Source	Rater	Type III Sum of Squares	df	Mean Square	F	Sig.	Partial Eta Squared	Noncent. Parameter	Observed Power[a]
Rater	Linear	189.225	1	189.225	103.685	.000	.937	103.685	1.000
	Quadratic	8.000	1	8.000	18.667	.003	.727	18.667	.957
	Cubic	.900	1	.900	2.032	.197	.225	2.032	.235
Error	Linear	12.775	7	1.825					
(rater)	Quadratic	3.000	7	.429					
	Cubic	3.100	7	.443					

[a] Computed using alpha = .05.

> The output from the "Tests of between-Subjects Effects" will not be used as there is no between-subjects factor.

Measure: MEASURE_1

Transformed Variable: Average   **Tests of between-Subjects Effects**

Source	Type III Sum of Squares	df	Mean Square	F	Sig.	Partial Eta Squared	Noncent. Parameter	Observed Power[a]
Intercept	946.125	1	946.125	445.235	.000	.985	445.235	1.000
Error	14.875	7	2.125					

[a] Computed using alpha = .05.

Estimated Marginal Means

1. Grand Mean

Measure: MEASURE_1

Mean	Std. Error	95% Confidence Interval	
		Lower Bound	Upper Bound
5.438	.258	4.828	6.047

> The "Grand Mean" (in this case, 5.438) represents the overall mean, regardless of the rater. The 95% CI represents the CI of the grand mean.

2. Rater

Measure: MEASURE_1   **Estimates**

Rater	Mean	Std. Error	95% Confidence Interval	
			Lower Bound	Upper Bound
1	2.750	.526	1.506	3.994
2	3.625	.324	2.859	4.391
3	6.250	.366	5.385	7.115
4	9.125	.295	8.427	9.823

> The table labeled **"Rater"** provides descriptive statistics for each of the four raters. In addition to means, the *SE* and 95% CI of the means are reported.

(continued)

TABLE 5.14 (continued)

One-Factor Repeated Measures ANOVA SPSS Results for the Writing Assessment Example

> "Mean Difference" is simply the difference between the means of the two raters being compared. For example, the mean difference of rater 1 and rater 2 is calculated as 2.750 − 3.625 = −.875.

Measure: MEASURE_1

Pairwise Comparisons

(I) Rater	(J) Rater	Mean Difference (I–J)	Std. Error	Sig.[a]	95% Confidence Interval for Difference[a] Lower Bound	Upper Bound
1	2	−.875	.295	.126	−1.948	.198
	3	−3.500[*]	.267	.000	−4.472	−2.528
	4	−6.375[*]	.706	.000	−8.940	−3.810
2	1	.875	.295	.126	−.198	1.948
	3	−2.625[*]	.263	.000	−3.581	−1.669
	4	−5.500[*]	.567	.000	−7.561	−3.439
3	1	3.500[*]	.267	.000	2.528	4.472
	2	2.625[*]	.263	.000	1.669	3.581
	4	−2.875[*]	.549	.007	−4.871	−.879
4	1	6.375[*]	.706	.000	3.810	8.940
	2	5.500[*]	.567	.000	3.439	7.561
	3	2.875[*]	.549	.007	.879	4.871

Based on estimated marginal means.
[a] Adjustment for multiple comparisons: Bonferroni.
*The mean difference is significant at the .05 level.

> "Sig." denotes the observed p value and provides the results of the Bonferroni post hoc procedure. There is a statistically significant mean difference between:
>
> 1. Rater 1 and rater 3
> 2. Rater 1 and rater 4
> 3. Rater 2 and rater 3
> 4. Rater 2 and rater 4
> 5. Rater 3 and rater 4
>
> The only groups for which there is not a statistically significant mean difference is between raters 1 and 2.
>
> Note there are redundant results presented in the table. The comparison of rater 1 and 2 (presented in results for rater 1) is the same as the comparison of rater 2 and 1 (presented in results for rater 2) and so forth.

Friedman Test: Nonparametric One-Factor Repeated Measures ANOVA

Step 1: The nonparametric version of the repeated measures ANOVA is the Friedman test. To compute the Friedman test, go to "Analyze" in the top pulldown menu and then select "Nonparametric Tests," then "Legacy Dialogs," and then finally "K Related Samples." Following the screenshot (step 1) as follows produces the "Tests for Several Related Samples" dialog box.

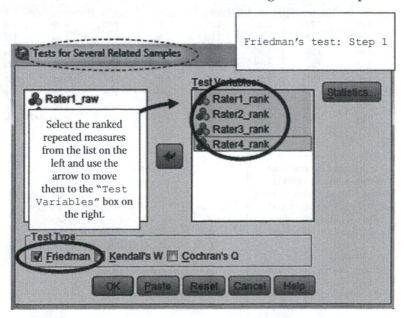

Step 2: Recall that the Friedman test operates using ranked data, not continuous raw scores as with the repeated measures ANOVA; thus, we will work with the ranked variables in our dataset for this test. From the "Tests for Several Related Samples" dialog box, click the variables representing the *ranked levels* of the repeated factor into the "Test Variables" box by using the arrow key in the middle of the dialog box. Under "Test Type" at the bottom left, check "Friedman." Then click on "Ok" to return to generate the output.

Interpreting the output: Annotated results are presented in Table 5.15.

TABLE 5.15

Friedman's Test SPSS Results for the Writing Assessment Example

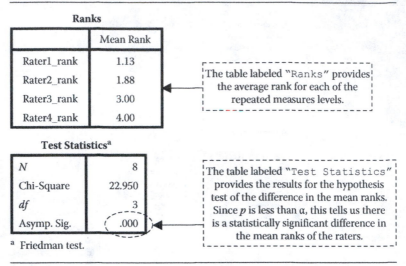

Ranks

	Mean Rank
Rater1_rank	1.13
Rater2_rank	1.88
Rater3_rank	3.00
Rater4_rank	4.00

The table labeled "Ranks" provides the average rank for each of the repeated measures levels.

Test Statistics[a]

N	8
Chi-Square	22.950
df	3
Asymp. Sig.	.000

[a] Friedman test.

The table labeled "Test Statistics" provides the results for the hypothesis test of the difference in the mean ranks. Since p is less than α, this tells us there is a statistically significant difference in the mean ranks of the raters.

Two-Factor Split-Plot ANOVA

To conduct the two-factor split-plot ANOVA, the dataset must include variables for each level of the repeated factor (as in the one-factor repeated measures ANOVA) and another variable for the nonrepeated factor. Here our repeated measures or within-subjects factor is reflected in the raw scores of the four raters, and the nonrepeated or between-subjects factor is the instructor.

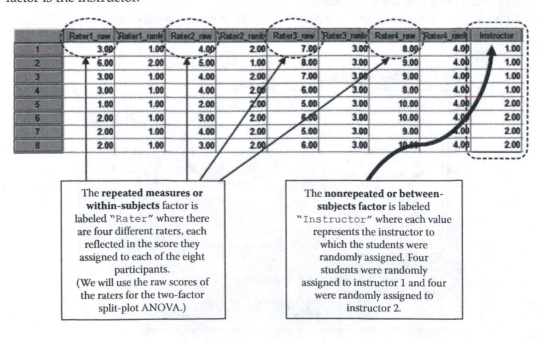

	Rater1_raw	Rater1_rank	Rater2_raw	Rater2_rank	Rater3_raw	Rater3_rank	Rater4_raw	Rater4_rank	Instructor
1	3.00	1.00	4.00	2.00	7.00	3.00	8.00	4.00	1.00
2	6.00	2.00	5.00	1.00	8.00	3.00	9.00	4.00	1.00
3	3.00	1.00	4.00	2.00	7.00	3.00	9.00	4.00	1.00
4	3.00	1.00	4.00	2.00	6.00	3.00	8.00	4.00	1.00
5	1.00	1.00	2.00	2.00	5.00	3.00	10.00	4.00	2.00
6	2.00	1.00	3.00	2.00	6.00	3.00	10.00	4.00	2.00
7	2.00	1.00	4.00	2.00	5.00	3.00	9.00	4.00	2.00
8	2.00	1.00	3.00	2.00	6.00	3.00	10.00	4.00	2.00

The **repeated measures or within-subjects** factor is labeled "Rater" where there are four different raters, each reflected in the score they assigned to each of the eight participants.
(We will use the raw scores of the raters for the two-factor split-plot ANOVA.)

The **nonrepeated or between-subjects factor** is labeled "Instructor" where each value represents the instructor to which the students were randomly assigned. Four students were randomly assigned to instructor 1 and four were randomly assigned to instructor 2.

Step 1: To conduct a two-factor split-plot ANOVA, go to "Analyze" in the top pulldown menu, then select "General Linear Model," and then select "Repeated Measures." This will produce the "Repeated Measures" dialog box. This step has been presented previously (see screenshot step 1 for the one-factor repeated measures design) and will not be reiterated here.

Step 2: The "Repeated Measures Define Factor(s)" dialog box will appear (see screenshot step 2 for the one-factor repeated measures design presented previously). In the box under "Within-Subjects Factor Name," enter the name you wish to call the repeated factor. For this example, we label the repeated factor "Rater." It is necessary to define a name for the repeated factor as there is no single variable representing this factor (recall that the columns in the dataset represent the repeated measures); in the dataset, there is one variable for each level of the factor (in other words, one variable for each different rater or measurement). Again, in our example, there are four levels of rater (i.e., four raters) and thus four variables. Let us name the within-subjects factor "Rater." The "Number of Levels" indicates the number of measurements of the repeated factor. Here there were four raters, and, thus, the "Number of Levels" of the factor is 4.

Step 3: After defining the "Within-Subjects Factor Name" and the "Number of Levels," then click on "Add" to move this information into the middle box. In screenshot step 3 for the one-factor repeated measures design presented previously, we see our newly defined repeated factor (i.e., Rater) with "4" indicating it was measured by four raters: Rater(4). Finally, click on "Define" to open the main "Repeated Measures" dialog box.

Step 4a: From the "Repeated Measures" dialog box (see screenshot steps 4a and b for the one-factor repeated measures design presented previously), we see a heading called "Within-Subjects Variables" with the newly defined factor rater in parentheses. Here the values of 1 through 4 represent each one of the four raters. Preceding each of the levels of the repeated factor are lines with question marks. This is the software's way of asking us to define which variable represents the first measurement (or the first rater in our illustration).

Step 4b: Move the appropriate variables from the variable list on the left into the "Within-Subjects Variables" box on the right. It is important to make sure that the first measurement is matched up with "1," the second measurement is matched with "2," and so forth so that the correct order of repeated measures is defined.

Step 5: Once the "Within-Subjects Variables" are defined, the next step is to define the between-subjects or nonrepeated factor, as we see in screenshot step 5 that follows. Move the appropriate variable from the variable list on the left into the "Between-Subjects Factors" box on the right. From this point, the options and selections work as we have seen when conducting other ANOVA models.

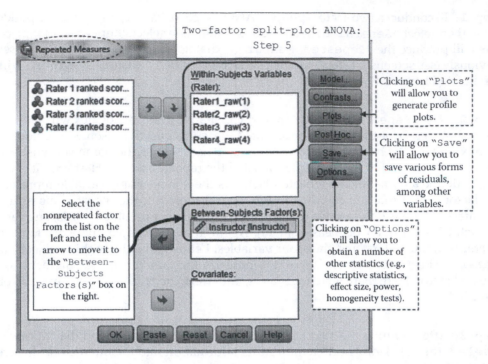

Step 6: From the "Repeated Measures" dialog box, clicking on "Options" will provide the option to select such information as "Descriptive Statistics," "Estimates of effect size," "Observed power," and "Homogeneity tests" (see screenshot step 6). For the two-factor split-plot ANOVA, the "Options" dialog box is the proper place to obtain post hoc MCPs for the *repeated measure*. Post hoc procedures include the Tukey LSD, Bonferroni, and Sidak procedures. Click on "Continue" to return to the original dialog box.

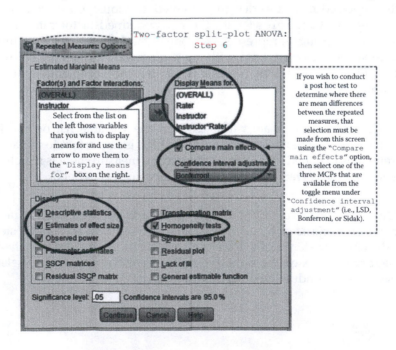

Step 7: Click on the name of the nonrepeated or between-subjects factor in the "Factor(s)" list box in the top left and move it to the "Post Hoc Tests for" box in the top right by clicking on the arrow key. Check an appropriate MCP for your situation by placing a checkmark in the box next to the desired MCP. In this example, we select Tukey (see screenshot step 7). Click on "Continue" to return to the original dialog box.

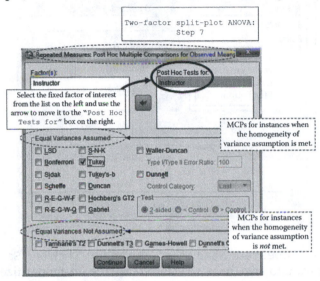

Step 8: From the "Repeated Measures" dialog box, click on "Plots" to obtain a profile plot of means. Click one independent variable (e.g., "Rater") and move it into the "Horizontal Axis" box by clicking the arrow button. Then click the other independent variable (e.g., instructor) and move it into the "Separate Lines" box by clicking the arrow button. Then click on "Add" to move this into the "Plots" box at the bottom of the dialog box (see screenshot steps 8a and b). Click on "Continue" to return to the original dialog box. (*Tip: Placing the factor that has the most categories or levels on the horizontal axis of the profile plot will make for easier interpretation of the graph. In this case, there were four raters and two instructors; thus, we placed "rater" on the horizontal axis.*)

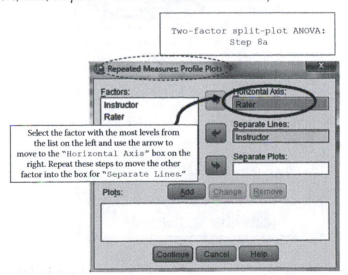

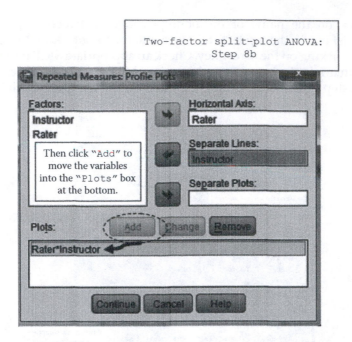

Step 9: From the "Repeated Measures" dialog box, click on "Save" to select those elements that you want to save (here we want to save the unstandardized residuals which will be used later to examine the extent to which normality and independence are met). To do this, place a checkmark next to "Unstandardized." Click "Continue" to return to the main "Repeated Measures" dialog box. From the "Repeated Measures" dialog box, click on "Ok" to generate the output.

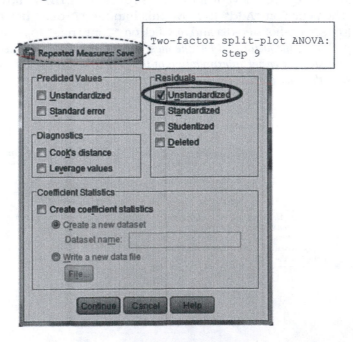

Interpreting the output: Annotated results are presented in Table 5.16.

TABLE 5.16

Two-Factor Split-Plot ANOVA SPSS Results for the Writing Assessment Example

Within-Subjects Factors

Measure: MEASURE_1

Rater	Dependent Variable
1	Rater1_raw
2	Rater2_raw
3	Rater3_raw
4	Rater4_raw

The table labeled "Within-Subjects Factors" lists the variable names for levels of the repeated factor.

Between-Subjects Factors

		Value Label	N
Instructor	1.00	Instructor 1	4
	2.00	Instructor 2	4

The table labeled "Between-Subjects Factors" lists the names and sample sizes for the levels of the nonrepeated factor.

Descriptive Statistics

Instructor		Mean	Std. Deviation	N
Rater 1 raw score	Instructor 1	3.7500	1.50000	4
	Instructor 2	1.7500	.50000	4
	Total	2.7500	1.48805	8
Rater 2 raw score	Instructor 1	4.2500	.50000	4
	Instructor 2	3.0000	.81650	4
	Total	3.6250	.91613	8
Rater 3 raw score	Instructor 1	7.0000	.81650	4
	Instructor 2	5.5000	.57735	4
	Total	6.2500	1.03510	8
Rater 4 raw score	Instructor 1	8.5000	.57735	4
	Instructor 2	9.7500	.50000	4
	Total	9.1250	.83452	8

The table labeled "Descriptive Statistics" lists the means, standard deviations, and sample sizes for each of the between-subjects factors (i.e., instructors) by each of the repeated measures (i.e., raters).

(continued)

TABLE 5.16 (continued)

Two-Factor Split-Plot ANOVA SPSS Results for the Writing Assessment Example

Multivariate Tests[a]

Effect		Value	F	Hypothesis df	Error df	Sig.	Partial Eta Squared	Noncent. Parameter	Observed Power[b]
Rater	Pillai's trace	.983	74.892[c]	3.000	4.000	.001	.983	224.677	1.000
	Wilks' lambda	.017	74.892[c]	3.000	4.000	.001	.983	224.677	1.000
	Hotelling's trace	56.169	74.892[c]	3.000	4.000	.001	.983	224.677	1.000
	Roy's largest root	56.169	74.892[c]	3.000	4.000	.001	.983	224.677	1.000
Rater* instructor	Pillai's trace	.899	11.925[c]	3.000	4.000	.018	.899	35.774	.860
	Wilks' lambda	.101	11.925[c]	3.000	4.000	.018	.899	35.774	.860
	Hotelling's trace	8.944	11.925[c]	3.000	4.000	.018	.899	35.774	.860
	Roy's largest root	8.944	11.925[c]	3.000	4.000	.018	.899	35.774	.860

[a] Design: intercept + instructor
[b] Computed using alpha = .05.
[c] Exact statistic.
Within-subjects design: rater.

The table labeled "Multivariate Tests" provides results for the multivariate test of mean differences for the repeated measures factor (i.e., "Rater"), and for the between-by within-subjects interaction (i.e., "Rater*Instructor"). Multivariate tests are provided when there are three or more levels of the within-subjects factor. These results are generally more conservative than the univariate results (in other words, you may be less likely to find statistically significant multivariate results as compared to univariate results). *Note that the multivariate tests do not require meeting the assumption of sphericity.* Thus if the assumption of sphericity is met, reporting univariate results is recommended.

If results for the multivariate tests are reported, of the four test criteria, Wilks' lambda is recommended. In this example, all four multivariate criteria produce the same results—specifically that there is a statistically significant multivariate mean difference for the repeated measures factor and a statistically significant between- by within-subjects interaction (as noted by p less than α).

"Mauchly's Test of Sphericity" can be reviewed to determine if the assumption of sphericity is met. If the p value is larger than α (as in this illustration), we have met the assumption of sphericity.

"Epsilon" is a gauge of differences in the variances of the repeated measures. The closer the epsilon value is to 1.0, the more homogenous are the variances. Complete heterogeneity of variances is specified by the "Lower bound" and is computed as $1/(K-1)$ where K is the number of within-subjects levels. For this example, with four raters, the lower bound is $1/(4-1)$ or .333.

Measure: MEASURE_1   **Mauchly's Test of Sphericity[a]**

Within Subject Effects	Mauchly's W	Approx. Chi-Square	df	Sig.	Epsilon[b]		
					Geisser–Greenhouse	Huynh–Feldt	Lower bound
Rater	.429	4.001	5	.557	.706	1.000	.333

Tests the null hypothesis that the error covariance matrix of the orthonormalized transformed dependent variables is proportional to an identity matrix.

[a] Design: intercept + instructor
[b] May be used to adjust the degrees of freedom for the averaged tests of significance. Corrected tests are displayed in the Tests of within-Subjects Effects table.
Within-subjects design: rater.

TABLE 5.16 (continued)

Two-Factor Split-Plot ANOVA SPSS Results for the Writing Assessment Example

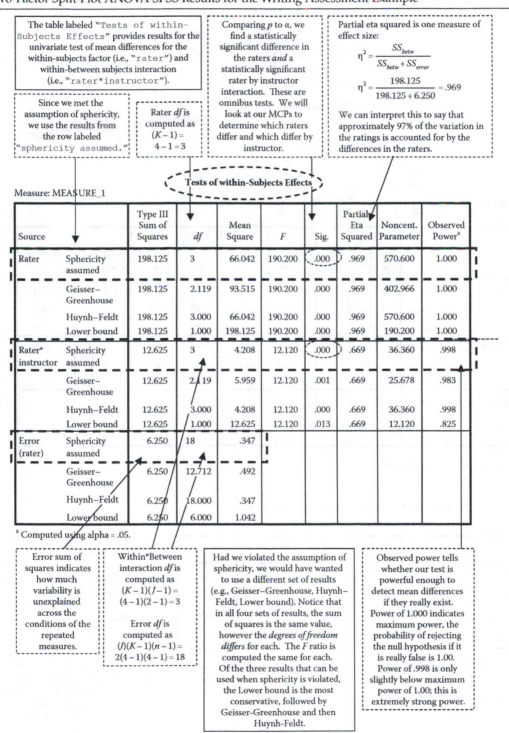

The table labeled "Tests of within-Subjects Effects" provides results for the univariate test of mean differences for the within-subjects factor (i.e., "rater") and within-between subjects interaction (i.e., "rater*instructor").

Comparing *p* to α, we find a statistically significant difference in the raters *and* a statistically significant rater by instructor interaction. These are omnibus tests. We will look at our MCPs to determine which raters differ and which differ by instructor.

Partial eta squared is one measure of effect size:

$$\eta^2 = \frac{SS_{betw}}{SS_{betw} + SS_{error}}$$

$$\eta^2 = \frac{198.125}{198.125 + 6.250} = .969$$

We can interpret this to say that approximately 97% of the variation in the ratings is accounted for by the differences in the raters.

Since we met the assumption of sphericity, we use the results from the row labeled "sphericity assumed."

Rater *df* is computed as $(K-1) = 4-1 = 3$

Tests of within-Subjects Effects

Measure: MEASURE_1

Source		Type III Sum of Squares	df	Mean Square	F	Sig.	Partial Eta Squared	Noncent. Parameter	Observed Power[a]
Rater	Sphericity assumed	198.125	3	66.042	190.200	.000	.969	570.600	1.000
	Geisser–Greenhouse	198.125	2.119	93.515	190.200	.000	.969	402.966	1.000
	Huynh–Feldt	198.125	3.000	66.042	190.200	.000	.969	570.600	1.000
	Lower bound	198.125	1.000	198.125	190.200	.000	.969	190.200	1.000
Rater* instructor	Sphericity assumed	12.625	3	4.208	12.120	.000	.669	36.360	.998
	Geisser–Greenhouse	12.625	2.119	5.959	12.120	.001	.669	25.678	.983
	Huynh–Feldt	12.625	3.000	4.208	12.120	.000	.669	36.360	.998
	Lower bound	12.625	1.000	12.625	12.120	.013	.669	12.120	.825
Error (rater)	Sphericity assumed	6.250	18	.347					
	Geisser–Greenhouse	6.250	12.712	.492					
	Huynh–Feldt	6.250	18.000	.347					
	Lower bound	6.250	6.000	1.042					

[a] Computed using alpha = .05.

Error sum of squares indicates how much variability is unexplained across the conditions of the repeated measures.

Within*Between interaction *df* is computed as $(K-1)(J-1) = (4-1)(2-1) = 3$

Error *df* is computed as $(J)(K-1)(n-1) = 2(4-1)(4-1) = 18$

Had we violated the assumption of sphericity, we would have wanted to use a different set of results (e.g., Geisser–Greenhouse, Huynh–Feldt, Lower bound). Notice that in all four sets of results, the sum of squares is the same value, however the *degrees of freedom differs* for each. The *F* ratio is computed the same for each. Of the three results that can be used when sphericity is violated, the Lower bound is the most conservative, followed by Geisser-Greenhouse and then Huynh-Feldt.

Observed power tells whether our test is powerful enough to detect mean differences if they really exist. Power of 1.000 indicates maximum power, the probability of rejecting the null hypothesis if it is really false is 1.00. Power of .998 is only slightly below maximum power of 1.00; this is extremely strong power.

(continued)

TABLE 5.16 (continued)

Two-Factor Split-Plot ANOVA SPSS Results for the Writing Assessment Example

```
The output from the
"Tests of within-Subjects
Contrasts" will
not be used as polynomial contrasts
do not make sense here.
```

Measure: MEASURE_1   **Tests of within-Subjects Contrasts**

Source	Rater	Type III Sum of Squares	df	Mean Square	F	Sig.	Partial Eta Squared	Noncent. Parameter	Observed Power[a]
Rater	Linear	189.225	1	189.225	302.760	.000	.981	302.760	1.000
	Quadratic	8.000	1	8.000	48.000	.000	.889	48.000	1.000
	Cubic	.900	1	.900	3.600	.107	.375	3.600	.359
Rater* instructor	Linear	9.025	1	9.025	14.440	.009	.706	14.440	.883
	Quadratic	2.000	1	2.000	12.000	.013	.667	12.000	.821
	Cubic	1.600	1	1.600	6.400	.045	.516	6.400	.563
Error(rater)	Linear	3.750	6	.625					
	Quadratic	1.000	6	.167					
	Cubic	1.500	6	.250					

[a] Computed using alpha = .05.

Levene's Test of Equality of Error Variances[a]

	F	df1	df2	Sig.
Rater 1 raw score	3.600	1	6	.107
Rater 2 raw score	.158	1	6	.705
Rater 3 raw score	.000	1	6	1.000
Rater 4 raw score	1.000	1	6	.356

```
The F test (and associated p
values) for Levene's Test for
Equality of Error Variances is
reviewed to determine if equal
variances can be assumed. In
this case, we meet the
assumption (as p is greater
than α).

Note that df1 is degrees of
freedom for the numerator
(calculated as J − 1 and df2
are the degrees of freedom for
the denominator
(calculated as N − J).
```

Tests the null hypothesis that the error variance of the dependent variable is equal across groups.

[a] Design: intercept + instructor

Within-subjects design: rater.

TABLE 5.16 (continued)

Two-Factor Split-Plot ANOVA SPSS Results for the Writing Assessment Example

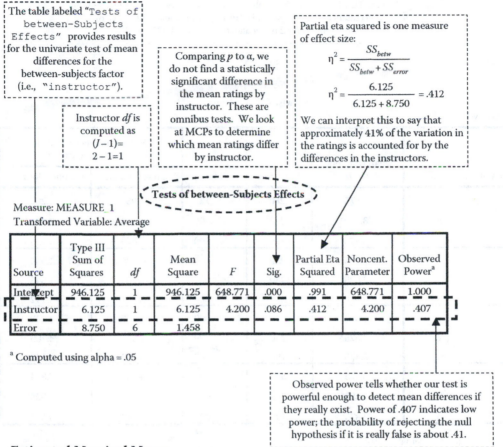

The table labeled "Tests of between-Subjects Effects" provides results for the univariate test of mean differences for the between-subjects factor (i.e., "instructor").

Instructor *df* is computed as $(J-1)= 2-1=1$

Comparing *p* to α, we do not find a statistically significant difference in the mean ratings by instructor. These are omnibus tests. We look at MCPs to determine which mean ratings differ by instructor.

Partial eta squared is one measure of effect size:

$$\eta^2 = \frac{SS_{betw}}{SS_{betw} + SS_{error}}$$

$$\eta^2 = \frac{6.125}{6.125 + 8.750} = .412$$

We can interpret this to say that approximately 41% of the variation in the ratings is accounted for by the differences in the instructors.

Tests of between-Subjects Effects

Measure: MEASURE_1
Transformed Variable: Average

Source	Type III Sum of Squares	df	Mean Square	F	Sig.	Partial Eta Squared	Noncent. Parameter	Observed Power[a]
Intercept	946.125	1	946.125	648.771	.000	.991	648.771	1.000
Instructor	6.125	1	6.125	4.200	.086	.412	4.200	.407
Error	8.750	6	1.458					

[a] Computed using alpha = .05

Observed power tells whether our test is powerful enough to detect mean differences if they really exist. Power of .407 indicates low power; the probability of rejecting the null hypothesis if it is really false is about .41.

Estimated Marginal Means

1. Grand Mean

Measure: MEASURE_1

Mean	Std. Error	95% Confidence Interval	
		Lower Bound	Upper Bound
5.438	.213	4.915	5.960

The "Grand Mean" (in this case, 5.438) represents the overall mean, regardless of the rater or instructor. The 95% CI represents the CI of the grand mean.

2. Rater

Estimates

Measure: MEASURE_1

Rater	Mean	Std. Error	95% Confidence Interval	
			Lower Bound	Upper Bound
1	2.750	.395	1.783	3.717
2	3.625	.239	3.039	4.211
3	6.250	.250	5.638	6.862
4	9.125	.191	8.658	9.592

The table labeled "Rater" provides descriptive statistics for each of the four raters. In addition to means, the *SE* and 95% CI of the means are reported.

(continued)

TABLE 5.16 (continued)

Two-Factor Split-Plot ANOVA SPSS Results for the Writing Assessment Example

> "Mean Difference" is simply the difference between the means of the two raters being compared. For example, the mean difference of rater 1 and rater 2 is calculated as $2.750 - 3.625 = -.875$.

Pairwise Comparisons

Measure: MEASURE_1

(*I*) Rater	(*J*) Rater	Mean Difference (*I – J*)	Std. Error	Sig.[a]	95% Confidence Interval for Difference[a] Lower Bound	95% Confidence Interval for Difference[a] Upper Bound
1	2	−.875	.280	.122	−1.955	.205
	3	−3.500*	.270	.000	−4.543	−2.457
	4	−6.375*	.375	.000	−7.824	−4.926
2	1	.875	.280	.122	−.205	1.955
	3	−2.625*	.280	.000	−3.705	−1.545
	4	−5.500*	.339	.000	−6.808	−4.192
3	1	3.500*	.270	.000	2.457	4.543
	2	2.625*	.280	.000	1.545	3.705
	4	−2.875*	.191	.000	−3.613	−2.137
4	1	6.375*	.375	.000	4.926	7.824
	2	5.500*	.339	.000	4.192	6.808
	3	2.875*	.191	.000	2.137	3.613

Based on estimated marginal means.

[a] Adjustment for multiple comparisons: Bonferroni.

*The mean difference is significant at the .05 level.

> "Sig." denotes the observed *p* value and provides the results of the Bonferroni *post hoc* procedure. There is a statistically significant mean difference in ratings of writing between:
>
> 1. Rater 1 and rater 3
> 2. Rater 1 and rater 4
> 3. Rater 2 and rater 3
> 4. Rater 2 and rater 4
> 5. Rater 3 and rater 4
>
> The only groups for which there is not a statistically significant mean difference is raters 1 and 2.
>
> Note there are redundant results presented in the table. The comparison of rater 1 and 2 (presented in results for rater 1) is the same as the comparison of rater 2 and 1 (presented in results for rater 2) and so forth.

TABLE 5.16 (continued)

Two-Factor Split-Plot ANOVA SPSS Results for the Writing Assessment Example

3. Instructor

Estimates

Measure: MEASURE_1

Instructor	Mean	Std. Error	95% Confidence Interval	
			Lower Bound	Upper Bound
Instructor 1	5.875	.302	5.136	6.614
Instructor 2	5.000	.302	4.261	5.739

> The table for "`Instructor`" provides descriptive statistics for each of the levels of our between-subjects factor. In addition to means, the *SE* and 95% CI of the means are reported.

> "`Mean difference`" is simply the difference between the means of the two categories of our between-subjects factor. For example, the mean difference of instructor 1 and instructor 2 is calculated as $5.875 - 5.000 = .875$

Pairwise Comparisons

Measure: MEASURE_1

(*I*) Instructor	(*J*) Instructor	Mean Difference (*I – J*)	Std. Error	Sig.[a]	95% Confidence Interval for Difference[a]	
					Lower Bound	Upper Bound
Instructor 1	Instructor 2	.875	.427	.086	−.170	1.920
Instructor 2	Instructor 1	−.875	.427	.086	−1.920	.170

Based on estimated marginal means.

[a] Adjustment for multiple comparisons: Bonferroni.

> "Sig." denotes the observed *p* value and provides the results of the Bonferroni *post hoc* procedure. There is not a statistically significant mean difference in ratings between instructor 1 and 2.
>
> Note there are redundant results presented in the table. The comparison of instructor 1 and 2 (presented in the first row) is the same as the comparison of instructor 2 and 1 (presented in the second row).

> The contrast output from the "`Univariate Tests`" will not be used here.

Univariate Tests

Measure: MEASURE_1

	Sum of Squares	*df*	Mean Square	*F*	Sig.	Partial Eta Squared	Noncent. Parameter	Observed Power[a]
Contrast	1.531	1	1.531	4.200	.086	.412	4.200	.407
Error	2.188	6	.365					

The *F* tests the effect of instructor. This test is based on the linearly independent pairwise comparisons among the estimated marginal means.

[a] Computed using alpha = .05.

(continued)

TABLE 5.16 (continued)

Two-Factor Split-Plot ANOVA SPSS Results for the Writing Assessment Example

4. Instructor*Rater

Measure: MEASURE_1

Instructor	Rater	Mean	Std. Error	95% Confidence Interval	
				Lower Bound	Upper Bound
Instructor 1	1	3.750	.559	2.382	5.118
	2	4.250	.339	3.422	5.078
	3	7.000	.354	6.135	7.865
	4	8.500	.270	7.839	9.161
Instructor 2	1	1.750	.559	.382	3.118
	2	3.000	.339	2.172	3.828
	3	5.500	.354	4.635	6.365
	4	9.750	.270	9.089	10.411

> The table for "**Instructor*Rater**" provides descriptive statistics for each of the combinations of instructor by rater (or cell). In addition to means, the *SE* and 95% CI of the means are reported.

Estimated marginal means of MEASURE_1

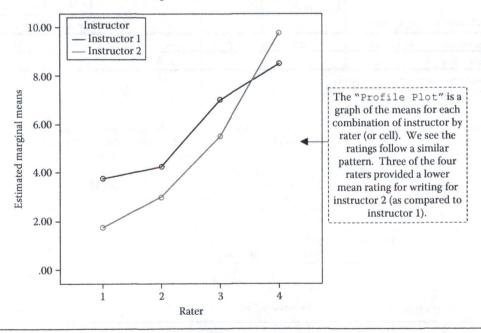

> The "Profile Plot" is a graph of the means for each combination of instructor by rater (or cell). We see the ratings follow a similar pattern. Three of the four raters provided a lower mean rating for writing for instructor 2 (as compared to instructor 1).

Examining Data for Assumptions for Two-Factor Split-Plot ANOVA

Normality

We use the residuals (which we requested and created through the "Save" option when generating our two-factor split-plot ANOVA) to examine the extent to which normality was met.

	Rater1_raw	Rater1_rank	Rater2_raw	Rater2_rank	Rater3_raw	Rater3_rank	Rater4_raw	Rater4_rank		RES_1	RES_2	RES_3	RES_4
1	3.00	1.00	4.00	2.00	7.00	3.00	8.00	4.00	1.00	-.75	-.25	.00	-.50
2	6.00	2.00	5.00	1.00	8.00	3.00	9.00	.00	1.00	2.25	.75	1.00	.50
3	3.00	1.00	4.00	2.00	7.00	3.00	9.00	4.00	1.00	-.75	-.25	.00	.50
4									.00	-.75	-.25	-1.00	-.50
5									.00	-.75	-1.00	-.50	.25
6									.00	.25	.00	.50	.25
7									.00	.25	1.00	-.50	-.75
8									.00	.25	.00	.50	.25

The residuals are computed by subtracting the cell mean from each observation. For example, the mean rating on writing for students assigned to instructor 1 and rated by rater 1 was 3.75. Person 1 was rated a "3" on writing by rater 1. Thus the residual for person 1 is

$$3.00 - 3.75 = -.75.$$

We see four new variables have been added to the dataset labeled **RES_1**, **RES_2**, and so forth. These are the residual used to review the normality assumption.

Generating normality evidence: As mentioned in previous chapters, understanding the distributional shape, specifically the extent to which normality is a reasonable assumption, is important. For the two-factor mixed design ANOVA, the distributional shape for the residuals should be a normal distribution. Because we have multiple residuals to reflect the multiple measurements, we need to examine normality for *each* residual. For brevity, we provide SPSS excerpts only for "RES_1," which reflects the residual for time 1; however, we will narratively discuss all of the residuals.

As in previous chapters, we can again use "Explore" to examine the extent to which the assumption of normality is met. The steps for accessing "Explore" have already been presented, and, thus, we only provide a basic overview of the process. Click the residual and move it into the "Dependent List" box by clicking on the arrow button. The procedures for selecting normality statistics are as follows: Click on "Plots" in the upper right corner. Place a checkmark in the boxes for "Normality plots with tests" and also for "Histogram." Then click "Continue" to return to the main "Explore" dialog box. Finally click "Ok" to generate the output.

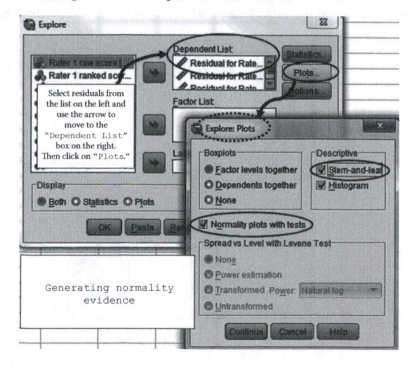

Generating normality evidence

Interpreting normality evidence: We have already developed a good understanding of how to interpret some forms of evidence of normality including skewness and
kurtosis, histograms, and boxplots. Next we see the output for this evidence.

Descriptives

			Statistic	Std. Error
Residual for Rater1_raw	Mean		.0000	.36596
	95% Confidence interval for mean	Lower bound	−.8654	
		Upper bound	.8654	
	5% Trimmed mean		−.0833	
	Median		−.2500	
	Variance		1.071	
	Std. deviation		1.03510	
	Minimum		−.75	
	Maximum		2.25	
	Range		3.00	
	Interquartile range		1.00	
	Skewness		1.675	.752
	Kurtosis		3.136	1.481

The skewness statistic of the residuals for rater 1 is 1.675 and kurtosis is 3.136—skewness
being within the range of an absolute value of 2.0, suggesting some evidence of normality.
However, kurtosis suggests some nonnormality. For the other three residuals, all skewness
and kurtosis statistics (not shown here) are within an absolute value of 2.0, suggesting evidence
of normality. As suggested by the skewness statistic, the histogram of residuals is positively
skewed, and the histogram also provides a visual display of the leptokurtic distribution.

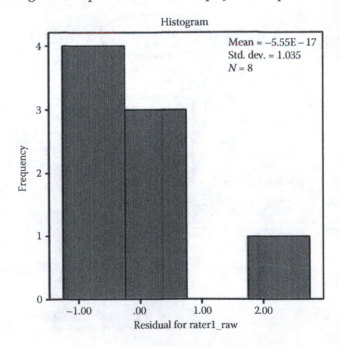

Histogram

Mean = −5.55E − 17
Std. dev. = 1.035
N = 8

There are a few other statistics that can be used to gauge normality. The formal test of normality, the Shapiro–Wilk (S–W) test (*SW*) (Shapiro & Wilk, 1965), provides evidence of the extent to which the sample distribution is statistically different from a normal distribution. The output for the S–W test is presented in the following and suggests that our sample distributions for three of the four residuals (specifically residuals for raters 2, 3, and 4) are not statistically significantly different than what would be expected from a normal distribution, as those *p* values are less than α. However, the distribution for the residual for rater 1 *is* statistically significantly different than a normal distribution (*SW* = .745, *df* = 8, *p* = .007).

Tests of Normality

	Kolmogorov–Smirnov[a]			Shapiro–Wilk		
	Statistic	*df*	Sig.	Statistic	*df*	Sig.
Residual for Rater1_raw	.280	8	.065	.745	8	.007
Residual for Rater2_raw	.250	8	.150	.913	8	.374
Residual for Rater3_raw	.152	8	.200*	.965	8	.857
Residual for Rater4_raw	.316	8	.018	.828	8	.057

[a] Lilliefors significance correction.
*This is a lower bound of the true significance.

Quantile–quantile (Q–Q) plots are also often examined to determine evidence of normality. These graphs plot quantiles of the theoretical normal distribution against quantiles of the sample distribution. Points that fall on or close to the diagonal line suggest evidence of normality. The Q–Q plot of residuals shown in the following suggests some nonnormality.

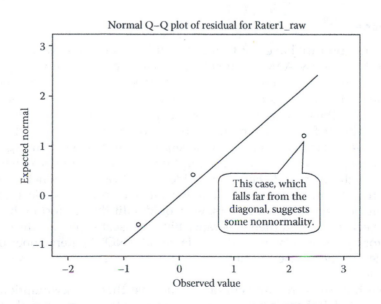

Normal Q–Q plot of residual for Rater1_raw

Examination of the following boxplot also suggests a nonnormal distributional shape of residuals with one outlier.

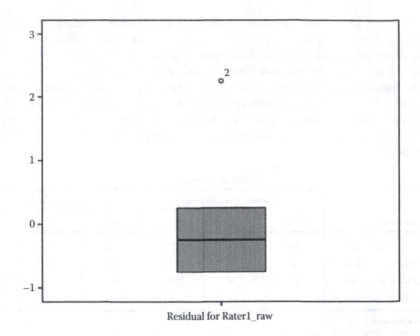

Residual for Rater1_raw

For three of the four residuals (residuals for raters 2, 3, and 4), the forms of evidence we have examined—skewness and kurtosis statistics, the S–W test, the Q–Q plot, and the boxplot—all suggest normality is a reasonable assumption. We can be reasonably assured we have met the assumption of normality for residuals for raters 2, 3, and 4. However, all forms of evidence suggest nonnormality for the residual for rater 1.

Independence

The only assumption we have not tested for yet is independence. As we discussed in reference to the one-way ANOVA, if subjects have been randomly assigned to conditions (in other words, the different levels of the between-subjects factor), the assumption of independence has been met. In this illustration, students were randomly assigned to instructor, and, thus, the assumption of independence was met. However, we often use between-subjects factors that do not allow random assignment, such as preexisting characteristics (e.g., gender or education level). We can plot residuals against levels of our between-subjects factor using a scatterplot to get an idea of whether or not there are patterns in the data and thereby provide an indication of whether we have met this assumption. In this illustration, we only have one between-subjects factor. If there were multiple between-subjects factors, we would split the scatterplot by levels of one between-subjects factor and then generate a bivariate scatterplot for the other between-subjects factor by residual (as we did with factorial ANOVA). Remember that the residual was added to the dataset by saving it when we generated the two-factor split-plot ANOVA model.

Please note that some researchers do not believe that the assumption of independence can be tested. If there is not random assignment to groups, then these researchers believe this assumption has been violated—period. The plot that we generate will give us a general idea of patterns, however, in situations where random assignment was not performed.

Generating the scatterplot: The general steps for generating a simple scatterplot through "Scatter/dot" have been presented in Chapter 10 of *An Introduction to Statistical Concepts*, Third Edition, and will not be reiterated here. From the "Simple Scatterplot" dialog screen, click the residual variable and move it into the "Y Axis" box by clicking on the arrow. Click the between-subjects factor (e.g., "Instructor") and move it into the "X Axis" box by clicking on the arrow. Then click "Ok." Repeat these steps for each of the four residuals.

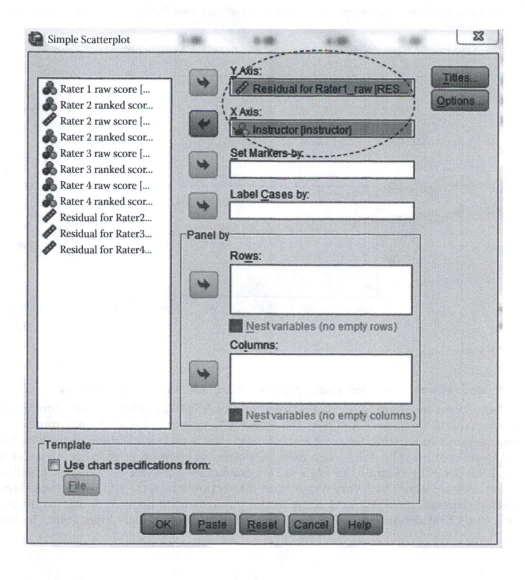

Interpreting independence evidence: In examining the scatterplots for evidence of independence, the points should fall relatively randomly above and below a horizontal line at 0. (You may recall in Chapter 1 that we added a reference line to the graph using Chart Editor. To add a reference line, double click on the graph in the output to activate the chart editor. Select "Options" in the top pulldown menu, then "Y axis reference line." This will bring up the "Properties" dialog box. Change the value of the position to be "0." Then click on "Apply" and "Close" to generate the graph with a horizontal line at 0.)

Here our scatterplot for each residual generally suggests evidence of independence with a relatively random display of residuals above and below the horizontal line at 0 for each category of time (note that only the scatterplot of the residual for rater 3 by instructor is presented). If we had not met the assumption of independence through random assignment of cases to groups, this provides evidence that independence was a reasonable assumption.

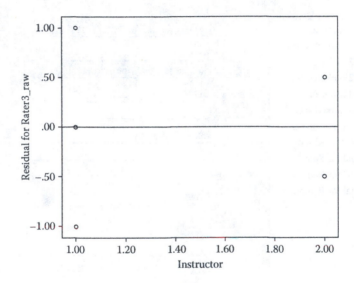

Post Hoc Power for Two-Factor Split-Plot ANOVA Using G*Power

Generating power analyses for two-factor split-plot ANOVA models follows similarly to that for ANOVA, factorial ANOVA, and ANCOVA. In particular, if there is more than one independent variable, we must test for main effects and interactions separately. The first thing that must be done when using G*Power for computing post hoc power is to select the correct test family. In our case, we conducted a two-factor split-plot ANOVA. Because we have both between, within, and interaction terms, the type of statistical test selected depends on which part of the model power is to be estimated. In this illustration, let us first determine power for the within-between subjects interaction. To find this design, we select "Tests" in the top pulldown menu, then "Means," and then "ANOVA: Repeated measures, within-between interactions." Once that selection is made, the "Test family" automatically changes to "F Tests." (Note that had we wanted to determine power for the between-subjects main effect, we would have selected "ANOVA: Repeated measures, between factors." For the within-subjects main effect, we would have selected "ANOVA: Repeated measures, within factors.")

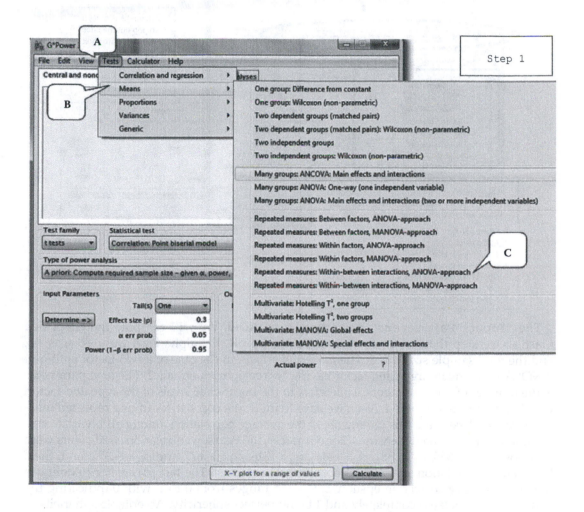

The "Type of Power Analysis" desired needs to be selected. To compute post hoc power, select "Post hoc: Compute achieved power—given α, sample size, and effect size."

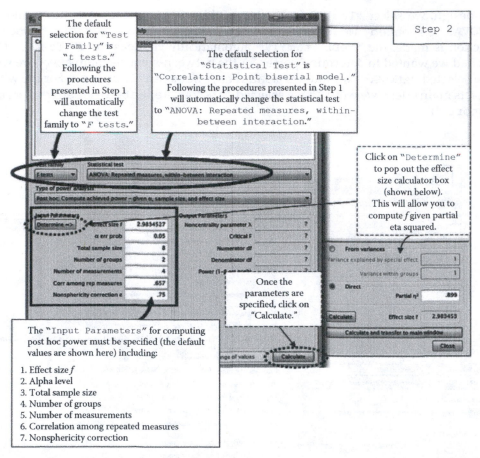

The "Input Parameters" must then be specified. We will compute the effect size *f* last, so we skip that for the moment. In our example, the alpha level we used was .05, and the total sample size was 8. The *number of groups*, in the case of a two-factor split-plot ANOVA with one nonrepeated factor having two categories, equals 2. The next parameter is the number of measurements. This refers to the number of levels of the repeated factor, which in this illustration is 4. Next, we have to input the correlation among repeated measures. We will estimate this parameter as the average correlation among all bivariate correlations of the repeated measures. For our raters, the Pearson correlation coefficients were as follows: $r_{12} = .865$, $r_{13} = .881$, $r_{14} = -.431$, $r_{23} = .716$, $r_{24} = -.677$, and $r_{34} = -.372$, and, thus, the average correlation was .657 (in absolute value terms). The last parameter to define is the nonsphericity correction epsilon, ε. Epsilon ranges from 0 to 1, with 0 indicating the assumption is violated completely and 1 being perfect sphericity. Acceptable sphericity is approximately .75 or higher. One option is to input an acceptable level of sphericity; thus, we input .75 here. Alternatively, we could input the epsilon values obtained for the usual, Geisser–Greenhouse, and Huynh–Feldt *F* tests.

We skipped filling in the first parameter, the effect size *f*, until all of the previous values were input. This is because SPSS only provides a partial eta squared effect size. We use the pop-out effect size calculator in G*Power to compute the effect size *f*. To pop out the effect size calculator, click on "Determine," which is displayed under "Input Parameters." In the pop-out effect size calculator, click on the radio button for "Direct" and then enter the partial eta squared value that was calculated in SPSS (i.e., .899). Clicking on

"Calculate" in the pop-out effect size calculator will calculate the effect size *f*. Then click on "Calculate and Transfer to Main Window" to transfer the calculated effect size (i.e., 2.9834527) to the "Input Parameters." Once the parameters are specified, click on "Calculate" to find the power statistics.

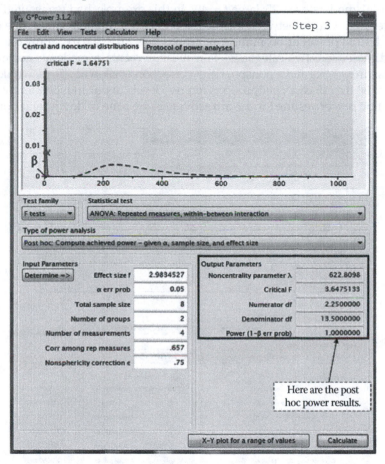

The "Output Parameters" provide the relevant statistics given the input just specified. In this example, we were interested in determining post hoc power for the within-between interaction in a two-factor split-plot ANOVA with a computed effect size *f* of 2.9834527, an alpha level of .05, total sample size of 8, two groups, four measurements, an average correlation among repeated measures of .657, and epsilon sphericity correction of .75. Based on those criteria, the post hoc power of our within-between interaction effect for this test was 1.000—the probability of rejecting the null hypothesis when it is really false (in this case, the probability that the means of the dependent variable would be equal for each level of the independent variable) was at the maximum (i.e., 100%) (sufficient power is often .80 or above). Note that this is the same value as that reported in SPSS. Keep in mind that conducting power analysis a priori is recommended so that you avoid a situation where, post hoc, you find that the sample size was not sufficient to reach the desired level of power (given the observed parameters).

A Priori Power for Two-Factor Split-Plot ANOVA Using G*Power

For a priori power, we can determine the total sample size needed for the main effects and/or interactions given an estimated effect size *f*, alpha level, desired power, number of groups (i.e., the number of categories of the independent variable *in the case of only one independent variable* OR the product of the number of levels of the independent variables *in the case of multiple independent variables*), number of measurements, correlation among repeated measures, and nonsphericity correction epsilon. We follow Cohen's (1988) convention for effect size (i.e., small $f = .10$; moderate $f = .25$; large $f = .40$). In this example, had we wanted to determine a priori power for a within-between interaction and had estimated a moderate effect f of .25, alpha of .05, desired power of .80, number of groups was 2 (i.e., we have only one independent variable, and there were two categories), four measurements, a moderate correlation among repeated measures of .50, and a nonsphericity correction epsilon of .75, we would need a total sample size of 30 (i.e., 15 cases per group given two levels to our independent variable). Here are the post hoc power results for the attractiveness by time of day interaction.

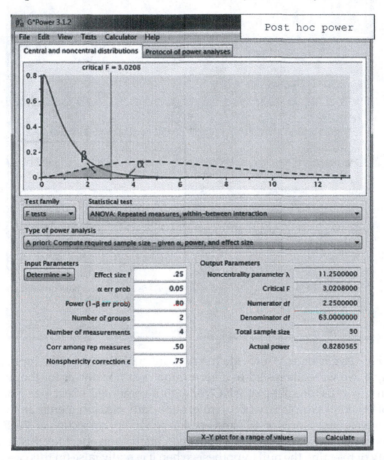

5.7 Template and APA-Style Write-Up

Finally, here is an example paragraph just for the results of the two-factor split-plot design (feel free to write similar paragraphs for the other models in this chapter). Recall that our graduate research assistant, Marie, was assisting the coordinator of the English program, Mark. Mark wanted to know the following: if there is a mean difference in writing based on instructor, if there is a mean difference in writing based on rater, and if there is a mean difference in writing based on rater by instructor. The research questions presented to Mark from Marie's work include the following:

- *Is there a mean difference in writing based on instructor?*
- *Is there a mean difference in writing based on rater?*
- *Is there a mean difference in writing based on rater by instructor?*

Marie then assisted Mark in generating a two-factor split-plot ANOVA as the test of inference, and a template for writing the research questions for this design is presented as follows. As we noted in previous chapters, it is important to ensure the reader understands the levels or groups of the factor(s). This may be done parenthetically in the actual research question, as an operational definition, or specified within the methods section:

- Is there a mean difference in [dependent variable] based on [between-subjects factor]?
- Is there a mean difference in [dependent variable] based on [within-subjects factor]?
- Is there a mean difference in [dependent variable] based on [between-subjects factor] by [within-subjects factor]?

It may be helpful to preface the results of the two-factor split-plot ANOVA with information on an examination of the extent to which the assumptions were met (recall there are several assumptions that we tested). For the between-subjects factor (i.e., the nonrepeated factor), assumptions include (a) independence of observations, (b) homogeneity of variance, and (c) normality. For the within-subjects factor (i.e., the repeated factor), we examine the assumption of sphericity.

A two-factor split-plot (one within-subjects factor and one between-subjects factor) ANOVA was conducted. The within-subjects factor was rater on a writing assessment task (four independent raters), and the between-subjects factor was instructor (two instructors). The null hypotheses tested include the following: (1) the mean writing scores were equal for each of the four different raters, (2) the mean writing scores for each instructor were equal, and (3) the mean writing scores by rater given instructor were equal.

There were no missing data and no univariate outliers. The assumption of sphericity was met ($\chi^2 = 4.001$, Mauchly's $W = .429$, $df = 5$, $p = .557$); therefore, the results reported reflect univariate results. The sphericity assumption was further upheld in that the same results were obtained for the usual, Geisser–Greenhouse, and Huynh–Feldt F tests. The assumption of homogeneity of variance was met for the writing scores of all raters [rater 1, $F(1, 6) = 3.600$, $p = .107$; rater 2, $F(1, 6) = .158$, $p = .705$; rater 3, $F(1, 6) = .000$, $p = 1.000$; and rater 4, $F(1, 6) = 1.000$, $p = .356$].

The assumption of normality was tested via examination of the residuals. Review of the S–W test for normality ($SW_{rater1} = .745$, $df = 8$, $p = .007$; $SW_{rater2} = .913$, $df = 8$, $p = .374$; $SW_{rater3} = .965$, $df = 8$, $p = .857$; $SW_{rater4} = .828$, $df = 8$, $p = .057$), and skewness (rater 1 = 1.675; rater

2 = .290; rater 3 = .000; rater 4 = −.571) and kurtosis (rater 1 = 3.136; rater 2 = .272; rater 3 = −.700; rater 4 = −1.729) statistics suggest that normality was a reasonable assumption for raters 2, 3, and 4, but nonnormality was suggested for rater 1. The boxplot suggested a relatively normal distributional shape (with no outliers) of the residuals for raters 2 through 4. The boxplot of the residuals for rater 1 suggested nonnormality with one outlier. The Q–Q plots suggested normality was reasonable for the residuals of raters 2, 3, and 4, but suggested nonnormality for rater 1. Thus, while there was nonnormality suggested by the residuals for rater 1, the two-factor split-plot ANOVA is robust to violations of normality with equal sample sizes of groups as is evident in this design.

Random assignment of individuals to instructors helped ensure that the assumption of independence was met. Additionally, a scatterplot of residuals against the levels of the between-subjects factors was reviewed. A relatively random display of points around 0 provided further evidence that the assumption of independence was met.

Here is an APA-style example paragraph of results for the two-factor split-plot ANOVA (remember that this will be prefaced by the previous paragraph reporting the extent to which the assumptions of the test were met).

From Table 5.16, the results for the univariate ANOVA indicate the following:

1. A statistically significant within-subjects main effect for rater (F_{rater} = 190.200, df = 3,18, p = .001) (rater 1, M = 2.750, SE = .395; rater 2, M = 3.625, SE = .239; rater 3, M = 6.250, SE = .250; rater 4, M = 9.125, SE = .191)

2. A statistically significant within-between subjects interaction effect between rater and instructor ($F_{rater \times instructor}$ = 12.120, df = 3,18, p = .001) (for brevity, we have not included the means and standard errors here; however, you may want to include those in the narrative or in tabular form)

3. A nonstatistically significant between-subjects main effect for instructor ($F_{instructor}$ = 4.200, df = 1,6, p = .086) (instructor 1, M = 5.875, SE = .302; instructor 2, M = 5.000, SE = .302)

Effect sizes were rather large for the significant effects (partial η^2_{rater} = .969, power = 1.000; partial $\eta^2_{rater \times instructor}$ = .669, power = .998) with more than sufficient observed power, but less so for the nonsignificant effect (partial $\eta^2_{instructor}$ = .412, power = .407) which had less than desired power.

The statistically significant *main effect for the within-subjects factor* suggests that there are mean differences in writing scores by rater. The raters were quite inconsistent in that Bonferroni MCPs revealed statistically significant differences among all pairs of raters except for rater 1 versus rater 2. The nonstatistically significant *main effect for the between-subjects factor* suggests that there are not differences, on average, in writing scores per instructor. In examining CIs of the *interaction for the between-within factor* (i.e., instructor by rater), nonoverlapping CIs suggest statistically significant differences. We see that the patterns evident for the within-subjects factors echo here as well. For both instructor 1 and instructor 2, there are statistically significant differences among all pairs of raters except for rater 1 versus rater 2. From the profile plot in Figure 5.2, we see that while rater 4 found the students of instructor 2 to have better essays, the other raters liked the essays written by the students of instructor 1. It is suggested that a more detailed plan for evaluating essays, including rater training, be implemented in the future.

5.8 Summary

In this chapter, methods involving the comparison of means for random- and mixed-effects models were considered. Five different models were examined; these included the one-factor random-effects model, the two-factor random- and mixed-effects models, the one-factor repeated measures model, and the two-factor split-plot or mixed design. Included for each design were the usual topics of model characteristics, the linear model, assumptions of the model and the effects of their violation, the ANOVA summary table and expected mean squares, and MCPs. Also included for particular designs was a discussion of the compound symmetry assumption and alternative ANOVA procedures.

At this point, you should have met the following objectives: (a) be able to understand the characteristics and concepts underlying random- and mixed-effects ANOVA models, (b) be able to determine and interpret the results of random- and mixed-effects ANOVA models, and (c) be able to understand and evaluate the assumptions of random- and mixed-effects ANOVA models. In Chapter 6, we continue our extended tour of the ANOVA by looking at hierarchical designs that involve one factor nested within another factor (i.e., nested or hierarchical designs), and randomized block designs, which we have very briefly introduced in this chapter.

Problems

Conceptual Problems

5.1 When an ANOVA design includes a random factor that is crossed with a fixed factor, the design illustrates which type of model?

   a. Fixed

   b. Mixed

   c. Random

   d. Crossed

5.2 The denominator of the F ratio used to test the interaction in a two-factor ANOVA is MS_{with} in which one of the following?

    a. Fixed-effects model

    b. Random-effects model ✓

    c. Mixed-effects model

    d. All of the above

5.3 A course consists of five units, the order of presentation of which is varied (counterbalanced). A researcher used a 5×2 ANOVA design with order (five different randomly selected orders) and gender serving as factors. Which ANOVA model is illustrated by this design?

    a. Fixed-effects model

    b. Random-effects model

    c. Mixed-effects model

    d. Nested model

5.4 A researcher conducts a study where children are measured on frequency of sharing at three different times over the course of the academic year. Which ANOVA model is most appropriate for analysis of these data?

    a. One-factor random-effects model

    b. Two-factor random-effects model

    c. Two-factor mixed-effects model

    d. One-factor repeated measures design

    e. Two-factor split-plot design

5.5 A health-care researcher wants to make generalizations about the number of patients served by after hour clinics in her region. She randomly samples clinics and collects data on the number of patients served. Which ANOVA model is most appropriate for analysis of these data?

    a. One-factor random-effects model

    b. Two-factor random-effects model

    c. Two-factor mixed-effects model

    d. One-factor repeated measures design

    e. Two-factor split-plot design

5.6 A preschool teacher randomly assigns children to classrooms—some with windows and some without windows. She wants to know if there is a mean difference in receptive vocabulary based on type of classroom (with and without windows) and whether this varies by classroom teacher. Which ANOVA model is most appropriate for analysis of these data?

    a. One-factor random-effects model

    b. Two-factor random-effects model

    c. Two-factor mixed-effects model ✗

    d. One-factor repeated measures design

    e. Two-factor split-plot design (this is mixed)

5.7 If a given set of data were analyzed with both a one-factor fixed-effects model and a one-factor random-effects model, the F ratio for the random-effects model will be greater than the F ratio for the fixed-effects model. True or false?

5.8 A repeated measures design is necessarily an example of the random-effects model. True or false?

5.9 Suppose researchers A and B perform a two-factor ANOVA on the same data, but that A assumes a fixed-effects model and B assumes a random-effects model. I assert that if A finds the interaction significant at the .05 level, B will also find the interaction significant at the .05 level. Am I correct?

5.10 I assert that MS_{with} should always be used as the denominator for all F ratios in any two-factor ANOVA. Am I correct?

5.11 I assert that in a one-factor repeated measures ANOVA and a two-factor split-plot ANOVA, the SS_{total} will be exactly the same when using the same data. Am I correct?

5.12 Football players are each exposed to all three different counterbalanced coaching strategies, one per month. This is an example of which type of model?

    a. One-factor fixed-effects ANOVA model

    b. One-factor repeated-measures ANOVA model

    c. One-factor random-effects ANOVA model X

    d. One-factor fixed-effects ANCOVA model ?

5.13 A two-factor split-plot design involves which of the following? (p. 210)

    a. Two repeated factors X

    b. Two nonrepeated factors X

    c. One repeated factor and one nonrepeated factor ✓

    d. Farmers splitting up their land into plots X

5.14 The interaction between factors L and M can be assessed only if which one of the following occurs?

    a. Both factors are crossed.

    b. Both factors are random.

    c. Both factors are fixed.

    d. Factor L is a repeated factor.

5.15 A student factor is almost always random. True or false?

5.16 In a two-factor split-plot design, there are two interaction terms. Hypotheses can actually be tested for how many of those interactions?

    a. 0

    b. 1

    c. 2

    d. Cannot be determined

5.17 In a one-factor repeated measures ANOVA design, the F test is quite robust to violation of the sphericity assumption, and, thus, we never need to worry about it. True or false?

Computational Problems

5.1   Complete the following ANOVA summary table for a two-factor model, where there are three levels of factor A (fixed method effect) and two levels of factor B (random teacher effect). Each cell of the design includes four students ($\alpha = .01$).

Source	SS	df	MS	F	Critical Value	Decision
A	3.64	—	—	—	—	—
B	.57	—	—	—	—	—
AB	2.07	—	—	—	—	—
Within	—	—	—			
Total	8.18	—				

5.2   A researcher tested whether aerobics increased the fitness level of eight undergraduate students participating over a 4-month period. Students were measured at the end of each month using a 10-point fitness measure (10 being most fit). The data are shown here. Conduct an ANOVA to determine the effectiveness of the program, using $\alpha = .05$. Use the Bonferroni method to detect exactly where the differences are among the time points (if they are different).

Subject	Time 1	Time 2	Time 3	Time 4
1	3	4	6	9
2	4	7	5	10
3	5	7	7	8
4	1	3	5	7
5	3	4	7	9
6	2	5	6	7
7	1	4	6	9
8	2	4	5	6

5.3   Using the same data as in Computational Problem 2, conduct a two-factor split-plot ANOVA, where the first four subjects participate in a step aerobics program and the last four subjects participate in a spinning program ($\alpha = 05$).

5.4   To examine changes in teaching self-efficacy, 10 teachers were measured on their self-efficacy toward teaching at the beginning of their teaching career and at the end of their 1st and 3rd years of teaching. The teaching self-efficacy scale ranged from 0 to 100 with higher scores reflecting greater teaching self-efficacy. The data are shown here. Conduct a one-factor repeated measures ANOVA to determine mean differences across time, using $\alpha = .05$. Use the Bonferroni method to detect if and/or where the differences are among the time points.

Subject	Beginning Year 1	End Year 1	End Year 3
1	35	50	45
2	50	75	82
3	42	51	56
4	70	72	71
5	65	50	81
6	92	42	69
7	80	82	88
8	78	76	79
9	85	60	83
10	64	71	89

5.5 Using the same data as in Computational Problem 4, conduct a two-factor split-plot ANOVA, where the first five subjects participate in a mentoring program and the last five subjects do not participate in a mentoring program ($\alpha = 05$).

5.6 As a statistical consultant, a researcher comes to you with the following partial SPSS output (sphericity assumed). In a two-factor split-plot ANOVA design, rater is the repeated (or within-subjects) factor, gender of the rater is the nonrepeated (or between-subjects) factor, and the dependent variable is history exam scores. (a) Are the effects significant (which you must determine, as significance is missing, using $\alpha = .05$)? (b) What are the implications of these results in terms of rating the history exam?

Tests of Within-Subjects Effects

Source	Type III SS	df	MS	F
Rater	298.38	3	99.46	30.47
Rater*gender	184.38	3	61.46	18.83
Error (rater)	58.75	18	3.26	✗

Tests of Between-Subjects Effects

Source	Type III SS	df	MS	F
Gender	153.13	1	153.13	20.76
Error	44.25	6	7.38	

Interpretive Problems

5.1 In Chapter 3, you built on the interpretive problem from Chapter 1 utilizing the survey 1 dataset from the website. SPSS was used to conduct a two-factor fixed-effects ANOVA, including effect size, where political view was factor A (as in Chapter 1, $J = 5$), gender is factor B (a new factor, $K = 2$), and the dependent variable was the same one you used previously in Chapter 1. Now, in addition to the two-factor fixed-effects ANOVA, conduct a random-effects and mixed-effects designs. Determine whether the nature of the factors makes any difference in the results.

5.2 In Chapter 3, you built on the interpretive problem from Chapter 1 utilizing the survey 1 dataset from the website. SPSS was used to conduct a two-factor fixed-effects ANOVA, including effect size, where hair color was factor A (i.e., one independent variable) ($J = 5$), gender was factor B (a new factor, $K = 2$), and the dependent variable was a variable of interest to you (the following variables look interesting: books, TV, exercise, drinks, GPA, GRE-Q, CDs, hair appointment). Now, in addition to the two-factor fixed-effects ANOVA, conduct a random-effects and mixed-effects designs. Determine whether the nature of the factors makes any difference in the results.

6

Hierarchical and Randomized Block Analysis of Variance Models

Chapter Outline

Key Concepts

1. Crossed designs and nested designs
2. Confounding
3. Randomized block designs
4. Methods of blocking

In the previous chapters, our discussion has dealt with different analysis of variance (ANOVA) models. In this chapter, we complete our discussion of ANOVA by considering models in which there are multiple factors, but where at least one of the factors is either a hierarchical (or nested) factor or a blocking factor. As we define these models, we shall see that this results in a hierarchical (or nested) design and a blocking design, respectively. In this chapter, we are mostly concerned with the two-factor hierarchical (or nested) model and the two-factor randomized block model, although these models can be generalized to designs with more than two factors. Most of the concepts used in this chapter are the same as those covered in previous chapters. In addition, new concepts include crossed and nested factors, confounding, blocking factors, and methods of blocking. Our objectives are that by the end of this chapter, you will be able to (a) understand the characteristics and concepts underlying hierarchical and randomized block ANOVA models, (b) determine and interpret the results of hierarchical and randomized block ANOVA models, (c) understand and evaluate the assumptions of hierarchical and randomized block ANOVA models, and (d) compare different ANOVA models and select an appropriate model.

6.1 Two-Factor Hierarchical Model

Throughout the text, we have followed Marie, a graduate student enrolled in an educational research program, on her statistical analysis adventures. In this chapter, we see her embarking on a new journey.

Seeing the success that Marie has had with more complex statistical analysis, Marie's faculty advisor has provided Marie with another challenging task. This time, Marie will be working with a reading faculty member (JoAnn) at their university. JoAnn has conducted an experiment in which children were randomly assigned to one of two reading approaches (basal or whole language) and one of four different teachers. There were 24 children who participated; thus, there were six children in each reading approach-teacher combination. Each student was assessed on reading comprehension at the conclusion of the study. JoAnn wants to know the following: if there is a mean difference in reading based on approach to reading and if there is a mean difference in reading between teachers. Marie suggests the following research questions to JoAnn:

- *Is there a mean difference in reading based on approach to reading?*
- *Is there a mean difference in reading based on teacher?*

With one between-subjects independent variable (i.e., approach to reading) and one hierarchical or nested factor (i.e., teacher), Marie determines that a two-factor hierarchical ANOVA is the best statistical procedure to use to answer JoAnn's question. Her next task is to assist JoAnn in analyzing the data.

In this section, we describe the distinguishing characteristics of the two-factor hierarchical ANOVA model, the layout of the data, the linear model, the ANOVA summary table and expected mean squares, and multiple comparison procedures (MCPs).

6.1.1 Characteristics of the Model

The characteristics of the two-factor fixed-, random-, and mixed-effects models have already been covered in Chapters 3 and 5. Here we consider a special form of the two-factor model where one factor is nested within another factor. The best introduction to this model is via an example. Suppose you are interested in which of several different major teaching pedagogies (e.g., worksheet, math manipulative, and computer-based approaches) results in the highest level of achievement in mathematics among second-grade students. Thus, math achievement is the dependent variable, and teaching pedagogy is one factor. A second factor is teacher. That is, you may also believe that some teachers are more effective than others, which results in different levels of student achievement. However, each teacher has only one class of students and thus only one major teaching pedagogy. In other words, all combinations of the pedagogy and teacher factors are not possible. This design is known as a **nested design, hierarchical design**, or **multilevel model** because the teacher factor is nested within the pedagogy factor. This is in contrast to a two-factor **crossed design** where all possible combinations of the two factors are included. The two-factor designs described in Chapters 3 and 5 were all crossed designs.

Let us give a more precise definition of crossed and nested designs. A two-factor completely crossed design (or **complete factorial design**) is one where every level of factor A occurs in combination with every level of factor B. A two-factor nested design (or **incomplete factorial design**) of factor B being nested within factor A is one where the levels of factor B occur for only one level of factor A. We denote this particular nested design as B(A), which is read as factor B being nested within factor A (in other references, you may see this written as B:A or as B|A). To return to our example, the teacher factor (factor B) is nested within the method factor (factor A), as each teacher utilizes only one major teaching pedagogy. The outcome measured is student performance. Thus, a researcher may select a nested design to examine the extent to which student performance in mathematics differs given that teachers are nested within teaching pedagogy. The researcher is likely most interested in the treatment (e.g., teaching pedagogy), but recognizes that the context (i.e., the classroom teacher) may contribute to differences in the outcome, and can model this statistically through a hierarchical ANOVA.

These models are shown graphically in Figure 6.1. In Figure 6.1a, a completely crossed or complete factorial design is shown where there are two levels of factor A and six levels of factor B. Thus, there are 12 possible factor combinations that would all be included in a completely crossed design. The shaded region indicates the combinations that might be included in a nested or incomplete factorial design where factor B (e.g., teacher) is nested within factor A (e.g., teaching pedagogy). Although the number of levels of each factor remains the same, factor B now has only three levels within each level of factor A. For A_1, we see only B_1, B_2, and B_3, whereas for A_2, we see only B_4, B_5, and B_6. Thus, only 6 of the possible 12 factor combinations are included in the nested design. For example, level 1 of factor B occurs only in combination with level 1 of factor A. In summary, Figure 6.1a shows that the nested or incomplete factorial design consists of only a portion of the completely crossed design (the shaded regions). In Figure 6.1b, we see the nested design depicted in its more traditional form. Here you see that the six factor combinations not included are not even shown (e.g., A_1 with B_4). Other examples of the two-factor nested design are as follows: (a) school is nested within school district, (b) faculty member is nested within department, (c) individual is nested within neighborhood, and (d) county is nested within state.

Thus, with this design, one factor is nested within another factor, rather than the two factors being crossed. As is shown in more detail later in this chapter, the nesting characteristic

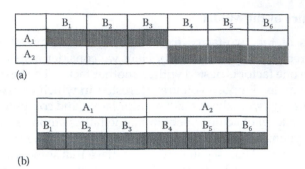

(a)

(b)

FIGURE 6.1

Two-factor completely crossed versus nested designs. (a) The *completely crossed design*: The shaded region indicates the cells that would be included in a nested design where factor B is nested within factor A. In the nested design, factor A has two levels, and factor B has three levels within each level of factor A. You see that only 6 of the 12 possible cells are filled in the nested design. (b) The same nested design in *traditional form*: The shaded region indicates the cells included in the nested design (i.e., the same six as shown in the first part).

has some interesting and distinct outcomes. For now, some brief mention should be made of these outcomes. **Nesting** is a particular type of confounding among the factors being investigated, where the AB interaction is part of the B effect (or is **confounded** with B) and therefore cannot be investigated. (Going back to the previous example, this means that the teacher by teaching pedagogy interaction effect is confounded with the teacher main effect, and thus teasing apart those effects is not possible.) In the ANOVA model and the ANOVA summary table, there will not be an interaction term or source of variation. This is due to the fact that each level of factor B (the nested factor, such as the teacher) occurs in combination with only one level of factor A (the nonnested factor, such as the teaching pedagogy). We cannot compare for a particular level of B (e.g., the classroom teacher) all levels of factor A (e.g., teaching pedagogy), as a certain level of B only occurs with one level of A.

Confounding may occur for two reasons. First, the confounding may be intentional due to practical reasons, such as a reduction in the number of individuals to be observed. Fewer individuals would be necessary in a nested design, as compared to a crossed design, due to the fact that there are fewer cells in the model. Second, the confounding may be absolutely necessary because crossing may not be possible. For example, school is nested within school district because a particular school can only be a member of one school district. The nested factor (here factor B) may be a nuisance variable that the researcher wants to take into account in terms of explaining or predicting the dependent variable Y. An error commonly made is to ignore the nuisance variable B and go ahead with a one-factor design using only factor A. This design may result in a biased test of factor A such that the F ratio is inflated. Thus, H_0 would be rejected more often than it should be, serving to increase the actual α level over that specified by the researcher and thereby increase the likelihood of a Type I error. The F test is then too liberal.

Let us make two further points about this first characteristic. First, in the one-factor design discussed in Chapter 1, we have already seen nesting going on in a different way. Here subjects were nested within factor A because each subject only responded to one level of factor A. It was only when we got to repeated measures designs in Chapter 5 that individuals were allowed to respond to more than one level of a factor. For the repeated measures design, we actually had a completely crossed design of subjects by factor A. Second, Glass and Hopkins (1996) give a nice conceptual example of a nested design with teachers being nested within schools, where each school is like a nest having multiple eggs or teachers.

The remaining characteristics should be familiar. These include the following: (a) two factors (or independent variables) that are nominal or ordinal in scale, each with two or more levels; (b) the levels of each of the factors may be either randomly sampled from the population of levels or fixed by the researcher (i.e., the model may be fixed, mixed, or random); (c) subjects are randomly assigned to only one combination of the levels of the two factors; and (d) the dependent variable is measured at least at the interval level. If individuals respond to more than one combination of the levels of the two factors, then this is a repeated measures design (see Chapter 5).

For simplicity, we again assume the design is balanced. For the two-factor nested design, a design is balanced if (a) the number of observations within each factor combination (or cell) is the same (in other words, the sample size for each cell of the design is the same), and (b) the number of levels of the nested factor within each level of the other factor is the same. The first portion of this statement should be quite familiar from factorial designs, so no further explanation is necessary. The second portion of this statement is unique to this design and requires a brief explanation. As an example, say factor B is nested within factor A and factor A has two levels. On the one hand, factor B may have the same number of levels for each level of factor A. This occurs if there are three levels of factor B under level 1 of factor A (i.e., A_1) and also three levels of factor B under level 2 of factor A (i.e., A_2). On the other hand, factor B may not have the same number of levels for each level of factor A. This occurs if there are three levels of factor B under A_1 and only two levels of factor B under A_2. If the design is unbalanced, see the discussion in Kirk (1982) and Dunn and Clark (1987), although most statistical software can seamlessly deal with this type of unbalanced design.

6.1.2 Layout of Data

The layout of the data for the two-factor nested design is shown in Table 6.1. To simplify matters, we have limited the number of levels of the factors to two levels of factor A (e.g., teaching pedagogy) and three levels of factor B (e.g., teacher). This only serves as an example layout because many other possibilities obviously exist. Here we see the major set of columns designated as the levels of factor A, the nonnested factor (e.g., teaching pedagogy), and for each level of A, the minor set of columns are the levels of factor B, the nested factor (e.g., teacher). Within each factor level combination or cell are the subjects. Means are shown for each cell, for the levels of factor A, and overall. Note that the means for the levels of factor B need not be shown, as they are the same as the cell means. For instance, $\bar{Y}_{.11}$ is the same as $\bar{Y}_{..1}$ (not shown) as B_1 only occurs once. This is another result of the nesting.

TABLE 6.1

Layout for the Two-Factor Nested Design

	A_1			A_2		
	B_1	B_2	B_3	B_4	B_5	B_6
	Y_{111}	Y_{112}	Y_{113}	Y_{124}	Y_{125}	Y_{126}
	.	.	.	.	.	.
	.	.	.	.	.	.
	.	.	.	.	.	.
	Y_{n11}	Y_{n12}	Y_{n13}	Y_{n24}	Y_{n25}	Y_{n26}
Cell means	$\bar{Y}_{.11}$	$\bar{Y}_{.12}$	$\bar{Y}_{.13}$	$\bar{Y}_{.24}$	$\bar{Y}_{.25}$	$\bar{Y}_{.26}$
A means		$\bar{Y}_{.1.}$			$\bar{Y}_{.2.}$	
Overall mean			$\bar{Y}_{...}$				

6.1.3 ANOVA Model

The nested factor is almost always random (Glass & Hopkins, 1996; Keppel & Wickens, 2004; Mickey, Dunn, & Clark, 2004; Page, Braver, & MacKinnon, 2003). In other words, the levels of the nested factor are a random sample of the population of levels. For example, in the case of teachers nested within teaching pedagogy, it is often the case that a random sample of the teachers is selected rather than specific teachers (which would be a fixed-effects factor). Thus, the nested factor (i.e., the teacher factor) is a random factor. As a result, the two-factor nested ANOVA is often a mixed-effects model where the nonnested factor is fixed (i.e., all the levels of interest for the nonnested factor are included in the model) and the nested factor is random. The two-factor mixed-effects nested ANOVA model is written in terms of population parameters as

$$Y_{ijk} = \mu + \alpha_j + b_{k(j)} + \varepsilon_{ijk}$$

where
  Y_{ijk} is the observed score on the dependent variable for individual i in level j of factor A
    and level k of factor B (or in the jk cell)
  μ is the overall or grand population mean (i.e., regardless of cell designation)
  α_j is the fixed effect for level j of factor A
  $b_{k(j)}$ is the random effect for level k of factor B
  ε_{ijk} is the random residual error for individual i in cell jk

Notice that there is no interaction term in the model and also that the effect for factor B is denoted by $b_{k(j)}$. *This tells us that factor B is nested within factor A.* The residual error can be due to individual differences, measurement error, and/or other factors not under investigation. We consider the fixed-, mixed-, and random-effects cases later in this chapter.

  For the two-factor mixed-effects nested ANOVA model, there are only two sets of hypotheses, one for each of the main effects, because there is no interaction effect. The null and alternative hypotheses, respectively, for testing the effect of factor A are as follows. The null hypothesis is similar to what we have seen in previous chapters for fixed-effects factors and written as the means of the levels of factor A are the same:

$$H_{01}\colon \mu_{.1.} = \mu_{.2.} = \cdots = \mu_{.J.}$$

$$H_{11}\colon \text{not all the } \mu_{.j.} \text{ are equal}$$

The hypotheses for testing the effect of factor B, because this is a random-effects factor, are written as the variation among the means, and are presented as follows:

$$H_{02}\colon \sigma_b^2 = 0$$

$$H_{12}\colon \sigma_b^2 > 0$$

These hypotheses reflect the inferences made in the fixed-, mixed-, and random-effects models (as fully described in Chapter 5). For fixed main effects, the null hypotheses are about means, whereas for random main effects, the null hypotheses are about variation among the means. As we already know, the difference in the models is also reflected in the MCPs. As before, we do need to pay particular attention to whether the model is fixed, mixed, or random. The assumptions about the two-factor nested model are exactly the same as with the two-factor crossed model (discussed in Chapters 3 and 5), and, thus, we need not provide any additional discussion other than to remind you of the assumptions regarding normality, homogeneity of variance, and independence (of observations within cells). In addition, procedures for determining power, confidence intervals (CIs), and effect size are the same as with the two-factor crossed model.

6.1.4 ANOVA Summary Table and Expected Mean Squares

The computations of the two-factor mixed-effects nested model are somewhat similar to those of the two-factor mixed-effects crossed model. The main difference lies in the fact that there is no interaction term. The ANOVA summary table is shown in Table 6.2, where we see the following sources of variation: A, B(A), within cells, and total. There we see that only two F ratios can be formed, one for each of the two main effects, because no interaction term is estimated (recall that this is because not all possible combinations of A and B occur).

If we take the total sum of squares and decompose it, we have the following:

$$SS_{total} = SS_A + SS_{B(A)} + SS_{with}$$

We leave the computations involving these terms to the statistical software. The degrees of freedom, mean squares, and F ratios are determined as shown in Table 6.2, assuming a mixed-effects model. The critical value for the test of factor A is $_{\alpha}F_{J-1, J(K(j)-1)}$ and for the test of factor B is $_{\alpha}F_{J(K(j)-1), JK(j)(n-1)}$. Let us explain something about the degrees of freedom. The degrees of freedom for B(A) are equal to $J(K_{(j)} - 1)$. This means that for a design with two levels of factor A (e.g., teaching pedagogy) and three levels of factor B (e.g., teacher) within each level of A (for a total of six levels of B), the degrees of freedom are equal to $2(3 - 1) = 4$. This is not the same as the degrees of freedom for a completely crossed design where df_B would be 5 (i.e., $6 - 1 = 5$). The degrees of freedom for within are equal to $JK_{(j)}(n - 1)$. For this same design with $n = 10$, then the degrees of freedom within are equal to $(2)(3)(10 - 1) = 54$ (i.e., six cells with nine degrees of freedom per cell).

The appropriate error terms for each of the fixed-, random-, and mixed-effects models are described in the following two paragraphs. For the fixed-effects model, both F ratios use the within source as the error term. For the random-effects model, the appropriate error term for the test of A is $MS_{B(A)}$ and for the test of B is MS_{with}. For the mixed-effects model where A is fixed and B is random, the appropriate error term for the test of A is $MS_{B(A)}$,

TABLE 6.2

Two-Factor Nested Design ANOVA Summary Table: Mixed-Effects Model

Source	SS	df	MS	F
A	SS_A	$J - 1$	MS_A	$MS_A/MS_{B(A)}$
B(A)	$SS_{B(A)}$	$J(K_{(j)} - 1)$	$MS_{B(A)}$	$MS_{B(A)}/MS_{with}$
Within	SS_{with}	$JK_{(j)}(n - 1)$	MS_{with}	
Total	SS_{total}	$N - 1$		

and for the test of B, is MS_{with}. As already mentioned, this is the predominant model in education and the behavioral sciences. Finally, for the mixed-effects model where A is random and B is fixed, both F ratios use the within source as the error term. These are now described by the expected mean squares.

The formation of the proper F ratios is again related to the expected mean squares. If H_0 is actually *true*, then the *expected mean squares* are as follows:

$$E(MS_A) = \sigma_\varepsilon^2$$

$$E(MS_{B(A)}) = \sigma_\varepsilon^2$$

$$E(MS_{\text{with}}) = \sigma_\varepsilon^2$$

If H_0 is actually *false*, then the expected mean squares for the *fixed-effects case* are as follows:

$$E(MS_A) = \sigma_\varepsilon^2 + nK_{(j)}\left[\sum_{j=1}^{J} \alpha_j^2/(J-1)\right]$$

$$E(MS_{B(A)}) = \sigma_\varepsilon^2 + n\left[\sum_{j=1}^{J}\sum_{k=1}^{K} \beta_{k(j)}^2/J(K_{(j)}-1)\right]$$

$$E(MS_{\text{with}}) = \sigma_\varepsilon^2$$

Thus, the appropriate F ratios both involve using the within source as the error term.

If H_0 is actually *false*, then the expected mean squares for the *random-effects case* are as follows:

$$E(MS_A) = \sigma_\varepsilon^2 + n\sigma_{b(a)}^2 + nK_{(j)}\sigma_a^2$$

$$E(MS_{B(A)}) = \sigma_\varepsilon^2 + n\sigma_{b(a)}^2$$

$$E(MS_{\text{with}}) = \sigma_\varepsilon^2$$

Thus, the appropriate error term for the test of A is $MS_{B(A)}$, and the appropriate error term for the test of B is MS_{with}.

If H_0 is actually *false*, then the expected mean squares for the *mixed-effects case where A is fixed and B is random* are as follows:

$$E(MS_A) = \sigma_\varepsilon^2 + n\sigma_{b(a)}^2 + nK_{(j)}\left[\sum_{j=1}^{J} \alpha_j^2/(J-1)\right]$$

$$E(MS_{B(A)}) = \sigma_\varepsilon^2 + n\sigma_{b(a)}^2$$

$$E(MS_{with}) = \sigma_\varepsilon^2$$

Thus, the appropriate error term for the test of A is $MS_{B(A)}$, and the appropriate error term for the test of B is MS_{with}.

Finally, if H_0 is actually *false*, then the expected mean squares for the *mixed-effects case where A is random and B is fixed* are as follows:

$$E(MS_A) = \sigma_\varepsilon^2 + nK_{(j)}\sigma_a^2$$

$$E(MS_{B(A)}) = \sigma_\varepsilon^2 + n\left[\sum_{j=1}^{J}\sum_{k=1}^{K}\beta_{k(j)}^2 / J(K_{(j)} - 1)\right]$$

$$E(MS_{with}) = \sigma_\varepsilon^2$$

Thus, the appropriate F ratios both involve using the within source as the error term.

6.1.5 Multiple Comparison Procedures

This section considers MCPs for the two-factor nested design. First of all, the researcher is usually not interested in making inferences about random effects. Second, for MCPs based on the levels of factor A (the nonnested factor), there is nothing new to report. Third, for MCPs based on the levels of factor B (the nested factor), this is a different situation. The researcher is not usually as interested in MCPs about the nested factor as compared to the nonnested factor because inferences about the levels of factor B are not even generalizable across the levels of factor A, due to the nesting. If you are nonetheless interested in MCPs for factor B, by necessity you have to look within a level of A to formulate a contrast. Otherwise MCPs are conducted as before. For more complex nested designs, see Myers (1979), Kirk (1982), Dunn and Clark (1987), Myers and Well (1995), or Keppel and Wickens (2004).

6.1.6 Example

Let us consider an example to illustrate the procedures in this section. The data are shown in Table 6.3. Factor A is approach to the teaching of reading (basal vs. whole language approaches), and factor B is teacher. Thus, there are two teachers using the basal approach and two different teachers using the whole language approach. The researcher is interested in the effects these factors have on student's reading comprehension in the first grade. Thus, the dependent variable is a measure of reading comprehension. Six students are randomly assigned to each approach-teacher combination for small-group instruction. This particular example is a mixed model, where factor A (teaching method) is a fixed effect and factor B (teacher) is a random effect. The results are shown in the ANOVA summary table of Table 6.4.

TABLE 6.3

Data for the Teaching Reading Example: Two-Factor
Nested Design

	\multicolumn{4}{c}{Reading Approaches}			
	\multicolumn{2}{c}{A_1 (Basal)}		\multicolumn{2}{c}{A_2 (Whole Language)}	
	Teacher B_1	Teacher B_2	Teacher B_3	Teacher B_4
	1	1	7	8
	1	3	8	9
	2	3	8	11
	4	4	10	13
	4	6	12	14
	5	6	15	15
Cell means	2.8333	3.8333	10.0000	11.6667
A means	\multicolumn{2}{c}{3.3333}		\multicolumn{2}{c}{10.8333}	
Overall mean	\multicolumn{4}{c}{7.0833}			

TABLE 6.4

Two-Factor Nested Design ANOVA
Summary Table: Teaching Reading Example

Source	SS	df	MS	F
A	337.5000	1	337.5000	59.5585[a]
B(A)	11.3333	2	5.6667	0.9524[b]
Within	119.0000	20	5.9500	
Total	467.8333	23		

[a] $_{.05}F_{1,2} = 18.51$.
[b] $_{.05}F_{2,20} = 3.49$.

From Table A.4, the critical value for the test of factor A is $_\alpha F_{J-1,\,J(K(j)-1)} = {}_{.05}F_{1,2} = 18.51$, and the critical value for the test of factor B is $_\alpha F_{J\,(K(j)-1),\,JK(j)\,(n-1)} = {}_{.05}F_{2,20} = 3.49$. Thus, there is a statistically significant difference between the two approaches to reading instruction at the .05 level of significance, and there is no significant difference between the teachers. When we look at the means for the levels of factor A, we see that the mean comprehension score for the whole language approach ($\overline{Y}_{.2.} = 10.8333$) is greater than the mean for the basal approach ($\overline{Y}_{.1.} = 3.3333$). Because there were only two levels of the reading approach tested (whole language and basal), no post hoc multiple comparisons are really necessary. Rather the mean reading comprehension scores for each approach can be merely examined to determine which mean was statistically significantly larger.

6.2 Two-Factor Randomized Block Design for $n = 1$

In this section, we describe the distinguishing characteristics of the two-factor random-ized block ANOVA model for one observation per cell, the layout of the data, the linear model, assumptions and their violation, the ANOVA summary table and expected mean squares, MCPs, and methods of block formation.

6.2.1 Characteristics of the Model

The characteristics of the two-factor randomized block ANOVA model are quite similar to those of the regular two-factor ANOVA model, as well as sharing a few characteristics with the one-factor repeated measures ANOVA design. There is one obvious exception, which has to do with the nature of the factors being used. Here there will be two factors, each with at least two levels. One factor is known as the **treatment factor** and is referred to here as factor A (a treatment factor is technically what we have been considering in Chapters 1 through 5). The second factor is known as the **blocking factor** and is referred to here as factor B. A blocking factor is a new concept and requires some discussion.

Take an ordinary one-factor ANOVA design, where the single factor is a treatment factor (e.g., method of exercising) and the researcher is interested in its effect on some dependent variable (e.g., percentage of body fat). Despite individuals being randomly assigned to a treatment group, the groups may be different due to a nuisance variable operating in a nonrandom way. For instance, group 1 may consist of mostly older adults and group 2 may consist of mostly younger adults. Thus, it is likely that group 2 will be favored over group 1 because age, the nuisance variable, has not been properly balanced out across the groups by the randomization process.

One way to deal with this problem is to control the effect of the nuisance variable by incorporating it into the design of the study. Including the blocking or nuisance variable as a factor in the design should result in a reduction in residual variation (due to some additional portion of individual differences being explained) and an increase in power (Glass & Hopkins, 1996; Keppel & Wickens, 2004). The blocking factor is selected based on the strength of its relationship to the dependent variable, where an unrelated blocking variable would not reduce residual variation. It would be reasonable to expect, then, that variability among individuals within a block (e.g., within younger adults) should be less than variability among individuals between blocks (e.g., between younger and older adults). Thus, each block represents the formation of a matched set of individuals, that is, matched on the blocking variable, but not necessarily matched on any other nuisance variable. Using our example, we expect that in general, adults within a particular age block (i.e., the older or younger blocks) will be more similar in terms of variables related to body fat than adults across blocks.

Let us consider several examples of blocking factors. Some blocking factors are naturally occurring blocks such as siblings, friends, neighbors, plots of land, and time. Other blocking factors are not naturally occurring but can be formulated by the researcher. Examples of this type include grade point average (GPA), age, weight, aptitude test scores, intelligence test scores, socioeconomic status, and school or district size. Note that the examples of blocking factors here represent a variety of measurement scales (categorical as well as continuous). Later we will discuss how to deal with the blocking factor based on its measurement scale.

Let us make some summary statements about characteristics of blocking designs. First, designs that include one or more blocking factors are known as **randomized block designs**, also known as matching designs or treatment by block designs. The researcher's main interest is in the treatment factor. The purpose of the blocking factor is to reduce residual variation. Thus, the researcher is not as much interested in the test of the blocking factor (possibly not at all) as compared to the treatment factor. Thus, there is at least one blocking factor and one treatment factor, each with two or more levels. Second, each subject falls into only one block in the design and is subsequently randomly assigned to one level of the treatment factor within that block. Thus, subjects within a block serve as their own controls such that some portion of their individual differences is taken into account. As a result, the scores of subjects are not independent within a particular block. Third, for purposes of this section, we assume there is only one subject for each treatment-block level combination. As a result, the model does not include an interaction term. Later in this chapter, we consider the multiple observations case, where there is an interaction term in the model. Finally, the dependent variable is measured at least at the interval level.

6.2.2 Layout of Data

The layout of the data for the two-factor randomized block model is shown in Table 6.5. Here we see the columns designated as the levels of the blocking factor B and the rows as the levels of the treatment factor A. Row, block, and overall means are also shown. Here you see that the layout of the data looks the same as the two-factor model, but with a single observation per cell.

6.2.3 ANOVA Model

The two-factor fixed-effects randomized block ANOVA model is written in terms of population parameters as

$$Y_{jk} = \mu + \alpha_j + \beta_k + \varepsilon_{jk}$$

where
$\quad Y_{jk}$ is the observed score on the dependent variable for the individual responding to level
$\quad\quad j$ of factor A and level k of block B
$\quad \mu$ is the overall or grand population mean
$\quad \alpha_j$ is the fixed effect for level j of factor A
$\quad \beta_k$ is the fixed effect for level k of the block B
$\quad \varepsilon_{jk}$ is the random residual error for the individual in cell jk

The residual error can be due to measurement error, individual differences, and/or other factors not under investigation. You can see this is similar to the two-factor fully crossed model with one observation per cell (i.e., $i = 1$, making the i subscript unnecessary) and with no interaction term included. Also, the effects are denoted by α and β given we have a fixed-effects model. Note that the row and column effects both sum to 0 in the fixed-effects model.

TABLE 6.5

Layout for the Two-Factor Randomized Block Design

Level of Factor A	Level of Factor B				Row Mean
	1	2	...	K	
1	Y_{11}	Y_{12}	...	Y_{1K}	$\bar{Y}_{1.}$
2	Y_{21}	Y_{22}	...	Y_{2K}	$\bar{Y}_{2.}$
.	.	.	...	.	.
.	.	.	...	.	.
.	.	.	...	.	.
J	Y_{J1}	Y_{J2}		Y_{JK}	$\bar{Y}_{J.}$
Block mean	$\bar{Y}_{.1}$	$\bar{Y}_{.2}$	...	$\bar{Y}_{.K}$	$\bar{Y}_{..}$ (overall mean)

The hypotheses for testing the effect of factor A are as follows, where the null indicates that the means of the levels of factor A are equal:

$$H_{01}: \mu_{1.} = \mu_{2.} = \cdots = \mu_{J.}$$

$$H_{11}: \text{not all the } \mu_{j.} \text{ are equal}$$

For testing the effect of factor B (the blocking factor), the hypotheses are presented here, where the null hypothesis is that the means of the levels of the blocking factor are equal:

$$H_{02}: \mu_{.1} = \mu_{.2} = \cdots = \mu_{.K}$$

$$H_{12}: \text{not all the } \mu_{.k} \text{ are equal}$$

The factors are both fixed, so the hypotheses are written in terms of means.

6.2.4 Assumptions and Violation of Assumptions

In Chapter 5, we described the assumptions for the one-factor repeated measures ANOVA model. The assumptions are nearly the same for the two-factor randomized block model, and we need not devote much attention to them here. As before, the assumptions are mainly concerned with independence, normality, and homogeneity of variance of the population scores on the dependent variable.

Another assumption is **compound symmetry** and is necessary because the observations within a block are not independent. The assumption states that the population covariances for all pairs of the levels of the treatment factor A (i.e., j and j') are equal. ANOVA is not particularly robust to a violation of this assumption. If the assumption is violated, three alternative procedures are available. The first is to limit the levels of factor A, either to those that meet the assumption or to two levels (in which case, there is only one covariance). The second, and more plausible, alternative is to use adjusted F tests. These are reported shortly. The third is to use multivariate ANOVA, which has no compound symmetry assumption but is slightly less powerful. This method is beyond the scope of this text.

Huynh and Feldt (1970) showed that the compound symmetry assumption is a sufficient but unnecessary condition for the test of treatment factor A to be F distributed. Thus, the F test may also be valid under less stringent conditions. The necessary and sufficient condition for the validity of the F test of A is known as **sphericity**. This assumes that the variance of the difference scores for each pair of factor levels is the same. Further discussion of sphericity is beyond the scope of this text (see Keppel, 1982; or Kirk, 1982), although we have previously discussed sphericity for repeated measures designs in Chapter 5.

A final assumption purports that there is no interaction between the treatment and blocking factors. This is obviously an assumption of the model because no interaction term is included. Such a model is often referred to as an **additive model**. As was mentioned previously, in this model, the interaction is confounded with the error term. Violation of the additivity assumption results in the test of factor A to be negatively biased; thus, there is an increased probability of committing a Type II error. As a result, if H_0 is rejected, then we are confident that H_0 is really false. If H_0 is not rejected, then

TABLE 6.6

Assumptions and Effects of Violations: Two-Factor Randomized Block ANOVA

Assumption	Effect of Assumption Violation
Independence	• Increased likelihood of a Type I and/or Type II error in F • Affects standard errors of means and inferences about those means
Homogeneity of variance	• Small effect with equal or nearly equal n's • Otherwise effect decreases as n increases
Normality	• Minimal effect with equal or nearly equal n's
Sphericity	• Fairly serious effect
No interaction between treatment and blocks	• Increased likelihood of a Type II error for the test of factor A and thus reduced power

our interpretation is ambiguous as H_0 may or may not be really true (due to an increased probability of a Type II error). Here you would not know whether H_0 was true or not, as there might really be a difference, but the test may not be powerful enough to detect it. Also, the power of the test of factor A is reduced by a violation of the additivity assumption. The assumption may be tested by Tukey's (1949) test of additivity (see Hays, 1988; Kirk, 1982; Timm, 2002), which generates an F test statistic that is compared to the critical value of $_\alpha F_{1,\ [(J-1)\ (K-1)-1]}$. If the test is not statistically significant, then the model is additive and the assumption has been met. If the test *is* significant, then the model is *not* additive and the assumption has *not* been met. A summary of the assumptions and the effects of their violation for this model is presented in Table 6.6.

6.2.5 ANOVA Summary Table and Expected Mean Squares

The sources of variation for this model are similar to those of the regular two-factor model, except that there is no interaction term. The ANOVA summary table is shown in Table 6.7, where we see the following sources of variation: A (treatments), B (blocks), residual, and total. The test of block differences is usually of no real interest. In general, we expect there to be differences between the blocks. From the table, we see that two F ratios can be formed.

If we take the total sum of squares and decompose it, we have

$$SS_{total} = SS_A + SS_B + SS_{res}$$

The remaining computations are determined by the statistical software. The degrees of freedom, mean squares, and F ratios are also shown in Table 6.7.

TABLE 6.7

Two-Factor Randomized Block Design ANOVA Summary Table

Source	SS	df	MS	F
A	SS_A	$J-1$	MS_A	MS_A/MS_{res}
B	SS_B	$K-1$	MS_B	MS_B/MS_{res}
Residual	SS_{res}	$(J-1)(K-1)$	MS_{res}	
Total	SS_{total}	$N-1$		

Earlier in our discussion of the two-factor randomized block design, we mentioned that the *F* test is not very robust to violation of the sphericity assumption. We again recommend the following sequential procedure be used in the test of factor A. First, perform the usual *F* test, which is quite liberal in terms of rejecting H_0 too often, where the degrees of freedom are $J - 1$ and $(J - 1)(K - 1)$. If H_0 is not rejected, then stop. If H_0 is rejected, then continue with step 2, which is to use the Geisser and Greenhouse (1958) conservative *F* test. For the model we are considering here, the degrees of freedom for the *F* critical value are adjusted to be 1 and $K - 1$. If H_0 is rejected, then stop. This would indicate that both the liberal and conservative tests reached the same conclusion, that is, to reject H_0. If H_0 is not rejected, then the two tests did not reach the same conclusion, and a further test should be undertaken. Thus, in step 3, an adjusted *F* test is conducted. The adjustment is known as Box's (1954b) correction [the Huynh and Feldt (1970) procedure]. Here the degrees of freedom are equal to $(J - 1)\varepsilon$ and $(J - 1)(K - 1)\varepsilon$, where ε is the correction factor (see Kirk, 1982). It is now fairly standard for the major statistical software to conduct the Geisser-Greenhouse and Huynh-Feldt tests.

Based on the expected mean squares (not shown here for simplicity), the residual is the proper error term for the fixed-, random-, and mixed-effects models. Thus, MS_{res} is the proper error term for every version of this model. One may also be interested in an assessment of the effect size for the treatment factor A; note that the effect size of the blocking factor B is usually not of interest. As in previously presented ANOVA models, effect size measures such as ω^2 and η^2 should be considered. Finally, the procedures for determining CIs and power are the same as in previous models.

6.2.6 Multiple Comparison Procedures

If the null hypothesis for either the A (treatment) or B (blocking) factor is rejected and there are more than two levels of the factor for which statistical significance was found, then the researcher may be interested in which means or combinations of means are different. This could be assessed, as put forth in previous chapters, by the use of some MCP. In general, the use of MCPs outlined in Chapter 2 is unchanged as long as the sphericity assumption is met. If the assumption is not met, then MS_{res} is not the appropriate error term, and the alternatives recommended in Chapter 5 should be considered (see Boik, 1981; Kirk, 1982; or Maxwell, 1980).

6.2.7 Methods of Block Formation

There are different methods available for the formation of blocks depending on the nature of the blocking variable. As we see, the methods have to do with whether the blocking factor is an ordinal or an interval/ratio variable and whether the blocking factor is a fixed or random effect. This discussion borrows heavily from the work of Pingel (1969) in defining five such methods. The first method is the **predefined value blocking method**, where the blocking factor is an ordinal variable. Here the researcher specifies *K* different population values of the blocking variable. For each of these values (i.e., a fixed effect), individuals are randomly assigned to the levels of the treatment factor. Thus, individuals within a block have the same value on the blocking variable. For example, if class rank is the blocking variable, the levels might be the top third, middle third, and bottom third of the class.

The second method is the **predefined range blocking method**, where the blocking factor is an interval or ratio variable. Here the researcher specifies *K* mutually exclusive ranges in the population distribution of the blocking variable, where the probability of obtaining a value of the blocking variable in each range may be specified as $1/K$. For each of these ranges (i.e., a fixed effect), individuals are randomly assigned to the levels of the treatment factor. Thus, individuals within a block are in the same range on the blocking variable. For example, if the Graduate Record Exam-Verbal (GRE-V) score is the blocking variable, the levels might be 200–400, 401–600, and 601–800.

The third method is the **sampled value blocking method**, where the blocking variable is an ordinal variable. Here the researcher randomly samples K population values of the blocking variable (i.e., a random effect). For each of these values, individuals are randomly assigned to the levels of the treatment factor. Thus, individuals within a block have the same value on the blocking variable. For example, if class rank is again the blocking variable, only this time measured in 10ths, the researcher might randomly select 3 levels from the population of 10 levels.

The fourth method is the **sampled range blocking method**, where the blocking variable is an interval or ratio variable. Here the researcher randomly samples N individuals from the population, such that $N = JK$, where K is the number of blocks desired (i.e., a fixed effect) and J is the number of treatment groups. These individuals are ranked according to their values on the blocking variable from 1 to N. The first block consists of those individuals ranked from 1 to J, the second block of those ranked from $J + 1$ to $2J$, and so on. Finally individuals within a block are randomly assigned to the J treatment groups. For example, consider the GRE-V score again as the blocking variable, where there are $J = 4$ treatment groups, $K = 10$ blocks, and thus $N = JK = 40$ individuals. The top four ranked individuals on the GRE-V exam would constitute the first block, and they would be randomly assigned to the four groups. The next four ranked individuals would constitute the second block, and so on.

The fifth method is the **post hoc blocking method**. Here the researcher has already designed the study and collected the data, without the benefit of a blocking variable. After the fact, a blocking variable is identified and incorporated into the analysis. It is possible to implement any of the four preceding procedures on a post hoc basis.

Based on the research of Pingel (1969), some statements can be made about the precision of these blocking methods in terms of a reduction in residual variability as well as better estimation of the treatment effect. In general, for an ordinal blocking variable, the predefined value blocking method is more precise than the sampled value blocking method. Likewise, for an interval or ratio blocking variable, the predefined range blocking method is more precise than the sampled range blocking method. Finally, the post hoc blocking method is the least precise of the methods discussed. For discussion of selecting an optimal number of blocks, we suggest you consider Feldt (1958; highly recommended), as well as Myers (1979), Myers and Well (1995), and Keppel and Wickens (2004). These researchers make the following recommendations about the optimal number of blocks (where r_{xy} is the correlation between the blocking factor X, in a randomized block design, and the dependent variable Y): if $r_{xy} = .2$, then use five blocks; if $r_{xy} = .4$, then use four blocks; if $r_{xy} = .6$, then use three blocks; and if $r_{xy} = .8$, then use two blocks.

6.2.8 Example

Let us consider an example to illustrate the procedures in this section. The data are shown in Table 6.8. The blocking factor is age (i.e., 20, 30, 40, and 50 years of age), the treatment factor is number of workouts per week (i.e., 1, 2, 3, and 4), and the dependent variable is amount of weight lost during the 1st month. Presume we have a fixed-effects model. Table 6.9 contains the resultant ANOVA summary table.

The test statistics are both compared to the usual F test critical value of $_{.05}F_{3,9} = 3.86$ (from Table A.4), so that both main effects tests are statistically significant. The Geisser-Greenhouse

TABLE 6.8

Data for the Exercise Example: Two-Factor Randomized Block Design

Exercise Program	Age				Row Means
	20	30	40	50	
1/week	3	2	1	0	1.5000
2/week	6	5	4	2	4.2500
3/week	10	8	7	6	7.7500
4/week	9	7	8	7	7.7500
Block means	7.0000	5.5000	5.0000	3.7500	5.3125 (*overall mean*)

TABLE 6.9

Two-Factor Randomized Block Design
ANOVA Summary Table: Exercise Example

Source	SS	df	MS	F
A	21.6875	3	7.2292	18.2648[a]
B	110.1875	3	36.7292	92.7974[a]
Residual	3.5625	9	0.3958	
Total	135.4375	15		

[a] $_{.05}F_{3,9} = 3.86$.

conservative procedure is necessary for the test of factor A; here the test statistic is compared to the critical value of $_{.05}F_{1,3} = 10.13$, which is also significant. The two procedures both yield a statistically significant result, so we need not be concerned with a violation of the sphericity assumption for the test of A. In summary, the effects of amount of exercise undertaken and age on amount of weight lost are both statistically significant at the .05 level of significance.

Next we need to test the additivity assumption using Tukey's (1949) test of additivity. The F test statistic is equal to 0.1010, which is compared to the critical value of $_{.05}F_{1,8} = 5.32$ from Table A.4. The test is nonsignificant, so the model is additive and the assumption has been met.

As an example of a MCP, the Tukey HSD procedure is used to test for the equivalence of exercising once a week ($j = 1$) and four times a week ($j = 4$), where the contrast is written as $\bar{Y}_{4.} - \bar{Y}_{1.}$. The mean amounts of weight lost for these groups are 1.5000 for the once a week program and 7.7500 for the four times a week program. The standard error is computed as follows:

$$s_{\psi'} = \sqrt{\frac{MS_{res}}{J}} = \sqrt{\frac{0.3958}{4}} = 0.3146$$

and the studentized range statistic is as follows:

$$q = \frac{\bar{Y}_{4.} - \bar{Y}_{1.}}{s_{\psi'}} = \frac{7.75 - 1.50}{0.3146} = 19.8665$$

The critical value is $_{\alpha}q_{9,4} = 4.415$ (from Table A.9). The test statistic exceeds the critical value; thus, we conclude that the mean amounts of weight lost for groups 1 (exercise once per week) and 4 (exercise four times per week) are statistically significantly different at the .05 level (i.e., more frequent exercise helps one to lose more weight).

6.3 Two-Factor Randomized Block Design for $n > 1$

For two-factor randomized block designs with more than one observation per cell, there is little that we have not already covered. First, the characteristics are exactly the same as with the $n = 1$ model, with the obvious exception that when $n > 1$, an interaction term exists. Second, the layout of the data, the model, the ANOVA summary table, and the MCPs are the same as in the regular two-factor model. Third, the assumptions are the same as with the $n = 1$ model, except the assumption of additivity is not necessary because an interaction term exists. The sphericity assumption is required for those tests using MS_{AB} as the error term. We do not mean to minimize the importance of this popular model; however, there really is no additional information to provide beyond what we have already presented. For a discussion of other randomized block designs, see Kirk (1982).

6.4 Friedman Test

There is a nonparametric equivalent to the two-factor randomized block ANOVA model. The test was developed by Friedman (1937) and is based on mean ranks. For the case of $n = 1$, the procedure is precisely the same as the Friedman test for the one-factor repeated measures model (see Chapter 5). For the case of $n > 1$, the procedure is slightly different. First, all of the scores within each block are ranked for that block. For instance, if there are $J = 4$ levels of factor A and $n = 10$ individuals per cell, then each block's scores would be ranked from 1 to 40. From this, a mean ranking can be determined for each level of factor A. The null hypothesis tests whether the mean rankings for each of the levels of A are equal. The test statistic is a χ^2, which is compared to the critical value of $_\alpha\chi^2_{J-1}$ (see Table A.3), where the null hypothesis is rejected if the test statistic exceeds the critical value.

In the case of tied ranks, either the available ranks can be averaged, or a correction factor can be used (see Chapter 5). You may also recall the problem with small n's in terms of the test statistic not being precisely distributed as a χ^2. For situations where $J < 6$ and $n < 6$, consult the table of critical values in Marascuilo and McSweeney (1977, Table A-22, p. 521). The Friedman test assumes that the population distributions have the same shape (although not necessarily normal) and the same variability and that the dependent measure is continuous. For alternative nonparametric procedures, see the discussion in Chapter 5.

Various MCPs can be used for the nonparametric two-factor randomized block model. For the most part, these MCPs are analogs to their parametric equivalents. In the case of planned pairwise comparisons, one may use multiple matched-pair Wilcoxon tests in a Bonferroni form (i.e., taking the number of contrasts into account by splitting up the α level). Due to the nature of planned comparisons, these are more powerful than the Friedman test. For post hoc comparisons, two example MCPs are the Tukey HSD analog for pairwise contrasts and the Scheffé analog for complex contrasts. For additional discussion about the use of MCPs for this model, see Marascuilo and McSweeney (1977). For an example of the Friedman test, return to Chapter 5. Finally, note that MCPs are not usually conducted on the blocking factor as they are rarely of interest to the applied researcher.

6.5 Comparison of Various ANOVA Models

How do some of the ANOVA models we have considered compare in terms of power and precision? Recall again that **power** is defined as the probability of rejecting H_0 when H_0 is false, and **precision** is defined as a measure of our ability to obtain good estimates of the treatment effects. The classic literature on this topic revolves around the correlation between the dependent variable Y and the concomitant variable X (i.e., r_{xy}), where the concomitant variable can be either a covariate or a blocking factor. First let us compare the one-factor ANOVA and one-factor ANCOVA models. If r_{xy}, the correlation between the covariate X and the dependent variable Y, is not statistically significantly different from 0, then the amount of unexplained variation will be the same in the two models. Thus, no statistical adjustment will be made on the group means. In this situation, the ANOVA model is more powerful, as we lose one degree of freedom for each covariate used in the ANCOVA model. If r_{xy} is significantly different from 0, then the amount of unexplained variation will be smaller in the ANCOVA model as compared to the ANOVA model. Here the ANCOVA model is more powerful and is more precise as compared to the ANOVA model. Second, compare the one-factor ANOVA and two-factor randomized block designs. If r_{xy}, the correlation between the blocking factor X and the dependent variable Y, is not statistically significantly different from 0, then the blocking factor will not account for much variability in the dependent variable. One rule of thumb states that if $r_{xy} < .2$, then ignore the concomitant variable (whether it is a covariate or a blocking factor), and use the one-factor ANOVA. Otherwise, take the concomitant variable into account somehow, either as a covariate or blocking factor.

How should we take the concomitant variable into account if it correlates with the dependent variable at greater than .20 (i.e., $r_{xy} > .2$)? The two best possibilities are the analysis of covariance design (ANCOVA, Chapter 4) and the randomized block ANOVA design (discussed in this chapter). That is, the concomitant variable can be used either as a covariate through a statistical form of control (i.e., ANCOVA) or as a blocking factor through an experimental design form of control (i.e., randomized block ANOVA). As suggested by the classic work of Feldt (1958), if $.2 < r_{xy} < .4$, then use the concomitant variable as a blocking factor in a randomized block design as it is the most powerful and precise design. If $r_{xy} > .6$, then use the concomitant variable as a covariate in an ANCOVA design as it is the most powerful and precise design. If $.4 < r_{xy} < .6$, then the randomized block and ANCOVA designs are about equal in terms of power and precision.

However, Maxwell, Delaney, and Dill (1984) showed that the correlation between the covariate and dependent variable should not be the ultimate criterion in deciding whether to use an ANCOVA or a randomized block design. These designs differ in the following two ways: (a) whether the concomitant variable is treated as continuous (ANCOVA) or categorical (randomized block) and (b) whether individuals are assigned to groups based on the concomitant variable (randomized blocks) or without regard to the concomitant variable (ANCOVA). Thus, the Feldt (1958) comparison of these particular models is not a fair one in that the models differ in these two ways. The ANCOVA model makes full use of the information contained in the concomitant variable, whereas in the randomized block model, some information is lost due to the categorization. In examining nine different models, Maxwell and colleagues suggest that r_{xy} should not be the sole factor in the choice of a design (given that r_{xy} is at least .3), but that two other factors be considered. The first factor is whether scores on the concomitant variable are available prior to the assignment of individuals to groups. If so, power will be increased by assigning individuals to groups based on the concomitant variable (i.e., blocking). The second factor is whether X (the concomitant variable) and Y (the dependent variable) are linearly related. If so, the use of ANCOVA with a continuous concomitant variable is more powerful because linearity is an assumption of the model (Keppel & Wickens, 2004; Myers & Well, 1995). If not, either the concomitant variable should be used as a blocking variable, or some sort of nonlinear ANCOVA model should be used.

There are a few other decision criteria you may want to consider in choosing between the randomized block and ANCOVA designs. First, in some situations, blocking may be difficult to carry out. For instance, we may not be able to find enough homogeneous individuals to constitute a block. If the blocks formed are not very homogeneous, this defeats the whole purpose of blocking. Second, the interaction of the independent variable and the concomitant variable may be an important effect to study. In this case, use the randomized block design with multiple individuals per cell. If the interaction is significant, this violates the assumption of homogeneity of regression slopes in the analysis of covariance design, but does not violate any assumption in the randomized block design with $n > 1$. Third, it should be obvious by now that the assumptions of the ANCOVA design are much more restrictive than in the randomized block design. Thus, when important assumptions are likely to be seriously violated, the randomized block design is preferable.

There are other alternative designs for incorporating the concomitant variable as a pretest, such as an ANOVA on gain (the difference between posttest and pretest), or a mixed (split-plot) design where the pretest and posttest measures are treated as the levels of a repeated factor. Based on the research of Huck and McLean (1975) and Jennings (1988), the ANCOVA model is generally preferred over these other two models. For further discussion, see Reichardt (1979), Huitema (1980), or Kirk (1982).

6.6 SPSS

In this section, we examine SPSS for the models presented in this chapter. We begin with the two-factor hierarchical ANOVA and then follow with the two-factor randomized block ANOVA.

Two-Factor Hierarchical ANOVA

To conduct a two-factor hierarchical (or nested) ANOVA, there are a few differences from other ANOVA models we have considered in this text. We will illustrate computation of the model that follows the point-and-click method as we have done in previous chapters. It is important to note, however, that while SPSS offers limited capability for estimating hierarchical ANOVA models, the most recent versions of SPSS offer increasing ability to generate multilevel regression models, and readers interested in more complex regression models are referred to Heck, Thomas, and Tabata (2010).

In terms of the form of the data, one column or variable indicates the levels or categories of the independent variable (i.e., the fixed factor), one column indicates the levels of the nested factor, and the one variable represents the outcome or the dependent variable. Each row represents one individual, indicating the level or group of the nonnested factor (basal or whole language, in our example), the level or group of the nested factor (teachers 1, 2, 3, or 4), and their score on the dependent variable. Thus, we have three columns which represent the nonnested factor, the nested factor, and the scores, as shown in the following screenshot.

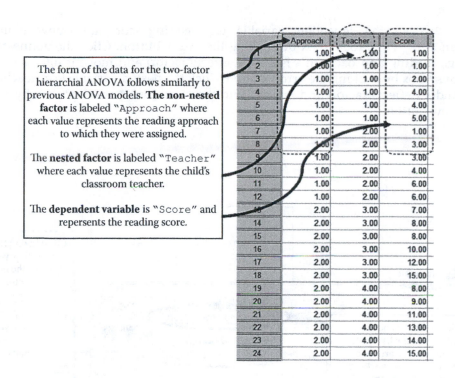

The form of the data for the two-factor hierarchial ANOVA follows similarly to previous ANOVA models. **The non-nested factor** is labeled "Approach" where each value represents the reading approach to which they were assigned.

The **nested factor** is labeled "Teacher" where each value represents the child's classroom teacher.

The **dependent variable** is "Score" and repersents the reading score.

	Approach	Teacher	Score
1	1.00	1.00	1.00
2	1.00	1.00	1.00
3	1.00	1.00	2.00
4	1.00	1.00	4.00
5	1.00	1.00	4.00
6	1.00	1.00	5.00
7	1.00	2.00	1.00
8	1.00	2.00	3.00
9	1.00	2.00	3.00
10	1.00	2.00	4.00
11	1.00	2.00	6.00
12	1.00	2.00	6.00
13	2.00	3.00	7.00
14	2.00	3.00	8.00
15	2.00	3.00	8.00
16	2.00	3.00	10.00
17	2.00	3.00	12.00
18	2.00	3.00	15.00
19	2.00	4.00	8.00
20	2.00	4.00	9.00
21	2.00	4.00	11.00
22	2.00	4.00	13.00
23	2.00	4.00	14.00
24	2.00	4.00	15.00

Step 1: To conduct a two-factor hierarchical ANOVA, go to "Analyze" in the top pulldown menu, then select "General Linear Model," and then select "Univariate." Following the screenshot (step 1) as follows produces the "Univariate" dialog box.

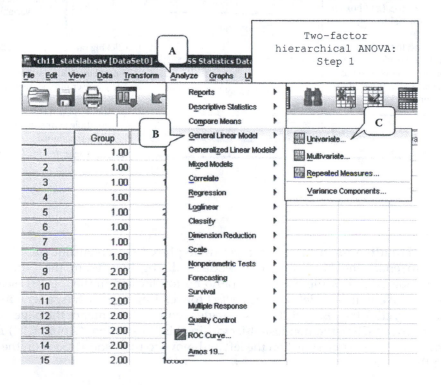

Two-factor hierarchical ANOVA: Step 1

Step 2: Click the dependent variable (e.g., reading score) and move it into the "Dependent Variable" box by clicking the arrow button. Click the nonnested factor (e.g., reading approach; this is a fixed-effects factor) and move it into the "Fixed Factors" box by clicking the arrow button. Click the nested variable (e.g., teacher; this is a random-effects factor) and move it into the "Random Factors" box by clicking the arrow button.

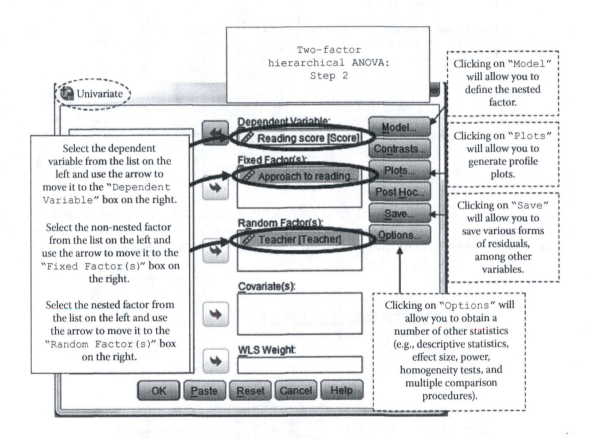

Step 3a: From the main "Univariate" dialog box (see screenshot step 2), click on "Model" to enact the "Univariate Model" dialog box. From the "Univariate Model" dialog box, click the "Custom" radio button located in the top left (see screenshot step 3a). We will now define a *main effect* for reading approach (see screenshot step 3a). To do this, click the "Build Terms" toggle menu in the center of the page and select "Main Effect." Click the nonnested factor (in this illustration, "Approach") from the "Factors & Covariates" list on the left and move to the "Model" box on the right by clicking the arrow.

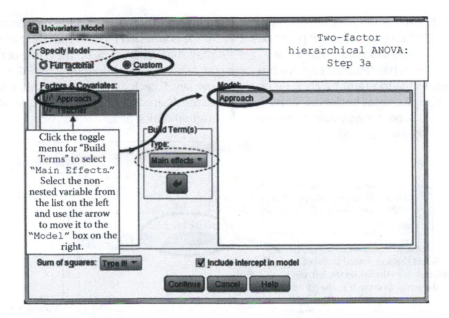

Step 3b: We will now define an *interaction effect* for reading approach by teacher (see screenshot step 3b). To do this, click the "Build Terms" toggle menu in the center of the page and select "Interaction." Click both the nonnested factor (e.g., "Approach") and nested factor (e.g., "Teacher") from the "Factors & Covariates" list on the left and move them to the "Model" box on the right by clicking the arrow. The interaction term is necessary to trick SPSS into computing the main effect of B(A) for the nested factor (which SPSS calls "method*teacher," but is actually "teacher") and thus generate the proper ANOVA summary table. Thus, the model should *not* include a main effect term for "Teacher."

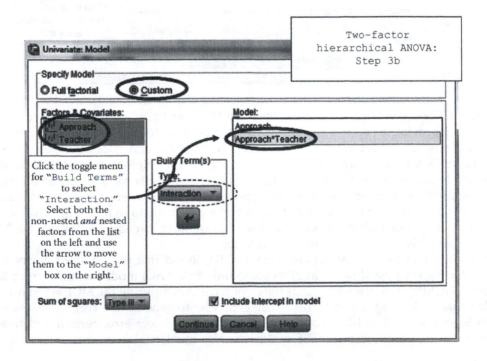

Step 4: From the "Univariate" dialog box (see screenshot step 2), clicking on "Post hoc" will provide the option to select post hoc MCPs for the nonnested factor. From the "Post Hoc Multiple Comparisons for Observed Means" dialog box, click on the name of the non-nested factor in the "Factor(s)" list box in the top left and move it to the "Post Hoc Tests for" box in the top right by clicking on the arrow key. Check an appropriate MCP for your situation by placing a checkmark in the box next to the desired MCP. In this example, we select "Tukey." Click on "Continue" to return to the original dialog box.

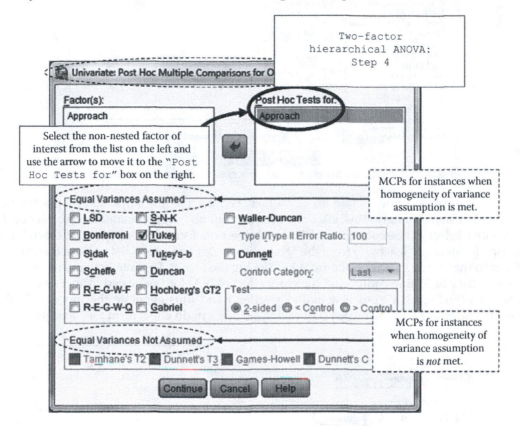

Step 5: Clicking on "Options" from the main "Univariate" dialog box (see screenshot step 2) will provide the option to select such information as "Descriptive Statistics," "Estimates of effect size," "Observed power," and "Homogeneity tests" (i.e., Levene's test). Click on "Continue" to return to the original dialog box. *Note that if you are interested in an MCP for the nested factor (although generally not of interest for this model), post hoc MCPs are only available from the "Options" screen.* To select a post hoc procedure, click on "Compare main effects" and use the toggle menu to reveal the Tukey LSD, Bonferroni, and Sidak procedures. However, we have already mentioned that MCPs are not generally of interest for the nested factor.

It is important to note that Li and Lomax (2011) found that the standard errors of the MCPs for the nonnested factor in SPSS point-and-click (PAC) mode are not correct. More specifically, SPSS PAC uses MS_{within} as the error term in computing the MCP standard error rather than $MS_{B(A)}$ as the error term. There is no way to generate the correct results solely with SPSS PAC, unless hand computations using the correct error term are utilized or other software programs (e.g., SPSS syntax) are also involved.

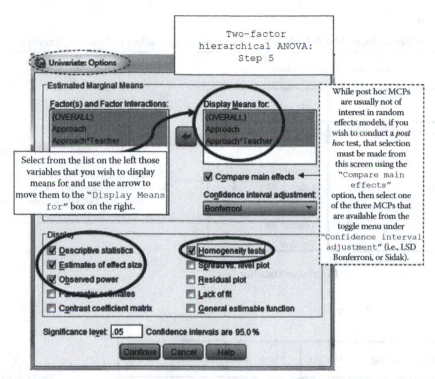

Two-factor
hierarchical ANOVA:
Step 5

Select from the list on the left those variables that you wish to display means for and use the arrow to move them to the "Display Means for" box on the right.

While post hoc MCPs are usually not of interest in random effects models, if you wish to conduct a *post hoc* test, that selection must be made from this screen using the "Compare main effects" option, then select one of the three MCPs that are available from the toggle menu under "Confidence interval adjustment" (i.e., LSD Bonferroni, or Sidak).

Step 6: From the "Univariate" dialog box (screenshot step 2), click on "Save" to select those elements you want to save. Here we want to save the unstandardized residuals to be used to examine the extent to which normality and independence are met. Thus, place a checkmark in the box next to "Unstandardized." Click "Continue" to return to the main "Univariate" dialog box. From the "Univariate" dialog box, click on "OK" to generate the output.

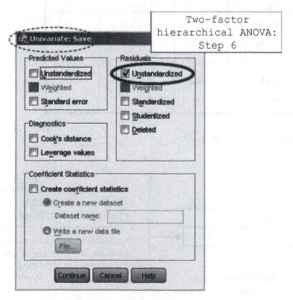

Two-factor
hierarchical ANOVA:
Step 6

Interpreting the output: Annotated results are presented in Table 6.10.

TABLE 6.10

Two-Factor Hierarchical ANOVA SPSS Results for the Approaches to Reading Example

Between-Subjects Factors

		Value Label	N
Approach to reading	1.00	Basal	12
	2.00	Whole language	12
Teacher	1.00	Teacher B1	6
	2.00	Teacher B2	6
	3.00	Teacher B3	6
	4.00	Teacher B4	6

> The table labeled "Between-Subjects Factors" lists the variable names and sample sizes for the non-nested factor (i.e. "Approach to reading") and the nested factor (i.e., "Teacher").

Descriptive Statistics

Dependent Variable: Reading Score

Approach to Reading	Teacher	Mean	Std. Deviation	N
Basal	Teacher B1	2.8333	1.72240	6
	Teacher B2	3.8333	1.94079	6
	Total	3.3333	1.82574	12
Whole language	Teacher B3	10.0000	3.03315	6
	Teacher B4	11.6667	2.80476	6
	Total	10.8333	2.91807	12
Total	Teacher B1	2.8333	1.72240	6
	Teacher B2	3.8333	1.94079	6
	Teacher B3	10.0000	3.03315	6
	Teacher B4	11.6667	2.80476	6
	Total	7.0833	4.51005	24

> The table labeled "Descriptive Statistics" provides basic descriptive statistics (means, standard deviations, and sample sizes) for each non-nested factor and nested factor combination (or cell).

Levene's Test of Equality of Error Variances[a]

Dependent Variable: Reading Score

F	df1	df2	Sig.
1.042	3	20	.396

> The F test (and associated p value) for Levene's Test for Equality of Error Variances is reviewed to determine if equal variances can be assumed. In this case, we meet the assumption (as p is greater than α).

[a] Tests the null hypothesis that the error variance of the dependent variable is equal across groups.

TABLE 6.10 (continued)

Two-Factor Hierarchical ANOVA SPSS Results for the Approaches to Reading Example

> Partial eta squared is one measure of effect size:
>
> $$\eta_p^2 = \frac{SS_{approach}}{SS_{approach} + SS_{approach\_error}}$$
>
> $$\eta_p^2 = \frac{337.500}{337.500 + 11.333} = .968$$
>
> We can interpret this to say that approximately 97% of the variation in reading score is accounted for by the differences in reading approach.

> Comparing p to α, we find a statistically significant difference in approach to reading. This is an omnibus test. We will look at our MCPs to determine which mean ratings differ.

Tests of Between-Subjects Effects

Dependent Variable: Reading Score

Source		Type III Sum of Squares	df	Mean Square	F	Sig.	Partial Eta Squared	Noncent. Parameter	Observed Power[a]
Intercept	Hypothesis	1204.167	1	1204.167	212.500	.005	.991	212.500	1.000
	Error	11.333	2	5.667[b]					
Approach	Hypothesis	337.500	1	337.500	59.559	.016	.968	59.559	.948
	Error	11.333	2	5.667[b]					
Approach*	Hypothesis	11.333	2	5.667	.952	.403	.087	1.905	.192
Teacher	Error	119.000	20	5.950[c]					

[a] Computed using alpha = .05.

[b] MS(Approach * Teacher).

[c] MS(Error).

> Observed power tells whether our test is powerful enough to detect mean differences if they really exist. power of .948 is strong. The probability of rejecting the null hypothesis, if it is really false, is about 95%.

Estimated Marginal Means

1. Grand Mean

Dependent Variable: Reading Score

Mean	Std. Error	95% Confidence Interval	
		Lower Bound	Upper Bound
7.083[a]	.498	6.045	8.122

[a] Based on modified population marginal mean.

> The "Grand Mean" (in this case, 7.083) represents the overall reading score mean, regardless of the reading approach or teacher. The 95% CI represents the CI of the grand mean.

(continued)

TABLE 6.10 (continued)

Two-Factor Hierarchical ANOVA SPSS Results for the Approaches to Reading Example

2. Approach to Reading

Estimates

Dependent Variable: Reading Score

Approach to Reading	Mean	Std. Error	95% Confidence Interval	
			Lower Bound	Upper Bound
Basal	3.333[a]	.704	1.864	4.802
Whole language	10.833[a]	.704	9.364	12.302

[a] Based on modified population marginal mean.

> The table for "Approach to Reading" provides descriptive statistics for each of the reading approaches. In addition to means, the *SE* and 95% CI of the means are reported.

Pairwise Comparisons

Dependent Variable: Reading Score

(*I*) Approach to Reading	(*J*) Approach to Reading	Mean Difference (*I – J*)	Std. Error	Sig.[c]	95% Confidence Interval for Difference[c]	
					Lower Bound	Upper Bound
Basal	Whole language	−7.500[*,a,b]	.996	.000	−9.577	−5.423
Whole language	Basal	7.500[*,a,b]	.996	.000	5.423	9.577

Based on estimated marginal means.

[a] An estimate of the modified population marginal mean (*I*).

[b] An estimate of the modified population marginal mean (*J*).

[c] Adjustment for multiple comparisons: Bonferroni.

[*] The mean difference is significant at the .05 level.

> "Mean Difference" is simply the difference between the means of the two categories of our reading approach factor. For example, the mean difference of basal reading and whole language is calculated as $3.333 - 10.833 = -7.500$.

> "Sig." is the observed *p* value for the results of the Bonferroni *post hoc* MCP. There is a statistically significant mean difference in reading scores between basal reading and whole language ($p < .001$). Note the redundant results in the table. The comparison of basal and whole language (row 1) is the same as the comparison of whole language and basal (row 2).

Univariate Tests

Dependent Variable: Reading Score

	Sum of Squares	df	Mean Square	F	Sig.	Partial eta Squared	Noncent. Parameter	Observed Power[a]
Contrast	337.500	1	337.500	56.723	.000	.739	56.723	1.000
Error	119.000	20	5.950					

The *F* tests the effect of approach to reading. This test is based on the linearly independent pairwise comparisons among the estimated marginal means.

[a] Computed using alpha = .05.

> The error term represents the within cells source of variation.

TABLE 6.10 (continued)

Two-Factor Hierarchical ANOVA SPSS Results for the Approaches to Reading Example

3. Approach to Reading * Teacher
Dependent Variable: Reading Score

Approach to Reading	Teacher	Mean	Std. Error	95% Confidence Interval	
				Lower Bound	Upper Bound
Basal	Teacher B1	2.833	.996	.756	4.911
	Teacher B2	3.833	.996	1.756	5.911
	Teacher B3	.[a]	.	.	.
[a]	Teacher B4	.[a]	.	.	.
Whole language	Teacher B1	.[a]	.	.	.
	Teacher B2	.[a]	.	.	.
	Teacher B3	10.000	.996	7.923	12.077
	Teacher B4	11.667	.996	9.589	13.744

[a] This level combination of factors is not observed, thus the corresponding population marginal mean is not estimable.

> The table for "Approach to Reading * Teacher" provides descriptive statistics for each of the approach-teacher combinations. In addition to means, the *SE* and 95% CI of the means are reported. Note the footnote in reference to the missing mean values. This is because this is not a completely crossed design (i.e., the teachers taught only one reading approach).

Examining Assumptions for Two-Factor Hierarchical ANOVA

Normality

We will use the residuals (which were requested and created through the "Save" option mentioned earlier) to examine the extent to which normality was met.

	Approach	Teacher	Score	RES_1
1	1.00	1.00	1.00	-1.83
2	1.00	1.00	1.00	-1.83
			2.00	-.83
			4.00	1.17
			4.00	1.17
			5.00	2.17
			1.00	-2.83
			3.00	-.83
			3.00	-.83
			4.00	.17
11	1.00	2.00	6.00	2.17
12	1.00	2.00	6.00	2.17
13	2.00	3.00	7.00	-3.00
14	2.00	3.00	8.00	-2.00
15	2.00	3.00	8.00	-2.00
16	2.00	3.00	10.00	.00
17	2.00	3.00	12.00	2.00
18	2.00	3.00	15.00	5.00
19	2.00	4.00	8.00	-3.67
20	2.00	4.00	9.00	-2.67
21	2.00	4.00	11.00	-.67
22	2.00	4.00	13.00	1.33
23	2.00	4.00	14.00	2.33
24	2.00	4.00	15.00	3.33

> The residuals are computed by subtracting the cell mean from each observation. For example, the mean reading score for students assigned to teacher 1 who received the basal approach to reading was 2.833. The first student scored 1 on reading comprehension. Thus the residual for the first person is 1.00 − 2.83 = −1.83. As we look at the raw data, we see one new variable has been added to our dataset labeled **RES_1**. These are the residuals and will be used to review the assumption of normality.

Generating normality evidence: As described in earlier ANOVA chapters, understanding the distributional shape, specifically whether normality is a reasonable assumption, is important. For the two-factor hierarchical ANOVA, the residuals should be normally distributed.

As in previous chapters, we use "Explore" to examine whether the assumption of normality is met. The general steps for accessing "Explore" have been presented in previous chapters and will not be repeated here. Click the residual and move it into the "Dependent List" box by clicking on the arrow button. The procedures for selecting normality statistics were presented in Chapter 6 of *An Introduction to Statistical Concepts*, Third Edition and remain the same here: Click on "Plots" in the upper right corner. Place a checkmark in the boxes for "Normality plots with tests" and also for "Histogram." Then click "Continue" to return to the main "Explore" dialog box and click "OK" to generate the output.

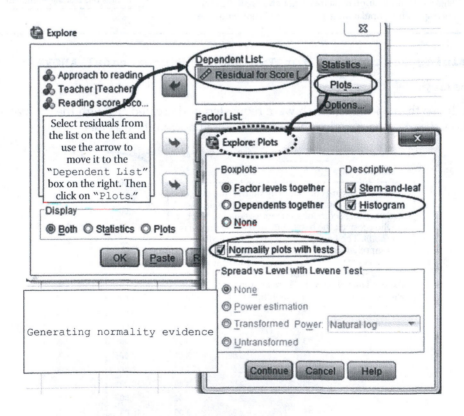

Interpreting normality evidence: By this point, we have had a substantial amount of practice in interpreting quite a range of normality statistics and interpret them again in reference to the hierarchical ANOVA model assumption of normality.

Descriptives

			Statistic	Std. Error
Residual for score	Mean		.0000	.46431
	95% Confidence interval	Lower bound	−.9605	
	for mean	Upper bound	.9605	
	5% Trimmed mean		−.0648	
	Median		−.3333	
	Variance		5.174	
	Std. deviation		2.27462	
	Minimum		−3.67	
	Maximum		5.00	
	Range		8.67	
	Interquartile range		4.08	
	Skewness		.284	.472
	Kurtosis		−.693	.918

The skewness statistic of the residuals is .284 and kurtosis is −.693—both being within the range of an absolute value of 2.0, suggesting some evidence of normality.

As suggested by the skewness statistic, the histogram of residuals is slightly positively skewed, and the histogram also provides a visual display of the slightly platykurtic distribution.

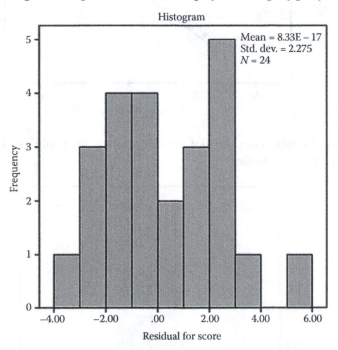

Histogram

There are a few other statistics that can be used to gauge normality. The formal test of normality, the Shapiro–Wilk (S–W) test (*SW*) (Shapiro & Wilk, 1965), provides evidence of the extent to which our sample distribution is statistically different from a normal distribution. The output for the S–W test is presented as follows and suggests that our sample distribution for the residual is not statistically significantly different than what would be expected from a normal distribution as the p value is greater than α.

Tests of Normality

	Kolmogorov–Smirnov[a]			Shapiro–Wilk		
	Statistic	df	Sig.	Statistic	df	Sig.
Residual for score	.123	24	.200*	.960	24	.442

[a] Lilliefors significance correction.
*This is a lower bound of the true significance.

Quantile–quantile (Q–Q) plots are also often examined to determine evidence of normality, where quantiles of the theoretical normal distribution are plotted against quantiles of the sample distribution. Points that fall on or close to the diagonal line suggest evidence of normality. The Q–Q plot of residuals shown in the following suggests relative normality.

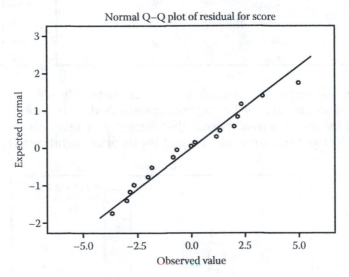

Normal Q–Q plot of residual for score

Examination of the following boxplot also suggests a relatively normal distributional shape of residuals with no outliers.

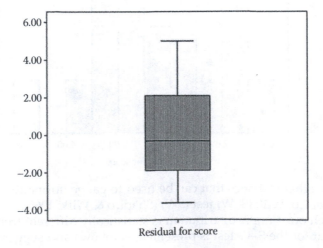

Residual for score

Considering the forms of evidence we have examined, skewness and kurtosis statistics, the S–W test, histogram, the Q–Q plot, and the boxplot, all suggest normality is a reasonable assumption. We can be reasonably assured we have met the assumption of normality.

Independence

The last assumption to test for is independence. As we have seen this tested in other designs, we do not consider it further here.

Two-Factor Fixed-Effects Randomized Block ANOVA for n = 1

To run a two-factor fixed-effects randomized block ANOVA for $n = 1$, there a few differences from the regular two-factor fixed-effects ANOVA that we see later as we build the model in SPSS. Additionally, the test of additivity is not available in SPSS, nor are the adjusted F tests (i.e., the Geisser–Greenhouse and Huynh–Feldt procedures). All other ANOVA procedures that you are familiar with will operate as before.

In terms of the form of the data, it looks just as we saw with the two-factor fixed-effects ANOVA with the exception that now we have one treatment factor and one blocking variable. The dataset must therefore consist of three variables or columns, one for the level of the treatment factor, second for the level of the blocking factor, and the third for the dependent variable. Each row still represents one individual, indicating the levels of the treatment and blocking factors to which the individual is a member, and their score on the dependent variable. As seen in the following screenshot, for a two-factor fixed-effects randomized block ANOVA, the SPSS data are in the form of two columns that represent the group values (i.e., the treatment and blocking factors) and one column that represents the scores on the dependent variable.

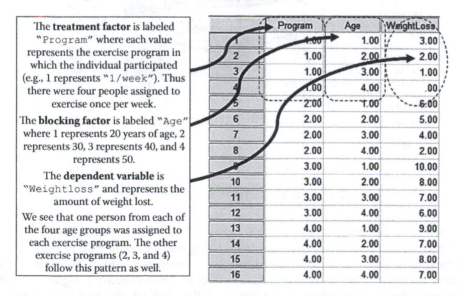

Step 1: To conduct a two-factor randomized block ANOVA for $n = 1$, go to "Analyze" in the top pulldown menu, then select "General Linear Model," and then select "Univariate." Following the screenshot (step 1) as follows produces the "Univariate" dialog box.

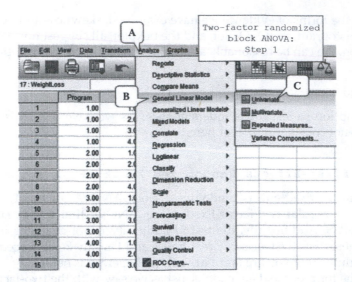

Step 2: Click the dependent variable (e.g., weight loss) and move it into the "Dependent Variable" box by clicking the arrow button. Click the treatment factor and the blocking factor and move them into the "Fixed Factors" box by clicking the arrow button.

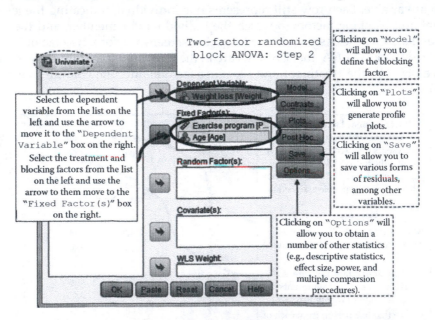

Step 3: From the main "Univariate" dialog box (see screenshot step 2), click on "Model" to enact the "Univariate Model" dialog box. From the "Univariate Model" dialog box, click the "Custom" radio button (see screenshot step 3). We will now define the effects necessary for this model, a main effect for both exercise program and for age. We will *not* define an interaction. To do this, click the "Build Terms" toggle menu in the center of the page and select "Main effect." Click the treatment factor (i.e., "Program") and the blocking factor (i.e., "Age") from the "Factors & Covariates" list on the left and move them to the "Model" box on the right by clicking the arrow. Thus, the model should *not* include an interaction effect for "Program*Age."

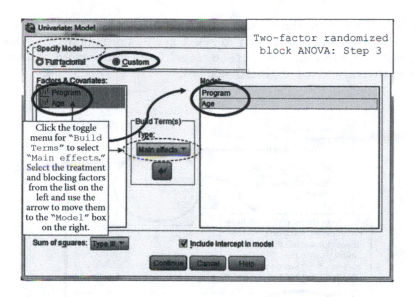

Step 4: From the "Univariate" dialog box (see screenshot step 2), clicking on "Post Hoc" will provide the option to select post hoc MCPs for both factors. From the "Post Hoc Multiple Comparisons for Observed Means" dialog box, click on the name of the factors (i.e., "Program" and "Age") in the "Factor(s)" list box in the top left and move to the "Post Hoc Tests for" box in the top right by clicking on the arrow key. Check an appropriate MCP for your situation by placing a checkmark in the box next to the desired MCP. In this example, we select "Tukey." Click on "Continue" to return to the original dialog box.

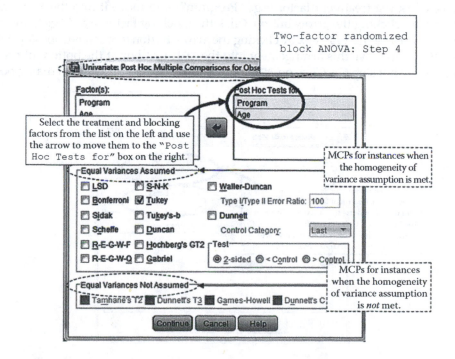

Step 5: Clicking on "Options" from the main "Univariate" dialog box (see screen-shot step 2) will provide the option to select such information as "Descriptive Statistics," "Estimates of effect size," and "Observed power." Click on "Continue" to return to the original dialog box.

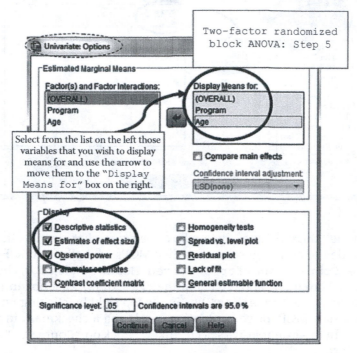

Step 6: From the "Univariate" dialog box, click on "Plots" to obtain a profile plot of means. Click the treatment factor (e.g., "Program") and move it into the "Horizontal Axis" box by clicking the arrow button. Click the blocking factor (e.g., "Age") and move it into the "Separate Lines" box by clicking the arrow button (see screenshot step 6a). Then click on "Add" to move this arrangement into the "Plots" box at the bottom of the dialog box (see screenshot step 6b). Click on "Continue" to return to the original dialog box.

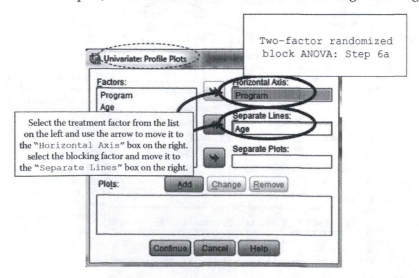

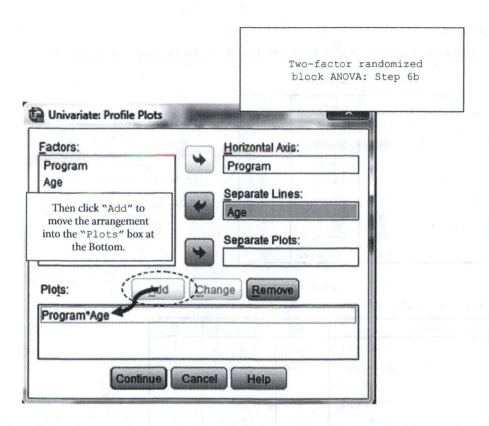

Two-factor randomized
block ANOVA: Step 6b

Step 7: From the "Univariate" dialog box (see screenshot step 2), click on "Save" to select those elements you want to save. Here we save the unstandardized residuals to use later to examine the extent to which normality and independence are met. Thus, place a checkmark in the box next to "Unstandardized." Click "Continue" to return to the main "Univariate" dialog box. From the "Univariate" dialog box, click on "OK" to return and generate the output.

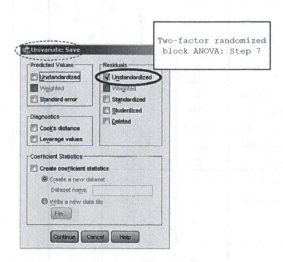

Two-factor randomized
block ANOVA: Step 7

Interpreting the output: Annotated results are presented in Table 6.11.

TABLE 6.11

Two-Factor Randomized Block ANOVA SPSS Results for the Exercise Program Example

Between-Subjects Factors

		Value Label	N
Exercise program	1.00	1/week	4
	2.00	2/week	4
	3.00	3/week	4
	4.00	4/week	4
Age	1.00	20 years old	4
	2.00	30 years old	4
	3.00	40 years old	4
	4.00	50 years old	4

The table labeled "Between-Subjects Factors" lists the variable names and sample sizes for the levels of treatment factor (i.e., "Exercise program") and the blocking factor (i.e., "Age").

Descriptive Statistics

Dependent Variable: Weight Loss

Exercise Program	Age	Mean	Std. Deviation	N
1/week	20 years old	3.0000	.	1
	30 years old	2.0000	.	1
	40 years old	1.0000	.	1
	50 years old	.0000	.	1
	Total	1.5000	1.29099	4
2/week	20 years old	6.0000	.	1
	30 years old	5.0000	.	1
	40 years old	4.0000	.	1
	50 years old	2.0000	.	1
	Total	4.2500	1.70783	4
3/week	20 years old	10.0000	.	1
	30 years old	8.0000	.	1
	40 years old	7.0000	.	1
	50 years old	6.0000	.	1
	Total	7.7500	1.70783	4
4/week	20 years old	9.0000	.	1
	30 years old	7.0000	.	1
	40 years old	8.0000	.	1
	50 years old	7.0000	.	1
	Total	7.7500	.95743	4
Total	20 years old	7.0000	3.16228	4
	30 years old	5.5000	2.64575	4
	40 years old	5.0000	3.16228	4
	50 years old	3.7500	3.30404	4
	Total	5.3125	3.00486	16

The table labeled "Descriptive Statistics" provides basic descriptive statistics (means, standard deviations, and sample sizes) for each treatment factor-blocking factor combination. Because there was only one individual per age group in each exercise program, there is no within cells variation to calculate (and thus missing values for the standard deviation).

TABLE 6.11 (continued)

Two-Factor Randomized Block ANOVA SPSS Results for the Exercise Program Example

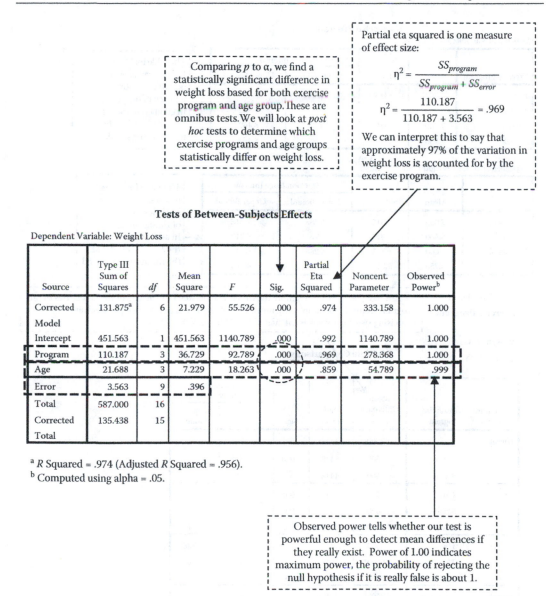

Partial eta squared is one measure of effect size:

$$\eta^2 = \frac{SS_{program}}{SS_{program} + SS_{error}}$$

$$\eta^2 = \frac{110.187}{110.187 + 3.563} = .969$$

We can interpret this to say that approximately 97% of the variation in weight loss is accounted for by the exercise program.

Comparing p to α, we find a statistically significant difference in weight loss based for both exercise program and age group. These are omnibus tests. We will look at *post hoc* tests to determine which exercise programs and age groups statistically differ on weight loss.

Tests of Between-Subjects Effects

Dependent Variable: Weight Loss

Source	Type III Sum of Squares	df	Mean Square	F	Sig.	Partial Eta Squared	Noncent. Parameter	Observed Power[b]
Corrected Model	131.875[a]	6	21.979	55.526	.000	.974	333.158	1.000
Intercept	451.563	1	451.563	1140.789	.000	.992	1140.789	1.000
Program	110.187	3	36.729	92.789	.000	.969	278.368	1.000
Age	21.688	3	7.229	18.263	.000	.859	54.789	.999
Error	3.563	9	.396					
Total	587.000	16						
Corrected Total	135.438	15						

[a] R Squared = .974 (Adjusted R Squared = .956).
[b] Computed using alpha = .05.

Observed power tells whether our test is powerful enough to detect mean differences if they really exist. Power of 1.00 indicates maximum power, the probability of rejecting the null hypothesis if it is really false is about 1.

Estimated Marginal Means

1. Grand Mean

Dependent Variable: Weight Loss

		95% Confidence Interval	
Mean	Std. Error	Lower Bound	Upper Bound
5.313	.157	4.957	5.668

The "Grand Mean" (in this case, 5.313) represents the overall mean, regardless of the exercise program or age. The 95% CI represents the CI of the grand mean.

(continued)

TABLE 6.11 (continued)

Two-Factor Randomized Block ANOVA SPSS Results for the Exercise Program Example

2. Exercise Program

Dependent Variable: Weight Loss

Exercise Program	Mean	Std. Error	95% Confidence Interval	
			Lower Bound	Upper Bound
1/week	1.500	.315	.788	2.212
2/week	4.250	.315	3.538	4.962
3/week	7.750	.315	7.038	8.462
4/week	7.750	.315	7.038	8.462

The table for "Exercise Program" provides descriptive statistics for each of the programs. In addition to means, the *SE* and 95% CI of the means are reported.

3. Age

Dependent Variable: Weight Loss

Age	Mean	Std. Error	95% Confidence Interval	
			Lower Bound	Upper Bound
20 years old	7.000	.315	6.288	7.712
30 years old	5.500	.315	4.788	6.212
40 years old	5.000	.315	4.288	5.712
50 years old	3.750	.315	3.038	4.462

The table for "Age" provides descriptive statistics for each of the age groups. In addition to means, the *SE* and 95% CI of the means are reported.

Post Hoc Tests
Exercise Program

"Mean Difference" is simply the difference between the means of the categories of our program factor. For example, the mean difference of exercising once per week and exercising twice per week is calculated as $1.500 - 4.250 = -2.750$.

Weight Loss

Tukey HSD

Multiple Comparisons

(I) Exercise Program	(J) Exercise Program	Mean Difference (I−J)	Std. Error	Sig.	95% Confidence Interval	
					Lower Bound	Upper Bound
1/week	2/week	−2.7500*	.44488	.001	−4.1388	−1.3612
	3/week	−6.2500*	.44488	.000	−7.6388	−4.8612
	4/week	−6.2500*	.44488	.000	−7.6388	−4.8612
2/week	1/week	2.7500*	.44488	.001	1.3612	4.1388
	3/week	−3.5000*	.44488	.000	−4.8888	−2.1112
	4/week	−3.5000*	.44488	.000	−4.8888	−2.1112
3/week	1/week	6.2500*	.44488	.000	4.8612	7.6388
	2/week	3.5000*	.44488	.000	2.1112	4.8888
	4/week	.0000	.44488	1.000	−1.3888	1.3888
4/week	1/week	6.2500*	.44488	.000	4.8612	7.6388
	2/week	3.5000*	.44488	.000	2.1112	4.8888
	3/week	.0000	.44488	1.000	−1.3888	1.3888

Based on observed means.
The error term is mean square(error) = .396.
*The mean difference is significant at the .05 level.

"Sig." denotes the observed *p* value and provides the results of the Tukey *post hoc* procedure. There is a statistically significant mean difference in weight loss for all exercise programs except for exercising 3 vs. 4 times per week ($p = 1.000$). Note there are redundant results presented in the table. The comparison of exercising 1/week vs. 2/week (row 1) is the same as the comparison of 2/week vs. 1/week (row 4).

TABLE 6.11 (continued)

Two-Factor Randomized Block ANOVA SPSS Results for the Exercise Program Example

Homogeneous Subsets

Tukey HSD[a,b]   **Weight Loss**

Exercise Program	N	Subset 1	2	3
1/week	4	1.5000		
2/week	4		4.2500	
3/week	4			7.7500
4/week	4			7.7500
Sig.		1.000	1.000	1.000

Means for groups in homogeneous subsets are displayed.
Based on observed means.
The error term is mean square(error) = .396.
[a] Uses harmonic mean sample size = 4.000.
[b] Alpha = .05.

"Homogenous Subsets" provides a visual representation of the MCP. For each subset, the means that are printed are homogeneous, or not significantly different. For example, in subset 1 the mean weight loss for exercising once per week (regardless of age group) is 1.50. This is statistically significantly different than the mean weight loss for exercising two, three, or four times per week (as reflected by empty cells in row 1). Similar interpretations are made for contrasts involving exercising two, three, and four times per week.

"Mean difference" is simply the difference between the means of the age groups (i.e., the blocking factor). For example, the mean weight loss difference of 20–30 year olds is calculated as 7.000 – 5.500 = 1.5000.

Age

Weight Loss
Tukey HSD

Multiple Comparisons

(I) Age	(J) Age	Mean Difference (I – J)	Std. Error	Sig.	95% Confidence Interval Lower Bound	Upper Bound
20 years old	30 years old	1.5000*	.44488	.034	.1112	2.8888
	40 years old	2.0000*	.44488	.007	.6112	3.3888
	50 years old	3.2500*	.44488	.000	1.8612	4.6388
30 years old	20 years old	−1.5000*	.44488	.034	−2.8888	−.1112
	40 years old	.5000	.44488	.685	−.8888	1.8888
	50 years old	1.7500*	.44488	.015	.3612	3.1388
40 years old	20 years old	−2.0000*	.44488	.007	−3.3888	−.6112
	30 years old	−.5000	.44488	.685	−1.8888	.8888
	50 years old	1.2500	.44488	.080	−.1388	2.6388
50 years old	20 years old	−3.2500*	.44488	.000	−4.6388	−1.8612
	30 years old	−1.7500*	.44488	.015	−3.1388	−.3612
	40 years old	−1.2500	.44488	.080	−2.6388	.1388

Based on observed means.
The error term is mean square(error) = .396.
*The mean difference is significant at the .05 level.

"Sig." denotes the observed p value and provides the results of the Tukey *post hoc* procedure. There is a statistically significant mean difference in weight loss for:
• 20 and 30 year olds ($p = .034$)
• 20 and 40 year olds ($p = .007$)
• 20 and 50 year olds ($p < .001$)
• 30 and 50 year olds ($p = .015$)
Note there are redundant results presented in the table. The comparison of 20–30 year olds is the same as the comparison of 30–20 year olds, and so forth.

(continued)

TABLE 6.11 (continued)

Two-Factor Randomized Block ANOVA SPSS Results for the Exercise Program Example

Homogeneous Subsets

Weight Loss

Tukey HSD[a,b]

Age	N	Subset 1	Subset 2	Subset 3
50 years old	4	3.7500		
40 years old	4	5.0000	5.0000	
30 years old	4		5.5000	
20 years old	4			7.0000
Sig.		.080	.685	1.000

Means for groups in homogeneous subsets are displayed.

Based on observed means.

The error term is mean square(error) = .396.

[a] Uses harmonic mean sample size = 4.000.

[b] Alpha = .05.

> "Homogenous Subsets" provides a visual representation of the MCP. For each subset, the means that are printed are homogeneous, or not significantly different. For example, in subset 1 the mean weight loss for 50 year olds (regardless of exercise program) is 3.750. This is statistically significantly different than the mean weight loss for individuals in the 30 and 20 year old age groups (as they are not printed in subset 1).

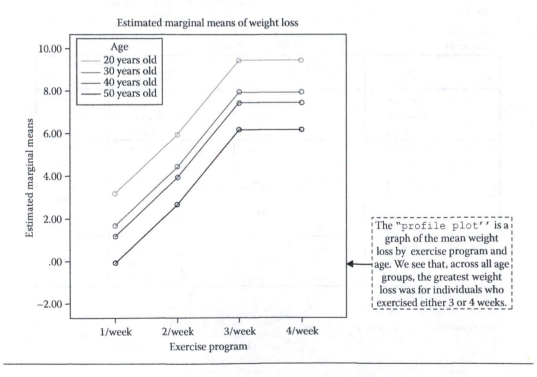

Estimated marginal means of weight loss

> The "profile plot" is a graph of the mean weight loss by exercise program and age. We see that, across all age groups, the greatest weight loss was for individuals who exercised either 3 or 4 weeks.

Examining Assumptions for Two-Factor Randomized Block ANOVA

Normality

We use the residuals (which were requested and created through the "Save" option when generating our model) to examine the extent to which normality was met.

Generating normality evidence: As shown in previous ANOVA chapters, understanding the distributional shape, specifically the extent to which normality is a reasonable assumption, is important. For the two-factor randomized block ANOVA, the residuals should be normally distributed. Because the steps for generating normality evidence were presented previously in the chapter for the two-factor hierarchical ANOVA model, they will not be reiterated here.

Interpreting normality evidence: By this point, we have had a substantial amount of practice in interpreting quite a range of normality statistics. Here we interpret them again, only now in reference to the two-factor randomized block ANOVA model.

Descriptives

			Statistic	Std. Error
Residual for weight loss	Mean		.0000	.12183
	95% Confidence interval for mean	Lower bound	−.2597	
		Upper bound	.2597	
	5% Trimmed mean		.0069	
	Median		.0625	
	Variance		.238	
	Std. deviation		.48734	
	Minimum		−.94	
	Maximum		.81	
	Range		1.75	
	Interquartile range		.87	
	Skewness		−.154	.564
	Kurtosis		−.496	1.091

The skewness statistic of the residuals is −.154 and kurtosis is −.496—both being within the range of an absolute value of 2.0, suggesting some evidence of normality.

As suggested by the skewness statistic, the histogram of residuals is slightly negatively skewed, and the histogram also provides a visual display of the slightly platykurtic distribution.

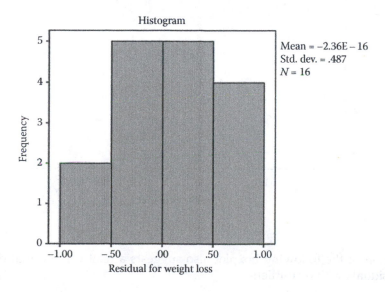

Histogram

Mean = −2.36E − 16
Std. dev. = .487
N = 16

There are a few other statistics that can be used to gauge normality. The formal test of normality, the S–W test (*SW*) (Shapiro & Wilk, 1965), provides evidence of the extent to which our sample distribution is statistically different from a normal distribution. The output for the S–W test is presented as follows and suggests that our sample distribution for the residuals is *not* statistically significantly different than what would be expected from a normal distribution as the *p* value is greater than α.

Tests of Normality

	Kolmogorov–Smirnov[a]			Shapiro–Wilk		
	Statistic	*df*	Sig.	Statistic	*df*	Sig.
Residual for weight loss	.136	16	.200*	.965	16	.757

[a] Lilliefors significance correction.
*This is a lower bound of the true significance.

Q–Q plots are also often examined to determine evidence of normality where quantiles of the theoretical normal distribution are plotted against quantiles of the sample distribution. Points that fall on or close to the diagonal line suggest evidence of normality. The Q–Q plot of residuals shown in the following suggests relative normality.

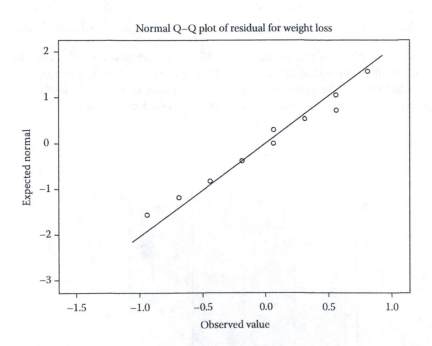

Normal Q–Q plot of residual for weight loss

Examination of the following boxplot also suggests a relatively normal distributional shape of residuals with no outliers.

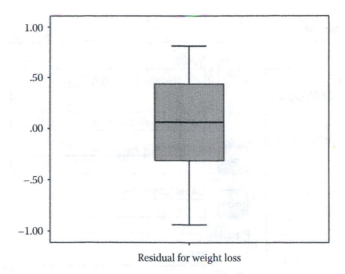

Residual for weight loss

Considering the forms of evidence we have examined, skewness and kurtosis statistics, the S–W test, histogram, the Q–Q plot, and the boxplot, all suggest normality is a reasonable assumption. We can be reasonably assured we have met the assumption of normality.

Independence

The only assumption we have not tested for yet is independence. As we discussed in reference to the one-way ANOVA, if subjects have been randomly assigned to conditions (in other words, the different levels of the treatment factor in a two-factor randomized block ANOVA), the assumption of independence has likely been met. In our example, individuals were randomly assigned to exercise program, and, thus, the assumption of independence was met. However, we often use independent variables that do not allow random assignment. We can plot residuals against levels of our treatment factor using a scatterplot to see whether or not there are patterns in the data and thereby provide an indication of whether we have met this assumption.

Please note that some researchers do not believe that the assumption of independence can be tested. If there is not random assignment to groups, then these researchers believe this assumption has been violated—period. The plot that we generate will give us a general idea of patterns, however, in situations where random assignment was not performed.

Generating the scatterplot: The general steps for generating a simple scatterplot through "Scatter/Dot" have been presented in Chapter 10 of *An Introduction to Statistical Concepts*, Third Edition, and they will not be reiterated here. From the "Simple Scatterplot" dialog screen, click the residual variable and move it into the "Y Axis" box by clicking on the arrow. Click the independent variable that we wish to display (e.g., "Exercise Program") and move it into the "X Axis" box by clicking on the arrow. Then click "OK."

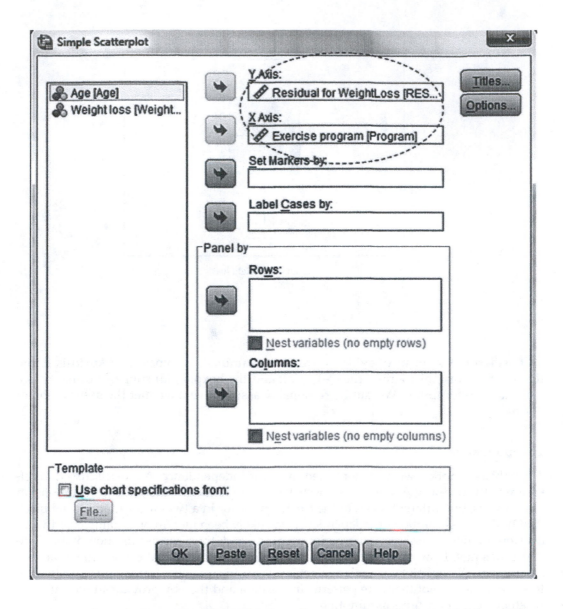

Interpreting independence evidence: In examining the scatterplot for evidence of independence, the points should fall relatively randomly above and below a horizontal line at 0. (You may recall in Chapter 1 that we added a reference line to the graph using Chart Editor. To add a reference line, double click on the graph in the output to activate the chart editor. Select "Options" in the top pulldown menu, then "Y axis reference line." This will bring up the "Properties" dialog box. Change the value of the position to be "0." Then click on "Apply" and "Close" to generate the graph with a horizontal line at 0.)

In this example, our scatterplot for exercise program by residual generally suggests evidence of independence with a relatively random display of residuals above and below the horizontal line at 0. Thus, had we not met the assumption of independence through random assignment of cases to groups, this would have provided evidence that independence was a reasonable assumption.

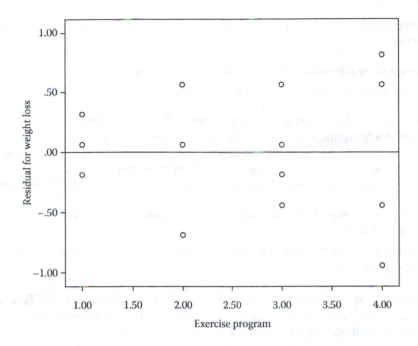

Two-Factor Fixed-Effects Randomized Block ANOVA *n* > 1

To run a two-factor randomized block ANOVA for *n* > 1, the procedures are exactly the same as with the regular two-factor ANOVA. However, the adjusted *F* tests are not available.

Friedman Test

Lastly, the Friedman test can be run as previously described in Chapter 5.

Post Hoc Power for Two-Factor Randomized Block ANOVA Using G*Power

G*Power provides power calculations for the two-factor randomized block ANOVA model. In G*Power, just treat this design as if it were a regular two-factor ANOVA model.

6.7 Template and APA-Style Write-Up

Finally, here is an example paragraph just for the results of the two-factor hierarchical ANOVA design (feel free to write a similar paragraph for the two-factor randomized block ANOVA example). Recall that our graduate research assistant, Marie, was assisting a reading faculty member, JoAnn. JoAnn wanted to know the following: if there is a mean difference in reading based on the approach to reading and if there is a mean difference in reading based on teacher. The research questions presented to JoAnn from Marie include the following:

- *Is there a mean difference in reading based on approach to reading?*
- *Is there a mean difference in reading based on teacher?*

Marie then assisted JoAnn in generating a two-factor hierarchical ANOVA as the test of inference, and a template for writing the research questions for this design is presented as follows. As we noted in previous chapters, it is important to ensure the reader understands the levels of the factor(s). This may be done parenthetically in the actual research question, as an operational definition, or specified within the methods section:

- Is there a mean difference in [dependent variable] based on [nonnested factor]?
- Is there a mean difference in [dependent variable] based on [nested factor]?

It may be helpful to preface the results of the two-factor hierarchical ANOVA with information on an examination of the extent to which the assumptions were met. The assumptions include (a) homogeneity of variance and (b) normality.

A two-factor hierarchical ANOVA was conducted. The nonrepeated factor was approach to reading (basal or whole language) and the nested factor was teacher (four teachers). The null hypotheses tested included the following: (1) the mean reading score was equal for each of the reading approaches, and (2) the mean reading score for each teacher was equal.

The data were screened for missingness and violation of assumptions prior to analysis. There were no missing data. The assumption of **homogeneity of variance** was met ($F(3, 20) = 1.042$, $p = .396$). The assumption of **normality** was tested via examination of the residuals. Review of the S–W test ($SW = .960$, $df = 24$, $p = .442$) and skewness (.284) and kurtosis (−.693) statistics suggested that normality was a reasonable assumption. The boxplot displayed a relatively normal distributional shape (with no outliers) of the residuals. The Q–Q plot and histogram suggested normality was tenable.

Here is an APA-style example paragraph of results for the two-factor hierarchical ANOVA (remember that this will be prefaced by the previous paragraph reporting the extent to which the assumptions of the test were met).

From Table 5.10, the results for the two-factor hierarchical ANOVA indicate the following:

1. A statistically significant main effect for approach to reading ($F_{approach} = 59.559$, $df = 1, 2$, $p = .016$)
2. A nonstatistically significant main effect for teacher ($F_{teacher} = .952$, $df = 2, 20$, $p = .403$)

Effect size was rather large for the effect of approach to reading (partial $\eta^2_{approach}$ = .968), with high observed power (.948), but expectedly less so for the nonsignificant teacher effect (partial $\eta^2_{teacher}$ = .087, power = .192). The results of this study provide evidence to suggest that reading comprehension scores are significantly higher for students taught by the whole language method (M = 10.833, SE = .704) as compared to the basal method (M = 3.333, SE = .704). The results also suggest that mean scores for reading are comparable for children regardless of the teacher who instructed them.

6.8 Summary

In this chapter, models involving nested and blocking factors for the two-factor case were considered. Three different models were examined; these included the two-factor hierarchical design, the two-factor randomized block design with one observation per cell, and the two-factor randomized block design with multiple observations per cell. Included for each design were the usual topics of model characteristics, the layout of the data, the linear model, assumptions of the model and dealing with their violation, the ANOVA summary table and expected mean squares, and MCPs. Also included for particular designs was a discussion of the compound symmetry/sphericity assumption and the Friedman test based on ranks. We concluded with a comparison of various ANOVA models on precision and power. At this point, you should have met the following objectives: (a) be able to understand the characteristics and concepts underlying hierarchical and randomized block ANOVA models, (b) be able to determine and interpret the results of hierarchical and randomized block ANOVA models, (c) be able to understand and evaluate the assumptions of hierarchical and randomized block ANOVA models, and (d) be able to compare different ANOVA models and select an appropriate model. This chapter concludes our extended discussion of ANOVA models. In the remaining three chapters of the text, we discuss regression models where the dependent variable is predicted by one or more independent variables or predictors.

Problems

Conceptual Problems

6.1   A researcher wants to know if the number of professional development courses that a teacher completes differs based on the format that the professional development is offered (online, mixed mode, face-to-face). The researcher randomly samples 100 teachers employed in the district. Believing that years of teaching experience may be a concomitant variable, the researcher ranks the teachers on years of experience and places them in categories that represent 5-year intervals. The researcher then randomly selects 4 years of experience blocks. The teachers within those blocks are then randomly assigned to professional development format. Which of the following methods of blocking is employed here?

a. Predefined value blocking

b. Predefined range blocking

c. Sampled value blocking

d. Sampled range blocking

6.2   To study the effectiveness of three spelling methods, 45 subjects are randomly selected from the fourth graders in a particular elementary school. Based on the order of their IQ scores, subjects are grouped into IQ groups (low = 75–99, average = 100–115, high = 116–130), 15 in each group. Subjects in each group are randomly assigned to one of the three methods of spelling, five each. Which of the following methods of blocking is employed here?

a. Predefined value blocking

b. Predefined range blocking

c. Sampled value blocking

d. Sampled range blocking

6.3   A researcher is examining preschoolers' knowledge of number identification. Fifty preschoolers are grouped based on socioeconomic status (low, moderate, high). Within each SES group, students are randomly assigned to one of two treatment groups: one which incorporates numbers through individual, small group, and whole group work with manipulatives, music, and art; and a second which incorporates numbers through whole group study only. Which of the following methods of blocking is employed here?

a. Predefined value blocking

b. Predefined range blocking

c. Sampled value blocking

d. Sampled range blocking

6.4   If three teachers employ method A and three other teachers employ method B, then which one of the following is suggested?

a. Teachers are nested within method.

b. Teachers are crossed with methods.

c. Methods are nested within teacher.

d. Cannot be determined.

6.5   The interaction of factors A and B can be assessed only if which one of the following occurs?

a. Both factors are fixed.

b. Both factors are random.

c. Factor A is nested within factor B.

d. Factors A and B are crossed.

6.6   In a two-factor design, factor A is nested within factor B for which one of the following?

a. At each level of A, each level of B appears.

b. At each level of A, unique levels of B appear.

c. At each level of B, unique levels of A appear.

d. Cannot be determined.

6.7   Five teachers use an experimental method of teaching statistics, and five other teachers use the traditional method. If factor M is method of teaching, and factor T is teacher, this design can be denoted by which one of the following?

    a. T(M)

    b. T × M

    c. M × T

    d. M(T)

6.8   If factor C is nested within factors A and B, this is denoted as AB(C). True or false?

6.9   A design in which all levels of each factor are found in combination with each level of every other factor is necessarily a nested design. True or false?

6.10 To determine if counseling method E is uniformly superior to method C for the population of counselors, from which random samples are taken to conduct a study, one needs a nested design with a mixed model. True or false?

6.11 I assert that the predefined value method of block formation is more effective than the sampled value method in reducing unexplained variability. Am I correct?

6.12 For the interaction to be tested in a two-factor randomized block design, it is required that which one of the following occurs?

    a. Both factors be fixed

    b. Both factors be random

    c. $n = 1$

    d. $n > 1$

6.13 Five medical professors use a computer-based method of teaching and five other medical professors use a lecture-based method of teaching. A researcher is interested in student outcomes for those enrolled in classes taught by these instructional methods. This is an example of which type of design?

    a. Completely crossed design

    b. Repeated measures design

    c. Hierarchical design

    d. Randomized block design

6.14 In a randomized block study, the correlation between the blocking factor and the dependent variable is .35. I assert that the residual variation will be smaller when using the blocking variable than without. Am I correct?

6.15 A researcher is interested in examining the number of suspensions of high school students based on random assignment participation in a series of self-awareness workshops. The researcher believes that age may be a concomitant variable. Applying a two-factor randomized block ANOVA design to the data, age is an appropriate blocking factor?

6.16 In a two-factor hierarchical design with two levels of factor A and three levels of factor B nested within each level of A, how many F ratios can be tested?

    a. 1

    b. 2

    c. 3

    d. Cannot be determined

6.17 If the correlation between the concomitant variable and dependent variable is −.80, which of the following designs is recommended?

    a. ANCOVA

    b. One-factor ANOVA

    c. Randomized block ANOVA

    d. All of the above

6.18 IQ must be used as a treatment factor. True or false?

6.19 Which of the following blocking methods best estimates the treatment effects?

    a. Predefined value blocking

    b. Post hoc predefined value blocking

    c. Sampled value blocking

    d. Sampled range blocking

Computational Problems

6.1 An experiment was conducted to compare three types of behavior modification (1, 2, and 3) using age as a blocking variable (4-, 6-, and 8-year-old children). The mean scores on the dependent variable, number of instances of disruptive behavior, are listed here for each cell. The intention of the treatments is to minimize the number of disruptions.

Type of Behavior Modification	Age		
	4 Years	6 Years	8 Years
1	20	40	40
2	50	30	20
3	50	40	30

Use these cell means to graph the interaction between type of behavior modification and age.

    a. Is there an interaction between type of behavior modification and age?

    b. What kind of recommendation would you make to teachers?

6.2 An experiment was conducted to compare four different preschool curricula that were adopted in four different classrooms. Reading readiness proficiency was used as a blocking variable (below proficient, at proficient, above proficient). The mean scores on the dependent variable, letter recognition, are listed here for each cell. The intention of the treatment (i.e., the curriculum) is to increase letter recognition.

Curriculum	Reading Readiness Proficiency		
	Below	At	Above
1	12	20	22
2	20	24	18
3	16	16	20
4	15	18	25

Use these cell means to graph the interaction between curriculum and reading readiness proficiency.

a. Is there an interaction between type of curriculum and reading readiness proficiency?

b. What kind of recommendation would you make to teachers?

6.3 An experimenter tested three types of perfume (or aftershave) (tame, sexy, and musk) when worn by light-haired and dark-haired women (or men). Thus, hair color is a blocking variable. The dependent measure was attractiveness defined as the number of times during a 2-week period that other persons complimented a subject on their perfume (or aftershave). There were five subjects in each cell. Complete the ANOVA summary table below, assuming a fixed-effects model, where $\alpha = .05$.

Source	SS	df	MS	F	Critical Value	Decision
Perfume (A)	200	—	—	—	—	—
Hair color (B)	100	—	—	—	—	—
Interaction (AB)	20	—	—	—	—	—
Within	240	—	—			
Total		—	—			

6.4 An experiment was conducted to determine if there was a mean difference in weight for women based on type of aerobics exercise program participated (low impact vs. high impact). Body mass index (BMI) was used as a blocking variable to represent below, at, or above recommended BMI. The data are shown as follows. Conduct a two-factor randomized block ANOVA ($\alpha = .05$) and Bonferroni MCPs using SPSS to determine the results of the study.

Subject	Exercise Program	BMI	Weight
1	1	1	100
2	1	2	135
3	1	3	200
4	1	1	95
5	1	2	140
6	1	3	180
7	2	1	120
8	2	2	152
9	2	3	176
10	2	1	128
11	2	2	142
12	2	3	220

6.5   A mathematics professor wants to know which of three approaches to teaching calculus resulted in the best test performance (Sections 6.1, 6.2, or 6.3). Scores on the GRE-Quantitative (GRE-Q) portion were used as a blocking variable (block 1: 200–400; block 2: 401–600; block 3: 601–800). The data are shown as follows. Conduct a two-factor randomized block ANOVA ($\alpha = .05$) and Bonferroni MCPs using SPSS to determine the results of the study.

Subject	Section	GRE-Q	Test Score
1	1	1	90
2	1	2	93
3	1	3	100
4	2	1	88
5	2	2	90
6	2	3	97
7	3	1	79
8	3	2	85
9	3	3	92

Interpretive Problems

6.1   The following is the first one-factor ANOVA interpretive problem you developed in Chapter 1: *Using the survey 1 dataset from the website, use SPSS to conduct a one-factor fixed-effects ANOVA, including effect size, where political view is the grouping variable (i.e., independent variable) ($J = 5$) and the dependent variable is a variable of interest to you (the following variables look interesting: books, TV, exercise, drinks, GPA, GRE-Q, CDs, hair appointment). Then write an APA-style paragraph describing the results.*

Take the one-factor ANOVA interpretive problem you developed in Chapter 1. What are some reasonable blocking variables to consider? Which type of blocking would be best in your situation? Select this blocking variable from the same dataset and conduct a two-factor randomized block ANOVA. Compare these results with the one-factor ANOVA results (without the blocking factor) to determine how useful the blocking variable was in terms of reducing residual variability.

6.2   The following is the second one-factor ANOVA interpretive problem you developed in Chapter 1: *Using the survey 1 dataset from the website, use SPSS to conduct a one-factor fixed-effects ANOVA, including effect size, where hair color is the grouping variable (i.e., independent variable) ($J = 5$) and the dependent variable is a variable of interest to you (the following variables look interesting: books, TV, exercise, drinks, GPA, GRE-Q, CDs, hair appointment). Then write an APA-style paragraph describing the results.*

Take this one-factor ANOVA interpretive problem you developed in Chapter 1. What are some reasonable blocking variables to consider? Which type of blocking would be best in your situation? Select this blocking variable from the same dataset and conduct a two-factor randomized ANOVA. Compare these results with the one-factor ANOVA results (without the blocking factor) to determine how useful the blocking variable was in terms of reducing residual variability.

7

Simple Linear Regression

Chapter Outline

Key Concepts

1. Slope and intercept of a straight line

2. Regression model

3. Prediction errors/residuals

4. Standardized and unstandardized regression coefficients

5. Proportion of variation accounted for; coefficient of determination

In Chapter 10 of *An Introduction to Statistical Concepts*, Third Edition, we considered various bivariate measures of association. Specifically, the chapter dealt with the topics of scatterplot, covariance, types of correlation coefficients, and their resulting inferential tests. Thus, the chapter was concerned with addressing the question of the extent to which two variables are associated or related. In this chapter, we extend our discussion of two variables to address the question of the extent to which one variable can be used to predict or explain another variable.

Beginning in Chapter 1, we examined various analysis of variance (ANOVA) models. It should be mentioned again that ANOVA and regression are both forms of the same general linear model (GLM), where the relationship between one or more independent variables

322   Statistical Concepts: A Second Course

and one dependent variable is evaluated. The major difference between the two procedures is that in ANOVA, the independent variables are discrete variables (i.e., nominal or ordinal), while in regression, the independent variables are continuous variables (i.e., interval or ratio; however, we will see later how we can apply dichotomous variables in regression models). Otherwise there is considerable overlap of these two procedures in terms of concepts and their implementation. Note that a continuous variable can be transformed into a discrete variable. For example, the Graduate Record Exam-Quantitative (GRE_Q) exam is a continuous variable scaled from 200 to 800 (albeit in 10-point score increments). It could be made into a discrete variable, such as low (200–400), average (401–600), and high (601–800).

When considering the relationship between two variables (say X and Y), the researcher usually determines some measure of relationship between those variables, such as a correlation coefficient (e.g., r_{XY}, the Pearson product–moment correlation coefficient), as we did in Chapter 10 of *An Introduction to Statistical Concepts*, Third Edition. Another way of looking at how two variables may be related is through regression analysis, in terms of prediction or explanation. That is, we evaluate the ability of one variable to predict or explain a second variable. Here we adopt the usual notation where X is defined as the **independent** or **predictor variable**, and Y as the **dependent** or **criterion variable**.

For example, an admissions officer might want to use GRE scores to predict graduate-level grade point averages (GPAs) to make admission decisions for a sample of applicants to a university or college. The research question of interest is how well does the GRE (the independent or predictor variable) predict or explain performance in graduate school (the dependent or criterion variable)? This is an example of simple linear regression where only a single predictor variable is included in the analysis. The utility of the GRE in predicting GPA requires that these variables have a correlation different from 0. Otherwise the GRE will not be very useful in predicting GPA. For education and the behavioral sciences, the use of a single predictor does not usually result in reasonable prediction or explanation. Thus, Chapter 8 considers the case of multiple predictor variables through multiple linear regression analysis.

In this chapter, we consider the concepts of slope, intercept, regression model, unstandardized and standardized regression coefficients, residuals, proportion of variation accounted for, tests of significance, and statistical assumptions. Our objectives are that by the end of this chapter, you will be able to (a) understand the concepts underlying simple linear regression, (b) determine and interpret the results of simple linear regression, and (c) understand and evaluate the assumptions of simple linear regression.

7.1 Concepts of Simple Linear Regression

In this chapter, we continue to follow Marie on yet another statistical analysis adventure.

Marie has developed excellent rapport with the faculty at her institution as she has assisted them in statistical analysis. Marie will now be working with Randall, an associate dean in the Graduate Student Services office. Randall wants to know if the required entrance exam for graduate school (specifically the GRE_Q) can be used to predict midterm grades. Marie suggests the following research question to Randall: *Can midterm exam scores be predicted from the GRE_Q?* Marie determines that a simple linear regression is the best statistical procedure to use to answer Randall's question. Her next task is to assist Randall in analyzing the data.

Let us consider the basic concepts involved in simple linear regression. Many years ago when you had algebra, you learned about an equation used to describe a straight line,

$$Y = bX + a$$

Here the predictor variable X is used to predict the criterion variable Y. The **slope** of the line is denoted by b and indicates the number of Y units the line changes for a one-unit change in X. You may find it easier to think about the slope as measuring tilt or steepness. The Y-intercept is denoted by a and is the point at which the line intersects or crosses the Y axis. To be more specific, a is the value of Y when X is equal to 0. Hereafter we use the term **intercept** rather than Y-intercept to keep it simple.

Consider the plot of the straight line $Y = 0.5X + 1.0$ as shown in Figure 7.1. Here we see that the line clearly intersects the Y axis at $Y = 1.0$; thus, the intercept is equal to 1. The slope of a line is defined, more specifically, as the change in Y (numerator) divided by the change in X (denominator).

$$b = \frac{\Delta Y}{\Delta X} = \frac{Y_2 - Y_1}{X_2 - X_1}$$

For instance, take two points shown in Figure 7.1, (X_1, Y_1) and (X_2, Y_2), that fall on the straight line with coordinates $(0, 1)$ and $(4, 3)$, respectively. We compute the slope for those two points to be $(3 - 1)/(4 - 0) = 0.5$. If we were to select any other two points that fall on the straight line, then the slope for those two points would also be equal to 0.5. That is, regardless of the two points on the line that we select, the slope will always be the same, constant value of 0.5. This is true because we only need two points to define a particular straight line. That is, with the points $(0, 1)$ and $(4, 3)$, we can draw only one straight line that passes through both of those points, and that line has a slope of 0.5 and an intercept of 1.0.

Let us take the concepts of slope, intercept, and straight line and apply them in the context of correlation so that we can study the relationship between the variables X and Y.

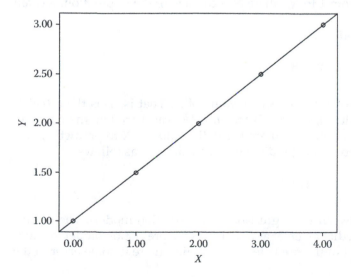

FIGURE 7.1
Plot of line: $Y = 0.5X + 1.0$.

If the slope of the line is a positive value (e.g., Figure 7.1), as X increases Y also increases, then the correlation will be positive. If the slope of the line is 0, such that the line is parallel or horizontal to the X axis, as X increases Y remains constant, then the correlation will be 0. If the slope of the line is a negative value, as X increases Y decreases (i.e., the line decreases from left to right), then the correlation will be negative. Thus, the sign of the slope corresponds to the sign of the correlation.

7.2 Population Simple Linear Regression Model

Let us take these concepts and apply them to simple linear regression. Consider the situation where we have the entire population of individual's scores on both variables X (the independent variable, such as GRE) and Y (the dependent variable, such as GPA). We define the linear regression model as the equation for a straight line. This yields an equation for the regression of Y the criterion, given X the predictor, often stated as the regression of Y on X, although more easily understood as Y being predicted by X.

The **population regression model** for Y being predicted by X is

$$Y_i = \beta_{YX} X_i + \alpha_{YX} + \varepsilon_i$$

where
  Y is the criterion variable
  X is the predictor variable
  β_{YX} is the population slope for Y predicted by X
  α_{YX} is the population intercept for Y predicted by X
  ε_i are the population residuals or errors of prediction (the part of Y_i not predicted from X_i)
  i represents an index for a particular case (an individual or object; in other words, the
     unit of analysis that has been measured)

The index i can take on values from 1 to N, where N is the size of the population, written as $i = 1,\ldots, N$.

The **population prediction model** is

$$Y_i' = \beta_{YX} X_i + \alpha_{YX}$$

where Y_i' is the predicted value of Y for a specific value of X. That is, Y_i is the *actual or observed score* obtained by individual i, while Y_i' is the *predicted score* based on their X score for that same individual (in other words, you are using the value of X to predict what Y will be). Thus, we see that the population prediction error is defined as follows:

$$\varepsilon_i = Y_i - Y_i'$$

There is only one difference between the regression and prediction models. The regression model explicitly includes prediction error as ε_i, whereas the prediction model includes prediction error implicitly as part of the predicted score Y'_i (i.e., there is some error in the predicted values).

Consider for a moment a practical application of the difference between the regression and prediction models. Frequently a researcher will develop a regression model for a population where X and Y are both known, and then use the prediction model to actually predict Y when only X is known (i.e., Y will not be known until later). Using the GRE example, the admissions officer first develops a regression model for a population of students currently attending the university so as to have a current measure of GPA. This yields the slope and intercept. Then the prediction model is used to predict future GPA and to help make admission decisions for next year's population of applicants based on their GRE scores.

A simple method for determining the population slope (β_{YX}) and intercept (α_{YX}) is computed as

$$\beta_{YX} = \rho_{XY} \frac{\sigma_Y}{\sigma_X}$$

and

$$\alpha_{YX} = \mu_Y - \beta_{YX} \mu_X$$

where

σ_Y and σ_X are the population standard deviations for Y and X respectively
ρ_{XY} is the population correlation between X and Y (simply the Pearson correlation coefficient, rho)
μ_Y and μ_X are the population means for Y and X respectively

Note that the previously used mathematical method for determining the slope and intercept of a straight line is not appropriate in regression analysis with real data.

7.3 Sample Simple Linear Regression Model

7.3.1 Unstandardized Regression Model

Let us return to the real world of sample statistics and consider the sample simple linear regression model. As usual, Greek letters refer to population parameters, and English letters refer to sample statistics. The **sample regression model** for predicting Y from X is computed as follows:

$$Y_i = b_{YX} X_i + a_{YX} + e_i$$

where
Y and X are as before (i.e., the dependent and independent variables, respectively)
b_{YX} is the sample slope for Y predicted by X
a_{YX} is the sample intercept for Y predicted by X
e_i are sample residuals or errors of prediction (the part of Y_i not predictable from X_i)
i represents an index for a case (an individual or object)

The index i can take on values from 1 to n, where n is the size of the sample, and is written as $i = 1,\ldots, n$.

The **sample prediction model** is computed as follows:

$$Y'_i = b_{YX}X_i + a_{YX}$$

where Y'_i is the predicted value of Y for a specific value of X. We define the sample prediction error as the difference between the *actual score* obtained by individual i (i.e., Y_i) and the *predicted score* based on the X score for that individual (i.e., Y'_i). In other words, the residual is that part of Y that is *not* predicted by X. The goal of the prediction model is to include an independent variable X that minimizes the residual; this means that the independent variable does a nice job of predicting the outcome. Computationally, the residual (or error) is computed as follows:

$$e_i = Y_i - Y'_i$$

The difference between the regression and prediction models is the same as previously discussed, except now we are dealing with a sample rather than a population.

The sample slope (b_{YX}) and intercept (a_{YX}) can be determined by

$$b_{YX} = r_{XY}\frac{s_Y}{s_X}$$

and

$$a_{YX} = \bar{Y} - b_{YX}\bar{X}$$

where

s_Y and s_X are the sample standard deviations for Y and X respectively

r_{XY} is the sample correlation between X and Y (again the Pearson correlation coefficient, rho)

$\bar{Y}$ and $\bar{X}$ are the sample means for Y and X, respectively

The sample slope (b_{YX}) is referred to alternately as (a) the expected or predicted change in Y for a one-unit change in X and (b) the unstandardized or raw regression coefficient. The sample intercept (a_{YX}) is referred to alternately as (a) the point at which the regression line intersects (or crosses) the Y axis and (b) the value of Y when X is 0.

Consider now the analysis of a realistic example to be followed throughout this chapter. Let us use the GRE_Q subtest to predict midterm scores of an introductory statistics course. The GRE_Q has a possible range of 20–80 points (if we remove the unnecessary last digit of zero), and the statistics midterm has a possible range of 0–50 points. Given the sample of 10 statistics students shown in Table 7.1, let us work through a simple linear regression analysis. The observation numbers ($i = 1,\ldots, 10$), and values for the GRE_Q (the independent variable, X) and midterm (the dependent variable, Y) variables are given in the first three columns of the table, respectively. The other columns are discussed as we go along.

TABLE 7.1

Statistics Midterm Example Regression Data

Student	GRE_Q (X)	Midterm (Y)	Residual (e)	Predicted Midterm (Y')
1	37	32	3.7125	28.2875
2	45	36	3.5125	32.4875
3	43	27	−4.4375	31.4375
4	50	34	−1.1125	35.1125
5	65	45	2.0125	42.9875
6	72	49	2.3375	46.6625
7	61	42	1.1125	40.8875
8	57	38	−0.7875	38.7875
9	48	30	−4.0625	34.0625
10	77	47	−2.2875	49.2875

The sample statistics for the GRE_Q (the independent variable) are $\bar{X} = 55.5$ and $s_X = 13.1339$, for the statistics midterm (the dependent variable) are $\bar{Y} = 38$ and $s_Y = 7.5130$, and the correlation r_{XY} is 0.9177. The sample slope (b_{YX}) and intercept (a_{YX}) are computed as follows:

$$b_{YX} = r_{XY}\frac{s_Y}{s_X} = 0.9177\frac{7.5130}{13.1339} = 0.5250$$

and

$$a_{YX} = \bar{Y} - b_{YX}\bar{X} = 38 - 0.5250(55.5) = 8.8625$$

Let us interpret the slope and intercept values. A slope of 0.5250 means that if your score on the GRE_Q is increased by one point, then your predicted score on the statistics midterm (i.e., the dependent variable) will be increased by 0.5250 points or about half a point. An intercept of 8.8625 means that if your score on the GRE_Q is 0 (although not possible as you receive 200 points just for showing up), then your score on the statistics midterm is 8.8625. The sample simple linear regression model, given these values, becomes

$$Y_i = b_{YX}X_i + a_{YX} + e_i = .5250X_i + 8.8625 + e_i$$

If your score on the GRE_Q is 63, then your predicted score on the statistics midterm is the following:

$$Y'_i = .5250(63) + 8.8625 = 41.9375$$

Thus, based on the prediction model developed, your predicted score on the midterm is approximately 42; however, as becomes evident, predictions are generally not perfect.

7.3.2 Standardized Regression Model

Up until now, the computations in simple linear regression have involved the use of raw scores. For this reason, we call this the *unstandardized regression model*. The slope estimate is an unstandardized or raw regression slope because it is the predicted change in Y raw score units for a one raw score unit change in X. We can also express regression in standard z score units for both X and Y as

$$z(X_i) = \frac{X_i - \bar{X}}{s_X}$$

and

$$z(Y_i) = \frac{Y_i - \bar{Y}}{s_Y}$$

In both cases, the numerator is the difference between the observed score and the mean, and the denominator is the standard deviation (and dividing by the standard deviation, standardizes the value). The means and variances of both standardized variables (i.e., z_X and z_Y) are 0 and 1, respectively.

The sample standardized linear prediction model becomes the following, where $z(Y_i')$ is the standardized predicted value of Y:

$$z(Y_i') = b_{YX}^* \, z(X_i) = r_{XY} \, z(X_i)$$

Thus, the standardized regression slope, b_{YX}^*, sometimes referred to as a **beta weight**, is equal to r_{XY}. No intercept term is necessary in the prediction model as the mean of the z scores for both X and Y is 0 (i.e., $a_{YX}^* = \bar{z}_Y - b_{YX}^* \, \bar{z}_X = 0$). In summary, *the standardized slope is equal to the correlation coefficient*, and *the standardized intercept is equal to 0*.

For our statistics midterm example, the sample standardized linear prediction model is

$$z(Y_i') = .9177 z(X_i)$$

The slope of .9177 would be interpreted as the expected increase in the statistics midterm in z score (i.e., standardized score) units for a one z score (i.e., standardized score) unit increase in the GRE_Q. A one z score unit increase is also the same as a one standard deviation increase because the standard deviation of z is equal to 1 (Chapter 4 of *An Introduction to Statistical Concepts*, Third Edition discusses that the mean of a standardized z score is 0 with a standard deviation of 1).

When should you consider use of the standardized versus unstandardized regression analyses? According to Pedhazur (1997), the standardized regression slope b^* is not very stable from sample to sample. For example, at Ivy-Covered University, the standardized regression slope b^* would vary across different graduating classes (or samples), whereas the unstandardized regression slope b would be much more consistent across classes. Thus, in simple regression, most researchers prefer the use of b. We see later that the standardized regression slope b^* has some utility in multiple regression analysis.

7.3.3 Prediction Errors

Previously we mentioned that perfect prediction of Y from X is extremely unlikely, only occurring with a perfect correlation between X and Y (i.e., $r_{XY} = \pm 1.0$). When developing the regression model, the values of the outcome, Y, are known. Once the slope and intercept have been estimated, we can then use the prediction model to predict the outcome (Y) from the independent variable (X) when the values of Y are unknown. We have already defined the predicted values of Y as Y'. In other words, a predicted value Y' can be computed by plugging the obtained value for X into the prediction model. It can be shown that $Y'_i = Y_i$ for all i only when there is perfect prediction. However, this is extremely unlikely in reality, particularly in simple linear regression using a single predictor.

We can determine a value of Y' for each of the i cases (individuals or objects) from the prediction model. In comparing the actual Y values to the predicted Y values, we obtain the *residuals* as the difference between the observed (Y_i) and predicted values (Y'_i), computed as follows:

$$e_i = Y_i - Y'_i$$

for all $i = 1,..., n$ individuals or objects in the sample. The residuals, e_i, are also known as **errors of estimate**, or **prediction errors**, and are that portion of Y_i that is not predictable from X_i. The residual terms are random values that are unique to each individual or object.

The residuals and predicted values for the statistics midterm example are shown in the last two columns of Table 7.1, respectively. Consider observation 2, where the observed GRE_Q score is 45 and the observed midterm score is 36. The predicted midterm score is 32.4875 and the residual is +3.5125. This indicates that person 2 had a higher observed midterm score than was predicted using the GRE_Q as a predictor. We see that a *positive* residual indicates the observed criterion score is larger than the predicted criterion score, whereas a *negative* residual (such as in observation 3) indicates the observed criterion score is smaller than the predicted criterion score. For observation 3, the observed GRE_Q score is 43, the observed midterm score is 27, the predicted midterm score is 31.4375, and, thus, the residual is −4.4375. Person 2 scored higher on the midterm than we predicted, and person 3 scored lower on the midterm than we predicted.

The regression example is shown graphically in the **scatterplot** of Figure 7.2, where the straight diagonal line represents the regression line. Individuals falling above the regression line have positive residuals (e.g., observation 1) (in other words, the difference between the observed score, represented as open circle 1 on the graph, is greater in value than the predicted value, which is represented by the regression line), and individuals falling below the regression line have negative residuals (e.g., observation 3) (in other words, the difference between the observed score, represented as open circle 3 on the graph, is less in value than the predicted value, which is represented by the regression line). The residual is, very simply, the vertical distance between the observed score [represented by the open circles or "dots" in the scatterplot (Figure 7.2)] and the regression line. In the residual column of Table 7.1, we see that half of the residuals are positive and half negative, and in Figure 7.2, that half of the points fall above the regression line and half below the regression line. It can be shown that the mean of the residuals is always 0 (i.e., $\bar{e} = 0$), as the sum of the residuals is always 0. This results from the fact that the mean of the observed criterion scores is equal to the mean of the predicted criterion scores (i.e., $\bar{Y} = \bar{Y}'$ 38 for the example data).

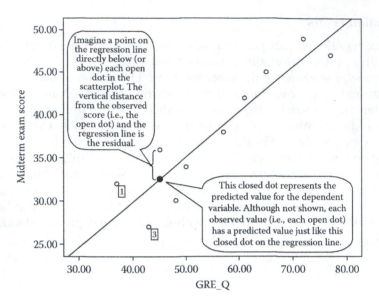

FIGURE 7.2
Scatterplot for midterm example.

7.3.4 Least Squares Criterion

How was one particular method selected for determining the slope and intercept? Obviously, some standard procedure has to be used. Thus, there are statistical criteria that help us decide which method to use in determining the slope and intercept. The criterion usually used in linear regression analysis (and in all GLMs, for that matter) is the **least squares criterion**. According to the least squares criterion, the sum of the squared prediction errors or residuals is smallest. That is, we want to find that regression line, defined by a particular slope and intercept, which results in the smallest sum of the squared residuals (recall that the residual is the difference between the observed and predicted values for the outcome). Since the residual is the vertical difference between the observed and predicted value, the regression line is simply the line that minimizes that vertical distance. Given the value that we place on the accuracy of prediction, this is the most logical choice of a method for estimating the slope and intercept.

In summary then, the least squares criterion gives us a particular slope and intercept, and thus a particular regression line, such that the sum of the squared residuals is smallest. We often refer to this particular method for determining the slope and intercept as **least squares estimation** because *b* and *a* represent sample estimates of the population parameters β and α obtained using the least squares criterion.

7.3.5 Proportion of Predictable Variation (Coefficient of Determination)

How well is the criterion variable *Y* predicted by the predictor variable *X*? For our example, we want to know how well the statistics midterm scores are predicted by the GRE_Q. Let us consider two possible situations with respect to this example. First, if the GRE_Q is found to be a really good predictor of statistics midterm scores, then instructors could use the GRE_Q information to individualize their instruction to the skill level of each student or class. They could, for example, provide special instruction to those students with low GRE_Q scores, or in general, adjust the level of instruction to fit the quantitative skills of their students.

Second, if the GRE_Q is not found to be a very good predictor of statistics midterm scores, then instructors would not find very much use for the GRE_Q in terms of their preparation for the statistics course. They could search for some other more useful predictor, such as prior grades in quantitatively oriented courses or the number of years since the student had taken algebra. In other words, if a predictor is not found to be particularly useful in predicting the criterion variable, then other relevant predictors should be considered.

How do we determine the utility of a predictor variable? The simplest method involves partitioning the total sum of squares in Y, which we denote as SS_{total} (sometimes written as SS_Y). This process is much like partitioning the sum of squares in ANOVA.

In simple linear regression, we can partition SS_{total} into

$$SS_{total} = SS_{reg} + SS_{res}$$

$$\sum_{i=1}^{n}(Y-\bar{Y})^2 = \sum_{i=1}^{n}(Y'-\bar{Y})^2 + \sum_{i=1}^{n}(Y-Y')^2$$

where
SS_{total} is the total sum of squares in Y

SS_{reg} is the sum of squares of the regression of Y predicted by X (sometimes written as $SS_{Y'}$) (and represented in the equation as $\sum_{i=1}^{n}(Y'-\bar{Y})^2$)

SS_{res} is the sum of squares of the residuals (and represented in the equation as $\sum_{i=1}^{n}(Y-Y')^2$), and the sums are taken over all observations from $i = 1,\ldots, n$

Thus, SS_{total} represents the total variation in the observed Y scores, SS_{reg} the variation in Y predicted by X, and SS_{res} the variation in Y not predicted by X.

The equation for SS_{reg} uses information about the difference between the predicted value of Y and the mean of Y: $\sum_{i=1}^{n}(Y'-\bar{Y})^2$. Thus, the SS_{reg} is essentially examining how much better the line of best fit (i.e., the predicted value of Y) is as compared to the mean of Y (recall that a slope of 0 is a horizontal line, which is the mean of Y). The equation for SS_{res} uses information about the difference between the observed value of Y and the predicted value of Y: $\sum_{i=1}^{n}(Y-Y')^2$. Thus, the SS_{res} is providing an indication of how "off" or inaccurate the model is. The closer SS_{res} is to 0, the better the model fit (as more variability of the dependent variable is being explained by the model; in other words, the independent variables are doing a good job of prediction when the SS_{res} is smaller). Since $r_{XY}^2 = SS_{reg}/SS_{total}$, we can write SS_{total}, SS_{reg}, and SS_{res} as follows:

$$SS_{total} = \frac{n\sum_{i=1}^{n}Y^2 - \left(\sum_{i=1}^{n}Y\right)^2}{n}$$

$$SS_{reg} = r_{XY}^2 SS_{total}$$

$$SS_{res} = (1 - r_{XY}^2)SS_{total}$$

where r_{XY}^2 is the squared sample correlation between X and Y, commonly referred to as the **coefficient of determination**. The coefficient of determination in simple linear regression is not only the squared simple bivariate Pearson correlation between X and Y but also $r_{XY}^2 = \dfrac{SS_{reg}}{SS_{total}}$, which tells us that it is the proportion of the total variation of the dependent variable (i.e., the denominator) that has been explained by the regression model (i.e., the numerator).

There is no objective gold standard as to how large the coefficient of determination needs to be in order to say a meaningful proportion of variation has been predicted. The coefficient is determined, not just by the quality of the one predictor variable included in the model, but also by the quality of relevant predictor variables not included in the model and by the amount of total variation in Y. However, the coefficient of determination can be used both as a measure of effect size and as a test of significance (described in the next section). According to the subjective standards of Cohen (1988), a small effect size is defined as $r = .10$ or $r^2 = .01$, a medium effect size as $r = .30$ or $r^2 = .09$, and a large effect size as $r = .50$ or $r^2 = .25$. For additional information on effect size measures in regression, we suggest you consider Steiger and Fouladi (1992), Mendoza and Stafford (2001), and Smithson (2001; which also includes some discussion of power).

With the sample data of predicting midterm statistics scores from the GRE_Q, let us determine the sums of squares. We can write SS_{total} as follows:

$$SS_{total} = \frac{n \sum_{i=1}^{n} Y^2 - \left(\sum_{i=1}^{n} Y \right)^2}{n} = \frac{10(14{,}948) - (380)^2}{10} = 508.0000$$

We already know that $r_{XY} = .9177$, so squaring it, we obtain $r_{XY}^2 = .8422$. Next we can determine SS_{reg} and SS_{res} as follows:

$$SS_{reg} = r_{XY}^2 SS_{total} = .8422(508.0000) = 427.8376$$

$$SS_{res} = (1 - r_{XY}^2)SS_{total} = (1 - .8422)(508.0000) = 80.1624$$

Given the squared correlation between X and Y ($r_{XY}^2 = .8422$), the GRE_Q predicts approximately 84% of the variation in the midterm statistics exam, which is clearly a large effect size. Significance tests are discussed in the next section.

7.3.6 Significance Tests and Confidence Intervals

This section describes four procedures used in the simple linear regression context. The first two are tests of statistical significance that generally involve testing whether or not X is a significant predictor of Y. Then we consider two confidence interval (CI) techniques.

7.3.6.1 Test of Significance of r^2_{XY}

The first test is the test of the significance of r^2_{XY} (alternatively known as the test of the proportion of variation in Y predicted or explained by X). It is important that r^2_{XY} be different from 0 in order to have reasonable prediction. The null and alternative hypotheses, respectively, are as follows, where the null indicates that the correlation between X and Y will be 0:

$$H_0: \rho^2_{XY} = 0$$

$$H_1: \rho^2_{XY} > 0$$

This test is based on the following test statistic:

$$F = \frac{r^2/m}{(1-r^2)/(n-m-1)}$$

where
 F indicates that this is an F statistic
 r^2 is the coefficient of determination
 $1 - r^2$ is the proportion of variation in Y that is not predicted by X
 m is the number of predictors (which in the case of simple linear regression is always 1)
 n is the sample size

The F test statistic is compared to the F critical value, always a one-tailed test (given that a squared value cannot be negative), and at the designated level of significance α, with degrees of freedom equal to m (i.e., the number of independent variables) and $(n - m - 1)$, as taken from the F table in Table A.4. That is, the tabled critical value is $_\alpha F_{m, (n-m-1)}$.
 For the statistics midterm example, we determine the test statistic to be the following:

$$F = \frac{r^2/m}{(1-r^2)/(n-m-1)} = \frac{.8422/1}{(1-.8422)/(10-1-1)} = 42.6971$$

From Table A.4, the critical value, at the .05 level of significance, with degrees of freedom of 1 (i.e., one predictor) and 8 (i.e., $n - m - 1 = 10 - 1 - 1 = 8$), is $_{.05}F_{1,8} = 5.32$. The test statistic exceeds the critical value; thus, we reject H_0 and conclude that ρ^2_{XY} is not equal to 0 at the .05 level of significance (i.e., GRE_Q does predict a significant proportion of the variation on the midterm exam).

7.3.6.2 Test of Significance of b_{YX}

The second test is the test of the significance of the slope or regression coefficient, b_{YX}. In other words, is the unstandardized regression coefficient statistically significantly different from 0? This is actually the same as the test of b^*, the standardized regression coefficient, so we need not develop a separate test for b^*. The null and alternative hypotheses, respectively, are as follows:

$$H_0: \beta_{YX} = 0$$

$$H_1: \beta_{YX} \neq 0$$

To test whether the regression coefficient is equal to 0, we need a standard error for the slope b. However, first we need to develop some new concepts. The first new concept is the **variance error of estimate**. Although this is the correct term, it is easier to consider this as the **variance of the residuals**. The variance error of estimate, or variance of the residuals, is defined as

$$s_{res}^2 = \Sigma e_i^2 / df_{res} = SS_{res} / df_{res} = MS_{res}$$

where the summation is taken from $i = 1,...,n$ and $df_{res} = (n - m - 1)$ (or $n - 2$ if there is only a single predictor). Two degrees of freedom are lost because we have to estimate the population slope and intercept, β and α, from the sample data. The variance error of estimate indicates the amount of variation among the residuals. If there are some extremely large residuals, this will result in a relatively large value of s_{res}^2, indicating poor prediction overall. If the residuals are generally small, this will result in a comparatively small value of s_{res}^2, indicating good prediction overall.

The next new concept is the **standard error of estimate** (sometimes known as the root mean square error). The standard error of estimate is simply the positive square root of the variance error of estimate and thus is the standard deviation of the residuals or errors of estimate. We denote the standard error of estimate as s_{res}.

The final new concept is the **standard error of b**. We denote the standard error of b as s_b and define it as

$$s_b = \frac{s_{res}}{\sqrt{\left[n \sum X^2 - \left(\sum X\right)^2\right] / n}} = \frac{s_{res}}{\sqrt{SS_X}}$$

where the summation is taken over $i = 1,...,n$. We want s_b to be small to reject H_0, so we need s_{res} to be small and SS_X to be large. In other words, we want there to be a large spread of scores in X. If the variability in X is small, it is difficult for X to be a significant predictor of Y.

Now we can put these concepts together into a test statistic to test the significance of the slope b. As in many significance tests, the test statistic is formed by the ratio of a parameter estimate divided by its respective standard error. A ratio of the parameter estimate of the slope b to its standard error s_b is formed as follows:

$$t = \frac{b}{s_b}$$

The test statistic t is compared to the critical values of t (in Table A.2), a two-tailed test for a nondirectional H_1, at the designated level of significance α, and with degrees of freedom of $(n - m - 1)$. That is, the tabled critical values are $\pm_{(\alpha/2)} t_{(n-m-1)}$ for a two-tailed test.

In addition, all other things being equal (i.e., same data, same degrees of freedom, same level of significance), both of these significance tests (i.e., the test of significance of the squared bivariate correlation between X and Y and the test of significance of the slope) will yield the exact same result. That is, if X is a significant predictor of Y, then H_0 will be rejected in both tests. If X *is not* a significant predictor of Y, then H_0 will not be rejected for either test. In simple linear regression, each of these tests is a method for testing the same general hypothesis and logically should lead the researcher to the exact same conclusion. Thus, there is no need to implement both tests.

We can also form a CI around the slope b. As in most CI procedures, it follows the form of the sample estimate plus or minus the tabled critical value multiplied by the standard error. The CI around b is formed as follows:

$$\text{CI}\,(b) = b \,\pm_{(\alpha/2)} t_{(n-m-1)} s_b$$

Recall that the null hypothesis was written as H_0: $\beta = 0$. Therefore, if the CI contains 0, then β is not significantly different from 0 at the specified α level. This is interpreted to mean that in $(1 - \alpha)\%$ of the sample CIs that would be formed from multiple samples, β will be included. This procedure assumes homogeneity of variance (discussed later in this chapter); for alternative procedures, see Wilcox (1996, 2003).

Now we can determine the second test statistic for the midterm statistics example. We specify H_0: $\beta = 0$ (i.e., the null hypothesis is that the slope is equal to 0; visually a slope of 0 is a horizontal line) and conduct a two-tailed test. First the variance error of estimate is

$$s^2_{res} = \Sigma\, e_i^2 / df_{res} = SS_{res} / df_{res} = MS_{res} = 80.1578/8 = 10.0197$$

The standard error of estimate, s_{res}, is $\sqrt{10.0197} = 3.1654$. Next the standard error of b is computed as follows:

$$s_b = \cfrac{s_{res}}{\sqrt{\left[n\Sigma\, X^2 - \left(\Sigma\, X\right)^2\right] \big/ n}} = \cfrac{s_{res}}{\sqrt{SS_X}} = \cfrac{3.1654}{\sqrt{1552.5000}} = .0803$$

Finally, we determine the test statistic to be as follows:

$$t = \frac{b}{s_b} = \frac{.5250}{.0803} = 6.5380$$

To evaluate the null hypothesis, we compare this test statistic to its critical values $\pm_{.025} t_8 = \pm 2.306$. The test statistic exceeds the critical value, so H_0 is rejected in favor of H_1. We conclude that the slope is indeed significantly different from 0, at the .05 level of significance.

Finally let us determine the CI for the slope b as follows:

$$\text{CI}\,(b) = b \,\pm_{(\alpha/2)} t_{(n-m-1)} s_b = b \,\pm_{.025} t_8 (s_b)$$

$$= 0.5250 \pm 2.306(0.0803) = (0.3398,\ 0.7102)$$

The interval does not contain 0, the value specified in H_0; thus, we conclude that the slope β is significantly different from 0, at the .05 level of significance.

7.3.6.3 Confidence Interval for the Predicted Mean Value of Y

The third procedure is to develop a CI for the predicted mean value of Y, denoted by $\bar{Y}_0'$, for a specific value of X_0. Alternatively, $\bar{Y}_0'$ is referred to as the conditional mean of Y given X_0 (more about conditional distributions in the next section). In other words, for a particular predictor score X_0, how confident can we be in the predicted mean for Y?

The standard error of $\bar{Y}_0'$ is

$$s(\bar{Y}_0') = s_{res}\sqrt{(1/n)+[(X_0 - \bar{X})^2/SS_X]}$$

In looking at this equation, the further X_0 is from $\bar{X}$, the larger the standard error. Thus, the standard error depends on the particular value of X_0 selected. In other words, we expect to make our best predictions at the center of the distribution of X scores and to make our poorest predictions for extreme values of X. Thus, the closer the value of the predictor is to the center of the distribution of the X scores, the better the prediction will be.

A CI around $\bar{Y}_0'$ is formed as follows:

$$CI(\bar{Y}_0') = \bar{Y}_0' \pm_{(\alpha/2)} t_{(n-2)} s(\bar{Y}_0')$$

Our interpretation is that in $(1 - \alpha)\%$ of the sample CIs that would be formed from multiple samples, the population mean value of Y for a given value of X will be included.

Let us consider an example of this CI procedure with the midterm statistics data. If we take a GRE_Q score of 50, the predicted score on the statistics midterm is 35.1125. A CI for the predicted mean value of 35.1125 is as follows:

$$s(\bar{Y}_0') = s_{res}\sqrt{(1/n)+[(X_0 - \bar{X})^2/SS_X]} = 3.1654\sqrt{(1/10)+[(50-55)^2/1552.5000]} = 1.0786$$

$$CI(\bar{Y}_0') = \bar{Y}_0' \pm_{(\alpha/2)} t_{(n-2)} s(\bar{Y}_0') = \bar{Y}_0' \pm_{.025} t_8 \, s(\bar{Y}_0')$$

$$= 35.1125 \pm (2.306)(1.0786) = (32.6252, \ 37.5998)$$

In Figure 7.3, the CI around $\bar{Y}_0'$ given X_0 is plotted as the pair of curved lines closest to the regression line. Here we see graphically that the width of the CI increases the further we move from $\bar{X}$ (where $\bar{X} = 55.5000$).

7.3.6.4 Prediction Interval for Individual Values of Y

The fourth and final procedure is to develop a prediction interval (PI) for an individual predicted value of Y_0' at a specific individual value of X_0. That is, the predictor score for a particular individual is known, but the criterion score for that individual has not yet been observed. This is in contrast to the CI just discussed where the individual Y scores have already been observed. Thus, the CI deals with the mean of the predicted values, while the PI deals with an individual predicted value not yet observed.

The standard error of Y_0' is

$$s(Y_0') = s_{res}\sqrt{1+(1/n)+[(X_0 - \bar{X})^2/SS_X]}$$

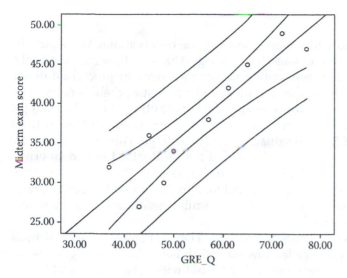

FIGURE 7.3
CIs for midterm example: the curved lines closest to the regression line are for the 95% CI; the curved lines furthest from the regression line are for the 95% PI.

The standard error of Y_0' is similar to the standard error of $\bar{Y}_0'$ with the addition of 1 to the equation. Thus, the standard error of Y_0' will always be greater than the standard error of $\bar{Y}_0'$ as there is more uncertainty about individual values than about the mean. The further X_0 is from $\bar{X}$, the larger the standard error. Thus, the standard error again depends on the particular value of X, where we have more confidence in predictions for values of X close to $\bar{X}$.

The PI around Y_0' is formed as follows:

$$PI(Y_0') = Y_0' \pm_{(\alpha/2)} t_{(n-2)} s(Y_0')$$

Our interpretation is that in $(1 - \alpha)\%$ of the sample PIs that would be formed from multiple samples, the new observation Y_0 for a given value of X will be included.

Consider an example of this PI procedure with the midterm statistics data. If we take a GRE_Q score of 50, the predicted score on the statistics midterm is 35.1125. A PI for the predicted individual value of 35.1125 is as follows:

$$s(Y_0') = s_{res}\sqrt{1+(1/n)+[(X_0 - \bar{X})^2/SS_X]} = 3.1654\sqrt{1+(1/10)+[(50-55)^2/1552.5000]} = .3.3441$$

$$PI\,(Y_0') = Y_0' \pm_{(\alpha/2)} t_{(n-2)} s(Y_0') = Y_0' \pm_{.025} t_8 s(Y_0')$$

$$= 35.1125 \pm (2.306)(3.3441) = (27.4010,\ 42.8240)$$

In Figure 7.3, the PI around Y_0' given X_0 is plotted as the pair of curved lines furthest from the regression line. Here we see graphically that the PI is always wider than its corresponding CI.

7.3.7 Assumptions and Violation of Assumptions

In this section, we consider the following assumptions involved in simple linear regression: (a) independence, (b) homogeneity, (c) normality, (d) linearity, and (e) fixed X. Some discussion is also devoted to the effects of assumption violations and how to detect them.

7.3.7.1 Independence

The first assumption is concerned with independence of the observations. We should be familiar with this assumption from previous chapters (e.g., ANOVA). In regression analysis, another way to think about this assumption is that the errors in prediction or the residuals (i.e., e_i) are assumed to be random and independent. That is, there is no systematic pattern about the errors, and each error is independent of the other errors. An example of a systematic pattern would be where for small values of X the residuals tended to be small, whereas for large values of X, the residuals tended to be large. Thus, there would be a relationship between the independent variable X and the residual e. Dependent errors occur when the error for one individual depends on or is related to the error for another individual as a result of some predictor not being included in the model. For our midterm statistics example, students similar in age might have similar residuals because age was not included as a predictor in the model.

Note that there are several different types of residuals. The e_i is known as **raw residuals** for the same reason that X_i and Y_i are called raw scores, all being in their original scale. The raw residuals are on the same raw score scale as Y but with a mean of 0 and a variance of s_{res}^2. Some researchers dislike raw residuals as their scale depends on the scale of Y, and, therefore, they must temper their interpretation of the residual values. Several different types of **standardized residuals** have been developed, including the original form of standardized residual e_i/s_{res}. These values are measured along the z score scale with a mean of 0 and a variance of 1, and approximately 95% of the values are within ±2 units of 0. Later in our illustration of SPSS, we will use **studentized residuals** for diagnostic checks. Studentized residuals are a type of standardized residual that are more sensitive to detecting outliers. Some researchers prefer these or other variants of standardized residuals over raw residuals because they find it easier to detect large residuals. However, if you really think about it, one can easily look at the middle 95% of the raw residuals by just considering the range of ±2 standard errors (i.e., $±2s_{res}$) around 0. Readers interested in learning more about other types of standardized residuals are referred to a number of excellent resources (see Atkinson, 1985; Cook & Weisberg, 1982; Dunn & Clark, 1987; Kleinbaum, Kupper, Muller, & Nizam, 1998; Weisberg, 1985).

The simplest procedure for assessing this assumption is to examine a scatterplot (Y vs. X) or a residual plot (e.g., e vs. X). If the independence assumption is satisfied, there should be a random display of points. If the assumption is violated, the plot will display some type of pattern; for example, the negative residuals tend to cluster together, and positive residuals tend to cluster together. As we know from ANOVA, violation of the independence assumption generally occurs in the following three situations: (a) when the observations are collected over time (the independent variable is a measure of time; consider using the Durbin and Watson test [1950, 1951, 1971]); (b) when observations are made within blocks, such that the observations within a particular block are more similar than observations in different blocks; or (c) when observation involves replication. Lack of independence affects the estimated standard errors, being under- or overestimated. For serious violations, one could consider using generalized or weighted least squares as the method of estimation.

7.3.7.2 Homogeneity

The second assumption is **homogeneity of variance**, which should also be a familiar assumption (e.g., ANOVA). This assumption must be reframed a bit in the regression context by examining the concept of a **conditional distribution**. In regression analysis, a conditional distribution is defined as the distribution of Y for a particular value of X. For instance, in the midterm statistics example, we could consider the conditional distribution of midterm scores when GRE_Q = 50; in other words, what the distribution of Y looks like for X = 50. We call this a conditional distribution because it represents the distribution of Y conditional on a particular value of X (sometimes denoted as Y|X, read as Y given X). Alternatively we could examine the conditional distribution of the prediction errors, that is, the distribution of the prediction errors conditional on a particular value of X (i.e., e|X, read as e given X). Thus, the homogeneity assumption is that the conditional distributions have a constant variance for all values of X.

In a plot of the Y scores or the residuals versus X, the consistency of the variance of the conditional distributions can be examined. A common violation of this assumption occurs when the conditional residual variance increases as X increases. Here the residual plot is cone- or fan-shaped, where the cone opens toward the right. An example of this violation would be where weight is predicted by age, as weight is more easily predicted for young children than it is for adults. Thus, residuals would tend to be larger for adults than for children.

If the homogeneity assumption is violated, estimates of the standard errors are larger, and although the regression coefficients remain unbiased, the validity of the significance tests is affected. In fact with larger standard errors, it is more difficult to reject H_0, therefore resulting in a larger number of Type II errors. Minor violations of this assumption will have a small net effect; more serious violations occur when the variances are greatly different. In addition, nonconstant variances may also result in the conditional distributions being nonnormal in shape.

If the homogeneity assumption is seriously violated, the simplest solution is to use some sort of transformation, known as **variance stabilizing transformations** (e.g., Weisberg, 1985). Commonly used transformations are the log or square root of Y (e.g., Kleinbaum et al., 1998). These transformations can also often improve on the nonnormality of the conditional distributions. However, this complicates things in terms of dealing with transformed variables rather than the original variables. A better solution is to use generalized or weighted least squares (e.g., Weisberg, 1985). A third solution is to use a form of robust estimation (e.g., Carroll & Ruppert, 1982; Kleinbaum et al., 1998; Wilcox, 1996, 2003).

7.3.7.3 Normality

The third assumption of **normality** should also be a familiar one. In regression, the normality assumption is that the conditional distributions of either Y or the prediction errors (i.e., residuals) are normal in shape. That is, for all values of X, the scores on Y or the prediction errors are normally distributed. Oftentimes nonnormal distributions are largely a function of one or a few extreme observations, known as **outliers**. Extreme values may cause nonnormality and seriously affect the regression results. The regression estimates are quite sensitive to outlying observations such that the precision of the estimates is affected, particularly the slope. Also the coefficient of determination can be affected. In general, the regression line will be pulled toward the outlier, because the least squares principle always attempts to find the line that best fits all of the points.

Various rules of thumb are used to crudely detect outliers from a residual plot or scatterplot. A commonly used rule is to define an outlier as an observation more than two or three standard errors from the mean (i.e., a large distance from the mean). The outlier observation may be a result of (a) a simple recording or data entry error, (b) an error in observation, (c) an improperly functioning instrument, (d) inappropriate use of administration instructions, or (e) a true outlier. If the outlier is the result of an error, correct the error if possible and redo the regression analysis. If the error cannot be corrected, then the observation could be deleted. If the outlier represents an accurate observation, then this observation may contain important theoretical information, and one would be more hesitant to delete it (or perhaps seek out similar observations).

A simple procedure to use for single case outliers (i.e., just one outlier) is to perform two regression analyses, both with and without the outlier being included. A comparison of the regression results will provide some indication of the effects of the outlier. Other methods for detecting and dealing with outliers are available, but are not described here (e.g., Andrews & Pregibon, 1978; Barnett & Lewis, 1978; Beckman & Cook, 1983; Cook, 1977; Hawkins, 1980; Kleinbaum et al., 1998; Mickey, Dunn, & Clark, 2004; Pedhazur, 1997; Rousseeuw & Leroy, 1987; Wilcox, 1996, 2003).

How does one go about detecting violation of the normality assumption? There are two commonly used procedures. The simplest procedure involves checking for symmetry in a histogram, frequency distribution, boxplot, or skewness and kurtosis statistics. Although **nonzero kurtosis** (i.e., a distribution that is either flat, platykurtic, or has a sharp peak, leptokurtic) will have minimal effect on the regression estimates, **nonzero skewness** (i.e., a distribution that is not symmetrical with either a positive or negative skew) will have much more impact on these estimates. Thus, finding asymmetrical distributions is a must. One rule of thumb is to be concerned if the skewness value is larger than 1.5 or 2.0 in magnitude. For the midterm statistics example, the skewness value for the raw residuals is −0.2692. Thus, there is evidence of normality in this illustration.

Another useful graphical technique is the normal probability plot [or quantile–quantile (Q–Q) plot]. With normally distributed data or residuals, the points on the normal probability plot will fall along a straight diagonal line, whereas nonnormal data will not. There is a difficulty with this plot because there is no criterion with which to judge deviation from linearity. A normal probability plot of the raw residuals for the midterm statistics example is shown in Figure 7.4. Together the skewness and normal probability plot results indicate that the normality assumption is satisfied. It is recommended that skewness and/ or the normal probability plot be considered at a minimum.

There are also several statistical procedures available for the detection of nonnormality (e.g., Andrews, 1971; Belsley, Kuh, & Welsch, 1980; Ruppert & Carroll, 1980; Wu, 1985). In addition, various transformations are available to transform a nonnormal distribution

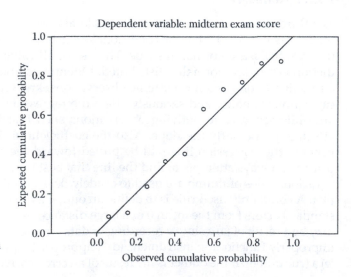

FIGURE 7.4
Normal probability plot for midterm example.

into a normal distribution. The most commonly used transformations to correct for non-normality in regression analysis are to transform the dependent variable using the log (to correct for positive skew) or the square root (to correct for positive or negative skew). However, again there is the problem of dealing with transformed variables measured along some other scale than that of the original variables.

7.3.7.4 Linearity

The fourth assumption is **linearity**. This assumption simply indicates that there is a linear relationship between X and Y, which is also assumed for most types of correlations. Consider the scatterplot and regression line in Figure 7.5 where X and Y are not linearly related. Here X and Y form a perfect curvilinear relationship as all of the points fall precisely on a curve. However, fitting a straight line to these points will result in a slope of 0 not useful at all for predicting Y from X (as the predicted score for all cases will be the mean of Y). For example, age and performance are not linearly related.

If the relationship between X and Y is linear, then the sample slope and intercept will be unbiased estimators of the population slope and intercept, respectively. The linearity assumption is important because, regardless of the value of X_i, we always expect Y_i to increase by b_{YX} units for a one-unit increase in X_i. If a nonlinear relationship exists, this means that the expected increase in Y_i depends on the value of X_i. Strictly speaking, linearity in a model refers to there being linearity in the parameters of the model (i.e., slope β and intercept α).

Detecting violation of the linearity assumption can often be done by looking at the scatterplot of Y versus X. If the linearity assumption is met, we expect to see no systematic pattern of points. While this plot is often satisfactory in simple linear regression, less obvious violations are more easily detected in a residual plot. If the linearity assumption is met, we expect to see a horizontal band of residuals mainly contained within ±2 or ±3s_{res} (or standard errors) across the values of X. If the assumption is violated, we expect to see a systematic pattern between e and X. Therefore, we recommend you examine both the scatterplot and the residual plot. A residual plot for the midterm statistics example is shown in Figure 7.6. Even with a very small sample, we see a fairly random display of residuals and therefore feel fairly confident that the linearity assumption has been satisfied.

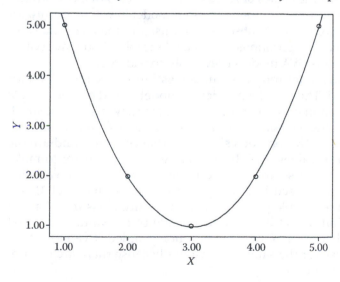

FIGURE 7.5
Nonlinear regression example.

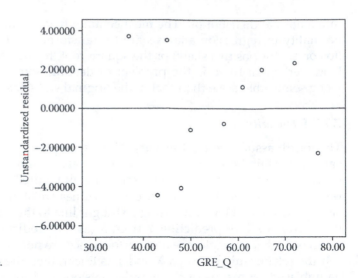

FIGURE 7.6
Residual plot for midterm example.

If a serious violation of the linearity assumption has been detected, how should we deal with it? There are two alternative procedures that the researcher can utilize, **transformations** or **nonlinear models**. The first option is to transform either one or both of the variables to achieve linearity. That is, the researcher selects a transformation that subsequently results in a linear relationship between the transformed variables. Then the method of least squares can be used to perform a linear regression analysis on the transformed variables. However, when dealing with transformed variables measured along a different scale, results need to be described in terms of the transformed rather than the original variables. A better option is to use a nonlinear model to examine the relationship between the variables in their original scale (see Wilcox, 1996, 2003; also discussed in Chapter 8).

7.3.7.5 Fixed X

The fifth and final assumption is that the values of X are **fixed**. That is, X is a fixed variable rather than a random variable. This results in the regression model being valid only for those particular values of X that were actually observed and used in the analysis. Thus, the same values of X would be used in replications or repeated samples. You may recall a similar concept in the fixed-effects ANOVA models previously considered.

Strictly speaking, the regression model and its parameter estimates are only valid for those values of X actually sampled. The use of a prediction model, based on one sample of individuals, to predict Y for another sample of individuals may also be suspect. Depending on the circumstances, the new sample of individuals may actually call for a different set of parameter estimates. Two obvious situations that come to mind are the **extrapolation** and **interpolation** of values of X. In general, we may not want to make predictions about individuals having X scores (i.e., scores on the independent variable) that are outside of the range of values used in developing the prediction model; this is defined as *extrapolating* beyond the sample predictor data. We cannot assume that the function defined by the prediction model is the same outside of the values of X that were initially sampled. The prediction errors for the new nonsampled X values would be expected to be larger than those for the sampled X values because there are no supportive prediction data for the former.

TABLE 7.2

Assumptions and Violation of Assumptions: Simple Linear Regression

Assumption	Effect of Assumption Violation
Independence	• Influences standard errors of the model
Homogeneity	• Bias in s_{res}^2 • May inflate standard errors and thus increase likelihood of a Type II error • May result in nonnormal conditional distributions
Normality	• Less precise slope, intercept, and R^2
Linearity	• Bias in slope and intercept • Expected change in Y is not a constant and depends on value of X • Reduced magnitude of coefficient of determination
Values of X fixed	• Extrapolating beyond the range of X: prediction errors larger, may also bias slope and intercept • Interpolating within the range of X: smaller effects than when extrapolating; if other assumptions met, negligible effect

On the other hand, we are not quite as concerned in making predictions about individuals having X scores within the range of values used in developing the prediction model; this is defined as *interpolating* within the range of the sample predictor data. We would feel somewhat more comfortable in assuming that the function defined by the prediction model is the same for other new values of X within the range of those initially sampled. For the most part, the fixed X assumption is satisfied if the new observations behave like those in the prediction sample. In the interpolation situation, we expect the prediction errors to be somewhat smaller as compared to the extrapolation situation because there are at least some similar supportive prediction data for the former. It has been shown that when other assumptions are met, regression analysis performs just as well when X is a random variable (e.g., Glass & Hopkins, 1996; Myers & Well, 1995; Pedhazur, 1997). There is no corresponding assumption about the nature of Y.

In our midterm statistics example, we have more confidence in our prediction for a GRE_Q value of 52 (which did not occur in the sample, but falls within the range of sampled values) than in a value of 20 (which also did not occur, but is much smaller than the smallest value sampled, 37). In fact, this is precisely the rationale underlying the PI previously developed, where the width of the interval increased as an individual's score on the predictor (X_i) moved away from the predictor mean ($\bar{X}$).

A summary of the assumptions and the effects of their violation for simple linear regression is presented in Table 7.2.

7.3.7.6 Summary

The simplest procedure for assessing assumptions is to plot the residuals and see what the plot tells you. Take the midterm statistics problem as an example. Although sample size is quite small in terms of looking at conditional distributions, it would appear that all of our assumptions have been satisfied. All of the residuals are within two standard errors of 0, and there does not seem to be any systematic pattern in the residuals. The distribution of the residuals is nearly symmetrical, and the normal probability plot looks good. The scatterplot also strongly suggests a linear relationship.

7.4 SPSS

Next we consider SPSS for the simple linear regression model. Before we conduct the analysis, let us review the data. With one independent variable and one dependent variable, the dataset must consist of two variables or columns, one for the independent variable and one for the dependent variable. Each row still represents one individual, with the value of the independent variable for that particular case and their score on the dependent variable. In the following screenshot, we see the SPSS dataset is in the form of two columns representing one independent variable (GRE_Q) and one dependent variable (midterm exam score).

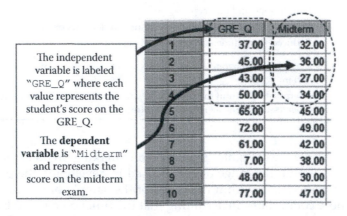

The independent variable is labeled "GRE_Q" where each value represents the student's score on the GRE_Q.

The **dependent variable** is "Midterm" and represents the score on the midterm exam.

Step 1: To conduct a simple linear regression, go to "Analyze" in the top pulldown menu, then select "Regression," and then select "Linear." Following the screenshot (step 1) as follows produces the "Linear Regression" dialog box.

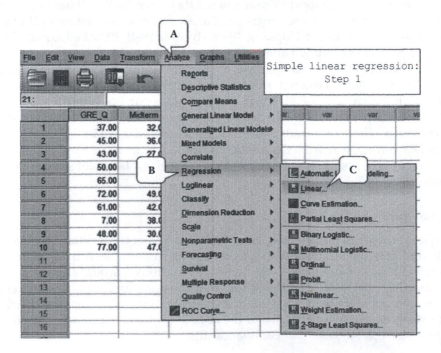

Step 2: Click the dependent variable (e.g., "Midterm") and move it into the "Dependent" box by clicking the arrow button. Click the independent variable and move it into the "Independent(s)" box by clicking the arrow button (see screenshot step 2).

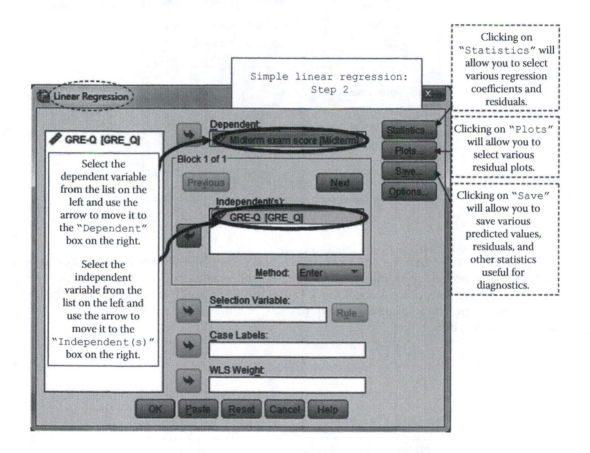

Step 3: From the "Linear Regression" dialog box (see screenshot step 2), clicking on "Statistics" will provide the option to select various regression coefficients and residuals. From the "Statistics" dialog box (see screenshot step 3), place a checkmark in the box next to the following: (1) estimates, (2) confidence intervals, (3) model fit, (4) descriptives, (5) Durbin–Watson, and (6) casewise diagnostics. Click on "Continue" to return to the original dialog box.

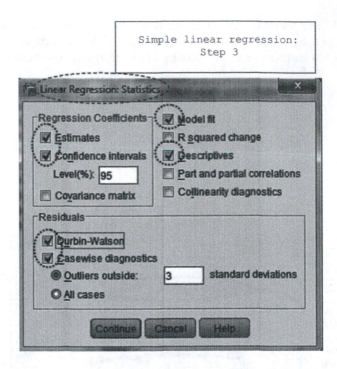

Step 4: From the "Linear Regression" dialog box (see screenshot step 2), click-ing on "Plots" will provide the option to select various residual plots. From the "Plots" dialog box, place a checkmark in the box next to the following: (1) histo-gram and (2) normal probability plot. Click on "Continue" to return to the original dialog box.

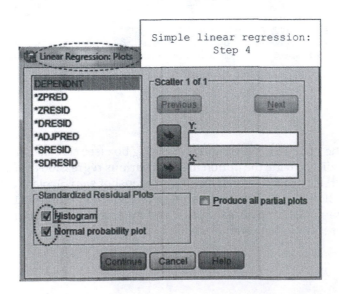

Step 5: From the "Linear Regression" dialog box (see screenshot step 2), clicking on "Save" will provide the option to save various predicted values, residuals, and statistics that can be used for diagnostic examination. From the "Save" dialog box under the heading of **Predicted Values**, place a checkmark in the box next to the following: unstandardized. Under the heading of **Residuals,** place a checkmark in the box next to the following: (1) unstandardized and (2) studentized. Under the heading of **Distances,** place a checkmark in the box next to the following: (1) Mahalanobis and (2) Cook's. Under the heading of **Influence Statistics,** place a checkmark in the box next to the following: (1) DFBETA(s) and (2) Standardized DFBETA(s). Click on "Continue" to return to the original dialog box. From the "Linear Regression" dialog box, click on "OK" to return to generate the output.

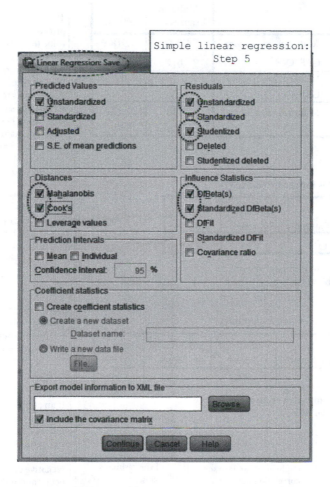

Simple linear regression: Step 5

Interpreting the output: Annotated results are presented in Table 7.3. In Chapters 8 and 9, we see other regression modules in SPSS which allow you to consider, for example, generalized or weighted least squares regression, nonlinear regression, and logistic regression. Additional information on regression analysis in SPSS is provided in texts such as Morgan and Griego (1998) and Meyers, Gamst, and Guarino (2006).

TABLE 7.3

Selected SPSS Results for the Midterm Example

Descriptive Statistics

	Mean	Std. Deviation	N
Midterm exam score	38.0000	7.51295	10
GRE_Q	55.5000	13.13393	10

> The table labeled "`Descriptive Statistics`" provides basic descriptive statistics (means, standard deviations, and sample sizes) for the independent and dependent variables.

Correlations

		Midterm Exam Score	GRE_Q
Pearson correlation	Midterm exam score	1.000	.918
	GRE_Q	.918	1.000
Sig. (One-tailed)	Midterm exam score	.	.000
	GRE_Q	.000	.
N	Midterm exam score	10	10
	GRE_Q	10	10

> The table labeled "`Correlations`" provides the correlation coefficient value ($r = .918$), p value ($<.001$), and sample size ($N = 10$) for the simple bivariate Pearson correlation between the independent and dependent variables. There is a statistically significant bivariate correlation between GRE_Q and midterm exam score.

Variables Entered/Removed[a]

Model	Variables Entered	Variables Removed	Method
1	GRE_Q[b]		Enter

> "`Variables Entered/ Removed`" lists the independent variables included in the model and the method by which they were entered (i.e., "`Enter`").

[a] Dependent variable: midterm exam score.
[b] All requested variables entered.

Model Summary[a]

Model	R	R Square	Adjusted R Square	Std. Error of the Estimate	Durbin–Watson
1	.918[b]	.842	.822	3.16540	1.287

[a] Dependent variable: midterm exam score.
[b] Predictors: (constant), GRE_Q.

> "`Adjusted R Square`" is an estimate of how well the model would fit other data from the same population and is calculated as:
>
> $$R_{adj}^2 = 1 - (1 - R^2)\left[\frac{n-1}{n-m-1}\right]$$
>
> If an additional independent variable were entered in the model, an increase in adjusted R^2 indicates the new variable is adding value to the model. Negative adjusted R^2 values can occur and indicate the model fits the data VERY poorly.

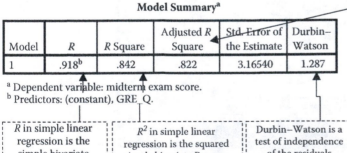

> R in simple linear regression is the simple bivariate Pearson correlation between X and Y.

> R^2 in simple linear regression is the squared simple bivariate Pearson correlation between X and Y. It represents the proportion of variance in the dependent variable that is explained by the independent variable.

> Durbin–Watson is a test of independence of the residuals. Ranging from 0 to 4, values of 2 indicate uncorrelated errors. Values less than 1 or greater than 3 indicate a likely assumption violation.

TABLE 7.3 (continued)

Selected SPSS Results for the Midterm Example

Total sum of squares is partitioned into *SS* regression and *SS* residual. When the regression *SS* equals 0, this indicates that the independent variable has provided no information in terms of explaining the dependent variable.

The *F* statistic is computed as

$$F = \frac{MS_{reg}}{MS_{res}} = \frac{427.842}{10.020}$$

The *p* value (.000) indicates we reject the null hypothesis. The prediction equation provides a better fit to the data than estimating the predicted value of *Y* to be equal to the mean of *Y*.

ANOVA[a]

Model		Sum of Squares	df	Mean Square	F	Sig.
1	Regression	427.842	1	427.842	42.700	.000[b]
	Residual	80.158	8	10.020		
	Total	508.000	9			

[a] Dependent variable: midterm exam score.
[b] Predictors: (constant), GRE-Q.

The "constant" is the intercept and tells us that if GRE_Q (the independent variable) was zero, the midterm exam score (the dependent variable) would be 8.865. The "GRE_Q" is the slope and tells us that for a one point increase in GRE_Q, the midterm exam score will increase by about one half of one point.

The test statistic, *t*, is calculated as the unstandardized coefficient divided by its standard error. Thus for the slope, the test statistic is:

$$t = \frac{b}{SE_b} = \frac{.525}{.080} = 6.535$$

The *p* value for the intercept (the "constant") (*p* = .088) indicates that the intercept is *not* statistically significantly different from 0 (this finding is usually of less interest than the slope). The *p* value for GRE_Q (the independent variable) (*p* = .000) indicates that the slope is statistically significantly different from 0.

Coefficients[a]

Model		Unstandardized Coefficients		Standardized Coefficients	t	Sig.	95.0% Confidence Interval for B	
		B	Std. Error	Beta			Lower Bound	Upper Bound
1	(Constant)	8.865	4.570		1.940	.088	−1.673	19.402
	GRE_Q	.525	.080	.918	6.535	.000	.340	.710

[a] Dependent variable: midterm exam score.

"Residuals statistics" and related graphs (histogram and Q–Q plot, not shown here) will be examined in our discussion of assumptions.

Residuals Statistics[a]

	Minimum	Maximum	Mean	Std. Deviation	N
Predicted value	28.2882	49.2866	38.0000	6.89478	10
Std. predicted value	−1.409	1.637	.000	1.000	10
Standard error of predicted value	1.008	1.996	1.380	.333	10
Adjusted predicted value	26.5379	50.7968	37.9612	7.24166	10
Residual	−4.43800	3.71176	.00000	2.98436	10
Std. residual	−1.402	1.173	.000	.943	10
Stud. residual	−1.568	1.422	.006	1.071	10
Deleted residual	−5.55197	5.46209	.03876	3.87616	10
Stud. deleted residual	−1.763	1.539	−.009	1.135	10
Mahal. distance	.013	2.680	.900	.893	10
Cook's distance	.004	.477	.159	.157	10
Centered leverage value	.001	.298	.100	.099	10

[a] Dependent variable: midterm exam score.

Examining Data for Assumptions in Simple Linear Regression

As you may recall, there were a number of assumptions associated with simple linear regression. These included the following: (a) independence, (b) homogeneity of variance, (c) linearity, and (d) normality. Although fixed values of X are assumed, this is not an assumption that can be tested but is instead related to the use of the results (i.e., extrapolation and interpolation).

Before we begin to examine assumptions, let us review the values that we requested to be saved to our data file (see dataset screenshot that follows).

1. **PRE _ 1** are the unstandardized predicted values (i.e., Y_i').

2. **RES _ 1** are the unstandardized residuals, simply the difference between the observed and predicted values. For student 1, for example, the observed value for the midterm (i.e., the dependent variable) was 32, and the predicted value was 28.28824. Thus, the unstandardized residual is simply $32 - 28.28824$, or 3.71176.

3. **SRE _ 1** are the studentized residuals, a type of standardized residual that is more sensitive to outliers as compared to standardized residuals. Studentized residuals are computed as the unstandardized residual divided by an estimate of the standard deviation with that case removed. As a rule of thumb, studentized residuals with an absolute value greater than 3 are considered outliers (Stevens, 1984).

4. **MAH _ 1** are Mahalanobis distance values that can be helpful in detecting outliers. These values can be reviewed to determine cases that are exerting leverage. Barnett and Lewis (1994) produced a table of critical values for evaluating Mahalanobis distance. Squared Mahalanobis distances divided by the number of variables (D^2/df) which are greater than 2.5 (for small samples) or 3–4 (for large samples) are suggestive of outliers (Hair, Black, Babin, Anderson, & Tatham, 2006). Later, we will follow another convention for examining these values using the chi-square distribution.

5. **COO _ 1** are Cook's distance values and provide an indication of influence of individual cases. As a rule of thumb, Cook's values greater than 1.0 suggest that case is potentially problematic.

6. **DFB0 _ 1** and **DFB1 _ 1** are unstandardized DFBETA values for the intercept and slope, respectively. These values provide estimates of the intercept and slope when the case is removed.

7. **SDB0 _ 1** and **SDB1 _ 1** are standardized DFBETA values for the intercept and slope, respectively, and are easier to interpret as compared to their unstandardized counterparts. Standardized DFBETA values greater than an absolute value of 2 suggest that the case may be exerting undue influence on the parameters of the model (i.e., the slope and intercept).

	GRE_Q	Midterm	PRE_1	RES_1	SRE_1	MAH_1	COO_1	DFB0_1	DFB1_1	SDB0_1	SDB1_1
1	37.00	32.00	28.28824	3.71176	1.42246	1.98406	.47708	4.15857	-.06509	.98488	-.87682
2	45.00	36.00	32.48792	3.51208	1.21860	.63913	.15317	2.01392	-.02865	.45683	-.36970
3	43.00	27.00	31.43800	-4.43800	-1.56816	.90580	.30863	-3.03615	.04470	-.74679	.62542
4	50.00	34.00	35.11272	-1.11272	-.37462	.17536	.00952	-.37484	.00448	-.07741	.05259
5	65.00	45.00	42.98712	2.01288	.69306	.52319	.04511	-.57291	.01463	-.12096	.17571
6	72.00	49.00	46.66184	2.33816	.86773	1.57826	.14306	-1.58060	.03429	-.33994	.41953
7	61.00	42.00	40.88728	1.11272	.37462	.17536	.00952	-.12210	.00448	-.02522	.05259
8	57.00	38.00	38.78744	-.78744	-.26243	.01304	.00389	-.04064	-.00085	-.00836	-.00990
9	48.00	30.00	34.06280	-4.06280	-1.38102	.32609	.15040	-1.73146	.02272	-.40614	.30317
10	47.00	47.00	49.28663	-2.28663	-.93085	2.67971	.28612	2.53853	-.05258	.55030	-.64835

Callouts: 1 → PRE_1; 2 → RES_1; 3 → SRE_1; 4 → MAH_1; 5 → COO_1; 6 → DFB0_1/DFB1_1; 7 → SDB0_1/SDB1_1

As we look at our raw data, we see nine new variables have been added to our dataset. These are our predicted values, residuals, and other diagnostic statistics. The residuals will be used as diagnostics to review the extent to which our data meet the assumptions of simple linear regression.

Independence

We now plot the studentized residuals (which were requested and created through the "Save" option mentioned earlier) against the values of X to examine the extent to which independence was met. The general steps for generating a simple scatterplot through "Scatter/dot" have been presented in Chapter 10 of *An Introduction to Statistical Concepts*, Third Edition, and they will not be reiterated here. From the "Simple Scatterplot" dialog screen, click the studentized residual variable and move it into the "Y Axis" box by clicking on the arrow. Click the independent variable X and move it into the "X Axis" box by clicking on the arrow. Then click "OK."

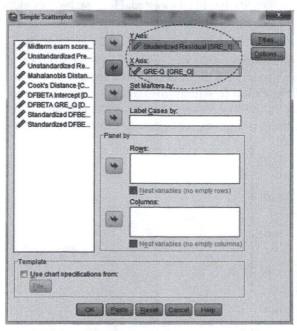

Interpreting independence evidence: If the assumption of independence is met, the points should fall randomly within a band of −2.0 to +2.0. Here we have evidence of independence, especially given the small sample size, as all points are within an absolute value of 2.0 and fall relatively randomly.

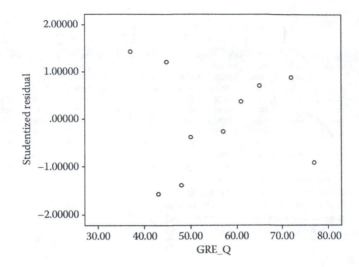

Homogeneity of Variance

We can use the same plot of studentized residuals against X values (used earlier for independence) to examine the extent to which homogeneity was met. Recall that homogeneity is when the dependent variable has the same variance for all values of the independent variable. Evidence of meeting the assumption of homogeneity is a plot where the spread of residuals appears fairly constant over the range of X values (i.e., a random display of points). If the spread of the residuals increases or decreases across the plot from left to right, this may indicate that the assumption of homogeneity has been violated. Here we have evidence of homogeneity.

Linearity

Since we have only one independent variable, a simple bivariate scatterplot of the dependent variable (on the Y axis) and the independent variable (on the X axis) will provide a visual indication of the extent to which linearity is reasonable. As those steps have been presented previously in the discussion of independence, they will not be repeated here. For this scatterplot, there is a general positive linear relationship between the variables.

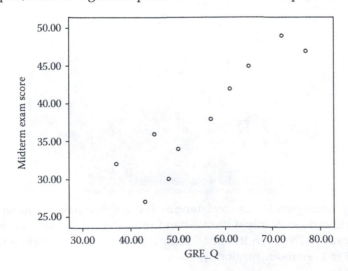

Additionally, the plot of studentized residuals against X values (used earlier for independence) can be used to examine the extent to which linearity was met. We highly recommend examining this residual plot as it is more sensitive to detecting independence violations. Here a random display of points within an absolute value of 2 or 3 suggests further evident of linearity.

Normality

Generating normality evidence: Understanding the distributional shape, specifically the extent to which normality is a reasonable assumption, is important in simple linear regression just as it was in ANOVA models. We again examine residuals for normality, following the same steps as with the previous ANOVA designs. We also use various diagnostics to examine our data for influential cases. Let us begin by examining the unstandardized residuals for normality. For simple linear regression, the distributional shape of the unstandardized residuals should be a normal distribution. Because the steps for generating normality evidence were presented previously in the chapters for ANOVA models, they will not be provided here.

Interpreting normality evidence: By now, we have had a substantial amount of practice in interpreting quite a range of normality statistics. We interpret them again in reference to the assumption of normality for the unstandardized residuals in simple linear regression.

Descriptives

			Statistic	Std. Error
Unstandardized residual	Mean		.0000000	.94373849
	95% Confidence interval for mean	Lower bound	−2.1348848	
		Upper bound	2.1348848	
	5% Trimmed mean		.0403471	
	Median		.1626409	
	Variance		8.906	
	Std. deviation		2.98436314	
	Minimum		−4.43800	
	Maximum		3.71176	
	Range		8.14976	
	Interquartile range		5.36232	
	Skewness		−.269	.687
	Kurtosis		−1.369	1.334

The skewness statistic of the residuals is −.269 and kurtosis is −1.369—both being within the range of an absolute value of 2.0, suggesting some evidence of normality.

While we have a very small sample size, the histogram reflects the skewness and kurtosis statistics.

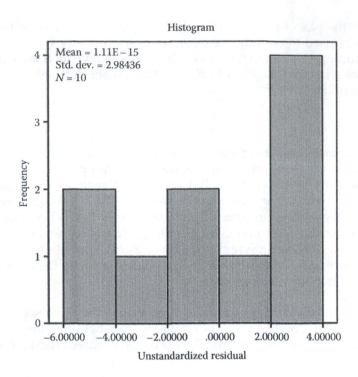

There are a few other statistics that can be used to gauge normality. The formal test of normality, the Shapiro–Wilk (S–W) test (*SW*) (Shapiro & Wilk, 1965), provides evidence of the extent to which our sample distribution is statistically different from a normal distribution. The output for the S–W test is presented as follows and suggests that our sample distribution for the residual is *not* statistically significantly different than what would be expected from a normal distribution as the *p* value is greater than α (*p* = .416).

Tests of Normality

	Kolmogorov–Smirnov[a]			Shapiro–Wilk		
	Statistic	*df*	Sig.	Statistic	*df*	Sig.
Unstandardized residual	.150	10	.200*	.927	10	.416

[a] Lilliefors significance correction.
* This is a lower bound of the true significance.

Q–Q plots are also often examined to determine evidence of normality. Q–Q plots graph quantiles of the theoretical normal distribution against quantiles of the sample distribution. Points that fall on or close to the diagonal line suggest evidence of normality. The Q–Q plot of residuals shown as follows suggests relative normality.

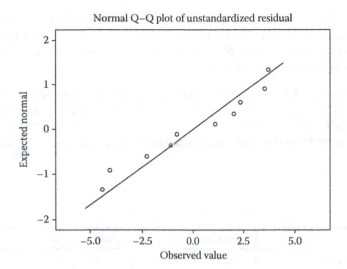

Normal Q–Q plot of unstandardized residual

Examination of the following boxplot also suggests a relatively normal distributional shape of residuals with no outliers.

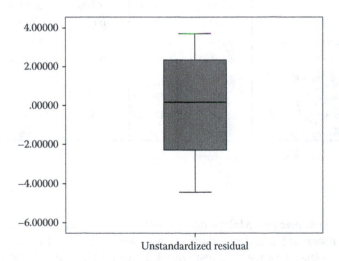

Unstandardized residual

Considering the forms of evidence we have examined, skewness and kurtosis statistics, the S–W test, histogram, the Q–Q plot, and the boxplot, all suggest normality is a reasonable assumption. We can be reasonably assured we have met the assumption of normality of the residuals.

Screening Data for Influential Points

Casewise diagnostics: Recall that we requested a number of statistics to help us in diagnostics and screening our data. One that we requested was for "Casewise diagnostics." If there were any cases with large values for the standardized residual (more than three standard deviations), there would have been information in our output to indicate the case number and values of the standardized residual, predicted value, and unstandardized residual. This information is useful for more closely examining case(s) with extreme standardized residuals.

Cook's distance: Cook's distance provides an overall measure for the influence of individual cases. Values greater than one suggest that the case may be problematic in terms of undue influence on the model. In examining the residual statistics provided in the following output, we see that the maximum value for Cook's distance is .477, well under the point at which we should be concerned.

Residuals Statistics[a]

	Minimum	Maximum	Mean	Std. Deviation	N
Predicted value	28.2882	49.2866	38.0000	6.89478	10
Std. predicted value	−1.409	1.637	.000	1.000	10
Standard error of predicted value	1.008	1.996	1.380	.333	10
Adjusted predicted value	26.5379	50.7968	37.9612	7.24166	10
Residual	−4.43800	3.71176	.00000	2.98436	10
Std. residual	−1.402	1.173	.000	.943	10
Stud. residual	−1.568	1.422	.006	1.071	10
Deleted residual	−5.55197	5.46209	.03876	3.87616	10
Stud. deleted residual	−1.763	1.539	−.009	1.135	10
Mahal. distance	.013	2.680	.900	.893	10
Cook's distance	.004	.477	.159	.157	10
Centered leverage value	.001	.298	.100	.099	10

[a] Dependent variable: midterm exam score.

Mahalanobis distances: Mahalanobis distances are measures of the distance from each case to the mean of the independent variable for the remaining cases. We can use the value of Mahalanobis distance as a test statistic value using the chi-square distribution. With only one independent variable and one dependent variable, we have two degrees of freedom. Given an alpha level of .05, the chi-square critical value is 5.99. Thus, any Mahalanobis distance greater than 5.99 suggests that case is an outlier. With a maximum distance of 2.680 (see previous table), there is no evidence to suggest there are outliers in our data.

DFBETA: We also asked to save DFBETA values. These values provide another indication of the influence of cases. The DFBETA provides information on the change in the predicted value when the case is deleted from the model. For standardized DFBETA values, values greater than an absolute value of 2.0 should be examined more closely. Looking at the minimum (−.87682) and maximum (.62542) DFBETA values for the slope (i.e., GRE_Q), we do not have any cases that suggest undue influence.

Descriptive Statistics

	N	Minimum	Maximum	Mean	Std. Deviation
DFBETA GRE_Q	10	−.06509	.04470	−.0021866	.03608593
Standardized DFBETA GRE_Q	10	−.87682	.62542	−.0275752	.47302980
Valid *N* (listwise)	10				

7.5 G*Power

A priori and post hoc power could again be determined using the specialized software described previously in this text (e.g., G*Power); alternatively, you can consult a priori power tables (e.g., Cohen, 1988). As an illustration, we use G*Power to compute the post hoc power of our test.

Post Hoc Power for Simple Linear Regression Using G*Power

The first thing that must be done when using G*Power to compute post hoc power is to select the correct test family. Here we conducted simple linear regression. To find regression, select "Tests" in the top pulldown menu, then "Correlation and regression," and then "Linear bivariate regression: One group, size of slope." Once that selection is made, the "Test family" automatically changes to "t tests."

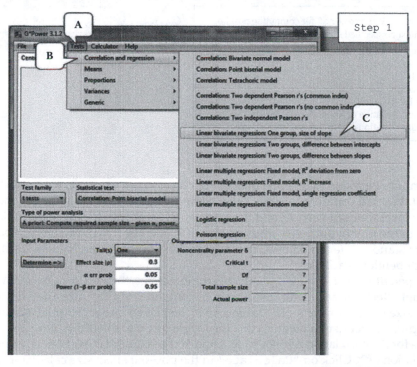

The "Type of Power Analysis" desired then needs to be selected. To compute post hoc power, select "Post hoc: Compute achieved power—given α, sample size, and effect size."

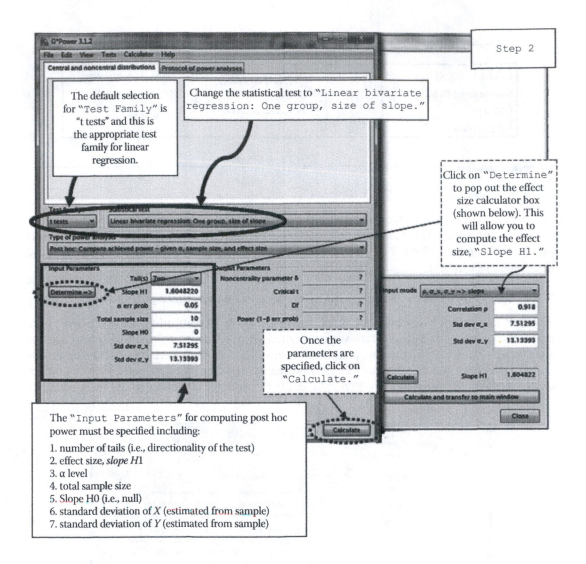

The "Input Parameters" must then be specified. In our example, we conducted a two-tailed test. We will compute the effect size, *Slope H1*, last, so we skip that for the moment. The alpha level we used was .05, and the total sample size was 10. The *Slope H0* is the slope specified in the null hypothesis—thus a value of 0. The last two parameters to be specified are for the standard deviation of *X*, the independent variable, and the standard deviation of *Y*, the dependent variable.

We skipped filling in the second parameter, the effect size, *Slope H1*, for a reason. We will use the pop-out effect size calculator in G*Power to compute the effect size *Slope H1*. To pop out the effect size calculator, click on "Determine" displayed under "Input Parameters." In the pop-out effect size calculator, click the toggle menu to select ρ, σ_x, σ_y => *slope*. Input the values for the correlation coefficient of *X* and *Y*, the standard deviation of *X*, and the standard deviation of *Y*. Click on "Calculate" in the pop-out effect size calculator to compute the effect size *Slope H1*. Then click on "Calculate and Transfer to Main Window" to transfer the calculated effect size (i.e., 1.604822) to the "Input Parameters." Once the parameters are specified, click on "Calculate" to find the power statistics.

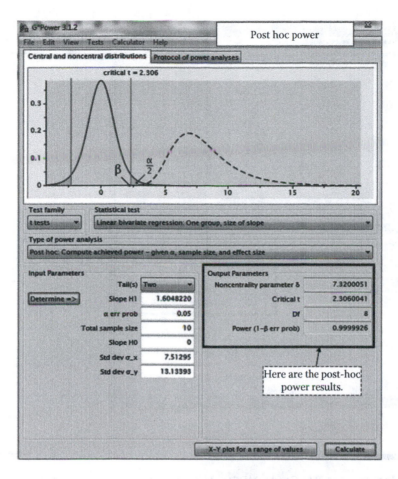

The "Output Parameters" provide the relevant statistics given the input just specified. Here we were interested in determining post hoc power for simple linear regression with a two-tailed test, a computed effect size *Slope H1* of 1.6048220, an alpha level of .05, total sample size of 10, a hypothesized null slope of 0, a standard deviation of X of 7.51295, and a standard deviation of Y of 13.13393. Based on those criteria, the post hoc power for the simple linear regression was .9999926. In other words, for these conditions the post hoc power of our simple linear regression was nearly 1.00—the probability of rejecting the null hypothesis when it is really false (in this case, the probability that the slope is 0) was around the maximum (i.e., 1.00) (sufficient power is often .80 or above). Keep in mind that conducting power analysis a priori is recommended so that you avoid a situation where, post hoc, you find that the sample size was not sufficient to reach the desired level of power (given the observed parameters).

A Priori Power for Simple Linear Regression Using G*Power

For a priori power, we can determine the total sample size needed for simple linear regression given the directionality of the test, an estimated effect size *Slope H1*, α level, desired power, slope for the null hypothesis (i.e., 0), and the standard deviations of X and Y. We follow Cohen's (1988) conventions for effect size (i.e., small $r = .10$; moderate $r = .30$; large $r = .50$). In this example, had we wanted to determine a priori power and had estimated a moderate effect r of .30, α of .05, desired power of .80, null slope of 0, and standard deviation of 5 for both the X and Y, we would need a total sample size of 82.

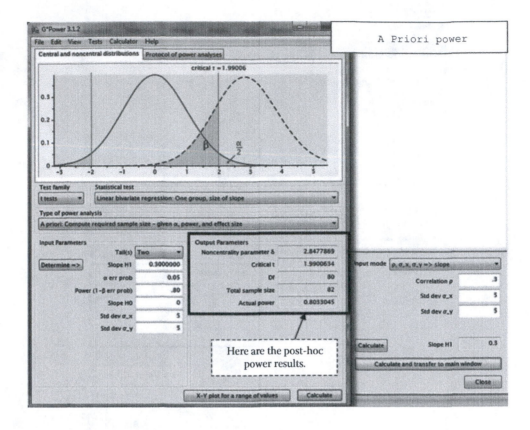

Here are the post-hoc power results.

A Priori power

7.6 Template and APA-Style Write-Up

Finally, here is an example paragraph for the results of the simple linear regression analysis. Recall that our graduate research assistant, Marie, was assisting the associate dean in Graduate Student Services, Randall. Randall wanted to know if midterm exam scores could be predicted by the quantitative subtest of the required graduate entrance exam, the GRE_Q. The research question presented to Randall from Marie included the following: *Can midterm exam scores be predicted from the GRE_Q?*

Marie then assisted Randall in generating a simple linear regression model as the test of inference. A template for writing the research question for this design is presented as follows:

- Can [dependent variable] be predicted from [independent variable]?

It may be helpful to preface the results of the simple linear regression with information on an examination of the extent to which the assumptions were met. The assumptions include (a) independence, (b) homogeneity of variance, (c) normality, (d) linearity, and (e) fixed values of X.

A simple linear regression analysis was conducted to determine if midterm exam scores (dependent variable) could be predicted from GRE _ Q scores (independent variable). The null hypothesis tested was that the regression coefficient (i.e., the slope) was equal to 0. The data were screened for missingness and violation of assumptions prior to analysis. There were no missing data.

Linearity: The scatterplot of the independent variable (GRE _ Q) and the dependent variable (midterm exam scores) indicates that the assumption of linearity is reasonable—as GRE _ Q increases, midterm exam scores generally increase as well. With a random display of points falling within an absolute value of 2, a scatterplot of unstandardized residuals against values of the independent variable provided further evidence of linearity.

Normality: The assumption of normality was tested via examination of the unstandardized residuals. Review of the S-W test for normality (SW = .927, df = 10, p = .416) and skewness (–.269) and kurtosis (–1.369) statistics suggested that normality was a reasonable assumption. The boxplot suggested a relatively normal distributional shape (with no outliers) of the residuals. The Q-Q plot and histogram suggested normality was reasonable.

Independence: A relatively random display of points in the scatterplot of studentized residuals against values of the independent variable provided evidence of independence. The Durbin–Watson statistic was computed to evaluate independence of errors and was 1.287, which is considered acceptable. This suggests that the assumption of independent errors has been met.

Homogeneity of variance: A relatively random display of points, where the spread of residuals appears fairly constant over the range of values of the independent variable (in the scatterplot of studentized residuals against values of the independent variable) provided evidence of homogeneity of variance.

Here is an APA-style example paragraph of results for the simple linear regression analysis (remember that this will be prefaced by the previous paragraph reporting the extent to which the assumptions of the test were met).

The results of the simple linear regression suggest that a significant proportion of the total variation in midterm scores was predicted by GRE _ Q. In other words, a student's score on the GRE _ Q is a good predictor of their midterm exam grade, $F(1, 8)$ = 42.700, p < .001. Additionally, we find the following: (a) the unstandardized slope (.525) and standardized slope (.918) are statistically significantly different from 0 (t = 6.535, df = 8, p < .001); with every one point increase in the GRE _ Q, midterm exam scores will increase by approximately one half of one point; (b) the CI around the unstandardized slope does not include 0 (.340, .710), further confirming that GRE _ Q is a statistically significant predictor of midterm scores; and (c) the intercept (or average midterm exam score when

GRE _ Q is 0) was 8.865. Multiple R squared indicates that approximately 84% of the variation in midterm scores was predicted by GRE _ Q scores. According to Cohen (1988), this suggests a large effect.

7.7 Summary

In this chapter, the method of simple linear regression was described. First we discussed the basic concepts of regression such as the slope and intercept. Next, a formal introduction to the population simple linear regression model was given. These concepts were then extended to the sample situation where a more detailed discussion was given. In the sample context, we considered unstandardized and standardized regression coefficients, errors in prediction, the least squares criterion, the coefficient of determination, tests of significance, and a discussion of statistical assumptions. At this point, you should have met the following objectives: (a) be able to understand the concepts underlying simple linear regression, (b) be able to determine and interpret the results of simple linear regression, and (c) be able to understand and evaluate the assumptions of simple linear regression. Chapter 8 follows up with a description of multiple regression analysis, where regression models are developed based on two or more predictors.

Problems

Conceptual Problems

7.1 A regression intercept represents which one of the following?
   a. The slope of the line
   b. The amount of change in Y given a one-unit change in X
   c. The value of Y when X is equal to 0
   d. The strength of the relationship between X and Y

7.2 The regression line for predicting final exam grades in history from midterm scores in the same course is found to be $Y' = .61 X + 3.12$. If the value of X increases from 74 to 75, the value of Y will do which one of the following?
   a. Increase by .61 points
   b. Increase by 1.00 points
   c. Increase by 3.12 points
   d. Decrease by .61 points

7.3 The regression line for predicting salary of principals from cumulative GPA in graduate school is found to be $Y' = 35,000 X + 37,000$. What does the value of 37,000 represent?
   a. Average cumulative GPA
   b. The criterion value
   c. The mean salary of principals when cumulative GPA is 0
   d. The standardized regression coefficient given an intercept of 0

7.4 The regression line for predicting salary of principals from cumulative GPA in graduate school is found to be $Y' = 35{,}000X + 37{,}000$. What does the value of 35,000 represent?

    a. The amount of change in Y given a one-unit change in X

    b. The correlation between X and Y

    c. The intercept value

    d. The value of Y when X is equal to 0

7.5 You are given that $\mu_X = 14$, $\sigma_X^2 = 36$, $\mu_Y = 14$, $\sigma_Y^2 = 49$, and $Y = 14$ is the prediction equation for predicting Y from X. Which of the following is the variance of the predicted values of Y'?

    a. 0

    b. 14

    c. 36

    d. 49

7.6 In regression analysis, the prediction of Y is *most* accurate for which of the following correlations between X and Y?

    a. −.90

    b. −.30

    c. +.20

    d. +.80

7.7 If the relationship between two variables is linear, then which one of the following is correct?

    a. All of the points must fall on a curved line.

    b. The relationship is best represented by a curved line.

    c. All of the points must fall on a straight line.

    d. The relationship is best represented by a straight line.

7.8 If both X and Y are measured on a z score scale, the regression line will have a slope of which one of the following?

    a. 0.00

    b. +1 or −1

    c. r_{XY}

    d. s_Y/s_X

7.9 If the simple linear regression equation for predicting Y from X is $Y' = 25$, then the correlation between X and Y is which one of the following?

    a. 0.00

    b. 0.25

    c. 0.50

    d. 1.00

7.10 Which one of the following is correct for the unstandardized regression slope?

    a. It may never be negative.

    b. It may never be greater than +1.00.

    c. It may never be greater than the correlation coefficient r_{XY}.

    d. None of the above.

7.11 If two individuals have the same score on the predictor, their residual scores will be which one of the following?

  a. Be necessarily equal

  b. Depend only on their observed scores on Y

  c. Depend only on their predicted scores on Y

  d. Depend only on the number of individuals that have the same predicted score

7.12 If $r_{XY} = .6$, the proportion of variation in Y that is *not* predictable from X is which one of the following?

  a. .36

  b. .40

  c. .60

  d. .64

7.13 Homogeneity assumes which one of the following?

  a. The range of Y is the same as the range of X.

  b. The X and Y distributions have the same mean values.

  c. The variability of the X and the Y distributions is the same.

  d. The conditional variability of Y is the same for all values of X.

7.14 Which one of the following is suggested to examine the extent to which homogeneity of variance has been met?

  a. Scatterplot of Mahalanobis distances against standardized residuals

  b. Scatterplot of studentized residuals against unstandardized predicted values

  c. Simple bivariate correlation between X and Y

  d. S–W test results for the unstandardized residuals

7.15 Which one of the following is suggested to examine the extent to which normality has been met?

  a. Scatterplot of Mahalanobis distances against standardized residuals

  b. Scatterplot of studentized residuals against unstandardized predicted values

  c. Simple bivariate correlation between X and Y

  d. S–W test results for the unstandardized residuals

7.16 The linear regression slope b_{YX} represents which one of the following?

  a. Amount of change in X expected from a one-unit change in Y

  b. Amount of change in Y expected from a one-unit change in X

  c. Correlation between X and Y

  d. Error of estimate of Y from X

7.17 If the correlation between X and Y is 0, then the best prediction of Y that can be made is the mean of Y. True or false?

7.18 If X and Y are highly nonlinear, linear regression is more useful than the situation where X and Y are highly linear. True or false?

7.19 If the pretest (X) and the posttest (Y) are positively correlated, and your friend receives a pretest score below the mean, then the regression equation would predict that your friend would have a posttest score that is above the mean. True or false?

7.20 Two variables are linearly related so that given X, Y can be predicted without error. I assert that r_{XY} must be equal to either +1.0 or –1.0. Am I correct?

7.21 I assert that the simple regression model is structured so that at least two of the actual data points will necessarily fall on the regression line. Am I correct?

Computational Problems

7.1 You are given the following pairs of scores on X (number of hours studied) and Y (quiz score).

X	Y
4	5
4	6
3	4
7	8
2	4

   a. Find the linear regression model for predicting Y from X.

   b. Use the prediction model obtained to predict the value of Y for a new person who has a value of 6 for X.

7.2 You are given the following pairs of scores on X (preschool social skills) and Y (receptive vocabulary at the end of kindergarten).

X	Y
25	60
30	45
42	56
45	58
36	42
50	38
38	35
47	45
32	47
28	57
31	56

   a. Find the linear regression model for predicting Y from X.

   b. Use the prediction model obtained to predict the value of Y for a new child who has a value of 48 for X.

7.3 The prediction equation for predicting Y (pain indicator) from X (drug dosage) is $Y = 2.5 X + 18$. What is the observed mean for Y if $\mu_X = 40$ and $\sigma_X^2 = 81$?

7.4 You are given the following pairs of scores on X (number of years working) and Y (number of raises).

X	Y
2	2
2	1
1	1
1	1
3	5
4	4
5	7
5	6
7	7
6	8
4	3
3	3
6	6
6	6
8	10
9	9
10	6
9	6
4	9
4	10

Perform the following computations using $\alpha = .05$.

a. The regression equation of Y predicted by X.

b. Test of the significance of X as a predictor.

c. Plot Y versus X.

d. Compute the residuals.

e. Plot residuals versus X.

Interpretive Problems

7.1 With the class survey 1 dataset on the website, your task is to use SPSS to find a suitable single predictor of current GPA. In other words, select several potential predictors that seem reasonable, and conduct a simple linear regression analysis for each of those predictors individually. Which of those is the best predictor of current GPA? What is the interpretation of the effect size? Write up the results following APA.

7.2 With the class survey 1 dataset on the website, your task is to use SPSS to find a suitable single predictor of the number of hours exercised per week. In other words, select several potential predictors that seem reasonable, and conduct a simple linear regression analysis for each of those predictors individually. Which of those is the best predictor of the number of hours of exercise? What is the interpretation of the effect size? Write up the results following APA.

8

Multiple Regression

Chapter Outline

Key Concepts

1. Partial and semipartial (part) correlations
2. Standardized and unstandardized regression coefficients
3. Coefficient of multiple determination and multiple correlation

In Chapter 7, our concern was with the prediction or explanation of a dependent or criterion variable (Y) by a single independent or predictor variable (X). However, given the types of phenomena we typically deal with in education and the behavioral sciences, the use of a single predictor variable is quite restrictive. In other words, given the complexity of most human, organizational, and animal behaviors, one predictor is usually not sufficient in terms of understanding the criterion. In order to account for a sufficient proportion of variability in the criterion, more than one predictor is necessary. This leads us to analyze the data via multiple regression analysis where two or more predictors are used to predict or explain the criterion variable. Here we adopt the usual notation where the X's are defined as the independent or predictor variables, and Y as the dependent or criterion variable.

For example, our admissions officer might want to use more than just Graduate Record Exam (GRE) scores to predict graduate-level grade point averages (GPAs) to make admissions decisions for a sample of applicants to your favorite local university or college. Other potentially useful predictors might be undergraduate grade point averages (UGPAs), recommendation letters, writing samples, and/or an evaluation from a personal interview. The research question of interest would now be, how well do the GRE, UGPAs, recommendations, writing samples, and/or interview scores (the independent or predictor variables) predict performance in graduate school (the dependent or criterion variable)? This is an example of a situation where multiple regression analysis using multiple predictor variables might be the method of choice.

Most of the concepts used in simple linear regression from Chapter 7 carry over to multiple regression analysis. This chapter considers the concepts of partial, semipartial, and multiple correlations, standardized and unstandardized regression coefficients, and the coefficient of multiple determination, as well as introduces a number of other types of regression models. Our objectives are that by the end of this chapter, you will be able to (a) determine and interpret the results of partial and semipartial correlations, (b) understand the concepts underlying multiple linear regression, (c) determine and interpret the results of multiple linear regression, (d) understand and evaluate the assumptions of multiple linear regression, and (e) have a basic understanding of other types of regression models.

8.1 Partial and Semipartial Correlations

Marie has developed into quite a statistics guru. We see in this chapter that her statistical prowess has garnered her repeat business.

As you may recall from the previous chapter, Randall, an associate dean in the Graduate Student Services office, was assisted by Marie in determining if the GRE-Quantitative (GRE-Q) can be used to predict midterm grades. Having had such a good experience in working with Marie, Randall has requested that Jennifer, the assistant dean in the Graduate Student Services office, seek advice from Marie on a special project. Jennifer is interested in estimating the extent to which GGPA can be predicted by scores on the overall GRE total and UGPA. Marie suggests the following research question to Jennifer: *Can GGPA be predicted by scores on the overall GRE total and UGPA?* Marie determines that a multiple linear regression is the appropriate statistical procedure to use to answer Jennifer's question. Marie then proceeds to assist Jennifer in analyzing the data.

Prior to a discussion of regression analysis, we need to consider two related concepts in correlational analysis, partial and semipartial correlations. Multiple regression analysis involves the use of two or more predictor variables and one criterion variable; thus, there are at a minimum three variables involved in the analysis. If we think about these variables in the context of the Pearson correlation, we have a problem because this correlation can only be used to relate two variables at a time. How do we incorporate additional variables into a correlational analysis? The answer is through partial and semipartial correlations, and later in this chapter, multiple correlations.

8.1.1 Partial Correlation

First we discuss the concept of **partial correlation**. The simplest situation consists of three variables, which we label X_1, X_2, and X_3. Here an example of a partial correlation would be the correlation between X_1 and X_2 where X_3 is held constant (i.e., controlled or partialled out). That is, the influence of X_3 is removed from both X_1 and X_2 (both have been adjusted for X_3). Thus, the partial correlation here represents the linear relationship between X_1 and X_2 independent of the linear influence of X_3. This particular partial correlation is denoted by $r_{12.3}$, where the X's are not shown for simplicity and the dot indicates that the variables preceding it are to be correlated and the variable(s) following it are to be partialled out. We compute $r_{12.3}$ as follows:

$$r_{12.3} = \frac{r_{12} - r_{13}r_{23}}{\sqrt{(1 - r_{13}^2)(1 - r_{23}^2)}}$$

Let us take an example of a situation where a partial correlation might be computed. Say a researcher is interested in the relationship between height (X_1) and weight (X_2). The sample consists of individuals ranging in age (X_3) from 6 months to 65 years. The sample correlations are for height (X_1) and weight (X_2), $r_{12} = .7$; height (X_1) and age (X_3), $r_{13} = .1$; and weight (X_2) and age (X_3), $r_{23} = .6$. We compute the correlation between height and weight, controlling for age, $r_{12.3}$, as follows:

$$r_{12.3} = \frac{r_{12} - r_{13}r_{23}}{\sqrt{(1 - r_{13}^2)(1 - r_{23}^2)}} = \frac{.7 - (.1)(.6)}{\sqrt{(1 - .01)(1 - .36)}} = .8040$$

We see here that the bivariate correlation between height and weight, ignoring age ($r_{12} = .7$), is smaller than the partial correlation between height and weight controlling for age ($r_{12.3} = .8040$). That is, the relationship between height and weight is stronger when age is held constant (i.e., for a particular age) than it is across all ages. Although we often talk about holding a particular variable constant, in reality variables such as age cannot be held constant artificially.

Some rather interesting partial correlation results can occur in particular situations. At one extreme, if both the correlation between height (X_1) and age (X_3), r_{13}, and weight (X_2) and age (X_3), r_{23}, equal 0, then the correlation between height (X_1) and weight (X_2) will equal the partial correlation between height and weight controlling for age, $r_{12} = r_{12.3}$. That is, if the variable being partialled out is uncorrelated with each of the other two variables, then the partialling process will logically not have any effect. At the other extreme, if either r_{13} or r_{23} equals 1, then $r_{12.3}$ cannot be calculated as the denominator is equal to 0 (in other words, at least one of the terms in the denominator is equal to 0 which results in the product of the two terms in the denominator equaling 0 and thus a denominator of 0—and you cannot divide by 0). Thus, in this situation (where either r_{13} or r_{23} is perfectly correlated at 1.0), the partial correlation (i.e., $r_{12.3}$, partial correlation between height and weight controlling for age) is not defined. Later in this chapter, we refer to this as perfect collinearity, which is a serious problem. In between these extremes, it is possible for the partial correlation to be greater than or less than its corresponding bivariate correlation (including a change in sign) and even for the partial correlation to be equal to 0 when its bivariate correlation is not. For significance tests of partial and semipartial correlations, we refer you to your favorite statistical software.

8.1.2 Semipartial (Part) Correlation

Next the concept of **semipartial correlation** (also called a **part correlation**) is discussed. The simplest situation consists again of three variables, which we label X_1, X_2, and X_3. Here an example of a semipartial correlation would be the correlation between X_1 and X_2 where X_3 is removed from X_2 only. That is, the influence of X_3 is removed from X_2 only. Thus, the semipartial correlation here represents the linear relationship between X_1 and X_2 after that portion of X_2 that can be linearly predicted from X_3 has been removed from X_2. This particular semipartial correlation is denoted by $r_{1(2.3)}$, where the X's are not shown for simplicity and within the parentheses, the dot indicates that the variable(s) following it are to be removed from the variable preceding it. Another use of the semipartial correlation is when we want to examine the predictive power in the prediction of Y from X_1 after removing X_2 from the prediction. A method for computing $r_{1(2.3)}$ is as follows:

$$r_{1(2.3)} = \frac{r_{12} - r_{13}r_{23}}{\sqrt{(1 - r_{23}^2)}}$$

Let us take an example of a situation where a semipartial correlation might be computed. Say a researcher is interested in the relationship between GPA (X_1) and GRE scores (X_2). The researcher would like to remove the influence of intelligence (IQ: X_3) from GRE scores but not from GPA. The simple bivariate correlation between GPA and GRE is $r_{12} = .5$; between GPA and IQ is $r_{13} = .3$; and between GRE and IQ is $r_{23} = .7$. We compute the semipartial correlation that removes the influence of intelligence (IQ: X_3) from GRE scores (X_2) but not from GPA (X_1) (i.e., $r_{1(2.3)}$) as follows:

$$r_{1(2.3)} = \frac{r_{12} - r_{13}r_{23}}{\sqrt{(1 - r_{23}^2)}} = \frac{.5 - (.3)(.7)}{\sqrt{1 - .49}} = .4061$$

Thus, the bivariate correlation between GPA (X_1) and GRE scores (X_2) ignoring IQ (X_3) ($r_{12} = .50$) is larger than the semipartial correlation between GPA and GRE controlling for IQ in GRE ($r_{1(2.3)} = .4061$). As was the case with partial correlations, various values of a semipartial correlation can be obtained depending on the combination of the bivariate correlations. For more information on partial and semipartial correlations, see Hays (1988), Glass and Hopkins (1996), or Pedhazur (1997).

Now that we have considered the correlational relationships among two or more variables (i.e., partial and semipartial correlations), let us move on to an examination of the multiple regression model where there are two or more predictor variables.

8.2 Multiple Linear Regression

Let us take the concepts we have learned in this and the previous chapter and place them into the context of multiple linear regression. For purposes of brevity, we do not consider the population situation because the sample situation is invoked 99.44% of the time. In this section, we discuss the unstandardized and standardized multiple regression models, the coefficient of multiple determination, multiple correlation, tests of significance, and statistical assumptions.

8.2.1 Unstandardized Regression Model

The sample multiple linear regression model for predicting Y from m predictors $X_{1,2,...,m}$ is

$$Y_i = b_1 X_{1i} + b_2 X_{2i} + \cdots + b_m X_{mi} + a + e_i$$

where
  Y is the criterion variable (also known as the dependent variable)
  X_k's are the predictor (or independent) variables where $k = 1,..., m$
  b_k is the sample partial slope of the regression line for Y as predicted by X_k
  a is the sample intercept of the regression line for Y as predicted by the set of X_k's
  e_i represents the residuals or errors of prediction (the part of Y not predictable from the X_k's)
  i represents an index for an individual or object. The index i can take on values from 1 to n where n is the size of the sample (i.e., $i = 1,..., n$)

The term **partial slope** is used because it represents the slope of Y for a particular X_k in which we have partialled out the influence of the other X_k's, much as we did with the partial correlation.

The sample prediction model is

$$Y_i' = b_1 X_{1i} + b_2 X_{2i} + \cdots + b_m X_{mi} + a$$

where Y_i' is the predicted value of Y for specific values of the X_k's, and the other terms are as before. The difference between the regression and prediction models is the same as in Chapter 7. We can compute residuals, the e_i, for each of the i individuals or objects by comparing the actual Y values with the predicted Y values as

$$e_i = Y_i - Y_i'$$

for all $i = 1,..., n$ individuals or objects in the sample.

Determining the sample partial slopes and the intercept in the multiple predictor case is rather complicated. To keep it simple, we use a two-predictor model for illustrative purposes. Generally we rely on statistical software for implementing multiple regression analysis. For the two-predictor case, the sample partial slopes (b_1 and b_2) and the intercept (a) can be determined as follows:

$$b_1 = \frac{(r_{Y1} - r_{Y2}r_{12})s_Y}{(1 - r_{12}^2)s_1}$$

$$b_2 = \frac{(r_{Y2} - r_{Y1}r_{12})s_Y}{(1 - r_{12}^2)s_2}$$

$$a = \bar{Y} - b_1\bar{X}_1 - b_2\bar{X}_2$$

The sample partial slope b_1 is referred to alternately as (a) the expected or predicted change in Y for a one-unit change in X_1 with X_2 held constant (or for individuals with the same score on X_2) and (b) the unstandardized or raw regression coefficient for X_1. Similar statements may be made for b_2. Note the similarity of the partial slope equation to the semipartial correlation. The sample intercept is referred to as the value of the dependent variable Y when the values of the independent variables X_1 and X_2 are both 0.

An alternative method for computing the sample partial slopes that involves the use of a partial correlation is as follows:

$$b_1 = r_{Y1.2}\frac{s_Y\sqrt{1 - r_{Y2}^2}}{s_1\sqrt{1 - r_{12}^2}}$$

$$b_2 = r_{Y2.1}\frac{s_Y\sqrt{1 - r_{Y1}^2}}{s_2\sqrt{1 - r_{12}^2}}$$

What statistical criterion is used to arrive at the particular values for the partial slopes and intercept? The criterion usually used in multiple linear regression analysis [and in all general linear models (GLM) for that matter] is the least squares criterion. The least squares criterion arrives at those values for the partial slopes and intercept such that the sum of the squared prediction errors or residuals is smallest. That is, we want to find that regression model, defined by a particular set of partial slopes and an intercept, which has the smallest sum of the squared residuals. We often refer to this particular method for calculating the slope and intercept as least squares estimation because a and the b_k's represent sample estimates of the population parameters α and the β_k's, which are obtained using the least squares criterion. Recall from simple linear regression that the residual is simply the vertical distance from the observed value of Y to the predicted value of Y, and the line of best fit minimizes this distance. This concept still applies to multiple linear regression with the exception that we are now in a three-dimensional (or more) plane given there are multiple independent variables.

Consider now the analysis of a realistic example we will follow in this chapter. We use the GRE Quantitative + Verbal Total (GRETOT) and undergraduate grade point average (UGPA) to predict graduate grade point average (GGPA). GRETOT has a possible range of 40–160 points (if we remove the unnecessary last digit of 0), and GPA is defined as having a possible range of 0.00–4.00 points. Given the sample of 11 statistics students as shown in Table 8.1, let us work through a multiple linear regression analysis.

TABLE 8.1

GRE–GPA Example Data

Student	GRE Total (X_1)	UGPA (X_2)	GGPA (Y)
1	145	3.2	4.0
2	120	3.7	3.9
3	125	3.6	3.8
4	130	2.9	3.7
5	110	3.5	3.6
6	100	3.3	3.5
7	95	3.0	3.4
8	115	2.7	3.3
9	105	3.1	3.2
10	90	2.8	3.1
11	105	2.4	3.0

As sample statistics, we compute for GRETOT (X_1 or subscript 1) that the mean is $\bar{X}_1 = 112.7273$ and the variance is $s_1^2 = 266.8182$, for UGPA (X_2 or subscript 2) that the mean is $\bar{X}_2 = 3.1091$ and the variance is $s_2^2 = 0.1609$, and for GGPA (Y), a mean of $\bar{Y} = 3.5000$ and variance of $s_Y^2 = 0.1100$. In addition, we compute the bivariate correlation between the dependent variable (GGPA) and GRE total, $r_{Y1} = .7845$; between the dependent variable (GGPA) and UGPA, $r_{Y2} = .7516$; and between GRE total and UGPA, $r_{12} = .3011$. The sample partial slopes (b_1 and b_2) and intercept (a) are determined as follows:

$$b_1 = \frac{(r_{Y1} - r_{Y2}r_{12})s_Y}{(1 - r_{12}^2)s_1} = \frac{[.7845 - (.7516)(.3011)].3317}{(1 - .3011^2)16.3346} = .0125$$

$$b_2 = \frac{(r_{Y2} - r_{Y1}r_{12})s_Y}{(1 - r_{12}^2)s_2} = \frac{[.7516 - (.7845)(.3011)].3317}{(1 - .3011^2).4011} = .4687$$

$$a = \bar{Y} - b_1\bar{X}_1 - b_2\bar{X}_2 = 3.5000 - (.0125)(112.7273) - (.4687)(3.1091) = .6337$$

Let us interpret the partial slope and intercept values. A partial slope of .0125 for GRETOT would mean that if your score on the GRETOT was increased by one point, then your GGPA would be increased by .0125 points, controlling for UGPA. Likewise, a partial slope of .4687 for UGPA would mean that if your UGPA was increased by one point, then your GGPA would be increased by .4687 points, controlling for GRETOT. An intercept of .6337 would mean that if your scores on the GRETOT and UGPA were both 0, then your GGPA would be .6337. However, it is impossible to obtain a GRETOT score of 0 because you receive 40 points for putting your name on the answer sheet. In a similar way, an undergraduate student could not obtain a UGPA of 0 and be admitted to graduate school. This is not to say that the regression equation is incorrect but just to point out how the interpretation of "GRETOT and UGPA were both 0" is a bit meaningless in context.

To put all of this together then, the sample multiple linear regression model is

$$Y_i = b_1 X_{1i} + b_2 X_{2i} + a + e_i = .0125 X_{1i} + .4687 X_{2i} + .6337 + e_i$$

If your score on the GRETOT was 130 and your UGPA was 3.5, then your predicted score on the GGPA would be computed as follows:

$$Y_i' = .0125(130) + .4687(3.5000) + .6337 = 3.8992$$

Based on the prediction equation, we predict your GGPA to be around 3.9; however, as we saw in Chapter 7, predictions are usually somewhat less than perfect, even with two predictors.

8.2.2 Standardized Regression Model

Up until this point in the chapter, everything in multiple linear regression analysis has involved the use of raw scores. For this reason, we referred to the model as the unstandard-ized regression model. Often we may want to express the regression in terms of standard z score units rather than in raw score units (as in Chapter 7). The means and variances of the standardized variables (e.g., z_1, z_2, z_Y) are 0 and 1, respectively. The sample standard-ized linear prediction model becomes the following:

$$z(Y_i') = b_1^* z_{1i} + b_2^* z_{2i} + ... + b_m^* z_{mi}$$

where b_k^* represents a sample standardized partial slope (sometimes called beta weights) and the other terms are as before. As was the case in simple linear regression, no intercept term is necessary in the standardized prediction model as the mean of the z scores for all variables is 0. (Recall that the intercept is the value of the dependent variable when the scores on the independent variables are all 0. Thus, in a standardized prediction model, the dependent variable will equal 0 when the values of the independent variables are equal to their means—i.e., 0.) The sample standardized partial slopes are, in general, computed by the following equation:

$$b_k^* = b_k \frac{s_k}{s_Y}$$

For the two-predictor case, the standardized partial slopes can be calculated by

$$b_1^* = b_1 \frac{s_1}{s_Y}$$

or

$$b_1^* = \frac{r_{Y1} - r_{Y2} r_{12}}{(1 - r_{12}^2)}$$

and

$$b_2^* = b_2 \frac{s_2}{s_Y}$$

or

$$b_2^* = \frac{r_{Y2} - r_{Y1}r_{12}}{(1 - r_{12}^2)}$$

If the two predictors are uncorrelated (i.e., $r_{12} = 0$), then the standardized partial slopes are equal to the simple bivariate correlations between the dependent variable and the independent variables (i.e., $b_1^* = r_{Y1}$ and $b_2^* = r_{Y2}$) because the rest of the equation goes away. For example,

$$b_1^* = \frac{r_{Y1} - r_{Y2}r_{12}}{(1 - r_{12}^2)} = \frac{r_{Y1} - r_{Y2}(0)}{(1 - 0)} = r_{Y1}$$

For our GGPA example, the standardized partial slopes are equal to

$$b_1^* = b_1 \frac{s_1}{s_Y} = .0125(16.3346 / .3317) = .6156$$

$$b_2^* = b_2 \frac{s_2}{s_Y} = .4687(.4011 / .3317) = .5668$$

The prediction model is then

$$z(Y_i') = .6156z_{1i} + .5668z_{2i}$$

The standardized partial slope of .6156 for GRETOT would be interpreted as the expected increase in GGPA in z score units for a one z score unit increase in the GRETOT, controlling for UGPA. A similar statement may be made for the standardized partial slope of UGPA. The b_k^* can also be interpreted as the expected standard deviation change in the dependent variable Y associated with a one standard deviation change in the independent variable X_k when the other X_k's are held constant.

When would you want to use the standardized versus unstandardized regression analyses? According to Pedhazur (1997), b_k^* is sample specific and is not very stable across different samples due to the variance of X_k changing (as the variance of X_k increases, the value of b_k^* also increases, all else being equal). For example, at Ivy-Covered University, b_k^* would vary across different graduating classes (or samples) while b_k would be much more consistent across classes. Thus, most researchers prefer the use of b_k to compare the influence of a particular predictor variable across different samples and/or populations. Pedhazur also states that the b_k^* is of "limited value" (p. 321), but could be reported along with the b_k. As Pedhazur and others have reported, the b_k^* can be deceptive in determining the relative importance of the predictors as they are affected by the variances and covariances of both the included predictors and the predictors not included in the model. Thus, we recommend the b_k for general purpose use.

8.2.3 Coefficient of Multiple Determination and Multiple Correlation

An obvious question now is, how well is the criterion variable predicted or explained by the set of predictor variables? For our example, we are interested in how well the GGPAs (the dependent variable) are predicted by the GRE total scores and the UGPAs. In other words, what is the utility of the set of predictor variables?

The simplest method involves the partitioning of the familiar total sum of squares in Y, which we denote as SS_{total}. In multiple linear regression analysis, we can write SS_{total} as follows:

$$SS_{total} = [n\Sigma Y_i^2 - (\Sigma Y_i)^2]/n$$

or

$$SS_{total} = (n-1)s_Y^2$$

where we sum over Y from $i = 1,\ldots, n$. Next we can conceptually partition SS_{total} as

$$SS_{total} = SS_{reg} + SS_{res}$$

$$\Sigma(Y_i - \bar{Y})^2 = \Sigma(Y_i' - \bar{Y})^2 + \Sigma(Y_i - Y_i')^2$$

where
  SS_{reg} is the regression sum of squares due to the prediction of Y from the X_k's (often written as $SS_{Y'}$)
  SS_{res} is the sum of squares due to the residuals

Before we consider computation of SS_{reg} and SS_{res}, let us look at the coefficient of multiple determination. Recall from Chapter 7 the coefficient of determination, r_{XY}^2. Now consider the multiple predictor version of r_{XY}^2, here denoted as $R_{Y.1,\ldots,m}^2$. The subscript tells us that Y is the criterion (or dependent) variable and that $X_{1,\ldots,m}$ are the predictor (or independent) variables. The simplest procedure for computing R^2 is as follows:

$$R_{Y.1,\ldots,m}^2 = b_1^* r_{Y1} + b_2^* r_{Y2} + \cdots + b_m^* r_{Ym}$$

The coefficient of multiple determination tells us the proportion of total variation in the dependent variable Y that is predicted from the set of predictor variables (i.e., $X_{1,\ldots,m}$'s). Often we see the coefficient in terms of SS as

$$R_{Y.1,\ldots,m}^2 = SS_{reg} / SS_{total}$$

Thus, one method for computing the sums of squares regression and residual, SS_{reg} and SS_{res}, is from the coefficient of multiple determination, R^2, as follows:

$$SS_{reg} = R^2 \, SS_{total}$$

$$SS_{res} = (1 - R^2)SS_{total} = SS_{total} - SS_{reg}$$

As discussed in Chapter 7, there is no objective gold standard as to how large the coefficient of determination needs to be in order to say a meaningful proportion of variation has been predicted. The coefficient is determined not just by the quality of the predictor variables included in the model but also by the quality of relevant predictor variables not included in the model, as well as by the amount of total variation in the dependent variable Y. However, the coefficient of determination can be used as a measure of effect size. According to the subjective standard of Cohen (1988), a small effect size is defined as $R^2 = .10$, a medium effect size as $R^2 = .30$, and a large effect size as $R^2 = .50$. For additional information on effect size measures in regression, we suggest you consider Steiger and Fouladi (1992), Mendoza and Stafford (2001), and Smithson (2001; which also includes some discussion of power). Note also that $R_{Y.1, ..., m}$ is referred to as the *multiple correlation coefficient* so as not to confuse it with a simple bivariate correlation coefficient.

With the example of predicting GGPA from GRETOT and UGPA, let us examine the partitioning of the total sum of squares SS_{total} as follows:

$$SS_{total} = (n-1)s_Y^2 = (10).1100 = 1.1000$$

Next, we can determine the multiple correlation coefficient R^2 as

$$R_{Y.1,...,m}^2 = b_1^* r_{Y1} + b_2^* r_{Y2} + ... + b_m^* r_{Ym} = .6156(.7845) + .5668(.7516) = .9089$$

We can also partition SS_{total} into SS_{reg} and SS_{res}, where

$$SS_{reg} = R^2 SS_{total} = .9089(1.1000) = 0.9998$$

$$SS_{res} = (1 - R^2)SS_{total} = (1 - .9089)1.1000 = .1002$$

Finally, let us summarize these results for the example data. We found that the coefficient of multiple determination (R^2) was equal to .9089. Thus, the GRE total score and the UGPA predict around 91% of the variation in the GGPA. This would be quite satisfactory for the college admissions officer in that there is little variation left to be explained, although this result is quite unlikely in actual research in education and the behavioral sciences. Obviously there is a large effect size here.

It should be noted that R^2 is sensitive to sample size and to the number of predictor variables. As sample size and/or the number of predictor variables increase, R^2 will increase as well. R is a biased estimate of the population multiple correlation due to sampling error in the bivariate correlations and in the standard deviations of X and Y. Because R systematically overestimates the population multiple correlation, an adjusted coefficient of multiple determination has been devised. The adjusted $R^2 (R_{adj}^2)$ is calculated as follows:

$$R_{adj}^2 = 1 - (1 - R^2)\left(\frac{n-1}{n-m-1}\right)$$

Thus, R_{adj}^2 adjusts for sample size and for the number of predictors in the model; this allows us to compare models fitted to the same set of data with different numbers of predictors or with different samples of data. The difference between R^2 and R_{adj}^2 is called **shrinkage**.

When n is small relative to m, the amount of bias can be large as R^2 can be expected to be large by chance alone. In this case, the adjustment will be quite large, as it should be. In addition, with small samples, the regression coefficients (i.e., the b_k's) may not be very good estimates of the population values. When n is large relative to m, bias will be minimized and generalizations are likely to be better about the population values.

With a large number of predictors, power is reduced, and there is an increased likelihood of a Type I error across the total number of significance tests (i.e., one for each predictor and overall, as we show in the next section). In multiple regression, power is a function of sample size, the number of predictors, the level of significance, and the size of the population effect (i.e., for a given predictor, or overall). To determine how large a sample you need relative to the number of predictors, we suggest that you consult power tables (e.g., Cohen, 1988) or power software (e.g., Murphy & Myors, 2004; Power and Precision; G*Power). Simple advice is to design your research such that the ratio of n to m is large.

For the example data, we determine the adjusted multiple coefficient of determination R^2_{adj} to be

$$R^2_{adj} = 1 - (1 - R^2)\left(\frac{n-1}{n-m-1}\right) = 1 - (1 - .9089)\left(\frac{11-1}{11-2-1}\right) = .8861$$

which, in this case, indicates a very small adjustment in comparison to R^2.

8.2.4 Significance Tests

Here we describe two procedures used in multiple linear regression analysis. These involve testing the significance of the overall regression model and of each individual partial slope (or regression coefficient).

8.2.4.1 Test of Significance of Overall Regression Model

The first test is the test of significance of the overall regression model, or alternatively the test of significance of the coefficient of multiple determination. This is a test of all of the b_k's simultaneously, an examination of overall model fit of the independent variables in aggregate. The null and alternative hypotheses, respectively, are as follows:

$$H_0: \beta_1 = \beta_2 = \cdots = \beta_k = 0$$

$$H_1: \text{not all the } \beta_k = 0$$

If H_0 is rejected, then one or more of the individual regression coefficients (i.e., the b_k) is statistically significantly different from 0 (if the assumptions are satisfied, as discussed later). If H_0 is not rejected, then none of the individual regression coefficients will be significantly different from 0.

The test is based on the following test statistic:

$$F = \frac{R^2/m}{(1 - R^2)/(n - m - 1)}$$

where

F indicates that this is an *F* statistic

m is the number of predictors or independent variables

n is the sample size

The *F* test statistic is compared to the *F* critical value, always a one-tailed test (by default, this value can never be negative given the terms in the equation, so this will always be a nondirectional test) and at the designated level of significance, with degrees of freedom being *m* and $(n - m - 1)$, as taken from the *F* table in Table A.4. That is, the tabled critical value is $_\alpha F_{m,(n-m-1)}$. The test statistic can also be written in equivalent form as

$$F = \frac{SS_{reg}/df_{reg}}{SS_{res}/df_{res}} = \frac{MS_{reg}}{MS_{res}}$$

where the degrees of freedom regression equals the number of independent variables, $df_{reg} = m$, and degrees of freedom residual equals the difference between the sample size, number of independent variables, and 1, $df_{res} = (n - m - 1)$.

For the GGPA example, we compute the overall *F* test statistic as the following:

$$F = \frac{R^2/m}{(1-R^2)/(n-m-1)} = \frac{.9089/2}{(1-.9089)/(11-2-1)} = 39.9078$$

or as

$$F = \frac{SS_{reg}/df_{reg}}{SS_{res}/df_{res}} = \frac{0.9998/2}{.1002/8} = 39.9122$$

The critical value, at the .05 level of significance, is $_{.05}F_{2,8} = 4.46$. The test statistic exceeds the critical value, so we reject H_0 and conclude that all of the partial slopes are not equal to 0 at the .05 level of significance (the two *F* test statistics differ slightly due to rounding error).

8.2.4.2 Test of Significance of b_k

The second test is the test of the statistical significance of each individual partial slope or regression coefficient, b_k. That is, are the individual unstandardized regression coefficients statistically significantly different from 0? This is actually the same as the test of b_k^*, so we need not develop a separate test for b_k^*. The null and alternative hypotheses, respectively, are as follows:

$$H_0: \beta_k = 0$$

$$H_1: \beta_k \neq 0$$

where β_k is the population partial slope for X_k.

In multiple regression, it is necessary to compute a standard error for each regression coefficient b_k. Recall from Chapter 7 the variance error of estimate concept. The variance error of estimate is similarly defined for multiple linear regression and computed as follows:

$$s_{res}^2 = \frac{SS_{res}}{df_{res}} = MS_{res}$$

where $df_{res} = (n - m - 1)$. Degrees of freedom are lost as we have to estimate the population partial slopes and intercept, the β_k's and α, respectively, from the sample data. The variance error of estimate indicates the amount of variation among the residuals. The standard error of estimate is simply the positive square root of the variance error of estimate and is the standard deviation of the residuals or errors of estimate. We call it the **standard error of estimate**, denoted as s_{res}.

Finally, we need to compute a standard error for each b_k. Denote the standard error of b_k as $s(b_k)$ and define it as

$$s(b_k) = \frac{s_{res}}{\sqrt{(n-1)s_k^2(1-R_k^2)}}$$

where
s_k^2 is the sample variance for predictor X_k
R_k^2 is the squared multiple correlation between X_k and the remaining X_k's
R_k^2 represents the overlap between that predictor (X_k) and the remaining predictors

In the case of two predictors, the squared multiple correlation, R_k^2, is equal to the simple bivariate correlation between the two independent variables, r_{12}^2.

The test statistic for testing the significance of the regression coefficients, b_k's, is as follows:

$$t = \frac{b_k}{s(b_k)}$$

The test statistic t is compared to the critical values of t, a two-tailed test for a nondirectional H_1, at the designated level of significance, and with degrees of freedom $(n - m - 1)$, as taken from the t table in Table A.2. Thus, the tabled critical values are $\pm_{(\alpha/2)} t_{(n-m-1)}$ for a two-tailed test.

We can also form a confidence interval (CI) around b_k as follows:

$$CI(b_k) = b_k \pm {}_{(\alpha/2)} t_{(n-m-1)} s(b_k)$$

Recall that the null hypothesis tested is H_0: $\beta_k = 0$. Therefore, if the CI contains 0, then the regression coefficient b_k is not statistically significantly different from 0 at the specified α level. This is interpreted to mean that in $(1 - \alpha)\%$ of the sample CIs that would be formed from multiple samples, β_k will be included.

Let us compute the second test statistic for the GGPA example. We specify the null hypothesis to be $\beta_k = 0$ (i.e., the slope is 0) and conduct two-tailed tests. First the variance error of estimate is

$$s_{res}^2 = \frac{SS_{res}}{df_{res}} = \frac{.1002}{8} = .0125$$

The standard error of estimate, s_{res}, is .1118. Next the standard errors of the b_k are found to be

$$s(b_1) = \frac{s_{res}}{\sqrt{(n-1)s_1^2(1-r_{12}^2)}} = \frac{.1118}{\sqrt{(10)266.8182(1-.3011^2)}} = .0023$$

$$s(b_2) = \frac{s_{res}}{\sqrt{(n-1)s_2^2(1-r_{12}^2)}} = \frac{.1118}{\sqrt{(10)0.1609(1-.3011^2)}} = .0924$$

Finally we find the t test statistics to be computed as follows:

$$t_1 = b_1/s(b_1) = .0125/.0023 = 5.4348$$

$$t_2 = b_2/s(b_2) = .4687/.0924 = 5.0725$$

To evaluate the null hypotheses, we compare these test statistics to the critical values of $\pm_{.025}t_8 = \pm 2.306$. Both test statistics exceed the critical value; consequently H_0 is rejected in favor of H_1 for both predictors. We conclude that both partial slopes are indeed statistically significantly different from 0 at the .05 level of significance.

Finally, let us compute the CIs for the b_k's as follows:

$$CI(b_1) = b_1 \pm_{(\alpha/2)} t_{(n-m-1)} s(b_1) = b_1 \pm_{.025} t_8 \, s(b_1) = .0125 \pm 2.306(.0023) = (.0072, \ .0178)$$

$$CI(b_2) = b_2 \pm_{(\alpha/2)} t_{(n-m-1)} s(b_2) = b_2 \pm_{.025} t_8 \, s(b_2) = .4687 \pm 2.306(.0924) = (.2556, \ .6818)$$

The intervals do not contain 0, the value specified in H_0; thus, we again conclude that both b_k's are significantly different from 0 at the .05 level of significance.

8.2.4.3 Other Tests

One can also form CIs for the predicted mean of Y and the prediction intervals for individual values of Y, as we described in Chapter 7.

8.2.5 Assumptions

A considerable amount of space in Chapter 7 was dedicated to the assumptions of simple linear regression. For the most part, the assumptions of multiple linear regression analysis are the same, and, thus, we need not devote as much space here. The assumptions are concerned with (a) independence, (b) homogeneity, (c) normality, (d) linearity, (e) fixed X, and (f) noncollinearity. This section also mentions those techniques appropriate for evaluating each assumption.

8.2.5.1 Independence

The first assumption is concerned with **independence** of the observations. The simplest procedure for assessing independence is to examine residual plots of e versus the predicted values of the dependent variable Y' and of e versus each independent variable X_k

(alternatively, one can look at plots of observed values of the dependent variable Y versus predicted values of the dependent variable Y' and of observed values of the dependent variable Y versus each independent variable X_k). If the independence assumption is satisfied, the residuals should fall into a random display of points. If the assumption is violated, the residuals will fall into some sort of pattern. Lack of independence affects the estimated standard errors of the model. For serious violations, one could consider generalized or weighted least squares as the method of estimation (e.g., Myers, 1986; Weisberg, 1985), or some type of transformation. The residual plots shown in Figure 8.1 do not suggest any independence problems for the GGPA example, where Figure 8.1a represents the residual e versus the predicted value of the dependent variable Y', Figure 8.1b represents e versus GRETOT, and Figure 8.1c represents e versus UGPA.

8.2.5.2 Homogeneity

The second assumption is **homogeneity of variance**, where the conditional distributions have the same constant variance for all values of X. In the residual plots, the consistency of the variance of the conditional distributions may be examined. If the homogeneity assumption is violated, estimates of the standard errors are larger, and the conditional distributions may also be nonnormal. As described in Chapter 7, solutions include variance-stabilizing transformations (such as the square root or log of Y), generalized or weighted least squares (e.g., Myers, 1986; Weisberg, 1985), or robust regression (Kleinbaum, Kupper, Muller, & Nizam, 1998; Myers, 1986; Wilcox, 1996, 2003; Wu, 1985). Due to the small sample size, homogeneity cannot really be assessed for the example data.

8.2.5.3 Normality

The third assumption is that the conditional distributions of the scores on Y, or the prediction errors, are **normal** in shape. Violation of the normality assumption may be the result of outliers. The simplest outlier detection procedure is to look for observations that are more than two standard errors from the mean. Other procedures were previously described in Chapter 7. Several methods for dealing with outliers are available, such as conducting regression analyses with and without suspected outliers, robust regression (Kleinbaum et al., 1998; Myers, 1986; Wilcox, 1996, 2003; Wu, 1985), and nonparametric regression (Miller, 1997; Rousseeuw & Leroy, 1987; Wu, 1985). The following can be used to detect normality violations: frequency distributions, normal probability [quantile–quantile (Q–Q)] plots, and skewness statistics. For the example data, the normal probability plot is shown in Figure 8.2, and even with a small sample looks good. Violation can lead to imprecision in the partial slopes and in the coefficient of determination. There are also several statistical procedures available for the detection of nonnormality (e.g., Andrews, 1971; Belsley, Kuh, & Welsch, 1980; D'Agostino, 1971; Ruppert & Carroll, 1980; Shapiro & Wilk, 1965; Wu, 1985); transformations can also be used to normalize the data. Review Chapter 7 for more details.

8.2.5.4 Linearity

The fourth assumption is **linearity**, that there is a linear relationship between the observed scores on the dependent variable Y and the values of the independent variables, X_k's. If satisfied, then the sample partial slopes and intercept are unbiased estimators of the population partial slopes and intercept, respectively. The linearity assumption is important

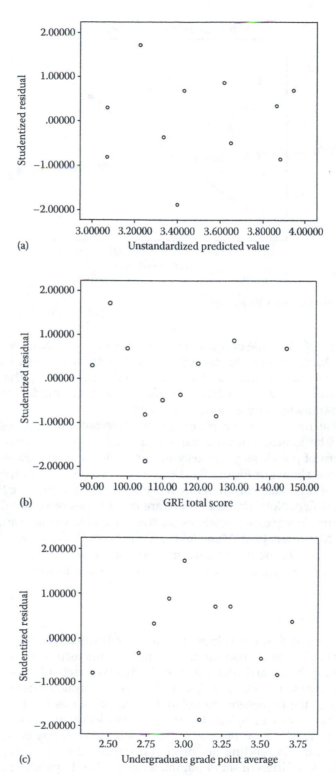

FIGURE 8.1
Residual plots for GRE–GPA example: (a), (b), and (c).

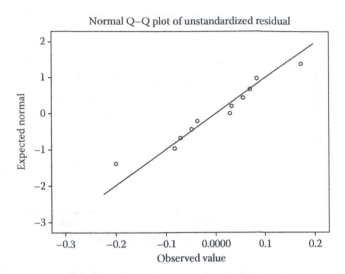

FIGURE 8.2
Normal probability plot for GRE–GPA example.

because regardless of the value of X_k, we always expect Y to increase by b_k units for a one-unit increase in X_k, controlling for the other X_k's. If a nonlinear relationship exists, this means that the expected increase in Y depends on the value of X_k; that is, the expected increase is not a constant value. Strictly speaking, linearity in a model refers to there being linearity in the parameters of the model (i.e., α and the β_k's).

Violation of the linearity assumption can be detected through residual plots. The residuals should be located within a band of $\pm 2 s_{res}$ (or standard errors), indicating no systematic pattern of points, as previously discussed in Chapter 7. Residual plots for the GGPA example are shown in Figure 8.1. Even with a very small sample, we see a fairly random pattern of residuals, and therefore feel fairly confident that the linearity assumption has been satisfied. Note also that there are other types of residual plots developed especially for multiple regression analysis, such as the added variable and partial residual plots (Larsen & McCleary, 1972; Mansfield & Conerly, 1987; Weisberg, 1985). Procedures to deal with nonlinearity include transformations (of one or more of the X_k's and/or of Y as described in Chapter 7) and other regression models (discussed later in this chapter).

8.2.5.5 Fixed X

The fifth assumption is that the values of X_k are **fixed**, where the independent variables, X_k's, are fixed variables rather than random variables. This results in the regression model being valid only for those particular values of X_k that were actually observed and used in the analysis. Thus, the same values of X_k would be used in replications or repeated samples.

Strictly speaking, the regression model and its parameter estimates are only valid for those values of X_k actually sampled. The use of a prediction model developed to predict the dependent variable Y, based on one sample of individuals, may be suspect for another sample of individuals. Depending on the circumstances, the new sample of individuals may actually call for a different set of parameter estimates. Expanding on our discussion in Chapter 7, generally we may not want to make predictions about individuals having combinations of X_k scores outside of the range of values used in developing the prediction model; this is defined as *extrapolating* beyond the sample predictor data. On the other hand, we may not be quite as concerned in making predictions about individuals having combinations of X_k scores within the range of values used in developing the prediction model; this is defined as *interpolating* within the range of the sample predictor data.

It has been shown that when other assumptions are met, regression analysis performs just as well when X is a random variable (e.g., Glass & Hopkins, 1996; Myers & Well, 1995; Pedhazur, 1997; Wonnacott & Wonnacott, 1981). There is no such assumption about Y.

8.2.5.6 Noncollinearity

The final assumption is unique to multiple linear regression analysis, being unnecessary in simple linear regression. A violation of this assumption is known as collinearity where there is a very strong linear relationship between two or more of the predictors. The presence of severe collinearity is problematic in several respects. First, it will lead to instability of the regression coefficients across samples, where the estimates will bounce around quite a bit in terms of magnitude and even occasionally result in changes in sign (perhaps opposite of expectation). This occurs because the standard errors of the regression coefficients become larger, thus making it more difficult to achieve statistical significance. Another result that may occur involves an overall regression that is significant, but none of the individual predictors are significant. Collinearity will also restrict the utility and generalizability of the estimated regression model.

Recall from earlier in the chapter the notion of partial regression coefficients, where the other predictors were held constant. In the presence of severe collinearity, the other predictors cannot really be held constant because they are so highly intercorrelated. Collinearity may be indicated when there are large changes in estimated coefficients due to (a) a variable being added or deleted and/or (b) an observation being added or deleted (Chatterjee & Price, 1977). Collinearity is also likely when a composite variable as well as its component variables are used as predictors in the same regression model (e.g., including GRETOT, GRE-Quantitative, and GRE-Verbal as predictors).

How do we detect violations of this assumption? The simplest procedure is to conduct a series of special regression analyses, one for each X, where that predictor is predicted by all of the remaining X's (i.e., the criterion variable is not involved). If any of the resultant R_k^2 values are close to 1 (greater than .9 is a good rule of thumb), then there may be a collinearity problem. However, the large R^2 value may also be due to small sample size; thus, more data would be useful. For the example data, $R_{12}^2 = .091$ and therefore collinearity is not a concern.

Also, if the number of predictors is greater than or equal to n, then perfect collinearity is a possibility. Another statistical method for detecting collinearity is to compute a variance inflation factor (VIF) for each predictor, which is equal to $1/(1 - R_k^2)$. The VIF is defined as the inflation that occurs for each regression coefficient above the ideal situation of uncorrelated predictors. Many suggest that the largest VIF should be less than 10 in order to satisfy this assumption (Myers, 1990; Stevens, 2009; Wetherill, 1986).

There are several possible methods for dealing with a collinearity problem. First, one can remove one or more of the correlated predictors. Second, ridge regression techniques can be used (e.g., Hoerl & Kennard, 1970a, 1970b; Marquardt & Snee, 1975; Myers, 1986; Wetherill, 1986). Third, principal component scores resulting from principal component analysis can be utilized rather than raw scores on each variable (e.g., Kleinbaum et al., 1998; Myers, 1986; Weisberg, 1985; Wetherill, 1986). Fourth, transformations of the variables can be used to remove or reduce the extent of the problem. The final solution, and probably our last choice, is to use simple linear regression, as collinearity cannot exist with a single predictor.

TABLE 8.2

Assumptions and Violation of Assumptions: Multiple Linear Regression Analysis

Assumption	Effect of Assumption Violation
Independence	• Influences standard errors of the model
Homogeneity	• Bias in s_{res}^2 • May inflate standard errors and thus increase likelihood of a Type II error • May result in nonnormal conditional distributions
Normality	• Less precise slopes, intercept, and R^2
Linearity	• Bias in slope and intercept • Expected change in Y is not a constant and depends on value of X
Fixed X values	• Extrapolating beyond the range of X combinations: prediction errors larger, may also bias slopes and intercept • Interpolating within the range of X combinations: smaller effects than earlier; if other assumptions met, negligible effect
Noncollinearity of X's	• Regression coefficients can be quite unstable across samples (as standard errors are larger) • R^2 may be significant, yet none of the predictors are significant • Restricted generalizability of the model

8.2.5.7 Summary

For the GGPA example, although sample size is quite small in terms of looking at conditional distributions, it would appear that all of our assumptions have been satisfied. All of the residuals are within two standard errors of 0, and there does not seem to be any systematic pattern in the residuals. The distribution of the residuals is nearly symmetric, and the normal probability plot looks good. A summary of the assumptions and the effects of their violation for multiple linear regression analysis is presented in Table 8.2.

8.3 Methods of Entering Predictors

The multiple predictor model which we have considered thus far can be viewed as **simultaneous regression**. That is, all of the predictors to be used are entered (or selected) simultaneously, such that all of the regression parameters are estimated simultaneously; here the set of predictors has been selected a priori. In computing these regression models, we have used the default setting in SPSS of the method of entry as "Enter," which enters the set of independent variables in aggregate. There are other methods of entering the independent variables where the predictor variables are entered (or selected) systematically; here the set of predictors has not been selected a priori. This class of models is referred to as **sequential regression** (also known as **variable selection procedures**). This section introduces a brief description of the following sequential regression procedures: backward elimination, forward selection, stepwise selection, all possible subsets regression, and hierarchical regression.

8.3.1 Backward Elimination

First consider the backward elimination procedure. Here variables are eliminated from the model based on their minimal contribution to the prediction of the criterion variable. In the first stage of the analysis, all potential predictors are included in the model. In the second stage, that predictor is deleted from the model that makes the smallest contribution to the prediction of the dependent variable. This can be done by eliminating that variable having the smallest t or F statistic such that it is making the smallest contribution to R^2_{adj}. In subsequent stages, that predictor is deleted that makes the next smallest contribution to the prediction of the outcome Y. The analysis continues until each of the remaining predictors in the model is a significant predictor of Y. This could be determined by comparing the t or F statistics for each predictor to the critical value, at a preselected level of significance. Some computer programs use as a stopping rule the maximum F-to-remove criterion, where the procedure is stopped when all of the selected predictors' F values are greater than the specified F criterion. Another stopping rule is where the researcher stops at a predetermined number of predictors (see Hocking, 1976; Thompson, 1978). In SPSS, this is the **backward** method of entering predictors.

8.3.2 Forward Selection

In the forward selection procedure, variables are added or selected into the model based on their maximal contribution to the prediction of the criterion variable. Initially, none of the potential predictors are included in the model. In the first stage, the predictor is added to the model that makes the largest contribution to the prediction of the dependent variable. This can be done by selecting that variable having the largest t or F statistic such that it is making the largest contribution to R^2_{adj}. In subsequent stages, the predictor is selected that makes the next largest contribution to the prediction of Y. The analysis continues until each of the selected predictors in the model is a significant predictor of the outcome Y, whereas none of the unselected predictors is a significant predictor. This could be determined by comparing the t or F statistics for each predictor to the critical value, at a preselected level of significance. Some computer programs use as a stopping rule the minimum F-to-enter criterion, where the procedure is stopped when all of the unselected predictors' F values are less than the specified F criterion. For the same set of data and at the same level of significance, the backward elimination and forward selection procedures may not necessarily result in the exact same final model due to the differences in how variables are selected. In SPSS, this is the **forward** method of entering predictors.

8.3.3 Stepwise Selection

The stepwise selection procedure is a modification of the forward selection procedure with one important difference. Predictors that have been selected into the model can, at a later step, be deleted from the model; thus, the modification conceptually involves a backward elimination mechanism. This situation can occur for a predictor when a significant contribution at an earlier step later becomes a nonsignificant contribution given the set of other predictors in the model. Thus, a predictor loses its significance due to new predictors being added to the model.

The stepwise selection procedure is as follows. Initially, none of the potential predictors are included in the model. In the first step, that predictor is added to the model that makes the largest contribution to the explanation of the dependent variable. This can be done by selecting that variable having the largest t or F statistic such that it is making the largest contribution to R^2_{adj}. In subsequent stages, the predictor is selected that makes the next largest contribution to the prediction of Y. Those predictors that have entered at earlier stages are also checked to see if their contribution remains significant. If not, then that predictor is eliminated from the model. The analysis continues until each of the predictors remaining in the model is a significant predictor of Y, while none of the other predictors is a significant predictor. This could be determined by comparing the t or F statistics for each predictor to the critical value, at a specified level of significance. Some computer programs use as stopping rules the minimum

F-to-enter and maximum F-to-remove criteria, where the F-to-enter value selected is usually equal to or slightly greater than the F-to-remove value selected (to prevent a predictor from continuously being entered and removed). For the same set of data and at the same level of significance, the backward elimination, forward selection, and stepwise selection procedures may not necessarily result in the exact same final model, due to differences in how variables are selected. In SPSS, this is the **stepwise** method of entering predictors.

8.3.4 All Possible Subsets Regression

Another sequential regression procedure is known as all possible subsets regression. Let us say, for example, that there are five potential predictors. In this procedure, all possible one-, two-, three-, and four-variable models are analyzed (with five predictors, there is only a single five-predictor model). Thus, there will be 5 one-predictor models, 10 two-predictor models, 10 three-predictor models, and 5 four-predictor models. The best k predictor model can be selected as the model that yields the largest R_{adj}^2. For example, the best 3-predictor model would be that model of the 10 estimated that yields the largest R_{adj}^2. With today's powerful computers, this procedure is easier and more cost efficient than in the past. However, the researcher is not advised to consider this procedure, or for that matter, any of the other sequential regression procedures, when the number of potential predictors is large. Here the researcher is allowing number crunching to take precedence over thoughtful analysis. Also, the number of models will be equal to 2^m, so that for 10 predictors, there are 1024 possible subsets. Obviously, examining that number of models is not a thoughtful analysis.

8.3.5 Hierarchical Regression

In hierarchical regression, the researcher specifies a priori a sequence for the individual predictor variables (not to be confused with hierarchical linear models, which is a regression approach for analyzing nested data collected at multiple levels, such as child, classroom, and school). The analysis proceeds in a forward selection, backward elimination, or stepwise selection mode according to a researcher-specified, theoretically based sequence, rather than an unspecified, statistically based sequence. This variable selection method is different from those previously discussed in that the researcher determines the order of entry from a careful consideration of the available theory and research, instead of the software dictating the sequence.

A type of hierarchical regression is known as **setwise regression** (also called **blockwise**, **chunkwise**, or **forced stepwise regression**). Here the researcher specifies a priori a sequence for sets of predictor variables. This procedure is similar to hierarchical regression in that the researcher determines the order of entry of the predictors. The difference is that the setwise method uses sets of predictor variables at each stage rather than one individual predictor variable at a time. The sets of variables are determined by the researcher so that variables within a set share some common theoretical ground (e.g., home background variables in one set and aptitude variables in another set). Variables within a set are selected according to one of the sequential regression procedures. The variables selected for a particular set are then entered in the specified theoretically based sequence. In SPSS, this is conducted by entering predictors in **blocks** and selecting their desired method of entering variables in each block (e.g., simultaneously, forward, backward, stepwise).

8.3.6 Commentary on Sequential Regression Procedures

Let us make some comments and recommendations about the sequential regression procedures. First, numerous statisticians have noted problems with stepwise methods (i.e., backward elimination, forward selection, and stepwise selection) (e.g., Derksen & Keselman, 1992; Huberty, 1989; Mickey, Dunn, & Clark, 2004; Miller, 1984, 1990; Wilcox, 2003). These problems include the following: (a) selecting noise rather than important predictors; (b) highly inflated R^2 and R^2_{adj} values; (c) CIs for partial slopes that are too narrow; (d) p values that are not trustworthy; (e) important predictors being barely edged out of the model, making it possible to miss the true model; and (f) potentially heavy capitalization on chance given the number of models analyzed. Second, theoretically based regression models have become the norm in many disciples (and the stepwise methods of entry are driven by mathematics of the models rather than theory). Thus, hierarchical regression either has or will dominate the landscape of the sequential regression procedures. Thus, we strongly encourage you to consider more extended discussions of hierarchical regression (e.g., Bernstein, 1988; Cohen & Cohen, 1983; Pedhazur, 1997; Schafer, 1991; Tabachnick & Fidell, 2007).

If you are working in an area of inquiry where research evidence is scarce or nonexistent, then you are conducting exploratory research. Thus, you are probably trying to simply identify the key variables. Here hierarchical regression is not appropriate, as a theoretically driven sequence cannot be developed and there is no theory to guide its development. Here we recommend the use of all possible subsets regression (e.g., Kleinbaum et al. 1998). For additional information on the sequential regression procedures, see Cohen and Cohen (1983), Weisberg (1985), Miller (1990), Pedhazur (1997), and Kleinbaum et al. (1998).

8.4 Nonlinear Relationships

Here we continue our discussion on how to deal with nonlinearity from Chapter 7. We formally introduce several multiple regression models for when the criterion variable does not have a linear relationship with the predictor variables.

First consider polynomial regression models. In polynomial models, powers of the predictor variables (e.g., squared, cubed) are used. In general, a sample polynomial regression model that includes one predictor is as follows:

$$Y = b_1 X + b_2 X^2 + \cdots + b_m X^m + a + e$$

where the independent variable X is taken from the first power through the mth power, and the i subscript for observations has been deleted to simplify matters. If the model consists only of X taken to the first power, then this is a **simple linear regression model** (or **first-degree polynomial**; this is a straight line and what we have studied to this point). A **second-degree polynomial** includes X taken to the second power (or **quadratic model**; this is a curve with one bend in it rather than a straight line). A **third-degree polynomial** includes X taken to the third power (or **cubic model**; this is a curve with two bends in it).

A polynomial model with multiple predictors can also be utilized. An example of a second-degree polynomial model with two predictors is illustrated in the following equation:

$$Y = b_1 X_1 + b_2 X_1^2 + b_3 X_2 + b_4 X_2^2 + a + e$$

It is important to note that whenever a higher-order polynomial is included in a model (e.g., quadratic, cubic, and more), the first-order polynomial must also be included in the model. In other words, it is not appropriate to include a quadratic term X^2 without also including the first-order polynomial X. For more information on polynomial regression models, see Weisberg (1985), Bates and Watts (1988), Seber and Wild (1989), Pedhazur (1997), and Kleinbaum et al. (1998). Alternatively, one might transform the criterion variable and/or the predictor variables to obtain a more linear form, as previously discussed.

8.5 Interactions

Another type of model involves the use of an interaction term, as previously discussed in factorial ANOVA (Chapter 3). These can be implemented in any type of regression model. We can write a simple two-predictor interaction-type model as

$$Y = b_1 X_1 + b_2 X_2 + b_3 X_1 X_2 + a + e$$

where $X_1 X_2$ represents the interaction of predictor variables 1 and 2. An interaction can be defined as occurring when the relationship between Y and X_1 depends on the level of X_2. In other words, X_2 is a **moderator variable**. For example, suppose one were to use years of education and age to predict political attitude. The relationship between education and attitude might be moderated by age. In other words, the relationship between education and attitude may be different for older versus younger individuals. If age were a moderator, we would expect there to be an interaction between age and education in a regression model. Note that if the predictors are very highly correlated, collinearity is likely. For more information on interaction models, see Cohen and Cohen (1983), Berry and Feldman (1985), Kleinbaum et al. (1998), Weinberg and Abramowitz (2002), and Meyers, Gamst, and Guarino (2006).

8.6 Categorical Predictors

So far, we have only considered continuous predictors—independent variables that are interval or ratio in scale. There may be times, however, that you wish to use a categorical predictor—an independent variable that is nominal or ordinal in scale. For example, gender, grade level (e.g., freshman, sophomore, junior, senior), and highest education earned (less than high school, high school graduate, etc.) are all categorical variables that may be very interesting and theoretically appropriate to include in either a simple or multiple regression model. Given their scale (i.e., nominal or ordinal), however, we must recode the values prior to analysis so that they are on a scale of 0 and 1. This is called "dummy coding" as this type of recoding makes the model work. For example, males might be coded as 0 and females coded as 1. When there are more than two categories to the categorical predictor, multiple dummy coded variables must be created—*specifically 1 minus the number of levels or categories of the categorical variable*. Thus, in the case of grade level where there are four categories (freshman, sophomore, junior, senior), three of the four categories would be dummy coded and included in the regression model as predictors. The category that is "left out" is the reference category, or that category to which all other levels are compared. The easiest way to understand this is perhaps to examine the data. In the screenshot that follows, the first column represents grade level where 1 = freshman, 2 = sophomore, 3 = junior, and 4 = senior. Dummy coding three of the four grade levels, with "senior" as the reference category, will result in three additional columns (columns 2, 3, and 4 in the screenshot).

		1	2	3	4
		Grade	Freshman	Sophomore	Junior
1		1.00	1.00	.0	.0
2		1.00	1.00	.0	.0
3		1.00	1.00	.0	.0
4		2.00	.0	1.00	.0
5		2.00	.0	1.00	.0
6		2.00	.0	1.00	.0
7		3.00	.0	.0	1.00
8		3.00	.0	.0	1.00
9		3.00	.0	.0	1.00
10		4.00	.0	.0	.0
11		4.00	.0	.0	.0
12		4.00	.0	.0	.0

In terms of generating the analysis and the point and click use of SPSS to compute the regression model, nothing changes. The steps are the same regardless of whether the predictors are continuous or categorical. Now let us discuss *why* dummy coding works in this situation. You may recall from Chapter 10 of *An Introduction to Statistical Concepts*, Third Edition our discussion of point biserial correlations. The point biserial correlation is a variant of the Pearson product–moment correlation, and we can use the Pearson as a variant of the point biserial. Thus, while we will not have a linear relationship between a continuous outcome and a binary variable, the mathematics that underlie the model will hold.

Consider an example output for predicting GPA based on grade level, where "senior" is the reference category. We see that the intercept (i.e., "constant") is statistically significant as is "freshman." The interpretation of the intercept remains the same regardless of the scale of the predictors. The intercept represents GPA (the dependent variable) when all the predictors are 0. In this case, this means that GPA is 3.267 for *seniors* (the reference category). The only statistically significant predictor is "freshman." This is interpreted to say that mean GPA decreases by .800 points for freshmen *as compared to seniors*. The nonstatistically significant regression coefficients for "sophomore" and "junior" indicate that mean GPA is similar for these grade levels as compared to seniors. The interpretation for dummy variable predictors is always in reference to the category that was "left out." In this case, that was "seniors."

Coefficients[a]

Model		Unstandardized Coefficients		Standardized Coefficients		
		B	Std. Error	Beta	t	Sig.
1	(Constant)	3.267	.183		17.892	.000
	Freshman	−.800	.258	−.704	−3.098	.015
	Sophomore	.233	.258	.205	.904	.393
	Junior	.200	.258	.176	.775	.461

[a] Dependent variable: GPA.

It is important to note that even though "sophomore" and "junior" were not statistically significant, they should be retained in the model as they represent (along with "freshman") a group. Dropping one or more dummy coded indicator variables that represent a group will change the reference category. For example, if "sophomore" and "junior" were dropped from the model, the interpretation would then become the mean GPA for freshmen *as compared to all other grade levels*. Thus, careful thought needs to be put into dropping one or more indicators that are part of a set.

8.7 SPSS

Next we consider SPSS for the multiple linear regression model. Before we conduct the analysis, let us review the data. With one dependent variable and two independent variables, the dataset must consist of three variables or columns, one for each independent variable and one for the dependent variable. Each row still represents one individual, indicating the value of the independent variables for that particular case and their score on the dependent variable. As seen in the following screenshot, for a multiple linear regression analysis therefore, the SPSS data are in the form of three columns that represent the two independent variables (GRE total score and UGPA) and one dependent variable (GGPA).

	GRE_Total	UGPA	GGPA
1	145.00	3.20	4.00
2	120.00	3.70	3.90
3	125.00	3.60	3.80
4	130.00	2.90	3.70
5	110.00	3.50	3.60
6	100.00	3.30	3.50
7	95.00	3.00	3.40
8	115.00	2.70	3.30
9	105.00	3.10	3.20
10	90.00	2.80	3.10
11	105.00	2.40	3.00

The independent variables are labeled "GRE Total" and "UGPA" where each value represents the student's total score on the GRE and their undergraduate GPA.

The **dependent variable** is "GGPA" and represents their graduate GPA.

Step 1: To conduct a simple linear regression, go to "Analyze" in the top pulldown menu, then select "Regression," and then select "Linear." Following the screenshot (step 1) as follows produces the "Linear Regression" dialog box.

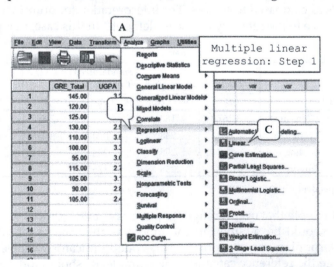

Step 2: Click the dependent variable (e.g., "GGPA") and move it into the "Dependent" box by clicking the arrow button. Click the independent variables and move them into the "Independent(s)" box by clicking the arrow button (see screenshot Step 2).

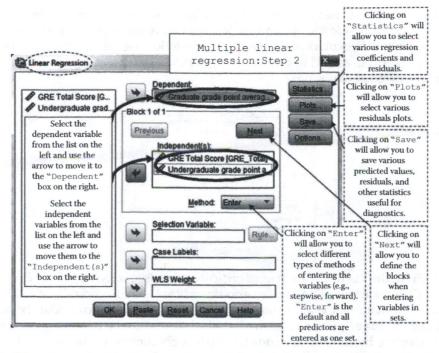

Step 3: From the "Linear Regression" dialog box (see screenshot Step 2), clicking on "Statistics" will provide the option to select various regression coefficients and residuals. From the "Statistics" dialog box (see screenshot Step 3), place a checkmark in the box next to the following: (a) estimates, (b) CIs, (c) model fit, (d) R squared change, (e) descriptives, (f) part and partial correlations, (g) collinearity diagnostics, (h) Durbin-Watson, and (i) casewise diagnostics. For this example, we apply an α level of .05; thus, we will leave the default CI percentage at 95. If we were using a different α, the CI would be the complement of alpha (e.g., α = .01, then CI = 1 − .01 = 99). We will also leave the default of "three standard deviations" for defining outliers for the casewise diagnostics. Click on "Continue" to return to the original dialog box.

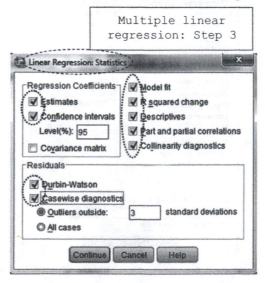

Step 4: From the "Linear Regression" dialog box (see screenshot Step 2), clicking on "Plots" will provide the option to select various residual plots. From the "Plots" dialog box, place a checkmark in the box next to the following: (a) histogram, (b) normal probability plot, and (c) produce all partial plots. Click on "Continue" to return to the original dialog box.

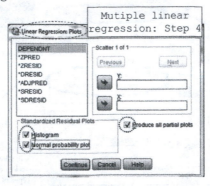

Step 5: From the "Linear Regression" dialog box (see screenshot Step 2), clicking on "Save" will provide the option to save various predicted values, residuals, and statistics that can be used for diagnostic examination. From the "Save" dialog box under the heading of **Predicted Values**, place a checkmark in the box next to the following: unstandardized. Under the heading of **Residuals**, place a checkmark in the box next to the following: (a) unstandardized and (b) studentized. Under the heading of **Distances**, place a checkmark in the box next to the following: (a) Mahalanobis, (b) Cook's, and (c) leverage values. Under the heading of **Influence Statistics**, place a checkmark in the box next to the following: standardized DfBeta(s). Click on "Continue" to return to the original dialog box. From the "Linear Regression" dialog box, click on "OK" to return and generate the output.

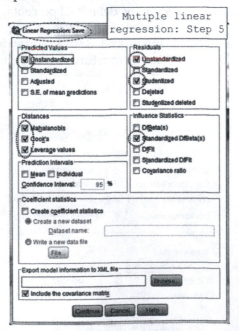

Interpreting the output: Annotated results are shown in Table 8.3.

TABLE 8.3

SPSS Results for the Multiple Regression GRE–GPA Example

Descriptive Statistics

	Mean	Std. Deviation	N
Graduate grade point average	3.5000	.33166	11
GRE total score	112.7273	16.33457	11
Undergraduate grade point average	3.1091	.40113	11

The table labeled "Descriptive Statistics" provides basic descriptive statistics (means, standard deviations, and sample sizes) for the independent and dependent variables.

Correlations

The table labeled "Correlations" provides the: Pearson correlation coefficient values, *p* values, and sample size, for the simple bivariate Pearson correlation between the independent and dependent variables.

		Graduate Grade Point Average	GRE Total Score	Undergraduate Grade Point Average
Pearson correlation	Graduate grade point average	1.000	.784	.752
	GRE total score	.784	1.000	.301
	Undergraduate grade point average	.752	.301	1.000
Sig. (1-tailed)	Graduate grade point average	.	.002	.004
	GRE total score	.002	.	.184
	Undergraduate grade point average	.004	.184	.
N	Graduate grade point average	11	11	11
	GRE total score	11	11	11
	Undergraduate grade point average	11	11	11

The correlation between graduate GPA and GRE-total (*p* = .002) and the correlation between graduate GPA and undergraduate GPA (*p* = .004) are statistically significant.

Variables Entered/Removed[b]

Model	Variables Entered	Variables Removed	Method
1	Undergraduate grade point average, GRE total score		Enter

"Variables Entered/Removed" lists the independent variables included in the model and the method they were entered (i.e., "Enter").

[a] All requested variables entered.
[b] Dependent variable: Graduate grade point average.

(*continued*)

TABLE 8.3 (continued)

SPSS Results for the Multiple Regression GRE–GPA Example

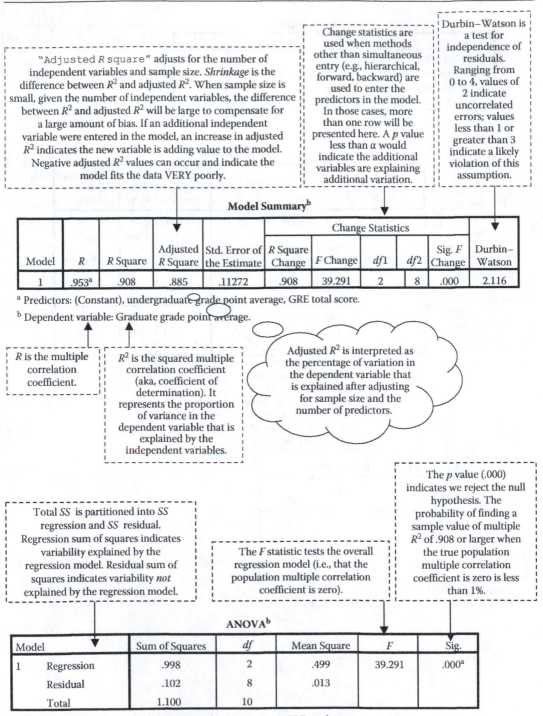

"Adjusted R square" adjusts for the number of independent variables and sample size. *Shrinkage* is the difference between R^2 and adjusted R^2. When sample size is small, given the number of independent variables, the difference between R^2 and adjusted R^2 will be large to compensate for a large amount of bias. If an additional independent variable were entered in the model, an increase in adjusted R^2 indicates the new variable is adding value to the model. Negative adjusted R^2 values can occur and indicate the model fits the data VERY poorly.

Change statistics are used when methods other than simultaneous entry (e.g., hierarchical, forward, backward) are used to enter the predictors in the model. In those cases, more than one row will be presented here. A p value less than α would indicate the additional variables are explaining additional variation.

Durbin–Watson is a test for independence of residuals. Ranging from 0 to 4, values of 2 indicate uncorrelated errors; values less than 1 or greater than 3 indicate a likely violation of this assumption.

Model Summary[b]

Model	R	R Square	Adjusted R Square	Std. Error of the Estimate	Change Statistics R Square Change	F Change	$df1$	$df2$	Sig. F Change	Durbin–Watson
1	.953[a]	.908	.885	.11272	.908	39.291	2	8	.000	2.116

[a] Predictors: (Constant), undergraduate grade point average, GRE total score.

[b] Dependent variable: Graduate grade point average.

R is the multiple correlation coefficient.

R^2 is the squared multiple correlation coefficient (aka, coefficient of determination). It represents the proportion of variance in the dependent variable that is explained by the independent variables.

Adjusted R^2 is interpreted as the percentage of variation in the dependent variable that is explained after adjusting for sample size and the number of predictors.

Total SS is partitioned into SS regression and SS residual. Regression sum of squares indicates variability explained by the regression model. Residual sum of squares indicates variability *not* explained by the regression model.

The F statistic tests the overall regression model (i.e., that the population multiple correlation coefficient is zero).

The p value (.000) indicates we reject the null hypothesis. The probability of finding a sample value of multiple R^2 of .908 or larger when the true population multiple correlation coefficient is zero is less than 1%.

ANOVA[b]

Model		Sum of Squares	df	Mean Square	F	Sig.
1	Regression	.998	2	.499	39.291	.000[a]
	Residual	.102	8	.013		
	Total	1.100	10			

[a] Predictors: (Constant), undergraduate grade point average, GRE total score.

[b] Dependent variable: Graduate grade point average.

TABLE 8.3 (continued)

SPSS Results for the Multiple Regression GRE–GPA Example

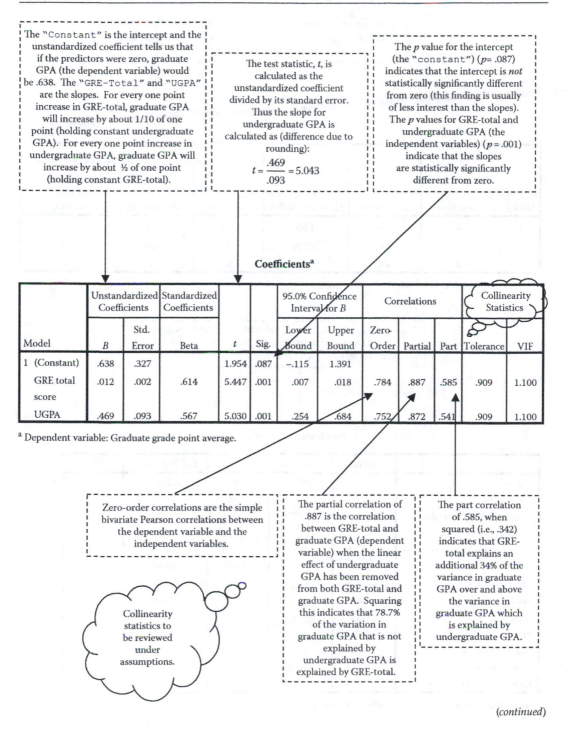

The "Constant" is the intercept and the unstandardized coefficient tells us that if the predictors were zero, graduate GPA (the dependent variable) would be .638. The "GRE-Total" and "UGPA" are the slopes. For every one point increase in GRE-total, graduate GPA will increase by about 1/10 of one point (holding constant undergraduate GPA). For every one point increase in undergraduate GPA, graduate GPA will increase by about ½ of one point (holding constant GRE-total).

The test statistic, t, is calculated as the unstandardized coefficient divided by its standard error. Thus the slope for undergraduate GPA is calculated as (difference due to rounding):

$$t = \frac{.469}{.093} = 5.043$$

The p value for the intercept (the "constant") ($p = .087$) indicates that the intercept is *not* statistically significantly different from zero (this finding is usually of less interest than the slopes). The p values for GRE-total and undergraduate GPA (the independent variables) ($p = .001$) indicate that the slopes are statistically significantly different from zero.

Coefficients[a]

Model	Unstandardized Coefficients B	Std. Error	Standardized Coefficients Beta	t	Sig.	95.0% Confidence Interval for B Lower Bound	Upper Bound	Correlations Zero-Order	Partial	Part	Collinearity Statistics Tolerance	VIF
1 (Constant)	.638	.327		1.954	.087	−.115	1.391					
GRE total score	.012	.002	.614	5.447	.001	.007	.018	.784	.887	.585	.909	1.100
UGPA	.469	.093	.567	5.030	.001	.254	.684	.752	.872	.541	.909	1.100

[a] Dependent variable: Graduate grade point average.

Zero-order correlations are the simple bivariate Pearson correlations between the dependent variable and the independent variables.

The partial correlation of .887 is the correlation between GRE-total and graduate GPA (dependent variable) when the linear effect of undergraduate GPA has been removed from both GRE-total and graduate GPA. Squaring this indicates that 78.7% of the variation in graduate GPA that is not explained by undergraduate GPA is explained by GRE-total.

The part correlation of .585, when squared (i.e., .342) indicates that GRE-total explains an additional 34% of the variance in graduate GPA over and above the variance in graduate GPA which is explained by undergraduate GPA.

Collinearity statistics to be reviewed under assumptions.

(continued)

TABLE 8.3 (continued)

SPSS Results for the Multiple Regression GRE–GPA Example

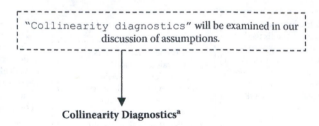

Collinearity Diagnostics[a]

Model	Dimension	Eigenvalue	Condition Index	Variance Proportions		
				(Constant)	GRE Total Score	Undergraduate Grade Point Average
1	1	2.981	1.000	.00	.00	.00
	2	.012	15.727	.03	.86	.40
	3	.007	20.537	.97	.13	.60

[a] Dependent variable: Graduate grade point average.

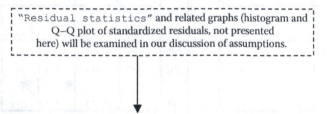

Residuals Statistics[a]

	Minimum	Maximum	Mean	Std. Deviation	N
Predicted value	3.0714	3.9448	3.5000	.31597	11
Std. predicted value	−1.357	1.408	.000	1.000	11
Standard error of predicted value	.038	.079	.058	.011	11
Adjusted predicted value	3.0599	3.9117	3.4954	.30917	11
Residual	−.19943	.17207	.00000	.10082	11
Std. residual	−1.769	1.527	.000	.894	11
Stud. residual	−1.881	1.716	.017	1.008	11
Deleted residual	−.22531	.21754	.00458	.12935	11
Stud. deleted residual	−2.355	2.020	.000	1.145	11
Mahal. distance	.240	4.053	1.818	1.048	11
Cook's distance	.012	.260	.092	.081	11
Centered leverage value	.024	.405	.182	.105	11

[a] Dependent variable: Graduate grade point average.

TABLE 8.3 (continued)

SPSS Results for the Multiple Regression GRE–GPA Example

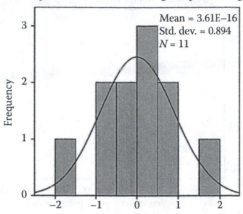

Histogram
Dependent variable: Graduate grade point average

Mean = 3.61E–16
Std. dev. = 0.894
$N = 11$

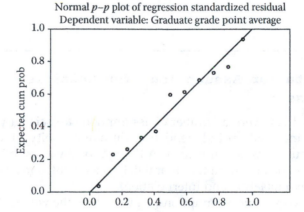

Normal p–p plot of regression standardized residual
Dependent variable: Graduate grade point average

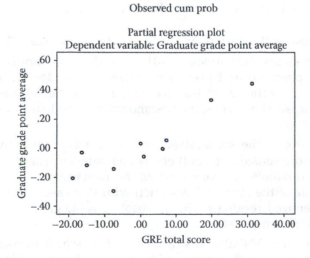

Partial regression plot
Dependent variable: Graduate grade point average

(continued)

TABLE 8.3 (continued)

SPSS Results for the Multiple Regression GRE–GPA Example

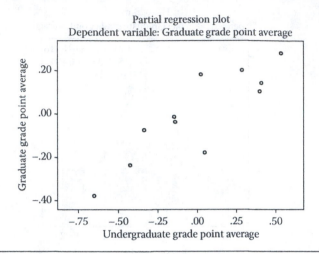

Examining Data for Assumptions for Multiple Linear Regression

As you may recall, there were a number of assumptions associated with multiple linear regression. These included (a) independence, (b) homogeneity of variance, (c) linearity, (d) normality, and (e) multicollinearity. Although fixed values of X were discussed in assumptions, this is not an assumption that will be tested but is instead related to the use of the results (i.e., extrapolation and interpolation).

Before we begin to examine assumptions, let us review the values that we requested to be saved to our dataset (see dataset screenshot that follows).

1. **PRE _ 1** represents the unstandardized predicted values (i.e., Y_i').

2. **RES _ 1** represents the unstandardized residuals, simply the difference between the observed and predicted values. For student 1, for example, the observed value for the GGPA (i.e., the dependent variable) was 4, and the predicted value was 3.94483. Thus, the unstandardized residual is simply 4 – 3.94483, or .05517.

3. **SRE _ 1** represents the studentized residuals, a type of standardized residual that is more sensitive to outliers as compared to standardized residuals. Studentized residuals are computed as the unstandardized residual divided by an estimate of the standard deviation with that case removed. As a rule of thumb, studentized residuals with an absolute value greater than 3 are considered outliers (Stevens, 1984).

4. **MAH _ 1** represents Mahalanobis distance values which measure how far that particular case is from the average of the independent variable and thus can be

helpful in detecting outliers. These values can be reviewed to determine cases that are exerting leverage. Barnett and Lewis (1978) produced a table of critical values for evaluating Mahalanobis distance. Squared Mahalanobis distances divided by the number of variables (D^2/df) which are greater than 2.5 (for small samples) or 3–4 (for large samples) are suggestive of outliers (Hair, Black, Babin, Anderson, & Tatham, 2006). Later, we follow another convention for examining these values using the chi-square distribution.

5. **COO _ 1** represents Cook's distance values and provide an indication of influence of individual cases. As a rule of thumb, Cook's values greater than 1 suggest that case is potentially problematic.

6. **LEV _ 1** represents leverage values, a measure of distance from a respective case to the average of the predictor.

7. **SDB0 _ 1, SDB1 _ 1,** and **SDB2 _ 1** are standardized DFBETA values for the intercept and slopes, respectively, and are easier to interpret as compared to their unstandardized counterparts. Standardized DFBETA values greater than an absolute value of 2 suggest that the case may be exerting undue influence on the calculation of the parameters in the model (i.e., the slopes and intercept).

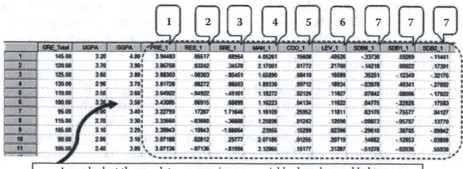

	GRE_Total	UGPA	GGPA	PRE_1	RES_1	SRE_1	MAH_1	COO_1	LEV_1	SDB0_1	SDB1_1	SDB2_1
1	145.00	3.20	4.00	3.94483	.05517	.68954	4.05261	.15608	.40526	-.33730	.59269	-.11441
2	120.00	3.70	3.90	3.86758	.03242	.34570	2.17001	.01772	.21700	-.14218	.00022	.17391
3	125.00	3.60	3.80	3.88303	-.08303	-.85451	1.65890	.08410	.16589	.35251	-.12349	-.32176
4	130.00	2.90	3.70	3.61728	.08272	.86503	1.89336	.09712	.18934	-.03978	.40341	-.27892
5	110.00	3.50	3.60	3.64922	-.04922	-.49101	1.18272	.02126	.11827	.07842	.08006	-.17822
6	100.00	3.30	3.50	3.43085	.06915	.68099	1.16223	.04134	.11622	.04775	-.22820	.17583
7	95.00	3.00	3.40	3.22793	.17207	1.71646	1.18109	.25952	.11811	.63170	-.75577	.04127
8	115.00	2.70	3.30	3.33660	-.03660	-.36688	1.25898	.01242	.12590	-.08873	-.05787	.13770
9	105.00	3.10	3.20	3.39943	-.19943	-1.88064	.23956	.15299	.02396	-.29610	.38705	-.09942
10	90.00	2.80	3.10	3.07188	.02812	.29777	2.07186	.01256	.20719	.14662	-.12853	-.03898
11	105.00	2.40	3.00	3.07136	-.07136	-.81994	3.12965	.15177	.31287	-.51278	-.02036	.55938

As we look at the raw data, we see nine new variables have been added to our dataset. These are our predicted values, residuals, and other diagnostic statistics. The residuals will be used to for diagnostics to review the extent to which our data meet the assumptions of multiple linear regression.

Independence

Here we will plot the following: (a) studentized residuals (which were requested and created through the "Save" option when generating our model) against unstandardized predicted values and (b) studentized residuals against each independent variable to examine the extent to which independence was met. The general steps for generating a simple scatterplot through "Scatter/dot" have been presented in Chapter 10 of *An Introduction to Statistical Concepts*, Third Edition, and they will not be reiterated here. From the "Simple Scatterplot" dialog screen, click the studentized residual variable and move it into the "Y Axis" box by clicking on the arrow. Click the unstandardized predicted values and move them into the "X Axis" box by clicking on the arrow. Then click "Ok." Repeat these steps to plot the studentized residual to each independent variable.

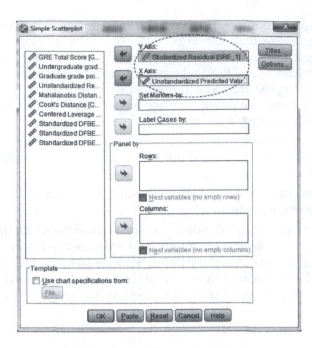

If the assumption of independence is met, the points should fall randomly within a band of −2.0 to +2.0. In this illustration (see Figure 8.1), we have evidence of independence as all points for all graphs are within an absolute value of 2.0 and fall relatively randomly.

Homogeneity of Variance

We can use the same plots that were used to examine independence. To examine the extent to which homogeneity was met, we plot (a) studentized residuals (which were requested and created through the "Save" option when generating our model) against unstandardized predicted values and (b) studentized residuals against each independent variable. Recall that homogeneity is when the dependent variable has the same variance for all values of the independent variable.

Evidence of meeting the assumption of homogeneity is a plot where the spread of residuals appears fairly constant over the range of unstandardized predicted values (i.e., a random display of points) and observed values of the independent variables. If the display of residuals increases or decreases across the plot, then there may be an indication that the assumption of homogeneity has been violated. Here we see evidence of homogeneity.

Linearity

Since we have more than one independent variable, we have to take a different approach to examining linearity than what was done with simple linear regression. However, we can use the same information gleaned from our examination of independence and homogeneity for reviewing the assumption of linearity. As those steps have been presented previously in the discussion of independence, they will not be repeated here. From the scatterplot, there is a general positive linear relationship between the variables, and, thus, we have evidence of linearity. We can also review the partial regression plots that we asked for when generating the regression model. A separate partial regression plot is provided for each independent variable, where we are looking for linearity (rather than some type of polynomial). Even with a small sample size, the partial regression plots suggest evidence of linearity.

Normality

Generating normality evidence: Understanding the distributional shape, specifically the extent to which normality is a reasonable assumption, is important in multiple linear regression just as it was in simple linear regression. We will examine residuals for normality, following the same steps as with the previous procedures. We will also use various diagnostics to examine our data for influential cases. Let us begin by examining the unstandardized residuals for normality. Just as we saw with simple linear regression, for multiple linear regression, the distributional shape of the unstandardized residuals should be normal. Because the steps for generating normality evidence were presented in previous chapters, they will not be repeated here.

Interpreting normality evidence: By this point, we are well versed in interpreting quite a range of normality statistics and will do the same for multiple linear regression.

Descriptives

			Statistic	Std. Error
Unstandardized residual	Mean		.0000000	.03039717
	95% Confidence interval for mean	Lower bound	−.0677291	
		Upper bound	.0677291	
	5% Trimmed mean		.0015202	
	Median		.0281190	
	Variance		.010	
	Std. deviation		.10081601	
	Minimum		−.19943	
	Maximum		.17207	
	Range		.37150	
	Interquartile range		.14051	
	Skewness		−.336	.661
	Kurtosis		.484	1.279

The skewness statistic of the residuals is −.336 and kurtosis is .484—both being within the range of an absolute value of 2.0, suggesting some evidence of normality. Given the very small sample size, the following histogram reflects as normal a distribution as might be expected.

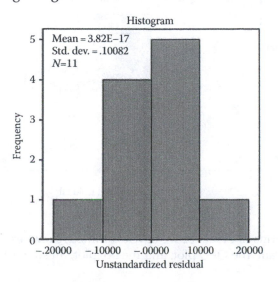

Histogram

Mean = 3.82E−17
Std. dev. = .10082
N=11

There are a few other statistics that can be used to gauge normality. The formal test of normality, the Shapiro–Wilk (S–W) test (*SW*) (Shapiro & Wilk, 1965), provides evidence of the extent to which our sample distribution is statistically different from a normal distribution. The output for the S–W test is presented as follows and suggests that our sample distribution for the residual is *not* statistically significantly different than what would be expected from a normal distribution as the *p* value is greater than α (*p* = .918).

Tests of Normality

	Kolmogorov–Smirnov[a]			Shapiro–Wilk		
	Statistic	df	Sig.	Statistic	df	Sig.
Unstandardized residual	.155	11	.200*	.973	11	.918

[a] Lilliefors significance correction.
*This is a lower bound of the true significance.

Q–Q plots are also often examined to determine evidence of normality. Q–Q plots graph quantiles of the theoretical normal distribution against quantiles of the sample distribution. Points that fall on or close to the diagonal line suggest evidence of normality. The Q–Q plot of residuals (see Figure 8.2) suggests relative normality. Examination of the following boxplot also suggests a relatively normal distribution of residuals with no outliers.

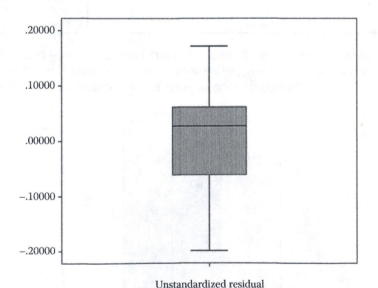

Unstandardized residual

Considering the forms of evidence we have examined, skewness and kurtosis statistics, the S–W test, histogram, the Q–Q plot, and the boxplot, all suggest normality is a reasonable assumption.

Screening Data for Influential Points

Casewise diagnostics: Recall that we requested a number of statistics to help in diagnostics. One that we requested was for "Casewise diagnostics." If we had any cases with large values for the standardized residual (outside three standard deviations), information would have been included in our output to indicate the case number, value of the standardized residual, predicted value, and unstandardized residual. This information can be used to more closely examine case(s) with the extreme values on the standardized residuals.

Cook's distance: Cook's distance provides an overall measure for the influence of individual cases. Values greater than 1 suggest that the case may be problematic in terms of undue influence on the model. Examining the residual statistics in our output (see following table), we see that the maximum value for Cook's distance is .260, well under the point at which we should be concerned.

Residuals Statistics[a]

	Minimum	Maximum	Mean	Std. Deviation	N
Predicted value	3.0714	3.9448	3.5000	.31597	11
Std. predicted value	−1.357	1.408	.000	1.000	11
Standard error of predicted value	.038	.079	.058	.011	11
Adjusted predicted value	3.0599	3.9117	3.4954	.30917	11
Residual	−.19943	.17207	.00000	.10082	11
Std. residual	−1.769	1.527	.000	.894	11
Stud. residual	−1.881	1.716	.017	1.008	11
Deleted residual	−.22531	.21754	.00458	.12935	11
Stud deleted residual	−2.355	2.020	.000	1.145	11
Mahal distance	.240	4.053	1.818	1.048	11
Cook's distance	.012	.260	.092	.081	11
Centered leverage value	.024	.405	.182	.105	11

[a] Dependent variable. Graduate grade point average.

Mahalanobis distances: Mahalanobis distances are measures of the distance from each case to the mean of the independent variable for the remaining cases. We can use the value of Mahalanobis distance as a test statistic value with the chi-square distribution. With two independent variables and one dependent variable, we have three degrees of freedom. Given an alpha level of .05, the chi-square critical value is 7.82. Thus, any Mahalanobis distance greater than 7.82 suggests that case is an outlier. With a maximum of 4.053 (see previous table), there is no evidence to suggest there are outliers in our data.

Centered leverage values: Centered leverage values less than .20 suggest there are no problems with cases that are exerting undue influence. Values greater than .5 indicate problems.

DFBETA: We also asked to save DFBETA values. These values provide another indication of the influence of cases. DFBETA provides information on the change in the predicted value when the case is deleted from the model. For standardized DFBETA values, values greater than an absolute value of 2.0 should be examined more closely. Looking at the minimum and maximum DFBETA values, there are no cases suggestive of undue influence.

Descriptive Statistics

	N	Minimum	Maximum
Standardized DFBETA intercept	11	−.51278	.63170
Standardized DFBETA GRE total	11	−.75577	.59269
Standardized DFBETA UGPA	11	−.32176	.55938
Valid N (listwise)	11		

Diagnostic plots: There are a number of diagnostic plots that can be generated from the values we saved. For example, a plot of Cook's distance against centered leverage values provides a way to identify influential cases (i.e., cases with leverage of .50 or above and Cook's distance of 1.0 or greater). Here there are no cases that suggest undue influence.

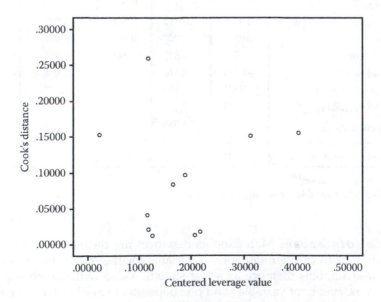

Multicollinearity

Generating multicollinearity evidence: Multicollinearity, as you recall, refers to strong correlations between the independent variables. Detecting multicollinearity can be done by reviewing the VIF and tolerance statistics. From the following table, we see tolerance and VIF values. Tolerance is calculated as $(1 − R^2)$, and values close to 0 (a rule of thumb is .10 or less) suggest potential multicollinearity problems. Why? A tolerance of .10 suggests that 90% (or more) of the variance in one of the independent variables can be explained by another independent variable. VIF is the "variance inflation factor" and is the reciprocal of tolerance where $VIF = \dfrac{1}{tolerance}$. VIF values greater than 10 (which correspond to a tolerance of .10) suggest potential multicollinearity.

Collinearity Statistics	
Tolerance	VIF
.909	1.100
.909	1.100

Collinearity diagnostics (see the following SPSS output) can also be reviewed. "Dimension 1" refers to the intercept; however, we are interested in reviewing data for "dimensions 2 and 3." Multiple eigenvalues close to 0 indicate independent variables that have strong intercorrelations. The condition index is calculated as the square root of the ratio of the largest eigenvalue to each preceding eigenvalue (e.g., $\sqrt{\dfrac{2.981}{.012}} = 15.76$). Condition indices greater than 15 suggest there is a possible problem with multicollinearity, and values greater than 30 indicate a substantial multicollinearity problem. In this case, both the eigenvalues and condition indices suggest possible problems with multicollinearity.

Collinearity Diagnostics[a]

Model	Dimension	Eigenvalue	Condition Index	(Constant)	GRE Total Score	Variance Proportions: Undergraduate Grade Point Average
1	1	2.981	1.000	.00	.00	.00
	2	.012	15.727	.03	.86	.40
	3	.007	20.537	.97	.13	.60

[a] Dependent variable: Graduate grade point average.

Multicollinearity can also be examined by computing regression models where each independent variable is considered the outcome and is predicted by the remaining independent variables (the dependent variable is not included in these models). Because the steps for conducting regression have already been presented, they will not be repeated again. Click one of the independent variables (e.g., "UGPA") and move it into the "Dependent" box by clicking the arrow button. Click the remaining independent variable(s) and move those into the "Independent(s)" box by clicking the arrow button.

Interpreting multicollinearity evidence: If any of the resultant R_k^2 values are close to 1 (greater than .9 is a good rule of thumb), then there may be a collinearity problem. For the example data, $R_{12}^2 = .091$ and therefore collinearity is not a concern. Note that in multiple regression situations where there are two independent variables (as in this example with GRE total and UGPA), only one regression needs to be conducted to check for multicollinearity as the results for regressing UGPA on GRE total are the same as regressing GRE total on UGPA.

Model	R	R Square	Adjusted R Square	Std. Error of the Estimate
1	.301[a]	.091	−.010	16.41926

8.8 G*Power

A priori and post hoc power could again be determined using the specialized software described previously in this text (e.g., G*Power), or you can consult a priori power tables (e.g., Cohen, 1988). As an illustration, we use G*Power to compute the post hoc power of our test.

Post Hoc Power for Multiple Linear Regression Using G*Power

The first thing that must be done when using G*Power for computing post hoc power is to select the correct test family. In our case, we conducted a multiple linear regression. To find regression, we select "Tests" in the top pulldown menu, then "Correlation and regression," and then "Linear multiple regression: Fixed model, R^2 deviation from zero." This will allow us to determine power for the hypothesis that the overall multiple R^2 is equal to 0 (i.e., power for the overall regression model). Once that selection is made, the "Test family" automatically changes to "F test."

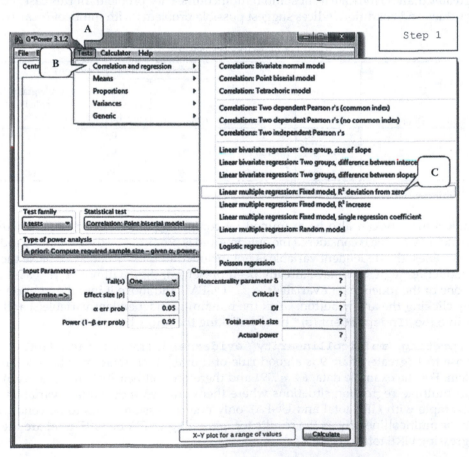

The "`Type of Power Analysis`" desired needs to be selected. To compute post hoc power, select "`Post hoc: Compute achieved power—given α, sample size, and effect size.`"

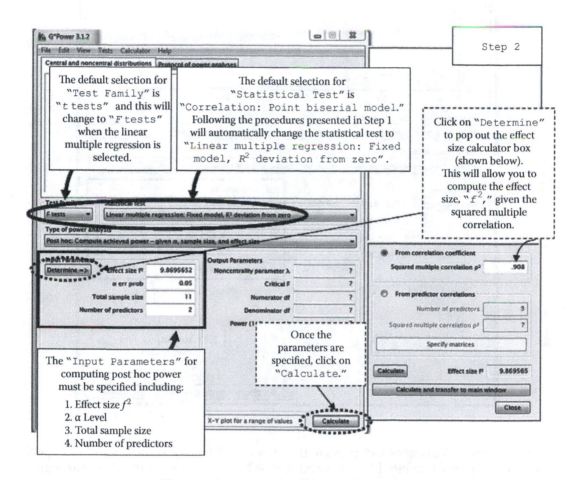

The "`Input Parameters`" must then be specified. We compute the effect size, f^2, last and so we skip that for the moment. The α level we used was .05, the total sample size was 11, and there were two independent variables. Next we use the pop-out effect size calculator in G*Power to compute the effect size f^2. To do this, click on "`Determine`" which is displayed under "`Input Parameters.`" In the pop-out effect size calculator, input the value for the squared multiple correlation. Click on "`Calculate`" to compute the effect size f^2. Then click on "`Calculate and Transfer to Main Window`" to transfer the calculated effect size (i.e., 9.8695652) to the "`Input Parameters.`" Once the parameters are specified, click on "`Calculate`" to find the power statistics.

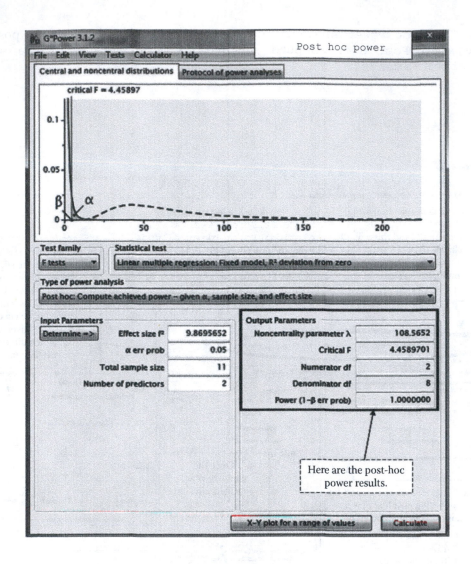

The "Output Parameters" provide the relevant statistics given the input just specified. Here we were interested in determining post hoc power for a multiple linear regression with a computed effect size f^2 of 9.8695652, an alpha level of .05, total sample size of 11, and two predictors. Based on those criteria, the post hoc power for the overall multiple linear regression model was 1.0000. In other words, given the input parameters, the probability of rejecting the null hypothesis when it is really false (in this case, the probability that the multiple correlation coefficient is 0) was at the maximum (i.e., 1.00) (sufficient power is often .80 or above). Do not forget that conducting power analysis a priori is recommended so that you avoid a situation where, post hoc, you find that the sample size was not sufficient to reach the desired level of power (given the observed parameters). Conducting power for change in R^2 and for the slopes can be conducted similarly by selecting the test family of "Linear multiple regression: Fixed model, R^2 increase" or "Linear multiple regression: Fixed model, single regression coefficient," respectively.

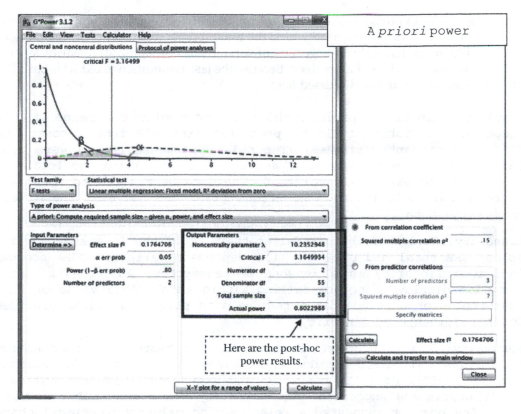

A Priori Power for Multiple Linear Regression Using G*Power

For a priori power, we can determine the total sample size needed for multiple linear regression given the estimated effect size f^2, α level, desired power, and number of predictors. We follow Cohen's (1988) conventions for effect size (i.e., small $r^2 = .02$; moderate $r^2 = .15$; large $r^2 = .35$). If we had estimated a moderate effect r^2 of .15, alpha of .05, observed power of .80, and two independent variables, we would need a total sample size of 58.

8.9 Template and APA-Style Write-Up

Finally, here is an example paragraph for the results of the multiple linear regression analysis. Recall that our graduate research assistant, Marie, was assisting the assistant dean in Graduate Student Services, Jennifer. Jennifer wanted to know if GGPA could be predicted by the total score on the required graduate entrance exam (GRE total) and by UGPA. The research question presented to Jennifer from Marie included the following: *Can GGPA be predicted from the GRE total and UGPA?*

Marie then assisted Jennifer in generating a multiple linear regression as the test of inference, and a template for writing the research question for this design is presented as follows:

- Can [dependent variable] be predicted from [list independent variables]?

It may be helpful to preface the results of the multiple linear regression with information on an examination of the extent to which the assumptions were met. The assumptions include (a) independence, (b) homogeneity of variance, (c) normality, (d) linearity, (e) non-collinearity, and (f) values of X are fixed. Because the last assumption (fixed X) is based on interpretation, it will not be discussed here.

A multiple linear regression model was conducted to determine if GGPA (dependent variable) could be predicted from GRE total scores and UGPA (independent variables). The null hypotheses tested were that the multiple R^2 was equal to 0 and that the regression coefficients (i.e., the slopes) were equal to 0. The data were screened for missingness and violation of assumptions prior to analysis. There were no missing data.

Linearity: Review of the partial scatterplot of the independent variables (GRE total and UGPA) and the dependent variable (GGPA scores) indicates linearity is a reasonable assumption. Additionally, with a random display of points falling within an absolute value of 2, a scatterplot of unstandardized residuals to predicted values provided further evidence of linearity.

Normality: The assumption of normality was tested via examination of the unstandardized residuals. Review of the S–W test for normality ($SW = .973$, $df = 11$, $p = .918$) and skewness (–.336) and kurtosis (.484) statistics suggested that normality was a reasonable assumption. The boxplot suggested a relatively normal distributional shape (with no outliers) of the residuals. The Q–Q plot and histogram suggested normality was reasonable. Examination of casewise diagnostics, including Mahalanobis distance, Cook's distance, DfBeta values, and centered leverage values, suggested there were no cases exerting undue influence on the model.

Independence: A relatively random display of points in the scatterplots of studentized residuals against values of the independent variables and studentized residuals against predicted values provided evidence of independence. The Durbin–Watson statistic was computed to evaluate independence of errors and was 2.116, which is considered acceptable. This suggests that the assumption of independent errors has been met.

Homogeneity of variance: A relatively random display of points, where the spread of residuals appears fairly constant over the range of values of the independent variables (in the scatterplots of studentized residuals against predicted values and studentized residuals against values of the independent variables) provided evidence of homogeneity of variance.

Multicollinearity: Tolerance was greater than .10 (.909), and the variance inflation factor was less than 10 (1.100), suggesting that multicollinearity was not an issue. However, the eigenvalues for the predictors were close to 0 (.012 and .007). A review of GRE total regressed on UGPA, however, produced a multiple R squared of .091, which suggests noncollinearity. In aggregate, therefore, the evidence suggests that multicollinearity is not an issue.

Here is an APA-style example paragraph of results for the multiple linear regression (remember that this will be prefaced by the previous paragraph reporting the extent to which the assumptions of the test were met).

The results of the multiple linear regression suggest that a significant proportion of the total variation in GGPA was predicted by GRE total and UGPA, $F(2, 8) = 39.291$, $p < .001$. Additionally, we find the following:

1. For GRE total, the unstandardized partial slope (.012) and standardized partial slope ·(.614) are statistically significantly different from 0 ($t = 5.447$, $df = 8$, $p < .001$); with every one-point increase in the GRE total, GGPA will increase by approximately 1/100 of one point when controlling for UGPA.

2. For UGPA, the unstandardized partial slope (.469) and standardized partial slope (.567) are statistically significantly different from 0 ($t = 5.030$, $df = 8$, $p < .001$); with every one-point increase in UGPA, GGPA will increase by approximately one-half of one point when controlling for GRE total.

3. The CI around the unstandardized partial slopes do not include 0 (GRE total, .007, .018; UGPA, .254, .684), further confirming that these variables are statistically significant predictors of GGPA. Thus, GRETOT and UGPA were shown to be statistically significant predictors of GGPA, both individually and collectively.

4. The intercept (or average GGPA when GRE total and UGPA is 0) was .638, not statistically significantly different from 0 ($t = 1.954$, $df = 8$, $p = .087$).

5. Multiple R^2 indicates that approximately 91% of the variation in GGPA was predicted by GRE total scores and UGPA. Interpreted according to Cohen (1988), this suggests a large effect.

6. Estimated power to predict multiple R^2 is at the maximum, 1.00.

We note that the more advanced regression models described in this chapter can all be conducted using SPSS. For further information on regression analysis with SPSS, see Morgan and Griego (1998), Weinberg and Abramowitz (2002), and Meyers et al. (2006).

8.10 Summary

In this chapter, methods involving multiple predictors in the regression context were considered. The chapter began with a look at partial and semipartial correlations. Next, a lengthy discussion of multiple linear regression analysis was conducted. Here we

extended many of the basic concepts of simple linear regression to the multiple predictor context. In addition, several new concepts were introduced, including the coefficient
of multiple determination, the multiple correlation, and tests of the individual regression
coefficients. Finally we examined a number of other regression models, such as forward
selection, backward elimination, stepwise selection, all possible subsets regression, hierarchical regression, and nonlinear regression. At this point, you should have met the following objectives: (a) be able to determine and interpret the results of part and semipartial
correlations, (b) be able to understand the concepts underlying multiple linear regression,
(c) be able to determine and interpret the results of multiple linear regression, (d) be able to
understand and evaluate the assumptions of multiple linear regression, and (e) be able to have
a basic understanding of other types of regression models. In Chapter 9, we conclude the
text by considering logistic regression analysis.

Problems

Conceptual Problems

8.1 The correlation of salary and cumulative GPA controlling for socioeconomic status
is an example of which one of the following?

a. Bivariate correlation

b. Partial correlation

c. Regression correlation

d. Semipartial correlation

8.2 Variable 1 is to be predicted from a combination of variable 2 and one of variables 3,
4, 5, and 6. The correlations of importance are as follows:

$r_{13} = .8$ $r_{23} = .2$

$r_{14} = .6$ $r_{24} = .5$

$r_{15} = .6$ $r_{25} = .2$

$r_{16} = .8$ $r_{26} = .5$

Which of the following multiple correlation coefficients will have the largest value?

a. $r_{1.23}$

b. $r_{1.24}$

c. $r_{1.25}$

d. $r_{1.26}$

8.3 The most accurate predictions are made when the standard error of estimate equals
which one of the following?

a. $\bar{Y}$

b. s_Y

c. 0

d. 1

8.4 The intercept can take on a positive value only. True or false?

8.5 Adding an additional predictor to a regression equation will necessarily result in an increase in R^2. True or false?

8.6 The best prediction in multiple regression analysis will result when each predictor has a high correlation with the other predictor variables and a high correlation with the dependent variable. True or false?

8.7 Consider the following two situations:

Situation 1 $r_{Y1} = .6$ $r_{Y2} = .5$ $r_{12} = .0$

Situation 2 $r_{Y1} = .6$ $r_{Y2} = .5$ $r_{12} = .2$

I assert that the value of R^2 will be greater in situation 2. Am I correct?

8.8 Values of variables X_1, X_2, and X_3 are available for a sample of 50 students. The value of $r_{12} = .6$. I assert that if the partial correlation $r_{12.3}$ were calculated, it would be larger than .6. Am I correct?

8.9 A researcher is building a regression model. There is theory to suggest that science ability can be predicted by literacy skills when controlling for child characteristics (e.g., age and socioeconomic status). Which one of the following variable selection procedures is suggested?

    a. Backward elimination

    b. Forward selection

    c. Hierarchical regression

    d. Stepwise selection

8.10 I assert that the forward selection, backward elimination, and stepwise regression methods will always arrive at the same final model, given the same dataset and level of significance? Am I correct?

8.11 I assert the R_{adj}^2 will always be larger for the model with the most predictors. Am I correct?

8.12 In a two-predictor regression model, if the correlation among the predictors is .95 and VIF is 20, then we should be concerned about collinearity. True or false?

Computational Problems

8.1 You are given the following data, where X_1 (hours of professional development) and X_2 (aptitude test scores) are used to predict Y (annual salary in thousands):

Y	X_1	X_2
40	100	10
50	200	20
50	300	10
70	400	30
65	500	20
65	600	20
80	700	30

Determine the following values: intercept, b_1, b_2, SS_{res}, SS_{reg}, F, s_{res}^2, $s(b_1)$, $s(b_2)$, t_1, t_2.

8.2   You are given the following data, where X_1 (final percentage in science class) and X_2 (number of absences) are used to predict Y (standardized science test score in third grade):

Y	X_1	X_2
300	65	7
480	98	0
350	70	3
420	80	2
400	82	0
335	70	3
370	75	4
390	80	1
485	99	0
415	95	2
375	88	3

Determine the following values: intercept, b_1, b_2, SS_{res}, SS_{reg}, F, s^2_{res}, $s(b_1)$, $s(b_2)$, t_1, t_2.

8.3   Complete the missing information for this regression model ($df = 23$).

Y'	=	25.1	+	1.2X_1	+	1.0X_2	−	.50X_3	
		(2.1)		(1.5)		(1.3)		(.06)	Standard errors
		(11.9)		()		()		()	t ratios
		()		()		()		()	Significant at .05?

8.4   Consider a sample of elementary school children. Given that r(strength, weight) = .6, r(strength, age) = .7, and r(weight, age) = .8, what is the first-order partial correlation coefficient between strength and weight holding age constant?

8.5   For a sample of 100 adults, you are given that r_{12} = .55, r_{13} = .80, and r_{23} = .70. What is the value of $r_{12(2.3)}$?

8.6   A researcher would like to predict salary from a set of four predictor variables for a sample of 45 subjects. Multiple linear regression analysis was utilized. Complete the following summary table (α = .05) for the test of significance of the overall regression model:

Source	SS	df	MS	F	Critical Value and Decision
Regression	—	—	20	—	
Residual	400	—	—		
Total	—	—			

8.7   Calculate the partial correlation $r_{12.3}$ and the part correlation $r_{1(2.3)}$ from the following bivariate correlations: r_{12} = .5, r_{13} = .8, r_{23} = .9.

8.8   Calculate the partial correlation $r_{13.2}$ and the part correlation $r_{1(3.2)}$ from the following bivariate correlations: r_{12} = .21, r_{13} = .40, r_{23} = −.38.

8.9 You are given the following data, where X_1 (verbal aptitude) and X_2 (prior reading achievement) are to be used to predict Y (reading achievement):

Y	X_1	X_2
2	2	5
1	2	4
1	1	5
1	1	3
5	3	6
4	4	4
7	5	6
6	5	4
7	7	3
8	6	3
3	4	3
3	3	6
6	6	9
6	6	8
10	8	9
9	9	6
6	10	4
6	9	5
9	4	8
10	4	9

Determine the following values: intercept, b_1, b_2, SS_{res}, SS_{reg}, F, s_{res}^2, $s(b_1)$, $s(b_2)$, t_1, t_2.

8.10 You are given the following data, where X_1 (years of teaching experience) and X_2 (salary in thousands) are to be used to predict Y (morale):

Y	X_1	X_2
125	1	24
130	2	30
145	3	32
115	2	28
170	6	40
180	7	38
165	5	48
150	4	42
195	9	56
180	10	52
120	2	33
190	8	50
170	7	49
175	9	53
160	6	49

Determine the following values: intercept, b_1, b_2, SS_{res}, SS_{reg}, F, s_{res}^2, $s(b_1)$, $s(b_2)$, t_1, t_2.

Interpretive Problems

8.1 Use SPSS to develop a multiple regression model with the example survey 1 dataset on the website. Utilize current GPA as the dependent variable and find at least two strong predictors from among the continuous variables in the dataset. Write up your results, including interpretation of effect size and testing of assumptions.

8.2 Use SPSS to develop a multiple regression model with the example survey 1 dataset on the website. Utilize how many hours of television watched per week as the dependent variable and find at least two strong predictors from among the continuous variables in the dataset. Write up your results, including interpretation of effect size and testing of assumptions.

9

Logistic Regression

Chapter Outline

Key Concepts

1. Logit
2. Odds
3. Odds ratio

In the past two chapters, we have examined ordinary least squares (OLS) regression—simple and multiple regression models—that allow us to examine the relationship between one or more predictors when the outcome is continuous. In this chapter, we are introduced to logistic regression, which can be used when the outcome is categorical. For the purposes of this chapter, we will concentrate on binary logistic regression which is used when the outcome has only two categories (i.e., dichotomous, binary, or sometimes referred to as a Bernoulli outcome). The logistic regression procedure appropriate for more than two categories is called multinomial (or polytomous) logistic regression. Readers interested in learning more about multinomial logistic regression will be provided some additional references later in this chapter. Also in this chapter, we discuss methods that can be used to enter predictors in logistic regression models. Our objectives are that by the end of this chapter, you will be able to (a) understand the concepts underlying logistic regression, (b) determine and interpret the results of logistic regression, (c) understand and evaluate the assumptions of logistic regression, and (d) have a basic understanding of methods of entering the covariates.

9.1 How Logistic Regression Works

We conclude the textbook as Marie embarks on her most challenging statistical project to date.

With excitement, Marie is finishing up her graduate program in educational research and has been assigned by her faculty advisor to one additional consultation. Malani is a faculty member in the early childhood department and has collected data on 20 children who will be entering kindergarten in the fall. Interested in kindergarten readiness issues, Malani wants to know if a teacher observation scale for social development and family structure (single family vs. two-family home) can predict whether children are prepared or unprepared to enter kindergarten. Marie suggests the following research question to Malani: *Can kindergarten readiness (prepared vs. unprepared) be predicted by social development and family structure (single family vs. two-family home)?* Given that the outcome is dichotomous, Marie determines that binary logistic regression is the appropriate statistical procedure to use to answer Malani's question. Marie then proceeds with assisting Malani in analyzing the data.

If the dependent variable is binary (i.e., dichotomous or having only two categories), then none of the regression methods described so far in this text are appropriate. Although simple and multiple regression can easily accommodate dichotomous independent variables through dummy coding (i.e., assignment of 1 and 0 to the categories), it is an entirely different case when the *outcome* is dichotomous. Applying OLS regression to a binary outcome creates problems. For example, a dichotomous outcome violates normality and homogeneity assumptions in OLS regression. In addition, OLS estimates are based on linear relationships between the independent and dependent variables, and forcing a linear relationship (as seen in Figure 9.1) in the case of a binary outcome is erroneous [although we found at least one author (Hellevik, 2009) who argues that OLS regression can be used with dichotomous outcomes].

As part of the regression family, logistic regression still allows a prediction to be made; however, now the prediction is whether or not the unit under investigation falls into one of the two categories of the dependent variable. Initially used mostly in the hard sciences, this method has become more broadly popular in recent years as there are many situations where researchers want to examine outcomes that are discrete, rather than continuous, in nature. Some examples of dichotomous dependent variables are pass/fail, surviving

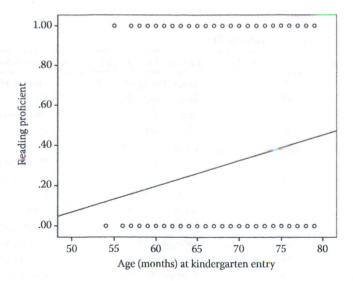

FIGURE 9.1
Nonlinearity of binary outcome.

surgery/not, admit/reject, vote for/against, employ/not, win/lose, or purchase/not. The idea of using a dichotomous variable was introduced in Chapter 8 as the concept of a *dummy variable*, where the first condition is indicated by a value of 1 (e.g., prepared for kindergarten), whereas a value of 0 indicates the opposite condition (e.g., unprepared for kindergarten). For the purposes of this text, our discussion will concentrate on dichotomous outcomes where logistic regression is appropriate (i.e., binary logistic regression, referred to throughout this chapter simply as logistic regression). Conditions for which there are more than two possible categories for the dependent variable (e.g., three categories, such as remain in the teaching profession, remain in teaching but change schools, or leave the teaching profession entirely), multinomial logistic regression may be appropriate. An example of the data structure for a logistic regression model with a binary outcome (prepared vs. unprepared for kindergarten), one continuous predictor (social development), and one dichotomous dummy coded predictor (family structure: single-parent vs. two-parent home) is presented in Table 9.1.

9.2 Logistic Regression Equation

As we learned previously with OLS regression, knowledge of the independent variable(s) provides the information necessary to be able to estimate a precise numerical value of the dependent variable, a predicted value. The following formula recaps the sample multiple regression equation where Y is the predicted outcome for individual i based on (a) the Y intercept, a, the value of Y when all predictor values are 0; (b) the product of the value of the independent variables, Xs, and the regression coefficients, b_k; and (c) the residual, ε_i:

$$Y_i = a + b_1X_1 + \dots + b_mX_m + \varepsilon_i$$

TABLE 9.1

Kindergarten Readiness Example Data

Child	Social Development (X_1)	Family Structure (X_2)	Kindergarten Readiness (Y)
1	15	Single family (0)	Unprepared (0)
2	12	Single family (0)	Unprepared (0)
3	18	Single family (0)	Prepared (1)
4	20	Single family (0)	Prepared (1)
5	11	Single family (0)	Unprepared (0)
6	17	Single family (0)	Prepared (1)
7	14	Single family (0)	Unprepared (0)
8	18	Single family (0)	Prepared (1)
9	13	Single family (0)	Unprepared (0)
10	10	Single family (0)	Unprepared (0)
11	22	Two-parent home (1)	Unprepared (0)
12	25	Two-parent home (1)	Prepared (1)
13	23	Two-parent home (1)	Prepared (1)
14	21	Two-parent home (1)	Prepared (1)
15	30	Two-parent home (1)	Prepared (1)
16	27	Two-parent home (1)	Prepared (1)
17	26	Two-parent home (1)	Prepared (1)
18	28	Two-parent home (1)	Prepared (1)
19	24	Two-parent home (1)	Unprepared (0)
20	30	Two-parent home (1)	Prepared (1)

As we see, the logistic regression equation is similar in concept to simple and multiple linear regression, but operates much differently. In logistic regression, the binary dependent variable is transformed into a logit variable (which is the natural log of the odds of the dependent variable occurring or not occurring), and the parameters are then estimated using maximum likelihood. The end result is that the odds of an event occurring are estimated through the logistic regression model (whereas OLS estimates a precise numerical value of the dependent variable).

To understand how the logistic regression equation operates, there are three primary computational concepts that must be understood: probability, odds, and the logit. These express the same thing, only in different ways (Menard, 2000). Let us first consider probability.

9.2.1 Probability

The overarching difference between OLS regression (i.e., simple and multiple linear regression) and logistic regression is the measurement scale of the outcome. With OLS regression, our outcome is continuous in scale (i.e., interval or ratio measurement scale). In binary logistic regression, our outcome is dichotomous—one of two categories. Let us use kindergarten readiness ("prepared for kindergarten" coded as "1" vs. unprepared coded as "0") as an example of our logistic regression outcome. Therefore, what the regression equation allows us to predict is substantially different for OLS as compared to logistic regression. In comparison to OLS, which allows us to compute a precise numerical value (e.g., a specific predicted score for the dependent variable), the logistic regression equation allows us to compute a *probability*—more specifically, the *probability* that the dependent variable will occur. The logistic regression equation, therefore, generates predicted probabilities that fall between values of 0 and 1. The probability of a case or unit being classified into the lowest numerical category [i.e., $P(Y = 0)$, or in the case of our example, the probability that a child will be unprepared for kindergarten] is equal to 1 minus the probability that it falls within the highest numerical category [i.e., $P(Y = 1)$, or the probability that a child will be prepared for kindergarten]. This equates to $P(Y = 0) = 1 - P(Y = 1)$. Applied to our example, the probability that a child will be unprepared for kindergarten is equal to 1 minus the probability that a child will be prepared for kindergarten. In other words, the knowledge of the probability of one category occurring (e.g., unprepared for kindergarten) allows us to easily determine the probability that the other category will occur (e.g., prepared) as the total probability must equal 1.0. Remember, however, that probabilities have to fall within the range of 0 to 1. As we know from Chapter 5 of *An Introduction to Statistical Concepts*, Third Edition, it is not possible to have a negative probability, nor is it possible to have a probability greater than 1 (i.e., greater than 100%). If we try to model the probability as the dependent variable in our OLS equation, it is mathematically possible that the predicted values would be negative or greater than 1—values that are outside the range of what is feasible when considering probabilities. Therefore this is where our logistic regression equation takes a turn from what we learned with linear regression.

9.2.2 Odds and Logit (or Log Odds)

So far, we have talked about the outcome of our logistic regression equation as being a probability, and we also know that predicted probabilities must be between 0 and 1. As we think about how to estimate probabilities, we will see that this takes a few steps to achieve. Rather than the dependent variable being a probability, if it were an *odds value*, then values greater than 1 would be possible and appropriate. **Odds** are simply the ratio of the probability of the dependent variable's two outcomes. The odds that the outcome of a binary variable is 1 (i.e., public school attendance) rather than 0 (or private school attendance) is simply the ratio of the odds that Y is equal 1 to the odds that Y does not equal 1. In mathematical terms, this can be written as follows:

$$Odds(Y = 1) = \frac{P(Y = 1)}{1 - P(Y = 1)}$$

As we see in Table 9.2, when the probability that $Y = 1$ (e.g., prepared for kindergarten) equals .50 (column 1 in Table 9.2), then $1 - P(Y = 1)$ (or unprepared for kindergarten) is .50 (column 2) and the odds are equal to 1.00 (column 3). When the probability of $Y = 1$

TABLE 9.2

Illustration of Logged Odds

$P(Y = 1)$	$1 - P(Y = 1)$	$Odds(Y = 1) = \dfrac{P(Y = 1)}{1 - P(Y = 1)}$	$\ln[Odds(Y = 1)] = \ln\left[\dfrac{P(Y = 1)}{1 - P(Y = 1)}\right]$
.001	.999	$.001/.999 = .001$	$ln(.001) = -6.908$
.100	.900	$.100/.900 = .111$	$ln(.111) = -2.198$
.300	.700	$.300/.700 = .429$	$ln(.429) = -.846$
.500	.500	$.500/.500 = 1.000$	$ln(1.000) = .000$
.700	.300	$.700/.300 = 2.333$	$ln(2.333) = .847$
.900	.100	$.900/.100 = 9.000$	$ln(9.000) = 2.197$
.999	.001	$.999/.001 = 999.000$	$ln(999) = 6.907$

(e.g., prepared) is very small (say, .100 or less), then the odds for being prepared for kindergarten are also very small and approach 0 the smaller the probability that $Y = 1$ (i.e., the smaller
the probability that a child is prepared for kindergarten). However, as the probability of $Y = 1$
(e.g., being prepared for kindergarten) increases, the odds (column 3) increase tremendously.
Thus, the issue that we are faced with when using odds is that while odds can be infinitely
large, we are still limited in that the minimum value is 0 and we still do not have data that can
be modeled linearly.

Changing the scale of the odds by taking the natural logarithm of the odds (also called
logit Y or *log odds*) provides us with a value of the dependent variable that can theoretically
range from negative infinity to positive infinity. Thus, taking the log odds of Y creates a
linear relationship between X and the probability of Y (Pampel, 2000). The natural log of
the odds is calculated as follows with the residual being the difference between the predicted probability and the actual value of the dependent variable (0 or 1):

$$\ln \frac{P(Y=1)}{1-P(Y=1)} = Logit(Y)$$

In column 4 of Table 9.2, we see what happens when the logit transformation is made. As
the odds increase from 1 to positive infinity, the logit (or log odds) of Y becomes larger and
larger (and remains positive). As the odds decrease from 1 to 0, the logit (or log odds) of
Y is negative and grows larger and larger (in absolute value).

The logit of Y equation is interpreted very similarly to that of OLS. For each one-unit
change in the independent variable, the logistic regression coefficients represent the change
in the predicted log odds of being in a category. In comparison to OLS regression, the
regression coefficients have the exact same interpretation. The difference in interpretation
with logistic regression is that the outcome now represents a *log odds* rather than a precise
numerical value as we saw with OLS regression. Linking the logit back to probabilities, a
one-unit change in the logit equals a bigger change in probabilities that are near the center
as compared to the extreme values. This happens because of the linearization once we
take the natural log. Taking the natural log stretches the S-shaped curve into a linear form;
thus, the values at the extreme are stretched less, so to speak, as compared to the values
in the middle (Pampel, 2000). By working with log odds, our familiar additive regression
equation is applicable:

$$\ln \frac{P(Y=1)}{1-P(Y=1)} = Logit(Y) = \alpha + \beta_1 X_1 + \beta_2 X_2 + ... + \beta_m X_m$$

It is important to note that although we were accustomed to examining standardized
regression coefficients in OLS regression, it is not the norm that standardized coefficients
are computed for logistic regression models by statistical software. Standardization is
ordinarily accomplished by taking the product of the unstandardized regression coefficient and the ratio of the standard deviation of X to the standard deviation of Y. The
interpretation of a standard deviation change in a continuous variable thus makes sense;
however, this is not the case for a dichotomous variable, nor is it the case for the log odds
(which is the predicted outcome and which does not have a standard deviation).

While interpretation of the logistic equation is relatively straightforward as it holds
many similarities to OLS regression, log odds are not a metric that we use often. Therefore
understanding what it means when a predictor, X, has some effect on the log odds, Y, can
be difficult. This is where odds come back into the picture.

If we exponentiate the logit (Y) (i.e., the outcome of our logistic regression equation), then it converts back to the odds (see the following equation). Now we can interpret the independent variables as affecting the odds (rather than log odds) of the outcome:

$$Odds(Y = 1) = e^{\text{logit}(Y)} = e^{\ln[Odds(Y=1)]} = e^{\alpha+\beta_1 X_1+\beta_2 X_2+...+\beta_m X_m} = (e^{\alpha})(e^{\beta_1 X_1})(e^{\beta_2 X_2})...(e^{\beta_m X_m})$$

As can be seen here, the exponentiation creates an equation that is multiplicative rather than additive, and this then changes the interpretation of the exponentiated coefficients. In previous regression equations we have studied, when the product of the regression coefficient and its predictor is 0, that variable adds nothing to the prediction of the dependent variable. In a multiplicative environment, a value of 0 corresponds to a coefficient of 1. In other words, a coefficient of 1 will not change the value of the odds (i.e., the outcome). Coefficients greater than 1 increase the odds, and coefficients less than 1 decrease the odds. In addition, the odds will change more the greater the distance the value is from 1.

Converting the odds back to a probability can be done through the following formula:

$$P(Y = 1) = \frac{Odds(Y = 1)}{1 + Odds(Y = 1)} = \frac{e^{\alpha+\beta_1 X_1+\beta_2 X_2+...+\beta_m X_m}}{1 + e^{\alpha+\beta_1 X_1+\beta_2 X_2+...+\beta_m X_m}}$$

Probability values close to 1 indicate increased likelihood of occurrence. In our example, since "1" indicates public school attendance, a probability close to 1 would indicate a child was more likely to attend public school. Children with probabilities close to 0 suggest a decreased probability of attending public school (and increased probability of attending private school).

9.3 Estimation and Model Fit

Now that we understand the logistic regression process and resulting equations a bit better, it is time to turn our attention to how the equation is estimated and how we can determine how well the model fits. We previously learned with simple and multiple regression that the data from the observed values of the independent variables in the sample were used to estimate or predict the values of the dependent variable. In logistic regression, we are also using the knowledge of the values of our predictor(s) to estimate the outcome (i.e., log odds). Now we are using a method called maximum likelihood estimation to estimate the values of the parameters (i.e., the logistic coefficients). As we just learned, the dependent variable in a logistic regression model is transformed into a logit value, which is the natural log of the odds of the dependent variable occurring or not occurring. Maximum likelihood estimation is then applied to the model and estimates the odds of occurrence after transformation into the logit. Very simply, maximum likelihood estimates the parameters most likely to occur given the patterns in the sample data. Whereas in OLS the sum of squared distance of the observed data to the regression line was minimized, in maximum likelihood the log likelihood is maximized.

The log of the likelihood function (sometimes abbreviated as *LL*) that results from ML estimation then reflects the likelihood of observing the sample statistics given the population parameters. The log likelihood provides an index of how much has not been explained in the model after the parameters have been estimated, and as such, the *LL* can be used as an indicator of model fit. The values of the log likelihood function vary from 0 to negative infinity, with values closer to 0 suggesting better model fit and larger values (in absolute value terms) indicating poorer fit. The log likelihood value will approach 0 the closer the likelihood value is to 1. When this happens, this suggests the observed data could be generated from these population parameters. In other words, the smaller the log likelihood, the better the model fit. It follows therefore, that the log likelihood value will grow more negative the closer the likelihood function is to 0. This suggests that the observed data are *less* likely to be generated from these population parameters.

Maximum likelihood estimation performed by statistical software usually begins the estimation process with all regression coefficients equal to the most conservative estimate (i.e., the least squares estimates). Better model fit is accomplished through the use of an algorithm which generates new sets of regression coefficients that produce larger log likelihoods. This is an iterative process that stops when the selection of new parameters creates very little change in the regression coefficients and very small increases in the log likelihood—so small that there is little value in any further estimation.

9.4 Significance Tests

As with multiple regression, there are two tests of significance in logistic regression. Specifically, these involve testing the significance of the overall logistic regression model and testing the significance of each of the logistic regression coefficients.

9.4.1 Test of Significance of Overall Regression Model

The first test is the test of statistical significance to determine overall model fit and provides evidence of the extent to which the predicted values accurately represent the observed values (Xie, Pendergast, & Clarke, 2008). We consider several overall model tests including (a) change in log likelihood, (b) Hosmer–Lemeshow goodness-of-fit test, (c) pseudovariance explained, and (d) predicted group membership. Additional work (e.g., Xie et al., 2008) has recently been conducted on new methods to assess model fit, but these are not currently available in statistical software nor easily computed. Also in this section, we briefly address sensitivity, specificity, false positive, false negative, and cross validation.

9.4.1.1 Change in Log Likelihood

One way to test overall model fit is the likelihood ratio test. This test is based on the change in the log likelihood function from a smaller model (often the baseline or intercept only model) to a larger model that includes one or more predictors (sometimes referred to as the fitted model). Although we indicate that the smaller model is often the intercept only model, this test can also be used to examine changes in model fit from one fitted model to another fitted model and we will discuss this in a bit. This likelihood ratio test is similar to the overall F test in OLS regression and tests the null hypothesis that all the regression coefficients are equal to 0. Using statistical notation, we can denote the null and alternative hypotheses for the regression coefficients as follows:

$$H_0: \beta_1 = \beta_2 = \cdots = \beta_m = 0$$

$$H_1: H_0 \text{ is false}$$

For explanation purposes, we assume the smaller model is the baseline or intercept only model. The baseline log likelihood is estimated from a logistic regression model that includes only the constant (i.e., intercept) term. The model log likelihood is estimated from the logistic regression model that includes the constant and the relevant predictor(s). By multiplying the difference in these log likelihood functions by -2, a chi-square test is produced with degrees of freedom equal to the difference in the degrees of freedom of the models ($df = df_{model} - df_{baseline}$) (where "model" refers to the fitted model that includes one or more predictors). In the case of the constant only model, there is only one parameter estimated (i.e., the intercept), so there is only one degree of freedom. In models that include independent variables, the degrees of freedom are equal to the number of independent variables in the model plus one for the constant. The larger the difference between the baseline and model LL values, the better the model fit. It is important to note that the log likelihood difference test assumes nested models. In other words, all elements that are included in the baseline or smallest model must also be included in the fitted model. As alluded to previously, the change in log likelihood test can be used for more than just comparing the intercept only model to a fitted model. Researchers often use this test in the model building process to determine if adding predictors (or sets of predictors) aids in model fit by comparing one fitted model to another fitted model. In general, the change in log likelihood is computed as follows:

$$\chi^2 = -2(LL_{model} - LL_{baseline})$$

9.4.1.2 Hosmer–Lemeshow Goodness-of-Fit Test

The Hosmer–Lemeshow goodness-of-fit test is another tool that can be used to examine overall model fit. The Hosmer–Lemeshow statistic is computed by dividing cases into deciles (i.e., 10 groups) based on their predicted probabilities. Then a chi-square value is computed based on the observed and expected frequencies. This is a chi-square test for which the researcher does *not* want to find statistical significance. Nonstatistically significant results for the Hosmer–Lemeshow test indicate the model has acceptable fit. In other words, the predicted or estimated model is not statistically significantly different from the observed values. Although the Hosmer–Lemeshow test can easily be requested in SPSS, it has been criticized for being conservative (i.e., lacking sufficient power to detect lack of fit in instances such as nonlinearity of an independent variable), too likely to indicate model fit when five or fewer groups (based on the decile groups created in computing the statistic) are used to calculate the statistic, and offers little diagnostics to assist the researcher when the test indicates poor model fit (Hosmer, Hosmer, LeCessie, & Lemeshow, 1997).

9.4.1.3 *Pseudovariance Explained*

Another overall model fit index for logistic regression is pseudovariance explained. This index is akin to multiple R^2 (or the coefficient of determination) in OLS regression, and can also be considered an effect size measure for the model. The reason these values are considered pseudovariance explained in logistic regression is that the variance in a dichotomous outcome, as evident in logistic regression, differs as compared to the variance of a continuous outcome, as present in OLS regression.

There are a number of multiple R^2 pseudovariance explained values that can be computed in logistic regression. We discuss the following: (a) Cox and Snell (1989), (b) Nagelkerke (1991), (c) Hosmer and Lemeshow (1989), (d) Aldrich and Nelson (1984), (e) Harrell (1986), and (f) traditional R^2. Of these, SPSS automatically computes the Cox and Snell and Nagelkerke indices. There is, however, no consensus on which (if any) of the pseudovariance explained indices are best, and many researchers choose not to report any of them in their published results. If you do choose to use and/or report one or more of these values, they should be used only as a guide "without attributing great importance to a precise figure" (Pampel, 2000, p. 50).

The Cox and Snell R^2 (1989) is computed as the ratio of the likelihood values raised to the power of $2/n$ (where n is sample size). A problem is that the computation is such that the theoretical maximum of 1 cannot be obtained, even when there is perfect prediction:

$$R_{CS}^2 = 1 - \left(\frac{LL_{baseline}}{LL_{model}} \right)^{2/n}$$

Nagelkerke (1991) adjusts the Cox and Snell value so that the maximum value of 1 can be achieved, and it is computed as follows:

$$R_N^2 = \frac{R_{CS}^2}{1 - (LL_{baseline})^{2/n}}$$

Hosmer and Lemeshow's (1989) R^2 is the proportional reduction in the log likelihood (in absolute value terms). Although not provided by SPSS, it can easily be computed by the ratio of the model to baseline $-2LL$. Ranging from 0 to 1, this value provides an indication of how much the badness of fit of the baseline model is improved by the inclusion of the predictors in the fitted model. Hosmer and Lemeshow's (1989) R^2 is computed as

$$R_L^2 = \frac{-2LL_{model}}{-2LL_{baseline}}$$

Harrell (1986) proposed that Hosmer and Lemeshow's R^2 be adjusted for the number of parameters (i.e., independent variables) in the model. This adjustment (where m equals the number of independent variables in the model) to the computation makes this R^2 value akin to the adjusted R^2 in OLS regression. It is computed as

$$R_{LA}^2 = \frac{(-2LL_{model}) - 2m}{-2LL_{baseline}}$$

Aldrich and Nelson (1984) provided an alternative to the R_L^2 that is equivalent to the squared contingency coefficient. This measure has the same problem as the Cox and Snell R^2; the theoretical maximum of 1 cannot be obtained even when the independent variable(s) perfectly predict the outcome. It is computed as

$$pseudo\ R^2 = \frac{-2LL_{model}}{-2LL_{model} + n}$$

The traditional R^2, the coefficient of determination as used in simple and multiple regression, can also be used in logistic regression (only with binary logistic regression, as the mean and variance of a dichotomous variable make sense; however the mean, for example, in a dummy coded variable situation, is equal to the proportion of cases in the category labeled as 1). R^2 can be computed by correlating the observed values of the binary dependent variable with the predicted values (i.e., predicted probabilities) obtained from the logistic regression model and then squaring the correlated value. Predicted probability values can easily be saved when generating logistic regression models in SPSS.

9.4.1.4 Predicted Group Membership

Another test of model fit for logistic regression can be accomplished by evaluating predicted to observed group membership. Assuming a cut value of .50, cases with predicted probabilities at .5 or above are predicted as 1 and predicted probabilities below .5 are predicted as 0. A crosstab table of predicted to observed predicted probabilities provides the frequency and percentage of cases correctly classified. Correct classification would be seen in cases that have the same value for both the predicted and observed values. A perfect model produces 100% correctly classified cases. A model that classifies no better than chance would provide 50% correctly classified cases. Press's Q is a chi-square statistic with one degree of freedom and can be used as a formal test of classification accuracy. It is computed as

$$Q = \frac{[N-(nK)]^2}{N(K-1)}$$

where
   N is the total sample size
   n represents the number of cases that were correctly classified
   K equals the number of groups

As with other chi-square statistics we have examined, this test is sensitive to sample size. Also, it is important to note that focusing solely on the correct classification overall (as is done with Press's Q) may result in overlooking one or more groups that have unacceptable classification. The researcher should evaluate the classification of each group in addition to the overall classification.

   Sensitivity is the probability that a case coded as 1 for the dependent variable (a.k.a. "positive") is classified correctly. In other words, sensitivity is the percentage of correct predictions of the cases that are coded as 1 for the dependent variable. In the kindergarten readiness example that we will review later, of those 12 children who were prepared for kindergarten (i.e., coded as 1 for the dependent variable), 11 were correctly classified. Thus, the sensitivity is 11/12 or about 92%.

Specificity is the probability that a case coded as 0 for the dependent variable (a.k.a. "negative") is classified correctly. In other words, specificity is the percentage of correct predictions of the cases that are coded as 0 for the dependent variable. In the kindergarten readiness example that we will review later, of those 8 children who were unprepared for kindergarten (i.e., coded as 0 for the dependent variable), 7 were correctly classified. Thus, the specificity is 7/8, or 87.5%.

False positive rate is the probability that a case coded as 0 for the dependent variable (a.k.a. "negative") is classified *incorrectly*. In other words, this is the percentage of cases in error where the dependent variable is predicted to be 1 (i.e., prepared), but in fact the observed value is 0 (i.e., unprepared). In the kindergarten readiness example that we will review later, of those 8 children who were unprepared for kindergarten (i.e., coded as 0 for the dependent variable), 1 was incorrectly classified. Thus, the false positive rate is 1/8, or 12.5%. The false positive rate is also computed as 1 minus specificity.

False negative rate is the probability that a case coded as 1 for the dependent variable (a.k.a. "positive") is classified *incorrectly*. In other words, this is the percentage of cases in error where the dependent variable is predicted to be 0 (i.e., unprepared), but in fact the observed value is 1 (i.e., prepared). In the kindergarten readiness example that we will review later, of those 12 children who were prepared for kindergarten (i.e., coded as 1 for the dependent variable), 1 was incorrectly classified. Thus, the false negative rate is 1/12, or about 8%. The false negative rate is also computed as 1 minus sensitivity.

9.4.1.5 Cross Validation

A recommended best practice in logistic regression is to cross validate the results. If the sample size is sufficient, this can be accomplished by using 75%–80% of the sample to derive the model and then use the remaining cases (the holdout sample) to determine its accuracy. With cross validation, you are in essence testing the model on two samples— a primary sample (which represents the largest percentage of the sample size) and a holdout sample (that which remains). If classification accuracy of the holdout sample is within 10% of the primary sample, this provides evidence of the utility of the logistic regression model.

9.4.2 Test of Significance of Logistic Regression Coefficients

The second test in logistic regression is the test of the statistical significance of each regression coefficient, b_k. This test allows us to determine if the individual coefficients are statistically significantly different from 0. The null and alternative hypotheses can be illustrated in the same mathematical notation as we used with OLS regression:

$$H_0: \beta_k = 0$$

$$H_1: \beta_k \neq 0$$

Interpreting the test provides evidence of the probability of obtaining the observed sample coefficient by chance if the null hypothesis was true (i.e., if the population regression coefficient value was 0). The Wald statistic, which follows a chi-square distribution, is used as the test statistic for regression coefficients in SPSS. For continuous predictors, this is calculated by squaring the ratio of the regression coefficient divided by its standard error:

$$W = \frac{\beta_k^2}{SE_{\beta_k^2}}$$

When the logistic regression coefficients are large (in absolute value), rounding error can create imprecision in estimation of the standard errors. This can result in inaccuracies in testing the null hypothesis, and more specifically, increased Type II errors (i.e., failing to reject the null hypothesis when the null hypothesis is false). An alternative to the Wald test, in situations such as this, is the difference in log likelihood test previously described to compare models with and without the variable of interest (Pampel, 2000).

Raferty (1995) proposed a Bayesian information criterion (BIC), computed as the difference between the chi-square value and the natural log of the sample size, that could also be applied to testing logistic regression coefficients:

$$BIC = \chi^2 - \ln n$$

To reject the null hypothesis, the BIC should be positive (i.e., greater than 0). That is, the chi-square value must be greater than the natural log of the sample size. BIC values below 0 suggest that the variable contributes little to the model. BIC values between 0 and +2 are considered weak; between 2 and 6, positive; between 6 and 10, strong; and more than 10, very strong.

Beyond determining statistical significance of the individual predictors, you may also want to assess which predictors are adding the most to the model. In OLS regression, we examined the standardized regression coefficients. There are no traditional standardized regression coefficients provided in SPSS for logistic regression, but they are easy to calculate. Simply standardize the predictors before generating the logistic regression model, and then run the model as desired. You can then interpret the logistic regression coefficients as standardized regression coefficients (if necessary, review Chapter 8).

We can also form a confidence interval (CI) around the logistic regression coefficient, b_k. The CI formula is the same as in OLS regression: the logistic regression coefficient plus or minus the product of the tabled critical value and the standard error:

$$CI(b_k) = b_k \pm {}_{(\alpha/2)}t_{(n-m-1)}s_b$$

The null hypothesis that we tested was H_0: $\beta_k = 0$. It follows that if our CI contains 0, then the logistic regression coefficient (b_k) is not statistically significantly different from 0 at the specified significance level. We can interpret this to say that β_k will be included in $(1 - \alpha)\%$ of the sample CIs formed from multiple samples.

9.5 Assumptions and Conditions

Compared to OLS regression, the assumptions of logistic regression are somewhat relaxed; however four primary assumptions must still be considered: (a) noncollinearity, (b) linearity, (c) independence of errors, and (d) values of X are fixed. In this section, we also discuss conditions that are needed in logistic regression as well as diagnostics that can be performed to more closely examine the data.

9.5.1 Assumptions

9.5.1.1 Noncollinearity

Noncollinearity is applicable to logistic regression models with multiple predictors just as it was in multiple regression (but is not applicable when there is only one predictor in any regression model). This assumption has already been explained in detail in Chapter 8 and thus will not be reiterated other than to explain tools that can be used to detect multicollinearity. Although SPSS does not provide an option to easily generate collinearity statistics in logistic regression, you can generate an OLS regression model (i.e., a traditional multiple linear regression) with the same variables used in the logistic regression model and request collinearity statistics there. Because it is only the collinearity statistics that are of interest, do not be concerned in generating an OLS regression model that violates some of OLS basic assumptions (e.g., normality). We have previously discussed tolerance and the variance inflation factor (VIF) as two collinearity diagnostics (where tolerance is computed as $1 - R_k^2$, where R_k^2 is the variance in each independent variable, X, explained by the other independent variables, and VIF is $\frac{1}{1 - R_k^2}$. In reviewing these statistics, tolerance values less than .20 suggest multicollinearity exists, and values less than .10 suggest serious multicollinearity. VIF values greater than 10 indicate a violation of noncollinearity.

The effects of a violation of noncollinearity in logistic regression are the same as that in Chapter 8. First, it will lead to instability of the regression coefficients across samples, where the estimates will bounce around quite a bit in terms of magnitude, and even occasionally result in changes in sign (perhaps opposite of expectation). This occurs because the standard errors of the regression coefficients become larger, thus making it more difficult to achieve statistical significance. Another result that may occur involves an overall regression that is significant, but none of the individual predictors are significant. Violation will also restrict the utility and generalizability of the estimated regression model.

9.5.1.2 Linearity

In OLS regression, the dependent variable is assumed to have a linear relationship with the continuous independent variable(s), but this does not hold in logistic regression. Because the outcome in logistic regression is a logit, the assumption of linearity in logistic regression refers to linearity between *logit of the dependent variable* and the continuous independent variable(s). Hosmer and Lemeshow (1989) suggest several strategies for detecting nonlinearity, the easiest of which to apply is likely the Box–Tidwell transformation. This strategy is also valuable as it is not overly sensitive to minor violations of linearity. This involves generating a logistic regression model that includes all independent variables of interest along with an interaction term for each—the interaction term being the product of the continuous independent variable and its natural log [i.e., $X*\ln(X)$]. Statistically significant interaction terms suggest nonlinearity. It is important to note that the assumption of linearity is applicable only for continuous predictors. A violation of linearity can result in biased parameter estimates, as well as the expected change in the logit of Y not being constant across the values of X.

9.5.1.3 Independence of Errors

Independence of errors is applicable to logistic regression models just as it was with OLS regression, and a violation of this assumption can result in underestimated standard errors (and thus overestimated test statistic values and perhaps finding statistical significance more often than is really viable, as well as affecting CIs). This assumption has already been explained in detail during the discussion of assumptions in Chapters 7 and 8, and, thus, additional information will not be provided here.

9.5.1.4 Fixed X

The last assumption is that the values of X_k are **fixed**, where the independent variables X_k are fixed variables rather than random variables. Because this assumption was discussed in detail in Chapters 7 and 8, we only summarize the main points. When X is fixed, the regression model is only valid for those particular values of X_k that were actually observed and used in the analysis. Thus, the same values of X_k would be used in replications or repeated samples. As discussed in the previous two chapters, generally we may not want to make predictions about individuals having combinations of X_k scores outside of the range of values used in developing the prediction model; this is defined as *extrapolating* beyond the sample predictor data. On the other hand, we may not be quite as concerned in making predictions about individuals having combinations of X_k scores within the range of values used in developing the prediction model; this is defined as *interpolating* within the range of the sample predictor data. Table 9.3 summarizes the assumptions of logistic regression and the impact of their violation.

9.5.2 Conditions

Although not assumptions, the following conditions should be met with logistic regression: nonzero cell counts, nonseparation of data, lack of influential points, and sufficient sample size.

9.5.2.1 Nonzero Cell Counts

The first condition is related to nonzero cell counts in the case of nominal independent variables. A zero cell count occurs when the outcome is constant for one or more categories

TABLE 9.3

Assumptions and Violation of Assumptions: Logistic Regression Analysis

Assumption	Effect of Assumption Violation
Noncollinearity of Xs	• Regression coefficients can be quite unstable across samples (as standard errors are larger) • Restricted generalizability of the model
Linearity	• Bias in slopes and intercept • Expected change in logit of Y is not a constant and depends on value of X
Independence	• Influences standard errors of the model and thus hypothesis tests and CIs
Values of Xs are fixed	• Extrapolating beyond the range of X combinations: prediction errors larger, may also bias slopes and intercept • Interpolating within the range of X combinations: smaller effects than when extrapolating; if other assumptions met, negligible effect

Statistical Concepts: A Second Course

of a nominal variable (e.g., all females pass the course). This results in high standard errors because entire groups of individuals have odds of 0 or 1. Strategies to remove zero cell counts include recoding the categories (e.g., collapsing categories) or adding a constant to each cell of the crosstab table. If the overall model fit is what is of primary interest, then you may choose not to do anything about zero cell counts. The overall relationship between the set of predictors and the dependent variable is not generally impacted by zero cell counts. However, if zero cell counts are retained and the results of the individual predictors are what is of interest, it would be wise to provide a limitation to your results recognizing higher standard errors that are produced due to zero cell counts as well as caution that the values of the individual regression coefficients may be affected. Careful review of the data prior to computing the logistic regression model can help thwart potential problems with zero cell counts.

9.5.2.2 Nonseparation of Data

Another condition that should be examined is that of complete or quasi-complete separation. Complete separation arises when the dependent variable is perfectly predicted and results in an inability to estimate the model. Quasi-complete separation occurs when there is less than complete separation and results in extremely large coefficients and standard errors. These conditions may occur when the number of variables equals (or nearly equals) the number of cases in the dataset, such that large coefficients and standard errors result.

9.5.2.3 Lack of Influential Points

Outliers and influential cases are problematic in logistic regression analysis just as with OLS regression. Severe outliers can cause the maximum likelihood estimator to reduce to 0 (Croux, Flandre, & Haesbroeck, 2002). Residual analysis and other diagnostic tests are equally beneficial for detecting miscoded data and unusual (and potentially influential) cases in logistic regression as it is in OLS regression. SPSS provides the option for saving a number of values including predicted values, residuals, and influence statistics. Both probabilities and group membership predicted values can be saved. Residuals that can be saved include (a) unstandardized, (b) logit, (c) studentized, (d) standardized, and (e) deviance. The three types of influence values that can be saved include Cook's, leverage values, and DfBeta.

The wide variety of values that can be saved suggests that there are many types of diagnostics that can be performed. Review should be conducted when standardized or studentized residuals are greater than an absolute value of 3.0 and DfBeta values are greater than 1. Leverage values greater than $(m + 1)/N$ (where m equals the number of independent variables) indicate an influential case (values closer to 1 suggest problems, while those closer to 0 suggest little influence). If outliers or influential cases are found, it is up to you to decide if removal of the case is warranted. It may be that they, while uncommon, are completely plausible so that they are retained in the model. If they are removed from the model, it is important to report the number of cases that were removed prior to analysis (and evidence to suggest what caused you to remove them). A review of Chapters 7 and 8 provides further details on diagnostic analysis of outliers and influential cases.

9.5.2.4 Sample Size

Simulation research suggests that logistic regression is best used with large samples. Samples of size 100 or greater are needed to accurately conduct tests of significance for logistic regression coefficients (Long, 1997). Note that for illustrative purposes, the example in this chapter uses a sample size of 20. We recognize this is insufficient in practice, but have used it for greater ease in presenting the data.

9.6 Effect Size

We have already talked about multiple R^2 pseudovariance explained values which can be used not only to gauge model fit but also as measures of effect size. Another important statistic in logistic regression is the **odds ratio** (*OR*), also an effect size index that is similar to R^2. The odds ratio is computed by exponentiating the logistic regression coefficient e^{b_k}. Conceptually this is the odds for one category (e.g., prepared for kindergarten) divided by the odds for the other category (e.g., unprepared for kindergarten). The null hypothesis to be tested is that $OR = 1$, which indicates that there is no relationship between a predictor variable and the dependent variable. Thus, we want to find *OR* to be significantly different from 1.

When the independent variable is continuous, the odds ratio represents the amount by which the odds change for a one-unit increase in the independent variable. When the odds ratio is greater than 1, the independent variable increases the odds of occurrence. When the odds ratio is less than 1, the independent variable decreases the odds of occurrence. The odds ratio is provided in SPSS output as "Exp(B)" in the table labeled "Variables in the Equation." In predicting kindergarten readiness, social development is a continuous covariate with a resulting odds ratio of 2.631. We can interpret this odds ratio to be that for every one-unit increase in social development, the odds of being ready for kindergarten (i.e., prepared) increase by 263%, controlling for the other variables in the model.

In the case of categorical variables, including dichotomous, multinomial, and ordinal variables, odds ratios are often interpreted in terms of their relative size or the change in odds ratios in comparing models. Consider first the case of a dichotomous variable. In the model predicting kindergarten readiness, type of household is one independent variable included in the model where a two-parent home is coded as "1" and a single-parent home as "0." An odds ratio of .002 indicates that the odds of being prepared for kindergarten (compared to unprepared for kindergarten) are decreased by a factor of .002 by being in a single-parent home (as opposed to living in a two-family home). We could also state that the odds that a child from a single-parent home will be prepared for kindergarten are .998 (i.e., 1 − .002).

In the case of a categorical variable with more than two categories, the odds ratio is interpreted relative to the reference (or left out) category. For example, say we have a predictor in our model that is mother's education level with categories that include (1) less than high school diploma, (2) high school diploma or GED, and (3) at least some college. Say we set the last category ("at least some college") as the reference category. An odds ratio of .86 for the category of "high school diploma or GED" for mother's education level suggests that the odds of being prepared for kindergarten (as compared to unprepared) decrease by a factor of .86 when the child's mother has a high school diploma or GED, relative to when the child's mother has at least some college, when the other variables in the model are controlled.

Odds ratio values can also be converted to Cohen's *d* using the following equation:

$$d = \frac{\ln(OR)}{1.81}$$

9.7 Methods of Predictor Entry

The three categories of model building that will be discussed include (a) simultaneous logistic regression, (b) stepwise logistic regression, and (c) hierarchical regression.

9.7.1 Simultaneous Logistic Regression

With simultaneous logistic regression, all the independent variables of interest are included in the model in one set. This method of model building is usually used when the researcher does not hypothesize that some predictors are more important than others. This method of entry allows you to evaluate the contribution of an independent variable over and above that of all other predictors in the model (i.e., each independent variable is evaluated as if it was the last one to enter the equation). One problem that may be encountered with this method of entry is related to strong correlations between the predictor and the outcome. An independent variable that has a strong bivariate correlation with the dependent variable may indicate a weak correlation when entered simultaneously with other predictors. In SPSS, this method of entry is referred to as "Enter."

9.7.2 Stepwise Logistic Regression

Stepwise logistic regression is a data-driven model building technique where the computer algorithms drive variable entry rather than theory. Issues with this type of technique have previously been outlined in the discussion associated with this method in multiple regression and thus are not rehashed here. If stepwise logistic regression is determined to be the most appropriate strategy to build your model, Hosmer and Lemeshow (2000) suggest setting a more liberal criterion for variable inclusion (e.g., α = .15 to .20). They also provide specific recommendations on dealing with interaction terms and scales of variables. Because it is only in unusual instances that this method of model building is appropriate (e.g., exploratory research), additional coverage of the suggestions by Hosmer and Lemeshow is not presented.

SPSS offers forward and backward stepwise methods. For both forward and backward methods, options include conditional, LR, and Wald. The differences between these options are mathematically driven. The LR method of entry uses the $-2LL$ for estimating entry of independent variables. The conditional method also uses the likelihood ratio test, but one that is considered to be computationally quicker. The Wald method applies the Wald test to determining entry of the independent variables. With forward stepwise methods, the model begins with a constant only, and based on some criterion, independent variables are added one at a time until a specified cutoff is achieved (e.g., all independent variables included in the model are statistically significant, and any additional variables not included in the model are not statistically significant). Backward stepwise methods work in the reverse fashion where initially all independent variables (and the constant) are included. Independent variables are then removed until only those that are statistically significant remain in the model, and including an omitted independent variable would not improve the model.

9.7.3 Hierarchical Regression

In hierarchical regression, the researcher specifies a priori a sequence for the individual predictor variables (not to be confused with hierarchical linear models, which is a regression approach for analyzing nested data collected at multiple levels, such as child, classroom, and school). The analysis proceeds in a forward selection, backward elimination, or stepwise selection mode according to a researcher-specified, theoretically based sequence, rather than an unspecified, statistically based sequence. In SPSS, this is conducted by entering predictors in **blocks** and selecting their desired method of entering variables in each block (e.g., simultaneously, forward, backward, stepwise). Because this method was explained in detail in Chapter 8 and operation of this method of variable selection is the same in logistic regression, additional information will not be presented.

9.8 SPSS

Next we consider SPSS for the logistic regression model. Before we conduct the analysis, let us review the data (note that we recognize the sample size of 20 does not meet minimum sample size criteria previously specified; however for illustrative purposes, we felt it important that we be able to show the entire dataset, and this would have been more difficult with the recommended sample size for logistic regression). With one dependent variable and two independent variables, the dataset must consist of three variables or columns, one for each independent variable and one for the dependent variable. Each row still represents one individual. As seen in the following screenshot, the SPSS data are in the form of three columns that represent the two independent variables (a continuous teacher-administered social development scale and household—a dichotomous variable, single- vs. two-adult household) and one binary dependent variable (kindergarten readiness screening test—prepared vs. not prepared). As our dependent variable is dichotomous, we will conduct binary logistic regression. When the dependent variable consists of more than two categories, multinomial logistic regression is appropriate (although not illustrated here).

		Social	Household	Readiness
The **independent variables** are labeled "Social" and "Household" where each value represents the child's score on the teacher reported social development scale (interval measurement) and whether the child lives with one or two parents (nominal measurement). A "1" for household indicates two-parents and "0" represents a single-parent family.	1	15.00	.00	.00
	2	12.00	.00	.00
	3	18.00	.00	1.00
	4	20.00	.00	1.00
	5	11.00	.00	.00
	6	17.00	.00	1.00
	7	14.00	.00	.00
The **dependent variable** is "Readiness" and represents whether or not the child is prepared for kindergarten. This is a binary variable where "1" represents "prepared" and "0" represents "unprepared."	8	18.00	.00	1.00
	9	13.00	.00	.00
	10	10.00	.00	.00
	11	22.00	1.00	.00
	12	25.00	1.00	1.00
	13	23.00	1.00	1.00
	14	21.00	1.00	1.00
	15	30.00	1.00	1.00
	16	27.00	1.00	1.00
	17	26.00	1.00	1.00
	18	28.00	1.00	1.00
	19	24.00	1.00	.00
	20	30.00	1.00	1.00

Step 1: To conduct a binary logistic regression, go to "Analyze" in the top pulldown menu, then select "Regression," and then select "Binary Logistic." Following the screenshot (step 1) that follows produces the "Logistic Regression" dialog box.

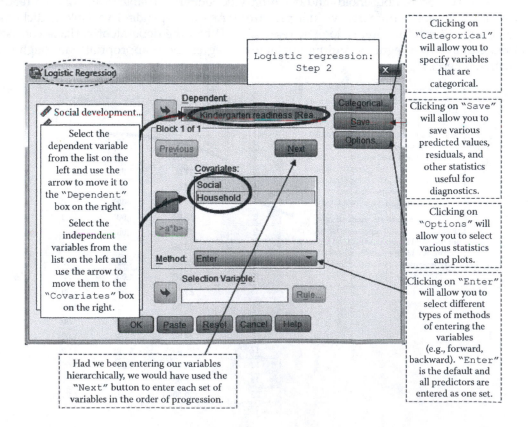

Step 2: Click the dependent variable (e.g., "Readiness") and move it into the "Dependent" box by clicking the arrow button. Click the independent variables and move them into the "Covariate(s)" box by clicking the arrow button (see screenshot step 2).

Step 3: From the "Logistics Regression" dialog box (see screenshot step 2), clicking on "Categorical" will provide the option to define as categorical those variables that are nominal or ordinal in scale as well as to select which category of the variable is the reference category through the "Define Categorical Variables" dialog box (see screenshot step 3a). From the list of covariates on the left, click the categorical covariate(s) (e.g., "Household") and move it into the "Categorical Covariates" box by clicking the arrow button. By default, "(Indicator)" will appear next to the variable name. Indicator refers to traditional dummy coding, and you have the option of selecting which value is the reference category. For binary variables (only two categories), using the "Last" value as the reference category means that the category coded with the largest value will be the category "left out" of the model (or referent), and using the "First" value as the reference category means that the category coded with the smallest value will be the category "left out" of the model. Here two-parent households were coded as 1 and single-parent households as 0. We use single-parent households (coded as 0) as the reference category. Thus, we select the radio button for "First" (see screenshot step 3a) to define single-parent households as the reference category.

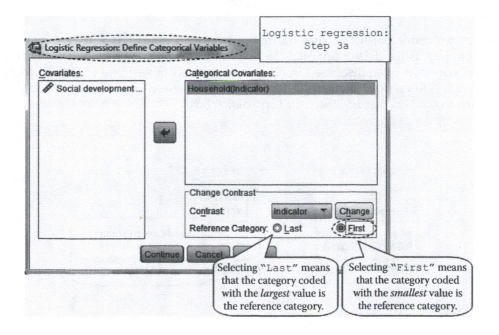

Next, we need to click the button labeled "Change" (see screenshot step 3b) to define the first value (i.e., 0 or single-parent household) as the reference (or "left out") category. By doing that, the name of our categorical covariate will now read Household(Indicator(first)). Had we had a categorical variable with more than two categories, we could just define the variable as categorical within logistic regression and select either the first or last value as the reference category. If neither the first or last were what you wanted as the reference category, then some recoding of the data is necessary.

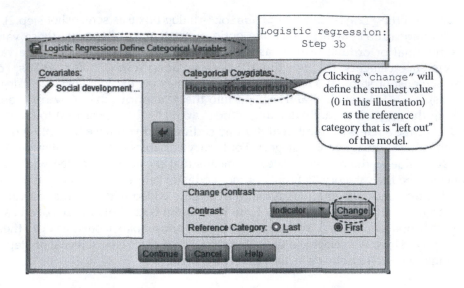

Before we move on, notice that the button for "Contrast" is a toggle menu with "Indicator" as the default option. Selecting the toggle menu allows you to select other types of contrasts often discussed in relation to analysis of variance (ANOVA) contrasts (e.g., Simple, Difference, Helmert). These will not be reviewed here. Click on "Continue" to return to the "Logistic Regression" dialog box.

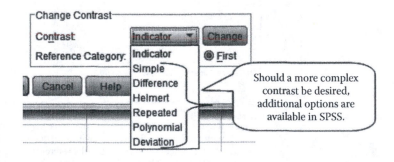

Step 4: From the "Logistic Regression" dialog box (see screenshot step 2), clicking on "Save" will provide the option to save various predicted values, residuals, and statistics that can be used for diagnostic examination. From the "Save" dialog box under the heading of **Predicted Values,** place a checkmark in the box next to the following: (1) probabilities and (2) group membership. Under the heading of **Residuals**, place a checkmark in the box next to the following: standardized. Under the heading of **Influences**, place a checkmark in the box next to the following: (1) Cook's, (2) Leverage values, and (3) DfBeta(s). Click on "Continue" to return to the original dialog box.

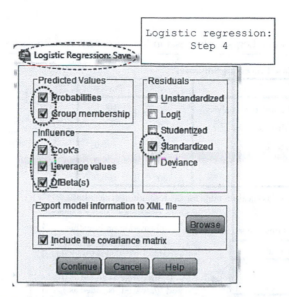

Step 5: From the "Logistic Regression" dialog box (see screenshot step 2), clicking on "Options" will allow you to generate various statistics and plots. From the "Options" dialog box under the heading of **Statistics and Plots**, place a checkmark in the box next to the following: (1) Classification plots, (2) Hosmer–Lemeshow goodness-of-fit, (3) casewise listing of residuals, (4) outliers outside, and (5) CI for exp(B). For Outliers outside, you must specify a numeric value of standard deviations to define what you consider to be an outlier. Common values may be 2 (in a normal distribution, 95% of cases will be within ±2 standard deviations), 3 (in a normal distribution, about 99% of cases will be within ±3 standard deviations), or 3.29 (in a normal distribution, about 99.9% of cases will be within ±3.29 standard deviations). For this illustration, we will use a value of 2. For CI for exp(B), you must specify a CI. This should be the complement of the alpha being tested. If you are using an alpha of .05, then the CI will be 1 − .05, or .95. All the remaining options in the "Options" dialog box will be left as the default settings. Click on "Continue" to return to the original dialog box. From the "Logistic Regression" dialog box, click on "OK" to generate the output.

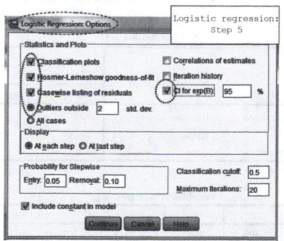

Interpreting the output: Annotated results are presented in Table 9.4.

TABLE 9.4

SPSS Results for the Binary Logistic Regression Kindergarten Readiness Example

Case Processing Summary

Unweighted Cases[a]		N	Percent
Selected cases	Included in analysis	20	100.0
	Missing cases	0	.0
	Total	20	100.0
Unselected cases		0	.0
Total		20	100.0

[a] If weight is in effect, see classification table for the total number of cases.

This table provides information on sample size and missing data. The sample size is 20 and we have no missing data.

Dependent Variables Encodings

Original Value	Internal Value
Unprepared	0
Prepared	1

Information on how the values of the dependent variable are coded is provided under "Internal Value." "Unprepared" is coded as 0 and "Prepared" is coded as 1.

Categorical Variables Codings

		Frequency	Parameter Coding (1)
Type of household	Single parent household	10	.000
	Two-parent household	10	1.000

Information on how the values of the categorical variable(s) are coded is provided as "Parameter Coding." "Single Parent Household" is coded as 0 and "Two-Parent Household" is coded as 1. The sample size per group is presented in the "Frequency" column.

Block 0: Beginning Block

Block 0 is a summary of the model with the constant only (i.e., none of the predictors are included). The classification table provides the percentage of cases correctly predicted given the constant only. Without including covariates, we can correctly predict children who are prepared for kindergarten 100% of the time but fail to predict any children (0%) who are unprepared. Here all children are predicted to be prepared.

Classification Table[a,b]

			Predicted		
			Kindergarten Readiness		Percentage Correct
Observed			Unprepared	Prepared	
Step 0	Kindergarten readiness	Unprepared	0	8	.0
		Prepared	0	12	100.0
	Overall percentage				60.0

[a] Constant is included in the model.
[b] The cut value is .500.

Variables in the Equation

		B	SE	Wald	df	Sig.	Exp(B)
Step 0	Constant	.405	.456	.789	1	.374	1.500

TABLE 9.4 (continued)

SPSS Results for the Binary Logistic Regression Kindergarten Readiness Example

Variables Not in the Equation

			Score	df	Sig.
Step 0	Variables	Social development	8.860	1	.003
		Household(1)	3.333	1	.068
	Overall statistics		11.168	2	.004

Variables not in the equation provides an indication of whether each covariate will statistically significantly contribute to predicting the outcome. Only social development ($p = .003$) is of value in the logistic model. The value of 11.168 for **overall statistics** is a residual chi-square statistic. Since the p value for it indicates statistical significance ($p = .004$), this indicates that including the two covariates improves the model as compared to the constant only model.

Block 1: Method = Enter

Method = Enter indicates that the method of entering the predictors was simultaneous entry (recall this is the default method in SPSS and is called "Enter").

Omnibus Tests of Model Coefficients

		Chi-Square	df	Sig.
Step 1	Step	15.793	2	.000
	Block	15.793	2	.000
	Model	15.793	2	.000

The $-2LL$ for the constant only model is computed as the sum of chi-square for the constant only model and $-2LL$ for the full model:

$$\chi^2_{Model} + -2LL = 15.793 + 11.128 = 26.921$$

Model Summary

Step	-2 Log Likelihood	Cox and Snell R Square	Nagelkerke R Square
1	11.128[a]	.546	.738

[a] Estimation terminated at iteration number 7 because parameter estimates changed by less than .001.

Model summary statistics provide overall model fit. For good model fit, the value of $-2LL$ for the full model (11.128) should be less than $-2LL$ for the constant only model (26.921). This is a chi-square value with degrees of freedom equal to the number of parameters in the full model (i.e., two predictors plus one constant) minus the number of parameters in the baseline model (i.e., 1). Thus there are two df using the chi-square table, with an alpha of .05 and two df, the critical value is 5.99. Since 11.128 is larger than the critical value, we reject the null hypothesis that the best prediction model is the constant only model. In other words, the full model (with predictors) is better at predicting kindergarten readiness than the constant only model.

The two R^2 values are pseudo R^2 and are interpreted similarly to multiple R^2. These can be used as effect size indices for logistic regression and Cohen's interpretations for correlation can be used to interpret. Both values indicate a large effect.

(continued)

TABLE 9.4 (continued)

SPSS Results for the Binary Logistic Regression Kindergarten Readiness Example

Hosmer and Lemeshow Test

Step	Chi-Square	df	Sig.
1	4.691	7	.698

As a measure of classification accuracy, non-statistical significance ($p= .698$) indicates good model fit for the Hosmer and Lemeshow test. This test is affected by small sample size, however; caution should be used when interpreting the results of this test when sample size is less than 50.

Contingency Table for Hosmer and Lemeshow Test

		Kindergarten Readiness = Unprepared		Kindergarten Readiness = Prepared		Total
		Observed	Expected	Observed	Expected	
Step 1	1	2	1.988	0	.012	2
	2	2	1.922	0	.078	2
	3	1	1.651	1	.349	2
	4	2	1.292	0	.708	2
	5	0	.607	2	1.393	2
	6	1	.404	2	2.596	3
	7	0	.100	2	1.900	2
	8	0	.030	2	1.970	2
	9	0	.005	3	2.995	3

The **classification table** provides information on how well group membership was predicted. Cells on the diagonal indicate correct classification. For example, children who were prepared for kindergarten were accurately classified 91.7% of the time as compared to unprepared children (87.5%). Overall, 90% of children were correctly classified. This is computed as the number of correctly classified cases divided by total sample size:

$$\frac{7+11}{20} = .90$$

Classification Table[a]

			Predicted		
			Kindergarten Readiness		Percentage Correct
Observed			Unprepared	Prepared	
Step 1	Kindergarten readiness	Unprepared	7	1	87.5
		Prepared	1	11	91.7
	Overall percentage				90.0

[a] The cut value is .500.

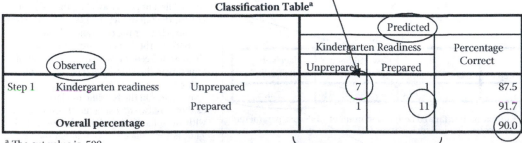

Using Press's Q and given the chi-square critical value of 3.841 ($df = 1$), we find:

$$Q = \frac{[N-(nK)]^2}{N(K-1)} = \frac{[20-(18)(2)]^2}{20(2-1)} = 12.8$$

We reject the null hypothesis. There is evidence to suggest that the predictions are statistically significantly better than chance.

TABLE 9.4 (continued)

SPSS Results for the Binary Logistic Regression Kindergarten Readiness Example

Exp(B) values are the odds ratios. The odds ratio of 2.631 for social indicates that the odds for being prepared for kindergarten are over 2–1/2 times greater (or 263%) for every one point increase in social development. The odds for household are nearly zero. This indicates that the odds for being prepared for kindergarten are about the same regardless of the child's household structure (single- versus two-parent home).

NOTE! Interpretations of *B* coefficients are usually done via odds ratios.

The *p* value for "Social" (*p*= .030) indicates that the slope is statistically significantly different from zero. This tells us that the independent variable is contributing to predicting kindergarten preparedness. The intercept (*p* = .032) is also statistically significantly different from zero.

The Wald statistic is used to test the statistical significance of each covariate.

Variables in the Equation

		B	SE	Wald	df	Sig.	Exp(B)	95% CI for Exp(B) Lower	Upper
Step 1ᵃ	Social development	.967	.446	4.696	1	.030	2.631	1.097	6.313
	Household(1)	−6.216	3.440	3.265	1	.071	.002	.000	1.693
	Constant	−15.404	7.195	4.584	1	.032	.000		

ᵃ Variable(s) entered on step 1: Social development, household.

The *B* coefficient is interpreted as the change in the logit of the dependent variable given a one-unit change in the independent variable. Recall that the logit is the natural log of the dependent variable occurring. With *B* equal to .967, this tells us that a one-unit change in social development will result in nearly a one-unit change in the logit of kindergarten preparedness. The constant is the expected value of the logit of kindergarten readiness for children of single parents (recall this was coded as 0) and when social development is zero.

Since the odds of 1.00 (which indicates similar odds for falling into either category of the outcome) are not contained within the interval for social development, this suggests the odds ratio is statistically significantly different from zero. Note that the odds ratio is only computed for the predictors and not for the intercept (i.e., constant).

A negative *B* indicates that an increase in value of that independent variable will result in an *decrease* in the predicted probability of the dependent variable.

A positive *B* indicates that an increase in value of that independent variable will result in an *increase* in the predicted probability of the dependent variable.

(continued)

TABLE 9.4 (continued)

SPSS Results for the Binary Logistic Regression Kindergarten Readiness Example

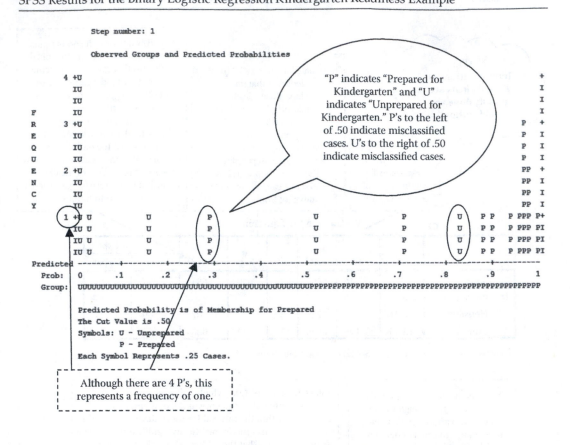

Step number: 1

Observed Groups and Predicted Probabilities

"P" indicates "Prepared for Kindergarten" and "U" indicates "Unprepared for Kindergarten." P's to the left of .50 indicate misclassified cases. U's to the right of .50 indicate misclassified cases.

Predicted Probability is of Membership for Prepared
The Cut Value is .50
Symbols: U - Unprepared
         P - Prepared
Each Symbol Represents .25 Cases.

Although there are 4 P's, this represents a frequency of one.

Casewise List[a]

Case	Selected Status[b]	Observed Kindergarten Readiness	Predicted	Predicted Group	Temporary Variable Resid	ZResid
8	S	U**	.832	P	−.832	−2.226
15	S	P**	.214	U	.786	1.918

[a] Cases with studentized residuals greater than 2.000 are listed.

[b] S = Selected, U = Unselected cases, and ** = Misclassified cases.

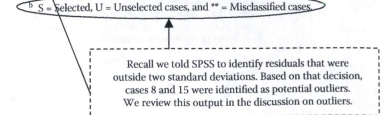

Recall we told SPSS to identify residuals that were outside two standard deviations. Based on that decision, cases 8 and 15 were identified as potential outliers. We review this output in the discussion on outliers.

Examining Data for Assumptions for Logistic Regression

Previously we described a number of assumptions used in logistic regression. These included (a) noncollinearity, (b) linearity between the predictors and logit of the dependent variable, and (c) independence of errors. We also review the data to ensure there are no outliers.

Before we begin to examine assumptions, let us review the values that we requested to be saved to our data file (see dataset screenshot that follows):

1. **PRE _ 1** represents the predicted probabilities.

2. **PGR _ 1** is the predicted group membership (here group membership is either prepared or unprepared for kindergarten).

3. **COO _ 1** represents Cook's influence statistics. As a rule of thumb, Cook's values greater than 1 suggest that case is potentially problematic.

4. **LEV _ 1** represents leverage values. As a general guide, leverage values less than .20 suggest there are no problems with cases exerting undue influence. Values greater than .5 indicate problems.

5. **ZRE _ 1** pertains to standardized residuals computed as the residual divided by an estimate of the standard deviation of the residual. Standardized residuals have a mean of 0 and standard deviation of 1.

6. **DFB0 _ 1, DFB1 _ 1,** and **DFB2 _ 1** are DfBeta values and indicate the difference in a beta coefficient if that particular case were excluded from the model.

As we look at the raw data, we see eight new variables have been added to our dataset. These are predicted values, residuals, and other diagnostic statistics.

Noncollinearity

It is not possible to request multicollinearity statistics, such as tolerance and VIF, using logistic regression in SPSS. We can, however, estimate those values by running the same variables in a multiple regression model (see Chapter 8) and requesting only the collinearity statistics. We are not interested in the parameter estimates of the model—only the collinearity statistics. Tolerance values less than .10 and VIF values greater than 10 indicate multicollinearity (Menard, 1995). Because the steps for generating multiple regression were presented in Chapter 8, we will not reiterate them here. Rather, we will merely present the applicable portion of the output of this model. From the output that follows with a tolerance of .248 and VIF of 4.037, we have evidence that we do not have multicollinearity. In examining collinearity diagnostics, condition index values that are substantially larger than others listed indicate potential problems with multicollinearity (although "substantially larger" is a subjective measure). Here the condition index of dimension 3(14.259) is about five times larger than the next largest condition index. The last three columns refer to variance proportions. Multiplying these values by 100 provides a percentage of the variance of the regression coefficient that is related to a particular eigenvalue. Multicollinearity is suggested when covariates have high percentages associated with a small eigenvalue. Thus, for purposes of reviewing for multicollinearity, concentrate only on the rows with small eigenvalues. In this example, 100% of the variance of the regression coefficient for social development and 73% for type of household are related to eigenvalue 3 (the dimension with the smallest eigenvalue). This suggests there may be some multicollinearity. In summary, we have met the assumption of noncollinearity with the tolerance and VIF values, but there is some suggestion of multicollinearity with the condition index and variance proportion values.

Coefficients[a]

Model		Collinearity Statistics	
		Tolerance	VIF
1	Social development	.248	4.037
	Type of household	.248	4.037

[a] Dependent Variable: Kindergarten readiness.

Collinearity Diagnostics[a]

Model	Dimension	Eigenvalue	Condition Index	Variance Proportions		
				(Constant)	Social Development	Type of Household
1	1	2.683	1.000	.00	.00	.01
	2	.303	2.974	.05	.00	.25
	3	.013	14.259	.95	1.00	.73

[a] Dependent Variable: Kindergarten readiness.

Linearity

Recall that the linearity assumption is applicable only to continuous variables. Thus, we will test this assumption only for social development. The Box-Tidwell transformation test can be used to test that the assumption of linearity has been met. To generate this test, for each *continuous* independent variable, we must first create an interaction term that is the product of the independent variable and its natural log (*ln*). Here we have only one continuous independent variable—social development. Thus, only one interaction term will be created.

Step 1: To create an interaction term of our continuous variable and the natural log of this variable, go to "Transform" in the top pulldown menu, then select "Compute Variable." Following the screenshot (step 1) that follows produces the "Compute Variable" dialog box.

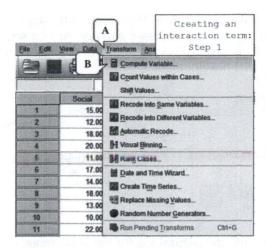

Creating an interaction term: Step 1

Step 2: In the "Target Variable" box in the upper left corner, enter the variable name that you want to appear as the column header. Since this is the column header name, this name cannot begin with special characters or numbers and cannot have any spaces. If you wish to define the label for this variable (i.e., what will appear on the output; this *can* include special characters, spaces, and numbers), then click on the "Type & Label" box directly underneath "Target Variable" where additional text to define the name of the variable can be included. Next, click on the continuous covariate (i.e., social development) and move it into the "Numeric Expression" box by clicking on the arrow in the middle of the screen. Using either the keyboard on screen or your keyboard, click on the asterisks key (i.e., *). This will be used as the multiplication sign. Next, under "Function group," click on arithmetic to display all of the basic mathematical functions. From this alphabetized list, click on "Ln" (natural log). To move this function into the "Numeric Expression" box, click on the arrow key in the right central part of the dialog box.

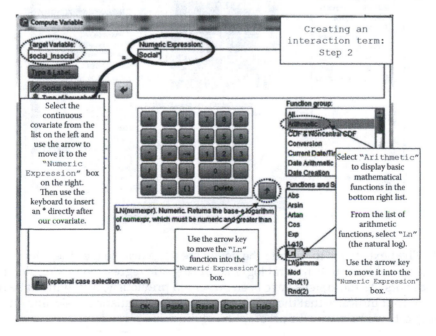

Creating an interaction term: Step 2

Step 3: Once the natural log function is displayed in the "Numeric Expression" box, a question mark enclosed inside parentheses will appear (see screenshot step 3a). This is SPSS's way of asking which variable you want the natural log computed for. Here it is the continuous covariate, social development.

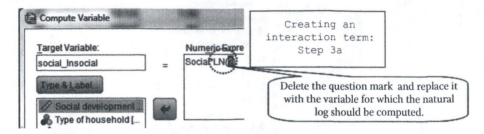

Here we want to compute the natural log for the continuous covariate, social development. To move this variable into the parentheses, use the backspace or delete key to remove the question mark. Then, click on the continuous covariate, social development, and move it into the parentheses next to LN in the "Numeric Expression" box by clicking on the arrow in the middle of the screen (see screenshot step 3b). The numeric expression should then read "Social*LN(Social)." Click "OK" to compute and create the new variable in the dataset.

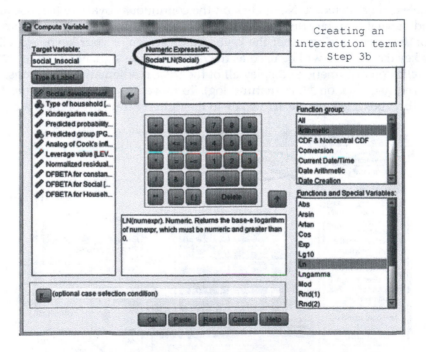

Step 4: The next step is to include the newly created variable (i.e., the interaction of the continuous variable with its natural log) into the logistic regression model, along with the other predictors. As those steps have been presented previously, they will not be reiterated here. The output indicates that the interaction term is not statistically significant ($p = .300$), which suggests we have met the assumption of linearity.

Variables in the Equation

		B	SE	Wald	df	Sig.	Exp(B)	95% CI for Exp(B) Lower	Upper
Step 1[a]	Social	12.953	11.897	1.185	1	.276	421981.259	.000	5.647E15
	Household(1)	−8.208	5.264	2.432	1	.119	.000	.000	8.236
	Social … Insocial	−2.948	2.845	1.074	1	.300	.052	.000	13.845
	Constant	−76.228	64.345	1.403	1	.236	.000		

[a] Variable(s) entered on step 1: Social, household, social … Insocial.

Independence

We plot the standardized residuals (which were requested and created through the "Save" option) against the values of X to examine the extent to which independence was met. The general steps for generating a simple scatterplot through "Scatter/dot" have been presented in Chapter 10 of *An Introduction to Statistical Concepts*, Third Edition, and they will not be repeated here. From the "Simple Scatterplot" dialog screen, click the standardized residual (called "normalized residual" in SPSS) variable and move it into the "Y Axis" box by clicking on the arrow. Click the independent variable X and move it into the "X Axis" box by clicking on the arrow. Then click "OK."

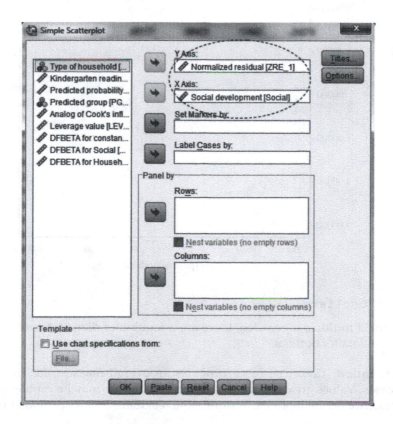

Interpreting independence evidence: If the assumption of independence is met, the points should fall randomly within a band of −2.0 to +2.0. Here we have pretty good evidence of independence, especially given the small sample size relative to logistic regression, as all but one point (case 19) are within an absolute value of 2.0.

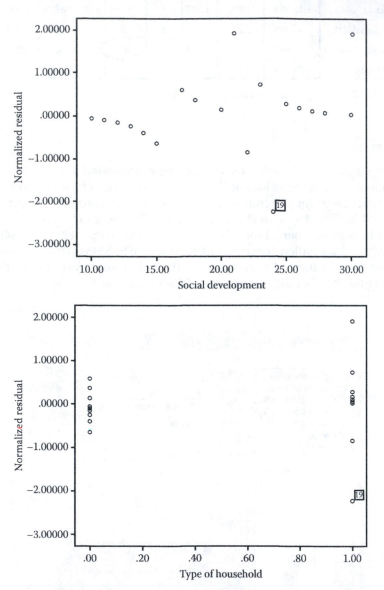

Absence of Outliers

Just as we saw in multiple regression, there are a number of diagnostics that can be used to examine the data for outliers.

Cook's distance: Cook's distance provides an overall measure for the influence of individual cases. Values greater than one suggest that a case may be problematic in terms of undue influence on the model. Examining the residual statistics provided in the binary logistic regression output (see following table), we see that the maximum value for Cook's distance is 1.58, which indicates at least one influential point.

Leverage values: These values range from 0 to 1, with values close to 1 indicating greater leverage. As a general rule, leverage values greater than $(m + 1)/n$ [where m equals the number of independent variables; here $(2 + 1)/20 = .15$] indicate an influential case. With a maximum of .307, there is evidence to suggest one or more cases are exerting leverage.

DfBeta: We saved the DfBeta values as another indication of the influence of a case. The DfBeta provide information on the change in the predicted value when the case is deleted from the model. For logistic regression, the DfBeta values should be smaller than 1. Looking at the minimum and maximum DfBeta values for the intercept (labeled "constant") and for household, we have at least one case that is suggestive of undue influence.

Descriptive Statistics

	N	Minimum	Maximum
Analog of Cook's influence statistics	20	.00000	1.58721
Leverage value	20	.00691	.30726
Normalized residual	20	−2.22568	1.91780
DfBeta for constant	20	−1.68367	6.53464
DfBeta for social	20	−.41034	.09948
DfBeta for household(1)	20	−1.36519	4.10130
Valid N (listwise)	20		

From our logistic regression output, we can review the "Casewise List" to determine cases with studentized residuals larger than two standard deviations (recall from the "Options" dialog box that we told SPSS to identify residuals outside two standard deviations). Here there were two cases (cases 8 and 15) that were identified as outliers, and the relevant statistics (e.g., observed group, predicted value, predicted group, residual, and standardized residual) are provided. We examine these cases to make sure there was not a data entry error. If the data are correct, then we determine whether to keep or filter out the case(s).

Casewise List[a]

Case	Selected Status[b]	Observed Kindergarten Readiness	Predicted	Predicted Group	Temporary Variable Resid	ZResid
8	S	U**	.832	P	−.832	−2.226
15	S	P**	.214	U	.786	1.918

[a] Cases with studentized residuals greater than 2.000 are listed.
[b] S = Selected, U = Unselected cases, and ** = Misclassified cases.

Since we have a small dataset, we can easily review the values of our diagnostics and see which cases are problematic in terms of exerting undue influence and/or outliers. Those that are circled are values that fall outside of the recommended guidelines and thus are suggestive of outlying or influential cases. Due to the already small sample size, we will not filter out any of these potentially problematic cases. However, in this situation (i.e., with diagnostics that suggest one or more influential cases), you may want to consider filtering out those cases or, at a minimum, reviewing the data to be sure that there was not a data entry error for that case.

	Social	Household	Readiness	PRE_1	PGR_1	COO_1	LEV_1	2RE_1	DFB0_1	DFB1_1	DFB2_1
1	15.00	.00	.00	.29087	.00	.16296	.28420	-.64046	-1.66367	.07492	-.02654
2	12.00	.00	.00	.02202	.00	.00228	.09212	-.15005	-.33145	.01897	-.10172
3	18.00	.00	1.00	.88150	1.00	.03665	.21502	.36580	-.80089	.06219	-.61089
4	20.00	.00	1.00	.98104	1.00	.00177	.00403	.13902	-.24278	.01681	-.14108
5	11.00	.00	.00	.00848	.00	.00046	.05082	-.09250	-.15052	.00877	-.04979
6	17.00	.00	1.00	.73959	1.00	.13483	.27690	.59338	-.79435	.07718	-.96766
7	14.00	.00	.00	.13486	.00	.04579	.22703	-.39482	-1.27676	.06695	-.25156
8	18.00	.00	1.00	.88150	1.00	.03665	.21502	.36580	-.80089	.06219	-.61089
9	13.00	.00	.00	.05593	.00	.01077	.15379	-.24340	-.69346	.03854	-.18626
10	10.00	.00	.00	.00324	.00	.00009	.02653	-.05702	-.06664	.00393	-.02313
11	22.00	1.00	.00	.41706	.00	.31732	.30726	-.84584	-1.58416	.09948	-1.36619
12	25.00	1.00	1.00	.92875	1.00	.01215	.13675	.27898	-.58887	.03572	-.15362
13	23.00	1.00	1.00	.65309	1.00	.18337	.25662	.72083	-.25348	.01592	-.41597
14	21.00	1.00	1.00	.21377	.00	1.58721	.30145	1.91780	6.53464	-.41034	4.19130
15	30.00	1.00	1.00	.99930	1.00	.00000	.00691	.02466	-.01393	.00087	-.00535
16	27.00	1.00	1.00	.98904	1.00	.00058	.04980	.10526	-.15271	.00959	-.05321
17	26.00	1.00	1.00	.97167	1.00	.00275	.08620	.17075	-.31209	.01960	-.10037
18	28.00	1.00	1.00	.99581	1.00	.00012	.02606	.06489	-.02074	.00444	-.02581
19	24.00	1.00	.00	.83204	1.00	1.20526	.19567	-2.22568	3.84582	-.24150	.50163
20	30.00	1.00	1.00	.99930	1.00	.00000	.00691	.02466	-.01393	.00087	-.00535

Assessing Classification Accuracy

In addition to examining Press's *Q* for classification accuracy, we can generate a kappa statistic. Kappa is the proportion of agreement above that expected by chance. A kappa statistic of 1.0 indicates perfect agreement, whereas a kappa of 0 indicates chance agreement. Negative values can occur and indicate weaker than chance agreement. General rules of interpretation for kappa are as follows: small, <.30; moderate, .30 to .50; large, >.50.

Step 1: Kappa statistics are generated through the "Crosstab" procedure. Because the process for creating a crosstab has been presented previously (see Chapter 8 of *An Introduction to Statistical Concepts*, Third Edition), it will not be reiterated here. Once the "Crosstab" dialog box is open, select the dependent variable from the list on the left and use the arrow key to move it to "Row(s)." Select the predicted group (PGR_1) from the list on the left and use the arrow key to move it to "Column(s)" (see step 1).

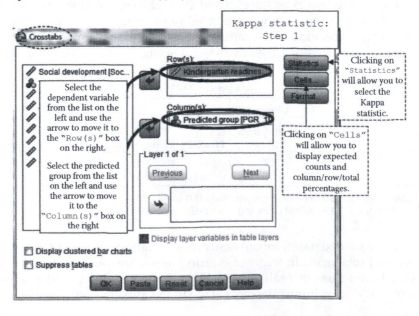

Step 2: Click on the "Statistics" option button. Place a checkmark in the box next to "Kappa" (step 2). Then click on "Continue" to return to the main dialog box.

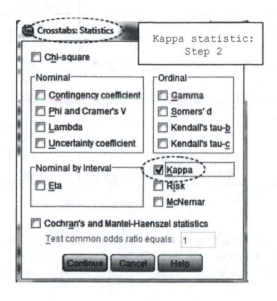

Step 3: Click on the "Cells" option button. In the "Cell Display" dialog box, place a checkmark in the box next to observed, expected, and row (step 3). Then click on "Continue" to return to the main dialog box. Then click "OK" to generate the output.

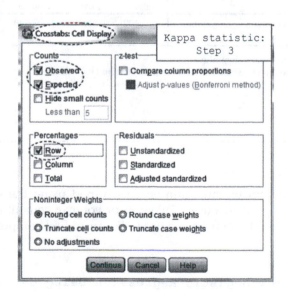

The crosstab table is interpreted as we have seen in the past. The columns represent the predicted group membership, and the rows represent the observed group membership. This table should look familiar to the one that was provided to us with the logistic regression results.

Kindergarten Readiness * Predicted Group Crosstabulation

			Predicted Group		
			Unprepared	Prepared	Total
Kindergarten readiness	Unprepared	Count	7	1	8
		Expected count	3.2	4.8	8.0
		% Within Kindergarten readiness	87.5%	12.5%	100.0%
	Prepared	Count	1	11	12
		Expected count	4.8	7.2	12.0
		% Within Kindergarten readiness	8.3%	91.7%	100.0%
Total		Count	8	12	20
		Expected count	8.0	12.0	20.0
		% Within Kindergarten readiness	40.0%	60.0%	100.0%

What is of most interest is the table labeled "Symmetric Measures," as this table contains the kappa statistic. With a kappa statistic of .792, and using our rules of thumb for interpretation, this is considered to be a large value, which suggests strong agreement.

Symmetric Measures

		Value	Asymp. Std. Error[a]	Approx. T[b]	Approx. Sig
Measure of agreement	Kappa	.792	.140	3.540	.000
N of valid cases		20			

[a] Not assuming the null hypothesis.
[b] Using the asymptotic standard error assuming the null hypothesis.

9.9 G*Power

A priori and post hoc power can again be determined using the specialized software described previously in this text (e.g., G*Power), or you can consult a priori power tables (e.g., Cohen, 1988). As an illustration, we use G*Power to first compute post hoc power of our example.

Post Hoc Power for Logistic Regression Using G*Power

The first thing that must be done when using G*Power for computing post hoc power is to select the correct test family. For logistic regression, we select "Tests" in the top pulldown menu, then "Correlation and regression," and finally "Logistic regression." Once that selection is made, the "Test family" automatically changes to "z tests."

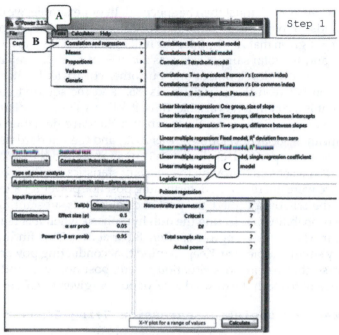

The "Type of Power Analysis" desired then needs to be selected. To compute post hoc power, select "Post hoc: Compute achieved power—given α, sample size, and effect size." For this illustration, we will compute power for the continuous covariate.

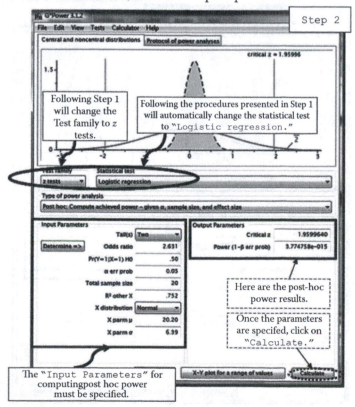

The "Input Parameters" must then be specified. In our example, we conducted a two-tailed test. The odds ratio for our continuous variable social development was 2.631. The probability that $Y = 1$ given that $X = 1$ under the null hypothesis is set to .50. The alpha level we used was .05, and the total sample size was 20. "R^2 other X" refers to the squared correlation between social development and our other covariate. In this case, the simple bivariate correlation between these variables is .867, and the squared correlation is .752. Social development is a continuous variable; thus, it follows a normal distribution. The last two parameters to be specified are for the mean and standard deviation of our covariate. In this case, the mean of social development was 20.20, and the standard deviation was 6.39. Once the parameters are specified, click on "Calculate" to find the power statistics.

The "Output Parameters" provide the relevant statistics for the input just specified. In this example, we were interested in determining post hoc power for a logistic regression model. Based on the criteria specified, the post hoc power was substantially less than 1. In other words, the probability of rejecting the null hypothesis when it is really false was significantly less than 1% (sufficient power is often .80 or above). This finding is not surprising given the very small sample size. Keep in mind that conducting power analysis a priori is recommended so that you avoid a situation where, post hoc, you find that the sample size was not sufficient to reach the desired level of power (given the observed parameters).

A Priori Power for Logistic Regression Using G*Power

For a priori power, we can determine the total sample size needed for logistic regression given the same parameters just discussed. In this example, had we wanted an a priori power of .80 given the same parameters just defined, we would need a total sample size of 7094.

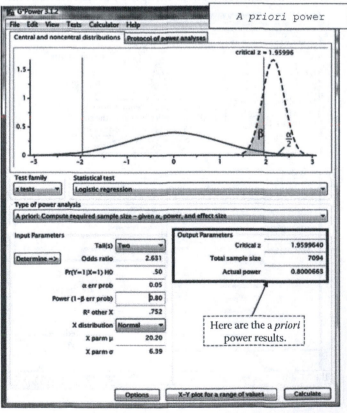

9.10 Template and APA-Style Write-Up

Finally, here is an example paragraph for the results of the logistic regression analysis. Recall that our graduate research assistant, Marie, was assisting Malani, a faculty member in the early childhood department. Malani wanted to know if kindergarten readiness (prepared vs. unprepared) could be predicted by social development (a continuous variable) and type of household (single- vs. two-parent home). The research question presented to Malani from Marie included the following: *Can kindergarten readiness be predicted from social development and type of household?*

Marie then assisted Malani in generating a logistic regression as the test of inference, and a template for writing the research question for this design is presented as follows:

- Can [dependent variable] be predicted from [list independent variables]?

It may be helpful to preface the results of the logistic regression with information on an examination of the extent to which the assumptions were met. The assumptions include (a) independence, (b) linearity, and (c) noncollinearity. We will also examine the data for outliers and influential points.

Logistic regression was conducted to determine whether social development and type of household (single- vs. two-parent home) could predict kindergarten readiness.

The assumptions of logistic regression were tested. Specifically, these include (a) noncollinearity, (b) linearity, and (c) independence of errors.

In terms of **noncollinearity**, a VIF value of 4.037 (below the value of 10.0 which indicates the point of concern) and tolerance of .248 (above the value of .10 which suggests multicollinearity) provided evidence of noncollinearity. However, there was some indication that multicollinearity existed. In examining the collinearity diagnostics, a condition index value of 14.259 was observed, about five times larger than the next largest condition index. Review of the variance proportions suggested that 100% of the variance of the regression coefficient for social development and 73% for type of household were related to the smallest eigenvalue. This also suggests multicollinearity.

Linearity was assessed by reestimating the model and including, along with the original predictors, an interaction term which was the product of the continuous independent variable (i.e., social development) and its natural logarithm. The interaction term was not statistically significant, thus providing evidence of linearity [social*ln(social), $B = -2.948$, $SE = 2.845$, Wald = 1.074, $df = 1$, $p = .300$].

Independence was assessed by examining a plot of the standardized residuals against values of each independent variable. With the exception of one case which was slightly outside the band, all cases were within an absolute value of 2.0, thus indicating the assumption of independence has been met.

In reviewing for **outliers and influential points**, Cook's distance values were generally within the recommended range of less than 1.0, although the maximum value was 1.587. Leverage values ranged from .007 to .307, well under the recommended .50, suggesting outliers were not problematic. DfBeta values beyond 1 also suggested cases that may be exerting influence on the model. Based on the evidence reviewed, there are some cases that are suggestive of outlying and influential points. Due to the small sample size, however, these cases were retained. Readers are urged to interpret the results with caution given the possible influence of outliers.

Here is an APA-style example paragraph of results for the logistic regression (remember that this will be prefaced by the previous paragraph reporting the extent to which the assumptions of the test were met).

Logistic regression analysis was then conducted to determine whether kindergarten readiness (prepared vs. unprepared) could be predicted from social development and type of household (single- vs. two-parent home). Good model fit was evidenced by nonstatistically significant results on the Hosmer–Lemeshow test, χ^2 ($n= 20$) = 4.691, $df = 7$, $p = .698$, and large effect size indices when interpreted using Cohen (1988) (Cox and Snell R^2 = .546; Nagelkerke R^2 = .738). These results suggest that the predictors, as a set, reliably distinguished between children who are ready for kindergarten (i.e., prepared) versus unprepared. Of the two predictors in the model, only social development was a statistically significant predictor of kindergarten readiness (Wald = 4.696, $df = 1$, $p = .030$). The odds ratio for social development suggests that for every one-point increase in social development, the odds are about two and two-thirds greater for being prepared for kindergarten as compared to unprepared. Type of household was not statistically significant, which suggests that the odds for being prepared for kindergarten (relative to unprepared) are similar regardless of being raised in a single-parent versus a two-parent household. The following table presents the results for the model including the regression coefficients, Wald statistics, odds ratios, and 95% CIs for the odds ratios. This is followed by a table which presents the group means and standard deviations of each predictor for both children who are prepared and unprepared for kindergarten.

Logistic Regression Results

	B	SE	Wald	p	Exp(B)	95% CI for Exp(B) Lower	Upper
Intercept (constant)	−15.404	7.195	4.584	.032	NA		
Social development	.967	.446	4.696	.030	2.631	1.097	6.313
Type of household (two-parent home)	−6.216	3.440	3.265	.071	.002	.000	1.693

Group Means (and Standard Deviations) of Predictors

Predictor	Prepared for Kindergarten	Unprepared for Kindergarten
Social development	23.58 (4.74)	15.13 (5.14)
Type of household (two-parent home)	.67 (.49)	.25 (.46)

Overall, the logistic regression model accurately predicted 90% of the children in our sample, with children who are prepared for kindergarten slightly more likely to be classified correctly (91.7% of children prepared for kindergarten and 87.5% of children unprepared correctly classified). To account for chance agreement in classification, the kappa coefficient was computed and found to be .792, a large value. Additionally, Press's Q was calculated to be 12.8, providing evidence that the predictions based on the logistic regression model are statistically significantly better than chance.

9.11 What Is Next?

As we conclude this text, the natural question to ask is, what do we consider next in statistics? There are two likely key alternatives. First, you could consider more advanced regression models such as multinomial logistic regression, propensity score analysis, or regression discontinuity. In terms of more advanced regression readings, consider Cohen and Cohen (1983), Grimm and Arnold (1995), Kleinbaum, Kupper, Muller, and Nizam, (1998), Meyers, Gamst, and Guarino (2006), and Pedhazur (1997). For more information on logistic regression, consider Christensen (1997), Glass and Hopkins (1996), Hosmer and Lemeshow (2000), Huck (2004), Kleinbaum et al. (1998), Meyers et al. (2006), Pampel (2000), Pedhazur (1997), and Wright (1995).

In the regression framework, one of the hottest topics relates to multilevel models that allow for the examination of nested cases (e.g., children within classrooms, employees within organizations, residents within states). There are a number of excellent resources for learning more about multilevel modeling including Heck and Thomas (2000), Kreft and de Leeuw (1998), O'Connell and McCoach (2008), Reise and Dunn (2003), and Snijders and Bosker (1999).

Alternatively you could consider multivariate analysis methods, either in terms of readings or in a multivariate course. Briefly, the major methods of multivariate analysis include multivariate analysis of variance (MANOVA), discriminant analysis, factor and principal components analysis, canonical correlation analysis, cluster analysis, multidimensional scaling, multivariate regression, and structural equation modeling. For multivariate readings, take a look at Grimm and Arnold (1995, 2000), Johnson and Wichern (1998), Kleinbaum et al. (1998), Manly (2004), Marcoulides and Hershberger (1997), Meyers et al. (2006), Stevens (2002), and Timm (2002).

9.12 Summary

In this chapter, a regression method appropriate for binary categorical outcomes was considered. The chapter began with an examination of how logistic regression works and the logistic regression equation. This was followed by estimation, model fit, significance tests, and assumptions within the context of logistic regression. Effect size indices of logistic regression models were also discussed. In addition, several new concepts were introduced, including logit, odds, and odds ratio. Finally we examined a number of methods of variable entry, such as simultaneous, stepwise selection, and hierarchical regression. At this point, you should have met the following objectives: (a) be able to understand the concepts underlying logistic regression, (b) be able to determine and interpret the results of logistic regression, (c) be able to understand and evaluate the assumptions of logistic regression, and (d) be able to have a basic understanding of methods of entering the covariates. This concludes our statistical concepts text. We wish you the best of luck in your future statistical adventures.

Problems

Conceptual Problems

9.1 Which one of the following represents the primary difference between OLS regression and logistic regression?

   a. Computer processing time to estimate the model

   b. The measurement scales of the independent variables that can be included in the model

   c. The measurement scale of the dependent variable

   d. The statistical software that must be used to estimate the model

9.2 Which one of the following is NOT an appropriate dependent variable for binary logistic regression?

   a. Bernoulli

   b. Dichotomous

   c. Multinomial

   d. One variable with two categories

9.3 Which of the following would NOT be appropriate outcomes to examine with binary logistic regression?

    a. Employment status (employed, unemployed not looking for work, unemployed looking for work)

    b. Enlisted member of the military (member vs. nonmember)

    c. Marital status (married vs. not married)

    d. Recreational athlete (athlete vs. nonathlete)

9.4 Which of the following represents what is being predicted in binary logistic regression?

    a. Mean difference between two groups

    b. Odds that the unit of analysis belongs to one of two groups

    c. Precise numerical value

    d. Relationship between one group compared to the other group

9.5 While probability, odds, and log odds may be computationally different, they all relay the same basic information.

    a. True

    b. False

9.6 A researcher is studying diet soda drinking habits and has coded "diet soda drinker" as "1" and "non-diet soda drinker" as "0." Which of the following is a correct interpretation given a probability value of .52?

    a. The odds of being a diet soda drinker are about equal to those of not being a diet soda drinker.

    b. The odds of being a diet soda drinker are substantially greater than not being a diet soda drinker.

    c. The odds of being a diet soda drinker are substantially less than not being a diet soda drinker.

    d. Cannot be determined from the information provided.

9.7 Which of the following is a correct interpretation of the logit?

    a. The log odds become larger as the odds increase from 1 to 100.

    b. The log odds become smaller as the odds increase from 1 to 100.

    c. The log odds stay relatively stable as the odds decrease from 1 to 0.

    d. The change in log odds becomes larger when the independent variables are categorical rather than continuous.

9.8 Which of the following correctly contrasts the estimation of OLS regression as compared to logistic regression?

    a. The sum of the squared distance of the observed data to the regression line is minimized in logistic regression. The log likelihood function is maximized in OLS regression.

    b. The sum of the squared distance of the observed data to the regression line is maximized in logistic regression. The log likelihood function is minimized in OLS regression.

c. The sum of the squared distance of the observed data to the regression line is maximized in OLS regression. The log likelihood function is minimized in logistic regression.

d. The sum of the squared distance of the observed data to the regression line is minimized in OLS regression. The log likelihood function is maximized in logistic regression.

9.9 Which of the following is NOT a test that can be used to evaluate overall model fit for logistic regression models?

a. Change in log likelihood

b. Hosmer–Lemeshow goodness-of-fit

c. Cox and Snell R squared

d. Wald test

9.10 A researcher is studying diet soda drinking habits and has coded "diet soda drinker" as "1" and "non-diet soda drinker" as "0." She has predicted drinking habits based on the individual's weight (measured in pounds). Given this scenario, which of the following is a correct interpretation of an odds ratio of 1.75?

a. For every one-unit increase in being a diet soda drinker, the odds of putting on an additional pound increase by 75%.

b. For every one-unit increase in being a diet soda drinker, the odds of putting on an additional pound decrease by 75%.

c. For every 1-pound increase in weight, the odds of being a diet soda drinker decrease by 75%.

d. For every 1-pound increase in weight, the odds of being a diet soda drinker increase by 75%.

Computational Problems

9.1 You are given the following data, where X_1 (high school cumulative grade point average) and X_2 (participation in school-sponsored athletics; 0 = nonathlete and 1 = athlete; use 0 as the reference category) are used to predict Y (college enrollment immediately after high school, "1," vs. delayed college enrollment or no enrollment, "0").

X_1	X_2	Y
4.15	1	1
2.72	0	1
3.16	0	0
3.89	1	1
4.02	1	1
1.89	0	0
2.10	0	1
2.36	1	1
3.55	0	0
1.70	0	0

Determine the following values based on simultaneous entry of independent variables: intercept, $-2LL$, constant, b_1, b_2, $se(b_1)$, $se(b_2)$, odds ratios, $Wald_1$, $Wald_2$.

9.2 You are given the following data, where X_1 (participation in high school honors classes; yes = 1, no = 0; use 0 as the reference category) and X_2 (participation in co-op program in college; yes = 1, no = 0; use 0 as the reference category) are used to predict Y (baccalaureate graduation with honors = 1 vs. graduation without honors = 0).

X_1	X_2	Y
0	1	1
0	0	1
1	0	0
1	1	1
1	1	1
0	0	0
1	0	1
0	1	1
1	0	0
0	0	0

Determine the following values based on simultaneous entry of independent variables: intercept, $-2LL$, constant, b_1, b_2, $se(b_1)$, $se(b_2)$, odds ratios, Wald$_1$, Wald$_2$.

Interpretive Problem

9.1 Use SPSS to develop a logistic regression model with the example survey 1 dataset on the website. Utilize "do you smoke" as the dependent (binary) variable to find at least two strong predictors from among the continuous and/or categorical variables in the dataset. Write up the results in APA style, including testing for the assumptions. Determine and interpret a measure of effect size.

Appendix: Tables

TABLE A.1

The Standard Unit Normal Distribution

z	P(z)	z	P(z)	z	P(z)	z	P(z)
.00	.5000000	.50	.6914625	1.00	.8413447	1.50	.9331928
.01	.5039894	.51	.6949743	1.01	.8437524	1.51	.9344783
.02	.5079783	.52	.6984682	1.02	.8461358	1.52	.9357445
.03	.5119665	.53	.7019440	1.03	.8484950	1.53	.9369916
.04	.5159534	.54	.7054015	1.04	.8508300	1.54	.9382198
.05	.5199388	.55	.7088403	1.05	.8531409	1.55	.9394292
.06	.5239222	.56	.7122603	1.06	.8554277	1.56	.9406201
.07	.5279032	.57	.7156612	1.07	.8576903	1.57	.9417924
.08	.5318814	.58	.7190427	1.08	.8599289	1.58	.9429466
.09	.5358564	.59	.7224047	1.09	.8621434	1.59	.9440826
.10	.5398278	.60	.7257469	1.10	.8643339	1.60	.9452007
.11	.5437953	.61	.7290691	1.11	.8665005	1.61	.9463011
.12	.5477584	.62	.7323711	1.12	.8686431	1.62	.9473839
.13	.5517168	.63	.7356527	1.13	.8707619	1.63	.9484493
.14	.5556700	.64	.7389137	1.14	.8728568	1.64	.9494974
.15	.5596177	.65	.7421539	1.15	.8749281	1.65	.9505285
.16	.5635595	.66	.7453731	1.16	.8769756	1.66	.9515428
.17	.5674949	.67	.7485711	1.17	.8789995	1.67	.9525403
.18	.5714237	.68	.7517478	1.18	.8809999	1.68	.9535213
.19	.5753454	.69	.7549029	1.19	.8829768	1.69	.9544860
.20	.5792597	.70	.7580363	1.20	.8849303	1.70	.9554345
.21	.5831662	.71	.7611479	1.21	.8868606	1.71	.9563671
.22	.5870644	.72	.7642375	1.22	.8887676	1.72	.9572838
.23	.5909541	.73	.7673049	1.23	.8906514	1.73	.9581849
.24	.5948349	.74	.7703500	1.24	.8925123	1.74	.9590705
.25	.5987063	.75	.7733726	1.25	.8943502	1.75	.9599408
.26	.6025681	.76	.7763727	1.26	.8961653	1.76	.9607961
.27	.6064199	.77	.7793501	1.27	.8979577	1.77	.9616364
.28	.6102612	.78	.7823046	1.28	.8997274	1.78	.9624620
.29	.6140919	.79	.7852361	1.29	.9014747	1.79	.9632730
.30	.6179114	.80	.7881446	1.30	.9031995	1.80	.9640697
.31	.6217195	.81	.7910299	1.31	.9049021	1.81	.9648521
.32	.6255158	.82	.7938919	1.32	.9065825	1.82	.9656205
.33	.6293000	.83	.7967306	1.33	.9082409	1.83	.9663750
.34	.6330717	.84	.7995458	1.34	.9098773	1.84	.9671159
.35	.6368307	.85	.8023375	1.35	.9114920	1.85	.9678432
.36	.6405764	.86	.8051055	1.36	.9130850	1.86	.9685572

(continued)

TABLE A.1 (continued)

The Standard Unit Normal Distribution

z	P(z)	z	P(z)	z	P(z)	z	P(z)
.37	.6443088	.87	.8078498	1.37	.9146565	1.87	.9692581
.38	.6480273	.88	.8105703	1.38	.9162067	1.88	.9699460
.39	.6517317	.89	.8132671	1.39	.9177356	1.89	.9706210
.40	.6554217	.90	.8159399	1.40	.9192433	1.90	.9712834
.41	.6590970	.91	.8185887	1.41	.9207302	1.91	.9719334
.42	.6627573	.92	.8212136	1.42	.9221962	1.92	.9725711
.43	.6664022	.93	.8238145	1.43	.9236415	1.93	.9731966
.44	.6700314	.94	.8263912	1.44	.9250663	1.94	.9738102
.45	.6736448	.95	.8289439	1.45	.9264707	1.95	.9744119
.46	.6772419	.96	.8314724	1.46	.9278550	1.96	.9750021
.47	.6808225	.97	.8339768	1.47	.9292191	1.97	.9755808
.48	.6843863	.98	.8364569	1.48	.9305634	1.98	.9761482
.49	.6879331	.99	.8389129	1.49	.9318879	1.99	.9767045
.50	.6914625	1.00	.8413447	1.50	.9331928	2.00	.9772499
2.00	.9772499	2.50	.9937903	3.00	.9986501	3.50	.9997674
2.01	.9777844	2.51	.9939634	3.01	.9986938	3.51	.9997759
2.02	.9783083	2.52	.9941323	3.02	.9987361	3.52	.9997842
2.03	.9788217	2.53	.9942969	3.03	.9987772	3.53	.9997922
2.04	.9793248	2.54	.9944574	3.04	.9988171	3.54	.9997999
2.05	.9798178	2.55	.9946139	3.05	.9988558	3.55	.9998074
2.06	.9803007	2.56	.9947664	3.06	.9988933	3.56	.9998146
2.07	.9807738	2.57	.9949151	3.07	.9989297	3.57	.9998215
2.08	.9812372	2.58	.9950600	3.08	.9989650	3.58	.9998282
2.09	.9816911	2.59	.9952012	3.09	.9989992	3.59	.9998347
2.10	.9821356	2.60	.9953388	3.10	.9990324	3.60	.9998409
2.11	.9825708	2.61	.9954729	3.11	.9990646	3.61	.9998469
2.12	.9829970	2.62	.9956035	3.12	.9990957	3.62	.9998527
2.13	.9834142	2.63	.9957308	3.13	.9991260	3.63	.9998583
2.14	.9838226	2.64	.9958547	3.14	.9991553	3.64	.9998637
2.15	.9842224	2.65	.9959754	3.15	.9991836	3.65	.9998689
2.16	.9846137	2.66	.9960930	3.16	.9992112	3.66	.9998739
2.17	.9849966	2.67	.9962074	3.17	.9992378	3.67	.9998787
2.18	.9853713	2.68	.9963189	3.18	.9992636	3.68	.9998834
2.19	.9857379	2.69	.9964274	3.19	.9992886	3.69	.9998879
2.20	.9860966	2.70	.9965330	3.20	.9993129	3.70	.9998922
2.21	.9864474	2.71	.9966358	3.21	.9993363	3.71	.9998964
2.22	.9867906	2.72	.9967359	3.22	.9993590	3.72	.9999004
2.23	.9871263	2.73	.9968333	3.23	.9993810	3.73	.9999043
2.24	.9874545	2.74	.9969280	3.24	.9994024	3.74	.9999080
2.25	.9877755	2.75	.9970202	3.25	.9994230	3.75	.9999116
2.26	.9880894	2.76	.9971099	3.26	.9994429	3.76	.9999150
2.27	.9883962	2.77	.9971972	3.27	.9994623	3.77	.9999184
2.28	.9886962	2.78	.9972821	3.28	.9994810	3.78	.9999216
2.29	.9889893	2.79	.9973646	3.29	.9994991	3.79	.9999247
2.30	.9892759	2.80	.9974449	3.30	.9995166	3.80	.9999277

TABLE A.1 (continued)

The Standard Unit Normal Distribution

z	P(z)	z	P(z)	z	P(z)	z	P(z)
2.31	.9895559	2.81	.9975229	3.31	.9995335	3.81	.9999305
2.32	.9898296	2.82	.9975988	3.32	.9995499	3.82	.9999333
2.33	.9900969	2.83	.9976726	3.33	.9995658	3.83	.9999359
2.34	.9903581	2.84	.9977443	3.34	.9995811	3.84	.9999385
2.35	.9906133	2.85	.9978140	3.35	.9995959	3.85	.9999409
2.36	.9908625	2.86	.9978818	3.36	.9996103	3.86	.9999433
2.37	.9911060	2.87	.9979476	3.37	.9996242	3.87	.9999456
2.38	.9913437	2.88	.9980116	3.88	.9996376	3.88	.9999478
2.39	.9915758	2.89	.9980738	3.39	.9996505	3.89	.9999499
2.40	.9918025	2.90	.9981342	3.40	.9996631	3.90	.9999519
2.41	.9920237	2.91	.9981929	3.41	.9996752	3.91	.9999539
2.42	.9922397	2.92	.9982498	3.42	.9996869	3.92	.9999557
2.43	.9924506	2.93	.9983052	3.43	.9996982	3.93	.9999575
2.44	.9926564	2.94	.9983589	3.44	.9997091	3.94	.9999593
2.45	.9928572	2.95	.9984111	3.45	.9997197	3.95	.9999609
2.46	.9930531	2.96	.9984618	3.46	.9997299	3.96	.9999625
2.47	.9932443	2.97	.9985110	3.47	.9997398	3.97	.9999641
2.48	.9934309	2.98	.9985588	3.48	.9997493	3.98	.9999655
2.49	.9936128	2.99	.9986051	3.49	.9997585	3.99	.9999670
2.50	.9937903	3.00	.9986501	3.50	.9997674	4.00	.9999683

Source: Reprinted from Pearson, E.S. and Hartley, H.O., *Biometrika Tables for Statisticians*, Cambridge University Press, Cambridge, U.K., 1966, Table 1. With permission of Biometrika Trustees.

P(z) represents the area below that value of z.

TABLE A.2

Percentage Points of the t Distribution

v	$\alpha_1 = .10$ / $\alpha_2 = .20$	.05 / .10	.025 / .050	.01 / .02	.005 / .010	.0025 / .0050	.001 / .002	.0005 / .0010
1	3.078	6.314	12.706	31.821	63.657	127.32	318.31	636.62
2	1.886	2.920	4.303	6.965	9.925	14.089	22.327	31.598
3	1.638	2.353	3.182	4.541	5.841	7.453	10.214	12.924
4	1.533	2.132	2.776	3.747	4.604	5.598	7.173	8.610
5	1.476	2.015	2.571	3.365	4.032	4.773	5.893	6.869
6	1.440	1.943	2.447	3.143	3.707	4.317	5.208	5.959
7	1.415	1.895	2.305	2.998	3.499	4.029	4.785	5.408
8	1.397	1.860	2.306	2.896	3.355	3.833	4.501	5.041
9	1.383	1.833	2.262	2.821	3.250	3.690	4.297	4.781
10	1.372	1.812	2.228	2.764	3.169	3.581	4.144	4.587
11	1.363	1.796	2.201	2.718	3.106	3.497	4.025	4.437
12	1.356	1.782	2.179	2.681	3.055	3.428	3.930	4.318
13	1.350	1.771	2.160	2.650	3.012	3.372	3.852	4.221
14	1.345	1.761	2.145	2.624	2.977	3.326	3.787	4.140
15	1.341	1.753	2.131	2.602	2.947	3.286	3.733	4.073
16	1.337	1.746	2.120	2.583	2.921	3.252	3.686	4.015
17	1.333	1.740	2.110	2.567	2.898	3.222	3.646	3.965
18	1.330	1.734	2.101	2.552	2.878	3.197	3.610	3.922
19	1.328	1.729	2.093	2.539	2.861	3.174	3.579	3.883
20	1.325	1.725	2.086	2.528	2.845	3.153	3.552	3.850
21	1.323	1.721	2.080	2.518	2.831	3.135	3.527	3.819
22	1.321	1.717	2.074	2.508	2.819	3.119	3.505	3.792
23	1.319	1.714	2.069	2.500	2.807	3.104	3.485	3.767
24	1.318	1.711	2.064	2.492	2.797	3.091	3.467	3.745
25	1.316	1.708	2.060	2.485	2.787	3.078	3.450	3.725
26	1.315	1.706	2.056	2.479	2.779	3.067	3.435	3.707
27	1.314	1.703	2.052	2.473	2.771	3.057	3.421	3.690
28	1.313	1.701	2.048	2.467	2.763	3.047	3.408	3.674
29	1.311	1.699	2.045	2.462	2.756	3.038	3.396	3.659
30	1.310	1.697	2.042	2.457	2.750	3.030	3.385	3.646
40	1.303	1.684	2.021	2.423	2.704	2.971	3.307	3.551
60	1.296	1.671	2.000	2.390	2.660	2.915	3.232	3.460
120	1.289	1.658	1.980	2.358	2.617	2.860	3.160	3.373
∞	1.282	1.645	1.960	2.326	2.576	2.807	3.090	3.291

Source: Reprinted from Pearson, E.S. and Hartley, H.O., *Biometrika Tables for Statisticians*, Cambridge University Press, Cambridge, U.K., 1966, Table 12. With permission of Biometrika Trustees.

α_t is the upper-tail value of the distribution with v degrees of freedom; appropriate for use in a one-tailed test.

Use α_2 for a two-tailed test.

TABLE A.3

Percentage Points of the χ^2 Distribution

v				α				
	0.990	0.975	0.950	0.900	0.100	0.050	0.025	0.010
1	$157088 \cdot 10^{-9}$	$982069 \cdot 10^{-8}$	$393214 \cdot 10^{-8}$	0.0157908	2.70554	3.84146	5.02389	6.63490
2	0.0201007	0.0506356	0.102587	0.210721	4.60517	5.99146	7.37776	9.21034
3	0.114832	0.215795	0.351846	0.584374	6.25139	7.81473	9.34840	11.3449
4	0.297109	0.484419	0.710723	1.063623	7.77944	9.48773	11.1433	13.2767
5	0.554298	0.831212	1.145476	1.61031	9.23636	11.0705	12.8325	15.0863
6	0.872090	1.23734	1.63538	2.20413	10.6446	12.5916	14.4494	16.8119
7	1.239043	1.68987	2.16735	2.83311	12.0170	14.0671	16.0128	18.4753
8	1.64650	2.17973	2.73264	3.48954	13.3616	15.5073	17.5345	20.0902
9	2.08790	2.70039	3.32511	4.16816	14.6837	16.9190	19.0228	21.6660
10	2.55821	3.24697	3.94030	4.86518	15.9872	18.3070	20.4832	23.2093
11	3.05348	3.81575	4.57481	5.57778	17.2750	19.6751	21.9200	24.7250
12	3.57057	4.40379	5.22603	6.30380	18.5493	21.0261	23.3367	26.2170
13	4.10692	5.00875	5.89186	7.04150	19.8119	22.3620	24.7356	27.6882
14	4.66043	5.62873	6.57063	7.78953	21.0641	23.6848	26.1189	29.1412
15	5.22935	6.26214	7.26094	8.54676	22.3071	24.9958	27.4884	30.5779
16	5.81221	6.90766	7.96165	9.31224	23.5418	26.2962	28.8454	31.9999
17	6.40776	7.56419	8.67176	10.0852	24.7690	27.5871	30.1910	33.4087
18	7.01491	8.23075	9.39046	10.8649	25.9894	28.8693	31.5264	34.8053
19	7.63273	8.90652	10.1170	11.6509	27.2036	30.1435	32.8523	36.1909
20	8.26040	9.59078	10.8508	12.4426	28.4120	31.4104	34.1696	37.5662
21	8.89720	10.28293	11.5913	13.2396	29.6151	32.6706	35.4789	38.9322
22	9.54249	10.9823	12.3380	14.0415	30.8133	33.9244	36.7807	40.2894
23	10.19567	11.6886	13.0905	14.8480	32.0069	35.1725	38.0756	41.6384
24	10.8564	12.4012	13.8484	15.6587	33.1962	36.4150	39.3641	42.9798
25	11.5240	13.1197	14.6114	16.4734	34.3816	37.6525	40.6465	44.3141
26	12.1981	13.8439	15.3792	17.2919	35.5632	38.8851	41.9232	45.6417
27	12.8785	14.5734	16.1514	18.1139	36.7412	40.1133	43.1945	46.9629
28	13.5647	15.3079	16.9279	18.9392	37.9159	41.3371	44.4608	48.2782
29	14.2565	16.0471	17.7084	19.7677	39.0875	42.5570	45.7223	49.5879
30	14.9535	16.7908	18.4927	20.5992	40.2560	43.7730	46.9792	50.8922
40	22.1643	24.4330	26.5093	29.0505	51.8051	55.7585	59.3417	63.6907
50	29.7067	32.3574	34.7643	37.6886	63.1671	67.5048	71.4202	76.1539
60	37.4849	40.4817	43.1880	46.4589	74.3970	79.0819	83.2977	88.3794
70	45.4417	48.7576	51.7393	55.3289	85.5270	90.5312	95.0232	100.425
80	53.5401	57.1532	60.3915	64.2778	96.5782	101.879	106.629	112.329
90	61.7541	66.6466	69.1260	73.2911	107.565	113.145	118.136	124.116
100	70.0649	74.2219	77.9295	82.3581	118.498	124.342	129.561	135.807

Source: Reprinted from Pearson, E.S. and Hartley, H.O., *Biometrika Tables for Statisticians*, Cambridge University Press, Cambridge, U.K., 1966, Table 8. With permission of Biometrika Trustees.

TABLE A.4

Percentage Points of the F Distribution

v_1

v_2	1	2	3	4	5	6	7	8	9	10	12	15	20	24	30	40	60	120	∞
$\alpha = .10$																			
1	39.86	49.50	53.59	55.83	57.24	58.20	58.91	59.44	59.86	60.19	60.71	61.22	61.74	62.00	62.26	62.53	62.79	63.06	63.33
2	8.53	9.00	9.16	9.24	9.29	9.33	9.35	9.37	9.38	9.39	9.41	9.42	9.44	9.45	9.46	9.47	9.47	9.48	9.49
3	5.54	5.46	5.39	5.34	5.31	5.28	5.27	5.25	5.24	5.23	5.22	5.20	5.18	5.18	5.17	5.16	5.15	5.14	5.13
4	4.54	4.32	4.19	4.11	4.05	4.01	3.98	3.95	3.94	3.92	3.90	3.87	3.84	3.83	3.82	3.80	3.79	3.78	3.76
5	4.06	3.78	3.62	3.52	3.45	3.40	3.37	3.34	3.32	3.30	3.27	3.24	3.21	3.19	3.17	3.16	3.14	3.12	3.10
6	3.78	3.46	3.29	3.18	3.11	3.05	3.01	2.98	2.96	2.94	2.90	2.87	2.84	2.82	2.80	2.78	2.76	2.74	2.72
7	3.59	3.26	3.07	2.96	2.88	2.83	2.78	2.75	2.72	2.70	2.67	2.63	2.59	2.58	2.56	2.54	2.51	2.49	2.47
8	3.46	3.11	2.92	2.81	2.73	2.67	2.62	2.59	2.56	2.54	2.50	2.46	2.42	2.40	2.38	2.36	2.34	2.32	2.29
9	3.36	3.01	2.81	2.69	2.61	2.55	2.51	2.47	2.44	2.42	2.38	2.34	2.30	2.28	2.25	2.23	2.21	2.18	2.16
10	3.29	2.92	2.73	2.61	2.52	2.46	2.41	2.38	2.35	2.32	2.28	2.24	2.20	2.18	2.16	2.13	2.11	2.08	2.06
11	3.23	2.86	2.66	2.54	2.45	2.39	2.34	2.30	2.27	2.25	2.21	2.17	2.12	2.10	2.08	2.05	2.03	2.00	1.97
12	3.18	2.81	2.61	2.48	2.39	2.33	2.28	2.24	2.21	2.19	2.15	2.10	2.06	2.04	2.01	1.99	1.96	1.93	1.90
13	3.14	2.76	2.56	2.43	2.35	2.28	2.23	2.20	2.16	2.14	2.10	2.05	2.01	1.98	1.96	1.93	1.90	1.88	1.85
14	3.10	2.73	2.52	2.39	2.31	2.24	2.19	2.15	2.12	2.10	2.05	2.01	1.96	1.94	1.91	1.89	1.86	1.83	1.80
15	3.07	2.70	2.49	2.36	2.27	2.21	2.16	2.12	2.09	2.06	2.02	1.97	1.92	1.90	1.87	1.85	1.82	1.79	1.76
16	3.05	2.67	2.46	2.33	2.24	2.18	2.13	2.09	2.06	2.03	1.99	1.94	1.89	1.87	1.84	1.81	1.78	1.75	1.72
17	3.03	2.64	2.44	2.31	2.22	2.15	2.10	2.06	2.03	2.00	1.96	1.91	1.86	1.84	1.81	1.78	1.75	1.72	1.69
18	3.01	2.62	2.42	2.29	2.20	2.13	2.08	2.04	2.00	1.98	1.93	1.89	1.84	1.81	1.78	1.75	1.72	1.69	1.66
19	2.99	2.61	2.40	2.27	2.18	2.11	2.06	2.02	1.98	1.96	1.91	1.86	1.81	1.79	1.76	1.73	1.70	1.67	1.63
20	2.97	2.59	2.38	2.25	2.16	2.09	2.04	2.00	1.96	1.94	1.89	1.84	1.79	1.77	1.74	1.71	1.68	1.64	1.61
21	2.96	2.57	2.36	2.23	2.14	2.08	2.02	1.98	1.95	1.92	1.87	1.83	1.78	1.75	1.72	1.69	1.66	1.62	1.59
22	2.95	2.56	2.35	2.22	2.13	2.06	2.01	1.97	1.93	1.90	1.86	1.81	1.76	1.73	1.70	1.67	1.64	1.60	1.57
23	2.94	2.55	2.34	2.21	2.11	2.05	1.99	1.95	1.92	1.89	1.84	1.80	1.74	1.72	1.69	1.66	1.62	1.59	1.55
24	2.93	2.54	2.33	2.19	2.10	2.04	1.98	1.94	1.91	1.88	1.83	1.78	1.73	1.70	1.67	1.64	1.61	1.57	1.53
25	2.92	2.53	2.32	2.18	2.09	2.02	1.97	1.93	1.89	1.87	1.82	1.77	1.72	1.69	1.66	1.63	1.59	1.56	1.52
26	2.91	2.52	2.31	2.17	2.08	2.01	1.96	1.92	1.88	1.86	1.81	1.76	1.71	1.68	1.65	1.61	1.58	1.54	1.50
27	2.90	2.51	2.30	2.17	2.07	2.00	1.95	1.91	1.87	1.85	1.80	1.75	1.70	1.67	1.64	1.60	1.57	1.53	1.49

(Handwritten annotation across top: "Degrees freedom (b)"; and "(lo)". Handwritten annotation at lower left: "degrees freedom (w)" and "(3)".)

Continuation of preceding table (numerator df across the top):

df	1	2	3	4	5	6	7	8	9	10	12	15	20	24	30	40	60	120	∞
28	2.89	2.50	2.29	2.16	2.06	2.00	1.94	1.90	1.87	1.84	1.79	1.74	1.69	1.66	1.63	1.59	1.56	1.52	1.48
29	2.89	2.50	2.28	2.15	2.06	1.99	1.93	1.89	1.86	1.83	1.78	1.73	1.68	1.65	1.62	1.58	1.55	1.51	1.47
30	2.88	2.49	2.28	2.14	2.05	1.98	1.93	1.88	1.85	1.82	1.77	1.72	1.67	1.64	1.61	1.57	1.54	1.50	1.46
40	2.84	2.44	2.23	2.09	2.00	1.93	1.87	1.83	1.79	1.76	1.71	1.66	1.61	1.57	1.54	1.51	1.47	1.42	1.38
60	2.79	2.39	2.18	2.04	1.95	1.87	1.82	1.77	1.74	1.71	1.66	1.60	1.54	1.51	1.48	1.44	1.40	1.35	1.29
120	2.75	2.35	2.13	1.99	1.90	1.82	1.77	1.72	1.68	1.65	1.60	1.55	1.48	1.45	1.41	1.37	1.32	1.26	1.19
∞	2.71	2.30	2.08	1.94	1.85	1.77	1.72	1.67	1.63	1.60	1.55	1.49	1.42	1.38	1.34	1.30	1.24	1.17	1.00

α = .05

df	1	2	3	4	5	6	7	8	9	10	12	15	20	24	30	40	60	120	∞
1	161.4	199.5	215.7	224.6	230.2	234.0	236.8	238.9	240.5	241.9	243.9	245.9	248.0	249.1	250.1	251.1	252.2	253.3	254.3
2	18.51	19.00	19.16	19.25	19.30	19.33	19.35	19.37	19.38	19.40	19.41	19.43	19.45	19.45	19.46	19.47	19.48	19.49	19.50
3	10.13	9.55	9.28	9.12	9.01	8.94	8.89	8.85	8.81	8.79	8.74	8.70	8.66	8.62	8.59	8.57	8.55	8.55	8.53
4	7.71	6.94	6.59	6.39	6.26	6.16	6.09	6.04	6.00	5.96	5.91	5.86	5.80	5.77	5.75	5.72	5.69	5.66	5.63
5	6.61	5.79	5.41	5.19	5.05	4.95	4.88	4.82	4.77	4.74	4.68	4.62	4.56	4.53	4.50	4.46	4.43	4.40	4.36
6	5.99	5.14	4.76	4.53	4.39	4.28	4.21	4.15	4.10	4.06	4.00	3.94	3.87	3.84	3.81	3.77	3.74	3.70	3.67
7	5.59	4.74	4.35	4.12	3.97	3.87	3.79	3.73	3.68	3.64	3.57	3.51	3.44	3.41	3.38	3.34	3.30	3.27	3.23
8	5.32	4.46	4.07	3.84	3.69	3.58	3.50	3.44	3.39	3.35	3.28	3.22	3.15	3.12	3.08	3.04	3.01	2.97	2.93
9	5.12	4.26	3.86	3.63	3.48	3.37	3.29	3.23	3.18	3.14	3.07	3.01	2.94	2.90	2.86	2.83	2.79	2.75	2.71
10	4.96	4.10	3.71	3.48	3.33	3.22	3.14	3.07	3.02	2.98	2.91	2.85	2.77	2.74	2.70	2.66	2.62	2.58	2.54
11	4.84	3.98	3.59	3.36	3.20	3.09	3.01	2.95	2.90	2.85	2.79	2.72	2.65	2.61	2.57	2.53	2.49	2.45	2.40
12	4.75	3.89	3.49	3.26	3.11	3.00	2.91	2.85	2.80	2.75	2.69	2.62	2.54	2.51	2.47	2.43	2.38	2.34	2.30
13	4.67	3.81	3.41	3.18	3.03	2.92	2.83	2.77	2.71	2.67	2.60	2.53	2.46	2.42	2.38	2.34	2.30	2.25	2.21
14	4.60	3.74	3.34	3.11	2.96	2.85	2.76	2.70	2.65	2.60	2.53	2.46	2.39	2.35	2.31	2.27	2.22	2.18	2.13
15	4.54	3.68	3.29	3.06	2.90	2.79	2.71	2.64	2.59	2.54	2.48	2.40	2.33	2.29	2.25	2.20	2.16	2.11	2.07
16	4.49	3.63	3.24	3.01	2.85	2.74	2.66	2.59	2.54	2.49	2.42	2.35	2.28	2.24	2.19	2.15	2.11	2.06	2.01
17	4.45	3.59	3.20	2.96	2.81	2.70	2.61	2.55	2.49	2.45	2.38	2.31	2.23	2.19	2.15	2.10	2.06	2.01	1.96
18	4.41	3.55	3.16	2.93	2.77	2.66	2.58	2.51	2.46	2.41	2.34	2.27	2.19	2.15	2.11	2.06	2.02	1.97	1.92
19	4.38	3.52	3.13	2.90	2.74	2.63	2.54	2.48	2.42	2.38	2.31	2.23	2.16	2.11	2.07	2.03	1.98	1.93	1.88
20	4.35	3.49	3.10	2.87	2.71	2.60	2.51	2.45	2.39	2.35	2.28	2.20	2.12	2.08	2.04	1.99	1.95	1.90	1.84
21	4.32	3.47	3.07	2.84	2.68	2.57	2.49	2.42	2.37	2.32	2.25	2.18	2.10	2.05	2.01	1.96	1.92	1.87	1.81
22	4.30	3.44	3.05	2.82	2.66	2.55	2.46	2.40	2.34	2.30	2.23	2.15	2.07	2.03	1.98	1.94	1.89	1.84	1.78
23	4.28	3.42	3.03	2.80	2.64	2.53	2.44	2.37	2.32	2.27	2.20	2.13	2.05	2.01	1.96	1.91	1.86	1.81	1.76
24	4.26	3.40	3.01	2.78	2.62	2.51	2.42	2.36	2.30	2.25	2.18	2.11	2.03	1.98	1.94	1.89	1.84	1.79	1.73

(continued)

TABLE A.4 (continued)

Percentage Points of the F Distribution

v_2		1	2	3	4	5	6	7	8	9	10	12	15	20	24	30	40	60	120	∞
$\alpha = .05$																				
25		4.24	3.39	2.99	2.76	2.60	2.49	2.40	2.34	2.28	2.24	2.16	2.09	2.01	1.96	1.92	1.87	1.82	1.77	1.71
26		4.23	3.37	2.98	2.74	2.59	2.47	2.39	2.32	2.27	2.22	2.15	2.07	1.99	1.95	1.90	1.85	1.80	1.75	1.69
27		4.21	3.35	2.96	2.73	2.57	2.46	2.37	2.31	2.25	2.20	2.13	2.06	1.97	1.93	1.88	1.84	1.79	1.73	1.67
28		4.20	3.34	2.95	2.71	2.56	2.45	2.36	2.29	2.24	2.19	2.12	2.04	1.96	1.91	1.87	1.82	1.77	1.71	1.65
29		4.18	3.33	2.93	2.70	2.55	2.43	2.35	2.28	2.22	2.18	2.10	2.03	1.94	1.90	1.85	1.81	1.75	1.70	1.64
30		4.17	3.32	2.92	2.69	2.53	2.42	2.33	2.27	2.21	2.16	2.09	2.01	1.93	1.89	1.84	1.79	1.74	1.68	1.62
40		4.08	3.23	2.84	2.61	2.45	2.34	2.25	2.18	2.12	2.08	2.00	1.92	1.84	1.79	1.74	1.69	1.64	1.58	1.51
60		4.00	3.15	2.76	2.53	2.37	2.25	2.17	2.10	2.04	1.99	1.92	1.84	1.75	1.70	1.65	1.59	1.53	1.47	1.39
120		3.92	3.07	2.68	2.45	2.29	2.17	2.09	2.02	1.96	1.91	1.83	1.75	1.66	1.61	1.55	1.50	1.43	1.35	1.25
∞		3.84	3.00	2.60	2.37	2.21	2.10	2.01	1.94	1.88	1.83	1.75	1.67	1.57	1.52	1.46	1.39	1.32	1.22	1.00
$\alpha = .01$																				
1		4052	4999.5	5403	5625	5764	5859	5928	5981	6022	6056	6106	6157	6209	6235	6261	6287	6313	6339	6366
2		98.50	99.00	99.17	99.25	99.30	99.33	99.36	99.37	99.39	99.40	99.42	99.43	99.45	99.46	99.47	99.47	99.48	99.49	99.50
3		34.12	30.82	29.46	28.71	28.24	27.91	27.67	27.49	27.35	27.23	27.05	26.87	26.69	26.60	26.50	26.41	26.32	25.22	26.13
4		21.20	18.00	16.69	15.98	15.52	15.21	14.98	14.80	14.66	14.55	14.37	14.20	14.02	13.93	13.84	13.75	13.55	13.56	13.46
5		16.26	13.27	12.06	11.39	10.97	10.67	10.46	10.29	10.16	10.05	9.89	9.72	9.55	9.47	9.38	9.29	9.20	9.11	9.02
6		13.75	10.92	9.78	9.15	8.75	8.47	8.26	8.10	7.98	7.87	7.72	7.56	7.40	7.31	7.23	7.14	7.06	6.97	6.88
7		12.25	9.55	8.45	7.85	7.46	7.19	6.99	6.84	6.72	6.62	6.47	6.31	6.16	6.07	5.99	5.91	5.82	5.74	5.65
8		11.26	8.65	7.59	7.01	6.63	6.37	6.18	6.03	5.91	5.81	5.67	5.52	5.36	5.28	5.20	5.12	5.03	4.95	4.86
9		10.56	8.02	6.99	6.42	6.06	5.80	5.61	5.47	5.35	5.26	5.11	4.96	4.81	4.73	4.65	4.57	4.48	4.40	4.31
10		10.04	7.56	6.55	5.99	5.64	5.39	5.20	5.06	4.94	4.85	4.71	4.56	4.41	4.33	4.25	4.17	4.08	4.00	3.91
11		9.65	7.21	6.22	5.67	5.32	5.07	4.89	4.74	4.63	4.54	4.40	4.25	4.10	4.02	3.94	3.86	3.78	3.69	3.60
12		9.33	6.93	5.95	5.41	5.06	4.82	4.64	4.50	4.39	4.30	4.16	4.01	3.86	3.78	3.70	3.62	3.54	3.45	3.36

v_1

v_2																			
13	9.07	6.70	5.74	5.21	4.86	4.62	4.44	4.30	4.19	4.10	3.96	3.82	3.66	3.59	3.51	3.43	3.34	3.25	3.17
14	8.86	6.51	5.56	5.04	4.69	4.46	4.28	4.14	4.03	3.94	3.80	3.66	3.51	3.43	3.35	3.27	3.18	3.09	3.00
15	8.68	6.36	5.42	4.89	4.56	4.32	4.14	4.00	3.89	3.80	3.67	3.52	3.37	3.29	3.21	3.13	3.05	2.96	2.87
16	8.53	6.23	5.29	4.77	4.44	4.20	4.03	3.89	3.78	3.69	3.55	3.41	3.26	3.18	3.10	3.02	2.93	2.84	2.75
17	8.40	6.11	5.18	4.67	4.34	4.10	3.93	3.79	3.68	3.59	3.46	3.31	3.16	3.08	3.00	2.92	2.83	2.75	2.65
18	8.29	6.01	5.09	4.58	4.25	4.01	3.84	3.71	3.60	3.51	3.37	3.23	3.08	3.00	2.92	2.84	2.75	2.66	2.57
19	8.18	5.93	5.01	4.50	4.17	3.94	3.77	3.63	3.52	3.43	3.30	3.15	3.00	2.92	2.84	2.76	2.67	2.58	2.49
20	8.10	5.85	4.94	4.43	4.10	3.87	3.70	3.56	3.46	3.37	3.23	3.09	2.94	2.86	2.78	2.69	2.61	2.52	2.42
21	8.02	5.78	4.87	4.37	4.04	3.81	3.64	3.51	3.40	3.31	3.17	3.03	2.88	2.80	2.72	2.64	2.55	2.46	2.36
22	7.95	5.72	4.82	4.31	3.99	3.76	3.59	3.45	3.35	3.26	3.12	2.98	2.83	2.75	2.67	2.58	2.50	2.40	2.31
23	7.88	5.66	4.76	4.26	3.94	3.71	3.54	3.41	3.30	3.21	3.07	2.93	2.78	2.70	2.62	2.54	2.45	2.35	2.26
24	7.82	5.61	4.72	4.22	3.90	3.67	3.50	3.36	3.26	3.17	3.03	2.89	2.74	2.66	2.58	2.49	2.40	2.31	2.21
25	7.77	5.57	4.68	4.18	3.85	3.63	3.46	3.32	3.22	3.13	2.99	2.85	2.70	2.62	2.54	2.45	2.36	2.27	2.17
26	7.72	5.53	4.64	4.14	3.82	3.59	3.42	3.29	3.18	3.09	2.96	2.81	2.66	2.58	2.50	2.42	2.33	2.23	2.18
27	7.68	5.49	4.60	4.11	3.78	3.56	3.39	3.26	3.15	3.06	2.93	2.78	2.63	2.55	2.47	2.38	2.29	2.20	2.10
28	7.64	5.45	4.57	4.07	3.75	3.53	3.36	3.23	3.12	3.03	2.90	2.75	2.60	2.52	2.44	2.35	2.26	2.17	2.06
29	7.60	5.42	4.54	4.04	3.73	3.50	3.33	3.20	3.09	3.00	2.87	2.73	2.57	2.49	2.41	2.33	2.23	2.14	2.03
30	7.56	5.39	4.51	4.02	3.70	3.47	3.30	3.17	3.07	2.98	2.84	2.70	2.55	2.47	2.39	2.30	2.21	2.11	2.01
40	7.31	5.18	4.31	3.83	3.51	3.29	3.12	2.99	2.89	2.80	2.66	2.52	2.37	2.29	2.20	2.11	2.02	1.92	1.80
60	7.08	4.98	4.13	3.65	3.34	3.12	2.95	2.82	2.72	2.63	2.50	2.35	2.20	2.12	2.03	1.94	1.84	1.73	1.60
120	6.85	4.79	3.95	3.48	3.17	2.96	2.79	2.66	2.56	2.47	2.34	2.19	2.03	1.95	1.86	1.76	1.66	1.53	1.38
∞	6.63	4.61	3.78	3.32	3.02	2.80	2.64	2.51	2.41	2.32	2.18	2.04	1.88	1.79	1.70	1.59	1.47	1.32	1.00

Source: Reprinted from Pearson, E.S. and Hartley, H.O., *Biometrika Tables for Statisticians*, Cambridge University Press, Cambridge, U.K., 1966, Table 18. With permission of Biometrika Trustees.

v_1 is the numerator degrees of freedom, and v_2 is the denominator degrees of freedom.

TABLE A.5

Fisher's Z Transformed Values

r	Z	r	Z
.00	.0000	.50	.5493
1	.0100	1	.5627
2	.0200	2	.5763
3	.0300	3	.5901
4	.0400	4	.6042
.05	.0500	.55	.6184
6	.0601	6	.6328
7	.0701	7	.6475
8	.0802	8	.6625
9	.0902	9	.6777
.10	.1003	.60	.6931
1	.1104	1	.7089
2	.1206	2	.7250
3	.1307	3	.7414
4	.1409	4	.7582
.15	.1511	.65	.7753
6	.1614	6	.7928
7	.1717	7	.8107
8	.1820	8	.8291
9	.1923	9	.8480
.20	.2027	.70	.8673
1	.2132	1	.8872
2	.2237	2	.9076
3	.2342	3	.9287
4	.2448	4	.9505
.25	.2554	.75	0.973
6	.2661	6	0.996
7	.2769	7	1.020
8	.2877	8	1.045
9	.2986	9	1.071
.30	.3095	.80	1.099
1	.3205	1	1.127
2	.3316	2	1.157
3	.3428	3	1.188
4	.3541	4	1.221
.35	.3654	.85	1.256
6	.3769	6	1.293
7	.3884	7	1.333
8	.4001	8	1.376
9	.4118	9	1.422

TABLE A.5 (continued)

Fisher's Z Transformed Values

r	Z	r	Z
.40	.4236	.90	1.472
1	.4356	1	1.528
2	.4477	2	1.589
3	.4599	3	1.658
4	.4722	4	1.738
.45	.4847	.95	1.832
6	.4973	6	1.946
7	.5101	7	2.092
8	.5230	8	2.298
9	.5361	9	2.647

Source: Reprinted from Pearson, E.S. and Hartley, H.O., *Biometrika Tables for Statisticians*, Cambridge University Press, Cambridge, U.K., 1966, Table 14. With permission of Biometrika Trustees.

TABLE A.6

Orthogonal Polynomials

J	Trend	j = 1	2	3	4	5	6	7	8	9	10	Σc_j^2
J = 3	Linear	−1	0	1								2
	Quadratic	1	−2	1								6
J = 4	Linear	−3	−1	1	3							20
	Quadratic	1	−1	−1	1							4
	Cubic	−1	3	−3	1							20
J = 5	Linear	−2	−1	0	1	2						10
	Quadratic	2	−1	−2	−1	2						14
	Cubic	−1	2	0	−2	1						10
	Quartic	1	−4	6	−4	1						70
J = 6	Linear	−5	−3	−1	1	3	5					70
	Quadratic	5	−1	−4	−4	−1	5					84
	Cubic	−5	7	4	−4	−7	5					180
	Quartic	1	−3	2	2	−3	1					28
	Quintic	−1	5	−10	10	−5	1					252
J = 7	Linear	−3	−2	−1	0	1	2	3				28
	Quadratic	5	0	−3	−4	−3	0	5				84
	Cubic	−1	1	1	0	−1	−1	1				6
	Quartic	3	−7	1	6	1	−7	3				154
	Quintic	−1	4	−5	0	5	−4	1				84
J = 8	Linear	−7	−5	−3	−1	1	3	5	7			168
	Quadratic	7	1	−3	−5	−5	−3	1	7			168
	Cubic	−7	5	7	3	−3	−7	−5	7			264
	Quartic	7	−13	−3	9	9	−3	−13	7			616
	Quintic	−7	23	−17	−15	15	17	−23	7			2184
J = 9	Linear	−4	−3	−2	−1	0	1	2	3	4		60
	Quadratic	28	7	−8	−17	−20	−17	−8	7	28		2772
	Cubic	−14	7	13	9	0	−9	−13	−7	14		990
	Quartic	14	−21	−11	9	18	9	−11	−21	14		2002
	Quintic	−4	11	−4	−9	0	9	4	−11	4		468
J = 10	Linear	−9	−7	−5	−3	−1	1	3	5	7	9	330
	Quadratic	6	2	−1	−3	−4	−4	−3	−1	2	6	132
	Cubic	−42	14	35	31	12	−12	−31	−35	−14	42	8580
	Quartic	18	−22	−17	3	18	18	3	−17	−22	18	2860
	Quintic	−6	14	−1	−11	−6	6	11	1	−14	6	780

Source: Reprinted from Pearson, E.S. and Hartley, H.O., *Biometrika Tables for Statisticians*, Cambridge University Press, Cambridge, U.K., 1966, Table 47. With permission of Biometrika Trustees.

TABLE A.7

Critical Values for Dunnett's Procedure

df	1	2	3	4	5	6	7	8	9
One tailed, α = .05									
5	2.02	2.44	2.68	2.85	2.98	3.08	3.16	3.24	3.30
6	1.94	2.34	2.56	2.71	2.83	2.92	3.00	3.07	3.12
7	1.89	2.27	2.48	2.62	2.73	2.82	2.89	2.95	3.01
8	1.86	2.22	2.42	2.55	2.66	2.74	2.81	2.87	2.92
9	1.83	2.18	2.37	2.50	2.60	2.68	2.75	2.81	2.86
10	1.81	2.15	2.34	2.47	2.56	2.64	2.70	2.76	2.81
11	1.80	2.13	2.31	2.44	2.53	2.60	2.67	2.72	2.77
12	1.78	2.11	2.29	2.41	2.50	2.58	2.64	2.69	2.74
13	1.77	2.09	2.27	2.39	2.48	2.55	2.61	2.66	2.71
14	1.76	2.08	2.25	2.37	2.46	2.53	2.59	2.64	2.69
15	1.75	2.07	2.24	2.36	2.44	2.51	2.57	2.62	2.67
16	1.75	2.06	2.23	2.34	2.43	2.50	2.56	2.61	2.65
17	1.74	2.05	2.22	2.33	2.42	2.49	2.54	2.59	2.64
18	1.73	2.04	2.21	2.32	2.41	2.48	2.53	2.58	2.62
19	1.73	2.03	2.20	2.31	2.40	2.47	2.52	2.57	2.61
20	1.72	2.03	2.19	2.30	2.39	2.46	2.51	2.56	2.60
24	1.71	2.01	2.17	2.28	2.36	2.43	2.48	2.53	2.57
30	1.70	1.99	2.15	2.25	2.33	2.40	2.45	2.50	2.54
40	1.68	1.97	2.13	2.23	2.31	2.37	2.42	2.47	2.51
60	1.67	1.95	2.10	2.21	2.28	2.35	2.39	2.44	2.48
120	1.66	1.93	2.08	2.18	2.26	2.32	2.37	2.41	2.45
∞	1.64	1.92	2.06	2.16	2.23	2.29	2.34	2.38	2.42
One tailed, α = .01									
5	3.37	3.90	4.21	4.43	4.60	4.73	4.85	4.94	5.03
6	3.14	3.61	3.88	4.07	4.21	4.33	4.43	4.51	4.59
7	3.00	3.42	3.66	3.83	3.96	4.07	4.15	4.23	4.30
8	2.90	3.29	3.51	3.67	3.79	3.88	3.96	4.03	4.09
9	2.82	3.19	3.40	3.55	3.66	3.75	3.82	3.89	3.94
10	2.76	3.11	3.31	3.45	3.56	3.64	3.71	3.78	3.83
11	2.72	3.06	3.25	3.38	3.48	3.56	3.63	3.69	3.74
12	2.68	3.01	3.19	3.32	3.42	3.50	3.56	3.62	3.67
13	2.65	2.97	3.15	3.27	3.37	3.44	3.51	3.56	3.61
14	2.62	2.94	3.11	3.23	3.32	3.40	3.46	3.51	3.56
15	2.60	2.91	3.08	3.20	3.29	3.36	3.42	3.47	3.52
16	2.58	2.88	3.05	3.17	3.26	3.33	3.39	3.44	3.48
17	2.57	2.86	3.03	3.14	3.23	3.30	3.36	3.41	3.45
18	2.55	2.84	3.01	3.12	3.21	3.27	3.33	3.38	3.42
19	2.54	2.83	2.99	3.10	3.18	3.25	3.31	3.36	3.40
20	2.53	2.81	2.97	3.08	3.17	3.23	3.29	3.34	3.38
24	2.49	2.77	2.92	3.03	3.11	3.17	3.22	3.27	3.31

(continued)

TABLE A.7 (continued)

Critical Values for Dunnett's Procedure

df	1	2	3	4	5	6	7	8	9
One tailed, $\alpha = .01$									
30	2.46	2.72	2.87	2.97	3.05	3.11	3.16	3.21	3.24
40	2.42	2.68	2.82	2.92	2.99	3.05	3.10	3.14	3.18
60	2.39	2.64	2.78	2.87	2.94	3.00	3.04	3.08	3.12
120	2.36	2.60	2.73	2.82	2.89	2.94	2.99	3.03	3.06
∞	2.33	2.56	2.68	2.77	2.84	2.89	2.93	2.97	3.00
Two tailed, $\alpha = .05$									
5	2.57	3.03	3.29	3.48	3.62	3.73	3.82	3.90	3.97
6	2.45	2.86	3.10	3.26	3.39	3.49	3.57	3.64	3.71
7	2.36	2.75	2.97	3.12	3.24	3.33	3.41	3.47	3.53
8	2.31	2.67	2.88	3.02	3.13	3.22	3.29	3.35	3.41
9	2.26	2.61	2.81	2.95	3.05	3.14	3.20	3.26	3.32
10	2.23	2.57	2.76	2.89	2.99	3.07	3.14	3.19	3.24
11	2.20	2.53	2.72	2.84	2.94	3.02	3.08	3.14	3.19
12	2.18	2.50	2.68	2.81	2.90	2.98	3.04	3.09	3.14
13	2.16	2.48	2.65	2.78	2.87	2.94	3.00	3.06	3.10
14	2.14	2.46	2.63	2.75	2.84	2.91	2.97	3.02	3.07
15	2.13	2.44	2.61	2.73	2.82	2.89	2.95	3.00	3.04
16	2.12	2.42	2.59	2.71	2.80	2.87	2.92	2.97	3.02
17	2.11	2.41	2.58	2.69	2.78	2.85	2.90	2.95	3.00
18	2.10	2.40	2.56	2.68	2.76	2.83	2.89	2.94	2.98
19	2.09	2.39	2.55	2.66	2.75	2.81	2.87	2.92	2.96
20	2.09	2.38	2.54	2.65	2.73	2.80	2.86	2.90	2.95
24	2.06	2.35	2.51	2.61	2.70	2.76	2.81	2.86	2.90
30	2.04	2.32	2.47	2.58	2.66	2.72	2.77	2.82	2.86
40	2.02	2.29	2.44	2.54	2.62	2.68	2.73	2.77	2.81
60	2.00	2.27	2.41	2.51	2.58	2.64	2.69	2.73	2.77
120	1.98	2.24	2.38	2.47	2.55	2.60	2.65	2.69	2.73
∞	1.96	2.21	2.35	2.44	2.51	2.57	2.61	2.65	2.69
Two tailed, $\alpha = .01$									
5	4.03	4.63	4.98	5.22	5.41	5.56	5.69	5.80	5.89
6	3.71	4.21	4.51	4.71	4.87	5.00	5.10	5.20	5.28
7	3.50	3.95	4.21	4.39	4.53	4.64	4.74	4.82	4.89
8	3.36	3.77	4.00	4.17	4.29	4.40	4.48	4.56	4.62
9	3.25	3.63	3.85	4.01	4.12	4.22	4.30	4.37	4.43
10	3.17	3.53	3.74	3.88	3.99	4.08	4.16	4.22	4.28
11	3.11	3.45	3.65	3.79	3.89	3.98	4.05	4.11	4.16
12	3.05	3.39	3.58	3.71	3.81	3.89	3.96	4.02	4.07
13	3.01	3.33	3.52	3.65	3.74	3.82	3.89	3.94	3.99
14	2.98	3.29	3.47	3.59	3.69	3.76	3.83	3.88	3.93
15	2.95	3.25	3.43	3.55	3.64	3.71	3.78	3.83	3.88
16	2.92	3.22	3.39	3.51	3.60	3.67	3.73	3.78	3.83

TABLE A.7 (continued)

Critical Values for Dunnett's Procedure

df	1	2	3	4	5	6	7	8	9
Two tailed, $\alpha = .01$									
17	2.90	3.19	3.36	3.47	3.56	3.63	3.69	3.74	3.79
18	2.88	3.17	3.33	3.44	3.53	3.60	3.66	3.71	3.75
19	2.86	3.15	3.31	3.42	3.50	3.57	3.63	3.68	3.72
20	2.85	3.13	3.29	3.40	3.48	3.55	3.60	3.65	3.69
24	2.80	3.07	3.22	3.32	3.40	3.47	3.52	3.57	3.61
30	2.75	3.01	3.15	3.25	3.33	3.39	3.44	3.49	3.52
40	2.70	2.95	3.09	3.19	3.26	3.32	3.37	3.41	3.44
60	2.66	2.90	3.03	3.12	3.19	3.25	3.29	3.33	3.37
120	2.62	2.85	2.97	3.06	3.12	3.18	3.22	3.26	3.29
∞	2.58	2.79	2.92	3.00	3.06	3.11	3.15	3.19	3.22

Sources: Reprinted from Dunnett, C.W., *J. Am. Stat. Assoc.*, 50, 1096, 1955, Table 1a and Table 1b. With permission of the American Statistical Association; Dunnett, C.W., *Biometrics*, 20, 482, 1964, Table II and Table III. With permission of the Biometric Society.

The columns represent J = number of treatment means (excluding the control).

TABLE A.8

Critical Values for Dunn's (Bonferroni's) Procedure

		Number of Contrasts										
ν	α	2	3	4	5	6	7	8	9	10	15	20
2	0.01	14.071	17.248	19.925	22.282	24.413	26.372	28.196	29.908	31.528	38.620	44.598
	0.05	6.164	7.582	8.774	9.823	10.769	11.639	12.449	13.208	13.927	17.072	19.721
	0.10	4.243	5.243	6.081	6.816	7.480	8.090	8.656	9.188	9.691	11.890	13.741
	0.20	2.828	3.531	4.116	4.628	5.089	5.512	5.904	6.272	6.620	8.138	9.414
3	0.01	7.447	8.565	9.453	10.201	10.853	11.436	11.966	12.453	12.904	14.796	16.300
	0.05	4.156	4.826	5.355	5.799	6.185	6.529	6.842	7.128	7.394	8.505	9.387
	0.10	3.149	3.690	4.115	4.471	4.780	5.055	5.304	5.532	5.744	6.627	7.326
	0.20	2.294	2.734	3.077	3.363	3.610	3.829	4.028	4.209	4.377	5.076	5.626
4	0.01	5.594	6.248	6.751	7.166	7.520	7.832	8.112	8.367	8.600	9.556	10.294
	0.05	3.481	3.941	4.290	4.577	4.822	5.036	5.228	5.402	5.562	6.214	6.714
	0.10	2.751	3.150	3.452	3.699	3.909	4.093	4.257	4.406	4.542	5.097	5.521
	0.20	2.084	2.434	2.697	2.911	3.092	3.250	3.391	3.518	3.635	4.107	4.468
5	0.01	4.771	5.243	5.599	5.888	6.133	6.346	6.535	6.706	6.862	7.491	7.968
	0.05	3.152	3.518	3.791	4.012	4.197	4.358	4.501	4.630	4.747	5.219	5.573
	0.10	2.549	2.882	3.129	3.327	3.493	3.638	3.765	3.880	3.985	4.403	4.718
	0.20	1.973	2.278	2.503	2.683	2.834	2.964	3.079	3.182	3.275	3.649	3.928
6	0.01	4.315	4.695	4.977	5.203	5.394	5.559	5.704	5.835	5.954	6.428	6.782
	0.05	2.959	3.274	3.505	3.690	3.845	3.978	4.095	4.200	4.296	4.675	4.956
	0.10	2.428	2.723	2.939	3.110	3.253	3.376	3.484	3.580	3.668	4.015	4.272
	0.20	1.904	2.184	2.387	2.547	2.681	2.795	2.895	2.985	3.066	3.385	3.620
7	0.01	4.027	4.353	4.591	4.782	4.941	5.078	5.198	5.306	5.404	5.791	6.077
	0.05	2.832	3.115	3.321	3.484	3.620	3.736	3.838	3.929	4.011	4.336	4.574
	0.10	2.347	2.618	2.814	2.969	3.097	3.206	3.302	3.388	3.465	3.768	3.990
	0.20	1.858	2.120	2.309	2.457	2.579	2.684	2.775	2.856	2.929	3.214	3.423
8	0.01	3.831	4.120	4.331	4.498	4.637	4.756	4.860	4.953	5.038	5.370	5.613
	0.05	2.743	3.005	3.193	3.342	3.464	3.589	3.661	3.743	3.816	4.105	4.316
	0.10	2.289	2.544	2.726	2.869	2.967	3.088	3.176	3.254	3.324	3.598	3.798
	0.20	1.824	2.075	2.254	2.393	2.508	2.605	2.690	2.765	2.832	3.095	3.286
9	0.01	3.688	3.952	4.143	4.294	4.419	4.526	4.619	4.703	4.778	5.072	5.287
	0.05	2.677	2.923	3.099	3.237	3.351	3.448	3.532	3.607	3.675	3.938	4.129
	0.10	2.246	2.488	2.661	2.796	2.907	3.001	3.083	3.155	3.221	3.474	3.658
	0.20	1.799	2.041	2.212	2.345	2.454	2.546	2.627	2.696	2.761	3.008	3.185
10	0.01	3.580	3.825	4.002	4.141	4.256	4.354	4.439	4.515	4.584	4.852	5.046
	0.05	2.626	2.860	3.027	3.157	3.264	3.355	3.434	3.505	3.568	3.813	3.989
	0.10	2.213	2.446	2.611	2.739	2.845	2.934	3.012	3.080	3.142	3.380	3.552
	0.20	1.779	2.014	2.180	2.308	2.413	2.501	2.578	2.646	2.706	2.941	3.106
11	0.01	3.495	3.726	3.892	4.022	4.129	4.221	4.300	4.371	4.434	4.682	4.860
	0.05	2.586	2.811	2.970	3.094	3.196	3.283	3.358	3.424	3.484	3.715	3.880
	0.10	2.166	2.412	2.571	2.695	2.796	2.881	2.955	3.021	3.079	3.306	3.468
	0.20	1.763	1.993	2.154	2.279	2.380	2.465	2.539	2.605	2.663	2.888	3.048
12	0.01	3.427	3.647	3.804	3.927	4.029	4.114	4.189	4.256	4.315	4.547	4.714
	0.05	2.553	2.770	2.924	3.044	3.141	3.224	3.296	3.359	3.416	3.636	3.793
	0.10	2.164	2.384	2.539	2.658	2.756	2.838	2.910	2.973	3.029	3.247	3.402
	0.20	1.750	1.975	2.133	2.254	2.353	2.436	2.508	2.571	2.628	2.845	2.999

TABLE A.8 (continued)

Critical Values for Dunn's (Bonferroni's) Procedure

		Number of Contrasts										
ν	α	2	3	4	5	6	7	8	9	10	15	20
13	0.01	3.371	3.582	3.733	3.850	3.946	4.028	4.099	4.162	4.218	4.438	4.595
	0.05	2.526	2.737	2.886	3.002	3.096	3.176	3.245	3.306	3.361	3.571	3.722
	0.10	2.146	2.361	2.512	2.628	2.723	2.803	2.872	2.933	2.988	3.198	3.347
	0.20	1.739	1.961	2.116	2.234	2.331	2.412	2.482	2.544	2.599	2.809	2.958
14	0.01	3.324	3.528	3.673	3.785	3.878	3.956	4.024	4.084	4.138	4.347	4.497
	0.05	2.503	2.709	2.854	2.967	3.058	3.135	3.202	3.261	3.314	3.518	3.662
	0.10	2.131	2.342	2.489	2.603	2.696	2.774	2.841	2.900	2.953	3.157	3.301
	0.20	1.730	1.949	2.101	2.217	2.312	2.392	2.460	2.520	2.574	2.779	2.924
15	0.01	3.285	3.482	3.622	3.731	3.820	3.895	3.961	4.019	4.071	4.271	4.414
	0.05	2.483	2.685	2.827	2.937	3.026	3.101	3.166	3.224	3.275	3.472	3.612
	0.10	2.118	2.325	2.470	2.582	2.672	2.748	2.814	2.872	2.924	3.122	3.262
	0.20	1.722	1.938	2.088	2.203	2.296	2.374	2.441	2.500	2.553	2.754	2.896
16	0.01	3.251	3.443	3.579	3.684	3.771	3.844	3.907	3.963	4.013	4.206	4.344
	0.05	2.467	2.665	2.804	2.911	2.998	3.072	3.135	3.191	3.241	3.433	3.569
	0.10	2.106	2.311	2.453	2.563	2.652	2.726	2.791	2.848	2.898	3.092	3.228
	0.20	1.715	1.929	2.077	2.190	2.282	2.359	2.425	2.483	2.535	2.732	2.871
17	0.01	3.221	3.409	3.541	3.644	3.728	3.799	3.860	3.914	3.963	4.150	4.284
	0.05	2.452	2.647	2.783	2.889	2.974	3.046	3.108	3.163	3.212	3.399	3.532
	0.10	2.096	2.296	2.439	2.547	2.634	2.706	2.771	2.826	2.876	3.066	3.199
	0.20	1.709	1.921	2.068	2.179	2.270	2.346	2.411	2.488	2.519	2.713	2.849
18	0.01	3.195	3.379	3.508	3.609	3.691	3.760	3.820	3.872	3.920	4.102	4.231
	0.05	2.439	2.631	2.766	2.869	2.953	3.024	3.085	3.138	3.186	3.370	3.499
	0.10	2.088	2.287	2.426	2.532	2.619	2.691	2.753	2.806	2.857	3.043	3.174
	0.20	1.704	1.914	2.059	2.170	2.259	2.334	2.399	2.455	2.505	2.696	2.830
19	0.01	3.173	3.353	3.479	3.578	3.658	3.725	3.784	3.835	3.881	4.059	4.185
	0.05	2.427	2.617	2.750	2.852	2.934	3.004	3.064	3.116	3.163	3.343	3.470
	0.10	2.080	2.277	2.415	2.520	2.605	2.676	2.738	2.791	2.839	3.023	3.152
	0.20	1.699	1.908	2.052	2.161	2.250	2.324	2.388	2.443	2.493	2.682	2.813
20	0.01	3.152	3.329	3.454	3.550	3.629	3.695	3.752	3.802	3.848	4.021	4.144
	0.05	2.417	2.605	2.736	2.836	2.918	2.986	3.045	3.097	3.143	3.320	3.445
	0.10	2.073	2.269	2.405	2.508	2.593	2.663	2.724	2.777	2.824	3.005	3.132
	0.20	1.695	1.902	2.045	2.154	2.241	2.315	2.378	2.433	2.482	2.668	2.798
21	0.01	3.134	3.308	3.431	3.525	3.602	3.667	3.724	3.773	3.817	3.987	4.108
	0.05	2.408	2.594	2.723	2.822	2.903	2.970	3.028	3.080	3.125	3.300	3.422
	0.10	2.067	2.261	2.396	2.498	2.581	2.651	2.711	2.764	2.810	2.989	3.114
	0.20	1.691	1.897	2.039	2.147	2.234	2.306	2.369	2.424	2.472	2.656	2.785
22	0.01	3.118	3.289	3.410	3.503	3.579	3.643	3.698	3.747	3.790	3.957	4.075
	0.05	2.400	2.584	2.712	2.810	2.889	2.956	3.014	3.064	3.109	3.281	3.402
	0.10	2.061	2.254	2.387	2.489	2.572	2.641	2.700	2.752	2.798	2.974	3.096
	0.20	1.688	1.892	2.033	2.141	2.227	2.299	2.361	2.415	2.463	2.646	2.773

(continued)

TABLE A.8 (continued)

Critical Values for Dunn's (Bonferroni's) Procedure

| ν | α | \multicolumn{11}{c}{Number of Contrasts} | | | | | | | | | | |
		2	3	4	5	6	7	8	9	10	15	20
23	0.01	3.103	3.272	3.392	3.483	3.558	3.621	3.675	3.723	3.766	3.930	4.046
	0.05	2.392	2.574	2.701	2.798	2.877	2.943	3.000	3.050	3.094	3.264	3.383
	0.10	2.056	2.247	2.380	2.481	2.563	2.631	2.690	2.741	2.787	2.961	3.083
	0.20	1.685	1.888	2.028	2.135	2.221	2.292	2.354	2.407	2.455	2.636	2.762
24	0.01	3.089	3.257	3.375	3.465	3.539	3.601	3.654	3.702	3.744	3.905	4.019
	0.05	2.385	2.566	2.692	2.788	2.866	2.931	2.988	3.037	3.081	3.249	3.366
	0.10	2.051	2.241	2.373	2.473	2.554	2.622	2.680	2.731	2.777	2.949	3.070
	0.20	1.682	1.884	2.024	2.130	2.215	2.286	2.347	2.400	2.448	2.627	2.752
25	0.01	3.077	3.243	3.359	3.449	3.521	3.583	3.635	3.682	3.723	3.882	3.995
	0.05	2.379	2.558	2.683	2.779	2.856	2.921	2.976	3.025	3.069	3.235	3.351
	0.10	2.047	2.236	2.367	2.466	2.547	2.614	2.672	2.722	2.767	2.938	3.058
	0.20	1.679	1.881	2.020	2.125	2.210	2.280	2.341	2.394	2.441	2.619	2.743
26	0.01	3.066	3.230	3.345	3.433	3.505	3.566	3.618	3.664	3.705	3.862	3.972
	0.05	2.373	2.551	2.675	2.770	2.847	2.911	2.966	3.014	3.058	3.222	3.337
	0.10	2.043	2.231	2.361	2.460	2.540	2.607	2.664	2.714	2.759	2.928	3.047
	0.20	1.677	1.878	2.016	2.121	2.205	2.275	2.335	2.388	2.435	2.612	2.735
27	0.01	3.056	3.218	3.332	3.419	3.491	3.550	3.602	3.647	3.688	3.843	3.952
	0.05	2.368	2.545	2.668	2.762	2.838	2.902	2.956	3.004	3.047	3.210	3.324
	0.10	2.039	2.227	2.356	2.454	2.534	2.600	2.657	2.707	2.751	2.919	3.036
	0.20	1.675	1.875	2.012	2.117	2.201	2.270	2.330	2.383	2.429	2.605	2.727
28	0.01	3.046	3.207	3.320	3.407	3.477	3.536	3.587	3.632	3.672	3.825	3.933
	0.05	2.383	2.539	2.661	2.755	2.830	2.893	2.948	2.995	3.038	3.199	3.312
	0.10	2.036	2.222	2.351	2.449	2.528	2.594	2.650	2.700	2.744	2.911	3.027
	0.20	1.672	1.872	2.009	2.113	2.196	2.266	2.326	2.378	2.424	2.599	2.720
29	0.01	3.037	3.197	3.309	3.395	3.464	3.523	3.574	3.618	3.658	3.809	3.916
	0.05	2.358	2.534	2.655	2.748	2.823	2.886	2.940	2.967	3.029	3.189	3.301
	0.10	2.033	2.218	2.346	2.444	2.522	2.588	2.644	2.693	2.737	2.903	3.018
	0.20	1.671	1.869	2.006	2.110	2.193	2.262	2.321	2.373	2.419	2.593	2.713
30	0.01	3.029	3.188	3.298	3.384	3.453	3.511	3.561	3.605	3.644	3.794	3.900
	0.05	2.354	2.528	2.649	2.742	2.816	2.878	2.932	2.979	3.021	3.180	3.291
	0.10	2.030	2.215	2.342	2.439	2.517	2.582	2.638	2.687	2.731	2.895	3.010
	0.20	1.669	1.867	2.003	2.106	2.189	2.258	2.317	2.369	2.414	2.587	2.707
40	0.01	2.970	3.121	3.225	3.305	3.370	3.425	3.472	3.513	3.549	3.689	3.787
	0.05	2.323	2.492	2.606	2.696	2.768	2.827	2.878	2.923	2.963	3.113	3.218
	0.10	2.009	2.189	2.312	2.406	2.481	2.544	2.597	2.644	2.686	2.843	2.952
	0.20	1.656	1.850	1.983	2.083	2.164	2.231	2.288	2.338	2.382	2.548	2.663
60	0.01	2.914	3.056	3.155	3.230	3.291	3.342	3.386	3.425	3.459	3.589	3.679
	0.05	2.294	2.456	2.568	2.653	2.721	2.777	2.826	2.869	2.906	3.049	3.146
	0.10	1.989	2.163	2.283	2.373	2.446	2.506	2.558	2.603	2.643	2.793	2.897
	0.20	1.643	1.834	1.963	2.061	2.139	2.204	2.259	2.308	2.350	2.511	2.621

TABLE A.8 (continued)

Critical Values for Dunn's (Bonferroni's) Procedure

ν	α	Number of Contrasts										
		2	3	4	5	6	7	8	9	10	15	20
120	0.01	2.859	2.994	3.067	3.158	3.215	3.263	3.304	3.340	3.372	3.493	3.577
	0.05	2.265	2.422	2.529	2.610	2.675	2.729	2.776	2.816	2.852	2.967	3.081
	0.10	1.968	2.138	2.254	2.342	2.411	2.469	2.519	2.562	2.600	2.744	2.843
	0.20	1.631	1.817	1.944	2.039	2.115	2.178	2.231	2.278	2.319	2.474	2.580
∞	0.01	2.806	2.934	3.022	3.089	3.143	3.188	3.226	3.260	3.289	3.402	3.480
	0.05	2.237	2.388	2.491	2.569	2.631	2.683	2.727	2.766	2.800	2.928	3.016
	0.10	1.949	2.114	2.226	2.311	2.378	2.434	2.482	2.523	2.560	2.697	2.791
	0.20	1.618	1.801	1.925	2.018	2.091	2.152	2.204	2.249	2.289	2.438	2.540

Source: Reprinted from Games, P.A., *J. Am. Stat. Asso.*, 72, 531, 1977, Table 1. With permission of the American Statistical Association.

TABLE A.9

Critical Values for the Studentized Range Statistic

					J or r				
v	2	3	4	5	6	7	8	9	10
α = .10									
1	8.929	13.44	16.36	18.49	20.15	21.51	22.64	23.62	24.48
2	4.130	5.733	6.773	7.538	8.139	8.633	9.049	9.409	9.725
3	3.328	4.467	5.199	5.738	6.162	6.511	6.806	7.062	7.287
4	3.015	3.976	4.586	5.035	5.388	5.679	5.926	6.139	6.327
5	2.850	3.717	4.264	4.664	4.979	5.238	5.458	5.648	5.816
6	2.748	3.559	4.065	4.435	4.726	4.966	5.168	5.344	5.499
7	2.680	3.451	3.931	4.280	4.555	4.780	4.972	5.137	5.283
8	2.630	3.374	3.834	4.169	4.431	4.646	4.829	4.987	5.126
9	2.592	3.316	3.761	4.084	4.337	4.545	4.721	4.873	5.007
10	2.563	3.270	3.704	4.018	4.264	4.465	4.636	4.783	4.913
11	2.540	3.234	3.658	3.965	4.205	4.401	4.568	4.711	4.838
12	2.521	3.204	3.621	3.922	4.156	4.349	4.511	4.652	4.776
13	2.505	3.179	3.589	3.885	4.116	4.305	4.464	4.602	4.724
14	2.491	3.158	3.563	3.854	4.081	4.267	4.424	4.560	4.680
15	2.479	3.140	3.540	3.828	4.052	4.235	4.390	4.524	4.641
16	2.469	3.124	3.520	3.804	4.026	4.207	4.360	4.492	4.608
17	2.460	3.110	3.503	3.784	4.004	4.183	4.334	4.464	4.579
18	2.452	3.098	3.488	3.767	3.984	4.161	4.311	4.440	4.554
19	2.445	3.087	3.474	3.751	3.966	4.142	4.290	4.418	4.531
20	2.439	3.078	3.462	3.736	3.950	4.124	4.271	4.398	4.510
24	2.420	3.047	3.423	3.692	3.900	4.070	4.213	4.336	4.445
30	2.400	3.017	3.386	3.648	3.851	4.016	4.155	4.275	4.381
40	2.381	2.988	3.349	3.605	3.803	3.963	4.099	4.215	4.317
60	2.363	2.959	3.312	3.562	3.755	3.911	4.042	4.155	4.254
120	2.344	2.930	3.276	3.520	3.707	3.859	3.987	4.096	4.191
∞	2.326	2.902	3.240	3.478	3.661	3.808	3.931	4.037	4.129

					J or r				
v	11	12	13	14	15	16	17	18	19
α = .10									
1	25.24	25.92	26.54	27.10	27.62	28.10	28.54	28.96	29.35
2	10.01	10.26	10.49	10.70	10.89	11.07	11.24	11.39	11.54
3	7.487	7.667	7.832	7.982	8.120	8.249	8.368	8.479	8.584
4	6.495	6.645	6.783	6.909	7.025	7.133	7.233	7.327	7.414
5	5.966	6.101	6.223	6.336	6.440	6.536	6.626	6.710	6.789
6	5.637	5.762	5.875	5.979	6.075	6.164	6.247	6.325	6.398
7	5.413	5.530	5.637	5.735	5.826	5.910	5.838	6.061	6.130
8	5.250	5.362	5.464	5.558	5.644	5.724	5.799	5.869	5.935
9	5.127	5.234	5.333	5.423	5.506	5.583	5.655	5.723	5.786
10	5.029	5.134	5.229	5.317	5.397	5.472	5.542	5.607	5.668
11	4.951	5.053	5.146	5.231	5.309	5.382	5.450	5.514	5.573
12	4.886	4.986	5.077	5.160	5.236	5.308	5.374	5.436	5.495
13	4.832	4.930	5.019	5.100	5.176	5.245	5.311	5.372	5.429

TABLE A.9 (continued)

Critical Values for the Studentized Range Statistic

	J or r								
v	11	12	13	14	15	16	17	18	19
$\alpha = .10$									
14	4.786	4.882	4.970	5.050	5.124	5.192	5.256	5.316	5.373
15	4.746	4.841	4.927	5.006	5.079	5.147	5.209	5.269	5.324
16	4.712	4.805	4.890	4.968	5.040	5.107	5.169	5.227	5.282
17	4.682	4.774	4.858	4.935	5.005	5.071	5.133	5.190	5.244
18	4.655	4.746	4.829	4.905	4.975	5.040	5.101	5.158	5.211
19	4.631	4.721	4.803	4.879	4.948	5.012	5.073	5.129	5.182
20	4.609	4.699	4.780	4.855	4.924	4.987	5.047	5.103	5.155
24	4.541	4.628	4.708	4.780	4.847	4.909	4.966	5.021	5.071
30	4.474	4.559	4.635	4.706	4.770	4.830	4.886	4.939	4.988
40	4.408	4.490	4.564	4.632	4.695	4.752	4.807	4.857	4.905
60	4.342	4.421	4.493	4.558	4.619	4.675	4.727	4.775	4.821
120	4.276	4.353	4.422	4.485	4.543	4.597	4.647	4.694	4.738
∞	4.211	4.285	4.351	4.412	4.468	4.519	4.568	4.612	4.654

	J or r								
v	2	3	4	5	6	7	8	9	10
$\alpha = .05$									
1	17.97	26.98	32.82	37.08	40.41	43.12	45.40	47.36	49.07
2	6.085	8.331	9.798	10.88	11.74	12.44	13.03	13.54	13.99
3	4.501	5.910	6.825	7.502	8.037	8.478	8.853	9.177	9.462
4	3.927	5.040	5.757	6.287	6.707	7.053	7.347	7.602	7.826
5	3.635	4.602	5.218	5.673	6.033	6.330	6.582	6.802	6.995
6	3.461	4.339	4.896	5.305	5.628	5.895	6.122	6.319	6.493
7	3.344	4.165	4.681	5.060	5.359	5.606	5.815	5.998	6.158
8	3.261	4.041	4.529	4.886	5.167	5.399	5.597	5.767	5.918
9	3.199	3.949	4.415	4.756	5.024	5.244	5.432	5.595	5.739
10	3.151	3.877	4.327	4.654	4.912	5.124	5.305	5.461	5.599
11	3.113	3.820	4.256	4.574	4.823	5.028	5.202	5.353	5.487
12	3.082	3.773	4.199	4.508	4.751	4.950	5.119	5.265	5.395
13	3.055	3.735	4.151	4.453	4.690	4.885	5.049	5.192	5.318
14	3.033	3.702	4.111	4.407	4.639	4.829	4.990	5.131	5.254
15	3.014	3.674	4.076	4.367	4.595	4.782	4.940	5.077	5.198
16	2.998	3.649	4.046	4.333	4.557	4.741	4.897	5.031	5.150
17	2.984	3.628	4.020	4.303	4.524	4.705	4.858	4.991	5.108
18	2.971	3.609	3.997	4.277	4.495	4.673	4.824	4.956	5.071
19	2.960	3.593	3.977	4.253	4.469	4.645	4.794	4.924	5.038
20	2.950	3.578	3.958	4.232	4.445	4.620	4.768	4.896	5.008
24	2.919	3.532	3.901	4.166	4.373	4.541	4.684	4.807	4.915
30	2.888	3.486	3.845	4.102	4.302	4.464	4.602	4.720	4.824
40	2.858	3.442	3.791	4.039	4.232	4.389	4.521	4.635	4.735
60	2.829	3.399	3.737	3.977	4.163	4.314	4.441	4.550	4.646
120	2.800	3.356	3.685	3.917	4.096	4.241	4.363	4.468	4.560
∞	2.772	3.314	3.633	3.858	4.030	4.170	4.286	4.387	4.474

(continued)

TABLE A.9 (continued)

Critical Values for the Studentized Range Statistic

					J or r				
v	11	12	13	14	15	16	17	18	19
$\alpha = .05$									
1	50.59	51.96	53.20	54.33	55.36	56.32	57.22	58.04	58.83
2	14.39	14.75	15.08	15.38	15.65	15.91	16.14	16.37	16.57
3	9.717	9.946	10.15	10.35	10.53	10.69	10.84	10.98	11.11
4	8.027	8.208	8.373	8.525	8.664	8.794	8.914	9.028	9.134
5	7.168	7.324	7.466	7.596	7.717	7.828	7.932	8.030	8.122
6	6.649	6.789	6.917	7.034	7.143	7.244	7.338	7.426	7.508
7	6.302	6.431	6.550	6.658	6.759	6.852	6.939	7.020	7.097
8	6.054	6.175	6.287	6.389	6.483	6.571	6.653	6.729	6.802
9	5.867	5.983	6.089	6.186	6.276	6.359	6.437	6.510	6.579
10	5.722	5.833	5.935	6.028	6.114	6.194	6.269	6.339	6.405
11	5.605	5.713	5.811	5.901	5.984	6.062	6.134	6.202	6.265
12	5.511	5.615	5.710	5.798	5.878	5.953	6.023	6.089	6.151
13	5.431	5.533	5.625	5.711	5.789	5.862	5.931	5.995	6.055
14	5.364	5.463	5.554	5.637	5.714	5.786	5.852	5.915	5.974
15	5.306	5.404	5.493	5.574	5.649	5.720	5.785	5.846	5.904
16	5.256	5.352	5.439	5.520	5.593	5.662	5.720	5.786	5.843
17	5.212	5.307	5.392	5.471	5.544	5.612	5.675	5.734	5.790
18	5.174	5.267	5.352	5.429	5.501	5.568	5.630	5.688	5.743
19	5.140	5.231	5.315	5.391	5.462	5.528	5.589	5.647	5.701
20	5.108	5.199	5.282	5.357	5.427	5.493	5.553	5.610	5.663
24	5.012	5.099	5.179	5.251	5.319	5.381	5.439	5.494	5.545
30	4.917	5.001	5.077	5.147	5.211	5.271	5.327	5.379	5.429
40	4.824	4.904	4.977	5.044	5.106	5.163	5.216	5.266	5.313
60	4.732	4.808	4.878	4.942	5.001	5.056	5.107	5.154	5.199
120	4.641	4.714	4.781	4.842	4.898	4.950	4.998	5.044	5.086
∞	4.552	4.622	4.685	4.743	4.796	4.845	4.891	4.934	4.974

					J or r				
v	2	3	4	5	6	7	8	9	10
$\alpha = .01$									
1	90.03	135.0	164.3	185.6	202.2	215.8	227.2	237.0	245.6
2	14.04	19.02	22.29	24.72	26.63	28.20	29.53	30.68	31.69
3	8.261	10.62	12.17	13.33	14.24	15.00	15.64	16.20	16.69
4	6.512	8.120	9.173	9.958	10.58	11.10	11.55	11.93	12.27
5	5.702	6.976	7.804	8.421	8.913	9.321	9.669	9.972	10.24
6	5.243	6.331	7.033	7.556	7.973	8.318	8.613	8.869	9.097
7	4.949	5.919	6.543	7.005	7.373	7.679	7.939	8.166	8.368
8	4.746	5.635	6.204	6.625	6.960	7.237	7.474	7.681	7.863
9	4.596	5.428	5.957	6.348	6.658	6.915	7.134	7.325	7.495
10	4.482	5.270	5.769	6.136	6.428	6.669	6.875	7.055	7.213
11	4.392	5.146	5.621	5.970	6.247	6.476	6.672	6.842	6.992
12	4.320	5.046	5.502	5.836	6.101	6.321	6.507	6.670	6.814
13	4.260	4.964	5.404	5.727	5.981	6.192	6.372	6.528	6.667

TABLE A.9 (continued)

Critical Values for the Studentized Range Statistic

					J or r				
v	2	3	4	5	6	7	8	9	10
$\alpha = .01$									
14	4.210	4.895	5.322	5.634	5.881	6.085	6.258	6.409	6.543
15	4.168	4.836	5.252	5.556	5.796	5.994	6.162	6.309	6.439
16	4.131	4.786	5.192	5.489	5.722	5.915	6.079	6.222	6.349
17	4.099	4.742	5.140	5.430	5.659	5.847	6.007	6.147	6.270
18	4.071	4.703	5.094	5.379	5.603	5.788	5.944	6.081	6.201
19	4.046	4.670	5.054	5.334	5.554	5.735	5.889	6.022	6.141
20	4.024	4.639	5.018	5.294	5.510	5.688	5.839	5.970	6.087
24	3.956	4.546	4.907	5.168	5.374	5.542	5.685	5.809	5.919
30	3.889	4.455	4.799	5.048	5.242	5.401	5.536	5.653	5.756
40	3.825	4.367	4.696	4.931	5.114	5.265	5.392	5.502	5.599
60	3.762	4.282	4.595	4.818	4.991	5.133	5.253	5.356	5.447
120	3.702	4.200	4.497	4.709	4.872	5.005	5.118	5.214	5.299
∞	3.643	4.120	4.403	4.603	4.757	4.882	4.987	5.078	5.157

					J or r				
v	11	12	13	14	15	16	17	18	19
$\alpha = .01$									
1	253.2	260.0	266.2	271.8	277.0	281.8	286.3	290.4	294.3
2	32.59	33.40	34.13	34.81	35.43	36.00	36.53	37.03	37.50
3	17.13	17.53	17.89	18.22	18.52	18.81	19.07	19.32	19.55
4	12.57	12.84	13.09	13.32	13.53	13.73	13.91	14.08	14.24
5	10.48	10.70	10.89	11.08	11.24	11.40	11.55	11.68	11.81
6	9.301	9.485	9.653	9.808	9.951	10.08	10.21	10.32	10.43
7	8.548	8.711	8.860	8.997	9.124	9.242	9.353	9.456	9.554
6	8.027	8.176	8.312	8.436	8.552	8.659	8.760	8.854	8.943
9	7.647	7.784	7.910	8.025	8.132	8.232	8.325	3.412	8.495
10	7.356	7.485	7.603	7.712	7.812	7.906	7.993	8.076	8.153
11	7.128	7.250	7.362	7.465	7.560	7.649	7.732	7.809	7.883
12	6.943	7.060	7.167	7.265	7.356	7.441	7.520	7.594	7.665
13	6.791	6.903	7.006	7.101	7.188	7.269	7.345	7.417	7.485
14	6.664	6.772	6.871	6.962	7.047	7.126	7.199	7.268	7.333
15	6.555	6.660	6.757	6.845	6.927	7.003	7.074	7.142	7.204
16	6.462	6.564	6.658	6.744	6.823	6.898	6.967	7.032	7.093
17	6.381	6.480	6.572	6.656	6.734	6.806	6.873	6.937	6.997
18	6.310	6.407	6.497	6.579	6.655	6.725	6.792	6.854	6.912
19	6.247	6.342	6.430	6.510	6.585	6.654	6.719	6.780	6.837
20	6.191	6.285	6.371	6.450	6.523	6.591	6.654	6.714	6.771
24	6.017	6.106	6.186	6.261	6.330	6.394	6.453	6.510	6.563
30	5.849	5.932	6.008	6.078	6.143	6.203	6.259	6.311	6.361
40	5.686	5.764	5.835	5.900	5.961	6.017	6.069	6.119	6.165
60	5.528	5.601	5.667	5.728	5.785	5.837	5.886	5.931	5.974
120	5.375	5.443	5.505	5.562	5.614	5.662	5.708	5.750	5.790
∞	5.227	5.290	5.348	5.400	5.448	5.493	5.535	5.574	5.611

Source: Reprinted from Harter, H.L., *Ann. Math. Statist.*, 31, 1122, 1960, Table 3. With permission of the Institute of Mathematical Statistics.

J for Tukey. r for Newman–Keuls.

TABLE A.10

Critical Values for the Bryant–Paulson Procedure

α = .05

v	$J = 2$	$J = 3$	$J = 4$	$J = 5$	$J = 6$	$J = 7$	$J = 8$	$J = 10$	$J = 12$	$J = 16$	$J = 20$
$X = 1$											
2	7.96	11.00	12.99	14.46	15.61	16.56	17.36	18.65	19.68	21.23	22.40
3	5.42	7.18	8.32	9.17	9.84	10.39	10.86	11.62	12.22	13.14	13.83
4	4.51	5.84	6.69	7.32	7.82	8.23	8.58	9.15	9.61	10.30	10.82
5	4.06	5.17	5.88	6.40	6.82	7.16	7.45	7.93	8.30	8.88	9.32
6	3.79	4.78	5.40	5.86	6.23	6.53	6.78	7.20	7.53	8.04	8.43
7	3.62	4.52	5.09	5.51	5.84	6.11	6.34	6.72	7.03	7.49	7.84
8	3.49	4.34	4.87	5.26	5.57	5.82	6.03	6.39	6.67	7.10	7.43
10	3.32	4.10	4.58	4.93	5.21	5.43	5.63	5.94	6.19	6.58	6.87
12	3.22	3.95	4.40	4.73	4.98	5.19	5.37	5.67	5.90	6.26	6.53
14	3.15	3.85	4.28	4.59	4.83	5.03	5.20	5.48	5.70	6.03	6.29
16	3.10	3.77	4.19	4.49	4.72	4.91	5.07	5.34	5.55	5.87	6.12
18	3.06	3.72	4.12	4.41	4.63	4.82	4.98	5.23	5.44	5.75	5.98
20	3.03	3.67	4.07	4.35	4.57	4.75	4.90	5.15	5.35	5.65	5.88
24	2.98	3.61	3.99	4.26	4.47	4.65	4.79	5.03	5.22	5.51	5.73
30	2.94	3.55	3.91	4.18	4.38	4.54	4.69	4.91	5.09	5.37	5.58
40	2.89	3.49	3.84	4.09	4.29	4.45	4.58	4.80	4.97	5.23	5.43
60	2.85	3.43	3.77	4.01	4.20	4.35	4.48	4.69	4.85	5.10	5.29
120	2.81	3.37	3.70	3.93	4.11	4.26	4.38	4.58	4.73	4.97	5.15
$X = 2$											
2	9.50	13.18	15.59	17.36	18.75	19.89	20.86	22.42	23.66	25.54	26.94
3	6.21	8.27	9.60	10.59	11.37	12.01	12.56	13.44	14.15	15.22	16.02
4	5.04	6.54	7.51	8.23	8.80	9.26	9.66	10.31	10.83	11.61	12.21
5	4.45	5.68	6.48	7.06	7.52	7.90	8.23	8.76	9.18	9.83	10.31
6	4.10	5.18	5.87	6.37	6.77	7.10	7.38	7.84	8.21	8.77	9.20
7	3.87	4.85	5.47	5.92	6.28	6.58	6.83	7.24	7.57	8.08	8.46
8	3.70	4.61	5.19	5.61	5.94	6.21	6.44	6.82	7.12	7.59	7.94
10	3.49	4.31	4.82	5.19	5.49	5.73	5.93	6.27	6.54	6.95	7.26
12	3.35	4.12	4.59	4.93	5.20	5.43	5.62	5.92	6.17	6.55	6.83
14	3.26	3.99	4.44	4.76	5.01	5.22	5.40	5.69	5.92	6.27	6.54
16	3.19	3.90	4.32	4.63	4.88	5.07	5.24	5.52	5.74	6.07	6.33
18	3.14	3.82	4.24	4.54	4.77	4.96	5.13	5.39	5.60	5.92	6.17
20	3.10	3.77	4.17	4.46	4.69	4.88	5.03	5.29	5.49	5.81	6.04
24	3.04	3.69	4.08	4.35	4.57	4.75	4.90	5.14	5.34	5.63	5.86
30	2.99	3.61	3.98	4.25	4.46	4.62	4.77	5.00	5.18	5.46	5.68
40	2.93	3.53	3.89	4.15	4.34	4.50	4.64	4.86	5.04	5.30	5.50
60	2.88	3.46	3.80	4.05	4.24	4.39	4.52	4.73	4.89	5.14	5.33
120	2.82	3.38	3.72	3.95	4.13	4.28	4.40	4.60	4.75	4.99	5.17

TABLE A.10 (continued)

Critical Values for the Bryant–Paulson Procedure

α = .05

v	$J = 2$	$J = 3$	$J = 4$	$J = 5$	$J = 6$	$J = 7$	$J = 8$	$J = 10$	$J = 12$	$J = 16$	$J = 20$
$X = 3$											
2	10.83	15.06	17.82	19.85	21.45	22.76	23.86	25.66	27.08	29.23	30.83
3	6.92	9.23	10.73	11.84	12.72	13.44	14.06	15.05	15.84	17.05	17.95
4	5.51	7.18	8.25	9.05	9.67	10.19	10.63	11.35	11.92	12.79	13.45
5	4.81	6.16	7.02	7.66	8.17	8.58	8.94	9.52	9.98	10.69	11.22
6	4.38	5.55	6.30	6.84	7.28	7.64	7.94	8.44	8.83	9.44	9.90
7	4.11	5.16	5.82	6.31	6.70	7.01	7.29	7.73	8.08	8.63	9.03
8	3.91	4.88	5.49	5.93	6.29	6.58	6.83	7.23	7.55	8.05	8.42
10	3.65	4.51	5.05	5.44	5.75	6.01	6.22	6.58	6.86	7.29	7.62
12	3.48	4.28	4.78	5.14	5.42	5.65	5.85	6.17	6.43	6.82	7.12
14	3.37	4.13	4.59	4.93	5.19	5.41	5.59	5.89	6.13	6.50	6.78
16	3.29	4.01	4.46	4.78	5.03	5.23	5.41	5.69	5.92	6.27	6.53
18	3.23	3.93	4.35	4.66	4.90	5.10	5.27	5.54	5.76	6.09	6.34
20	3.18	3.86	4.28	4.57	4.81	5.00	5.16	5.42	5.63	5.96	6.20
24	3.11	3.76	4.16	4.44	4.67	4.85	5.00	5.25	5.45	5.75	5.98
30	3.04	3.67	4.05	4.32	4.53	4.70	4.85	5.08	5.27	5.56	5.78
40	2.97	3.57	3.94	4.20	4.40	4.56	4.70	4.92	5.10	5.37	5.57
60	2.90	3.49	3.83	4.08	4.27	4.43	4.56	4.77	4.93	5.19	5.38
120	2.84	3.40	3.73	3.97	4.15	4.30	4.42	4.62	4.77	5.01	5.19

α = .01

v	$J = 2$	$J = 3$	$J = 4$	$J = 5$	$J = 6$	$J = 7$	$J = 8$	$J = 10$	$J = 12$	$J = 16$	$J = 20$
$X = 1$											
2	19.09	26.02	30.57	33.93	36.58	38.76	40.60	43.59	45.95	49.55	52.24
3	10.28	13.32	15.32	16.80	17.98	18.95	19.77	21.12	22.19	23.82	25.05
4	7.68	9.64	10.93	11.89	12.65	13.28	13.82	14.70	15.40	16.48	17.29
5	6.49	7.99	8.97	9.70	10.28	10.76	11.17	11.84	12.38	13.20	13.83
6	5.83	7.08	7.88	8.48	8.96	9.36	9.70	10.25	10.70	11.38	11.90
7	5.41	6.50	7.20	7.72	8.14	8.48	8.77	9.26	9.64	10.24	10.69
8	5.12	6.11	6.74	7.20	7.58	7.88	8.15	8.58	8.92	9.46	9.87
10	4.76	5.61	6.15	6.55	6.86	7.13	7.35	7.72	8.01	8.47	8.82
12	4.54	5.31	5.79	6.15	6.48	6.67	6.87	7.20	7.46	7.87	8.18
14	4.39	5.11	5.56	5.89	6.15	6.36	6.55	6.85	7.09	7.47	7.75
16	4.28	4.96	5.39	5.70	5.95	6.15	6.32	6.60	6.83	7.18	7.45
18	4.20	4.86	5.26	5.56	5.79	5.99	6.15	6.42	6.63	6.96	7.22
20	4.14	4.77	5.17	5.45	5.68	5.86	6.02	6.27	6.48	6.80	7.04
24	4.05	4.65	5.02	5.29	5.50	5.68	5.83	6.07	6.26	6.56	6.78
30	3.96	4.54	4.89	5.14	5.34	5.50	5.64	5.87	6.05	6.32	6.53
40	3.88	4.43	4.76	5.00	5.19	5.34	5.47	5.68	5.85	6.10	6.30
60	3.79	4.32	4.64	4.86	5.04	5.18	5.30	5.50	5.65	5.89	6.07
120	3.72	4.22	4.52	4.73	4.89	5.03	5.14	5.32	5.47	5.69	5.85

(continued)

TABLE A.10 (continued)

Critical Values for the Bryant–Paulson Procedure

$\alpha = .01$

v	$J = 2$	$J = 3$	$J = 4$	$J = 5$	$J = 6$	$J = 7$	$J = 8$	$J = 10$	$J = 12$	$J = 16$	$J = 20$
$X = 2$											
2	23.11	31.55	37.09	41.19	44.41	47.06	49.31	52.94	55.82	60.20	63.47
3	11.97	15.56	17.91	19.66	21.05	22.19	23.16	24.75	26.01	27.93	29.38
4	8.69	10.95	12.43	13.54	14.41	15.14	15.76	16.77	17.58	18.81	19.74
5	7.20	8.89	9.99	10.81	11.47	12.01	12.47	13.23	13.84	14.77	15.47
6	6.36	7.75	8.64	9.31	9.85	10.29	10.66	11.28	11.77	12.54	13.11
7	5.84	7.03	7.80	8.37	8.83	9.21	9.53	10.06	10.49	11.14	11.64
8	5.48	6.54	7.23	7.74	8.14	8.48	8.76	9.23	9.61	10.19	10.63
10	5.02	5.93	6.51	6.93	7.27	7.55	7.79	8.19	8.50	8.99	9.36
12	4.74	5.56	6.07	6.45	6.75	7.00	7.21	7.56	7.84	8.27	8.60
14	4.56	5.31	5.78	6.13	6.40	6.63	6.82	7.14	7.40	7.79	8.09
16	4.42	5.14	5.58	5.90	6.16	6.37	6.55	6.85	7.08	7.45	7.73
18	4.32	5.00	5.43	5.73	5.98	6.18	6.35	6.63	6.85	7.19	7.46
20	4.25	4.90	5.31	5.60	5.84	6.03	6.19	6.46	6.67	7.00	7.25
24	4.14	4.76	5.14	5.42	5.63	5.81	5.96	6.21	6.41	6.71	6.95
30	4.03	4.62	4.98	5.24	5.44	5.61	5.75	5.98	6.16	6.44	6.66
40	3.93	4.48	4.82	5.07	5.26	5.41	5 54	5.76	5.93	6.19	6.38
60	3.83	4.36	4.68	4.90	5.08	5.22	5.35	5.54	5.70	5.94	6.12
120	3.73	4.24	4.54	4.75	4.91	5.05	5.16	5.35	5.49	5.71	5.88
$X = 3$											
2	26.54	36.26	42.64	47.36	51.07	54.13	56.71	60.90	64.21	69.25	73.01
3	13.45	17.51	20.17	22.15	23.72	25.01	26.11	27.90	29.32	31.50	33.13
4	9.59	12.11	13.77	15.00	15.98	16.79	17.47	18.60	19.50	20.87	21.91
5	7.83	9.70	10.92	11.82	12.54	13.14	13.65	14.48	15.15	10.17	16.95
6	6.85	8.36	9.34	10.07	10.65	11.13	11.54	12.22	12.75	13.59	14.21
7	6.23	7.52	8.36	8.98	9.47	9.88	10.23	10.80	11.26	11.97	12.51
8	5.81	6.95	7.69	8.23	8.67	9.03	9.33	9.84	10.24	10.87	11.34
10	5.27	6.23	6.84	7.30	7.66	7.96	8.21	8.63	8.96	9.48	9.88
12	4.94	5.80	6.34	6.74	7.05	7.31	7.54	7.90	8.20	8.65	9.00
14	4.72	5.51	6.00	6.36	6.65	6.89	7.09	7.42	7.69	8.10	8.41
16	4.56	5.30	5.76	6.10	6.37	6.59	6.77	7.08	7.33	7.71	8.00
18	4.44	5.15	5.59	5.90	6.16	6.36	6.54	6.83	7.06	7.42	7.69
20	4.35	5.03	5.45	5.75	5.99	6.19	6.36	6.63	6.85	7.19	7.45
24	4.22	4.86	5.25	5.54	5.76	5.94	6.10	6.35	6.55	6.87	7.11
30	4.10	4.70	5.06	5.33	5.54	5.71	5.85	6.08	6.27	6.56	6.78
40	3.98	4.54	4.88	5.13	5.32	5.48	5.61	5.83	6.00	6.27	6.47
60	3.86	4.39	4.72	4.95	5.12	5.27	5.39	5.59	5.75	6.00	6.18
120	3.75	4.25	4.55	4.77	4.94	5.07	5.18	5.37	5.51	5.74	5.90

Source: Reprinted from Bryant, J.L. and Paulson, A.S., *Biometrika*, 63, 631, 1976, Table 1(a) and Table 1(b). With permission of Biometrika Trustees.

X is the number of covariates.

References

Agresti, A., & Finlay, B. (1986). *Statistical methods for the social sciences* (2nd ed.). San Francisco: Dellen.

Agresti, A., & Pendergast, J. (1986). Comparing mean ranks for repeated measures data. *Communications in Statistics—Theory and Methods, 15*, 1417–1433.

Aldrich, J. H., & Nelson, F. D. (1984). *Linear probability, logit, and probit models*. Beverly Hills, CA: Sage.

Andrews, D. F. (1971). Significance tests based on residuals. *Biometrika, 58*, 139–148.

Andrews, D. F., & Pregibon, D. (1978). Finding the outliers that matter. *Journal of the Royal Statistical Society, Series B, 40*, 85–93.

Applebaum, M. I., & Cramer, E. M. (1974). Some problems in the nonorthogonal analysis of variance. *Psychological Bulletin, 81*, 335–343.

Atiqullah, M. (1964). The robustness of the covariance analysis of a one-way classification. *Biometrika, 51*, 365–373.

Atkinson, A. C. (1985). *Plots, transformations, and regression*. Oxford, U.K.: Oxford University Press.

Barnett, V., & Lewis, T. (1978). *Outliers in statistical data*. New York: Wiley.

Barnett, V., & Lewis, T. (1994). *Outliers in statistical data* (3rd ed.). New York: Wiley.

Bates, D. M., & Watts, D. G. (1988). *Nonlinear regression analysis and its applications*. New York: Wiley.

Beckman, R., & Cook, R. D. (1983). Outliers... s. *Technometrics, 25*, 119–149.

Belsley, D. A., Kuh, E., & Welsch, R. E. (1980). *Regression diagnostics*. New York: Wiley.

Benjamini, Y., & Hochberg, Y. (1995). Controlling the false discovery rate: A practical and powerful approach to multiple testing. *Journal of the Royal Statistical Society, B, 57*, 289–300.

Bernstein, I. H. (1988). *Applied multivariate analysis*. New York: Springer-Verlag.

Berry, W. D., & Feldman, S. (1985). *Multiple regression in practice*. Beverly Hills, CA: Sage.

Boik, R. J. (1979). Interactions, partial interactions, and interaction contrasts in the analysis of variance. *Psychological Bulletin, 86*, 1084–1089.

Boik, R. J. (1981). A priori tests in repeated measures designs: Effects of nonsphericity. *Psychometrika, 46*, 241–255.

Box, G. E. P. (1954a). Some theorems on quadratic forms applied in the study of analysis of variance problems, I: Effects of inequality of variance in the one-way model. *Annals of Mathematical Statistics, 25*, 290–302.

Box, G. E. P. (1954b). Some theorems on quadratic forms applied in the study of analysis of variance problems, II: Effects of inequality of variance and of correlation between errors in the two-way classification. *Annals of Mathematical Statistics, 25*, 484–498.

Box, G. E. P., & Anderson, S. L. (1962). *Robust tests for variances and effect of non-normality and variance heterogeneity on standard tests*. Tech. Rep. No. 7, Ordinance Project No. TB 2-0001 (832), Dept. of Army Project No. 599-01-004.

Bradley, J. V. (1978). Robustness? *British Journal of Mathematical and Statistical Psychology, 31*, 144–152.

Brown, M. B., & Forsythe, A. (1974). The ANOVA and multiple comparisons for data with heterogeneous variances. *Biometrics, 30*, 719–724.

Brunner, E., Detta, H., & Munk, A. (1997). Box-type approximations in nonparametric factorial designs. *Journal of the American Statistical Association, 92*, 1494–1502.

Bryant, J. L., & Paulson, A. S. (1976). An extension of Tukey's method of multiple comparisons to experimental designs with random concomitant variables. *Biometrika, 63*, 631–638.

Campbell, D. T., & Stanley, J. C. (1966). *Experimental and quasi-experimental designs for research*. Chicago: Rand McNally.

Carlson, J. E., & Timm, N. H. (1974). Analysis of nonorthogonal fixed-effects designs. *Psychological Bulletin, 81*, 563–570.

Carroll, R. J., & Ruppert, D. (1982). Robust estimation in heteroscedastic linear models. *Annals of Statistics, 10*, 429–441.

Chatterjee, S., & Price, B. (1977). *Regression analysis by example*. New York: Wiley.

Christensen, R. (1997). *Log-linear models and logistic regression* (2nd ed.). New York: Springer-Verlag.

Clinch, J. J., & Keselman, H. J. (1982). Parametric alternatives to the analysis of variance. *Journal of Educational Statistics, 7*, 207–214.

Cohen, J. (1988). *Statistical power analysis for the behavioral sciences* (2nd ed.). Hillsdale, NJ: Erlbaum.

Cohen, J., & Cohen, P. (1983). *Applied multiple regression/correlation analysis for the behavioral sciences* (2nd ed.). Hillsdale, NJ: Erlbaum.

Coombs, W. T., Algina, J., & Ottman, D. O. (1996). Univariate and multivariate omnibus hypothesis tests selected to control Type I error rates when population variances are not necessarily equal. *Review of Educational Research, 66*, 137–179.

Conover, W., & Iman, R. (1982). Analysis of covariance using the rank transformation. *Biometrics, 38*, 715–724.

Cotton, J. W. (1998). *Analyzing within-subjects experiments*. Mahwah, NJ: Lawrence Erlbaum Associates.

Cook, R. D. (1977). Detection of influential observations in linear regression. *Technometrics, 19*, 15–18.

Cook, T. D., & Campbell, D. T. (1979). *Quasi-experimentation: Design and analysis issues for field settings*. Chicago: Rand McNally.

Cook, R. D., & Weisberg, S. (1982). *Residuals and influence in regression*. London: Chapman & Hall.

Cox, D. R., & Snell, E. J. (1989). *Analysis of binary data* (2nd ed.). London: Chapman & Hall.

Cramer, E. M., & Applebaum, M. I. (1980). Nonorthogonal analysis of variance—Once again. *Psychological Bulletin, 87*, 51–57.

Croux, C., Flandre, C., & Haesbroeck, G. (2002). The breakdown behavior of the maximum likelihood estimator in the logistic regression model. *Statistics and Probability Letters, 60*, 377–386.

D'Agostino, R. B. (1971). An omnibus test of normality for moderate and large size samples. *Biometrika, 58*, 341–348.

Derksen, S., & Keselman, H. J. (1992). Backward, forward and stepwise automated subset selection algorithms: Frequency of obtaining authentic and noise variables. *British Journal of Mathematical and Statistical Psychology, 45*, 265–282.

Dunn, O. J. (1961). Multiple comparisons among means. *Journal of the American Statistical Association, 56*, 52–64.

Dunn, O. J. (1974). On multiple tests and confidence intervals. *Communications in Statistics, 3*, 101–103.

Dunn, O. J., & Clark, V. A. (1987). *Applied statistics: Analysis of variance and regression* (2nd ed.). New York: Wiley.

Dunnett, C. W. (1955). A multiple comparison procedure for comparing several treatments with a control. *Journal of the American Statistical Association, 50*, 1096–1121.

Dunnett, C. W. (1964). New tables for multiple comparisons with a control. *Biometrics, 20*, 482–491.

Dunnett, C. W. (1980). Pairwise multiple comparisons in the unequal variance case. *Journal of the American Statistical Association, 75*, 796–800.

Durbin, J., & Watson, G. S. (1950). Testing for serial correlation in least squares regression, I. *Biometrika, 37*, 409–428.

Durbin, J., & Watson, G. S. (1951). Testing for serial correlation in least squares regression, II. *Biometrika, 38*, 159–178.

Durbin, J., & Watson, G. S. (1971). Testing for serial correlation in least squares regression, III. *Biometrika, 58*, 1–19.

Elashoff, J. D. (1969). Analysis of covariance: A delicate instrument. *American Educational Research Journal, 6*, 383–401.

Feldt, L. S. (1958). A comparison of the precision of three experimental designs employing a concomitant variable. *Psychometrika, 23*, 335–354.

Ferguson, G. A., & Takane, Y. (1989). *Statistical analysis in psychology and education* (6th ed.). New York: McGraw-Hill.

Fidler, F., & Thompson, B. (2001). Computing correct confidence intervals for ANOVA fixed- and random-effects effect sizes. *Educational and Psychological Measurement, 61*, 575–604.

Fisher, R. A. (1949). *The design of experiments*. Edinburgh, U.K.: Oliver & Boyd, Ltd.

Friedman, M. (1937). The use of ranks to avoid the assumption of normality implicit in the analysis of variance. *Journal of the American Statistical Association, 32*, 675–701.

Games, P. A., & Howell, J. F. (1976). Pairwise multiple comparison procedures with unequal n's and/or variances: A Monte Carlo study. *Journal of Educational Statistics, 1*, 113–125.

Geisser, S., & Greenhouse, S. (1958). Extension of Box's results on the use of the F distribution in multivariate analysis. *Annals of Mathematical Statistics, 29*, 855–891.

Glass, G. V., & Hopkins, K. D. (1996). *Statistical methods in education and psychology* (3rd ed.). Boston: Allyn & Bacon.

Glass, G. V., Peckham, P. D., & Sanders, J. R. (1972). Consequences of failure to meet assumptions underlying the fixed effects analyses of variance and covariance. *Review of Educational Research, 42*, 237–288.

Grimm, L. G., & Arnold, P. R. (Eds.). (1995). *Reading and understanding multivariate statistics.* Washington, DC: American Psychological Association.

Hair, J. F., Black, W. C., Babin, B. J., Anderson, R. E., & Tatham, R. L. (2006). *Multivariate data analysis* (6th ed.). Upper Saddle River, NJ: Pearson Prentice Hall.

Harrell, F. E. J. (1986). The LOGIST procedure. In I. SAS Institute (Ed.), *SUGI supplemental library user's guide* (5th ed., pp. 269–293). Cary, NC: SAS Institute, Inc.

Harwell, M. (2003). Summarizing Monte Carlo results in methodological research: The single- factor, fixed-effects ANCOVA case. *Journal of Educational and Behavioral Statistics, 28*, 45–70.

Hawkins, D. M. (1980). *Identification of outliers.* London: Chapman & Hall.

Hays, W. L. (1988). *Statistics* (4th ed.). New York: Holt, Rinehart and Winston.

Hayter, A. J. (1986). The maximum familywise error rate of Fisher's least significant difference test. *Journal of the American Statistical Association, 81*, 1000–1004.

Heck, R. H., & Thomas, S. L. (2000). *An introduction to multilevel modeling techniques.* Mahwah, NJ: Lawrence Erlbaum.

Heck, R. H., Thomas, S. L., & Tabata, L. N. (2010). *Multilevel and longitudinal modeling with IBM SPSS.* New York: Routledge.

Hellevik, O. (2009). Linear versus logistic regression when the dependent variable is a dichotomy. *Quality & Quantity, 43*(1), 59–74.

Hochberg, Y. (1988). A sharper Bonferroni procedure for multiple tests of significance. *Biometrika, 75*, 800–802.

Hochberg, Y., & Tamhane, A. C. (1987). *Multiple comparison procedures.* New York: Wiley.

Hochberg, Y., & Varon-Salomon, Y. (1984). On simultaneous pairwise comparisons in analysis of covariance. *Journal of the American Statistical Association, 79*, 863–866.

Hocking, R. R. (1976). The analysis and selection of variables in linear regression. *Biometrics, 32*, 1–49.

Hoerl, A. E., & Kennard, R. W. (1970a). Ridge regression: Biased estimation for non-orthogonal models. *Technometrics, 12*, 55–67.

Hoerl, A. E., & Kennard, R. W. (1970b). Ridge regression: Application to non-orthogonal models. *Technometrics, 12*, 591–612.

Hosmer, D. W., Hosmer, T., LeCessie, S., & Lemeshow, S. (1997). A comparison of goodness-of-fit tests for the logistic regression model. *Statistics in Medicine, 16*, 965–980.

Hosmer, D. W., & Lemeshow, S. (1989). *Applied logistic regression,* New York: Wiley.

Hosmer, D. W., & Lemeshow, S. (2000). *Applied logistic regression* (2nd ed.). New York: Wiley.

Huberty, C. J. (1989). Problems with stepwise methods—Better alternatives. In B. Thompson (Ed.), *Advances in social science methodology* (Vol. 1, pp. 43–70). Greenwich, CT: JAI Press.

Huck, S. W. (2004). *Reading statistics and research* (4th ed.). Boston: Allyn & Bacon.

Huck, S. W., & McLean, R. A. (1975). Using a repeated measures ANOVA to analyze data from a pretest-posttest design: A potentially confusing task. *Psychological Bulletin, 82*, 511–518.

Huitema, B. E. (1980). *The analysis of covariance and alternatives.* New York: Wiley.

Huynh, H., & Feldt, L. S. (1970). Conditions under which mean square ratios in repeated measurement designs have exact F-distributions. *Journal of the American Statistical Association, 65*, 1582–1589.

James, G. S. (1951). The comparison of several groups of observations when the ratios of the population variances are unknown. *Biometrika, 38*, 324–329.

Jennings, E. (1988). Models for pretest-posttest data: Repeated measures ANOVA revisited. *Journal of Educational Statistics, 13*, 273–280.

Johansen, S. (1980). The Welch-James approximation to the distribution of the residual sum of squares in a weighted linear regression. *Biometrika, 67*, 85–93.

Johnson, P. O., & Neyman, J. (1936). Tests of certain linear hypotheses and their application to some educational problems. *Statistical Research Memoirs, 1*, 57–93.

Johnson, R. A., & Wichern, D. W. (1998). *Applied multivariate statistical analysis* (4th ed.). Upper Saddle River, NJ: Prentice Hall.

Kaiser, L., & Bowden, D. (1983). Simultaneous confidence intervals for all linear contrasts of means with heterogeneous variances. *Communications in Statistics—Theory and Methods, 12*, 73–88.

Keppel, G. (1982). *Design and analysis: A researcher's handbook* (2nd ed.). Englewood Cliffs, NJ: Prentice-Hall.

Keppel, G., & Wickens, T. D. (2004). *Design and analysis: A researcher's handbook* (3rd ed.). Upper Saddle River, NJ: Pearson.

Kirk, R. E. (1982). *Experimental design: Procedures for the behavioral sciences* (2nd ed.). Monterey, CA: Brooks/Cole.

Kleinbaum, D. G., Kupper, L. L., Muller, K. E., & Nizam, A. (1998). *Applied regression analysis and other multivariable methods* (3rd ed.). Pacific Grove, CA: Duxbury.

Kramer, C. Y. (1956). Extension of multiple range test to group means with unequal numbers of replications. *Biometrics, 12*, 307–310.

Kreft, I., & de Leeuw, J. (1998). *Introducing multilevel modeling.* Thousand Oaks, CA: Sage.

Kruskal, W. H., & Wallis, W. A. (1952). Use of ranks on one-criterion variance analysis. *Journal of the American Statistical Association, 47*, 583–621 (with corrections in *48*, 907–911).

Larsen, W. A., & McCleary, S. J. (1972). The use of partial residual plots in regression analysis. *Technometrics, 14*, 781–790.

Li, J., & Lomax, R. G. (2011). Analysis of variance: What is your statistical software actually doing? *Journal of Experimental Education, 73*, 279–294.

Lomax, R. G., & Surman, S. H. (2007). Factorial ANOVA in SPSS: Fixed-, random-, and mixed-effects models. In S. S. Sawilowsky (Ed.), *Real data analysis.* Greenwich, CT: Information Age.

Long, J. S. (1997). *Regression models for categorical and limited dependent variables.* Thousand Oaks, CA: Sage.

Lord, F. M. (1960). Large-sample covariance analysis when the control variable is fallible. *Journal of the American Statistical Association, 55*, 307–321.

Lord, F. M. (1967). A paradox in the interpretation of group comparisons. *Psychological Bulletin, 68*, 304–305.

Lord, F. M. (1969). Statistical adjustments when comparing preexisting groups. *Psychological Bulletin, 72*, 336–337.

Manly, B. F. J. (2004). *Multivariate statistical methods: A primer* (3rd ed.). London: Chapman & Hall.

Mansfield, E. R., & Conerly, M. D. (1987). Diagnostic value of residual and partial residual plots. *The American Statistician, 41*, 107–116.

Marascuilo, L. A., & Levin, J. R. (1970). Appropriate post hoc comparisons for interactions and nested hypotheses in analysis of variance designs: The elimination of type IV errors. *American Educational Research Journal, 7*, 397–421.

Marascuilo, L. A., & Levin, J. R. (1976). The simultaneous investigation of interaction and nested hypotheses in two-factor analysis of variance designs. *American Educational Research Journal, 13*, 61–65.

Marascuilo, L. A., & McSweeney, M. (1977). *Nonparametric and distribution-free methods for the social sciences.* Monterey, CA: Brooks/Cole.

Marascuilo, L. A., & Serlin, R. C. (1988). *Statistical methods for the social and behavioral sciences.* New York: Freeman.

Marcoulides, G. A., & Hershberger, S. L. (1997). *Multivariate statistical methods: A first course.* Mahwah, NJ: Lawrence Erlbaum Associates.

Marquardt, D. W., & Snee, R. D. (1975). Ridge regression in practice. *The American Statistician, 29,* 3–19.

Maxwell, S. E. (1980). Pairwise multiple comparisons in repeated measures designs. *Journal of Educational Statistics, 5,* 269–287.

Maxwell, S. E., & Delaney, H. D. (1990). *Designing experiments and analyzing data: A model comparison perspective.* Belmont, CA: Wadsworth.

Maxwell, S. E., Delaney, H. D., & Dill, C. A. (1984). Another look at ANOVA versus blocking. *Psychological Bulletin, 95,* 136–147.

McCulloch, C. E. (2005). Repeated measures ANOVA, RIP? *Chance, 18,* 29–33.

Menard, S. (1995). *Applied logistic regression analysis.* Thousand Oaks, CA: Sage.

Menard, S. (2000). *Applied logistic regression analysis* (2nd ed.). Thousand Oaks, CA: Sage.

Mendoza, J. L., & Stafford, K. L. (2001). Confidence intervals, power calculation, and sample size estimation for the squared multiple correlation coefficient under the fixed and random regression models: A computer program and useful standard tables. *Educational and Psychological Measurement, 61,* 650–667.

Meyers, L. S., Gamst, G., & Guarino, A. J. (2006). *Applied multivariate research: Design and interpretation.* Thousand Oaks, CA: Sage.

Mickey, R. M., Dunn, O. J., & Clark, V. A. (2004). *Applied statistics: Analysis of variance and regression* (3rd ed.). Hoboken, NJ: Wiley.

Miller, A. J. (1984). Selection of subsets of regression variables (with discussion). *Journal of the Royal Statistical Society, A, 147,* 389–425.

Miller, A. J. (1990). *Subset selection in regression.* New York: Chapman & Hall.

Miller, R. G. (1997). *Beyond ANOVA, Basics of applied statistics.* Boca Raton, FL: CRC Press.

Morgan, G. A., & Griego, O. V. (1998). *Easy use and interpretation of SPSS for Windows: Answering research questions with statistics.* Mahwah, NJ: Lawrence Erlbaum Associates.

Morgan, G. A., Leech, N. L., Gloeckner, & Barrett, K. C. (2011). *IBM SPSS for introductory statistics: Use and interpretation* (4th edition). New York: Routledge.

Mosteller, F., & Tukey, J.W. (1977). *Data analysis and regression.* Reading, MA: Addision-Wesley.

Murphy, K. R., & Myors, B. (2004). *Statistical power analysis: A simple and general model for traditional and modern hypothesis tests* (2nd ed.). Mahwah, NJ: Lawrence Erlbaum Associates.

Myers, R. H. (1979). *Fundamentals of experimental design* (3rd ed.). Boston: Allyn and Bacon.

Myers, R. H. (1986). *Classical and modern regression with applications.* Boston: Duxbury.

Myers, R. H. (1990). *Classical and modern regression with applications* (2nd ed.). Boston: Duxbury.

Myers, J. L., & Well, A. D. (1995). *Research design and statistical analysis.* Mahwah, NJ: Lawrence Erlbaum Associates.

Nagelkerke, N. J. D. (1991). A note on a general definition of the coefficient of determination. *Biometrika, 78,* 691–692.

O'Connell, A. A., & McCoach, D. B. (Eds.). (2008). *Multilevel modeling of educational data.* Charlotte, NC: Information Age Publishing.

O'Grady, K. E. (1982). Measures of explained variance: Cautions and limitations. *Psychological Bulletin, 92,* 766–777.

Overall, J. E., Lee, D. M., & Hornick, C. W. (1981). Comparison of two strategies for analysis of variance in nonorthogonal designs. *Psychological Bulletin, 90,* 367–375.

Overall, J. E., & Spiegel, D. K. (1969). Concerning least squares analysis of experimental data. *Psychological Bulletin, 72,* 311–322.

Page, M. C., Braver, S. L., & MacKinnon, D. P. (2003). *Levine's guide to SPSS for analysis of variance.* Mahwah, NJ: Lawrence Erlbaum Associates.

Pampel, F. C. (2000). *Logistic regression: A primer.* Thousand Oaks, CA: Sage.

Pavur, R. (1988). Type I error rates for multiple comparison procedures with dependent data. *The American Statistician, 42,* 171–173.

Peckham, P. D. (1968). *An investigation of the effects of non-homogeneity of regression slopes upon the F-test of analysis of covariance*. Laboratory of Educational Research, Rep. No. 16, University of Colorado, Boulder, CO.

Pedhazur, E. J. (1997). *Multiple regression in behavioral research* (3rd ed.). Fort Worth, TX: Harcourt Brace.

Pingel, L. A. (1969). *A comparison of the effects of two methods of block formation on design precision*. Paper presented at the annual meeting of the American Educational Research Association, Los Angeles, CA.

Porter, A. C. (1967). *The effects of using fallible variables in the analysis of covariance*. Unpublished doctoral dissertation, University of Wisconsin, Madison, WI.

Porter, A. C., & Raudenbush, S. W. (1987). Analysis of covariance: Its model and use in psychological research. *Journal of Counseling Psychology, 34*, 383–392.

Puri, M. L., & Sen, P. K. (1969). Analysis of covariance based on general rank scores. *Annals of Mathematical Statistic, 40*, 610–618.

Quade, D. (1967). Rank analysis of covariance. *Journal of the American Statistical Association, 62*, 1187–1200.

Raferty, A. E. (1995). Bayesian model selection in social research. In P. V. Marsden (Ed.), *Sociological methodology 1995* (pp. 111–163). London: Tavistock.

Reichardt, C. S. (1979). The statistical analysis of data from nonequivalent control group designs. In T. D. Cook & D. T. Campbell (Eds.), *Quasi-experimentation: Design and analysis issues for field settings*. Chicago: Rand McNally.

Reise, S. P., & Duan, N. (Eds.). (2003). *Multilevel modeling: Methodological advances, issues, and applications*. Mahwah, NJ: Lawrence Erlbaum.

Rogosa, D. R. (1980). Comparing non-parallel regression lines. *Psychological Bulletin, 88*, 307–321.

Rosenthal, R., & Rosnow, R. L. (1985). *Contrast analysis: Focused comparisons in the analysis of variance*. Cambridge, U.K.: Cambridge University Press.

Rousseeuw, P. J., & Leroy, A. M. (1987). *Robust regression and outlier detection*. New York: Wiley.

Ruppert, D., & Carroll, R. J. (1980). Trimmed least squares estimation in the linear model. *Journal of the American Statistical Association, 75*, 828–838.

Rutherford, A. (1992). Alternatives to traditional analysis of covariance. *British Journal of Mathematical and Statistical Psychology, 45*, 197–223.

Scariano, S. M., & Davenport, J. M. (1987). The effects of violations of independence assumptions in the one-way ANOVA. *The American Statistician, 41*, 123–129.

Schafer, W. D. (1991). Reporting hierarchical regression results. *Measurement and Evaluation in Counseling and Development, 24*, 98–100.

Scheffe', H. (1953). A method for judging all contrasts in the analysis of variance. *Biometrika, 40*, 87–104.

Seber, G. A. F., & Wild, C. J. (1989). *Nonlinear regression*. New York: Wiley.

Shadish, W. R., Cook, T. D., & Campbell, D. T. (2002). *Experimental and quasi-experimental designs for generalized causal inference*. Boston: Houston Mifflin.

Shapiro, S. S., & Wilk, M. B. (1965). An analysis of variance test for normality (complete samples). *Biometrika, 52*, 591–611.

Shavelson, R. J. (1988). *Statistical reasoning for the behavioral sciences* (2nd ed.). Boston: Allyn & Bacon.

Sidak, Z. (1967). Rectangular confidence regions for the means of multivariate normal distributions. *Journal of the American Statistical Association, 62*, 626–633.

Smithson, M. (2001). Correct confidence intervals for various regression effect sizes and parameters: The importance of noncentral distributions in computing intervals. *Educational and Psychological Measurement, 61*, 605–632.

Snijders, T. A. B., & Bosker, R. J. (1999). *Multilevel analysis: An introduction to basic and advanced multilevel modeling*. Thousand Oaks, CA: Sage.

Steiger, J. H., & Fouladi, R. T. (1992). R2: A computer program in interval estimation, power calculation, and hypothesis testing for the squared multiple correlation. *Behavior Research Methods, Instruments, and Computers, 4*, 581–582.

Stevens, J. P. (1984). Outliers and influential data points in regression analysis. *Psychological Bulletin*, *95*(2), 334–344.

Stevens, J. P. (2009). *Applied multivariate statistics for the social sciences* (5th ed.). New York: Routledge.

Tabachnick, B. G., & Fidell, L. S. (2007). *Using multivariate statistics* (5th ed.). Boston: Pearson.

Tabatabai, M., & Tan, W. (1985). Some comparative studies on testing parallelism of several straight lines under heteroscedastic variances. *Communications in Statistics—Simulation and Computation*, *14*, 837–844.

Thompson, M. L. (1978). Selection of variables in multiple regression. Part I: A review and evaluation. Part II: Chosen procedures, computations and examples. *International Statistical Review*, *46*, 1–19 and 129–146.

Timm, N. H. (2002). *Applied multivariate analysis*. New York: Springer-Verlag.

Timm, N. H., & Carlson, J. E. (1975). Analysis of variance through full rank models. *Multivariate Behavioral Research Monographs*, No. 75-1.

Tomarken, A., & Serlin, R. (1986). Comparison of ANOVA alternatives under variance heterogeneity and specific noncentrality structures. *Psychological Bulletin*, *99*, 90–99.

Tukey, J. W. (1949). One degree of freedom for nonadditivity. *Biometrics*, *5*, 232–242.

Tukey, J. W. (1953). *The problem of multiple comparisons* (396pp). Ditto: Princeton University.

Weinberg, S. L., & Abramowitz, S. K. (2002). *Data analysis for the behavioral sciences using SPSS*. Cambridge, U.K.: Cambridge University Press.

Weisberg, H. I. (1979). Statistical adjustments and uncontrolled studies. *Psychological Bulletin*, *86*, 1149–1164.

Weisberg, S. (1985). *Applied linear regression* (2nd ed.). New York: Wiley.

Welch, B. L. (1951). On the comparison of several mean values: An alternative approach. *Biometrika*, *38*, 330–336.

Wetherill, G. B. (1986). *Regression analysis with applications*. London: Chapman & Hall.

Wilcox, R. R. (1986). Controlling power in a heteroscedastic ANOVA procedure. *British Journal of Mathematical and Statistical Psychology*, *39*, 65–68.

Wilcox, R. R. (1987). *New statistical procedures for the social sciences: Modern solutions to basic problems*. Hillsdale, NJ: Lawrence Erlbaum Associates.

Wilcox, R. R. (1988). A new alternative to the ANOVA F and new results on James' second- order method. *British Journal of Mathematical and Statistical Psychology*, *41*, 109–117

Wilcox, R. R. (1989). Adjusting for unequal variances when comparing means in one-way and two-way fixed effects ANOVA models. *Journal of Educational Statistics*, *14*, 269–278.

Wilcox, R. R. (1996). *Statistics for the social sciences*. San Diego, CA: Academic.

Wilcox, R. R. (2003). *Applying contemporary statistical procedures*. San Diego, CA: Academic.

Wonnacott, T. H., & Wonnacott, R. J. (1981). *Regression: A second course in statistics*. New York: Wiley.

Wright, R. E. (1995). Logistic regression. In L. G. Grimm & P. R. Arnold (Eds.). *Reading and understanding multivariate statistics* (pp. 217–244). Washington, DC: American Psychological Association.

Wu, L. L. (1985). Robust M-estimation of location and regression. In N. B. Tuma (Ed.), *Sociological methodology, 1985*. San Francisco: Jossey-Bass.

Xie, X.-J., Pendergast, J., & Clarke, W. (2008). Increasing the power: A practical approach to goodness-of-fit test for logistic regression models with continuous predictors. *Computational Statistics & Data Analysis*, *52*(5), 2703–2713.

Zimmerman, D. W. (1997). A note of interpretation of the paired-samples t-test. *Journal of Educational and Behavioral Statistics*, *22*, 349–360.

Odd-Numbered Answers to Problems

Chapter 1
Conceptual Problems

1.1 a (if the sample means are all equal, then MS_{betw} is 0).

1.3 c (lose 1 df from each group; $63 - 3 = 60$).

1.5 d (equals the $df_{betw} + df_{with} = df_{total}$; $60 + 2 = 62$).

1.7 d (null hypothesis does not consider SS values).

1.9 a (for between source = $5 - 1 = 4$ and for within source = $250 - 5 = 245$).

1.11 c (an F ratio of 1.0 implies that between- and within-groups variations are the same).

1.13 True (mean square is a variance estimate).

1.15 True (F ratio must be greater than or equal to 0).

1.17 No (rejecting the null hypothesis in ANOVA only indicates that there is some difference among the means, not that all of the means are different).

1.19 c (the more t tests conducted, the more likely a Type I error for the set of tests).

1.21 True (basically the definition of independence).

1.23 No (find a new statistician as a negative F value is not possible in this context).

Computational Problems

1.1 $df_{betw} = 3$, $df_{with} = 60$, $df_{total} = 63$, $SS_{with} = 9.00$, $MS_{betw} = 3.25$, $MS_{with} = 0.15$, $F = 21.6666$, critical value = 2.76 (reject H_0).

1.3 $SS_{betw} = 150$, $SS_{total} = 1110$, $df_{betw} = 3$, $df_{with} = 96$, $df_{total} = 99$, $MS_{betw} = 50$, $MS_{with} = 10$, critical value approximately 2.7 (reject H_0).

1.5 $SS_{betw} = 25.333$, $SS_{with} = 27.625$, $SS_{total} = 52.958$, $df_{betw} = 2$, $df_{with} = 21$, $df_{total} = 23$, $MS_{betw} = 12.667$, $MS_{with} = 1.315$, $F = 9.629$, critical value = 3.47 (reject H_0).

Chapter 2
Conceptual Problems

2.1 False (requires equal n = s and equal variances; we hope the means are different).

2.3 c (c is not legitimate as the contrast coefficients do not sum to 0).

2.5 a (see flowchart of MCPs in Figure 2.2).

2.7 False (use Dunnett procedure).

2.9 e (Scheffe' is most flexible of all MCPs; can test simple and complex contrasts).

2.11 False (conducted to determine why null has been rejected).

2.13 True (see characteristics of Tukey HSD).

2.15 a (see Figure 2.2).

2.17 Yes (each contrast is orthogonal to the others as they rely on independent information).

2.19 d (see Figure 2.2).

2.21 No (do not know the values of the standard error, t, critical value, etc.).

Computational Problems

2.1 Contrast $= -5$, standard error $= 1$; $t = -5$, critical values are 5.10 and -5.10, fail to reject.

2.3 Standard error $= \sqrt{60/20} = \sqrt{3} = 1.7321$:

- $q_1 = (85 - 50)/1.7321 = 20.2073$.
- $q_2 = (85 - 70)/1.7321 = 8.6603$.
- $q_3 = (70 - 50)/1.7321 = 11.5470$.
- Critical values approximately 3.39 and -3.39; all contrasts are statistically significant.

2.5 (a) $\mu_{.1} - \mu_{.2}$, $\mu_{.3} - \mu_{.4}$, $(\mu_{.1} + \mu_{.2})/2 - (\mu_{.3} + \mu_{.4})/2$; all of the Σc_j are equal to 0.

(b) No, as Σc_j is not equal to 0.

(c) $H_0: \mu_{.1} - [(\mu_{.2} + \mu_{.3} + \mu_{.4})/3]$.

Chapter 3
Conceptual Problems

3.1 c (a plot of the cell means reveals an interaction).

3.3 b (product of number of degrees of freedom for each main effect; $(J - 1)(K - 1) = (2)(2) = 4$).

3.5 d (p less than alpha only for the interaction term).

3.7 c (c is one definition of an interaction).

3.9 b (interaction df = product of main effects df).

3.11 d (the effect of one factor depends on the second factor; see definition of interaction as well as example profile plots in Figure 3.1).

3.13 False (when the interaction is significant, this implies nothing about the main effects).

3.15 No (the numerator degrees of freedom for factor B can be anything).

3.17 e (3 levels of A, 2 levels of B, thus 6 cells).

3.19 a (check F table for critical values; only reject main effect for factor A).

3.21 b (as $df_{total} = 14$, then total sample size $= 15$).

Computational Problems

3.1 $SS_{with} = 225$; $df_A = 1$; $df_B = 2$; $df_{AB} = 2$; $df_{with} = 150$; $df_{total} = 155$; $MS_A = 6.15$; $MS_B = 5.30$; $MS_{AB} = 4.55$; $MS_{with} = 1.50$; $F_A = 4.10$; $F_B = 3.5333$; $F_{AB} = 3.0333$; critical value for A is approximately 3.91, thus reject H_0 for A; critical value for B and AB approximately 3.06, thus reject H_0 for B and fail to reject H_0 for AB.

3.3 See the following completed table:

Source	SS	df	MS	F	Critical Value	Decision
A	14.06	1	14.06	.25	4.75	Fail to reject H_0
B	39.06	1	39.06	.70	4.75	Fail to reject H_0
AB	1.56	1	1.56	.03	4.75	Fail to reject H_0
Within	668.75	12	55.73			
Total	723.43	15				

3.5 $F_A = 4.0541$, $F_B = 210.1622$, $F_C = 31.7838$, $F_{AB} = 7.9459$, $F_{AC} = 13.1351$, $F_{BC} = 10.3784$, $F_{ABC} = 4.0541$, all but ABC and A are significant.

Chapter 4

Conceptual Problems

4.1 No (there is no covariate mentioned for which to control).

4.3 c (evidence of meeting the assumption of independence can be examined by a scatter-plot of residuals by group or category of the independent variable; a random display of points suggests the assumption is met).

4.5 b (see discussion on homogeneity of regression slopes).

4.7 b (14 *df* per group, 3 groups, 42 *df* – 2 *df* for covariates = 40).

4.9 c (want covariate having a high correlation with the dependent variable).

4.11 c (the covariate and dependent variable need not be the same measure; could be pre-test and posttest, but does not have to be).

4.13 b (an interaction indicates that the regression lines are not parallel across the groups).

4.15 c (a post hoc covariate typically results in an underestimate of the treatment effect, due to confounding or interference of the covariate).

4.17 No (if the correlation is substantial, then error variance will be reduced in ANCOVA regardless of its sign).

4.19 b (11 *df* per group, 6 groups, 66 *df* – 1 *df* for covariate = 65).

4.21 No (there will be no adjustment due to the covariate and one *df* will be lost from the error term).

Computational Problems

4.1 The adjusted group means are all equal to 150; this resulted because the adjustment moved the mean for Group 1 up to 150 and the mean for Group 3 down to 150.

4.3 ANOVA results: $SS_{betw} = 4{,}763.275$, $SS_{with} = 9{,}636.7$, $df_{betw} = 3$, $df_{with} = 36$, $MS_{betw} = 1{,}587.758$, $MS_{with} = 267.686$, $F = 5.931$, critical value approximately 2.88 (reject H_0). Unadjusted means in order: 32.5, 60.4, 53.1, 39.9.

ANCOVA results: $SS_{betw} = 5402.046$, $SS_{with} = 3880.115$, $df_{betw} = 3$, $df_{with} = 35$, $MS_{betw} = 1800.682$, $MS_{with} = 110.8604$, $F = 16.24$, critical value approximately 2.88 (reject H_0), $SS_{cov} = 5117.815$, $F_{cov} = 46.164$, critical value approximately 4.12 (reject H_0).

Adjusted means in order: 30.7617, 61.2544, 53.1295, 40.7544.

Chapter 5
Conceptual Problems

5.1 b (when there are both random and fixed factors, then the design is mixed).

5.3 c (gender is fixed, order is random, thus a mixed-effects model).

5.5 a (clinics were randomly selected from the population; thus, the one-factor random-effects model is appropriate).

5.7 False (the F ratio will be the same for both the one-factor random- and fixed-effects models).

5.9 Yes (the test of the interaction is exactly the same for both models yielding the same F ratio).

5.11 Yes (SS_{total} is the same for both models; the total amount of variation is the same; it is just divided up in different ways; review the example dataset in this chapter).

5.13 c (see definition of design).

5.15 True (rarely is one interested in particular students; thus, students are usually random).

5.17 False (the F test is not very robust in this situation and we should be concerned about it).

Computational Problems

5.1 $SS_{with} = 1.9$, $df_A = 2$, $df_B = 1$, $df_{AB} = 2$, $df_{with} = 18$, $df_{total} = 23$, $MS_A = 1.82$, $MS_B = .57$, $MS_{AB} = 1.035$, $MS_{with} = .1056$, $F_A = 1.7585$, $F_B = 5.3977$, $F_{AB} = 9.8011$, critical value for AB = 6.01 (reject H_0 for AB), critical value for B = 8.29 (fail to reject H_0 for B), critical value for A = 99 (fail to reject H_0 for A).

5.3 $SS_{time} = 126.094$, $SS_{time \times program} = 2.594$, $SS_{program} = 3.781$, $MS_{time} = 42.031$, $MS_{time \times program} = 0.865$, $MS_{program} = 3.781$, $F_{time} = 43.078$ ($p < .001$), $F_{time \times program} = 0.886$ ($p > .05$), $F_{program} = 0.978$ ($p > .05$).

5.5 $SS_{time} = 691.467$, $SS_{time \times mentor} = 550.400$, $SS_{mentor} = 1968.300$, $MS_{time} = 345.733$, $MS_{time \times mentor} = 275.200$, $MS_{mentor} = 1968.300$, $F_{time} = 2.719$ ($p = .096$), $F_{time \times mentor} = 2.164$ ($p = .147$), $F_{mentor} = 7.073$ ($p < .001$).

Chapter 6
Conceptual Problems

6.1 d (teachers are ranked according to a ratio blocking variable; a random sample of blocks are drawn; then teachers within the blocks are assigned to treatment).

6.3 a (children are randomly assigned to treatment based on ordinal SES value).

6.5 d (interactions only occur among factors that are crossed).

6.7 a (this is the notation for teachers nested within methods; see also Problem 6.2).

6.9 False (cannot be a nested design; must be a crossed design).

6.11 Yes (see the discussion on the types of blocking).

6.13 c (physician is nested within method).

6.15 Yes (age is an appropriate blocking factor here).

6.17 a (use of a covariate is best for large correlations).

6.19 a (see the summary of the blocking methods).

Computational Problems

6.1 (a) Yes (b) at age 4 type 1 is most effective, at age 6 type 2 is most effective, and at age 8 type 2 is most effective.

6.3 $SS_{total} = 560$, $df_A = 2$, $df_B = 1$, $df_{AB} = 2$, $df_{with} = 24$, $df_{total} = 29$, $MS_A = 100$, $MS_B = 100$, $MS_{AB} = 10$, $MS_{with} = 10$, $F_A = 10$, $F_B = 10$, $F_{AB} = 1$, critical value for B = 4.26 (reject H_0 for B), critical value for A and AB = 3.40 (reject H_0 for A and fail to reject H_0 for AB).

6.5 $F_{section} = 44.385$, $p = .002$; $F_{GRE-Q} = 61.000$, $p = .001$; thus reject H_0 for both effects; Bonferroni results: all but sections 1 and 2 are different, and all but blocks 1 and 2 are statistically different.

Chapter 7
Conceptual Problems

7.1 c (see definition of intercept; a and b refer to the slope and d to the correlation).

7.3 c (the intercept is 37,000 which represents average salary when cumulative GPA is zero).

7.5 a (the predicted value is a constant mean value of 14 regardless of X; thus, the variance of the predicted values is 0).

7.7 d (linear relationships are best represented by a straight line, although all of the points need not fall on the line).

7.9 a (if the slope = 0, then the correlation = 0).

7.11 b (with the same predictor score, they will have the same residual score; whether the residuals are the same will only depend on the observed Y).

7.13 d (see definition of homogeneity).

7.15 d (various pieces of evidence for normality can be assessed, including formal tests such as the Shapiro–Wilk test).

7.17 True (the value of Y is irrelevant when the correlation = 0, so the mean of Y is the best prediction).

7.19 False (if the variables are positively correlated, then the slope would be positive and a low score on the pretest would predict a low score on the posttest).

7.21 No (the regression equation may generate any number of points on the regression line).

Computational Problems

7.1 $a - b$ (slope) = .8571, a (intercept) = 1.9716; $b - Y$ (outcome) = 7.1142.

7.3 118.

Chapter 8
Conceptual Problems

8.1 b (partial correlations correlate two variables while holding constant a third).

8.3 c (perfect prediction when the standard error = 0).

8.5 False (adding an additional predictor can result in the same R^2).

8.7   No (R^2 is higher when the predictors are uncorrelated).

8.9   c (given there is theoretical support, the best method of selection is hierarchical regression).

8.11 No (the purpose of the adjustment is to take the number of predictors into account; thus R^2_{adj} may actually be smaller for the most predictors).

Computational Problems

8.1   Intercept = 28.0952, b_1 = .0381, b_2 = .8333, SS_{res} = 21.4294, SS_{reg} = 1128.5706, F = 105.3292 (reject at .01), s^2_{res} = 5.3574, $s(b_1)$ = .0058, $s(b_2)$ = .1545, t_1 = 6.5343 (reject at .01), t_2 = 5.3923 (reject at .01).

8.3   In order, the t values are 0.8 (not significant), 0.77 (not significant), −8.33 (significant).

8.5 $r_{1(2.3)}$ = −.0140.

8.7 $r_{12.3}$ = −.8412, $r_{1(2.3)}$ = −.5047.

8.9   Intercept = −1.2360, b_1 = .6737, b_2 = .6184, SS_{res} = 58.3275, SS_{reg} = 106.6725, F = 15.5453 (reject at .05), s^2_{res} = 3.4310, $s(b_1)$ = .1611, $s(b_2)$ = .2030, t_1 = 4.1819 (reject at .05), t_2 = 3.0463 (reject at .05).

Chapter 9

Conceptual Problems

9.1   c—The measurement scale of the dependent variable.

9.3   a—Employment status (employed; unemployed, not looking for work; unemployed, looking for work) as there are more than two groups or categories.

9.5   a—True.

9.7   a—The log odds become larger as the odds increase from 1 to 100.

9.9   d—Wald test (assesses significance of individual predictors).

Computational Problems

9.1 $-2LL$ = 7.558, b_{HSGPA} = −.366, $b_{athlete}$ = 22.327, $b_{cons\,tan\,t}$ = .219, $se(b_{HSGPA})$ = 1.309, $se(b_{athlete})$ = 20006.861, odds ratio$_{HSGPA}$ = .693, odds ratio$_{athlete}$ < .001, $Wald_{HSGPA}$ = .078, $Wald_{athlete}$ = .000.

Author Index

Subject Index